APPLIED
HUMAN
RELATIONS

Douglas Benton

Colorado State University

Jack Halloran

Fourth Edition

APPLIED HUMAN RELATIONS

An Organizational Approach

 Prentice Hall, Englewood Cliffs, New Jersey 07632

Library of Congress Cataloging-in-Publication Data

Benton, Douglas,
    Applied human relations : an organizational approach / Douglas Benton, Jack
Halloran. — 4th ed.
        p.   cm.
    Authors' names in reverse order on previous edition.
    Includes bibliographical references.
    ISBN 0-13-040981-2
    1. Organizational behavior.   2. Management.   3. Personnel
management.   I. Halloran, Jack   II. Title.
    HD58.7.B463   1991
    658.3—dc20
                                                          90-34946
                                                          CIP

Editorial/production supervision: **Janet M. DiBlasi**
Interior design: **Cover to Cover Inc.**
Cover design: **Jannette Jacobs**
Manufacturing buyer: **Ed O'Dougherty/Ilene Levy**
Cover art: **Diana Ong**
Photo Editor: **Rona Tuccillo**
Photo Research: **Barbara Scott**

Chapter opening photographs with the permission of Laima Druskis; Bob
Daemmrich/The Image Works; Robert A. Isaacs/Photo Researchers; Jeffrey
Dunn Studios/The Picture Cube; Margaret Kois/The Stock Market; Michael
Kagan/Monkmeyer Press; Catherine Ursillo/Photo Researchers; Paul
Conklin/Uniphoto Picture Agency; Mimi Forsyth/Monkmeyer Press; Jeffrey
Blackman/The Stock Market; Arthur Tress/Photo Researchers; Bill
Anderson/Monkmeyer Press; United Nations/Saw Lwin

 © 1991, 1987, 1983, 1978 by Prentice-Hall, Inc.
A Division of Simon & Schuster
Englewood Cliffs, New Jersey 07632

Printed in the United States of America

10   9   8   7   6   5   4   3   2

ISBN 0-13-040981-2

Prentice-Hall International (UK) Limited, *London*
Prentice-Hall of Australia Pty. Limited, *Sydney*
Prentice-Hall Canada Inc., *Toronto*
Prentice-Hall Hispanoamericana, S.A., *Mexico*
Prentice-Hall of India Private Limited, *New Delhi*
Prentice-Hall of Japan, Inc., *Tokyo*
Simon & Schuster Asia Pte. Ltd., *Singapore*
Editora Prentice-Hall do Brasil, Ltda., *Rio de Janeiro*

CONTENTS

Preface —————————————————————————— **xxii**

PART ONE Introduction

People Are Human

1 *Fundamentals of Human Relations* ————————— **1**

Definitions and Purposes   3

The Interdisciplinary Aspect of Human Relations   4
A Brief History of the Human Relations Movement   5
  Scientific Management   5
  The Development of Unions   7
  Elton Mayo's Hawthorne Experiment   8
  The Informal Organization   8
  More Influences for Human Relations During Following Decades   9
  Quality Circles—Not a Fad   10
Organizational Values   10
  Business Ethics   11
  Commitment   12
  Honesty/Integrity   12
  Loyalty   12
  Mutual Trust/Mutual Respect   13
  Courtesy   13
  Work/Leisure Attitudes   13
  Visionary Leadership   13
  Action Orientation   13
  Quality Products and Services   14
Recurrent Themes in Human Relations   14
  Human Dignity   14
  Empathy   14
  Individual Differences   15
  Communications   15
  Motivation   15
  Leadership   16
  Responsibility   16

v

The Whole Person   16
Constant Change   17
What Is Required to "Run" Our Organizations?   17
Management Skills   18
Human Relations Skills   19
Technical Skills Versus Conceptual Skills   19
Human Relations Problems   19
Summary   21
Case Study 1   You, Human Relations, and This Book   22
Case Study 2   The Aerobics Instructor   23
Terms and Concepts   24
Notes   24
Recommended Reading   24

PART TWO Individual Challenges

Getting to Know Ourselves and Our Opportunities

2 *Personal and Career Development* _____ 26
Plans for Personal Development   27
Stress and Tension   28
Holistic Health   28
Types A, H, and B Behavior   28
Workaholics: Fortune's Favorite Children   30
Make Tension Work for You   30
The Cost of Stress   31
How to Cope with Stress   31
Anger and Stress   32
Stress and Illness   33
Time Management   34
We All Have the Same Amount of Time   35
Set Priorities on Your Time   37
The Telephone Paradox   37
Manage Your Own Time   38
Your Desk or Other Workplace   39
Meetings—Time Wasters or Communication Tools   39
Where to Meet—Your Place or Mine?   39
Formal Meetings   39
Career Development   40
Individual Responsibility   40
Organizational Responsibility   41
Demand   42

Career Pathing   43
Career Advancement   44
"Mommy Track" or Alternative Schedule Choice   46
Success   46
Success Is Respect   47
Maturity   48
You Don't Have to Be Perfect to Be Successful   48
Summary   49
Case Study 3   Is There Life After College?   50
Case Study 4   I Don't Have Enough Time   51
Terms and Concepts   51
Notes   52
Recommended Reading   52

3   Human Motivation _____ 54

What Is Motivation All About?   55

Motivation and Behavior   56
Motivation and Organizations   57
Schools of Psychology and Impact on Motivation   58
Psychoanalytic School   58
Behaviorist School   59
Humanist School   59
Other Approaches to Motivation   60
Maslow's Basic Needs   61
Physiological Needs   62
Safety or Security Needs   62
Social or Belonging Needs   62
Esteem Needs   63
Self-Actualization Needs   63
The Hierarchy of Needs   63
Can You Recognize the Need?   64
Herzberg's Hygiene Theory   65
Satisfiers and Dissatisfiers   65
Motivation-Maintenance Approach   65
Incentives   67
The Nature of Incentives   67
When Does an Incentive Become a Right?   67
Intrinsic and Extrinsic Motivators   67
Barriers to Achievement   68
Common Defense Mechanisms   69
Job Design   70
Horizontal Job Loading   70
Vertical Job Loading   71
Job Enrichment   72
Job Rotation   72
Delegation   72

Flexibility Gives Self-Direction   72
Let Workers See the End Product of Their Efforts   73
Listening Supervisors   73
Summary   73
Case Study 5   How Do You Motivate Motel Maids   74
Case Study 6   The "Hooky" Case   75
Terms and Concepts   76
Notes   77
Recommended Reading   77

4   **Job Performance and Morale**   78

Job Performance, the Key to Morale and Productivity   79
The Job Description   80
Performance Standards   80
Performance Measurement   83
Rewarding Results   83
Determinants of Job Performance   84
Job Satisfaction and Morale   86
The Variables of Job Satisfaction   86
Blue-Collar Challenge   88
Job Satisfaction in the White-Collar World   89
Morale and the Work Force   89
The Changing Work Force   90
Job Performance, Morale, and Productivity   91
Effective Job Performance Results in Job Satisfaction   91
Making Dull Jobs More Interesting   92
Diagnosing and Maintaining Morale   93
Analysis of Records   93
Informal Questions and Answers   93
Formal Surveys   94
Employee Responses and Follow-through   94
Physical Environment and Morale   95
Ergonomics   95
Noise Pollution Affects Morale   95
Visual Pollution   96
Lighting   97
Colors and Space   98
Summary   98
Case Study 7   Theft in the Service Station   99
Case Study 8   Morale Pollution   100
Terms and Concepts   101
Notes   101
Recommended Reading   102

5 *Personal Problems: Alcohol, Drugs and Sex* _____ 103

Types of Personal Problems   104
How to Identify Someone with a Problem   105
   Exaggerated Behavior   105
   Distress Symptoms   105
   Radical Change Symptoms   105
Alcoholism   106
   How Widespread Is the Problem?   106
   Problem Drinkers and Industry   106
   Spotting an Alcoholic   107
   Dealing with Alcoholics   108
The Drug Abusers   108
   Marijuana   109
   Cocaine   109
   Hard Drugs   110
   Depressants   110
   Stimulants   110
   Hallucinogens   111
   Designer Drugs   111
   Addicts on the Job   111
   Confronting Drug Abuse   111
Sex and the Workplace   112
Sexual Harassment   113
   Preventing Sexual Harassment   114
Who Can Help with Problems?   114
   Friends   114
   Supervisors   115
   Specialists or Counselors   116
   Comparisons of Supervisors and Trained Counselors   116
How to Counsel   117
   Directive Method   117
   Nondirective Method   117
   Cooperative Counseling   118
   Comparisons of Counseling Methods   119
Company Programs   119
   A Guide for Managers and Supervisors   120
Employee Assistance Programs   121

Posttreatment Procedures   122
   Follow-up—If the Employee Improves   122
   Follow-up—If the Employee Does Not Improve   122
Summary   122
Case Study 9   The Sweet Smell of Grass   123
Case Study 10   Just a Little Larceny—I'll Drink to That   124
Case Study 11   Love in Bloom or . . . ?   124
Terms and Concepts   125

Notes   125
Recommended Reading   126

PART THREE Group Challenges

Getting to Know and Interacting With Others

6 *Group and Role Behavior* ——————————— **127**

Group Dynamics   128
  What Is a Group?   128
  Norms   129
  Group Composition   130
  Size of Group   130
  Group Cohesiveness   131
How to Obtain Group Consensus   131
Changing Social Values   132
  Early Career Changes   133
  Midcareer Adjustments   133
The Fixed or Impermeable Social Class   134
  Inherited Class   134
  Social Class and Economic Success   134
The Striver and the Permeable Society   135
  Economic Prosperity   135
  Facilitates Creativity   135
  Less Discriminatory and Narrow-Minded Attitudes   136
  Increases Individualism   136
Group Behavior and Upward Mobility   136
  Intelligence and Success   137
Strivers Fall Prey to the "Peter Principle"   137
Disadvantages of a Permeable Class Society   138
  Diminished Intimacy   138
  Disruption of Primary Group Relationships   138
  Marriage Disruption   138
Group Roles   139
  Role Prescriptions and Role Behaviors   139
  Role Conflict and Ambiguity   140
Behavior of Small Groups   140
  Groupthink   140
  Task Leaders or Social Leaders?   141
Summary   141

Case Study 12   Who's the Boss?   142
Case Study 13   Charlie Has a Chance to Get Ahead   143
Terms and Concepts   144
Notes   144
Recommended Reading   144

7   *Interpersonal Communication* _____ 146

The Meaning of Communciation   148
  Meanings Are Within Us   148
The Communication Process   149
  Models   150
Perception   151
Speaking   151
  Voice Tone   152
  Emotions   152
  Sensitivity to Others   153
  Self-Disclosure   153
Listening   153
Barriers to Communication   155
  Distortion   155
  Language/Semantics   157
  Defensiveness   157
  Noise   158
  Mistrust   159
Feedback   159
  Silence   160
Levels of Verbal Communication   160
Nonverbal Communications   162
  Body Language   162
  Posture   162
  Eye Contact   162
  Space or Proxemics   163
  Touching   164
  Neurolinguistic Programming   164
Written Word   164
Visual Symbols   165
Summary   166
Case Study 14   There's a Rumor About My Promotion   167
Case Study 15   Visual Communications Speak Loudly in the Escrow
                    Office   168
Terms and Concepts   169
Notes   170
Recommended Reading   170

8 Organizational Design and Communication _____ **171**

Communicating in Organizations   173
The Need for Organizational Structure   173
Tall and Flat Organizational Structures   173
   Span of Management   175
   Limiting the Span of Management   175
   Stretching the Span of Management   175
Staff and Line Organizations   175
   Line Structure   176
   General Staff and Specialized Staff   176
Project Management   177
   Project Teams or Matrix Organizations   177
   Problems and Their Prevention in Matrix Organizations   178
Communication Channels   178
Formal Channels   178
   Organization Charts   179
   Chain of Command   179
Horizontal Channels   179
Vertical Channels   181
Downward Communications   181
   Written Versus Oral Downward Communications   183
   Self-Fulfilling Prophecy   183
   How to Handle Bad News   184
Upward Communication   184
   The Open-Door Policy   185
Informal Channels   186
   The Grapevine   186
   Rumor   187
Small-Group Communications   187
Electronic Communication   188
   Electronic Mail   188
   Facsimile and Other Telecommunications Machines   188
Summary   189
Case Study 16   How Can the Staff Communicate More Effectively with Line Personnel   190
Case Study 17   Work Delegation and Dual Command   191
Terms and Concepts   191
Notes   192
Recommended Reading   192

9 Power and Status _____ **193**

Definition of Power   195
Who Are the Powerful?   195
Power and Perception   197

      Leadership Power Is Derived   197
Sources and Types of Power   198
      Expert Power   198
      Information Power   199
      Referent Power   199
      Legitimate Power   199
      Reward Power   199
      Connection Power   200
      Coercive Power   200
Politics   201
      Office Politics   201
      Organizational Politics   201
      Power Plays   201
Power Relationships   202
      External Power Is Derived   202
Power Measurements   203
The Social Basis of Status   203
      Definition   203
      Social Stratification   204
Status Symbols   204
      Hours and Pay   205
      Work Environment   205
      Clothing and Cars   207
How Status Affects Communication   208
Job Status   209
      Titles and Positions   209
      Professionalism   210
      Status Inconsistency and Ambiguities   210
Success and Failure   211
Summary   212
Case Study 18 The Powerful Professor   212
Case Study 19 Status Reversal   213
Terms and Concepts   214
Notes   214
Recommended Reading   214

PART FOUR Organizational Challenges

We Lead, Develop, and Decide

10   ***Leadership***   **216**
What Is Leadership?   218
      Breaking Through the Myths   218

Defining Leadership   218
Following Leaders   218
Being a Leader   219
Leadership Traits   220
Social Popularity   220
Group Relationships   222
Functional Roles   222
Leadership Styles   222
Theory X and Theory Y Leaders   225
Autocratic Leaders   225
Participative and Democratic Leaders   225
Free-Rein Leaders   227
Theory Z   227
Long-Range Planning   228
Consensus Decision Making   228
Mutual Trust and Loyalty   228
Nonspecialized Careers   228
Strong Company Image and Direction   228
Quality over Quantity   229
Subsistence-Level Wages, but Real Bonuses   229
Few Promotions and Lifetime Employment   229
Contingency Model   230
Identifying the Style   230
Analyzing the Job—Matching the Style   231
Companies Are Selecting Personalities to Fit Positions   232
The Path-Goal Approach   232
Management by Objectives   233
Delegation   234
Delegation of Authority   234
Leadership Communication   234
Speech Patterns   234
Leadership Training   235
"Leaderless" Groups   235
Summary   236
Case Study 20   Conflict Between Two Styles of Supervision   236
Case Study 21   Who Leads: The Chosen Leader or the Informal
Leader?   238
Terms and Concepts   239
Notes   239
Recommended Reading   240

11   *Discipline and Training*   241
Discipline Defined   243
Emphasize Positive Discipline and Performance   243
Commitment   243
Training and Development Relationships   244

What Is Training?   244
What Is Development?   245
What Is Learning?   246
Goals and Methods   246
Orientation   248
Policy Orientation   248
Procedural Orientation   248
Two Approaches to Orientation   248
Developing Managers   250
Instructional Methods   250
On-the-Job Training   251
Written Material   251
Lectures   251
Programmed Instruction   252
Computer-Assisted Instruction   252
Videotape   253
Simulation Methods   253
In-Basket Method   253
Case Study   254
Management Games   255
Experiential Methods   256
Role Playing   257
Sensitivity Training   258
Transactional Analysis   259
Assertiveness Training   261
How to Be Assertive   262
Transcendental Meditation   262
Benefits of Meditation   263
Summary   264
Case Study 22 Training Gary for Promotion   264
Case Study 23 Should Training Be Required   265
Terms and Concepts   266
Notes   267
Recommended Reading   267

12 *Appraisals, Promotions, and Dismissals* _____ **269**

Appraisal of Performance   271
Purposes of an Appraisal   271
The Administrative Purpose   271
The Informative Purpose   272
A Developmental Purpose   272
Job Description   272
The Appraisal Interview   273
Preparing for the Interview   273
How to Open the Interview   274
Discussion Methods   274

Ending the Interview   275
Techniques of Appraisals   275
   Essay Appraisal   275
   Graphic Rating Scale   275
   Critical Incident Technique   276
   Ranking   279
   Field Review   279
   Peer and Subordinate Appraisal   280
   Self-Evaluation   280
   Management by Objectives   281
   Behaviorally Anchored Rating Scales   282
Frequent Errors Made in Rating Employees   282
   Halo Effect   282
   Personal Bias   283
   Central Tendency   283
   Recency Bias   283
Promotions   283
   What Promotion Means   284
   Promotion Based on Merit or Ability   284
   The Employee Who Doesn't Want to Be Promoted   284
Disciplinary Action   285
Demotions and Dismissals   285
   Warnings   285
   How to Handle a Demotion   286
   How Do You Fire an Employee?   286
   Layoffs   288
Salaries and Wages as Rewards   289
Incentive Plans   290
   Commissions   291
   Profit-Sharing Plans   291
   Merit Increases   291
   Cash Bonuses   291
Employee Benefits   291
Summary   292
Case Study 24   What Rewards Should Be Given Now?   294
Case Study 25   Promotion Based upon Supervisory Characteristics   295
Terms and Concepts   296
Notes   296
Recommended Reading   297

---

13   ***Innovation in Decision Making*** ———————————— **298**
What Is Innovation?   300
What Is Creativity?   300
   How Is Creativity Defined?   300
   Who Has It?   301
The Four P's of Creativity   301

The Person   302
    Approach   302
    Intelligence   303
    Age and Gender   303
    Behavior   304
    Inhibitors   304
The Process   305
    Perception   305
    Incubation   306
    Inspiration   306
    Verification   306
Pressure of Society   307
    Social Direction and Necessity   307
    Social Pressure   308
The Product   308
Business and the Creative Employee   309
    Management Attitudes   309
    Entrepreneurial Characteristics   310
    Brainstorming   310
    Rewards   311
What Is Decision Making?   311
    Problem Definition   312
    Analyze the Problem   313
    Consider the Alternative Solutions   313
    Take Action—a Solution   315
    Implement the Solution   315
    Ongoing Evaluation   316
    Need for Change   317
Long- and Short-Range Decisions   317
Traits That Influence Decisions   317
    Taking Risks   318
    Success and Failure Attitudes   318
    Decisiveness   319
    Personal Biases and Experience   319
    Intuition   319
    Seeking and Giving Advice   320
Who Makes the Decisions?   320
    Individual Decisions   320
    Decisions by a Powerful Few   320
    Decisions by Groups   321
    Problems of "Groupthink"   323
    Key People in Decision Making   324
Making Decisions During Conflict   324
    Polarizations   325
    Real Communication Leads to a Resolution   325
Summary   326
Case Study 26   Achievement—Accomplished by Individual Creativity or by
        "Groupthink" Team Effort   327

Case Study 27   Missing Company Property   327
Terms and Concepts   328
Notes   329
Recommended Reading   329

PART FIVE   Organizational Dynamics and Culture

We Change and Get to Know Our Organizations, Societies, and Culture

14   Managing Change Through Teamwork _____ 330

Innovative Decisions Invoke Change   332
Patterns of Change   332
    When to Expect Resistance   334
Changing the Individual   334
Psychological Resistance   336
    Occupational Identity and Security   336
    Fear of Unknown Future   336
    Status Consideration   337
Economic Resistance   337
Social Resistance   338
    The Theory of Homeostasis   338
    Driving Forces and Restraining Forces   338
    Balancing the Forces   339
    Change in Technology and "Quality of Life"   339
    Work Environment Change   340
Overcoming Resistance   341
    Participation   341
    Behavior Modification   342
    Mandating Change   343
    Time Allowance   345
    Group Dynamics of Change   345
Keys to Successful Change   345
Organization Development   346
    Teamwork and Trust   347
Murphy's Laws   347
Summary   349
Case Study 28   Group Pressure—"Rate Busting"   351
Case Study 29   The Overqualified Employee's Dilemma   352
Terms and Concepts   352
Notes   353
Recommended Reading   353

15 *Job and Pay Discrimination* _____ 354

Background to Prejudice and Discrimination   356
    Prejudgments   356
    What Is Prejudice?   356
    What Is Discrimination?   357
    Prejudice Works Both Ways   357
    Prejudice and Self-Image   357

Religious Discrimination   358

Racial Discrimination   359
    Afro-Americans   360
    Hispanic Americans   361
    The Indian Nation   361
    Oriental View   361
    Social Problems of Race Mixing   362

The Older Worker   362
    How Old is Old?   362
    When to Retire   363
    Supervising the Older Worker   363
    Age Discrimination in Employment Act   363
    How the Company Can Help the Older Worker   364

The Employment of Women   365
    Social Changes Have Altered Women's Roles   366
    Aims of Women's Action Groups   367
    Problems for the Businesswoman   368
    Dual Careers   369

Employment of the Handicapped   370
    AIDS   370

Psychological Roots of Prejudice   370

Economic Roots of Prejudice   371

Fighting Discrimination   371
    Education   371
    Programs of Awareness   372
    More Intergroup Contact   372
    Legal and Legislative Action   372
    Job Restructuring   373
    What Is Affirmative Action?   373
    Work Force Diversity   374
    Termination at Will   374

Summary   375
Case Study 30   Discrimination against a Female Account Executive   376
Case Study 31   Problems in Promoting a Minority   377
Terms and Concepts   378
Notes   378
Recommended Reading   379

16 *Employees and Unions* _____ **380**

Where Are Unions Going?   381
Who Are Union Members   382
A Clash of Goals   383
Management's Attitudes Toward Unions   384
Union Development   384
Dual Loyalty   386
    Why Do People Join Unions?   386
    How Nonunion Companies Keep Unions Out   387
    What Can Unions Promise?   387
An Election Can Vote a Union In or Out   388
Union Interaction with Management   388
The Two Personalities in the Middle   389
    Shop Steward   389
    Company Supervisor   390
Collective Bargaining   391
    Management and Union Preparation   391
    Negotiating Procedures   392
A Gripe Can Become a Grievance   393
How to Prevent Grievances   393
The Grievance Procedure   393
Tactics of the Union and Management   395
Today's Unions   396
    Wages and Benefits   396
    Mergers   397
    Social and Technological Change   397
    Quality of Work Life   397
    Union Losses   398
    Union Gains   398
    Internationalism and Unions   399
Spirit of Cooperation   399
Summary   399
Case Study 32   Firehouse Union   401
Case Study 33   Unions Versus Minority Rights   402
Terms and Concepts   403
Notes   403
Recommended Reading   404

17 *Intercultural Relations* _____ **405**

A Look at a Shrinking World   407
    The Wave of New Americans   408
Our Cultural Attitudes Toward Foreigners   408
The Ugly American or the Protective Father Image?   409
    Subtle Differences   410
    The Political Frame of Reference   410

The Economic Frame of Reference   411
Foreigners Are Bullish on America   412
Economic Tips for American Business Managers   412
The Cultural Frame of Reference   413
A Look at Two Cultures   415
Japan, Another Look at Theory Z   415
Arabs Influence So Much, Yet We Know So Little   417
The Changing European Community   418
Hidden Languages   418
The Language of Time   419
From Microseconds to Antiquity   419
The Language of Space   420
The Language of Touch   421
The Language of Context   422
The Language of Friendship   423
The Language of Agreements   424
Summary   426
Case Study 34   International Bribery   427
Case Study 35   A Problem of Cultural Communication   428
Terms and Concepts   429
Notes   429
Recommended Reading   430
Index   431

PREFACE

"If it's not broke, fix it anyway before it breaks" was the assumption followed in making revisions for this fourth edition. The previous editions have been very successful in applying human relations skills to various organizations. The revisions are intended to develop further these applications.

The late Jack Halloran and I have dedicated our lives to making learning about human relationships easier. The intention is not to bury the reader in "gobbledegook" but to provide practical human relations guidelines for the reader. We are all students and we all learn from one another. Reading and studying this book, it is hoped, will generate interest and point the way for further study.

This text is designed to meet the needs of popular courses taught in junior colleges, four-year colleges, universities, adult education and extension programs, and management training seminars. The direct, straightforward language used in this book attempts to emphasize the person in the organization rather than the traditional theories of management philosophy. It is not a book on organizational theory, office management, or elements of supervision. Rather, it is about the daily interactions between managers and other employees.

FEATURES OF THE BOOK

The material was written to develop thinking. To this end each chapter is introduced with objectives that the reader is intended to meet after studying the chapter. Following the *Objectives* are questions *To Start You Thinking . . .* Some can be answered only with personal opinions and are popular ways to start class discussions after the chapter has been read. Others are based on material that will be covered in the chapter, and they provide clues to the topics in the chapter. Throughout the chapters are self-quizzes (*Test Yourself*) and experiential exercises (*Express Your Opinion*). Since human relations means self-discovery and interchange among persons, the more participative the class can become, the more the students can learn from each experience.

At the close of each chapter are summaries, endnotes, and recommended readings, as well as case studies that can be done during class or as outside assignments. All the case studies are based on real-life experiences. Marginal notes identify important information within the paragraphs. They are ideal for reviewing the chapter or finding necessary material.

In addition to relevant examples and illustrative anecdotes, each chapter features:

1. Objectives
2. To Start You Thinking. . .

3. Express Your Opinion
4. Test Yourself ("self-quizzes" on human development)
5. Marginal Notes
6. Summary
7. Case Studies
8. Terms and Concepts
9. Notes
10. Recommended Reading

NEW AND EXPANDED FEATURES AND LEARNING AIDS

Well over 25 percent of the Fourth Edition is new or updated information. The new material includes:

1. Organizational values, including ethics, commitment, honesty and integrity, among others
2. A reexamination of "scientific management" and other outdated strategies
3. Visionary leadership
4. Constancy and desirability of change
5. Expanded coverage on stress and time management
6. Expanded coverage on loyalty and trust
7. Expanded coverage on motivation and incentives
8. Group dynamics and consensus
9. Barriers to communication
10. Electronic communication
11. Power and status
12. Discipline (a positive state of order and readiness)
13. Disciplinary action
14. Expanded coverage on innovation and decision making
15. Updated information on labor unions and discrimination, including handicapped and AIDS
16. Changing intercultural relations, including Asia and European Economic Communities

There are also several new, combined, or modified cases.

An updated *Activity Guide* is available that has a variety of objective, essay, and other review questions designed for each chapter. Experiential exercises, included for each chapter, can be done in or outside the classroom. Use of this *Activity Guide* is encouraged to permit greater understanding of the principles and ideas put forth in the book.

An *Instructor's Manual* with new classroom–tested questions, suggestions for other learning aids, and transparency masters are also available.

DEDICATION AND THANKS

This edition is dedicated to my wife Dorothy, daughter Sheryl, and son Bill, who all helped in its preparation and for whom my loves grows continually. I am particularly indebted to them and to the many practitioners from whom I have learned through years of private business, consulting, teaching, and management development work.

My colleagues at Colorado State University, and other institutions of higher education, including the University of Pittsburgh, the University of Wyoming and the Autonomous University of Guadalajara in Mexico, have been supportive. Constructive review and suggestions were also received from users at the U.S. Chamber of Commerce, Indiana Vocational Technical Colleges, Manatee Community College, and Phillips College of Atlanta, among many others. Special thanks go to Professor Ray Hogler and Mohan Limaye at CSU for their help with Chapters 15, 16, and 17.

Janet DiBlasi, the production editor, Maureen Hull, editor, Sally Ann Bailey, copyeditor, and Cover to Cover, designer, all provided outstanding professional assistance in preparing this edition. My writing is a labor of love. I enjoy writing as well as teaching, researching, and consulting and hope the enjoyment shows through in this revision. Comments from readers are welcome. Please let me hear from you in care of Prentice-Hall or write me directly at Colorado State University in Fort Collins, Colorado.

Finally, and most important, is my gratitude to the past, present, and future students and faculty who use this book as a reference and learning device. The book begins and ends with you, your individual challenges and opportunities, because we want you to perform as well in your job and other responsibilities as you possibly can.

In summary, it is important to get to know. . .

Yourself—you alone will have the most influence over your human relations

Your peers—you and an intimate group of others including coworkers

Your boss—you and selected others in leadership situations

Your organization—you and many others will share common concerns

Your business—your industry and your organization's role in it

Your society—you and all others in your culture share common characteristics

Your world—you and all others will share intercultural relationships

Have a pleasant journey in getting to know yourself and others!

Doug Benton

1

Fundamentals of Human Relations

After studying this chapter, you should be able to:

1. Explain why there is a need for an interdisciplinary approach to human relations in business.

2. Define human relations as it is used in business and its importance to the individual.

3. Discuss both the goals and results of "scientific management" today in light of almost a century of experience with the concept, including the comments of Konosuke Matsushita.

4. Explain applications and similarities of human relations concepts to "quality circles."

5. List and discuss basic themes in the human relations literature.

6. Discuss organizational values and perspectives on organization of work.

7. Describe the technical, human relations, and conceptual skills of management.

8. Distinguish among leadership, management, administration, and supervision.

TO START YOU THINKING . . .

Before you read this or any other chapter in the book, you will read questions that are designed to stimulate your thinking. Some of the answers will be found in the readings; others will depend upon your own personal opinion or experiences. Such open-ended questions are written to generate discussions and an exchange of ideas.

◆ What is your definition of human relations?

◆ Why would the study of human relations be more important to the supervisor than to the average worker?

◆ Has "scientific management" helped or hindered human relations?

◆ How may Waterman's attributes of corporate renewal be applied to people within organizations?

◆ How can you explain that responsibility is a two-way street between the company and the employee? Between management and employee?

◆ Are the skills required of managers changing?

◆ Are business values changing?

◆ What values do we put on loyalty, commitment, creativity, integrity, responsibility, trust?

◆ How are Deming's and Waterman's principles helping to transform organizations?

DEFINITIONS AND PURPOSES

Human relations is the study of interaction among people

Human relations, in its most general sense, refers to all the interactions that can occur among people, whether organizational or personal, conflicting or cooperating. The main focus of this book is organizational behavior and relationships, but because organizations are the sum of their parts, we also focus on personal behavior and relationships.

By the time most people reach college age, they have developed a system of human relations in their social and personal exchanges that satisfies most of their needs. Frequently, however, people who feel confident and secure in their personal relationships lack confidence and are insecure in their business relationships.

The book is arranged so that we take on the challenges of human relations and management as we come to them as individuals, groups, organizations, and systems. We cannot communicate effectively with others until we confront our individual challenges of career development, motivation, job performance, and personal problems.

When people work together in groups to achieve a common objective, there is a strong possibility that the differences among their individual viewpoints will cause conflicts. Many people do not know how to resolve business conflicts in a constructive manner. But, clearly, the person who does know how to work harmoniously even with those who hold different views or are motivated by different goals has found an important clue to successful human relations in the world of work.

Human relations is a discipline within business

Most employers agree that the majority of those who fail in managerial positions do so because they lack skill in human relations, even though they may be competent in technical matters. The need to find new solutions to the day-to-day problems associated with modern job responsibilities has led to the development of human relations as a separate field of study, a discipline within the business curriculum.

A key to success in business is satisfying company objectives and personal goals.

From both the managerial and workers' points of view, good human relations are necessary if people are to achieve economic, social, and psychological satisfaction from the work they do. *The study of human relations in business and industry is the study of how people can work effectively in groups to satisfy both (1) organizational objectives and (2) personal goals.* We prefer the terms *objectives* for organizations and *goals* for people.

One of the tests of a good manager is the ability to meet organizational objectives and to fulfill workers' personal needs at the same time. Another test is how well a manager balances efficiency and effectiveness. These relationships are the chief subject matter of this book.

Human goals are often recognition and job satisfaction

Human goals such as job satisfaction, recognition, and career advancement are influenced by many different kinds of social and psychological factors as well as by the organizational condition of the work environment. Consequently, because human goals are affected by so many more variables than are organizational objectives, they are far more complex to deal with and more difficult to satisfy.

Short-term solutions do not solve long-term human relations problems

The practices and relationships are not simple. The variety of causes of human relations problems leads inevitably to the conclusion that no one program or approach can create conditions for good human relations. Since so many different factors can be shown to cause trouble, many different kinds of programs are necessary to deal with different sets of problems. The work of the past several years has demonstrated conclusively that short-term solutions, no matter how popular they may be, do not solve complex human relations problems. Such problems demand carefully thought-out measures that must be given enough time in actual practice to prove or disprove their worth.

The study of human relations in the world of work is the study of practical attempts to achieve two separate goals: (1) greater productivity at work and (2) greater human satisfaction within the organization. (Figure 1-1). Patterns of behavior develop within groups of all kinds. For instance, parents and children interact in a special kind of group called the family; people jammed together at a football game are interacting in still another kind of human group. The focus of this book is on the *patterns of human behavior at work within organizations.*

THE INTERDISCIPLINARY ASPECT OF HUMAN RELATIONS

Human relations is an interdisciplinary field because the study of human behavior in an industrial or business setting must include the research of several social and physical sciences if it is to be coherent. The interdisciplinary approach requires an

FIGURE 1-1 Human relations is a study of how people can achieve satisfaction within an organization. Ed Wheeler/The Stock Market

understanding of the separate contributions made by other disciplines and then the integration of that information into a unified whole.

Psychologists and sociologists have contributed to human relations

For example, psychologists have done extensive research and experimentation on the relation of the individual to the work environment. They have conducted many valuable studies on job satisfaction, job placement, incentives, testing, training, counseling, and various other work-related areas. Sociologists, anthropologists, and social psychologists have made major contributions to human relations with their studies of group behavior and group dynamics. Their concepts of role behavior, status effects, and the influence of informal groupings have proved invaluable in understanding behavior in work environments. Political science has contributed useful information about the relationships between organizational structure, power struggles, and the processes of leadership, management, administration, and supervision.

These fields and others have added separate elements to our knowledge of human relations. Consequently, following a brief history of the human relations movement, we will consider aspects of communication, motivation, leadership, decision making, among others, keeping in mind that they are important not only in and of themselves but also as parts, or elements, of an integrated, interdisciplinary field of study.

A BRIEF HISTORY OF THE HUMAN RELATIONS MOVEMENT

Movement started after 1850

It is impossible to specify the exact date on which the human relations movement came into being, but it is fair to say that it was not until the second half of the nineteenth century that much attention was paid to workers' needs, nor was there much understanding of how those needs affect total productivity. Prior to that time, most managers and employers viewed the labor force as a commodity—to be bought and sold like any other commodity. Long hours, low wages, and miserable working conditions were the commonplace realities of the average worker's life. Labor unions were still struggling for existence and had not yet won the right to represent the labor force.

Scientific Management

Frederick Taylor developed the theory of scientific management

Then, at about the turn of the century, Frederick Taylor and other less famous but equally important figures introduced and developed the theory and practice of *scientific management*. This approach held that greater productivity could be achieved by breaking down work into isolated, specific, specialized tasks. Not too surprisingly, this theory became popular at approximately the same time that mass production became feasible, and it helped to pave the way for the assembly line.

Scientific management has often been described as a series of techniques for increasing production rates through the means of better cost accounting procedures, premium and incentive payments, time and motion studies, and so on. But Taylor himself lodged a vigorous protest against this interpretation. In his view, utilizing these techniques did not in itself constitute scientific management, because, as he put it, the main objective of scientific management was "to remove the causes for antagonism between the boss and the men who were under him."[1] Ironically, at times during his experimentation, Taylor achieved the opposite effect by creating antagonism, and conditions became so bad that it was necessary for Pinkerton guards to escort him home.

Taylor and followers like Frank and Lillian Gilbreth were criticized on the grounds that scientific management tended to exploit workers more than it benefited them. Early critics held that the theory emphasized control and discipline to the detriment of workers' morale. Critics said that scientific management paid no attention to the complex social networks created by workers within the work environment. These critics held that it was precisely those complex social networks that had the greatest influence on production rates.

A new view of scientific management

The new view of scientific management held that all workers were complex, unique beings whose individual skills and abilities could be measured, tested, and applied. The individual worker came to be seen as a combination of various traits, traits that could be measured accurately and improved by appropriate training. During this decade, many managers came to believe that testing could solve most if not all of the problems related to job selection, placement, and promotion.

Recently, "scientific" management has come under even further attack. Figure 1-2 is a revealing and slashing indictment of the concept.

A 1989 study by leaders at MIT also faults outdated strategies of mass production, parochialism, and neglect of human resources in U.S. manufacturing. They are very specific in faulting educational institutions for productivity problems:

Have Americans lost the work ethic? What has happened to the energy, mechanical genius, inventiveness, and willingness to work hard that drove American economic progress in the past? The idea that workers and managers are to blame for the trends in U.S. productivity is widespread today. Many

Konosuke Matsushita, founder of and executive advisor for Matsushita Electric Industrial Co. (Osaka, Japan), is certain that his country will win the manufacturing war. Not only that, but he thinks he knows just why that will be. "We will win and you will lose," he says. "You cannot do anything about it because your failure is an internal disease. Your companies are based on Taylor's principles. Worse, your heads are Taylorized too. You firmly believe that sound management means executives on one side and workers on the other, on one side men who think and on the other side men who can only work. For you, management is the art of smoothly transferring the executives' ideas to the workers' hands.

"We have passed the Taylor stage. We are aware that business has become terribly complex. Survival is very uncertain in an environment increasingly filled with risk, the unexpected, and competition. Therefore, a company must have the constant commitment of the minds of all of its employees to survive. For us, management is the entire work force's intellectual commitment at the service of the company . . . without self-imposed functional or class barriers.

"We have measured—better than you—the new technological and economic challenges. We know that the intelligence of a few technocrats—even very bright ones—has become totally inadequate to face these challenges. Only the intellects of all employees can permit a company to live with the ups and downs and the requirements of its new environment. Yes, we will win and you will lose. For you are not able to rid your minds of the obsolete Taylorisms that we never had."

FIGURE 1-2 "A Secret Is Shared". Source: "A Secret is Shared," *Manufacturing Engineering*, February 1988, p. 15.

people believe that America produces less well than the Japanese or the West Germans because American workers have become too affluent, lazy, and secure.

Our research on productivity and the quality of the work force suggests a very different explanation. We think the origins of the problem lie not in the disappearance or weakening of basic American values and capabilities but in the institutions that educate Americans for work. We have concluded that without major changes in the ways schools and firms train workers over the course of a lifetime, no amount of macroeconomic fine-tuning or technological innovation will be able to produce significantly improved economic performance and a rising standard of living.[2]

They suggest several imperatives for a more productive America:

1. Focus on new fundamentals of manufacturing.

   a. Put products and manufacturing processes ahead of finance.
   b. Establish new measures of productive performance.
   c. Focus on effective use of technology in manufacturing.
   d. Embrace product customization and production flexibility.
   e. Innovate in production processes.

2. Cultivate a new economic citizenship in the work force.

   a. Learn for work and at work.
   b. Increase employee breadth, responsibility, and involvement.
   c. Provide greater employment stability and new rewards.

3. Blend cooperation and individualism.

   a. Organize for both cooperation and individualism.
   b. Promote better intra- and interfirm relations.
   c. Expand partnerships.
   d. Strengthen cooperation between labor and management.

4. Learn to live in the world economy.

   a. Understand foreign languages, cultures, and practices.
   b. Shop internationally.
   c. Enhance distribution and service.
   d. Develop internationally conscious policies.

5. Provide for the future.

   a. Invest in basic education and technical literacy.
   b. Develop long-term business strategies.
   c. Establish policies that stimulate productive investment.
   d. Invest in infrastructure for productive performance.[3]

The Development of Unions

Membership in unions increased at the start of the twentieth century

At the same time that the new image of the worker was gaining popularity among employers, unions were becoming an increasingly powerful force in industrial affairs. During the years from 1897 to 1904, membership in trade unions grew from 400,000 to 2 million. And unions kept on growing. By 1920 trade unions throughout the nation had received a large measure of recognition from the owners and managers of industry.

Changes in management, unions, and testing pointed out workers' needs

Thus three separate developments—the emergence of scientific management techniques, the struggles of the trade unionists, and testing—all led to increased acceptance of the idea of the worker as a person with multiple needs. The same three developments also led large numbers of managers to reexamine their own image. They took a fresh look at themselves and began to question the wisdom of their traditional views of hard-line management and decision making. But it has taken 50 years or more for much of the new-found knowledge of human behavior to be recognized. Much of the good advice is still largely unheeded despite some excellent efforts in recent years such as Peters and Waterman's *In Search of Excellence* and Peters's *Thriving on Chaos*.

Elton Mayo's Hawthorne Experiment

Elton Mayo's famous Hawthorne experiment was the focus of human research

In the mid-1920s the focal point for the human relations approach in business and industry was the famous Hawthorne studies conducted by Elton Mayo and his colleagues. Mayo's group began its work by studying the effects of illumination, ventilation, and fatigue on the workers of the Hawthorne plant of Western Electric.

The greater the intensity of light, the greater the production—not necessarily

In one area of study, two groups of employees working under similar conditions and doing similar types of work were selected and output records were kept for each group. The intensity of the light under which one group worked was varied systematically; the light was held constant for the second group. The intensity of the light of the first group was increased. The general result was that the productivity of the group increased each time that the intensity of the light increased. This fact was anticipated. However, decreasing the intensity of the light under which employees worked also increased productivity. In fact, the productivity of the group continued to increase as the level of illumination was lowered and one of the highest levels of productivity was recorded during an extremely low level of illumination. Obviously some other variables were contaminating the effects of the experiment.

The employees themselves provided a clue to the changes in the output. They stated that it was easier to work faster because work in the test room was fun and there was little regular supervisory control. In effect, the employees were saying that their productivity increases were attributable to greater freedom and a feeling of importance.

Personal attention can affect production and morale

After a few years of experimentation, it became clear to the researchers that group morale and personal motivation factors were so important that they completely obscured the effects of the illumination, ventilation, and fatigue factors under investigation.

The Informal Organization

The informal group can have as much influence as the formal organization

The Hawthorne studies showed conclusively, by quantitative measurements, that normal interactions of workers at work *always* create a social network called the *informal organization*, which exerts tremendous influence over workers' behavior patterns. These particular studies also showed that the informal organization frequently countermanded official orders passed down through the formal organization and consequently played a determining role in setting production rates.

From that point on, it was no longer possible for management to view workers as mere economic tools or as isolated units in the production process. They had to be seen as complex human beings whose normal human interactions were bound to affect total production output, no matter how sophisticated the technological processes employed were. Mayo's findings developed the image of workers as whole persons, creatures of sentiment, whose basic human desires often resulted in complex outcomes, outcomes that cannot be predicted in a purely technological framework.

More Influences for Human Relations During Following Decades

Interest in human
relations decreased
during the Depression

Interest in human relations diminished in the 1930s during the early part of the Great Depression. With the passage of the Wagner Act in 1935 however, and the reemergence of militant unionism, business leaders turned again toward meeting workers' needs—particularly as those needs influenced total productivity. The industrial and business expansion during World War II and the prosperous postwar period stimulated and encouraged a deeper understanding of the relationship between productivity and worker satisfaction.

Countless studies were published by business theorists and social scientists. Three of the most important were Douglas McGregor's paper on traditional theory, which he called *Theory X,* as opposed to his humanistic approach to management called *Theory Y;* Abraham Maslow's studies on the hierarchy of human needs; and Frederick Herzberg's motivation-hygiene theory. All of these were milestones in human relations studies and still exert considerable influence.

New interest in human
relations reappeared in
1940 to 1970

Contributions to the fast-growing discipline increased greatly during the 1940s and 1950s. Studies were done by such psychologists as Carl Rogers and Kurt Lewin and sociologists Daniel Bell and C. Wright Mills. In the 1960s and 1970s, both by choice and necessity, corporate employers and managers in the developed nations came to value the importance of these theoretical and experimental contributions.

By the beginning of 1980, we were observing management theories and human relation concepts in other countries. *Theory Z,* originated by William Ouchi, focuses on Japan's work philosophy, which includes belief in lifetime employment, strong company loyalty, and group consensus.

Japan's loyalty, high productivity, group decision making, and efficient production has been based on long-term planning, not on short-term plans designed to head off a crisis. Theirs is not a business of "activity" but of commitment—commitment that is expected from, and given to, their employees, suppliers, and customers.[4]

Can Japanese workers
produce three times
more than U.S. workers?

Some business studies have stated that a steelworker in Japan can produce three times more steel than the same worker in Gary, Indiana. The "new American breed" wants to work, but not all that hard. If the job isn't satisfying, the worker is not motivated to do it well for the sake of his or her family's advancement. It is not surprising, therefore, to find a study that showed the average U.S. worker is productive only about 55 percent of the time. Any good business manager knows that productivity should be maintained at an 85 percent level for a fair return on the investment.

Lack of loyalty to a company is seen in the number of years that a person stays on the job, which has decreased steadily, indicating that there is unrest in the work force. Further, at times it seems that we live in an absenteeism culture. What does this culture cost us? Estimates are that absenteeism costs U.S. business over $40 billion a year.[5]

In contrast, some progressive firms in Japan, unable to convince their employees to go on vacation, have shut down factories for a week or two to force the workers to take a holiday. By comparison, it is little wonder that a steelworker in Japan may produce three times more product than his counterpart in the United States.

Note that how we treat our employees, customers, and others is no longer a management prerogative subject to unilateral or even a national decision. These human relations decisions affect us all. The actual decision-making process in Japan is less efficient than is that in the United States, but it produces a companywide consensus on the best course of action. Human relations has become a body of knowledge that no student of business or other organizations can afford to ignore.

Quality Circles—Not a Fad

Quality circles are voluntary groups of employees engaged in decision making at the lowest practical level of the organization. They show concern for the individual's life-style as well as problem solving in work-related areas. Quality circles have been in existence in the United States since the early 1970s and continue to be used extensively under various names.

Participation plans in Europe during 1970s

People want to be part of the solution. They want to use their minds. A good manager asks his or her staff, "How can we do this better?" and "How can we achieve this goal?" Workers are being asked to help make decisions about their jobs through a process often called *industrial democracy*, which is also leading to basic changes in the worker-boss relationships. During the 1970s, several European countries adopted laws mandating worker participation plans that ranged from worker representatives on corporate boards of directors to shop-floor workers' councils to help make daily decisions.

American workers just won't accept regimentation any more. A vice president of labor relations for the American Telephone & Telegraph Company stated, "We are going to have to give workers a piece of the action and stop treating them like children, or even worse, like machines with nothing to contribute to their jobs but their bodies."[6] Figure 1-3 is a poem from the auto workers' underground and illustrates the childlike approach of some American businesses.

Ford's "employee involvement"

The use of small problem-solving groups of workers at GM is typical of the revolutionary changes taking place between workers and managers across the nation. Now Ford, like GM, is fully committed to what Ford calls "employee involvement," with worker-management committees jointly considering decisions at every level of the corporation from the highest executive suite to the shop floor.

ORGANIZATIONAL VALUES

To turn around the long-term decline in America's productivity level requires implementation and adherence to a set of values, and the use of valid behavioral science principles in decision making and problem solving.[7]

Among the values and principles to be considered are:

- Business ethics
- Commitment

- Honesty/integrity
- Loyalty
- Mutual trust/mutual respect
- Courtesy
- Work/leisure attitudes
- Visionary leadership
- Action orientation
- Quality products and services

Business Ethics

Ethics in business may be defined as taking into consideration the effects of one's decisions on many publics—employees, customers, even competitors. Failure to consider these diverse publics results in unnecessary firings, reorganizations, and personal frustrations that stifle an organization. Professor Mark Pastin writes that "the ethics of a person or firm is simply *the most fundamental ground rules by which the person or firm acts.* Understanding these ground rules is the key to understanding how organizations function and to changing the way they function."[8]

Are these men and women
Workers of the world?
or is it an overgrown nursery
with children—goosing, slapping, boys
giggling, snotty girls?

What is it about that entrance way,
those gates to the plant? Is it the
guard, the showing of your badge—the smell?
is there some invisible eye
that pierces you through and
transforms your being? Some aura
or ether, that brain and spirit washes you
and commands, "For eight hours
you shall be different."
What is it that instantaneously makes
a child out of a man?
Moments before he was a father, a husband,
an owner of property,
a voter, a lover, an adult.

When he spoke at least some listened.
Salesmen courted his favor.
Insurance men appealed to his family responsibility
and by chance the church sought his help. . . .

But that was before he shuffled past the guard,
climbed the step,
hung up his coat and
took his place along the line.

FIGURE 1-3 The Immaturity of the American Management Approach. Source: Thomas J. Peters and Robert H. Waterman, Jr., *In Search of Excellence* (New York: Harper & Row, Pub., 1982). pp. 235–236.

Robert Waterman cites eight major attributes of corporate renewal. Those same eight factors may be applied to people in the renewing organizations:

1. Informed opportunism based on information and opportunity
2. Direction and empowerment within defined boundaries and delegated control
3. Familiar facts and congenial controls within existing contexts
4. External, different ideas from others (customers, competitors, etc.)
5. High value placed on teamwork and trust but inevitably politics and power are in the workplace
6. Stability, consistency, and norms within ever-changing conditions
7. Visible management backed by symbolic behavior and rules
8. Commitment to act toward a central purpose[9]

Waterman's renewal factors apply to people as well as organizations. In summary, what the attributes say for people to do is to be prepared for diverse opportunities through (1) both internal and external information; (2) seeking stability in our relationships in the form of teamwork and trust, adaptability, and flexibility; and (3) decisive and visible commitment to achieve goals.

Commitment

Honoring a commitment to one's job, word, and each other, including employees, employers, and customers, is another fundamental value to which we must return. Waterman's definition that "commitment results from management's ability to turn grand causes into small actions so that everyone can contribute to the central purpose" is a good one. Everyone is pulling for the same purpose regardless of how small the task may be or seem.

Honesty/Integrity

Fundamental principles such as "honesty is the best policy" and "giving a fair day's work for a fair day's pay" and the preeminence of truth are still worthwhile values that can help to strengthen our organizations. Even when the truth hurts, it is best in the long run to be open and honest with others in our human relationships. Failure to do so simply allows us to dig ourselves deeper into a hole—whether that be an employment or a personal relationship.

Loyalty

Employee loyalty is a two-way street. Who begins on the street is not as important as knowing that there is a reciprocal relationship. Management usually begins the relationship with an offer of employment but then may cease to honor its side of the contract, preferring instead to expect the employee to be eternally loyal. Many would argue that management loses considerable credibility and productivity with its employees because of this cavalier, take-the-employees-for-granted attitude.

William Werther writes that:

> Employee loyalty can do wonders for a company if it's channeled in the right direction. Yet, not only do executives perceive employee loyalty in their organizations as low, but they are not quite sure how to raise it. . . . For loyalty

at work to flow freely, however, it must begin somewhere. That place is senior management, whose members realize that the loyalty they earn for the organization reflects the loyalty the organization gives to its members.[10]

Employee loyalty means being aware, having the foresight to appreciate and involve employees, rewarding and being responsive to employee needs. Like the other values and principles discussed here, loyalty is fundamental to long-term success in an employer-employee relationship.

Mutual Trust/Mutual Respect

Like courtesy and loyalty, mutual trust and mutual respect are dominating factors in achieving the proper balance between employers and employees. But respect and trust go beyond courtesy and loyalty, which are by definition more related to customers. Respect and trust are the cornerstones of employees' relationships. Without them the relationships are destined to be short-lived—in spirit if not in time. Of course, mutual trust and respect like loyalty are appropriate in personal as well as organizational relationships. Our primary focus in this book, however, is determining how we can be more productive in our organizations.

Courtesy

Closely related to mutual respect is handling all publics—especially customers and coworkers—with courtesy. Courtesy goes beyond politeness or kindness. It means being civil to other people—customers, coworkers, subordinates, even the boss! Life is too short not to be courteous, not so short but that there is always time enough for courtesy.

Work/Leisure Attitudes

There is nothing wrong with the person who takes time off from his or her work to enjoy family, hobbies, and leisurely relaxation activities. In fact, the converse is true—there *is* something wrong with the workaholic who feels guilty about being "away from work." Many managers put in 60-hour work weeks and it may be hard for them to distinguish between working hard and workaholism.[11]

Visionary Leadership

We must continue to improve our visions for the future—and then act upon them; that's what leadership is all about. Organizations that do business as usual suffer in the long term. Tom Peters, Nancy Austin, and many others point out the importance of having that vision and leadership if we are to succeed. Organizations and individuals both need to know what their objectives and goals are. People need time to reflect—and plan. Organizations like Disney, Ford, IBM, McDonald's, Wal-Mart, among others, are where they are today because their founders and successive leaders had entrepreneurial spirit and vision, and demonstrated the leadership necessary to be successful.

Action Orientation

One could argue that inaction does less harm than some limited, albeit well-intentioned, action. But there are certainly cases where inaction has caused irreparable harm. The 1989 Exxon-Valdez fiasco on the part of the company, or the state and federal governments' inaction or inability to act rapidly enough, is a classic example of an inaction orientation.

There are many excellent examples of what the action orientation really means. They usually emphasize concepts such as "Try it, at least," "Ready! Fire! Aim!," "Do it now," and other quick-response mechanisms such as ad hoc teams.

Quality Products and Services

For retail and other types of business firms, courtesy and good manners increasingly mean good business. "It's a matter of survival. Customers are demanding quality service, and the business environment is extremely competitive. . . . Companies realize quality service is a significant way of doing business now."[12] Clearly, providing quality products and services is not just a matter of "being nice" to customers and employees. In fact, it means showing and acting upon real, substantial concern for employees and providing real, substantive service for customers.

All these values and principles have the following as common elements: goal accomplishment, that they are performed under highly competitive conditions, and with genuine concern for employees and customers. There is evidence that better managed employees provide better service to customers or constituents who are the ultimate purposes of being in business or a not-for-profit organization.

Despite significant progress in managing our organizations better, widespread realizations of the internationally competitive business environment and business failures suggest that there is still room for improvement. Professor Ricky Griffin writes that:

> The behavioral sciences have enormous potential to add to organizational effectiveness. Carefully managed interventions like quality circles have the potential to aid managers as they attempt to compete in both domestic and international arenas. The key to effectiveness may be to avoid a faddish, bandwagon approach and, instead, to develop an appropriate menu of interventions that we have some basis for recommending and some understanding of how to manage.[13]

RECURRENT THEMES IN HUMAN RELATIONS

There are many fundamentals of human relations that help define and can help reduce human relations problems. Foremost among these fundamentals are human dignity, empathy, individual differences, communications, motivation, leadership, responsible job behavior, and the whole person.

Human Dignity

The basic premise of all human relations is the dignity and worth of humans. People are not like other factors of production. *We are born, learn, love, live, retire, and die.* These activities form a challenging cycle for humans and especially for managers. Managers and employees must balance individual concerns in their private lives with the demands of their jobs. There are both personal and professional management responsibilities associated with each phase of the cycle.

Empathy

Empathy is the ability to put yourself in someone else's place and to understand that person's motives, point of view, needs, and reasons for their actions. Lack of empathy is a primary cause of conflict in organizations. Empathy is the chief quality that mediators of labor disputes must have, and successful salespersons are usually empathic to a very high degree. Empathy is an important element in leadership, and its absence can create insurmountable barriers to communication.

The theme of empathy, in the form of understanding and making allowances for other people's needs and desires, is *the* integrating and unifying theme of this book. It is stressed particularly in the chapter on interpersonal communication, and it is basic to the discussions in the chapters on creativity, unions, discrimination, and intercultural relations.

Individual Differences

The psychological concept of individual differences states that for any given variable, such as mental ability, there are marked differences among people. These differences have important impact on organizations in the selection of applicants for employment and in their motivation in various jobs. Individual differences need to be considered in three contexts: (1) differences among individuals in terms of job potential (e.g., abilities to learn a job), (2) the effects of training on individuals, and (3) differences in job performance after training. All are the concern of managers who are responsible for others' job performance.

Each person is different, but most are also the same in many ways, including the need for respect, recognition, socialization, and trust. It is the individual differences that really make the management of human relationships a challenge. Some people have more need for recognition; others want more respect.

According to Alvin Toffler's *The Third Wave,* people are more diverse now than ever before. These differences introduce the art as well as the scientific aspects of managing human relationships.

Communications

In modern organizations, all other functions depend on communication. It is the way in which information and understanding are transmitted, it unifies group behavior, and it provides the basis for group cooperation. Without effective communication procedures, no business can survive, much less prosper. If managers cannot communicate effectively with employees, neither can they motivate them nor exercise the functions of leadership. If workers cannot communicate well with management, neither can they perform their jobs properly nor receive adequate recognition for their work. If communication in an organization is not good, then there is no way in which the human relations in that organization can satisfy the people who work there.

Chapters 7 and 8 deal exclusively with communication principles and processes, first on the interpersonal, face-to-face level and then on the organizational plane. Chapter 7 presents a number of principles and communication behavior patterns, the mastery of which will lead to more effective communication behavior. Chapter 8 describes the interlocking relationships that exist between an organization's structural forms and its communication procedures. The importance of effective communication is implicit throughout this text.

Motivation

Although human relations is a vast and complicated subject composed of and influenced by many variables, it can be described simply as the total response of individuals to various motivating forces. In other words, people in organizations relate to each other in the ways that they do because they are driven by psychological, social, and economic forces that have the power to motivate them to behave in particular ways. The way in which people behave when they experience conflicting motives within and among themselves is a major source of organizational strife. It is well established that in most circumstances proper motivation on the part of leadership can increase overall productivity.

All performance is a function of motivation and ability. When someone's abilities and ambitions match the demands of a particular job, the job will be done well if the person has the motivation to do the job. If the demands of the job exceed a person's abilities or ambitions, the job will not be done well and personal frustration will result no matter how hard the individual tries. If the drives and abilities of the person far outdistance the job demands, he or she may experience boredom and the job may be done carelessly.

Chapter 3, "Human Motivation," introduces some of the theoretical and experimental approaches to motivation that have been influential in the human relations movement. As with communication, motivation is a pervasive theme in this book, most notably in the chapters on job performance and morale, change, status, appraisals, and creativity.

Leadership

In a very real sense, the history of the human relations movement is the history of leadership. A leader's fundamental responsibility in any kind of work organization is to get work done through the combined cooperative efforts of others.

A leader must communicate with and motivate his or her subordinates in a just and satisfactory manner or the work will not get done. The human relations function is not, of course, the only responsibility a leader must discharge. Planning, coordinating, and controling the organization's affairs from finances to work flow are equally, if not more, important. But good human relations with subordinates is necessary if leaders are to handle these other functions well.

Responsibility

The exercise of responsibility in a satisfactory and just manner is discussed from the managerial point of view in the chapters on job performance, leadership, change, and making decisions. The focus of the theme shifts to the worker's point of view in the chapter on morale. In "Personal Problems" (Chapter 5), the theme is expressed in terms of the reciprocal responsibilities that workers practice with each other to achieve good human relations. And, as with the themes of communication and motivation, the notion of responsibility underlies many of the concepts and practices discussed elsewhere in the text.

The Whole Person

As much as business might like to hire only a person's physical *or* mental skills, it must "take the bitter with the sweet" and employ the whole person. As much as a company might like to hire only Joe's brawn or Jill's brain, it gets both their brawn *and* brain, and all the infirmities associated with each. If something at home is bothering the employee, it might be desirable from the organization's viewpoint to have them leave that concern at home, but it is just not possible to separate people from their problems that easily. We bring with us our family problems, frustrations, and perhaps bad tempers. The whole person refers to the interrelationships of the mind and the body, and their total effect on the individual.

In a prophetic article, "More than Just a Paycheck," predicting workplace behavior for the remainder of this decade and the next century, Carol Clurman writes: "Essentially, employers are being forced to have a stake in the professional *and* personal well-being of their employees, realizing single parents and dual-income duos must be able to juggle things at home in order to hack it at work."[14] Pat Aburdene, coauthor of *Megatrends 2000,* with John Naisbitt, adds: "This most certainly is the new model of the corporate form that we will see created in the 1990s and into the 21st century."[15]

Constant Change

Leadership, management, and organizational human relationships are changing. No longer can organizations conduct business as usual. Peoples' economic, social, and psychological needs are changing. We will put these changes into perspective throughout the book.

In 1985, *Business Week* featured an article on the changing nature of American managers. It states:

> In the recent past, the American economy was run by a professional class of faceless managers willing to submerge their personalities in exchange for the safety and rewards of corporate bureaucracy. . . . [Today] the elite [of American business] strongly believes in leadership, personality and intuition. . . . rhetoric exalting individual initiative, teamwork and creativity pervade the corporate culture not only of Apple Computer but also of General Electric.[16]

Others extol the virtues of analysis, judgment, and problem-solving skills in an age of high technology. These are basic skills that all managers must have.

Express Your Opinion	Should all people: 1. Have human dignity? 2. Experience empathy? 3. Recognize individual differences? 4. Be motivated, led, and communicated within different ways? 5. Exercise responsibility within the constraints of the whole person concept?

WHAT IS REQUIRED TO ''RUN'' OUR ORGANIZATIONS?

One of the earlier quotations says that our economy is run by professional managers. How successful are they? What is really required of the people who run our organizations? Are they managers? leaders? caretakers? administrators? automatons?

Figure 1-4 shows a hierarchy of skills required to conduct operations within organizations. Notice that the top echelon must provide the greater part of organizational leadership but there is room for administrators and middle managers and supervisors to also provide leadership. Similarly, supervisors are charged primarily with running day-to-day operations, but the top leaders may also "get down and dirty" in their organizations by first hand involvement.

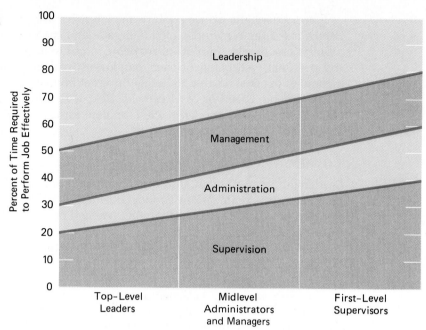

FIGURE 1-4 **Hierarchy of skills required to ``run'' organizations.**

MANAGEMENT SKILLS

Technical, human relations, and conceptual aspects

Management has three broad aspects: technical, human relations, and conceptual. The technical aspect is the easiest to understand. Most people obtain their jobs because of their ability to do certain tasks. Their first promotion may be based on how much they know about the department and the technical aspects related to their particular positions. However, as a person is promoted up the ranks, the technical aspects become less important, and the ability to work with people, and to handle abstract ideas becomes more important. Figure 1-5 illustrates the varying mix of these three types of abilities.

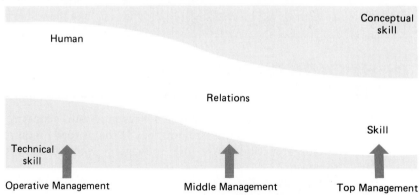

FIGURE 1-5 **Three skills are necessary in management. Technical skills are more important to the first-line supervisor. Conceptual skills are more important to the company president. Human relations skills are equally important to all levels.**

Human Relations Skills

The human relations aspect, or the ability to work well with people, will be important at any level, regardless of how many promotions one receives. More important at the upper levels is the conceptual skill—the ability to take many unrelated ideas and put them together to form new approaches to operating a department or a company. A company president spends time studying not only the firm's problems but also new laws, lobbying groups, the community reaction to the company, and, of course, the competition. Information on all these outside groups, as well as actions taking place inside the firm, is used by the president in deciding on the best direction for the company to travel. The president's direction may seem intuitive, but it is based on information and feelings developed over a broad base of input.

Technical Skills Versus Conceptual Skills

First-line bosses deal mostly with technical problems

In general, we see that, along with human relations problems, the important type of problem to the line supervisor is the technical one. A supervisor may deal with such contingencies as

1. Variations in the product or raw material
2. Shortages of raw materials
3. Breakdowns of machines
4. Shortages and variations of tools and equipment
5. Shortages of space

Top management deals with broad problems

Top management, on the other hand, might have to deal with more broadly conceptual problems, such as

1. Failure of a bank to grant a needed loan
2. Community objections to a new plant
3. Failure to receive a large sales contract that was expected
4. An unexpected wildcat strike

W. Edwards Deming, best known for his work that created a revolution in quality and economic production, postulated 14 principles for the transformation of management. Included in Deming's points are "drive out fear, so that everyone may work effectively for the company," "institute a vigorous program of education and self-improvement," and "break down the barriers between departments."[17]

HUMAN RELATIONS PROBLEMS

Human relations problems have many different causes. Five of the most common are:

Your talents

1. Every person brings a unique set of talents, ambitions, and work experience to a job. These personal attitudes change over time, often as a result of the degree of success or failure the person experiences in the work world. Matching so many unique sets of personal qualities to a standardized technology can create problems.

Company needs

2. The organizational aspects of a company, such as its size, geographic location, economic health, and degree of automation, define the scope of work and the activity in each work division. Frequent arbitrary structural definitions often cause difficulties in human relations.

Growth of technology

3. Innovations in technology and production methods generally require the restructuring of job roles and responsibilities. Radical changes in basic organizational structure can cause severe strains between workers and management and thus create intense problems in human relations.

Need for responsibility

4. Promotions of individuals to positions of greater responsibility and authority generally create a need for changed behavior patterns between the new supervisors and their former peers, which, in turn, can create human relations problems.

Young, inexperienced workers

5. Inexperienced or young workers may not be able to perform their roles or tasks in work groups in a competent manner. The time they require to adjust can not only create problems with production schedules but can also lead to particular kinds of human relations problems between them and their coworkers and supervisors.

TEST YOURSELF

Since human relations problems have many different causes and perspectives, it might be interesting to identify your feelings about these five causes. Then, it might be interesting to share them with members of your class. Listing your immediate feelings may help you to develop your own value clarifications as well as to determine your place in the working world.

1. Every person brings a unique set of talent, ambitions, and experience to a job. What three outstanding things do you feel that you can bring to a job?

   a. _____

   b. _____

   c. _____

2. With regard to the organizational aspects of a company,

   a. In what size company would you like to work? (1) 10–50 employees (2) 50–150 employees (3) over 150

   b. Where would you like your company located? (1) locally (2) within 100 miles of home (3) anywhere in the United States (4) outside the United States

3. Do you enjoy changes at work?

   a. Look forward to change.

   b. Occasionally enjoy changes.

   c. Seldom like to see change.

   d. Change makes it difficult to get the work done.

4. Promotions mean greater responsibility and authority. In my next job I would like to see a promotion

   a. In three months.

   b. In six months.

   c. In one year.

   d. When I deserve it.

5. One way to handle untrained and inexperienced workers is to

   a. Have training classes frequently for new employees.

b. Hire only experienced employees.

c. Have a trainee work with you to learn the trade.

Your ideas may change in a few months or remain the same. In any case, if you compare your answers with others and share your feelings about your answers, you may clarify some of your attitudes about work and discover some of your expectations of a career.

Summary

The study of human relations begins with you. Human relations refers to all the interactions that can occur among people, including organizational and personal, conflicting or cooperative relationships. How you and others interact determines the quality of your work and personal lives.

The history of human relations is colorful because of the ironies and personalities of individuals involved. Frederick Taylor, the father of scientific management, and his followers were responsible for structuring management and allowing it to be studied as a science. Surprisingly, he antagonized many of the people he was trying to help. And now, there is a backlash against scientific management. Elton Mayo, one of the principals responsible for the Hawthorne experiment, learned that the social aspects of the job were as important, if not more so, than the technical aspects. Unions play an important part in pointing out the inadequacies of management efforts.

An interdisciplinary approach to human relations is required because of the tasks of integrating diverse knowledge from different disciplines. No science can explain all of the complex interrelationships of human behavior. There is also an art to the management of human relationships because of the diversity and differences among people.

All of the changes that have been taking place in management and employee human relations have been accelerated in recent years. We continue to learn more about motivation, job performance, communications, leadership, and labor relations, among others. A major contributing factor to this knowledge has been the importance of intercultural relations and what we have learned about management from the Japanese and others. All these subjects are to be covered in subsequent chapters.

Organizational values worthy of our attention include business ethics, commitment, integrity, loyalty, mutual trust and respect, visionary leadership, and action orientation, among many others. These values and their implementation are fundamental to our successful transformation out of a productivity decline.

Fundamental concepts of human relations include the concepts of human dignity, empathy, individual differences, communications, motivation, leadership, and responsibility. How we relate to one another as human beings, how we put ourselves in others' places, and how we recognize individual needs make the management of human relations truly challenging.

People are hired primarily because of their technical and human relations skills. As a person is promoted to higher levels of management, the conceptual ability to handle abstract ideas becomes more important. Human relations skills are equally applicable to all levels of work and life. There is currently a deemphasis of the administrative/caretaker role, giving way to the catalytic leadership role.

There are major opportunities available today. We are more diverse as a culture than ever before and that creates both opportunities and challenges. Managing in this dynamic environment will be fun. Enjoy it and your life!

Case Study 1

You, Human Relations, and This Book

Of the basic themes mentioned in this chapter, which one do you feel most adept at performing? (1) Do you feel that you can communicate your ideas, feelings, and thoughts to others best? (2) Or do you feel that you are best at giving "pep talks," encouraging people to pursue their personal goals, and have a strong sense of direction and goal in life? (3) Or perhaps responsibility and the desire for leadership are some of your strongest characteristics? Do you feel that you could, with a little time, lead a group of five students in a group discussion? (4) Finally, is the ability to empathize one of your assets? Do you feel that you really know how others feel and can place "yourself in their shoes"? Do people come to you for counsel and help on personal matters?

It is always exciting to see how you feel about the attitudes you expressed at the beginning of a course. At the end of the course look back and see if your feelings about certain ideas on life have changed. These questions will be hard to answer, but put the first ideas that come to mind down on paper. This will be a study of value clarifications that will have you thinking about these questions long after you have answered them.

1 & 2. Which are your *strongest and weakest areas* in the human relations discipline?
   a. Ability to communicate _____
   b. Ability to motivate yourself and others _____
   c. Ability to accept responsibility and lead others _____
   d. Ability to empathize with others and understand their problems _____
   e. Loyalty _____
   f. Courtesy _____
   g. Commitment to task _____
   h. Commitment to people (boss, coworkers, customers, subordinates, etc.)
   _____

3. Which is more important, "team spirit" or individual achievement? _____
   _____

4. Is today's fun more important than future accomplishments? _____

5. What do you regard as your greatest personal achievement to date? _____

6. What do you regard as your greatest personal failure to date? _____

7. What two things would you most like to be said of you if you died today?

The Aerobics Instructor

Jill Greenwood is the head aerobics instructor for the HealthCare Club. Jill and several other instructors conduct both high- and low-impact aerobics classes for men and women of different age groups. Jill recognizes that there are differences in the abilities of the various groups and even differences within the groups.

All the participants have a different "agenda" or reason for attending the aerobics classes: most primarily want to attain and maintain a level of physical fitness; others enjoy a socialization process within the classes. Within any given class, some individuals desire autonomy—to be left alone—to perform their exercises; others want continual praise, recognition, and feedback; still others increase their self-esteem.

Similarly, Jill finds that all the instructors are different in their abilities to communicate with, motivate, and lead their classes. Jill wants to know how to help her instructors better meet the needs of the participants.

One of the instructors working with high-impact groups is Fred Billingsley. Fred likes to get the group "pumped up" and energized. He is a dynamic performer. The people in his class expect a tough workout, but they also expect a fun, entertaining time and they don't want to have to think. Fred attracts such a large following that it is difficult for him to pay attention to newcomers' and other individuals' aerobic needs.

Another instructor who desires recognition from her classes is Jan Grossman. Sometimes Jan has a great class, but other times it is a drag. Jan feeds off the mood of the class; if they are down, she is down. She takes her cues from the class instead of the other way around. Jan is not as confident in her own aerobic and leadership skills as she would like to be.

Jack Helmsley is very popular with students, but he is not keeping abreast of changes in the fitness industry. Some of his biomechanical moves are not as safe as they should be. HealthCare offers quarterly in-house training opportunities at no cost to all its aerobics instructors, but Jack very seldom takes advantage of the training.

1. What can Jill do to help her instructors better meet the needs of the participants?

2. Would you recommend training? If so, what specifically would you include in the training and how long would you recommend the training last? How would you structure any training?

3. Empathize with Jill—put yourself in her place—and try to communicate with Fred, Jan, and others in helping them perform their jobs better.

Terms and Concepts

company objectives the objectives listed most often are profit, production, and growth. Employee satisfaction may be listed for some companies' major objectives.

empathy the ability to put yourself in someone else's place and to understand that person's motives and point of view.

Hawthorne study a study conducted by Elton Mayo in the 1920s to see if workers could produce more if more lighting was used. The workers produced more when there was more light *and* less light. The reason that the workers produced more had nothing to do with the environment but everything to do with the attention they were receiving.

human goals in the business sense, goals that relate to job satisfaction, recognition, and career advancement. Pay is not always on the top of the list.

human relations the interaction among people, both in terms of conflict and cooperation. Good human relations exist when people work together in groups to achieve a common goal. Cooperation is needed to achieve individual and company goals.

individual differences the unique emotional, physical, and social qualities about each individual human being.

quality life circles the concern for the individual's life-style and the development of group decision making at the lowest level.

scientific management a method of breaking down a job into individual steps to see if there are easier ways of performing each task.

values fundamental guides that direct individuals and organizations in the conduct of activities (e.g., ethics, commitment, honesty/integrity).

whole person the interrelationships of the mind and the body and their total effect on the individual.

Notes

1. Frederick Taylor, *Scientific Management* (New York: Harper, 1947), pp. 128–129.
2. Michael L. Dertouzos et al., *Made in America: Regaining the Productive Edge* (Cambridge, Mass.: The MIT Press, 1989), p. 81.
3. Ibid., pp. 132–146.
4. Peter F. Drucker, "Business in Japan Isn't Just 'Done'," *The Wall Street Journal*, July 18, 1985, p. 22.
5. "Expensive Absenteeism," *The Wall Street Journal*, July 29, 1986, p. 1.
6. Harry Bernstein, "Democracy Moves Into the Workplace," *Los Angeles Times*, October 23, 1980, pp. 1, 14, 15, 16.
7. Robert R. Blake and Jane S. Mouton, "Increasing Productivity Through Behavioral Science," *Personnel*, May–June 1981, p. 59.
8. Mark Pastin, *The Hard Problems of Management: Gaining the Ethics Edge* (San Francisco: Jossey-Bass, 1986), p. xii.
9. "How the Best Get Better," *Business Week*, September 14, 1987, p. 99.
10. William B. Werther, Jr., "Loyalty at Work," *Harvard Business Review*, March–April 1988, pp. 28, 35.
11. "Detecting the Signs of Workaholic Behavior," *The Wall Street Journal*, August 31, 1989, p. B1.
12. "The New Etiquette: Be Nice for the '90s," *USA Weekend*, June 16–18, 1989, p. 12.
13. Ricky W. Griffin, "Consequences of Quality Circles in an Industrial Setting: A Longitudinal Assessment," *Academy of Management Journal*, June 1988, pp. 356–357.
14. Carol Clurman, "More than Just a Paycheck," *USA Weekend*, January 19–21, 1990, p. 4.
15. Ibid.
16. "The New Corporate Elite," *Business Week*, January 21, 1985, pp. 65, 69–70.
17. W. Edwards Deming, *Out of the Crisis* (Cambridge, Massachusetts Institute of Technology, 1986), pp. 23–24.

Recommended Reading

Bahrami, Bahman. "Productivity Improvement Through Cooperation of Employees and Employers," *Labor Law Journal*, March 1988, pp. 167–178.

Blanchard, Kenneth H., and Norman Vincent Peale. *The Power of Ethical Management.* New York: William A. Morrow, 1988.

Cohen, Allan R., and David L. Bradford. *Influence Without Authority.* New York: John Wiley, 1990.

Deming, W. Edwards. *Out of the Crisis.* Cambridge, Mass.: Massachusetts Institute of Technology, Center for Advanced Engineering Study, 1986.

Dertouzos, Michael, et al. *Made in America: Regaining the Productive Edge.* Cambridge, Mass.: The MIT Press, 1989.

Drucker, Peter. *The New Realities: In Government and Politics/In Economics and Business/In Society and*

World View. New York: Harper & Row, 1989.

Francis, Dave, and Mike Woodcock. *Unblocking Organizational Values.* Glenview, Ill.: Scott, Foresman, 1990.

Hoerr, John P. *And the Wolf Finally Came: The Decline of the American Steel Industry,* Pittsburgh: University of Pittsburgh Press, 1988.

Korn, Lester. *The Success Profile: A Leading Headhunter Tells You How to Get to the Top.* New York: Simon & Schuster, 1988.

Naisbitt, John, and Pat Aburdene. *Megatrends 2000.* New York: William A. Morrow, 1990.

Pastin, Mark. *The Hard Problems of Management: Gaining the Ethics Edge.* San Francisco: Jossey-Bass, 1986.

Peters, Tom. *Thriving on Chaos: Handbook for a Management Revolution.* New York: Alfred A. Knopf, 1988.

2

Personal and Career Development

After studying this chapter, you should be able to:

1. Describe the differences between Type A, H, and B behaviors.
2. Distinguish between anger and stress.
3. List at least four ways to manage stress.
4. Set time priorities consistent with goals.
5. Use various tools and techniques of time control.
6. Improve work habits including reading, paperwork, telephone, and workplace habits.
7. Discuss the stages in career development and career advancement.
8. Develop your own personal action plans.
9. Define "success" in your own terms.

TO START YOU THINKING . . .

Here are a few questions that you might want to think about before starting to read this chapter. In fact, these questions need to be answered before you can make a meaningful career. Talk with classmates and others about your answers.

- Is stress good or bad? What types of stress are good? What types are bad?
- What role does stress play in personal development?
- What role does time play in your personal development?
- How can you better manage your time? Who manages your time—you or others?
- Whose responsibility is career development?
- What do you want to be doing five years from now? ten? twenty?
- How many times do you anticipate changing jobs before then?
- How do you measure success?

PLANS FOR PERSONAL DEVELOPMENT

Introducing the concepts of career and other types of personal development early in this book helps to put the rest of the book in perspective. How we meet individual, group, and organizational challenges and adapt to change and different cultures can be personally rewarding.

Work—purposeful activity—is as natural as other life relationships. People thrive on things they do well, and work can be one of those things. The virtue of work is fulfilling one's purpose by activity. To make work and life truly rewarding, it is necessary to have personal development and career plans. Certainly those plans will change as you develop. Having a goal and charted course of action enables planning for all of the other human relations opportunities that arise in life.

STRESS AND TENSION

Among the factors impacting one's personal development is stress. Not all stress is bad. Positive stress and tension, in large part, create and play major roles in personal development. Stress and tension also help us learn how to cope with multiple demands and develop our personal skills.

Stress means pressure, strain, or force on a system. Human stress includes physical and psychological stress. Too much of either can lead to fatigue or damage of the affected system.

Eustress

According to Hans Selye, an expert on stress, there are two types of stress. *Eustress* is the positive type that has its foundations in meeting the challenges of a task or job. This type of stress manifests itself in achievement and accomplishment. The effects of eustress are beneficial in that they help us to overcome obstacles.

Distress

Distress is negative in that it allows us to be overpowered. Anger, loss of control, and feelings of inadequacy and insecurity are all manifestations of distress. We teeter on the edge of collapse because of these phenomena. If not restrained, serious physical and psychological health problems may result.

Stress and tension are natural. We need them to do our best work. We need them to get the adrenalin flowing. And so we cannot hope to, nor would we want to, eliminate all excitement and accompanying stress from our jobs.

Most stress is created by the person, not the job

Too much stress and tension on or off the job, however, can have a negative effect. In most cases the person, not the job, creates the tension. Many causes of stress originate off the job and only disrupt it.

Holistic Health

Holistic health

One means of controlling stress and tension is through the practice of holistic health, a comprehensive method of controlling stress and tension that deals with the complete life-style of the individual. It incorporates simultaneous interventions at several levels—physical, psychological, and social.

Negative stressors result in lower and poorer production, difficult relationships with other workers, inadequate attention and concentration, memory lapses, tardiness, and absenteeism. About 80 percent of the emotional problems of employees are of this nature; yet the good supervisor must be prepared to help with problems no matter what their cause.

Promotions frequently add stress

A promotion frequently will create added stress that can ruin a person's work and spill over into his or her home life. Some persons welcome and thrive on heavy stress and pressure at work. Some recognize when they have had enough and refuse an advancement—which often confounds people in management. Most people want the promotion, but don't want the added headaches, stresses, and responsibilities that accompany it.

Types A, H, and B Behavior

Type A is impatient, goal oriented

Different types of people are predisposed to different medical problems when under stress. Their different behavior can to some degree be cataloged. Some *Type A* persons are highly competitive, feel the pressure for time, and may react to frustration with hostility. For example, the Type A person is likely to set deadlines or quotas for himself or herself at work or at home at least once a week. The Type A person frequently brings work home. Such a person is highly achievement oriented and pushes himself or herself to near capacity. Hard-driving Type A students earn more academic honors than do their peers.

Type H stands for hostility

Some Type A persons are at more health risk than other Type A's. Recent research has shown that it is not being a hard worker that puts a person at high risk of having a heart attack. It is being an angry and hostile hard worker.[1] Type H is a subset of Type A behavior. The H refers to hostility, and some Type A people show a lot of hostility. Recent studies show that hostility alone is a risk factor for heart disease.

Doctor Redford Williams, a Duke University psychiatrist, told an American Heart Association forum that they could now state with some confidence that of all the aspects originally associated with the Type A personality, only those traits related to hostility and anger really contribute to coronary disease. The heartbeat is much quicker to slow down after mental stress in the Type B person than in the hostile Type A.[2]

Type B enjoys leisure activities

Type B persons put their time in at work and seldom bring work home. They are more inclined to have interests in sports or leisure activities. Time is not a master, and proving their worth to themselves or to others is not a strong requirement of their personalities. They can be as intelligent as Type A, but they don't work hard to prove it. Type B persons are less likely to demand strong control of their lives and environments. Sometimes it is fashionable just to be "busy" for busyness sake. Other times, people play the one-up-manship game of "I'm busier than you are."[3] Many of those people are benign (and unproductive!) Type A's.

TEST YOURSELF

Are You a Type H? Measure Your Hostility

1. Do you think you have to yell at subordinates so they don't mess up? _____
2. Do you assume cashiers will shortchange you if they can? _____
3. If your child spills milk, do you immediately yell? _____
4. After an irritating encounter, do you feel shaky or breathless? _____
5. Do you feel your anger is justified? Do you feel an urge to punish people? _____
6. Do you get angry every time you stand in line? get behind the wheel? _____

"Yes" answers show you're Type H, but check here to see how far it's progressed (a "Yes" to question 6 shows highest level of hostility; to question 1 the lowest):

- A "Yes" to questions 1 or 2 indicates cynical mistrust—that you expect the worst from people and take it personally.
- A "Yes" to question 3 shows that you're expressing anger—whether your responses are automatic or slightly disguised.
- A "Yes" to question 4 shows that your body is experiencing the effects of hostility.
- A "Yes" to question 5 indicates reactions that are aggressively hostile.
- A "Yes" to question 6 means that hostility has become a habit.[4]

Workaholics: Fortune's Favorite Children

Since the mid-1970s, thousands of articles have been written about the workaholic, stressing that there must be ways to slow down and become a Type B person. Recently, the emphasis has moved away from trying to change basic personality traits to modifying behavior. Hans Selye, an expert in the field, has said that a race horse cannot become a snail; the best it can become is a slow trotter. It is usually part of the person's makeup and is difficult to change—the trait is even noticed in childhood. Workaholics enjoy their work; it is not a sacrifice or an imposition. What sets them apart is their attitude toward work, not the number of hours they work. Work is the dominant role in life, and the mate and family may seem to suffer; inactivity is intolerable and having free time means boredom. Even vacations are hard to take.

Workaholism in all probability is permanent and can only be modified. Yet as Winston Churchill stated, "Those whose work and pleasures are one are fortune's favorite children." But at times, workaholism can become a problem for individuals and organizations. Fig. 2-1 shows some of the symptoms and tips on coping with workaholism.

Make Tension Work for You

Don't fight tension

Don't fight tension—use it. Built-up tensions can cause grave trouble, and telling ourselves not to be tense rarely works. There are not always times when we can remove the source of our tensions. However, when you are tense, you are temporarily more energetic, alert, and aggressive. Start doing a job you have been putting off for a long time or one that seems to be a tremendous task. You will

---

Symptoms
- Rigid, inflexible, narrow, and overfocused in their thinking.
- Need to be in control and often engage in ritualistic behavior.
- Unable to delegate work; overly concerned about details.
- Can't say no; poor at setting priorities.
- Intolerant, impatient, and demanding of others, poor personal relationships.
- Not team players, uncooperative.
- Can't handle criticism; need constant approval of work.
- Can't rest or relax; constant feelings of inadequacy, guilt, and loneliness.

Tips
- Focus on results, not hours at the workplace; manage by objective.
- Restructure jobs that carry too much responsibility.
- Find a steady pace at work; create challenges that don't involve crises.
- Don't deliberate over minor decisions; use time wisely.
- Learn to delegate tasks and do so without interfering.
- Schedule time away from the office or workplace.
- Develop friends and relationships outside of work.
- Determine what you are avoiding by overworking.
- Do not take work home and avoid thinking about work at home.[5]

FIGURE 2-1 **How to Detect and Treat Workaholism.**

enjoy the feeling of accomplishment that such drive can give; your tension will ease and perhaps even disappear.

Tackle one thing at a time

Tackle one thing at a time. Anxiety gives us a restless dissatisfaction with ourselves when we attempt to do too many things at once. For example, you find that you are not as successful at work as you would like so you decide to go to night school to work on your degree. You barely get started and you are asked to join a civic club that would provide some good contacts. You wish you had more money to buy better clothes, and you think of moonlighting to buy a new wardrobe. If you suffer persistent anxiety by starting things, dropping them, and becoming hopelessly distracted, then tackle one thing at a time. Stick with it until you have done all you can do about it.

Laugh at yourself

Finally, laugh at yourself on occasion. The way to tell whether you are leaning too heavily toward role playing or pretense is to ask yourself, "When was the last time I had a good belly laugh at my own expense?"

THE COST OF STRESS

Stress can be expensive for the employer

Stress is more than a matter of emotional problems and personality conflicts: it is a problem affecting the corporate balance sheet. Stress-related diseases such as ulcers, stroke, heart attack, alcoholism, drug addiction, and social breakdowns can also lead to low productivity, absenteeism, hospitalization, and premature death.

Several corporate programs are designed to take stress out of the job, or at least to minimize distress and reduce costs. Texas Instruments and John Hancock Mutual Life Insurance companies hold sessions that teach relaxation and coping skills. Several companies have built gyms and wellness centers. PepsiCo provides worker incentives that include rebates on fees for programs for losing weight and keeping it off. Adolph Coors Company holds stress classes, including one on the stress of child rearing.

How to Cope with Stress

A person undergoing stress feels "keyed up." Stress is usually accompanied by feelings of arousal or agitation. The problem is that when such arousal occurs, thoughts and action become more primitive. As people become more and more agitated, their thoughts become more simplistic; they notice less in the environment, revert to older habits, and all complicated responses in their repertoire disappear.

When it is said that a piece of metal is "stressed," it means that the stationary metal is acted upon. Strain is the result of this stress. Notice that stress occurs when something external has been applied. The implication for us is that if an individual sees himself or herself as passive and his or her fate as being controlled by others, that person is more susceptible to stress in the form of unplanned external events. On the other hand, a person whose self-concept is more active is less susceptible to stress.

TEST YOURSELF

Answer the following questions "Yes" or "No" to see how much stress you are undergoing. (Answers are evaluated on page 51.)

1. Do you worry about the future? _____

2. Do you sometimes have trouble falling asleep? _____

3. Do you often reach for a cigarette, a drink, or a tranquilizer? _____

4. Do you become irritated over everyday matters? _____

5. Do you have less energy than you seem to need or would like to have? _____

6. Do you have too many things to do and not enough time to do them? _____

7. Do you have headaches or stomach problems? _____

8. Are you very concerned about being either well liked or successful? _____

9. Do you perform well enough in life to satisfy yourself? _____

10. Do you get satisfaction from the small joys or simple pleasures of life? _____

11. Are you able to relax and really have fun? _____

Situations are not inherently stressful

We have to get away from the assumption that a situation is inherently stressful or nonstressful. We are the ones who put the labels there. We can also remove them. The feeling is often that stress will go on forever. It is not the stress itself that is painful and disabling but the impression that it will never end. It is this erroneous projection of a feeling, rather than the pain itself, that reduces the executive's ability to cope.

"Writer's block"

Suppose that you're trying to write a five-year plan for your department and you get stalled. You experience what some people would call a "writer's block." One way in which to handle that block is to imagine that it is now six years later. Then write yourself a letter from your boss congratulating you in great detail on how well your five-year plan worked. Be as specific as possible in the congratulatory letter. Although you are writing a letter for a set of activities that has not yet occurred, you may clarify things that you want to accomplish in those five years.

People like to control their own fate

People like to see themselves as able to control their own fate. A primary contributor to stress is the feeling of "losing control." The painfulness of the subsequent stress may result not from the actual fact of losing control, but from the individual's unwillingness to admit that he or she is capable of losing control.

If people can accept both their strengths and their weaknesses, they can control stress. If they regard themselves as persons who are capable of controlling events, even while recognizing that there are occasions when they cannot, then they will be in a much better position to manage stress. If they are unable to adapt, a physical or mental breakdown may result.

Anger and Stress

Anger may be a manifestation of stress. But it is not a productive result. All jobs have or maybe should have an element of at least positive stress. Anger and loss of control because of the stress can have fatal consequences.

Two psychology professors advise that "controlling your emotions at the office is an important skill new graduates should master. . . . Anger is an important emotion on the job. It signals that something is wrong, and it's often a sign of faulty communications. Anger doesn't always have negative consequences for the parties involved.[6] Plas and Hoover-Dempsey advocate that everyone should plan in advance how to react to negative feedback.

> Learning to understand your emotions and coping with them when problems arise can make a tremendous difference in how you are perceived by others. . . .

Whenever anger flares at work, remember that good communication often makes hostility disappear. So even if a conversation is interrupted, make sure you get back to it. When you can effectively replace anger with good communication, you've learned one of the hardest but most important lessons of building effective interoffice relationships.[7]

Stress and Illness

Watch for "overloading the human system"

Alvin Toffler popularized in *Future Shock* the phrase *overloading the human system.* He defines it as "the distress, both physical and psychological, that arises from the overload of the human organism's physical adaptive systems and its decision-making processes."[8]

"Life charts"

This idea has been around for many years. Adolf Meyer, professor of psychiatry at Johns Hopkins, recognized this idea around the turn of the century and began keeping "life charts" of his patients. Dr. Thomas Holmes began to apply Dr. Meyer's life chart to case histories of more than 5,000 patients.[9] The items listed in Table 2-1 show some of the changes in life styles that are socially desirable and some that are undesirable. We are all aware of the drain on energy and resources associated with such stressful events as divorce, troubles with the boss, and death of a spouse.

The numbers in the right-hand column represent the amount, duration, and severity of change required to cope with each item, averaged from the responses of

How to Survive Stress	Here is a seven-step survival plan. Remember to PLEASE yourself to a "T."
P	*Plan.* Disorganization can breed stress. Having too many projects going on simultaneously often leads to confusion and forgetfulness when uncompleted projects are hanging over your head. When possible, take on projects one at a time and work on them until completed.
L	*Learn to tolerate.* Many of us set unreasonable goals, and, since we can never be perfect, we often have a sense of failure no matter how well we perform. So set reasonable goals for yourself.
E	*Enjoy life.* You need to escape occasionally from the pressures of life and have fun. Find activities that are absorbing and enjoyable no matter what your level of ability or skill at doing them.
A	*Assert positive attitudes.* Learn to praise the things you like in others. Focus upon the good qualities that those around you possess.
S	*Set tolerance limits.* Intolerance of others leads to frustration and anger. An attempt to really understand the way other people feel can make you more accepting of them.
E	*Exercise.* First, check with your doctor before beginning any exercise program. Then, select an exercise program you will enjoy. You will be more likely to stay with a program you yourself chose, especially if you pick one that you really enjoy rather than one that is drudgery.
T	*Talk out tensions.* Find a friend, a member of the clergy, a counselor, or a psychologist with whom you can be open. Expressing your bottled-up tension to a sympathetic ear can be incredibly helpful in relieving it. Even if no solutions are reached, you may feel better about addressing your problems after releasing these tensions.

TABLE 2-1 The Social
Readjustment Rating Scale

LIFE EVENT	MEAN VALUE
Death of a spouse	100
Divorce	73
Jail term	63
Death of close family member	63
Personal injury or illness	53
Marriage	50
Fired at work	47
Retirement	45
Pregnancy	40
Sex difficulties	39
Gain of new family member	39
Son or daughter leaving home	29
Wife begins or stops work	26
Change in living conditions	25
Change in sleeping habits	16
Vacation	13
Christmas	12
Minor violation of the law	11

See T. H. Holmes and R. H. Rahe, "The Social
Readjustment Rating Scale," *Journal of
Psychosomatic Research,* Vol. 11 (1967), pp.
213–218.

hundreds of people. The more changes you undergo in a given period of time, the more points you accumulate. The higher the score, the more likely you are to have a health change of one kind or another; for example, a serious illness, possible physical injuries, surgical operations, psychiatric disorders. And the higher your score, the more serious the health change will likely be.

A recently recognized syndrome related to stress is job burnout, which follows a period of self-induced stress. Individuals in the counseling occupations such as lawyers, nurses, teachers, and mental health professionals are especially prone to burnout. As we increase the number of professional workers in counseling occupations, the opportunities for burnout will increase. Recognizing the symptoms, phases, and methods of overcoming burnout will help reduce its impact.

TIME MANAGEMENT

Another potentially positive and negative stressor is time. Time can be a positive stressor if *we* manage *it*, rather than letting it manage us. But if we become constantly rushed for time, always having to take our work home with us and working all of the time, then time becomes a negative stressor.

How we manage our time is also a major determinant of our personal development. All of us have the same amount of time in any given day. What we do with that time can determine our priorities, our future opportunities, our career options, and can help determine how successful we are.

Symptoms of Burnout (Beyond Stress)	1. Chronic fatigue and low energy.
	2. Irritability and negative attitude.
	3. Idealistic, inflexible, and indecisive viewpoints.

Four Phases of Burnout	1. Emotional exhaustion.
	2. Cynicism and defensiveness.
	3. Isolation, tendency to eat alone and act antisocial.
	4. Defeatism, feeling of having been unsuccessful with all job effort having been fruitless.

How to Overcome Burnout	1. List priorities. Schedule yourself to do less.
	2. Make goals that are achievable.
	3. Compartmentalize by focusing on one job at a time.
	4. Make changes in your job routine. Even schedule fun times.
	5. Listen to your body. Your listless feeling may indicate you need more exercise, a better diet, or more sleep.
	6. Develop a detached concern. Be concerned with your clients, but don't make them your problems. Build support groups by having contacts with people outside of work.

We All Have the Same Amount of Time

Keep a "to do" list

It makes good business sense to keep a calendar of appointments and a "to do" list. There will be a big payoff for a small amount of time spent each morning or evening in planning for the upcoming day. In addition to this planning time, we all need some "quiet" time during the day to get organized, to set priorities, and to think.

Some people's internal clocks and habits allow them to do their planning and organizing early in the morning; others prefer late evening. Regardless, we all have the same amount of time per day and planning it can help us maximize its use.

If you have difficulty losing or keeping track of time, it might be helpful to keep a detailed sample log of your time for a week or two. Only a time fanatic would keep this kind of detailed time log more than a week or two during a year. To see how you are doing, record your time in 10- or 15-minute intervals and, then, at the end of the week categorize and tabulate how you spent your time. (See Figure 2-2.)

Some experts advocate keeping a perpetual daily log. Paul Hawken, cofounder of Smith and Hawken, and author of *Growing a Business,* says "The best time to start keeping a daily log is when you first launch your company.

"Unfortunately, most people don't do that. Instead, they delegate the task to experts—and wind up hopelessly out of touch with their business."[10]

Another expert also advocates the use of a daily log to quit wasting time on telephone calls. Larry Baker, president of Time Management Center, Inc., of St. Louis, suggests keeping track of a week's worth of incoming calls, then going over the calls and classifying them so the secretary sees the principles behind the decision he or she has to make. Baker uses four basic classifications: calls that need

DAY OF THE WEEK _____   **DATE** _____

Time*	Activity	Interruptions:
6:00 A.M.		
6:10		
6:20		
6:30		
6:40		
6:50		
7:00		
7:10		
7:20		
{		
5:10 P.M.		
5:20		
5:30		
5:40		
5:50		
6:00		
{		
7:00		
{		
8:00		
{		
8:50		
9:00		
9:10		
9:20		
9:30		
9:40		
9:50		
10:00 P.M.		

*Ten-minute intervals, working hours and evening hours indicated by brackets as a repeat during normal day.

FIGURE 2-2 Log for Intermittent Time Analysis.

to be put through directly, those that should be referred elsewhere, those the secretary can handle, and calls that need returning. "The key," he says, "is basing the system on the real-world experience of calls that actually came in one week."[11]

Set Priorities on Your Time

The key to time management is setting priorities. Most time management authorities recommend keeping a prioritized "to do" list. Tasks to be accomplished on a given day are listed with a space for assigning a priority code. One long list would be too much to prioritize.

Alan Lakein suggests using an ABC priority system.[12] The "A" is for activities with the highest priority, "B" for medium priority, and "C" for low priority. After this "first cut" at prioritizing the list, the As can be prioritized as A_1, A_2, A_3, etc. Likewise for the Bs and Cs. Work on the As first or at least during your peak hours of performance. Lakein explains:

> Some people do as many items as possible on their lists. They get a very high percentage of tasks done, but their effectiveness is low because the tasks they've done are mostly of C-priority. Others like to start at the top of the list and go right down it, again with little regard to what's important. The best way is to take your list and label each item according to ABC priority, delegate as much as you can, and then polish off the list accordingly.[13]

Figure 2-3 shows a prioritized daily "to do" list. Using a prioritized list allows us to spend 80 percent of our time on the most important items rather than the all-too-common practice of spending 80 percent of our time on routine activities.

Table 2-2 presents eight essentials for effective time management.

The Telephone Paradox

Being put on "hold" is not all bad

Avoid "telephone tag"

The telephone can be a tremendous time saver. A quick call can answer questions that must be determined before you can proceed on an A-priority project. On the other hand, if you are put on "hold," the telephone *can* be a time waster. It need not be. Have work such as reading in front of you to do while on hold. Stay on hold, reading and working on papers, if *you* want to so that you and the person you are calling do not get into a game of "telephone tag," or calling each other back.

TABLE 2-2 Essentials for Effective Management of Time

1. Know how your time is spent.
2. Set priorities.
3. Schedule your time realistically.
4. Delegate effectively.
5. Lead meetings effectively.
6. Control interruptions.
7. Manage your reading load.
8. Improve communications skills.

SOURCE: Sterling H. Schoen and Douglas E. Durand, *Supervision: The Management of Organizational Resources* (Englewood Cliffs, N.J.: Prentice-Hall, 1979), p. 310.

C_2	_____	Call Morgan about Reardon project
B_1	_____	Complete paper on "Tech Transfer" for next month
A_1	_____	Finish report due next Friday
A_2	_____	Work on proposal for SBA
C_3	_____	Arrange itinerary for next month's trip—alert secretary
B_2	_____	Plan local travel and appointments for next week
A_4	_____	Letter to Bill Jones (fire problem)
A_3	_____	Refine goals with boss (make appointment)
B_4	_____	Call Johnsen about maintenance service
B_5	_____	Call City of Greeley engineer about new process they want
C_1	_____	Revise filing system (discuss with secretary)
B_3	_____	Recreation time

FIGURE 2-3 Abbreviated Example of Daily "To Do" List.

If you are away from your workplace, try to group the return of telephone calls. Again, be in control of your own time where possible. And, like Robert Townsend recommended in *Up the Organization,* there is nothing wrong in answering your own telephone—when *you* want to do so.

Manage Your Own Time

While it is not possible to *make* time for certain activities, it is essential to *take* time for yourself. Be in control of your own schedule so that you can work on A-priority projects. Organize your schedule and workplace to the point that they work for you.

Iacocca's time planning

On a longer-term scale, it is necessary to set priorities on an annual basis. Planning time for major projects and also for major relaxation are equally important. Lee Iacocca, in his autobiography, tells about the importance of planning and time.

> The ability to concentrate and to use your time well is everything if you want to succeed in business—or almost anywhere else, for that matter. Ever since college I've always worked hard during the week while trying to keep my weekends free for family and recreation. . . . Every Sunday night I get the adrenalin going again by making an outline of what I want to accomplish during the upcoming week. . . .
> I'm constantly amazed by the number of people who can't seem to control their own schedules. Over the years, I've had many executives come to me and

say with pride: "Boy, last year I worked so hard that I didn't take any vacation." . . . I always feel like responding: "You dummy. You mean to tell me that you can take responsibility for an $80 million project and you can't plan two weeks out of the year to go off with your family and have some fun?[14]

Most managers—increasingly, even Japanese bosses—want their subordinates to take vacations to avoid burnout. Of course, the vacation has to be planned so that it is not a bad time for the business.

Your Desk or Other Workplace

There has always been a running battle between the "clean-desk" and the "cluttered-desk" advocates. The former say that "a cluttered desk is a sign of a cluttered mind" while the latter argue that "a cluttered desk is a sign of genius." Regardless, the work area should be arranged comfortably for the principal workers. They should have close access to their tools and machines of production.

People with clean desks get ahead

A survey of 100 executives by Accountemps, a temporary employment service, found that "people with neat desks stand a much better chance of promotion than co-workers with messy desks."[15] But there were perceived differences between top executives and middle managers. Desks used by middle managers were much more likely to be cluttered than those of the top executives, according to the survey. But, as a representative of Accountemps noted, "We really don't know just how cluttered and crowded some of those desk drawers might be."[16]

Today, there is nothing wrong with using your own word processor. For years, we were admonished that only clerical people should type, but the computer changed that. Now, both efficiency and effectiveness dictate that even the chief executive may want to *draft* some material at a word processor or on a lap-top computer.

MEETINGS—TIME WASTERS OR COMMUNICATION TOOLS

Where to Meet—Your Place or Mine?

Management by Walking Around (MBWA)

Like the telephone, meetings and where to have them are a dilemma. Tradition suggests that the subordinate goes to the boss' office—out of deference to status and to "save" the boss time in getting to the meeting. Techniques such as "Management by Walking (or Wandering) Around," practiced at Hewlett-Packard and other companies, have changed that.

There is some benefit to be gained by going to the other person's office. You usually remain in control of your time by being able to exit more freely than if someone is in your workplace. That doesn't always work, but it's worth a try. Even if someone is in your office or workplace, you can still control the meeting and their departure by your summary of the meeting and movement away from or out of your workplace.

Formal Meetings

Use an agenda

Meeting convenors should solicit agenda items from participants, distribute the agenda in advance, and begin and end the meeting at a prestated time. A further dilemma about meetings is how often to have them. Having meetings just because they are routinely scheduled at that time is a time waster if there are no agenda items to be discussed. The irony of not having regular meetings is that the people who complain the most about meetings are the same ones who, in the absence of meetings, complain that they don't know what is going on in their organization.

Meetings also provide an opportunity for significant participation, a topic to be discussed later in this book. Obtain balanced participation; control the long-winded and draw out the silent.

Several Rules for Effective Meetings and Their Leadership

A. Preparation for meeting

1. Limit the number of participants to those persons who are needed to reach a decision on the topic confronting the group.
2. Schedule the meeting properly: (a) allocate time according to the relative importance of each topic, (b) schedule meetings before natural quitting time, such as lunch.
3. Determine the specific purpose of the meeting in your own mind.
4. Develop and distribute the agenda in advance.

B. Leading the meeting

5. Start the meeting on time. Do not wait for latecomers.
6. Start with the most important item on the agenda. Then stick to the agenda; permit only emergency interruptions.
7. Be sensitive to hidden agendas and the social-emotional needs of members.
8. Summarize group progress and restate conclusions to ensure agreement.
9. Make specific assignments for the next meeting.
10. End the meeting on time to allow participants to plan their own time effectively.

C. Follow-up meeting

11. Distribute the minutes or a summary of the proceedings. It is especially important to communicate group decisions to the group members.

Unless you know what your time is worth and how to evaluate the time cost of what you do, it is almost impossible to make a correct decision or to evaluate properly what action to take in a given situation. Too many people spend $5 worth of time on a 5 cent job.

Table 2-3 illustrates what your time is worth by the hour, based on 244 eight-hour working days per year (a five-day week less vacation and holidays).

CAREER DEVELOPMENT

Individual Responsibility

The individual has the primary responsibility for his or her career development. Career development includes all of the activities necessary to help individuals become aware of and acquire the knowledge, skills, and competence to perform different jobs. Career development, like time management and success to come, is a very personal and goal-oriented activity. No one can set your goals or plan your career for you.

TABLE 2-3 What Is Your Time Worth?

IF YOUR ANNUAL EARNINGS ARE	EVERY HOUR IS WORTH
$ 5,000	$ 2.56
6,000	3.07
8,000	4.10
10,000	5.12
12,000	6.15
15,000	7.68
18,000	9.22
20,000	10.25
25,000	12.81
30,000	15.37
35,000	17.93
40,000	20.49
50,000	25.61
60,000	30.74
75,000	38.42
100,000	51.23

The chart shows the broad average of the entire day based on annual income. You should also decide what your priority of time is for each activity in which you are engaged. Some things you do are more important, and more profitable, than others.

Career development starts with self-awareness

No matter how sophisticated an organization's training program or job rotation system might be, you will usually have to take the initiative in planning your career. Career development starts with a self-awareness—knowing where you are and where you want to be 5, 10, or 20 years from now. Any gaps between your present situation and your future goals provide the basis for career planning.

There are several stages in a person's career and life development. Become aware of career opportunities by talking with job counselors and researching literature such as the *Occupational Outlook Handbook* published by the U.S. Department of Labor. Current job opportunities as well as longer-term forecasts of job demands are available in current periodicals, such as *The Wall Street Journal, USA Today*, and industry-specific journals.

One way of looking at a person's career and life development is:

Ages	*Career Phases*	*Manifestations*
less than 25	Pulling up roots	Break with parents; establish own identity
25–31	Provisional adulthood	A period of trial and autonomy
32–40	Transitional period	Questioning of self, life, values
40–49	Settling down	Resolved to own/others' infallibility/ mortality
50–60	Potential plateauing/midlife crisis	Career reassessment; ``what will be, will be''
Over 60	Reestablishment	Maturity/late career changes; continued growth, retirement, or decline

Organizational Responsibility

Organizations can help you in various stages of the career development process. Many organizations are involved in some type of career development activity, ranging from one-on-one counseling to announcing available training and development seminars. If you are to capitalize on an employer's help, you should recognize the stages in a career development program.

Stages in Career Development	1. Job search
	2. Settling down and settling in
	3. Changing with the organization
	4. Midcareer changes and personal crises (burnout, lack of job challenge, plateauing, etc.)
	5. Changing jobs within and outside of the organization
	6. Preparing for retirement; identifying and grooming potential successors
	7. Continuing to work, but at a reduced rate, in retirement

Career development is a part of an organization's human resources planning

An organization's career development program will be more meaningful if it is a formalized process included in the organization's human resources planning. That means that your manager as well as a centralized data base have knowledge of your skills, training, and career aspirations and that they use these data in making personnel decisions. It pays to take the initiative in discussing these items with your manager and, if appropriate, personnel and career counselors in your organization.

Career patterns within an organization provide solutions to critical business problems before they become problems. Karen Gaertner writes that:

> Career patterns can be an integral part of any relatively large organization's strategy, culture, and structure. As such, careers will reflect and reinforce the dominant themes in the organization. Far from being an inhibitor of change, career patterns can be structured to be both concrete and incremental, both firm in purpose and flexible in execution. They can encourage an orientation of adaptability and flexibility among employees through commitment to ongoing training and development, while still providing a reasonably secure work environment for employees. Thus, career patterns contribute to the organization's ability to change, transform, evolve as the need arises, and provide a developmental context within which individuals may pursue their own career objectives.[17]

Whether or not an organization incorporates career planning into its human resources development process may be a determinant in where you decide to work. In recent years, many organizations have taken on part of the responsibility for helping employees grow and prepare for lateral, upward, and sometimes retrenchment moves. Human resources planning and proper assessment of abilities and skills are the keystones in a comprehensive career planning program.[18] Such programs also include demand analysis, career pathing, and career advancement.

Demand

Many careers are cyclical. Engineers, lawyers, and medical doctors are classic examples of fluctuating but fairly constant high-demand careers.

Demand for certain occupations is cyclical

Demand for nurses and teachers has also fluctuated heavily in recent years, partly because of increased technology and population. As health care services rely on more sophisticated technology, there is less demand for nurses who do not have technical skills, and more demand for clinical nursing specialists and other technologists.

Secondary school teachers

The demand for secondary school teachers, once considered a glutted market, is again increasing. School districts now recruit teachers the way businesses recruit managers—with elaborate hotel suites and other perquisites.

"Always room for a good manager"

Businesses, too, have their opportunity areas. Demand for sales and marketing jobs, and for data processors continues to grow. The outlook for first-level and middle managers may continue to be less than optimal because of the "lean-and-mean" approach to management advocated in the 1980s. By definition, there will always be a shortage of *really* good managers—or any other occupation. The primary factor in individual career advancement is the quality of current job performance.

Career Pathing

Career planning involves making detailed plans relating to career goals. Included in these plans will be career options and potential career paths. Career paths are alternative progressions planned by both the individual and the organization through jobs in an organization. Figure 2-4 shows an example of possible career paths in a savings and loan or bank branch office. Titles may vary and there may be

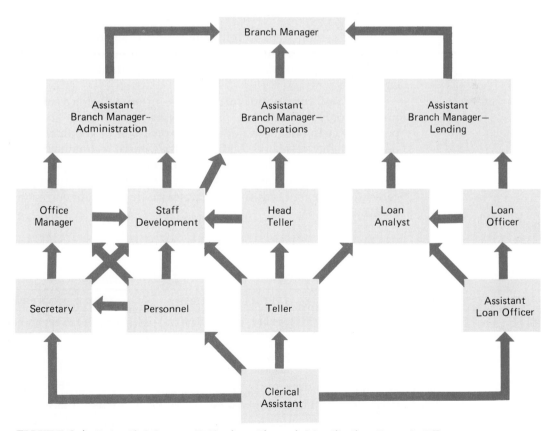

FIGURE 2-4 Potential Career Paths in a Financial Institution Branch Office.

additional steps, such as assistant cashier or administrative assistant. The point is to indicate alternative paths in promotion within an organization.

Career paths point out skills, knowledge, abilities, and training needed

Once the career paths are known, it is necessary to determine what skills, knowledge, and abilities a person needs in order to follow those paths. If analysis shows that a person does not have certain skills or training, then another career decision point and training needs analysis are immediately available. The individual and the organization are in a position to take action to move the person through the alternative career paths.

Check career paths with reality

Acquiring necessary skills for certain careers and possibilities for future action must be

> "reality checked" to assure that they have been drawn up realistically and that possibilities, missed by the individual, have been brought out. Reality checking is carried out with supervisors, colleagues, friends, family members and others. Future possibilities and alternatives are sketched out along with the needed training, experience or education build up to bring these about.[19]

Type Z career paths

There is a major difference in treatment of career paths in American and Japanese organizations. American, or type A, organizations follow more specialized career paths. Japanese, or type J, organizations are characterized by more general career paths.[20] A combination organizational type, type Z, suggests a moderately specialized career path. (See Table 2-4.)

Career Advancement

Learn how to learn

There are certain steps to follow in order to be successful in pursuing a career. Learning your current job well, learning how to learn, and identifying and understanding potential "next jobs" are important first steps in the pursuit of a career.

Do your current job well

How well you do your current job—including being a student—is the best but not the only indicator of promotability and success in another job. Good performance in one job is not a perfect predictor of good performance in another, perhaps higher-level, job. Additional assessment techniques are needed to predict success. But poor performance in the current job is a very good predictor of nonpromotability or failure in another job. One of the truest pieces of advice on career development is this: "you have to produce in your current job in order to get ahead."[21]

TABLE 2-4 Characteristics of Type A, Type J, and Type Z Organizations

TYPE A (AMERICAN)	TYPE J (JAPANESE)	TYPE Z (MODIFIED AMERICAN)
Short-term employment	Lifetime employment	Long-term employment
Individual decision-making	Consensual decision making	Consensual decision making
Individual responsibility	Collective responsibility	Individual responsibility
Rapid evaluation and promotion	Slow evaluation and promotion	Slow evaluation and promotion
Explicit, formalized control	Implicit, informal control	Implicit, informal control with explicit, formalized measures
Specialized career path	Nonspecialized career path	Moderately specialized career path
Segmented concern	Holistic concern	Holistic concern, including family

SOURCE: Adapted from William G. Ouchi and Alfred M. Jaeger, "Type Z Organization: Stability in the Midst of Mobility," *Academy of Management Review*, April 1978, pp. 308, 311.

Plan your career

Obtain help from mentors and networks

Have a career plan. The plan may change, but if you don't have a goal or a career plan, then anything will do, won't it? Seek the help of mentors and networks. A mentor is an advocate of yours who takes you under his or her wing to advise, encourage, and facilitate contacts for you. Networking is the construction and nurturing of information networks for business and social use in and outside of an organization. Mentoring and networking are not gender-based anymore. For years men have networked via the "good ol' boy" circuit. Team sports and other athletic activities have been one basis for these networks. Now women are also formalizing networks as well as capitalizing on informal activities such as aerobics classes and health clubs.

Build a performance base

In addition to doing your current job well, it is necessary that it be well documented for performance appraisal and promotion purposes. Build your own

data base or record of your achievements even if management doesn't require it.

Finally, make clear career choices. Poor career choices are summarized by the garbage collector who thought he was going to work as an environmental engineer.

Ask others in a job about the demands, expectations, and frustrations of the job before taking it. Jobs change but it is important for the job applicant to learn as much as possible before making a career commitment.

"Mommy Track" or Alternative Schedule Choice

During the late 1980s "mommy track" became a familiar term for career women who also wanted to have more time for motherhood. The term itself is unfortunate because it may be deemed patronizing. But the concept can help women make a comfortable and productive reconciliation of the roles if employers make effective use of talented women's skills.

Several alternatives exist for accomplishing alternative schedule choices.

1. *Alternative career paths.* Individuals work part time for a salary and may receive longevity credit for part-time work, but they lower their odds of becoming partners or other senior-level managers.
2. *Extended leave.* Employees can take up to three years off—with benefits and the guarantee of a comparable job on return.
3. *Flexible scheduling.* Employees create customized schedules and work at home, allowing a "phase-in" after maternity or other leave.
4. *Flextime.* Any employee has the right to shift the standard workday forward or back as long as they work a "common core" of hours.
5. *Job sharing.* Where two or more employees share a title, work load, salary, benefits, and vacation.
6. *Telecommuting.* Employees are allowed to limit the time they spend in the office by using personal computers, fax machines, and electronic mail at home.[22]

The American Medical Association provides interesting statistics advising when to stop work for mothers-to-be. The data in Figure 2-5 assume a normal, healthy 40-week pregnancy. Each individual's personal situation will vary and should be modified by the advice of a doctor.

Another consideration in career advancement is created by opportunities for dual-career couples and geographic transfer. Many career opportunities arise for one individual where it is not possible for the other half of the couple to secure meaningful employment. Taylor and Lounsbury recommend "that companies should show a greater awareness of transfer-related problems to reduce possible bias against employees planning a commuter marriage."[23]

SUCCESS

Being ready to act is the key to capitalizing on opportunities; and opportunities, along with hard work, are the keys to success. Success is not just a destination—it is a journey.

The concepts of "success" and "failure" as fundamental motivating forces are constantly being redefined. More and more, people are realizing that success can

If the job involves:	Last week of work (approx.)
Desk sitting (most professional/secretarial jobs)	40
Standing:	
More than 4 hours	24
More than 30 minutes/hour	32
Less than 30 minutes/hour	40
Stooping and bending below knees:	
More than 10 times/hour	20
Fewer than 2 times/hour	40
Climbing ladders and poles during 8 hour shift	28
Climbing stairs:	
Four or more times per 8 hours	28
Fewer than 4 times per 8 hours	40
Intermittent lifting: up to 31 pounds	40
Repetitive lifting:	
Twenty-four to 51 pounds	24
Less than 24 pounds	40

FIGURE 2-5 When to stop working for normal, healthy mothers-to-be. Source: Adapted from ''Effects of Pregnancy on Work Performance,'' *Informational Report of the Council on Scientific Affairs* (Chicago: American Medical Association, December 1988), p. 3.

be measured by personal standards as well as by public ones. Some people listen to different drummers.

Success may be defined in terms of one's attitudes or material wealth. But is material wealth an adequate dimension by itself? Does it depend on how and why you acquire wealth?

Success depends on your goals

Success is goal oriented. If you set demanding but attainable goals and achieve them, you are successful. If you perform well in your job, as well as in other relationships within your family and other social institutions, you are successful.

Success Is Respect

Success is attitudinal

A more universal meaning of success relates to the attitudes of others. Respect from others is a more recognized dimension of success than any other. People need to be accepted by others.

Success is not a popularity contest

A person is successful who has gained the respect of intelligent men and women. Respect does not necessarily imply admiration nor popularity. Respect means that a person is recognized and given consideration. The person doesn't have to be loved, or even liked, to be successful. It does mean that individuals should have respect from some, preferably a majority, of their coworkers, customers, and others with whom they interact.

Maturity

A mature attitude is another sign of respect. Magnanimity, or the ability to rise above petty matters, is in itself a sign of maturity and success. The art of being successful includes being concerned with the important rather than the petty. Positive attitudes have a profound effect on success. The foundation for a simple strategy for success is giving top priority to positive rewards and support.[24]

Negative attitudes and preoccupation with what is wrong with one's self, others, the organization, or society, can drain energies away from the important and one's ultimate success. We may spend our time tilting at windmills in a Don Quixotic manner while success is getting away. Or we win the battle and lose the war.

Whether applied to international relations, national politics, or interoffice squabbles, magnanimity is a means of translating hostility into harmony and success. There are times when it is better to "turn the other cheek." Obviously there is also a limit beyond which we cannot go in both international and interpersonal relations.

No suggestion is made of not taking a firm stand on major issues. But, as in time management, it is important to make sure the issues are really important issues before we spend the majority of our time and emotional energies on the least important items. From a likeability viewpoint, magnanimity does much to facilitate human relationships.

Magnanimity How delightful is the company of generous people, who overlook trifles and keep their minds instinctively fixed on whatever is good and positive in the world about them. People of small caliber are always carping. They are bent on showing their own superiority, their knowledge or prowess or good breeding. But magnanimous people have no vanity, they have no jealousy, they have no reserves, and they feed on the true and the solid wherever they find it. And what is more, they find it everywhere.

Van Wyck Brooks

You Don't Have to Be Perfect to Be Successful

Success does not necessarily imply perfection. David D. Burns, M.D., encourages us to aim for success, not perfection. "In fact, the discouragement and pressure that so often plague perfectionists can lead to decreases in creativity and productivity."[25] Finally, then, success is a matter of feeling that we are doing our very best, and having our boss, coworkers, customers, and others respect, acknowledge, and accept our efforts.

TEST YOURSELF
Perfection Versus Satisfaction

If you are a compulsive perfectionist, you may find it hard to believe that you can enjoy life to the maximum or find true happiness without aiming for perfection. You can put this notion to the test. On a piece of paper, list a wide range of activities such as mowing the lawn, preparing a meal, writing a report for work. Record the actual satisfaction you get from each activity by scoring it from 0 to 100 percent. Now estimate how perfectly you do each activity, again using a scale of 0 to 100. I call this an Antiperfectionism Sheet. It will help you break the illusory connection between perfection and satisfaction.

Here's how it works: A physician I know was convinced he had to be perfect at all times. No matter how much he accomplished he would always raise his standards slightly higher and then he'd feel miserable. I persuaded him to do some research on his moods and accomplishments, using the Antiperfectionism Sheet. One weekend a pipe broke at his home and flooded the kitchen. It took a long time but he did manage to stop the leak. Since he was such a novice at plumbing, had taken a long time and required considerable guidance from a neighbor, he recorded his expertise as only 20 percent. On the other hand, he estimated his level of satisfaction with the job as 99 percent. By contrast, he received low degrees of satisfaction from some activities on which he did an outstanding job.

This experience with the Antiperfectionism Sheet persuaded him that he did not have to be perfect at something to enjoy it. Furthermore, striving for perfection and performing exceptionally did not guarantee happiness, but tended, rather, to be associated with less satisfaction. He concluded he could either give up his compulsive drive for perfection and settle for joyous living and high productivity, or cling to it and settle for emotional anguish and modest productivity. Which would you choose? Put yourself to the test.

SOURCE: Excerpts abridged from pp. 303–304 in *Feeling Good* by David D. Burns, M.D., as it appeared in "Aim for Success, *Not* Perfection," *Reader's Digest*. Copyright © 1980 by David D. Burns, M.D. By permission of William Morrow & Company.

A quote from President Theodore Roosevelt is appropriate to close this chapter on personal and career development:

> It is not the critic who counts, nor the man who points out how the strong man stumbles or where the doer of deeds could have done them better. The credit belongs to the man who is actually in the arena, whose face is marred by dust and sweat and blood. And who strives valiantly. Who errs and comes short again and again. Who knows the great enthusiasms, the great devotions and spends himself in a worthy cause. Who at the best knows in the end the triumph of high achievement and who at the worst, if he fails, at least fails while daring greatly. So that his place will never be with those cold and timid souls who knew neither victory nor defeat."

Summary

Our personal and career development is our own primary responsibility. We need the eustress—positive stress—to help us to develop personally and professionally. However, the distress, or negative stress, can be dysfunctional.

Tension is natural but can be our worst enemy when it leads to emotional and physical ills. People with Type A behavior seem to be compulsive, hard-working achievers and are more likely to experience associated physical ailments.

Negative stress, or even too much positive stress, can lead to burnout. People who are fatigued and irritable express negative attitudes and make "missteaks." Feelings of burnout can be overcome in part by managing time.

Time management is largely a matter of scheduling activities and setting priorities. If we are in control of our own time, we manage our schedule and take time for ourselves. Telephones and meetings can be either time savers or time wasters depending on how we manage them and get them to work for us.

Both stress and time factors contribute to career development and success. The types of jobs, environment, and lifestyle work together to create an ambience that allows us to be successful. By not letting the petty things bother us, we give ourselves more time to concentrate on our important goals. Success should not be confused with perfection.

Focus on one job at a time and even schedule fun times; this helps to overcome the failure syndrome. Build support groups by having contacts with people outside of work. Finally, develop a somewhat detached concern for problems at work; this helps and can spell success in life as well as work. Success depends in large measure on how well we (1) cope with stress and tension; (2) manage our time, meetings, and other human interactions; and (3) plan and otherwise manage our personal careers.

Case Study 3

Is There Life after College?

Bill Kuck graduated from the Business Division of Andaluska County Community College three years ago. He is a very personable individual and was well-liked by fellow students, teachers, and coworkers—when he was working! But Bill has not worked more than a total of four months since he graduated, living on dwindling family income and inheritances.

His first position was salesperson in a shoe store near his college. He had worked there part time while in school, but his full-time job fell apart. The reasons are not entirely clear. The Andaluska economy was deteriorating, but others in the store had survived. Bill knew he would have to work harder under these economic circumstances, but did not; so he was laid off. He spent a lot of time talking with customers, but just wasn't able to make sales.

Bill thought about going to the state university for further education, but did not have the "bucks" to do it; so he took a temporary job as custodian at the college. His hours were late nights and he had a hard time getting to work on time. His supervisor was critical of his performance and his job was not extended.

At this point Bill began to experience some health problems including headaches, lethargy, and fatigue. He tried to get another job by talking with his buddies at the gym, but was not successful. He was getting very depressed.

1. What do you think Bill's problem is?
2. Is there a place for stress in this case? What kind of stress?
3. Has Bill planned out a career?
4. What other factors might influence Bill?

I Don't Have Enough Time

Joan Flickinger is branch manager of the Home Savings and Loan Association branch in the growing suburban community of Sylvan Dale. Ten years ago she had started at another suburban branch as teller, and was gradually promoted to assistant manager. When the Sylvan Dale office opened, she was promoted to branch manager.

Joan sat in her office at 6:15 P.M. wondering why she had not accomplished more that day. She had arrived just after 8 A.M. as usual. Her day had been filled by appointments with subordinates and customers, and was fairly typical, she thought, insofar as day-to-day operations were concerned.

She was frustrated because she had not spent any time on the report that the main office expected from her next week on expansion plans for Home in Sylvan Dale. She knew that she would have to take that work home with her again tonight. It was difficult to work on it, in addition to spending time with her family—her husband and two teenage daughters. Joan had never really had any training in staff development positions and found it difficult to write such reports.

Joan's secretary schedules appointments for her. The last meeting for the day was scheduled for 4:30, right after the office closed, with the secretary herself. The secretary wanted to talk about a raise because of her normal responsibilities in answering the phone, scheduling appointments, working for other branch officers, as well as typing correspondence and reports to the main office. The request for a raise had been unexpected by Joan, and the meeting was a little tense at times. It lasted over an hour and a half. No resolution was achieved.

1. What is Joan's problem?
2. Could career development and a career path help alleviate some of Joan's problem?
3. What should Joan do about her problem?

ANSWERS TO TEST YOURSELF: Test Your Stress Level (pages 31–32)   Score one point for each "Yes" answer to questions 1 through 8 and one point for each "No" answer to questions 9 through 11. A score of four or more suggests you may be under significant stress.

Terms and Concepts

career development activities necessary to help individuals become aware of and acquire the knowledge, skills, and competence to perform a job.

career paths alternative planned progressions through jobs in an organization.

distress a negative stressor that allows loss of touch with reality and may result in temper tantrums and loss of control.

eustress a positive type of stress that results in achievement and accomplishment.

holistic health comprehensive method of controlling stress and tension that deals with the complete life-style of the individual; incorporates physical, psychological, and social dimensions.

magnanimity the ability to rise above petty matters; generosity in overlooking insult or injury.

"mommy track" a familiar term for career women who also want to have more time for motherhood.

success primarily attitudinal, or goal-oriented, feeling of accomplishment.

time management the actions required to control events.

time waster any activity that detracts from your main goals.

Type A person a striving, goal-oriented person more likely to experience certain ailments; work is central to his or her life.

Type B person a person who has more interests in leisure activities than does the Type A individual; the Type B person may be more productive in the long run.

Type H person a person who is probably Type A, but also hostile and manifests angry behavior.

Notes

1. Jerry E. Bishop, "Hostility, Distrust May Put Type A's at Coronary Risk," *The Wall Street Journal*, January 17, 1989, p. B1.
2. Ibid.
3. Diane Cole, "Busy as You Are, Consider the Business of Busyness," *The Wall Street Journal*, October 17, 1988, p. A14.
4. "Are You a Type H?" *USA Weekend*, July 7–9, 1989, p. 8.
5. Adapted from "Workaholics Die Young: How to Detect and Then Treat Workaholism," *The Coloradoan*, December 12, 1987, p. D6.
6. Jeanne M. Plas and Kathleen V. Hoover-Dempsey, "Keeping Anger in Check," *National Business Employment Weekly*, Spring 1989, p. 18.
7. Ibid., pp. 18, 20.
8. Alvin Toffler, *Future Shock* (New York: Bantam, 1971), pp. 93–94.
9. *Stress*, a report from Blue Cross of Northern California, 1974, pp. 66–75.
10. Paul Hawken, "Mastering the Numbers," *Inc.*, October 1987, p. 20.
11. Michael Moran, "Efficient Phone Habits Can Make Work Day More Productive," *The Coloradoan*, August 13, 1989, p. E6.
12. Alan Lakein, *How to Get Control of Your Time and Your Life* (New York: Signet, 1973), p. 28.
13. Ibid., pp. 65–66.
14. Lee Iacocca with William Novak, *Iacocca: An Autobiography* (New York: Bantam, 1984), p. 20.
15. "Clean Desk for Success," *USA Today*, June 28, 1985, p. 1.
16. Ibid.
17. Karen N. Gaertner, "Manager's Careers and Organizational Change," *The Academy of Management Executive*, November 1988, p. 318.
18. Stephen L. Cohen and Herbert H. Meyer, "Toward a More Comprehensive Career Planning Program," *Personnel Journal*, September 1979, pp. 611–615.
19. Elmer H. Burack and Nicholas Mathys, "Career Ladders, Pathing and Planning: Some Neglected Basics," *Human Resource Management*, Summer 1979, p. 7.
20. William G. Ouchi and Alfred M. Jaeger, "Type Z Organization: Stability in the Midst of Mobility," *Academy of Management Review*, April 1978, p. 308.
21. Robert S. Burnett and James A. Waters, "The Action Profile: A Practical Aid to Career Development and Succession Planning," *Business Horizons*, May–June 1984, p. 21.
22. "The Mommy Track," *Business Week*, March 20, 1989, pp. 128–129.
23. Ann Siegris Taylor and John W. Lounsbury, "Dual-Career Couples and Geographic Transfer: Executives' Reactions to Commuter Marriage and Attitude Toward the Move," *Human Relations*, May 1988, p. 407.
24. Jack Falvey, "A Simple Strategy for Success," *Reader's Digest*, May 1986, pp. 133–135.
25. David D. Burns, "Aim for Success, *Not* Perfection," *Reader's Digest*, March 1985, p. 71.

Recommended Reading

"Are You a Type H?" *USA Weekend*, July 7–9, 1989, p. 8.

Blanchard, Kenneth, and Spencer Johnson. *The One-Minute Manager.* LaJolla, Calif.: Blanchard-Johnson, 1981.

Burnett, Robert S., and James A. Waters. "The Action Profile: A Practical Aid to Career Development and Succession Planning." *Business Horizons*, May–June 1984, p. 21.

Christensen, Donna R. "Organizational Involvement: The Key to Employee Career Development." *Management Solutions*, May 1987, pp. 38–41.

Clawson, James G., and others. *Self-assessment and Career Development*, 2nd ed. Englewood Cliffs, N.J.: Prentice-Hall, 1985.

Cohen, Stephen L., and Herbert H. Meyer. "Toward a More Comprehensive Career Planning Program." *Personnel Journal*, September 1979, pp. 611–615.

D'Arcy, Carl. "Perceived Job Attributes, Job Satisfaction, and Psychological Distress: A Comparison of Working Men and Women." *Human Relations*, August 1984, pp. 603–611.

Edelson, Nathan. "Business Meetings on the Run." *The Wall Street Journal*, March 13, 1989, p. A14.

Freudenberger, Herbert J., with Geraldine Richelson. *Burn-out: The High Cost of High Achievement*. New York: Bantam, 1980.

Gaertner, Karen N. "Manager's Careers and Organizational Change." *The Academy of Management Executive*, November 1988, pp. 311–318.

Iacocca, Lee, with William Novak. *Iacocca: An Autobiography*. New York: Bantam, 1984.

Kirkland, Richard I., Jr. "Are Service Jobs Good Jobs?" *Fortune*, June 10, 1985, pp. 38–43.

Korn, Lester. *The Success Profile: A Leading Headhunter Tells You How to Get to the Top*. New York: Simon & Schuster, 1988.

Lakein, Alan. *How to Get Control of Your Time and Your Life*. New York: Signet, 1973.

Naisbitt, John. *Megatrends: Ten New Directions Transforming Our Lives*. New York: Warner, 1982.

Ouchi, William. *Theory Z: How American Business Can Meet the Japanese Challenge*. Reading, Mass.: Addison-Wesley, 1981.

Russell, Mary. "Career Planning in a Blue Collar Company." *Training and Development Journal*, January 1984, pp. 87–88.

Selye, Hans. *Stress Without Distress*. Philadelphia: J. B. Lippincott, 1974. Reprinted by Signet, 1975.

Skrzycki, Cindy. "'Plateauing' Forces Career Assessment." *The Washington Post*, April 6, 1989, p. Cl.

Taylor, Ann Siegris, and John W. Lounsbury. "Dual-Career Couples and Geographic Transfer: Executives' Reactions to Commuter Marriage and Attitude Toward the Move." *Human Relations*, May 1988, pp. 407–424.

Williams, Redford. *The Trusting Heart: Great News About Type A Behavior*. New York: Times Books, 1989.

Human Motivation

After studying this chapter, you should be able to:

1. Describe what motivation means to you.
2. Explain how the individual's need to be motivated may differ from the company's and supervisor's need to motivate.
3. Describe the schools of psychology and how they relate to motivation.
4. Discuss the various behavior defense mechanisms we exhibit when we cannot achieve our goals easily.
5. Describe the five elements of Maslow's hierarchy of needs.
6. Contrast the differences between Herzberg's hygiene or maintenance theory and motivators.
7. Contrast intrinsic motivators from extrinsic motivators and list several of each type.
8. Describe the nature of incentives and their relationship to motivation.
9. Summarize some of the important methods of job enrichment.
10. Describe barriers to achievement and how to overcome them.

TO START YOU THINKING . . .

Here are some questions that may stimulate your thinking. The answers to some will be found in the readings; other answers will come from your experiences and personal opinions.

♦ How are you motivated? What "turns you on"?
♦ How are the growth and humanist schools of motivation similar?
♦ Hedonistic and behaviorist? tensional and psychoanalytic?
♦ Why do people work when they don't need the money?
♦ Is money the most important incentive, or are there other incentives equally important?
♦ What makes some people work harder than others?
♦ Does everyone have the same needs?
♦ Are people motivated internally or externally?
♦ How can routine jobs be redesigned to be more productive and satisfying?
♦ Do managers motivate subordinates by listening to them?

WHAT IS MOTIVATION ALL ABOUT? _____

Motivation is an internal concept based on a person's needs and the fulfillment of those needs. Too often, we think of motivating another person. But, as we shall see, it is not something that we do *to* or *for* another person, nor is it externally imposing a set of needs on that other person. In its simplest sense, motivation is need fulfillment.

Motivation is what inspires people to act. It instills a belief that what people are doing on the job is important. At work, motivation is achieved naturally because work is defined as any activity or effort undertaken to accomplish a goal. All workers are motivated to some degree. Some are more motivated than others.

A motivated person wants to work

In the business world, *motivation* is used to describe the drive that impels an individual to work. A truly motivated person is one who *wants* to work. Both employees and employers are interested in understanding motivation. If workers know what strengthens and what weakens their motivation, they can often perform more effectively to find more satisfaction in their jobs. Employers want to know what motivates the employees so that they can get them to work harder. The motivation to work is integral both to successful organizations and to employee job satisfaction. Thus, both employees and employers must understand it better.

Motivation and Behavior

Motivation is an internal need satisfied by external expression

A psychologist who uses the word "motivation" thinks of it as something stemming from *within* a person. Motivation is an internal need that is satisfied through an external expression. The achievement of the goal or the obtaining of the incentive is the external factor that the public sees, but the reason why people are moved or motivated to achieve it may not always be obvious.

Concept of individual differences

People are motivated to perform similar actions by very different internal drives. The concept of individual differences is illustrated by the fact that two employees work hard to get raises but for different reasons. To one, the raise is important because it will provide more money; to the other, the higher status that the raise signifies is a stronger motivation than the money.

Also, similar internal motivations can have different results. Two employees who feel a strong need for job security may handle their needs in very different ways. One might decide to work hard but never to "rock the boat" for fear of being fired. The other chooses to be innovative, even at the risk of being controversial, as a way of becoming indispensable.

Motivation and Organizations

Management may try to manipulate motivation

Management often refers to employees as "resources" or "assets," which means that employees are valuable, profit-making parts of a business organization. Studies of motivation try to discover what incentives will cause workers to work and increase their value as assets. Managers care about their workers' personal motivations as they affect production rates. Therefore, they try to structure, by incentive systems, the motivations of workers. They cannot motivate the workers —only the workers themselves can do that.

Management can facilitate achievement of workers' goals, such as personal salary maximization, while at the same time accomplishing organizational objectives. (See Figure 3-1). Chris Argyris examined the proposition that individual growth needs and organizational objectives are often in conflict. He found that as people mature, they grow more independent and want to make more decisions for themselves. They want to take on more responsibility, to become more competent. He also found that some organizations exert pressures that directly oppose these patterns of self-actualization. In the interest of efficiency, organizations require employees to submit to rigid forms of authority, demand few skills of them, and make as many decisions as possible for them.

Argyris believes that the "incongruence between the individual and the organization can provide the basis for a continued challenge that, as it is fulfilled, will tend to help people to enhance their own growth and to develop organizations that will tend to be viable and effective."[1] Earlier, Argyris had stated that organizations are willing to pay high wages and provide adequate seniority if mature adults will, for eight hours a day, behave in a less than mature manner!

Motivation can be understood in its simplest form as a three-step process: (1) an internal need exists, (2) a behavioral action or direction is taken to satisfy that need, and (3) the satisfaction of that need is accomplished. Note that the need is

Organization
Objectives

Individuals'
Goals

FIGURE 3-1 Goal congruency. The objective is to make the shaded area as congruent as possible.

internally, not externally, imposed. The need may be economic, social, or psychological. For example, you may have a desire for food which can be satisfied by various actions: grabbing a snack or waiting several hours for a more substantial meal. Another example would be a social or psychological need to be the top salesperson in a division.

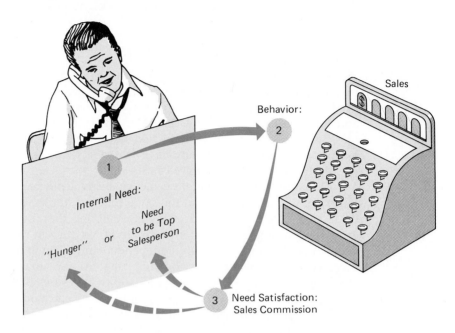

The achievement of a goal is very satisfying and the tension release is gratifying, but the feeling of satisfaction is usually short-lived. The "glow" of achieving a goal lasts but a few minutes to an hour, and seldom more than a day. Thus, how can the individual's motivation become more long lasting? The answer in part is in different schools of psychology and concepts of motivation.

SCHOOLS OF PSYCHOLOGY AND IMPACT ON MOTIVATION

Three schools of psychology have had a great impact on people's beliefs about motivation. None of the ideas is more right than others; they only represent different ways of perceiving motivation and how to motivate. They are the psychoanalytic, the behaviorist, and the humanistic schools of behavior.

Psychoanalytic School

"Iceberg" theory

Sigmund Freud, the founder of the psychoanalytic process, stressed the complexity of human motivation and pointed out that the outward manifestation of an individual's psyche is like the tip of a submerged iceberg (Figure 3-2). Freud believed that the interpersonal and social environments determined the outcome of the individual's life and death efforts. To Freud, the physical environment is experienced rather than observed; that is, we may hit the submerged iceberg without knowing it. On the other hand, it may be necessary for us to hit or feel the iceberg if we are to know what our true motivations are.

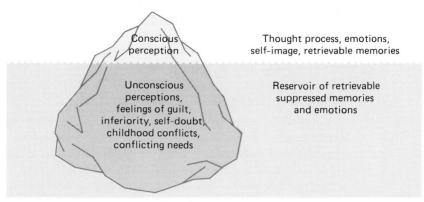

FIGURE 3-2 **Iceberg theory: a large portion of our personality is hidden from our conscious perception.**

Behaviorist School

Behavior modification

Over 30 years ago, psychologist B. F. Skinner developed a behavior modification theory that is relatively easy to understand but is sometimes difficult to implement. It involves the principle of conditioning and the principle of reinforcement. *Conditioning* involves rewarding desired behavior and not rewarding undesirable behavior.

Principle of reinforcement

Repeated rewards are called *reinforcement.* Skinner found that, for effective reinforcement, a carefully planned schedule must be followed. Rewards must be timed properly to be effective. The most effective rewards are those that immediately follow the desired behavior.

Positive rewards, such as praise or food, are generally more effective than negative reinforcement, such as punishment. The basic approach is to reinforce desired behavior and ignore undesirable actions. Over a period of time, the reinforced behavior will tend to be repeated, and the unrewarded will tend to disappear. Punishment of undesired behavior is to be avoided as contributing to feelings of restraint and actions of rebellion.

Emery Air Freight used behavior modification

Behavior modification has some intriguing possibilities for motivation. One of the best documented examples of the potential of behavior modification in industry is at the Emery Air Freight Company. The supervisors at the company were trained to praise work done correctly by the employees, such as keeping records of all their activities, improving delivery times, or responding quickly to telephone requests.

Humanist School

Classical organizational theory

There are many people who search for universal guidelines and principles that are applicable to all organizations. They seem to believe in the "classical organizational theory." By this theory, one believes employees are lazy, work only for money, and need to be supervised closely if they are to produce up to standard.

Humanist school looks to people

Informal groups, leadership, and morale are part of the humanist school

The humanist school, on the other hand, was developed by a contrasting or opposite viewpoint. Its supporters believe in looking to people rather than to the organization.

There is a heavy emphasis on the study of informal groups, group decision making, employee satisfaction, and leadership styles. People have many different feelings and collectively develop a group personality that should be managed differently from that of other groups. From an academic point of view, the human relations theory is now being classified as neoclassical when compared with the classical (rigid) organizational theory.

Other Approaches to Motivation

Considerable research has been done on the other specific needs including achievement, affiliation, and power. The *achievement* approach holds that a person's performance is a function of the strength of that individual's need for achievement. The *affiliation* approach measures the need to be with other people in meaningful relationships including business. The *power* approach measures the need for control and influence over others.

The *expectancy approach* relates to the strength of an individual's belief that a particular course of action will result in a given outcome (reward). That belief is a function of expectation itself (expectancy), the method for making it happen (instrumentality), and the degree of attractiveness of a behavioral goal (valence) that the individual places on the outcome (reward). A good example is the grade that you expect to get in a class influences how hard you work and the value you place on the outcome.

The formula for the relationship is:

motivation = (or is a function of) expectancy × instrumentality × valence

where

expectancy = the person's belief that effort will result in performance
instrumentality = the person's belief that performance will be rewarded
valence = the perceived strength or value of receiving the rewards

The *equity* approach places emphasis for motivation on perceived fairness. Its basis is that workers strive to maintain balance between their own inputs and their rewards in comparison to other workers with whom they compare themselves.

The concept is comparative in that our perception of fairness is based on how we see others rewarded for more or less effort. If individuals perceive inequity, they can reduce that inequity by working harder, by seeking other rewards, or by a variety of other actions. Can you think of other ways to reduce inequity?

Another modern model is *ERG theory*, based on the work of Clayton Alderfer.[2] Like other need-based models, Alderfer's model looks at three sets of needs: (1) existence (subsistence) needs, (2) relatedness (social) needs, and (3) growth needs. This approach recognizes that while there is no one best way to motivate all employees, there are some broad guidelines or models to follow and some recognizable hierarchy that make motivation problems easier to resolve. Managers need to learn to know employees and tailor motivation techniques to meet their needs.[3]

Other types of motivation are (1) tensional or deficiency motivation; (2) hedonistic motivation; (3) the "pull" or positive stick-and-carrot approach; (4) the "push" or negative K.I.T.A. (kick in the "pants") approach; or (5) the growth, self-actualization ("be everything you can be") approach.

In essence, Freud's approach is the tensional or "a-deficiency-must-exist-before-you-can-have-a-motivating-situation" approach. The hedonists believe that an individual will try to attain or maintain a pleasant state, and strive to change or leave an unpleasant state: "If it feels good, do it; if it hurts, don't do it."

Growth motivation is a more positive type that puts emphasis on the individual and psychological growth of the human being.

The carrot dangled on a stick in front of a donkey encourages the animal to move forward. People, too, will move if the reward is big enough, the incentive not too distant, and the goal strong enough.

Management by objectives is an example of motivation that is practiced in industry. The supervisor and the employee together develop realistic goals for the employee to accomplish by some future date, usually six months to a year.

The employee's next appraisal or review is based on how well he or she has met the established goals. In some firms, it becomes a method by which employees can set their own goals and recognize how they will be evaluated later.

There is a time and place for all approaches. Try the Test Yourself exercise. It will probably lead you toward establishing internal motivation. Develop a determination to accomplish your goals and focus on your strengths, not on your weaknesses.

TEST YOURSELF

Goal-setting Exercise

Here is an exercise that will help you zero in on goal setting. Write down something you personally would like to accomplish in three months.

MY GOAL FOR THREE MONTHS _____

By writing something down you have committed yourself and established a deadline. Don't procrastinate—work for it. Now list something you would like to accomplish in three years.

MY GOAL FOR THREE YEARS _____

Neither goal should be so easy that you will naturally reach it through the course of events. You should have to make a few sacrifices to achieve them. If you have enough stamina, you will write your goals on the cover of your notebook as a constant reminder of what you are striving for. If you have enough self-confidence, you will share your goals, not dreams, with others in your class.

MASLOW'S BASIC NEEDS

Internal need fulfillment is the basis for motivation. Whether those motives arise out of fear, determination, goal setting, or whatever source, the identification and fulfillment of individuals' needs congruent with organizational objectives become an important management task.

Abraham Maslow conjectured that basic needs are the same for all human beings.[4] He found that, although different cultures satisfy these needs in different ways, the needs themselves remain the same. What are these basic needs or instincts that motivate people to act in the ways that they do?

Identifying needs in one's self and in others can be difficult for a variety of reasons. First, while five basic needs have been defined, they result in endlessly varying activities. The expression of these needs is influenced by both a person's present surroundings and by past experiences and is different in different individuals. To complicate matters further, basic needs are often more unconscious than conscious. For example, someone who feels hungry and eats to satisfy that ''felt'' hunger may actually be needing love or security. (See Figure 3-3.)

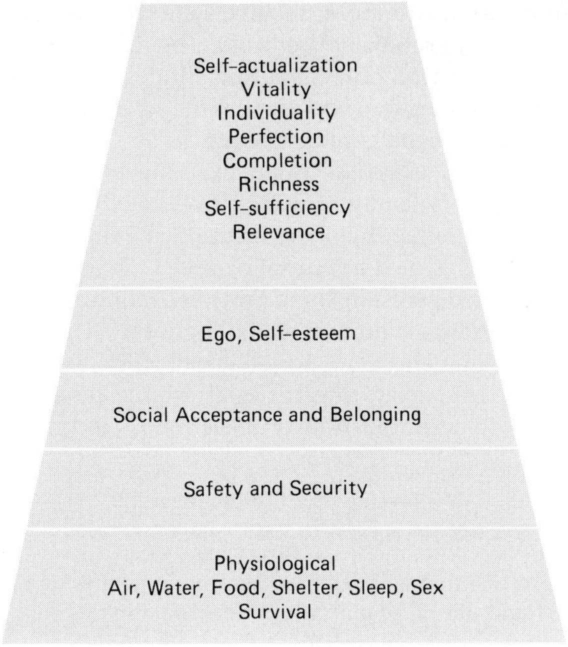

FIGURE 3-3 Maslow's hierarchy of needs.

Physiological Needs _____

Maslow's five basic needs start with the physiological needs

Not much can motivate a person who has not reasonably satisfied his or her basic physiological needs. Maslow suggested that when a person is starving, the only need that is important is food. Gandhi put it another way, "Even God cannot talk to a hungry man except in terms of bread."

The physiological needs include such basics as food and drink, sleep, clean air, satisfactory temperature, and protection from the elements by clothing and shelter. When the primary physical needs are satisfied, other physical instincts may take their place, such as sexual desires, and the sensual desires of taste, smell, and touch. For most people, the physical needs are indirectly satisfied with the money earned from the work they do.

Safety or Security Needs _____

People also want to feel safe from harm. In most adults, the safety needs are expressed by the desire to be stable and secure. To prefer the familiar and the known to the unfamiliar and the unknown reflects the basic need for safety.

Your chosen career may reflect your need for security

The type of career we choose may reflect our need for security. Such careers might be teaching, accounting, or civil service. Are you thinking of working for a large, stable company whose growth and future is predictable? Is your choice in the changing fields of aerospace or electronics, or is it in a more stable area, such as food processing or the fire department? If you find that these stabilizing factors fit your outlook on a career, then your need for security is very strong.

Social or Belonging Needs _____

People need a sense of belonging

Once people have basically satisfied their physiological and safety needs, they feel an urge for acceptance, affection, and the feeling of belonging. This need expresses itself in a desire to be loved by someone and to have someone to love. It is important to remember that a person needs to *give* as well as to *receive* affection. Supervisors can see the strength of the social need by observing cliques during coffee breaks or groups leaving work together. What management needs to do is capitalize on this need during work hours.

The social need may more aptly be called the "belongingness" or team spirit need. Teamwork and team spirit are often more important than individual achievement, but many leaders and administrators underestimate their importance. We want to be successful as a group or team as well as individually.

Esteem Needs

Maslow classifies the needs for esteem into two categories: (1) the desire for a sense of internal worth and (2) the desire for prestige or reputation that can only be conferred by other people. People who value themselves have highly developed feelings of confidence, worth, strength, capability, and adequacy. Lack of self-esteem produces feelings of inferiority, inadequacy, weakness, and helplessness. These feelings of self-dislike lead to discouragement and a sense of failure.

Management often recognizes that individual needs can be satisfied better with "status" symbols than with money. The executives have their "status" symbols in forms of private dining rooms, carpeted offices, and the key to the executive washroom.

Status symbols satisfy the self-esteem need

Supervisors also recognize that individual needs often can be satisfied better with "status" symbols than with money. Blue-collar workers, although they may sneer at executive symbols, have many status symbols of their own. The shop foreman or union boss may rate the end locker or wear some distinctive symbol, such as a jacket or badge, to denote his or her position. A word processor may gain self-esteem by serving as a private secretary rather than as a member of the word processing section. A salesperson gains status by driving a company car or by receiving a new car from the company every three years.

Belonging need can be in conflict with the esteem need

Sometimes our needs are in conflict. The need to be an integrated, accepted member of a group may conflict with the need to be a leader. A good worker who is selected as a supervisor may become an ambivalent leader, because the need to be an accepted member of the group proves stronger than the ego drive to be a supervisor.

Self-Actualization Needs

The need for self-fulfillment, the realization of one's fullest potential, is called self-actualization. Needs for self-fulfillment are demonstrated by doing a job well for the sake of doing it well and by striving toward more creative endeavors of all kinds. Maslow distinguishes the needs concerned with physiology, safety, belonging, and esteem as "deficiency" needs—without their satisfaction, people lack the necessary components for developing healthy personalities. Self-actualization is a "growth" need. Healthy people are those who are free to concern themselves mainly with satisfying their needs for continual growth and fulfillment including on the job.

The Hierarchy of Needs

Maslow explains the five categories of needs in terms of a hierarchy and says that one need must be relatively well satisfied before the next in line can become a driving force. Although this description of a hierarchy of needs is convenient, it is

Express Your Opinion

You have now read Maslow's hierarchy of needs. Let us assume that most of your physiological needs are satisfied and concentrate on your psychological needs. Sometimes, the self-esteem need seems to prevail, as when you need considerable recognition as an individual. Other times, there may be a strong need for social acceptance to overcome a loneliness in your daily life. Which need seems to be the strongest and most desirable need to satisfy in the next few months? Can you say why? What one accomplishment could satisfy it most?

What do you think is the strongest need of your closest friend? Is it the same as yours? What is the strongest need of your parents? Do you think that people may go through life cycles that at different stages reflect the importance of different needs?

slightly misleading. One need does not require full satisfaction before the next need on the hierarchical ladder makes itself felt.

People are constantly driven by internal forces—they are unceasingly motivated toward new goals. One of the chief reasons for the pleasurable feelings accompanying the achievement of a goal being short-lived is that another goal, based on the same or a different need, soon takes its place. *When a need is satisfied, it no longer motivates.* The ever-changing nature of needs plays an important role in the theory and practice of incentive systems and job development programs. The truly motivated person will look for opportunities to satisfy his or her desires, as demonstrated in "To the Kid on the End of the Bench" (Figure 3-4).

To the Kid on the End of the Bench

Champions once sat where you're sitting, kid.
The Football Hall of Fame (and every other Hall of Fame) is filled with names of people who sat, week after week, without getting a spot of mud on their well-laundered uniforms.
Generals, senators, surgeons, prize-winning novelists, professors, business executives started on the end of a bench, too.
Don't sit and study your shoe tops. Keep your eye on the game.
Watch for defensive lapses.
Look for offensive opportunities.
If you don't think you're in a great spot, wait until you see how many would like to take it away from you at next spring practice.
What you do from the bench this season could put you on the field next season, as a player, or back in the grandstand as a spectator.

FIGURE 3-4 To be motivated to long-term goals means determination, sacrifice, and strong desire. Compliments of United Technologies, Box 360, Hartford, Conn. 06141

Can You Recognize the Need?

TEST YOURSELF

Each of the following work situations stresses the denial of one of four basic needs: (1) security, (2) social, (3) self-esteem, and (4) self-actualization. After each situation write the number of the need being denied. Refer to the text if necessary. (Answers are given at the end of the chapter.)

1. A rumor of imminent layoffs is being circulated in the company, and the employees are upset. ______________________

2. A new employee felt "left out" when she was not asked to join her fellow workers for coffee. _____

3. A machine operator developed a way to cut production time. His supervisor adopted the plan for operators on similar machines without giving him credit. The man was resentful. _____

4. A man who had worked hard on behalf of the union wished to be elected shop steward. At the last election, he was not nominated, and he felt let down by his friends. _____

5. A worker received $15 extra in his weekly paycheck. He felt ashamed that he did not report the mistake. _____

6. A group of employees liked to go for coffee together. The boss divided them into two groups and made them go at different times. The employees were unhappy about the ruling. _____

7. An employee who felt he could not work smoothly with others wanted to take a human relations course. The course required him to leave work 15 minutes early once a week, and he offered to make up the loss by coming in 15 minutes early on those days. The supervisor denied his request, thereby causing the employee a setback in his planning. _____

8. A store manager set a goal of a 15 percent sales increase in the next six months. She failed to attain her goal, but she did increase sales by 5 percent. She was keenly disappointed. _____

9. A salesman is worried because he has experienced a substantial drop in sales for no apparent reason. _____

10. A manager resented having to cancel, at the last minute, elaborate plans for a camping trip with his family. _____

HERZBERG'S HYGIENE THEORY

Another, but complementary, approach to motivation by need fulfillment is provided by Frederick Herzberg. In an attempt to provide global satisfaction for an organization's work force, Herzberg classified needs into two categories.

Satisfiers and Dissatisfiers

Herzberg found that the factors that make a job satisfying are separate from the factors that make it dissatisfying. For example, offering workers more money can lead to less *dis*satisfaction, but not to true job satisfaction. Employees who hold jobs that they consider intrinsically rewarding are satisfied with their jobs: with less rewarding work, they become *less* satisfied. Offering them more money does not *replace* the opportunity of doing fulfilling work.

Workers are often in a neutral position—neither happy nor unhappy, but simply doing their jobs. Certain negative job factors decrease job satisfaction, and alleviating them brings employees back to a neutral position. Other positive factors can create employee satisfaction on the job. Without them, the employees again drop back to neutral, without turning into dissatisfied employees.

Motivation-Maintenance Approach

Satisfying a hygiene factor keeps us from being unhappy

Herzberg believes certain factors are used to keep a person from being unhappy (Table 3-1), much in the same way that food keeps us from being hungry. Having a fine breakfast in the morning does not keep us from being hungry in the afternoon.

TABLE 3-1 Hygiene Factors and Growth Needs

HYGIENE MAINTENANCE FACTORS	MOTIVATORS AND GROWTH NEEDS
Salary, status, and security	Growth and advancement to higher-level tasks
Good factors keep one from being unhappy	
	Achievement
Company policies and administration	Recognition for achievement
Supervision	Interest in the task
Work environment and interpersonal relations	Responsibility for enlarged task

SOURCE: Adapted from Frederick Herzberg and others, *The Motivation to Work* (New York: John Wiley, 1959), p. 81.

Such is the case of motivation in industry. For example, a salary raise makes us happy, but not forever. Six months or a year later, we feel that we are deserving of a raise again, for one of many reasons. In Herzberg's terminology, money and fringe benefits are known as "negative motivators." Their absence from a job unquestionably will make people unhappy, but their presence doesn't necessarily make them happier or more productive.

But . . . satisfying a hygiene factor does not make us happy or productive

Hygiene factors are conditions conducive to maintaining mental and physical health. Satisfying the hygiene maintenance factors only keeps us from being unhappy. Whether a man's behavior is motivated by his physical needs, security needs, or social needs, once his "appetites" are satisfied, he ceases to be motivated, but he will become "hungry" again. We find that more money in routine amounts, such as the annual raise, is largely taken for granted, anticipated before it arrives, and viewed as a justly deserved reward for past services, not as a stimulus to a new effort.

Another way of viewing Herzberg's approach is that, once certain maintenance factors are present, they are adequate and keep a person from being unhappy. Such factors are company policies, supervision, interpersonal relationships, status, money, and security. However, the strong factors that motivate persons to do more on the job are really the opportunities for professional growth, responsibility, work itself, recognition, and achievement.

Dissatisfiers relate more to hygiene factors

When employees are asked what is dissatisfying in their jobs, they usually complain about things that are not associated with the actual work itself but rather with the work environment. These complaints include such matters as supervision, relations with others, physical conditions, organizational policies, administrative practices, pay, fringe benefits, status, and job security. Such complaints suggest that the context within which the work is done "is unfair or disorganized and as such represents . . . an unhealthy psychological work environment.[5]

Satisfiers relate more to the job itself

When employees are asked what satisfies them about their work, they will describe aspects of the job itself. Employees are satisfied when the work they do interests them, when they achieve job goals and receive recognition for their achievements, and when they grow or advance in responsibility. The factors that lead to job satisfaction are directly related to the need for self-actualization.

Both hygiene and growth needs must be satisfied

In summary, Herzberg believes that both hygiene and growth needs must be satisfied. Employees with exciting jobs will usually be willing to tolerate unpleasant circumstances, such as low pay or an unfriendly supervisor. However, the fewer the possibilities for growth and personal fulfillment on a job, the greater the number of hygiene factors that must be offered in compensation. Workers want something back for what they give. If they can't get personal satisfaction, then they will seek satisfaction in other ways.

INCENTIVES

The Nature of Incentives

An incentive is anything other than the job itself that motivates employees to produce. Incentive systems, which are based on external manipulation, are products of an external control management philosophy. According to this approach people are viewed as passive and must be persuaded, rewarded, pushed, punished, or otherwise externally controlled into action.

When Does an Incentive Become a Right?

Some past incentives have become today's rights

Today, about the only plan left that can be called a true incentive plan is the monetary reward offered to workers if they increase their standard output. Most other rewards offered as incentives are today considered workers' rights. Rights do not have incentive value; they are taken for granted. Employees who feel underpaid do not work any harder when their wages are raised—their responses are to feel less dissatisfied and to feel that deficiencies have been remedied.

Managers want rewards as incentives

Most managers also want to see rewards as incentives. However, many of these incentive schemes have been a source of frustration, because they have not increased output consistently. One reason for this disappointing state of affairs can be explained by Maslow's principle: a need that is satisfied ceases to motivate. Employees adjust rapidly to changing conditions, particularly when they are for the better.

Management is thus in the awkward position of offering incentives that are basically irrelevant. As Douglas McGregor said:

> . . . the carrot and stick theory does not work at all once man has reached an adequate subsistance level and is motivated primarily by higher needs. Management cannot provide a man with self-respect, or with the respect of his fellows, or with the satisfaction of needs for self-fulfillment. It can create conditions such that he is encouraged and enabled to seek such satisfaction *for himself,* or it can thwart him by failing to create those conditions.[6]

But to create these conditions the manager must know a great deal about human nature.

INTRINSIC AND EXTRINSIC MOTIVATORS

During the past 40 years, the growth of employee benefits has become an important aspect of the payroll. They are no longer "fringes." In some organizations, they amount to 50 percent of payroll. Companies provide sick leave, paid vacations, medical and dental plans, and free legal aid. All these plans were established in hopes that employees would show more loyalty and more motivation. Ironically, in most cases an employee can enjoy the fringe benefits only when off the job. These are called extrinsic motivators.

Extrinsic motivators may undermine intrinsic motivators

Often extrinsic motivators are needed to prod people into doing new or more difficult jobs or into acquiring rudimentary skills. In fact, there is a danger that extrinsic rewards may undermine intrinsic motivation—that we may undermine a person's intrinsic interest in an activity by inducing him or her to engage in it only as a means to some extrinsic goal. The joy of performing a task for itself may disappear when it is done simply for the reward offered by the supervisor.

Intrinsic motivators benefit employees on the job. Logically, people work harder when they are provided with comforts and when work is enjoyable.

In one University of Michigan survey, a sample of 1,533 workers were asked to rate the importance of various aspects of work and intrinsic motivators led the list. Of the five top-ranked features, only the fifth had to do with tangible economic benefits:

1. Interesting work
2. Enough help and equipment to get the job done
3. Sufficient information to get the job done
4. Enough authority to do the job
5. Good pay

Express Your Opinion

During your working career you may have held many or only a few jobs, but within a short time you were able to state that you enjoyed the job or were looking eagerly for another. Concentrate on one company and list the major extrinsic motivators. Now list the company's intrinsic motivators.

Now ask yourself, if you enjoyed the job, was it because of the extrinsic or the intrinsic motivators? If you disliked the job, was it because of the extrinsic or the intrinsic motivators?

By your own experience and the experiences that might be shared by others in the class, which seems to be the most important? Which motivators do companies tend to advertise and spend most of their time developing? Why?

BARRIERS TO ACHIEVEMENT

Regardless of the type of motivation, the end result of motivation should be performance. A formula for performance is:

$$\text{performance} = \text{function (ability} \times \text{motivation)}.$$

It is necessary to have both the ability and motivation to perform. If either ability or motivation is low, the performance will be low.

Even if motivation and ability are high, some personal goals and needs may not be met. Certainly when we have an internal need and decide consciously or unconsciously to satisfy that need, we may exhibit certain behavior to reduce tension. Notice in Figure 3-5 that barriers can deter us from reaching our goals.

Barriers cause frustrations that persist and become stronger. Some external barriers encountered by employees are discriminatory practices, hostile supervisors, monotonous jobs, and economic insecurity. Some internal barriers that frustrate employees are poor work habits, a dysfunctional personality, or a poor aptitude to do a particular job.

In some cases, by strengthening motivation (e.g., internal drive or external reward systems), it is possible to overcome the barrier. In other cases, it is not possible to overcome the barriers and behavior defense mechanisms are the result.

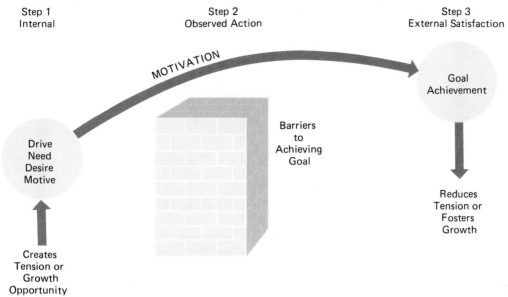

Step 1
Internal

Step 2
Observed Action

Step 3
External Satisfaction

MOTIVATION

Goal
Achievement

Drive
Need
Desire
Motive

Barriers
to
Achieving
Goal

Reduces
Tension or
Fosters
Growth

Creates
Tension or
Growth
Opportunity

FIGURE 3-5 **Barriers to the motivation process.**

Common Defense Mechanisms

Aggression

Aggression or hostility may be of a direct verbal or a physical type that is expressed in the form of attacks against persons perceived to be the cause of frustration. *Displaced aggression* can be observed in a supervisor who feels that he or she is not able to communicate with a superior and in turn will take it out on his or her subordinates with strong verbal abuse.

Individuals who can tolerate a high degree of abuse or aggression by others are said to have a high degree of tolerance to frustration. People with an "inner calm" are able to handle their own frustrations as well as those of others more easily.

Regression

Regression is defined as reverting to an earlier form of behavior to find satisfaction. It can be seen best through "childish actions," such as temper tantrums or pouting. We can even see this in the case of a newly appointed supervisor who starts doing segments of the old job he or she enjoyed because he or she cannot master the duties of the new position.

Fixation

Fixation behavior is the persistence of doing the same thing over and over again in the same way. Have you known a mechanic who is determined to put a bolt in a particular hole? He continues to force it until he strips the threads. Such behavior can continue even when several demonstrations show that it won't work. This type of stubbornness can also be seen when a salesperson has been taught to use several sales techniques but slips back into an old worn-out technique that he or she has learned will not work with a particular client.

Resignation

Resignation is displayed when someone gives up all sense of emotional or personal involvement. By failing to achieve some goal, a person may lose any positive concern about his or her job and adopt an apathetic attitude toward the situation.

Withdrawal

Such behavior can lead to *withdrawal*, in which the frustrated individual simply removes himself or herself from the situation in question—either physically or psychologically. A person who is not able to cope with a business adversary may avoid situations that would put him in contact with certain individuals. A person who becomes the butt of jibes and jokes may become a loner by adopting withdrawal behavior.

Repressive behavior is exhibited by the person who blocks out from the conscious mind those cognitive associations that are disturbing. It is an unrealistic form of behavior, since it implies that the problem will simply go away if one doesn't think about it.

Other common reactions are *compensation, rationalization,* and *projection.* The office clerk who is frustrated with his limited education may try to compensate by using multisyllable words and complicated language to impress others. Or the manager who is frustrated with having little or no authority may attempt to impress others by her "bossiness," which is really a form of rationalization. Or an employee may compensate when he has been passed over several times for a promotion by saying, "It would hardly have been worth the small difference in pay; I can find other good ways to spend my time." Projection is the act of subscribing to someone else's attitudes or thoughts. It can take the form of blaming others for their own thoughts, feelings, and behaviors. Some employees continually blame others because they sincerely believe that they themselves are not at fault for their own actions.

Defense mechanisms are common in all of us and very often unconscious. Unless used to an extreme degree, defensive behavior is considered quite normal; perhaps not acceptable at all times, but certainly normal.

Repression (margin note)

Compensation, rationalization, projection (margin note)

JOB DESIGN

The world is filled with boring jobs. Managers must rely on incentives to encourage workers to perform their jobs well because many jobs cannot be made satisfying to all people. But managers can have a great influence on the design of even the dullest jobs. Ideally, jobs should be structured to expand workers' capabilities. Workers can be motivated most effectively when managers allow employees to assume responsibility and participate in a productive way in making decisions. (See Figure 3-6).

Create a job where the person is self-motivated (margin note)

Jim Tunney, motivational speaker and NFL referee, says: "Most of the time people go through life doing the things they do because they're supposed to do them. They've been conditioned."[7] The management challenge is to get people to motivate themselves by helping them realize their own strengths and weaknesses, helping them achieve self-confidence and belief in themselves and their capabilities. Although the following approaches are not equally effective, they give a solid foundation for understanding how jobs can be designed to be challenging.

Horizontal Job Loading

Horizontal job loading assumes that, if employees are given more work to do at the *same level* at which they are currently performing, they will be motivated to work harder and also be more satisfied with their work. For example, an assembler is told to put together 1,000 parts instead of the 500 previously required. Horizontal job loading does not motivate.

FIGURE 3-6 Workers can be motivated most effectively when managers allow employees to assume responsibility and to participate in a productive way in making decisions. Michael Mayman/Photo Researchers

Vertical Job Loading

More work doesn't motivate; greater challenge or responsibility does

Vertical job loading changes jobs to include larger areas of responsibility. Jobs are restructured so that they will become *intrinsically* more interesting. The worker is motivated because the job is more challenging and more meaningful. For instance, a dishwasher's job would be changed vertically if he or she were also made responsible for keeping track of worn and broken dishes and for reporting defects to a supervisor.

Vertical loading implies that employees should be given as much responsibility as possible. Employees should be encouraged to be accountable for their work, with little supervision. Vertical job loading includes the idea of "closure": employees have an understanding of the organization of which they are a part. They are no longer just cogs in a wheel but instead can participate in and contribute to the entire work process. To provide for closure, tasks that belong together logically are grouped into one job—steps that one employee can carry through from beginning to end.

Thus, vertical job loading means:

1. Less direct control of the employee
2. Increased personal accountability
3. Assignment of complete tasks
4. Greater freedom on the job
5. Better skill utilization

Bank employee has control; she is not told what to do

A clerk at a bank remembers her job well. Even a machine would have grown bored with it. "My job was to pull invoices and checks out of envelopes and stack them into three piles: one under $10, another between $10 and $25, and a third over $25. Then I passed the piles on to the next person. After two months of this I was so bored I would have quit within another month." After two more years she was still at the bank, but instead of performing a tiny task in the paper mill, she handled all the processing for 22 corporate accounts. "Handling your own accounts is a lot more interesting, and you feel like you have accomplished something."

Job Enrichment

The term *enrichment* gained popularity when *job enlargement* began to be mistaken for horizontal job loading. *Job development* is another term in current use. Job enrichment and development indicate the fundamental principles of vertical job loading.

Overspecializing leads to boredom

For at least 50 years, industry has been committed to breaking down jobs into their smallest possible components and to stringing them out along assembly lines. Managers, assuming that work was inevitably boring, tried to boost morale and productivity by improving benefits and working conditions. We are now finding that the impact of boredom on productivity outweighs the benefits of extreme specialization.

Job Rotation

Change of tasks relieves the monotony

In job rotation, workers learn to do all the different activities necessary in one operation or unit of work. Teams that are used to working together adapt well to the rotation method. Job rotation can be subjected easily to horizontal loading. The monotony may be relieved by rotating similarly meaningless tasks, but this does not help to make the job more significant. However, it is quite possible to arrange for vertical job rotation, where both routine and complex tasks are passed around and new skills have to be applied to each job in the operation.

Delegation

One way to satisfy the needs for achievement, recognition, and responsibility is to give employees a task and the authority to carry it out. Authority is one of the most important positive motivators delegated to employees by supervisors. If workers are allowed to have it, they may be willing to take on new challenges.

Some leaders, however, are afraid to grant such authority, because an employee may make a poor decision that would embarrass the supervisor. Or worse, they are afraid that delegation will lessen their own authority. In fact, there is a logarithmic effect that permits the boss's authority to expand.

You should be looking for new ways in which to expand, rather than to limit, your subordinates' scope of activities. Many supervisors do not use their time wisely because they are not delegating enough duties to their employees.

Secretaries sign their own letters

One company that does try new methods is Polaroid. It allows its scientists to pursue their own projects and order their own materials without checking with a supervisor. Film-assembly workers are allowed to run their machines at their own pace. At another company, marketing correspondents are allowed to send letters affixed with their signatures rather than with those of their executives.

Flexibility Gives Self-Direction

"Sliding time" or "flexitime" helps employees decide for themselves

Such giants as General Foods and Motorola banished time clocks years ago. Other companies have staggered the working hours to best fit the parking lot traffic flow. One company has five shifts starting every 15 minutes. The morning shifts start at

8:00, 8:15, 8:30, 8:45, and 9:00 A.M. The evening shifts end at 4:00, 4:15, 4:30, 4:45 and 5:00 P.M. Each group puts in an 8-hour shift. But the employee can pick his or her time schedule. The factory or office workers can come in any time they like, provided that they are around for "core time," from 10:00 A.M. to 3:00 P.M., and that they put in a 40-hour week. Supervisors must trust their workers to maintain or increase productivity under decreased supervision, and supervisors must be prepared to deal with those few who abuse the system.[8]

Let Workers See the End Product of Their Efforts

Tour of the factory helps workers see the "whole picture"

In today's automated society, too often do employees work on parts for pieces of equipment that they never see. It is common that employees have no idea of the type of equipment that will hold their handiwork. Such a limiting view of the product can lead to a more complacent, bored attitude on the job. Some manufacturing firms have sent employees from their supply plants to assembly plants to see where their parts fit into the finished product. Other firms put the assembly-line workers on inspection jobs for one-week stints. Said one welder, "I now see metal damage, missing welds, and framing fits that I never would have noticed before." The employee who sees more of the company as a whole can identify with it in more positive terms. There is a great chance of loyalty and motivation under these conditions.

Listening Supervisors

Listening motivates more than talking

Studies seem to indicate that employees who have listening supervisors have higher morale than those who do not. To be an effective communicator, it is necessary to know far more than the rules for writing memos or making effective speeches. It is important to develop an insight into human motives and aspirations of employees to interact effectively. Xerox and the American Management Society have developed and conducted listening clinics.

As one manager said, "I don't understand why the employees don't perform better." In reply another manager commented: "Perhaps they don't want to be treated better, but want to be used better, and the only way we can find out how to use them better is to listen to them."

Summary

Motivation is an internal need

Motivation refers to any activity with a goal toward which the action is oriented. In business, that motivational action is called work. To want to act is true motivation.

Motivation is an internal state, which may be triggered by incentives. We all have highly individualized reasons for acting in the ways that we do. Therefore, while some generalizations can be made safely about the nature of motivation, it is inadvisable to judge the reasons for motivation on behavior alone.

Because organizations are responsible for job structure and content, they are largely responsible for workers' responsibilities to satisfy their personal needs— needs that provide the motivating force for their work. Organizations and individuals must constantly reevaluate their mutual satisfactions and dissatisfactions in an attempt to balance each other's needs.

There are at least three schools of psychology that might be studied as they relate to motivation. Sigmund Freud founded the psychoanalytic school of thought that states that much of a person's motivational thrust is hidden in the unconscious realm of the brain. Therefore the reason for a person's motivation is hard to discover. B. F. Skinner believes that people can be motivated to act through behavior modification, which involves the rewarding of desired behavior and the ignoring of undesirable behavior. Any attention to a behavior, either positive or negative, will enforce such a behavior. The third school of thought was developed by Abraham Maslow. Maslow widened the scope of motivational theory with his observations on the hierarchy of needs.

Carrot-and-stick management

Incentives are punishments and rewards that are *ex*trinsic to the job itself. They are used to try to motivate people to work better or harder. The carrot-and-stick management philosophy is a way of describing incentives. Basically, incentives are designed to push or pull employees to perform their jobs even better.

Motivating factors are *in*trinsic to the job. True motivation must come from the job itself—only the job can be satisfying. Part of feeling self-fulfilled is having the sense of utilizing one's energy in a fruitful way. Only when workers feel that they are achieving something in spite of the routine nature of the work are their jobs satisfying. Managers cannot always change the structures of jobs so that they give more responsibility and decision-making power to employees.

Horizontal job loading

Vertical job loading

Horizontal job loading only increases workers' duties at the same level, without giving workers higher levels of responsibility. Vertical job loading, on the other hand, adds dimension to jobs. Employees are made responsible for entire operations, including many levels of tasks and skills. Job rotation is the concept of trading jobs, which often relieves monotony and can increase responsibility. Through job enlargement programs, assembly lines have been disbanded and teams formed that build entire assemblies together. Job enrichment or job development are the terms now used to indicate vertical job loading methods.

Job enrichment

Case Study 5

How Do You Motivate Motel Maids?

All Western Motels are part of a franchise operation with six interests in the San Diego area. For the last several years, employee turnover, especially among the lower-salaried workers, has been a major problem. The turnover rate for maids alone reached the level of three employees per month per motel. This computes to the staggering figure of 45 percent on an annual basis.

The maid is probably the most potent representative of a motel, even though she is seldom, if ever, seen by the guests. It is the way in which she performs her work that will determine, to a large extent, whether a guest will return to the motel for a second stay; and motels survive on repeat business. "Repeaters" make a house's reputation—especially through word-of-mouth advertising, which is the best and the cheapest kind! Not only were the motels faced with the expense of hiring, processing, and bonding employees, but low morale was producing a low-grade, careless approach to the job. In several instances, a complete refund of rent monies had to be made. In addition, maids quit without notice, and the cost to train a new applicant was becoming intolerable.

The maids for the Western concerns were being paid the top wages in the area for related employment. These wages were not at all high, however, as no motel can afford to increase its overhead appreciably. The working conditions seemed good. The women were allowed one meal per shift "gratis" at the motel's coffee shops, and they were allowed to use the pool facilities during their "off-hours" at four of the locations.

The managers tried to interview the workers who had left their employ, but they could get no useful information from them. They spoke in generalities, such as "I'm just tired of working here." Finally, the operators approached the franchise's main office in Phoenix, and a general meeting of the concerned managers was called. You were chosen as the franchise representative to the conference.

The meeting was held on September 19 and 20 at one of the San Diego locations. Five of the motels sent representatives. One manager claimed that the whole thing was "just a waste of time and money." After lunch, on the first day, your group sat down to discuss the situation.

It was the general consensus of the group that the fidelity of the employees toward the company should be increased. Personal identity and pride in their jobs seemed to be the ingredients most lacking. But how to induce these feelings into a role such as that of a maid?

1. Put yourself in the role of the motel maid. What physical changes could be made to enhance the job?

2. Personal identity and pride in the job should be given top priority in redesigning the position. Can changes be made in uniform, job functions, reporting times, personal recognition, or "off-duty privileges" to enhance the employees' personal identity?

3. What psychological factors can be developed to help the maids' personal images?

4. What intrinsic motivators can help the situation?

Case Study 6

The "Hooky" Case

The XYZ Corporation of Midland, Nebraska, manufactures and distributes water pumps for irrigation systems. Its products are outstanding and are much sought after by individual farmers and agricultural corporations. The company is well financed and its products are marketed through the company's own marketing and sales organizations rather than manufacturers' representatives. Because its pumps are so well accepted, the marketing function is less demanding than that in similar companies.

Nevertheless, XYZ has an extensive geographical marketing organization throughout the United States as well as international operations. Similar to other organizations, they have a fairly extensive hierarchy in both production, marketing, finance, personnel, and other staff departments. Their marketing function is organized with geographical regions, divisions, and departments.

Frank Taylor, Midwest division manager for XYZ, has been selected to attend an all-expense-paid two-week course on management development at a state university. Frank is 49 years old and has been with the company for 20 years. He has held several sales and marketing positions with XYZ and other employers before XYZ.

While in these jobs, Frank attended many technical, marketing, and management development courses and seminars. Consequently, he is not sure whether he needs to attend the present course, but he did want to visit the city and other organizations in the area where the course is being held. In fact, Frank takes his family with him to the city where the course is held but does not actually attend the class meetings.

1. What is the problem here?
2. What do you need to know that you don't know before you can recommend a solution?
3. What are several alternatives that you see?
4. What, if anything, should be done about Frank?

Terms and Concepts

belonging need part of Maslow's hierarchy of needs theory. We all need to be accepted and be a member of a group. This need may be satisfied with a group of friends, the family, a mate, or a community organization.

ego need the desire to satisfy basic self-esteem or ego needs. Being a leader or obtaining status can satisfy this need.

equity theory workers try to maintain balance between their own inputs and their rewards in comparison to other workers.

expectancy theory based on the strength of an individual's belief that a course of action will result in a given performance and reward.

growth motivation positive type of motivation that puts emphasis on the individual and psychological growth of employees.

hygiene-maintenance theory the Herzberg theory that states that some factors only prompt us to keep from being dissatisfied and are not self-motivating. Such factors only keep us from being unhappy.

intrinsic motivators motivators that take place on the job that help us to enjoy working, as contrasted to extrinsic motivators that can only be enjoyed off the job.

job design variables in a job that will increase the quality and quantity of worker performance.

job enlargement enlargement of a position to include more duties. Such action does not necessarily motivate workers.

job enrichment the view that a job may include more duties that are more complex and hence grant more responsibility and authority.

job rotation performance of several different positions to learn a whole system and alleviate boredom. It provides variety and sometimes opportunity for promotion.

physiological needs the basic needs according to Maslow's theory of motivation. Most workers in the United States find that they can satisfy most of their needs for food, shelter, clothing, and comforts.

security need the second need described by Maslow. It can be satisfied by physical and psychological factors, such as safety belts, insurance, and pensions.

self-actualization knowing the zenith of your ability and achieving it.

Notes

1. Chris Argyris, *Integrating the Individual and the Organization* (New York: John Wiley, 1964), p. 7.

2. Clayton Alderfer, *Existence, Relatedness, and Growth* (New York: Free Press, 1972).

3. Pat Buhler, "Motivation: What Is Behind the Motivation of Employees?" *Supervision*, June 1988, pp. 18–20.

4. A. H. Maslow, *Motivation and Personality* (New York: Harper & Row, 1954).

5. Frederick Herzberg, Bernard Mausner, and Barbara Bloch Snyderman, *The Motivation to Work* (New York: John Wiley, 1959), p. 113.

6. Douglas McGregor, *The Human Side of Enterprise* (New York: McGraw-Hill, 1960), pp. 121–122.

7. Jim Tunney, "Motivating People," *USA Today*, June 7, 1985, p. 13A.

8. David Hull, "No More 9 to 5?" *Computer Decisions*, June 1982, pp. 160–178.

Recommended Reading

Alderfer, Clayton. *Existence, Relatedness, and Growth.* New York: Free Press, 1972.

Argyris, Chris. *Integrating the Individual and the Organization.* New York: John Wiley, 1964.

Charsley, Walter F. "Management, Morale, and Motivation." *Management World*, July–August 1988, pp. 27–28.

Fleishman, Edwin A., Marilyn K. Quaintance, and Laurie A. Broedling. *Taxonomies of Human Performance.* Orlando, Fla.: Academic Press, 1984.

Hackman, J. Richard, and Greg R. Oldham. *Work Redesign.* Reading, Mass.: Addison-Wesley, 1980.

Herzberg, Frederick. *Work and the Nature of Man.* New York: Collins, 1966.

Latham, G. P., and E. A. Locke. "Goal Setting: A Motivational Technique That Works." *Organizational Dynamics*, March–April 1979, pp. 68–80.

Lawler, Edward E., III. *High Involvement Management.* San Francisco: Jossey-Bass, 1986.

Maslow, A. H. *Motivation and Personality.* New York: Harper & Row, 1954.

McGregor, Douglas. *The Human Side of Enterprise.* New York: McGraw-Hill, 1960.

Mitchell, Terrence R. "Motivation: New Directions for Theory, Research and Practice." *Academy of Management Review*, January 1982, pp. 80–88.

Raven, John. "Toward Measures of High-Level Competencies: A Re-examination of McClelland's Distinction Between Needs and Values." *Human Relations*, April 1988, pp. 281–284.

Skinner, B. F. *Beyond Freedom and Dignity.* New York: Alfred A. Knopf, 1971.

Steers, Richard M., and Lyman W. Porter. *Motivation and Work Behavior*, 4th ed. New York: McGraw-Hill, 1987.

Vroom, Victor H. *Work and Motivation.* New York: John Wiley, 1964.

Job Performance and Morale

OBJECTIVES

After studying this chapter, you should be able to:

1. Define job performance, performance standards, and performance measurement.

2. Argue the merits and disadvantages of job descriptions.

3. Understand the determinants of effective job performance.

4. Define the terms *morale* and *job satisfaction.* Understand the relationships among job performance, morale, and job satisfaction.

5. Discuss the general attitudes of the following groups toward their jobs in today's society:

   a. Blue-collar workers

   b. White-collar workers

6. Explain how and why employee surveys can be useful in studying morale.

7. Explain how reviewing the company's records can tell us something about the employees' morale.

8. Describe how the physical environment can affect employees' morale.

TO START YOU THINKING . . .

This chapter will help you discover certain feelings about your work. Begin by considering the following questions:

◆ How do human needs affect work performance?

◆ What is the ultimate goal of work activity—job satisfaction? high morale? job performance?

◆ What makes a job satisfying or dissatisfying?

◆ Do you like the people you work with? Do you socialize with them on and off the job? If not, what prevents this exchange? With whom do you enjoy working most?

◆ Are you treated as part of a team or as an employee with only specific duties to perform?

◆ Is your job boring or challenging? If you had your way, how would you change your job to make it more meaningful?

◆ How do you feel about your organization's goals? Do you think that the organization is interested in profits only, or does it have the interests of its employees and society in mind?

JOB PERFORMANCE, THE KEY TO MORALE AND PRODUCTIVITY

The study of human relations involves the practical attempt to achieve the two separate goals of greater productivity at work and greater human satisfaction within the organization. Job performance provides the key to these two goals and the key to organizational effectiveness. What employees and management do in setting and meeting standards of performance determines organizational effectiveness. Arthur Pell writes that preparation before beginning a job assignment will help to bring successful results. Steps that lead to performance success include becoming technically competent by learning as much as possible about a subject, receiving training, and teaching skills to others.[1]

Human satisfaction within the organization can be broken down into two aspects. Job satisfaction relates to the individual, whereas morale reflects the feelings of the group. After years of research on motivation, job satisfaction, and productivity, we still do not have agreement regarding a cause-and-effect relationship between any of these variables. Herzberg, Lawler, Porter, and many others have studied and written extensively on job satisfaction and related subjects for decades.[2] The results regarding the relationship of job satisfaction and productivity are not always clear nor well established.

What does seem clear is that there is a greater probability of job satisfaction resulting from effective job performance than the opposite. This finding is contrary to the thrust of the research in the 1960s and 1970s, which tried to establish job satisfaction as a cause of good performance.

A beginning in determining the relationship between productivity and satisfaction is the source of both concepts—job performance. Effective job performance is best defined by determining (1) the job to be done, (2) the standards by which job completion is to be measured, and (3) tying results to a reward system.

The Job Description

The job description is the definition of the job to be done. The manner of preparing and updating job descriptions is changing with computer applications of human resource information systems (HRIS). They are much easier to keep up-to-date and therefore more useful to both employees and managers. The use of job descriptions as orientation devices and as the first step in job analysis remains important for all human resources managers. More importantly, they are a means of defining the expectations of job incumbents.

Some of the factors included in the job description are responsibilities, relationships, duties (tasks), and performance elements. The last two, tasks and performance elements, are relatively new additions. They add meaning to the description allowing the incumbent to know what is expected, what is to be done, and how the performance standards will be applied—that is, how the performance will be evaluated.

The Office of Personnel Management and other federal government agencies have made significant progress in recognizing the importance of setting performance standards for performance appraisals. The performance elements, tasks, and performance standards are utilized actively in goal setting, counseling, and evaluation. Figure 4-1 shows how tasks, performance elements, and standards can be built into the job description.

Performance Standards

In addition to the use of job descriptions to define job performance expectations, there must be specific standards and criteria for performance. The standards can be

Job satisfaction is a function of job performance

Job descriptions are fundamental

Job descriptions are changing with computer applications

New additions to job descriptions

Federal government's use of performance standards

Behaviorally based, results-oriented standards

Express Your Opinion

Some experts, including Tom Peters, argue that job descriptions are archaic and ought to be scrapped. Peters makes a strong case that:

> The job description is a cop-out, pure and simple. But it is more (or less) than that. It is imperative today that managers and nonmanagers be induced to cross "uncrossable" boundaries as a matter of course, day after day. Standing on the formality of a written job description (as an excuse for inaction, or the reason you have to "check up—and up and up—the line") is a guaranteed strategy for disaster.[3]

On the other hand, if the job description is well written as described and gives general guidance as well as specific direction, can you argue with the utility of having these guidelines? Another recent study puts emphasis on job analysis to develop better job descriptions.[4]

What do you think about job descriptions? Do you think you will need one during your first few days on a job? during your first few jobs? How about senior managers—do they need job descriptions?

arrived at through the management by objectives (MBO) process, or any other behaviorally based, results-oriented system. Participation by the employee in setting the standards is a key aspect of this process.

People should be able to set their own targets of performance within organizational constraints. That does not mean "do your own thing"! It means setting your own standards of performance within organizational constraints and mission. The manager determines what must be done, when, and by whom. Other requirements in setting performance standards include determining quantity and quality of work to be done, setting time schedules, and establishing cost and other budgetary constraints.

At a fully acceptable level of performance, a performance standard should have the following characteristics:

1. Enable the user to differentiate between acceptable and unacceptable results.

2. Present some challenge to the employee.

3. Be realistic—that is, be attainable by any qualified, proficient, and fully trained employee who has the necessary authority and resources.

4. Be a statement of the conditions that will exist and will measure a job activity when it is performed acceptably, expressed in terms of quantity, quality, time cost, effect obtained, manner of performance, or method of doing.

5. Relate to or express a time frame for accomplishment.

6. Be observable.[5]

People-oriented standards

If the criteria are behaviorally oriented, as in Behaviorally Anchored Rating Scales (BARS), they provide standards that are people oriented. The scales (expected behavioral outcomes) are worded in terms of actual behavioral expectations and become part of a graphic scale. Multiple levels (usually 7 or 9) on the scales correspond to expected behaviors at various levels of performance. The

PERFORMANCE ELEMENT	TASK	PERFORMANCE STANDARD* FULLY SATISFACTORY
I. Program Planning	1. Consult and interact with higher management research leader, scientists, cooperators, industry groups, etc., in order to identify research gaps, needs and priorities.	1. a. Essential internal and external groups are consulted prior to submission of program planning information to RA.
		b. Any sensitive program issues are communicated and/or documented in submission to RA.
	2. Develop implementation plan/proposal including justification statement and financial plans.	2. a. Research program and project priorities are communicated to RA on a timely basis.
		b. Annual Position Resource Management Plans sent to RA no later than (date).
		c. New or revised research proposals, including budget increase requests, sent to RA consistent with the budgetary cycle.
		d. Research proposals, documentation, etc., responding to emergencies submitted on a timely basis.
II. Program Management	1. Provide program leadership.	1. a. Assures that new ideas, stimuli, etc. are provided to research units/programs.
		b. Resources have been shifted, where appropriate, to support new or redirected research efforts.
		c. Multidisciplinary research efforts have been increased.
		d. Internal and external interest in the new or redirected research effort have been increased.
	2. Promote research productivity	2. a. Publications (1) Referred journals _____ (2) Department series _____ (3) Trade publications _____ (4) Proceedings _____ (5) Book chapters _____ (6) Citation index _____ (7) Reviews _____ (8) Abstracts _____ (9) Mimeographed releases _____ (10) Popular publications _____

*This agency has three performance rating levels: meets standard, exceeds standard, does not meet standard; therefore, one performance standard is sufficient.
SOURCE: U.S. Office of Personnel Management, *Performance Standards Handbook*, April 1981, p. 11–23.

subordinates play a key role in establishing the BARS. In Chapter 12 there is further discussion and examples of both MBO and BARS.

Andrall Pearson, former president of PepsiCo, says the secret to building a company is "raising standards relentlessly. That means identifying and grooming talent at every level, and cutting the dead wood." He dispels the myth that this type of scrutiny—and inevitable firings—will demoralize employees. His experience suggests the opposite: "Top performers relish the challenge of ever-higher goals. What demoralizes them is a climate that rewards mediocrity and excellence equally."[6]

Performance Measurement _____

Set standards in advance of performance

If desired performance has not been defined in advance of performance measurement—that is, if objective standards are lacking—how can the employee and the manager know when performance has been achieved? How can the subordinate know if he or she has performed well and thereby be satisfied with the job? Effort alone may influence one's job performance but is less important than measuring results. Both quality and quantity dimensions must be used in measuring results. The active participation of employees in setting their performance standards contributes to better job performance.

Feedback should be immediate, precise, and specific

We all like to know how we are doing. To know that, we must have feedback. Performance measurement systems are based on feedback. That feedback should be available *immediately*, *precisely*, and *specifically*. Most performance appraisal techniques currently in practice disregard the immediacy. Many performance evaluations are still performed only annually, if then. Monthly, weekly, or even daily feedback is preferred to provide employees with the necessary information to perform their jobs better. Likewise, the feedback should relate to precise behavior, specific performance, and desired behavioral outcomes.

Most job performance is difficult to measure objectively. There are external variables such as economic conditions that may influence job performance but these are usually noncontrollable by the individual. The measurement of performance is easier and more precise given predetermined criteria and standards.

A recent study by Graham Kenny and Alan Dunk shows several performance measures that are useful to production managers:

Performance Measure	Related Element
Variance between planned "output" and actual "output"	Product
Machine output rates	Machines
Variance between standard amounts of materials required for jobs and actual amounts used	Machines
Incidence of quality control problems	Product
Rate at which delivery schedules are met	Customers
Variance between standard times allowed for jobs and actual times taken	Employees
Scrap or waste levels	Material
Absenteeism levels of employees in department	Employees
Incidence of customer complaints	Customers
General "output" per employee	Employees
Accident levels of employees in department	Employees[7]

Rewarding Results _____

There has been difficulty in making the connection between performance and rewards. Jan Muczyk and Robert Hastings write that:

The sad truth of the matter is that in many organizations with productivity problems, the below-average, average, and above-average employees at all levels of the organization receive roughly identical rewards—and this applies to nonunionized organizations as well. Therefore, the extrinsic incentives for performing at high levels are absent from the workplace.[8]

Rewards should be timely and effective

Tying both monetary and nonmonetary rewards to performance is important. The ties should be both causative and timely; that is, a cause-and-effect relationship should be present as well as a timely reward. If the reward only comes once a year, it is too late to be considered a reward for performance. It is possible to have monetary reward increments more frequently if they are based on a computerized Human Resource Information System.

Nonmonetary rewards

Of course, the monetary reward cannot always be tied immediately to performance, but nonmonetary praise and recognition can. Nonmonetary rewards can occur as often as necessary to reinforce feedback on job performance. *One of the most overlooked factors in rewarding performance is communicating recognition and praise for a job well done.* Praise and recognition can be frequently communicated orally and sometimes in writing for both public media and individual personnel files.

Determinants of Job Performance

Job performance is multidimensional

Job performance is more complicated than a uridimensional variable such as job satisfaction would suggest. The ability to perform on the job is based on such variables as rewards, coworkers, management competence, the intrinsic quality of the work itself, promotion opportunities, and other social and external conditions.

Pay and job

Rewards. Monetary and nonmonetary rewards, such as recognition and job security, are usually at the top of the lists of variables affecting job performance. The overall tie between pay and performance has always been present but the relationships between an employee's behavioral performance and pay have too frequently been ignored.

Pay-for-performance

Pay-for-performance plans provide a more direct link between good performance and its reward than do salary and wage levels. Regardless of whether the pay plan is for blue-collar piecework or rate of return on the balance sheet for executives, there is more of a cause-and-effect relationship between pay and performance than if a straight salary or wage is paid. Nevertheless, the relationship of pay to job performance is often complicated by age, education, and occupational level. Further, there is evidence that the importance of pay is overestimated and that performance is not solely contingent upon pay but on social and intrinsic factors as well.

The social environment

Coworkers. The place of the work group in contributing to effective job performance has been well established by the Hawthorne and other studies. The importance of being continuously associated with fellow workers is stronger for some employees than the more direct monetary rewards.

From "day one," new employees form impressions about coworkers that affect their job performance for the duration of their careers with that organization. Managers and supervisors, inasmuch as they are also coworkers, contribute to the social environment affecting job performance.

Expectations of management

Management and Supervisory Competence. The expectations of employees about the competence of their supervisors and managers have increased with higher levels of education and with each generation. If managers do not have the technical and interpersonal competence expected by the employees, then the employees will not be as diligent in performing their jobs.

Interpersonal contact

There is no substitute for interpersonal job contact and relationships by managers to ensure the commitment necessary for effective job performance. At least one company, Hewlett-Packard, achieves this by following a philosophy of "Management by Walking (or Wandering) Around."

Job design

Intrinsic Factors of the Work Itself. Regardless of the extrinsic factors such as quality of management, coworkers, and pay, the internal aspects of how the job is designed are important determinants in how effectively the job is performed. (See Figure 4-2.) Job design and the autonomy and responsibility of employees are critical areas for most individuals. When jobs are too structured, employees lose interest in performing to maximum levels.

Recognition

Recognition is another factor contributing to how "good" the job is and consequently how well the employee performs the job. The amount of recognition provided for individuals is a significant force having a direct bearing on how intensely they work.

FIGURE 4-2 How well the job is designed determines how effectively the job is performed. Source: Gerard Fritz/Monkmeyer Press

Promotion opportunities subject to individual differences

Promotion opportunities must be present whether used or not

Promotion Opportunities. Not all employees want promotions, but the opportunities for promotion must be present. Unlike most of the foregoing factors where there is general commonality among most individuals, there are considerable individual differences regarding promotion opportunities.

Whether or not the promotion actually takes place is not as important for some employees as the opportunity. There is an analogy to Herzberg's dual-factor approach to motivation: the opportunity for promotion must be present to avoid dissatisfaction but satisfaction is still not guaranteed. The "neutral" point of at least having the opportunities available is preferable to dissatisfaction and negative job attitudes and performance.

Similarities of Job Performance to Job Satisfaction. Not too surprisingly, these factors of pay, working conditions, promotion opportunities, and others are the same items that have been considered the determinants of job satisfaction by Herzberg and others. The variables are not means to an end of job satisfaction, but are effects of the end itself—effective job performance. Job satisfaction, on the other hand, is influenced by job performance itself, along with other variables.

JOB SATISFACTION AND MORALE

Job satisfaction is an individual perception

Morale is a composite of all individuals' job satisfactions

Most career choices involve consideration or reconsideration of what one expects to get out of a job, that is, job satisfaction. Job satisfaction is a personal matter based on each individual's value system and attitudes about the job. Morale, on the other hand, is a group concept—a composite of all individuals' job satisfactions. Both job satisfaction and morale are based on attitude. Both are subjective, but it is essential that both be measured and heeded if the organization is to be highly productive.

Job satisfaction in relationship to "referent others"

Job satisfaction is relative. Only when an individual considers his or her situation in relationship to others can job satisfaction be determined. This is the important "referent others" concept. The referent others concept is that individuals compare their rewards with others who have similar backgrounds, abilities, and responsibilities.

Morale is a composite of feelings

Morale, that composite state of mind and emotions, affects our attitudes and willingness to work, which in turn, affect those of others. People with high morale have confidence in themselves, in the future, and in others. High morale permits taking minor irritations in stride and working under pressure without blowing up.

Maintaining high morale is a continuous task

Raising morale to a high level and maintaining it there is a continuous process that cannot be achieved simply through short-run devices such as pep talks or contests. High morale is usually slow to develop and difficult to maintain. Low morale develops more rapidly and is even more difficult to overcome. A positive outlook on life is contagious to the workplace. A simple explanation of individual job satisfaction and morale is fulfillment of one's own expectations.

Whereas satisfaction is a person's attitude toward job or life, morale reflects the general tone or *esprit de corps* of a collective group of personalities. Each person either heightens the prospect for *esprit de corps* or lowers the outlook for cooperative effort.

The Variables of Job Satisfaction

Classifications of job satisfaction

Knowing what to expect regarding the variables of job satisfaction will help managers predict and be prepared for changes in both individual job satisfaction and the morale of the entire organization. These variables are helpful in explaining job performance variances among various groups. Primary variables include age, years on the job, occupational field, organizational level, education, and gender.

Aggregate relationships

All the variable relationships discussed are aggregates. There are many individual exceptions, but on balance the relationships represent the work force population. Many researchers have observed and studied the relationships in various organizational settings.[9] (See Figure 4-3.)

Generally a positive but U-shaped relationship

Age. Generally, there is a positive correlation between age and job perform-ance/satisfaction, but the specific effects remain uncertain. Unique relationships exist for certain age groups such as the very young (19 or younger) who are relatively high performers and well satisfied, and for individuals nearing retire-ment who experience some downturn in performance and satisfaction.

Fluctuations in attitudes of younger workers occur because of a new interest in work and a change in workplace. Young people will perform well and experience high job satisfaction on initial employment. However, both performance and satisfaction can fall off rapidly and dramatically for several years until they reach their late twenties. Then, performance and satisfaction increase gradually with age—eventually surpassing the levels of initial employment.

Another positive but U-shaped curve

Years on the Job. Tenure on a particular job follows a very similar pattern. That is, the initial high performance and satisfaction are followed by a steep falling off or falling out during the first year of employment on any job. Both remain low for several years before turning upward.

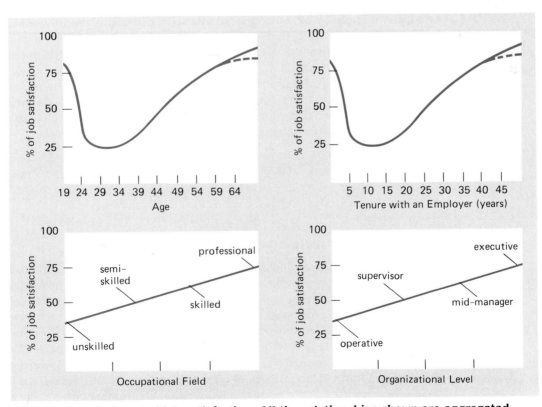

FIGURE 4-3 Variables of job satisfaction. All the relationships shown are aggregated. Individual differences will exist.

If individuals repeatedly leave organizations during this falling-off period and take different jobs, they are perpetually in flux: initially feeling almost euphoric about their jobs, and a short time later feeling dissatisfied and unproductive. Absenteeism and turnover are manifested in this situation. If employees keep moving through this cycle from job to job, they become "job-hoppers" and experience personal costs as well as the costs of turnover to their organizations.

Occupational Field. There are differences in job performance and satisfaction among various occupational groups, but there is generally a positive relationship between complexity of the job and performance/satisfaction. Historically, less skilled workers need more job security than the cosmopolitan or professional workers. Unskilled workers are less mobile and more dependent on local organizations including, in some cases, their unions.

One encouraging fact emerges from studies of job satisfaction: the higher the level of occupation, the higher the morale. Laborers and other nontechnical employees are generally lower performers and are less satisfied than technical, skilled, and professional workers.

Organizational Level. There is a positive relationship between job performance and satisfaction and organizational level. The performance and satisfaction levels of individuals are probably as much a function of level as they are a function of occupational field. As an individual ascends a hierarchical organization, he or she experiences opportunities for higher job performance and consequently opportunities for higher job satisfaction.

Education. Higher educational level does not necessarily mean greater job satisfaction. This may be due in part to increased expectations prompted by higher levels of education. Exceptions to this trend may be found at the level of graduate education, especially at the doctoral and postdoctoral levels in medicine and other disciplines.

The increased expectations brought about by higher education may be offset somewhat by the increase in promotions based on occupational and organizational levels. Similarly, the rising educational level of the general population may account for the relative dissatisfaction of younger, but more educated, workers.

Gender. In the past, men have reported a higher degree of job satisfaction than women. More recently, differences have diminished due in part to more equal opportunities for employment and advancement. Women have placed higher priorities on coworkers and working conditions than men.

Blue-Collar Challenge

Today's jobs are not as likely to bring the same satisfaction earned by such craftsmen as the cabinetmaker or blacksmith of the last century. Work skills are now linked to machine operations, and what we make is mostly the product of other machines and other workers. The mechanized worker stands at a psychological distance from his or her work and is not identified with the end product. Often this type of employee is confined to a fixed workstation and is expected to leave it only with permission. Such restrictions can affect one's attitude toward work.

An important determinant of job satisfaction is the length of the job cycle—how long it takes to perform an operation before starting over. For a college professor, the work cycle is often a semester. For a skilled craftsman, it may be weeks. For the worker on the assembly line, it may last only a minute: "The job can get sickening, if it is only plugging in ignition wires. You get through with one motor, turn around, and there's another motor staring you in the face."

The machine can be more of a taskmaster than the supervisor

Most people like variety in their work rhythm; they may work fast for a while and then slow down gradually as the day wears on. Such change of pace helps to reduce both fatigue and job boredom. The assembly line offers few provisions for worker preference. The pace is set and the worker may never change it. Therefore, the machine may be a worse autocrat than any supervisor.

Employees invent games to add "spice" to the workplace

To make work more enjoyable, many employees invent games that supply new goals. When job pressure is not tightly paced, the worker may experiment with various speeds and set various output goals. Social games frequently provide another form of diversion. Flipping coins to see who buys the coffee, World Series pools, numbers games, and other gambling games provide variety in the workplace.

Job Satisfaction in the White-Collar World

A change in title can mean higher job satisfaction

Banks, retail stores, hospitals, and service industries are providing more white-collar jobs than ever before. Even in the factories, the ratio of managers and engineers to production workers is growing. Research, design, marketing, and finance also provide more opportunities for white-collar people. Universally, white-collar work provides more prestige than does blue collar. The white-collar jobs are thought to give more individuality and are more likely to provide status. Industrial psychology has found that a job title such as "staff assistant" may provide a sense of advancement to an employee who was doing almost the same job when it was called "chief clerk."

Jobs in the white-collar area demand more intellectual than physical effort. Copywriters, programmers, and laboratory technicians all must exhibit initiative and creativity. Such positions require a deep concentration and present a varied work pace, both of which tend to raise employee morale.

White-collar jobs are more flexible

White-collar jobs are usually more flexible than blue-collar jobs because they are not as tied to strict production quotas. Working hours are often more flexible, and the procedures for doing a job are usually not as rigid. Even so, white-collar workers also often feel dead-ended in their work.

Blue-collar workers achieve earning plateau before white-collar workers

The big problem for collar color seems to occur in the "middle years." At this stage of their lives, nearly twice as many blue-collar as white-collar workers were dissatisfied with their jobs. One reason for this overall dissatisfaction with work may be that blue-collar workers may experience an "economic squeeze" during their middle years. Blue-collar workers usually achieve their top earnings earlier in life, whereas white-collar workers do not plateau early, but begin to reap the rewards of their greater education in their thirties.

Pink-collar workers are dissatisfied

An increasing number of pink-collar workers, including paraprofessionals in health care and other fields, are experiencing both pay and status dissatisfactions. Pink-collar workers also include waitresses, nurses' aides, and many office workers.

Morale and the Work Force

The more successful the company, the higher the workers' morale
Small companies enjoy higher morale

The more successful the company, the more likely will the employee show loyalty. If a company is showing a fine production record and good profits, it is wise to share such information with employees. Several firms send a copy of the annual report to each employee.

Second, the employees of today seem to demonstrate a higher morale in small companies than in large ones. An employee from a multinational company commented, "Oh, I am only one of a thousand employees; they don't care what my name is as long as I turn out so many parts an hour." Or the statement, "I am lost in this joint; the management only knows me as employee number 456."

Absenteeism—headache

Every day from 3 to 7 percent of the work force is missing, representing a loss of $100 million a year in absentee wages. Absenteeism also incurs the significant expenses of training workers to fill in for absentees, disruption of production, and overstaffing to minimize the impact of absenteeism. Companies most apt to have no-shows are those that offer sick-leave pay and those that keep scant records and are lax about employee absences.

Problems arise when the employee's salary comes close to the supervisor's

It may seem to employees that the longer they work, the higher their salaries become, but the closer their salaries come to their supervisors' salaries, the more likely their morale will drop. The reason for this is, "Why should I work to become a supervisor when I will only receive 3 or 4 cents more an hour for that much more responsibility. It isn't worth it." Likewise, the supervisor may feel that he or she is underpaid, because there is no wage premium attached to responsibility. As an employer, be sure to make that span of earnings between the employee and the supervisor enough, roughly 30 percent, to make it seem worthwhile to both of them. An employee should see a substantial monetary increase in accepting a supervisory role, and the supervisor should feel compensated for the task.

"Wellness programs"

A large number of companies are changing their attitudes toward employee health. They are taking a stance of "wellness" and illness prevention rather than health insurance and rehabilitation. Many companies are actively helping employees to maintain and improve their health through "wellness programs." Such firms are building swimming pools, gymnasiums, jogging tracks, squash and tennis courts, locker rooms, and saunas to keep employees healthy. Low-calorie menus in company cafeterias promote workers' health as well. Some companies give bonuses to employees who do not take any sick days.

"Third place," or social center

Some psychologists are saying the Americans need a third place, a hangout, a social center, where employees are free from social pressures.[10] Neighborhood taverns survive because of their ability to promote freewheeling sociability and status-free communication. This benefit is now available at gyms, sports and health programs offered by some companies, and in health clubs and fitness centers across the nation.

The Changing Work Force

Autonomy and creative opportunities are important variables for younger, better educated workers. Younger workers expect and are required to have greater creativity and decision-making abilities in high-tech and other contemporary organizations. Research in hospitals and other health care organizations confirms the expectations and demands of a younger changing work force. Younger, better educated doctors and nurses as well as paraprofessionals expect autonomy and independent decision-making ability along with a cooperative team effort.

Apple Computer permits autonomy and responsibility

Apple Computer permits its employees to perform with autonomy and responsibility. On task forces and their production lines as well as in their "think tanks," Apple employees strive for effective performance as an end in itself.

GE's appraisal system puts emphasis on performance

General Electric's performance appraisal system also puts emphasis on performance results. A guide for expected behavior is an important part of their system where behavior and results are evaluated separately. The system is viewed as a tool to be used in managing business performance, not as a personnel program.[11]

A commitment-based approach

A commitment-based approach where jobs are designed to be dynamic rather than static is advocated by Richard Walton.[12] Following this commitment strategy, individuals and teams are expected to be accountable for their job performance. Cooperative job performance rather than formal accountability is the important factor in determining effective management.

JOB PERFORMANCE, MORALE, AND PRODUCTIVITY

Effective Job Performance Results in Job Satisfaction

No direct link between job satisfaction and production

If employees don't have the tools and managerial latitude to perform, they can be neither satisfied nor productive. Efforts have been made for years to establish a link between job satisfaction, morale, and productivity—largely to no avail. There is not a direct link because the relationship between job satisfaction and productivity is more a matter of perception than direct link.

Relative job satisfaction must be present but does not ensure productivity

Again, there is an analogy to Herzberg's dual-factor theory: if relative job satisfaction is present, higher productivity is still not guaranteed because of other variables such as job design, organizational hierarchy, and age of the organization. But if relative job satisfaction is not present, long-term productivity gains are very difficult to achieve.

Performance and productivity relationship

The relationship between high-quality job performance and productivity is more direct. The whole point of job performance is to accomplish useful, productive jobs. Total organizational effectiveness is based on how productive as well as efficient each individual is in the organization. Enabling individuals to perform well and to be satisfied in their jobs contributes to accomplishment of organizational objectives.

A delicate balance

There is a delicate balance between too much pressure for productivity and high morale. Too little pressure results in a goof-off organization. Too much pressure results in a damn-the-organization, I'll-only-do-what's-necessary attitude. When management shows consideration and concern for individual differences of workers, increased job performance and consequently increased job satisfaction are the results. (See Figure 4-4.)

Turnarounds at American companies

American car manufacturers continue to struggle with the ragged reputation that they turn out cars inferior to those made by Asian or European manufacturers, and that American workers are not sufficiently productive. Nevertheless, there have been stunning turn-arounds at American manufacturers. By increasing

Too much pressure	*Balanced pressure*	*Too little pressure*
results in: • up-tight organization • I'll-do-only-what's necessary attitude • too little productivity	results in: • concern for individual differences • high morale • optimal productivity	results in: • goof-off organization • too little productivity

FIGURE 4-4 The delicate balance for productivity pressure.

participation of the blue-collar employees through informal discussions, GM reversed declines in production and morale at its Tarrytown plant. Within a few months, the percentage of bad welds, for example, dropped from 35 percent to 1.5 percent. And when the small voluntary program of worker participation was expanded to the plant's 3,800 employees, 95 percent of them took part. Giving workers a greater voice in their jobs can improve productivity by bringing about declines in grievances, absenteeism, and waste. Similar advances are anticipated at GM's new Saturn plant in Tennessee.

The Saab/Scania experience

Another approach to maintaining high morale and high productivity is used at the Saab/Scania automobile engine assembly plant in Sweden. Saab engineers had experienced difficulties in keeping their assembly line moving without boredom to the workers. Their solution was to accomplish assembly work on a group basis. Each worker as a part of the group has more autonomy over the pace of the assembly process. Within weekly quotas, the workers have considerable freedom in organizing their work. How successful they are depends on their abilities to communicate and work together.[13]

Positive motivational aspects

The positive motivational aspects of the Saab/Scania approach include (1) reducing boredom, (2) making work more meaningful, (3) imparting feelings of personal competence and responsibility. A worker who assembles an entire engine can experience all of these qualities.[14]

Negative aspects of the approach

There are negative aspects of the approach used at Saab. Six American workers who observed this operation were reluctant to adopt the group methods. Many believed, at least initially, that the job enrichment efforts were too tightly structured. The structure required considerable concentration, cooperation, and peer pressure. One American union worker lamented, "If I've got to bust my (expletive) to be meaningful, forget it. I'd rather be monotonous."[15]

Despite the American workers' reluctance to accept the changes, they concluded that the physical environment of the Swedish plant was superior to that of American plants. Cultural differences and other variables are bound to influence the workers' perceptions and preferences.

Making Dull Jobs More Interesting

Industry is trying to inject interest and incentive into jobs that have been monotonous. The trend toward "job enrichment" is constantly evolving because of innovations in many areas, but consider the following ways to combat monotony:

1. Allow workers to form natural work units. Work is distributed so that each person performing a task is identified with the job.
2. Combine tasks both horizontally and vertically where appropriate to allow workers to perform an entire job.
3. Where possible allow workers to establish direct relationships with their clients or ultimate users of their products or services.
4. Communicate end product or service feedback to workers so that workers know how they are performing.

The "whole-job" concept

The "whole-job" concept holds the worker responsible for the assembling, finishing, and testing of a complete unit instead of for one small, repetitive task. In one plant, rejects dropped from 23 percent to 1 percent in the six months following the change from assembly-line concept to whole-job concept. The company also found that absenteeism dropped from 8 percent to 1 percent and that productivity increased.

Encouraging job participation is another method of job enrichment—helping hourly employees to realize that they are not part of a machine and challenging employees to use their thinking abilities. The worker is involved in problem solving and planning instead of routinely performing duties. Decision making leads to expansion of responsibilities, and work teams hold regular "rap" sessions to express complaints. Likewise, voluntary quality circles meet regularly to solve problems. Most employees opt for and participate actively in quality circles.

Express Your Opinion   **Does everyone want to have challenging, enriched jobs?**

DIAGNOSING AND MAINTAINING MORALE

Organizations, like any organisms, are subject to inertia and stasis; that is, they can become resistant to any kind of change or innovation. They easily accumulate practices and policies that can overload their systems. Checking up on morale can be preventive medicine as well as a way to begin a cure for a diseased corporate body. And when treatment is given, further checkups are often useful to reveal whether it has been successful or not.

Morale is not static, and because it is constantly changing, it must be assessed continuously. There are several methods of diagnosing and maintaining morale, including records analysis, informal and formal surveys, and above all listening.

Analysis of Records

Check company records first

Turnover can indicate morale problems

The first method of analysis to ascertain employee morale is examination of company records. Heavy absenteeism, excessive tardiness, long lunch hours, quitting early, and poor safety records all could indicate low morale. Low production and a high rate of spoilage may be another indication. Finally, personnel records show the percentage of employee turnover, which in some industries can be expected to be 10 to 20 percent, or even higher.

The following records should be maintained and give some indication of employee morale. These should be reviewed before a company survey is attempted:

1. Labor turnover
2. Production records
3. Waste and spoilage
4. Absenteeism
5. Tardiness
6. Grievance reports
7. Exit interviews
8. Safety records
9. Medical reports
10. Suggestion boxes

Informal Questions and Answers

The personnel department and supervisors can learn much from employees and one another about morale. They can ask questions and listen to employees and other managers. One pitfall is for supervisors and management to assume that morale is high or low. They can easily be mistaken in their understanding of what employees are really thinking and feeling.

Personal interviews discover personal feelings

One method of finding out what employees think is for human resource specialists to hold confidential, informal interviews with employees. The success of this method depends on the impartiality of the interviewer and the degree of trust that the employee feels. Employees with complaints often prefer to remain anonymous for fear of reprisals.

Employees who are leaving the company are often more than willing to talk about the negative aspects of their jobs. Some companies conduct "exit interviews" or send letters to elicit such information. Opinions from former employees can be helpful, but companies that wait to ask questions until employees leave may already have serious trouble with morale.

Formal Surveys

Employee surveys are the most comprehensive way in which to study morale. In a survey, everyone is asked to respond to the same questions so that management can get an accurate view of the general level of morale. Surveys can be conducted by impartial interviewers or by questionnaires. One common way of combining survey approaches is to distribute a questionnaire to pinpoint problem areas and then use the interview technique to find out more details.

The basic approach has a great deal to do with how valid a survey is. Indifference, resistance, or fear on the part of management is easily sensed by employees. The approach should always be, "What can be learned from the study?" rather than "Who can we blame?" If management wants to know whether employees are content with their working hours, it should ask, "Do you like your working hours? What hours would you prefer?" An example of a poor question is "How do you like your pay and benefits?" It asks for too much information at once, and the answers cannot be interpreted precisely.

Multiple-choice questions are popular on questionnaires because, with standardized responses, overall and longitudinal trends can be measured. Objective surveys generally use a direct approach, asking specific questions and categorizing the answers. The chief advantages to these types of surveys are that they can be administered and analyzed very easily and they can be scored by a computer, if desired. The results can give statistical data that can be measured easily.

Descriptive surveys encourage employees to express their feelings on a topic in their own words. Such questions as "How fairly do you feel the company treats you?" and "In what positive ways could the company improve its employee-employer relationships?" require the employee to express his or her feelings. Usually, the first questions of a descriptive survey are an attempt to get employees to express their own attitudes about the company and their work stations. The last part of the survey usually attempts to ask in a participative way how employees would improve the employer-employee relationship if they had an opportunity. Such surveys may be conducted by interview or individual questionnaire. The important considerations are that employees are assured that what they think is important and that their responses will not be identified by management except in a positive way, perhaps as a part of a suggestion system.

Employee Responses and Follow-through

Just conducting a morale survey tends to boost morale because it indicates to employees that the company is interested in what they think. Questionnaires that don't require employees to identify themselves add to the validity of the answers. Surveys conducted by mail do not generate as much response as do surveys conducted personally on the job.

Morale surveys may raise morale, but only for as long as employees believe their opinions are contributing to change. Surveys irritate employees when they feel that their answers are not given true consideration. Employers who are afraid to publish findings because they do not want to attract attention to problem areas take the chance of actually causing problems by encouraging only negative rumors. Management should be prepared to follow through with remedies for the problem areas the survey indicates. If management cannot effect change, it must be prepared to explain to employees why change is not possible at that time.

PHYSICAL ENVIRONMENT AND MORALE

It is worthwhile to study the effects of the environment on individuals. The explosion tragedies and mass fatalities in Mexico City and in Bhopal, India, and the potential for reoccurrence are matters for concern. Hazardous conditions can obviously have a negative effect on workers.

Ergonomics

Ergonomics is the study of work, focusing on the dynamics of "man-machine" interfaces and the best design to accommodate humans. Ergonomic specialists focus on the relationship of people to uses of work space. In addition, emphasis is being placed on intrinsic motivators in industrial circles. Much is said these days about noise, visual and toxic pollution, and the emotional fatigue that results from a poor working environment. Witness the increasing focus on ergonomics. Once called "human engineering," ergonomics involves designing workstations for maximum performance and in a way that makes the job more suitable to the employee. This requires studying not only size and shape of chairs and workbenches, but areas of lighting, music, sound, color, and temperature as well.

Many people spend major portions of their workdays seated. Men's bodies require a different kind of chair than most women's postures, but little attention is usually given to this kind of detail.[16]

Noise Pollution Affects Morale

There are two effects of noise: biological and psychosociological. Both can adversely affect morale. It has been suspected for some time that as many as 10 million workers may have suffered hearing loss due to excessive noise. A number of physicians are certain that job noises are a factor in some neurotic and psychotic illnesses.

Noise can be a source of psychological and physical stress

In a study entitled, "Affectiveness of Noise on People," prepared for the Environmental Protection Agency, Dr. James D. Miller of the Center Institute for the Deaf in Saint Louis wrote, "There is no definite evidence that noise can induce either neurotic or psychotic illness." However, his report added, "But all the facts show speech interference, hearing loss, annoyance, and the arousal and distraction clearly support the contention that noises can act as sources of psychological distress."[17] Such distress in turn can contribute to "such unpleasant symptoms as nausea, headaches, instability, argumentativeness, sexual impotence, change in general mood and general anxiety." Other studies show that noise contributes to a breakdown in communications and can produce irritable and depressed feelings, as well as a short attention span and hyperactivity.

Decibels measure noise

50 decibels for a normal chat

The difficulties in controlling sound are to find acceptable standards and feasible ways of controlling it. The limits are measured in decibels on a logarithmic scale that runs from the threshold of hearing 1 dB(A) (one decibel on the A audiometric scale) through normal conversation (about 50 decibels), to the level of hearing impairment (85 decibels, if continuous) to that of acute pain (135 decibels). (See Figure 4-5.)

Visual Pollution

Eye strain from CRTs and VDTs

Eye strain from cathode-ray tubes (CRTs), video-display terminals (VDTs), and other close work is of increasing concern to employees, unions, and managers. Office workers especially are bombarded by "visual shock" and monotony from viewing VDTs. In some cases, the bombardment is literally from hazardous radiation of unshielded CRTs. Pregnant women may be especially at risk in using VDTs. Miscarriage rates are higher than normal among women who work with VDTs.[18]

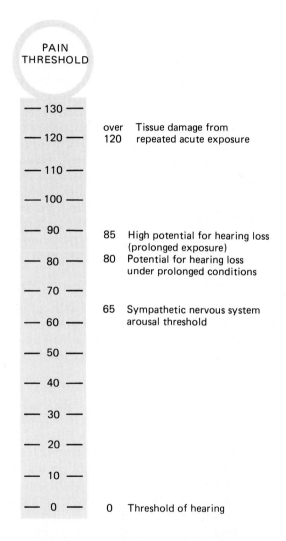

FIGURE 4-5 **Average hourly noise level scale.**
Source: Daniel A. Girdano and George S. Everly, *Controlling Stress and Tension: A Holistic Approach* (Englewood Cliffs, N.J.: Prentice-Hall, 1979). p. 99.

The following show the noise levels for common activities we are exposed to daily. They are measured in decibels. Calculate your average hourly level of noise exposure for a typical eight-hour day.

ACTIVITY	dB(A)		HRS./DAY	
Rocket engine	180 ×			=
Jet plane takeoff	150 ×			=
Police/fire sirens at 100 feet	138 ×			=
Pneumatic (air) drill at 5 feet	125 ×			=
Live rock concert	125 ×			=
Loud rock music (recorded)	115 ×			=
Train passing at 10 feet	108 ×			=
Heavy manufacturing plant	100 ×			=
Large truck at 90 feet	98 ×			=
10-hp outboard motor at 50 feet	88 ×			=
Heavy freeway or city traffic at 5 feet	85 ×			=
Bus ride	85 ×			=
Average assembly line	75 ×			=
Department store	65 ×			=
Average office	65 ×			=
Classroom	64 ×			=
Conversation at 3 feet	63 ×			=
Average residential street	55 ×			=
Air conditioner	55 ×			=
Average domestic noises	48 ×			=
Quiet radio at home	42 ×			=
Library	38 ×			=
Quiet auditorium	30 ×			=
Whisper at 5 feet	20 ×			=

Add 10 minutes for each time a noise or sound annoys you or disrupts your concentration on a task.

Total noise level = _____

Total noise level ÷ 8 = _____

This is your average hourly noise level.

SOURCE: Adapted from Daniel A. Girdano and George S. Everly, *Controlling Stress and Tension: A Holistic Approach* (Englewood Cliffs, N.J.: Prentice-Hall, 1979), p. 99.

Lighting

Lighting is expressed in footcandles

Lighting levels are generally expressed in footcandles. One footcandle is equal to the light of 1 candle at a distance of 1 foot, as established by Illuminating Engineering Society (an industry group that publishes lighting standards that are widely followed by electrical contractors when lighting is installed). The average level of light nationally in commercial buildings is 125 footcandles. It is estimated that candle power runs from 10 for a hotel lobby to 150 for proofreading activity.

Incandescent versus fluorescent fixtures; problems of glare

Supervisors should be aware that incandescent lighting is more economical to install, but more expensive to maintain than is fluorescent lighting. Perhaps the greatest problem is not the lack of candle power or the illumination of direct glare from lighting fixtures or windows; rather, it is the reflected glare from furniture and contrasting dark shadows that usually cause more eye fatigue and low production than lack of lighting.

In considering the adequacy of illumination, it is necessary to take into account the lighting of the total "visual field" rather than the light of the "field of observation." For instance, the light from the outside may be brighter than that at the desk; thus, if a person is facing a window, he or she must adjust visually to the combined value of the light rather than to that of the work space alone. If one eye receives more light than the other, the adjustment is similarly disturbing. The implication is that the whole area should be illuminated uniformly. Fatigue and low morale also are experienced when the illumination changes too rapidly for the pupil to contract and relax comfortably.

Increasing use of computers is a matter of concern because some arrangements and lighting thwart employee productivity. There is a need to combine adjustable task lighting with indirect, ceiling-mounted or ambient light. Workers at computer terminals should also have a visual path enabling them to focus on objects at least 10 feet away while taking breaks.[19]

Colors and Space

Color exerts a definite psychological effect, but it also has reflective quality. Light green and sky blue, for example, reflect approximately 40 percent of the light they receive, but dark red only about 16 percent. The lighting of a factory can be improved by the use of pastel colored paint.

Red encourages movement

In analyzing the color spectrum we find that red increases restlessness, attracts attention, and speeds decisions. As a result, bright red is a poor choice for large office areas in which people will be working continuously but is a good choice for areas in which people meet to enter and exit and where fast movement is encouraged. Pale blue is the most restful of the colors, whereas green slows muscular responses, steadies the nerves, and encourages reflective thinking.

Green is best for reflective thinking

Exit doors are hard to find in large factories, but the exit door in one factory is plainly marked by bright colors high above the door and, as a guide to finding the door, a 30-foot-tall arrow reinforces the identification. (See Figure 4-6.) Research indicates that proper use of color tones and combinations reduces fatigue, increases efficiency, decreases accidents, and improves housekeeping.

Employees need their space whether in the office or factory. Attention needs to be given to designing flexibility into work space to accommodate changes in technology and company growth. Long-term planning can minimize the costs of growth and change.

Summary

How individuals perform is a function of how well their jobs are defined, how they fit in with their work groups, and how adaptive the organization can be in accommodating their abilities and skills. High-tech and white-collar workers especially need considerable latitude in adapting to their organizations.

Effective job performance is a key to job satisfaction and morale. Life satisfaction is also influenced by job satisfaction. Employees experience relative job satisfaction—not as an end in itself but as a means to job performance. We need to identify and facilitate job performance as both the means and the end of organizational effectiveness.

Morale, like health, requires attention. It is a composite of feelings, and

FIGURE 4-6 Supergraphics add color, show the way, and help morale.

maintaining high morale is a continuous task for management. It appears that younger workers are more dissatisfied with work because they have higher expectations.

Conducting surveys and exit interviews are two ways in which to determine employee morale. Descriptive surveys ask respondents to write down how they feel.

Noise pollution, lighting, and colors all affect the attitudes of employees. Color has become more important than before in personalizing one's work space.

If employees are to perform at optimal levels, they need autonomy and other intrinsic job qualities in order to contribute to overall organizational effectiveness. Well-managed companies build in creative opportunities for their employees. They allow them to perform dynamic jobs and grow in a safe environment.

Case Study 7

Theft in the Service Station

Scott Hays is owner and manager of a service station in the downtown area of a large city. He employs 12 men, 4 of whom he hired just a month ago when he decided to extend the business hours.

When Scott conducted an inventory this morning of the tires that the station had in stock, he discovered that four tires were missing. His first thought was that someone had broken in when the station was closed, but he could find no evidence of this. Scott also discounted the idea that someone had managed to sneak into the garage and steal the tires while the station was open. Surely someone would have seen that happen. The only possibility left was employee theft.

Scott had conducted his last inventory just a few days before he had hired the new men. Since that time he had a sales slip for every tire sold, except for the four missing tires. Scott began considering his men. Could one of them have stolen the tires? This had never happened before! Two of his men Scott began to suspect in earnest.

Pete, who is the station mechanic, has worked for Scott for a number of years. Until recently Pete's performance has been good. But a few weeks ago, Scott caught Pete in the process of overbilling a customer for work done on his car. Scott corrected Pete's error without much thought until later, when he found that Pete had written two bills. There was a higher amount listed for the customer and the lower one for the station, thus enabling him to pocket the difference. When Scott confronted Pete, he apologized. Pete said he had never done it before and would never do it again. His reason was that temptation was too strong.

The other man Scott suspected was Dave. Dave had to be corrected on more than one occasion for not giving the proper change back to customers. Were these shortchanges honest mistakes? They only seemed to happen when Scott would be away from the station. Dave is apparently in financial trouble, because last week he requested an advance on his next paycheck. Yesterday he found out that Dave had been asking some of the men if he could borrow money. Scott wonders if Dave stole the tires for the money he would get for them?

If you were Scott, what steps would you now take?

1. Would you fire Dave and Pete? Would you release all four new men?
2. Would you call a meeting of all the employees and discuss the matter? Would you tell them that you felt one of them was a thief?
3. Would you demand that they all take a polygraph test?
4. Would you tell them that if it didn't happen again you would forget it?

Case Study 8

Morale Pollution

Have you ever experienced an increasing foul odor from your refrigerator and on inspection been unable to locate the source? In such cases it becomes necessary to investigate, to find the curdled milk or spoiled fruit. There is sometimes a parallel in organizations—in a person who over the years has soured in attitude to the point where the radiation from him pollutes the system's morale.

In one such case, the member was an original employee in a large and successful organization. He had been a central figure in the top management groups and had the perquisites that go with the status. But he had not, in his own eyes, kept pace with the upward mobility of his peers. So far as position was concerned, James Whitmore, 55, had been put in charge of an essential, but to him peripheral, component of the business. He sulks unhappily. His subordinates know that they have a discontented, demoralized boss and they do not feel represented properly to the rest of the company.

1. What options are available to solve this morale problem that has affected Whitmore's division?
2. What do you believe is the best option, considering the company? Considering the employee?

Terms and Concepts

blue-collar jobs principally physical jobs, including construction, manufacturing, and some service industries.

decibel a measure of noise; 50 decibels is the measure of a normal conversation.

descriptive survey a survey that asks employees to complete statements or to write out how they feel about conditions.

ergonomics study of work, focusing on dynamics of "man-machine" interfaces and best design to accommodate humans.

footcandle a measure of light intensity.

job cycle the length of time required to perform an operation before starting the task again.

job description the beginning point in defining what is to be done on a job; should include responsibilities, relationships, duties (tasks), and performance elements.

job performance both the beginning and ending point in determining how effective people are in their jobs.

job satisfaction a personal matter based on each individual's value system and attitudes held about the job.

morale a reflection of the general tone or *esprit de corps* of a collective group of personalities; the mental condition of a group with respect to cheerfulness or confidence.

objective survey a survey that asks employees true-false or multiple-choice questions.

referent others concept individuals compare their job satisfaction and rewards with others who have similar backgrounds, abilities, and responsibilities.

wellness programs programs of health, diet, and exercise that help to keep employees healthy and happy. Often paid for by the company.

white-collar workers principally office workers, managers, and some professionals. White-collar workers have more flexibility and receive their top pay later than do blue-collar workers.

"whole-job" concept the view that the employee is responsible for completing the entire assembly rather than a small portion of the task.

Notes

1. Arthur R. Pell, "Teeing Up for Superb Performance," *Managers Magazine*, December 1988, pp. 23–24.
2. Frederick Herzberg, *Work and the Nature of Man* (Cleveland: World Publishing, 1966); Edward E. Lawler III and Lyman W. Porter, "The Effect of Performance on Job Satisfaction," *Industrial Relations*, October 1967, pp. 20–28.
3. Tom Peters, *Thriving on Chaos: Handbook for a Management Revolution* (New York: Alfred A. Knopf, 1988), p. 501.
4. Philip C. Grant, "What Use Is a Job Description?" *Personnel Journal*, February 1988, pp. 45–53.
5. Richard Henderson, *Compensation Management: Rewarding Performance*, 5th ed. (Englewood Cliffs, N.J.: Prentice-Hall, 1989), p. 314.
6. Andrall E. Pearson, "Muscle-Build Your Company: Raise Standards Relentlessly," *Success*, July–August 1989, p. 10.
7. Graham Kenny and Alan Dunk, "The Utility of Perfor-

mance Measures: Production Managers' Perceptions," *IEEE Transactions on Engineering Management*, February 1989, pp. 47–48.

8. Jan Muczyk and Robert Hastings, "In Defense of Enlightened Hardball Management," *Business Horizons*, July–August 1985, p. 24.

9. Douglas Benton and Harold White, "Satisfaction of Job Factors," *The Journal of Nursing Administration*, November–December, 1972, pp. 55–63; Herzberg, *Work and the Nature of Man*.

10. Ramon Oldenberg and Dennis Brisset, "The Essential Hangout: A Third Place," *Psychology Today*, April 1980, pp. 83–84.

11. Robert J. Butler and Lyle Yorks, "A New Appraisal System as Organizational Change: GE's Task Force Approach," *Personnel*, January–February 1984, pp. 31–42.

12. Richard E. Walton, "From Control to Commitment in the Workplace," *Harvard Business Review*, March–April 1985, pp. 76–84.

13. Kim Hayes, "My Own Engine," *Sweden Now*, April 1976, pp. 24–27.

14. Lex Donaldson, "Job Enrichment: A Multidimensional Approach," *Human Relations*, September 1975.

15. *A Work Experiment: Six Americans in a Swedish Plant* (New York: Ford Foundation, 1976), p. 42.

16. "The Chair Ain't Broke, But They Fixed It," *The Wall Street Journal*, May 2, 1988, p. 25.

17. Sheldon Cohen, "Sound Effects on Behavior," *Psychology Today*, October 1981, pp. 38–49.

18. "Latest Study on VDTs Adds to Safety Fears," *The Wall Street Journal*, October 20, 1988, p. B1.

19. Jeffrey L. Skeggs, "Effective Lighting Needed Now for Computers to Come," *The Office*, October 1988, pp. 74–75.

Recommended Reading

Alexander, John O. "Toward Real Performance: The Circuit-Breaker Technique." *Supervisory Management*, April 1989, pp. 5–13.

Ariss, Sonny S., and Sherman A. Timmins. "Employee Education and Job Performance: Does Education Matter?" *Public Personnel Management*, Spring 1989, pp. 1–9.

Davis, Tim R. V. "The Influence of the Physical Environment in Offices." *Academy of Management Review*, April 1984, pp. 271–283.

Fisher, Cynthia D. "On the Dubious Wisdom of Expecting Job Satisfaction to Correlate with Performance." *Academy of Management Review*, October 1980, pp. 607–612.

Greene, Charles N. "The Satisfaction-Performance Controversy." *Business Horizons*, October 1972, pp. 31–41.

Herzberg, Frederick. *Work and the Nature of Man.* Cleveland: World Publishing, 1966.

Lawler, Edward E., and Lyman W. Porter. "The Effect of Performance on Job Satisfaction." *Industrial Relations*, October 1967, pp. 20–28.

Mackenzie, Susan T. *Noise and Office Work: Employee and Employer Concerns.* Ithaca, N.Y.: Cornell University, New York State School of Industrial and Labor Relations, 1975.

Magee, Richard H., Mary Finn Magee, and Melinda Magee Davies. "A Performance Planning Primer." *Training*, May 1985, pp. 99–101, 129–131.

Novak, Alys. "A Vision for the Future: Ergonomics." *Colorado Business Magazine*, March 1988, pp. 56–61.

Smith, Robert F., and Kerry Tucker. "Measuring Individual Performance." *Public Relations Journal*, October 1982, pp. 27–28.

Trunzo, James. "Office Computers Create Glaring Problems." *The Wall Street Journal*, October 5, 1987, p. 24.

Walton, Richard E. "From Control to Commitment in the Workplace." *Harvard Business Review*, March–April 1985, pp. 76–84.

Weiss, Alan. *Managing for Peak Performance: A Guide to the Power (and Pitfalls) of Personal Style.* New York: Harper & Row, 1989.

5

Personal Problems: Alcohol, Drugs, and Sex

After studying this chapter, you should be able to:

1. Identify personal problems that impact work.
2. Determine the extent of the problems.
3. Discuss the growing problems of alcoholism and drug addiction in business as well as be able to:

    a. Recognize some symptoms of alcoholics and drug abusers.

    b. Recognize some "slang" terms used by drug abusers.

    c. Develop some background in how to deal with alcoholics and drug abusers in the work scene.
4. Recognize the legal and moral aspects of sexual harassment.
5. Discuss the pros and cons of supervisors being trained to act as counselors on the job.
6. Compare the differences between directive and nondirective counseling.
7. Identify what company and posttreatment programs can do to help affected employees.

TO START YOU THINKING . . .

Again here are some questions to start you thinking about topics in the chapter. You know the answers to some already and you will find answers to the others in the chapter.

♦ To whom would you go with a personal problem at work? to a friend, your supervisor, or a counselor?

♦ Do you think that people should vent their feelings or try to keep themselves under control?

♦ Which is better, to get rid of problem employees or try to rehabilitate them?

♦ What can you do for the employee who is an alcoholic or drug abuser?

♦ Is drug testing "fair" at the workplace?

♦ Do you think that you could recognize the point at which the alcoholic or drug abuser was performing his or her job ineffectively?

♦ Does sexual liaison on or off the job create problems in the workplace?

♦ What is sexual harassment?

♦ Who can help counsel with personal problems?

TYPES OF PERSONAL PROBLEMS

This chapter addresses recognition, counseling, and treatment for the problems of employees. Emphasis is given to problems of alcohol, other drugs, and sexism/

sexual harassment in the workplace. More important, attention is given to counseling and the organization's response to employees who have these problems.

Everybody has problems! The magnitude of the problems and what, if anything, to do about them become challenges for management. How extensive are the problems and how do they manifest themselves? Only a recluse would not recognize the alcohol, drug, and sexism problems that exist in society and the workplace today. There are also more subtle problems that keep members of the work force from being as productive as they could be.

Most dealings with people do not involve unpleasant experiences or misunderstandings, but things do happen that are disturbing enough to cause management to become interested in some of the basic concepts of counseling employees.

Home problems enter the workplace

Problems that take place in the home are increasingly becoming felt in companies. There is the problem of nepotism (hiring of relatives) since the emergence of equal rights activities. There are certain pleasures, but also problems that face companies that hire married couples.

HOW TO IDENTIFY SOMEONE WITH A PROBLEM _____

Sudden behavior changes may signal distress

People who are coping with personal problems at work frequently show signs of emotional distress. Harry Levinson identified three behavioral changes that signal to coworkers and friends that emotional first aid is needed.[1] These behaviors are discussed in the following paragraphs.

Exaggerated Behavior _____

An emotionally disturbed person's behavior patterns may become highly exaggerated. For example, an orderly person will become excessively meticulous. Or a quiet person will become extremely withdrawn. Or a friendly person will appear to be in a perpetual life-of-the-party mood.

When ordinary behavior is exaggerated in this fashion, it is often a sign of stress. The troubled person tries to hide stress symptoms by *acting* as if everything were normal. In fact, everything is not normal; and because such behavior *is* an *act*, it will be discernible to those who are familiar with the person's normal behavior.

Distress Symptoms _____

A number of distress symptoms are apparent even to nonprofessional eyes. Disturbed persons are seldom able to concentrate and may be highly agitated. If they are worried and fearful, they may be jittery and perspire freely. They may be startled by loud noises or by the sudden appearance of the boss. If they are depressed or grieving, they may speak in dejected, exhausted tones. They may lose weight or seem to be suffering from lack of sleep. Some are likely to be constantly irritable; others will cry for the slightest reason.

Radical Change Symptoms _____

When someone's behavior at work changes radically, it may indicate severe stress. In such cases, irrational thoughts and actions will become apparent. For example, a quiet unassuming clerk with no official authority to do so might begin to issue orders to coworkers in an authoritarian manner. Or an ordinarily controlled and sober person might return from lunch drunk for several days in a row. Or an executive noted for forceful decision making might become incapable of deciding even the most trivial matters.

ALCOHOLISM

It is almost a cliché that the increased complexities of modern life have added to nearly everyone's share of tensions, guilts, anxieties, and inhibitions. Alcohol consumption can increase tension as well as guilt, anxiety, and inhibition. Excessive alcohol consumption also reduces efficiency, sensitivity, and caution—three essential qualities for good job performance.

How Widespread is the Problem?

The problem of alcoholism for business is not just with chronic alcoholics, but with the social drinker as well. Nevertheless, some progress in reducing alcoholism is being made. Organizations like MADD (Mothers Against Drunk Driving) and SADD (Students Against Drunk Driving) have begun to have an impact nationally in reducing drunk driving and in reducing overall alcohol consumption. The introduction of wine coolers, and low- and nonalcohol beers are also examples of the reduction in alcohol consumption.

Ten percent of drinkers are alcoholics; few obtain help

The National Council on Alcoholism estimates that 10 percent of the 110 million people who drink alcohol in the United States suffer from alcoholism. Of that 11 million, only about 700,000 to 1 million are in treatment by Alcoholics Anonymous or similar organizations. That means that there are about 10 million alcoholics who are not being treated.

Problem Drinkers and Industry

Alcoholism is a personal problem of many employees that affects job performance. "The National Institute on Alcohol Abuse and Alcoholism estimates 25 percent of employed alcoholics are white-collar workers, 30 percent are manual workers and 45 percent are from the professional and managerial ranks."[2] Many companies are getting tougher about drinking during the work day—at lunch, for example. In fact, drinking off the job and its influence on workers has become a matter of corporate policy.

Whether or not alcoholism is a disease or a bad habit, it generally progresses from a mild social or psychological dependence, to a physiological dependence, and finally to a true addictive state. The entire process can take from 10 to 20 years to develop, and, consequently, most early- and middle-stage alcoholics in business and industry are between 45 and 55 years of age.[3] Relatively few full-blown, late-stage alcoholics are employed because the symptoms at this stage are completely unsupportable in a work environment.

The National Council on Alcoholism lists some of the costs:

1. The alcoholic employee is absent approximately three times as often as the nonalcoholic employee.
2. On-the-job accidents for alcoholic employees are two to four times more frequent than among nonalcoholic employees, and off-the-job accidents for alcoholics are four to six times as numerous.
3. Sickness and accident benefits paid out for alcoholic employees are three times greater than for nonalcoholic employees.

4. In one auto assembly plant, 363 out of 746 grievances filed during one year, or 48.6 percent, were alcohol related.

To these costs we must add intangibles such as loss of experienced employees, job friction, lower morale, waste of supervisory time, bad decisions, and damaged customer and public relations.

Substance abuse costs industry $258 billion a year

The Research Triangle Institute has determined that the cost of substance abuse in the American workplace is over $258 *billion* a year.[4] Other estimates do not run quite so high, but there is agreement that alcoholism is a major cost factor to American industry: 88 percent of U. S. corporations surveyed by Wells Fargo Bank viewed substance abuse as a major problem, and drug abuse at Wells Fargo remains only one-third as big a problem as alcoholism.[5]

Spotting an Alcoholic

Watch for decrease in quantity or quality of work

Supervisors should keep records of absenteeism and investigate causes of on-the-job accidents. They should be suspicious if there is a decline in the quality or amount of work produced by a usually competent individual. Figure 5-1 outlines several signs that will indicate if the problem is due to excessive drinking.

These are some of the more common signs of alcohol (and certain drug) intoxication.

1. *Physical signs.* Bloodshot or bleary eyes, trembling hands, flushed face, irritability, nervousness, alcohol smell on breath or as body odor. Slurred or sloppy speech.

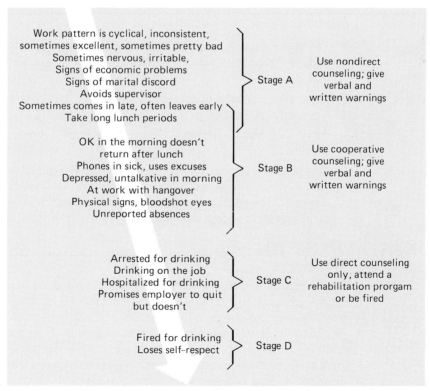

FIGURE 5-1 Signs of alcoholism and stages that the alcoholic passes through from inconsistent performance to the time of termination.

2. *Behavioral signs.* Impaired judgment, argumentative and insulting attitude, sudden changes of mood, fluctuating work output, avoidance of supervisor, use of breath purifiers, lowered work quality, increased absenteeism and lateness, longer lunch hours, early departures from work.

Dealing with Alcoholics

The manager becomes concerned when employee drinking interferes with doing a good job

It cannot be stated too strongly that it is only when the use of alcohol *interferes* with work that the supervisor is obligated to recognize the problem and come to grips with it. When employees' drinking habits create no problems at work, they are *not* any concern of the supervisor. The sensible managerial view is the one that says, "What my employees do during their leisure time is no business of mine. It becomes my business when drinking prevents them from doing their jobs properly."

Early identification of alcoholism is important, and the earliest cause for action is poor work performance. Supervisors who suspect that an employee's work difficulties may be due to problem drinking should discuss the matter with the employee. The matter should be treated *confidentially* and discussed with no one else except counseling or medical personnel.

Once the problem has been identified and admitted by the employee, neither the supervisor nor the employee should entertain any notions that the problem will cure itself. If there is no company program, it will be necessary to work out some kind of personal rehabilitation plan. Advice on how to do this can be obtained from doctors, counseling personnel, psychiatrists, governmental agencies, or Alcoholics Anonymous. There is no one "best" way in which to handle an employee with a drinking problem. But there are some general rules worth observing.

Exact no promises

1. The supervisor should not exact or demand any promise the employee might make to stop drinking. Alcoholics are often incapable of keeping promises of that nature.

Don't moralize

2. Supervisors should not moralize or lecture. It's a waste of time.

Shape up or ship out

3. It is not a waste of time to threaten dismissal if the threat is sincere. "Shape up or ship out!" is the best threat. They must continue to work in order to survive.

Keep it confidential

4. The problem should be kept confidential. There is nothing to gain and much to lose when someone's personal problems are broadcast to the world at large. Also, it makes good sense to try to assist someone in whom the company has made a substantial investment of time and money by training.

THE DRUG ABUSERS

Drug abuse is a critical problem in the workplace for many U.S. businesses. It is estimated that 10 to 30 percent of the work force uses drugs, and around 10 million workers use the drugs while working.[6] Companies face reduced revenue and productivity, theft, insurance costs, and low morale as a result. Some recommendations to erase or at least reduce drug use in the work force include implementing an employee assistance program, firing employees for drug trafficking, and developing drug training seminars for managers.

A major problem of drug abuse is that only a few people are aware of the complexity of the issue. Medical reports, state laws, and psychological opinions differ widely from state to state. Despite the federal government's Comprehensive Drug Abuse Prevention and Control Act of 1970, Controlled Substances Act, and legislation on "designer drugs," the increase in drug abuse is startling. One difficulty that companies face is that often supervisors and management cannot understand the "lingo," what the drugs look like, or even the symptoms exhibited by the user.

Four out of five drug abusers are recovering

Companies that are working with drug abusers under behavior medical treatment plans found that four out of five people are recovering. These data were released after surveying 2,400 companies. A motto used is "Try to get to people with problems before they become problem people."

Many people are polydrug users

One West Coast representative for a rehabilitation program stated that half the people in the program between the ages of 20 and 35 are *polydrug users;* that is, the employee is taking more than one drug. Therefore it is not uncommon to have people in the program who are alcoholics and drug addicts. People responsible for rehabilitation programs often used the word "drug" to refer to both alcohol and drugs, because the treatment is often similar.

High-level executives are major drug abusers

According to one study, the substances most abused by white-collar workers were alcohol (39 percent), cocaine (31 percent), and heroin (22 percent). More than 90 percent of the "addicts with briefcases" used these substances daily.[7]

We must dissuade ourselves of the notion that the ordinary stresses of life constitute a disease that needs medication. We cannot expect stress-free, pain-free existence. Americans sometimes become conditioned from infancy to believe there is a pill for every ill. A contrasting view is credited to Winston Churchill: "Most of the world's work is done by people who do not feel very well all of the time."

There are many social and political ambiguities related to drug laws

Today a high percentage of arrests throughout the nation are for drugs or drug-related charges. Thus the ambiguities of the political and social situation have not made drugs any less illegal.

Marijuana

Marijuana and other, much stronger, more dangerous drugs are hawked openly and competitively at rock concerts and at other gatherings of young people, and the vendors are not hassled by police. But the ambiguities of the political and social situation do not make drugs any less dangerous, and not just in terms of getting arrested.

Most researchers agree that frequent use of marijuana, or its use in combination with other drugs or alcohol, is hazardous. In addition, researchers say that regular pot smoking during the day at school plays havoc with learning. Studies show that reasoning is impaired after a joint is smoked, and this is a major problem for certain students.

Researchers know that not all the answers are in on marijuana. But they add that evidence is growing that it makes good sense to avoid heavy use of this controversial substance.

Cocaine

Cocaine is the alkaloid derived from the leaves of the coca plant. Its source is the eastern slopes of the Andes mountains, and it is available anywhere in the United States for about five times the price of gold per ounce.

But for whatever the price, cocaine and some of its derivatives, including "crack" and "crank," have become even more addictive, universally used, and dangerous. Today it is the drug of choice for perhaps millions of upwardly mobile citizens.

The pattern of constant use can lead to a psychological dependence, the effects of which are not all that different from addiction. Moreover, there is growing clinical evidence that, when coke is taken in the most potent and dangerous forms—injected in a solution or chemically converted and smoked in the process called freebasing, it may indeed become addictive. Cocaine can damage the liver, cause malnutrition, and, especially among those with cardiac problems, increase the risk of heart attack.

Hard Drugs

Heroin and opium are hard drugs

Heroin and opium belong to that class of drugs known as narcotics, or "hard drugs." Hard drugs cause physical addiction in the user. Physical addiction means that the body develops a tolerance for the chemical and alters its activities to correspond to the amount of the drug used. As a result, the user has to use more and more of the drug to get any kicks or the pleasure of what addicts call "the rush."

The more of the drug that is consumed, the greater the physical dependency that develops. The greater the dependency, the harder it becomes to stop usage.

Depressants

Depressants

Other kinds of dangerous drugs are called soft drugs, but not because they are any mellower than the hard ones. *Barbiturates* (sleeping pills) are physically addicting, and the body develops a tolerance to barbiturates that is similar to narcotics tolerance. Some doctors believe that it is more difficult to cure a barbiturate addiction than it is to cure heroin addiction. The sudden cessation of barbiturates can cause convulsions and has been known to cause death, particularly when alcohol has been consumed. Large doses of barbiturates and alcohol, taken together, can kill.

Symptoms of use include confusion, difficulty in thinking, impairment of judgment, and marked swings in mood between elation and depression. There may be increased irritability and inability to control fighting or weeping.

Stimulants

"Pep pills" help users go for long periods without sleep

Amphetamines or diet pills are stimulants

Stimulants

"Crashing down" can cause psychological depression

Stimulants act directly on the central nervous system, producing a feeling of excitation, energy, and the ability to go without sleep for prolonged periods. There is often a loss of appetite, and during such periods the user's body expends its reserve of energy, thus resulting in a "blackout." *Amphetamines* or methamphetamines are stimulants that are known as "speed," "dexies," "pep pills," "uppers," "bennies," or any of several other street names.

Besides causing the blackouts, amphetamines can also present withdrawal problems. When someone has become addicted to amphetamines and is suddenly cut off from them, withdrawal will result in severe psychological depression, laced with bouts of paranoia. "Crashing" or coming down from an amphetamine high may cause weeks of psychological distress. The abuser may exhibit nervousness, tremors of the hands, dilated pupils, dryness of the mouth, and heavy perspiration. In short, the person abusing stimulants may exhibit dangerous, aggressive behavior that resembles paranoid schizophrenia.

Hallucinogens

LSD can alter time and space perception

Mescaline, peyote, mushrooms, "Angel Dust" (P.C.P), and LSD cause hallucinations as well as alter time and space perceptions. Some people have reported very unpleasant hallucinations; others have described their "trips" as very pleasant. In the early days of LSD experimentation, great success was reported concerning its use with terminal cancer patients. However, its use in the United States is prohibited for many legal and medical reasons.

Designer Drugs

Synthetic drugs are dangerous, too

Designer drugs are tailor-made, synthetic drugs. The degree of potency and duration of their effect can be laboratory controlled. Because one or two minor changes in the molecular structure of the chemical compounds can change the overall effect of the drugs, they are especially dangerous.

We know little about designer drugs

Gary L. Henderson, pharmacologist and toxicologist at the University of California at Davis (the individual who coined the term *designer drugs*), says that we face an enormous challenge because of the synthetics. "Designer drugs can be made cheaply and easily and sold for enormous profits. They are very difficult to detect and we know little about their biological effects and side effects. More important, they seem to be proliferating at an alarming rate. They are the drugs of abuse of the future."[8]

Addicts on the Job

Symptoms and drug taking can be concealed

It appears not only that drug addicts hold a wide variety of jobs but that their drug use goes undetected for long periods. According to the subjects interviewed in one study, heroin addiction on the job can be masked through careful manipulation of the "high" by shooting only enough heroin to prevent withdrawal symptoms. If the worker-addict begins to feel drowsy, he simply moves about a great deal to reduce this effect.

If any questions about unusual behavior are asked by supervisors or fellow workers, subjects give a wide variety of excuses, the major ones being fatigue caused by family problems, anxiety, night school, or noisy neighbors. Another excuse, usually offered by older addicts, is that their unusual behavior results from either a hangover or a drink on the job. Drug abuse is usually not the stated reason for dismissal. Instead, poor job performance, lateness, absenteeism, among other reasons, are cited.

Confronting Drug Abuse

Listed now are specific recommendations for supervisors to consider in handling the drug problem.

1. The first step is education. Consider establishing programs for managers and employees to arm them with the facts and heighten their consciousness of alcohol- and drug-related behavior.

2. Establish a program and develop a company policy. Include members of security, the legal department, personnel, the union, supervisory personnel, the work force, medical specialists, and top management. If the problem is perceived as the sole responsibility of a single group, policy and program will inevitably be slanted and biased.

3. Consider employing recovered (or "recovering") former addicts from certified treatment programs. In addition to the fulfillment of their regular duties, they can lend a personal expertise to your company program.

According to some experts, first offenders should be offered counseling through EAPs.[9] Drug abuse and alcoholism in the workplace can be counteracted. Job applications and drug testing can help screen job applicants. Workers who abuse drugs or alcohol may be detected through searches, but all these activities must be handled carefully to avoid legal action. Drug testing by private employers has received a chilly reception in some courts, although the U.S. Supreme Court has ruled that the federal government may test workers in sensitive or safety-related jobs.

Express Your Opinion	Many companies are now using urinalysis to detect for traces of drugs including alcohol. Abstinence for a period of time before the test will throw off the results of the test. But some companies use spot-checks or unannounced tests.
	What do you think? Are these tests an invasion of privacy? What are the arguments for and against corporate prohibition of drug usage even off the job? Does it make a difference if the job is in a "sensitive" industry such as nuclear power generation, air traffic control, or law enforcement?

SEX AND THE WORKPLACE

Human sexuality probably doesn't need a lot of definition for most readers of this book. I am reminded of the young daughter who is an exceptionally good student but was very satisfied with a C in her sex education class. She was afraid if she got a better grade, her dad would worry! And, if she got a poorer grade, she would worry!

Sexual liaisons in the workplace may cause organizational grief

Sexual liaisons in the workplace are another concern because of the impact they may have on other employees. This is especially true if there is a boss-subordinate relationship involved. The parties concerned are probably setting themselves up for embarassment and grief, if not worse. Regardless of the emotions and feelings—or whether everything is highly moral—there may be organizational repercussions.

Mary Cunningham was a staff assistant–strategic planner at Bendix where Bill Agee was a senior executive. Agee sought the professional advice of Cunningham and because of that came to be viewed by others in management as weak and subject to easy influence. After they left the company, they were married but considerable personal damage had been inflicted on both.

The fact of two people falling in love does not mean they lose their business judgment. But when the relationship is between boss and subordinate, coworkers may feel uncomfortable, suspicious, or threatened.

As more couples enter the workplace the battered mate is seen more often with bruises and with feelings of guilt and shame. Such an employee can be your coworker or an employee under your supervision.

It is impossible for us all to be in optimal emotional balance all the time. We all occasionally "blow up," and we depend on others to help us overcome our moments of stress; management depends on supervisors to see that it is done.

SEXUAL HARASSMENT

Sexual harassment is offensive to at least one party

Sexual harassment is any unwanted attention of a sexual nature that occurs in the process of working or seeking work that interferes with a person's work ability. Unlike sexual liaisons, which are a function of mutual consent, sexual harassment is offensive to at least one of the parties. It may be blatant, involving physical touch, but is often verbally or visually offensive because of innuendo, jokes, or stares.

> Section 703 of Title VII of the Civil Rights Act of 1964 makes sexual harassment illegal. The final amendment to the EEOC Guidelines states that sexual harassment includes unwelcome sexual advances, request for sexual favors, and other verbal or physical conduct of a sexual nature made as a condition of employment or advancement.[10]

Case law holds that "sexist remarks" and "insistent and vicious looks" are sexual harassment. Specifically, the following situations have been found to be sexual harassment.

- A boss says to his secretary, "You deserve a pat on the fanny for a good job."
- Joking about sex in regard to women's bodies. The women employees get very uncomfortable, and the men enjoy every minute of it.
- Requiring a female lobby attendant to wear a skimpy uniform that the company claimed was part of its dress code.
- A female employee has been having an affair with the head of her division. She tells him she wants to break it off. He replies that she will lose out on the promotion she has been expecting.
- The company has a number of vending machines which require service twice a week. An outside male services these machines. Every time he comes to the company he remarks to the female receptionist that she looks sexy and asks her to go on dates with him. The receptionist is fed up with his behavior and tells her boss how she feels.[11]

As you can see from the examples, sexual harassment includes acts of outside vendors as well as employees. Companies such as Hewlett-Packard have posted notices in their lobbies asking that the company be made aware of improper advances or remarks between vendors and employees.

The supervisor *is* the company

The courts and the Equal Employment Opportunity Commission now hold the employer responsible for acts of sexual harassment in the workplace regardless of whether or not the employer knew of the conduct. Unless the company can show that it took "immediate and appropriate corrective action," it is liable for its employees' actions—even if it had a policy against harassment.[12] The U.S. Court of Appeals for the 7th Circuit has held that an employer is liable for sexual harassment by a supervisor even if it can show that no one in upper management knew of the misconduct. The court said: "Where a supervisory employee is given absolute authority to hire and fire, and uses this authority to extort sexual favors from subordinate employees, the supervisor is, for all intents and purposes, the company."[13]

Men may be sexually harassed too

Sexual harassment victims are not always women. Young men are sometimes sexually harassed in industries such as hotel/hospitality and food service. Physical, visual, and verbal acts may be just as offensive and unwelcome to men as they are to women. Would it make any difference if the roles were reversed in the incidents above (that is, if the "harasser" was a woman, and the "harassee" was a man)?

Preventing Sexual Harassment

According to a 1987 survey conducted by *Personnel* magazine, the majority of medium and large companies have a formal policy on sexual harassment. The survey found that confidentiality is a major concern of employees who are hesitant to report an incident of sexual harassment. Companies use dress codes to prevent incidents and surveys, hot lines, and complaint boxes to encourage employees to report harassment.[14]

The key to eliminating or at least reducing sexual harassment is prevention. The EEOC guidelines make a strong claim that prevention is the best tool for controlling sexual harassment. Their guidelines suggest that the employer should:

1. Affirmatively raise the subject of sexual harassment.
2. Express strong disapproval.
3. Develop an appropriate sanction.
4. Inform employees of their right to raise and how to raise the issue of harassment under Title VII.
5. Develop methods to sensitize all concerned.[15]

Prevention requires active management support

For a program to prevent sexual harassment to be effective, it must have the full understanding and support of management. Written policies that are distributed throughout the organization are also important preventive measures. Sanctions and mechanisms for complaint procedures should be a part of those policies. Finally, counseling should be available to individuals who have been victims of harassment.

WHO CAN HELP WITH PROBLEMS?

The main purpose of counseling is to discover an employee's principal problem and to find a way of decreasing it. First, one must find a way to understand the employee, to help him or her recognize that area of concern and deal with it objectively. An empathetic supervisor may condemn the problem but not the employee. Perhaps the hardest part of counseling is for the employee to accept help and the counselor to give it.

Remember the advice from Chapter 2 to make tension work *for* you—to not fight it, but use it in a positive sense. Suggestions there included a type of self-counseling to prioritize our activities to tackle one thing at a time and to enjoy an occasional laugh at our own expense. But there are also other sources of help: friends, supervisors, and professional counselors.

Sometimes we can be the source of help to solve our own problems, but frequently we need outside help. Who can we turn to? Regardless of our answer, we need someone who will listen to and help us act upon our problems.

Friends

Friends, supervisors, or specialists can help those under stress

Perhaps the closest confidant an employee can find to discuss a situation is a friend at the plant or office. A friend will tend to be receptive, open, and willing to listen without passing judgment. These qualities can be found in some, but not all, superiors. In the informal setting the "counselor-friend" can give empathy and friendly advice. Usually there is little pressure for the employee to follow the friend's advice, and the problem does not become public knowledge.

When some people recognize that a coworker is upset, they may be reluctant to speak to the person about their perceptions. They may feel that it is a private affair and that discussing it will only add to the distress. But there are circumstances in which it is permissible to intrude on another person's privacy at work. The first is when help is requested, which is certainly not an intrusion. The second is when two people have worked well together and one has strong evidence that the other's job performance is falling down. Calling attention to work-related problems often enables disturbed people to open up and talk about their personal problems. What is needed is a "listening" friend who can keep a confidence.

Supervisors

A listening supervisor may become a counselor

An employee's most logical step is to go to a listening supervisor with his or her minor problems. Good supervisors will soon discover whether they are capable of handling particular situations. If the supervisors are inexperienced, they should consult with their superiors or an expert in the field before having an interview with the disturbed employee. It is wise to call in an expert's opinion early in a case involving drugs, alcohol, or legal entanglements.

Beginning supervisors are often reluctant to discuss subordinates' personal problems because they feel poorly equipped to deal with such matters. Nevertheless, the longer they work in supervisory positions, the more practice they get in dealing with personal problems because, inevitably, some employees will need to talk about disturbing aspects of their lives and jobs.

WE ALL NEED **LISTENING** EARS — AND INDIVIDUALS WHO CAN ACT UPON WHAT THEY HEAR.

Counseling takes time but so does finding and training replacements

Experienced supervisors know that well-conducted counseling is hard and tiring work, especially when they have to deal with hostile and critical subordinates. They learn how to avoid being pushed into defensive postures and how to remain calm. But no matter how good they get, such encounters always use up a lot of energy.

The major limitation that most supervisors experience in counseling is time. Follow-up is often essential for effective counseling, and that can consume a great deal of time. In the long run, if insufficient time is set aside for counseling, more problems may result with an even greater loss of time.

Suppose that a supervisor never took the time to counsel an employee with problems but that employee's inefficiencies resulted in the loss of an hour's worth of work every day for three weeks. Wouldn't three or four hours of counseling be a better investment of time?

Specialists or Counselors

Counselors, attorneys, physicians, personnel directors, and ministers can act as specialists

Calling in specialists is often advisable in cases of abortion, adoption, and marital strife

The personnel counselor, the attorney, the physician all become counselors in one circumstance or another. Personnel directors by their very role can act as uninvolved third parties in labor disputes, salary placements, and job transfers. Because company physicians or attorneys are not labeled "counselors," they can perform the role of a counselor very effectively. Some company psychologists give yearly emotional checkups. An emotional checkup might discover undue tension and nervousness that need attention in the same way that a physical examination would detect the danger of high blood pressure.

Some companies have instituted various kinds of counseling programs to deal with specific personal needs. Companies hire specialists mostly in hopes that they will improve employee performance and free managers from trying to deal with problems beyond their expertise. Employees with serious problems don't leave them at home, which can render a worker practically useless.

Company counselors should either help solve the problems themselves or refer the employees to local resources. People should learn what services are available in their own communities.

Comparisons of Supervisors and Trained Counselors

Specialists help to free managers

The relative advantages of training supervisory staff as counselors or hiring expert personnel to handle the task are compared in Table 5-1.

It is clear from the table that both approaches have distinct advantages. One *dis*advantage of hiring experts is that programs using experts have had great

TABLE 5-1
Comparisons of Trained Supervisors and Specialists as Counselors

ADVANTAGES OF TRAINED SUPERVISORS	ADVANTAGES OF EXPERTS[1]
1. More available to employees	1. Usually more skillful
2. More natural relationship	2. Less bias and more confidential
3. More aware of the employee's job performance	3. Less conflict with other employee roles
4. No need to introduce the outside person to conflict	4. Less emotional involvement

[1]Personnel directors, psychologists, medical specialists.

difficulties winning the acceptance of supervisory personnel. Apparently, many supervisors feel threatened by such programs because they fear that employees will criticize them unjustly.

HOW TO COUNSEL

Directive Method

The traditional method of counseling is called directive because the counselor directs and controls the form, flow, and content of the exchange between counselor and counselee.

Even though it may be impossible for one person to understand exactly the attitudes of another, there are times when a person in a confused state wants concrete advice that can be given by such guidance. Asking questions, making a diagnosis, and giving advice are characteristic of the direct counseling approach. Counseling is often expected in an organization with a strong formal chain of command.

Directive methods usually appeal to novice supervisors, because they often seem to be the easiest paths to follow in troubled situations. These methods are fast and seem to require little skill, but are relied on much too heavily.

Directive method gives advice and reassurance

Advice. This is the most common type of counseling available. It is easy to give good advice—if you know what is suitable.

This doesn't mean the counselor should not answer direct questions requiring factual answers. Factual answers and opinions clearly labeled as opinions are often necessary and helpful. But when emotional problems are under consideration, direct advice seldom is helpful unless solicited.

Reassurance. There is nothing wrong with reassurance—in the right place and at the right time. It especially encourages new and timid workers.

Nondirective Method

Nondirective method requires active listening

Nondirective counseling, also known as "client-centered therapy," is the method that often lends itself to current human relations practices in industry. In large measure, it is the way in which professionally trained people practice active listening as a counseling technique. Nondirective counseling is so named because, up to a point, the counselor lets the client determine the direction of the discussion. The counselor listens without making judgments and helps the client to clarify alternatives.

Cartharsis is talking out one's feeling

The basic concept of nondirective counseling holds that by skillful, active listening a counselor can help a client to release pent-up emotions. The process of obtaining relief from psychic and emotional tensions by talking about deeply felt emotions is called *catharsis.* Only after the client experiences catharsis and feels free of the weight of locked-in emotions can he or she then identify and solve personal problems in a rational frame of mind, and with minimum direction or advice from the counselor.

A person can solve his or her own problems

The ultimate goal of nondirective counseling is to stimulate the growth of self-recognition and self-knowledge. The theory and the goal are based on the belief that clients are responsible for their own behaviors and that they will solve their own problems once these problems are recognized fully. It holds further that self-recognition can develop only when the counselor establishes what professionals call a "permissive atmosphere," one in which the counselor remains neutral and accepts all statements and actions without passing judgment. In this method there is a belief that the client can solve personal problems if given the opportunity to do so and that every person basically is interested in doing the right thing.

There are four basic practices that nondirective counselors follow when conducting counseling interviews.

Readiness.   They know that it pays to learn as much as possible about the client before the initial appointment. In most companies, personnel files will be open for counselors' inspection.

Active Listening.   Nondirective counselors listen for all positive and negative feelings. They don't interrupt. Often they repeat statements they don't understand to the client until both understand the intended meaning.

No Advice.   They can answer questions about company policies and procedures, but if the client asks, "What should I do?" about a personal problem, they will not answer it. They believe that, if the client expresses everything he or she thinks and feels about the problem, sooner or later the client will come up with self-generated advice. Further, they believe that the best advice is always self-generated.

One inquiry that works well is "Would you like to tell me about it?" Do not pursue lines of inquiry that can be answered with "yes" or "no." An occasional contradiction by the employee himself or herself usually indicates confusion, which is often a preliminary step in the clarification process.

Clarification.   When the client does begin to arrive at solutions, the nondirective counselor encourages the exploration of the ideas through to their logical consequences. Counselors may offer occasional questions and suggestions at this stage. They help to clarify alternative courses of action as clearly as possible, but they require the client to make the decisions.

What a troubled employee needs to do is let it all out and stimulate self-help. What a counselor needs to do is try to empathize—and, in some cases, sympathize. Finally, at the risk of being redundant, the counselor needs to listen.

Cooperative Counseling

Somewhere between directive and nondirective counseling lies the style called cooperative. It is a blend of the direct guidance and authority typical of directive counseling and the nonjudgmental, active listening behavior typical of nondirective techniques. This form of counseling is especially effective during appraisal and evaluation interviews, but it also has been useful in counseling employees with personal problems. When using this method, the counselor's role is neither that of a judge nor of a sympathetic listener, but a complex mixture of the two.

In cooperative counseling, the counselor tries to stimulate the client's thinking by asking specific, *nonthreatening* questions at the beginning of the interview. (See Figure 5-2.) These questions are directive in that they determine the subject of the interview, but they are also nondirective in that the client is encouraged to express emotions as well as thoughts and attitudes. If the expression of these emotions brings tears or anger, the counselor should remain sympathetic and patient until the outburst is over. When nonthreatening questioning works, it stimulates honest, deeply felt communication very quickly.

This style also uses the nondirective device called "mirroring," that is,

A nondirective counselor does not give advice

Cooperative counseling blends direct and nondirect counseling

"Mirroring"

FIGURE 5-2 In cooperative counseling the counselor stimulates the client's thinking by asking *nonthreatening* questions at the beginning of the interview.
Rhoda Sidney/Monkmeyer Press

restating a client's own words not only to reflect and clarify the client's feelings but as material from which to form nonthreatening questions. Silences and pauses for thought are also customary in cooperative counseling, but they are not as long lasting or as frequent as in nondirective practice.

Because of its combination of directive and nondirective features, cooperative counseling is particularly effective in dealing with some alcoholics and drug addicts. Its nondirective aspects encourage and stimulate honest communication quickly; its directive features allow the counselor to set realistic behavior limits for troublesome employees.

Comparisons of Counseling Methods

Table 5-2 summarizes the different features of directive, nondirective, and cooperative counseling.

COMPANY PROGRAMS

Companies can institute programs to help deal with problems of alcohol and drug abuse, and sexual harassment. Programs are best developed quietly without "fanfare." Since alcoholism and drug abuse are medical-personnel matters, all the safeguards of confidentiality should be observed.

When employees are referred by their supervisors, or when they come on their own, they are given a series of physical and psychological tests and are then referred to various agencies, such as Alcoholics Anonymous, the Employee Assistance Program, or the local chapter of the National Council on Alcohol. Employees select a rehabilitation agency of their own choice, and weekly consultations with the company's medical staff are held thereafter.

TABLE 5-2 Comparisons of Various Counseling Techniques

METHOD	DIRECTIVE COUNSELING:	COOPERATIVE COUNSELING:	NONDIRECTIVE COUNSELING:
	Judge	*Judge-helper*	*Helper*
Objective	To communicate, to evaluate, to persuade the employee	To communicate, to evaluate, to stimulate self-help	To stimulate growth and self-help
Assumptions	Employee desires to correct known weaknesses	People will change if defensive feelings are removed	Growth can occur without correcting faults
Attitude	People profit from criticism, appreciate help	One can respect the feelings of others if one understands them	Discussion develops new and mutual trust
Motivation	Use positive or negative incentives	Help overcome resistance to change; use positive incentives	Increase freedom: increase responsibility
Risk	Loss of loyalty; inhibition of independence; face-saving problems created	Need for change may not develop	Employee may lack ideas; change may be other than what the superior had in mind
Gains	Success is most probable when employee respects interviewer	Develops favorable attitude toward superior that increases probability of success	Almost assured of improvement in some respects

A Guide for Managers and Supervisors

Be alert to changes in the work and behavioral patterns of all personnel under your supervision. Document particular instances in which an employee's job performance fails to meet minimum established standards. Do not attempt to diagnose medical or behavioral causes for work deterioration.

Corrective interviews

Conduct a corrective interview with the employee when the documented record of his or her unsatisfactory performance warrants. At the end of the interview, inform the employee that the services of the Employee Assistance Program are available if a personal problem is causing the poor performance. Such programs are frequently available in areas served by the National Council on Alcoholism.

If the employee's performance continues to deteriorate, conduct a second interview and take whatever first-step disciplinary action is warranted. Inform the employee that failure to improve job performance will result in further disciplinary action up to and including termination. Conclude with a strong recommendation that the individual use the services of the Employee Assistance Program on a confidential basis. If deterioration of performance continues, conduct a third interview. Conclude by offering the employee the choice between accepting the services of the Employee Assistance Program or being terminated because of unsatisfactory job performance. Avoid diagnosing a problem or confronting the employee with what you may suspect might be the problem. Termination is always for a cause related to job performance standards.

Give complete documentation of the employee's job performance problems and arrange for referral to the counselor as soon as possible if the employee chooses that alternative.

If the employee refuses help or if his or her performance remains unsatisfactory, the manager will take the appropriate disciplinary action or dismiss the individual from employment.

Any deviation from firm and consistent administration of these procedures because of misguided feelings of sympathy or other reasons will delay needed treatment and create an extreme risk to the employee's health and ultimate recovery. It is important that the supervisor not focus his or her attention on a "witch hunt" for alcoholism or other problems. The only criterion used for referral to the Employee Assistance Program (EAP) is a deteriorating job performance. The program places the responsibility for needed diagnosis, counseling, and treatment in the hands of qualified professionals.

Management can minimize the impact of sex in the workplace by maintaining an open environment where affected parties may talk about the situation. The same type of counseling that is available for extensive alcohol and drug users should be available for the individual caught up in a potential sex involvement. And remember: in the workplace, a couple falling in love and getting married poses less of a problem than a couple getting "unmarried" or divorced and still trying to work together.

A modified view of the company's role in changing work behavior is offered by Andrew Grove, president of Intel. Grove concludes that managers must resist the temptation to be drawn into disagreements among employees about non-work related matters.[16]

EMPLOYEE ASSISTANCE PROGRAMS

Because poor employee performance can mean substantial economic losses, companies have turned increasingly to various forms of employee assistance programs in an effort to step up production and reduce costs. The first step in an EAP involves the maintenance of performance records and the application of corrective measures when performance falls below standard. The second phase constitutes the link between the work context and community treatment resources. Two experts recommend that management should address (1) the effect of program participation on disciplinary procedures, (2) the disposition of information about employees' participation in the program, and (3) the evaluation of results over time.[17]

Employee assistance programs can help employers cope with the effects that personal employee problems such as drug abuse and alcoholism have on job performance. One survey of 68 companies found that the responding firms provided EAPs in the areas of alcohol, drugs, family-emotional crises, finance, legal matters, and psychiatric concerns. Another survey showed that about 37 percent of EAP problems concern alcoholism or alcohol abuse, family problems account for 28 percent, emotional problems 18 percent, drug abuse about 8 percent, and financial or legal difficulties about 5 percent. Successful EAPs depend on top management support, a framework suited to the individual company's structure and needs, training for appropriate referral personnel, confidentiality in recordkeeping and program evaluation, and participation by mental health care professionals.[18]

POSTTREATMENT PROCEDURES

Follow-Up—If the Employee Improves

The employee must be assured that job security will not be jeopardized if he or she obtains the recommended treatment, progresses toward control of the illness, and job performance improves.

The employee should also be advised not to expect any special privileges or exemptions from standard personnel administration practices.

If a relapse occurs, close follow-up and coordination between the supervisor and the plant medical director is of utmost importance. In spite of relapses, many persons ultimately control their disease.

Follow-Up—If the Employee Does Not Improve

If the employee refuses help or accepts treatment but makes no progress toward rehabilitation, and job performance remains poor or deteriorates further, supervisors must take the action they would normally take in cases of unsatisfactory job performance.

Of course, many approaches to rehabilitation are possible. It is important to remember that alcoholism, drug abuse, or sexual misconduct are usually symptoms of other deeper social and psychological problems and that, for rehabilitation to actually work, these problems must be taken into account.

Summary

Personal problems cannot always be left at home. Sometimes they travel to work. At work personal problems are reflected in (1) exaggerated behavior, (2) specific distress, and (3) radical changes. Once distress is recognized, friends and coworkers can often help each other through the rough times. Their main counseling tool is the practice of active listening. Effective self-counseling is also a technique that can be learned to good advantage.

Both professionally trained counselors and supervisory staff perform counseling functions. These functions are very tiring and time consuming but necessary, and sometimes rewarding. The three major counseling styles are (1) the traditional directive, (2) the newer nondirective, and (3) the cooperative, a combination of the first two. In directive counseling, the counselor directs the subject matter; in nondirective counseling, the subject is allowed to develop spontaneously. Cooperative counseling combines features of both and is particularly useful when dealing with alcoholics and drug addicts.

Alcoholism is a major disease that does great damage to our national productivity and results in great waste of human resources. Drug addiction, although perhaps not as prevalent, is increasing throughout the entire population, and some companies have instituted counseling programs to help their afflicted employees lick these disabling problems. Sexual liaisons and sexual harassment are also becoming more significant problems in the workplace.

When a case of alcoholism, drug abuse, or sexual harassment is encountered, company policy often recognizes the problem as an illness that can be cured and offers the employee help through an employee assistance program. Such a program is based on counseling. If, after many trials, the employee refuses help and his or her job performance does not improve, two choices are left—leave the company or undertake self-cure, which is very difficult.

The Sweet Smell of Grass

Tom Nowak walked to his office on Monday morning to find Dan Porter waiting for him at his door. "Tom, I would like to see you right away in my office." Tom was surprised at the sudden approach that his boss had used and the first thing on a Monday morning. It must be serious, he thought, as they walked down the hall together. He thought that they had always had a stable, amicable relationship.

"What's up?" asked Tom, trying to keep from sounding too apprehensive as they arrived at Dan's office.

"Sit down, Tom, it's important. It involves some of the men in your department." Dan was obviously disturbed. "You have been responsible for the shipping room for several years, and I haven't had any serious reason to doubt how you handle your men or the decisions you make in that department. But this new development upsets me."

Dan continued, "I've heard, and occasionally seen, a group of your boys, a clique, seem to take their breaks surreptitiously in out-of-the-way places, the restroom, and behind the loading dock. I've heard the reason is because they're smoking marijuana. Is that true, Tom?"

"You might be right, Dan. I really don't know, but I suspect it."

"Have you ever confronted them with the idea? Have you asked them outright?"

"No," said Tom quietly, "and I am not sure it's a good idea."

"Why not," replied Dan quickly and rather irately, "do you have a better idea?"

"The first reason is that they would probably lie if I asked them outright if they were smoking pot. They would lie for fear of losing their jobs. Another is I am not their mother or guardian of their morals. Their break time is strictly their own. Oh, I know it's illegal, and the company could get into trouble even though we don't control their breaks. However, we might be opening 'Pandora's box' if we approach it head on."

"What do you mean by a crack like that, Tom?" inquired Dan.

"You know as well as I do," said Tom, "that there are some guys under you that have openly discussed the effects of pot and who have admitted trying it. I don't have to name them, you know them."

Dan looked perplexed. "You're right, but they haven't stepped out of line at work to my knowledge. If we condone its use at work we have a problem. It is illegal, you know. We just can't take the risk that it is being done on company time."

1. What would be your approach to solve the immediate problem?

2. If you were to counsel any of the employees, which counseling approach would you use?

3. Should Tom and Dan try to solve the problem between themselves or should they confer with others?
4. There is no company policy on the matter; should they develop one?

Case Study 10

Just a Little Larceny—I'll Drink to That

In the opinion of Bob Ruppert, hospital administrator, the theft of various items ranging in value from $1 to $100 has become a major problem at the Bisbee Memorial Hospital. And it is increasing. At the recent monthly supervisors' meeting, Ruppert stated, "All the evidence we have been able to gather seems to indicate that the problem is serious and the loss is quite large. We must take steps to stop our loss. Hopefully, we can take care of it on an individual basis. I hope so. I have no idea whether it is the problem of a few or many."

A few days later you are in the home of a long-time friend who works at the hospital with you, but not under your supervision. Darryl Gossage has been with the company as a maintenance man for more than 15 years and has been considered one of the company's most competent men in his field. You also knew his drinking habits were getting worse, and some of your friends say that he had become an alcoholic. This particular Saturday Darryl has imbibed rather heavily and as you chat with him in the garage you notice a microscope in his garage with the initials BMH marked on the side. You mention to him, "Isn't that one of our microscopes, Darryl?" "Yah," Darryl replies hesitantly, "it needs fixing." Casually, you go over to the microscope and check it out. It appears to be in good order. You say, "_____"

1. What would you say? Do you make an accusation or let it pass?
2. Do you ignore it and ask Darryl for suggestions on what can be done about theft of hospital property?
3. What is the best way to handle Darryl's possible "light finger" problem?
4. If you think Darryl's drinking is now a serious problem, how would you handle it?

Case Study 11

Love in Bloom or . . . ?

Fran is a good-looking 19-year-old student who works full time at a small fast-food restaurant. Fran is working to accumulate enough money for college and a new car.

The manager of the restaurant, Pat, is also a college student and about four years older than Fran. There is an assistant manager for each of the work shifts and Fran would like to be promoted to that position for the extra pay and status.

Pat likes Fran and has made no secret about it. In fact, several times Pat has asked Fran out to movies after work, and suggested that they take their breaks in Pat's car. Pat has openly commented on Fran's attractive qualities.

Fran has rejected Pat's advances. Pat appears to be "hurt" and has told Fran that unless they can take breaks together and date, Fran doesn't stand a chance of becoming an assistant manager.

1. What do you think—is this sexual harassment or just "love in bloom"?
2. What can Fran do?
3. Would it make a difference to know that Fran is a young man and Pat a young woman? Go back through the case and see if there are any differences.

Terms and Concepts

alcoholic (industrial definition) any employee whose repeated overindulgence in alcohol sharply reduces job effectiveness and dependability.

cooperative counseling a combination of some aspects of direct and non-direct counseling, such as the direct advice and authority typical of directive, and the nonjudgmental and active listening of the nondirective method.

depressants drugs obtained legally by prescription or illegally on the street. They are designed to relax a person, but they can become addicting. Barbiturates (sleeping pills), Valium (the most prescribed drug), and other tranquilizers are depressants.

designer drugs tailor-made, synthetic drugs. The degree of potency and duration of their effect can be laboratory controlled.

directive counseling the most common type of counseling. In such a method, advice and reassurance is given.

drug abuse the condition of individuals who are "hooked" on drugs of any type to the point that they cannot function without them.

employee assistance programs provide counseling and other remedies to employees having substance abuse, emotional, or other personal problems.

hallucinogens mescaline, peyote, mushrooms, "Angel Dust" (P.C.P.), and LSD. They alter time and space perceptions. The "trips" can be pleasant or disastrous.

nondirective counseling a method that allows people to talk out their own problems, via catharsis. The counselor listens, helps in clarifying the problem, but gives no advice. The client solves the personal problem.

polydrug user a person who uses more than one drug in a given time, such as alcohol and depressants or alcohol and marijuana.

sexual harassment any unwanted attention of a sexual nature that occurs in the process of working or seeking work, and that interferes with a person's work ability.

stimulants any pill that will induce a feeling of excitement and energy and permits going without sleep for prolonged periods. Amphetamines, diet pills, Benzedrine, and "pep pills" are all stimulants.

Notes

1. Harry Levinson, *Emotional Health in the World of Work* (New York: Harper & Row 1964), p. 222.

2. Steven H. Applebaum, "A Human Resource Counseling Model: The Alcoholic Employee," *Personnel Administrator*, August 1982, p. 35.

3. "Ways Employers Can Help Drinkers and Drug Addicts," *U.S. News and World Report*, August 27, 1979, p. 61.

4. Victor Schachter and Thomas E. Geidt, "Cracking Down on Drugs," *Across the Board*, November 1985, p. 28.

5. Marshall Christy, "Getting the Drugs Out," *Business Month*, May 1989, pp. 66–69.

6. Joseph H. Lodge, "Drugs: Abuse Is an Economic Issue," *Credit*, November–December 1987, pp. 28–29.

7. "Labor Letter: Substances Most Abused," *The Wall Street Journal*, July 2, 1985, p. 1.

8. Gary L. Henderson, "They're Cheap and Easy to Make," *USA Today*, July 29, 1985, p. 8A.

9. John Tanner, Peter Wright, and Jerry Kinard, "Controlling Substance Abuse in the Workplace." *Business*, October–December 1987, pp. 25–27.

10. "Final Amendment to Guidelines in Discrimination Because of Sex (EEOC)," *Federal Register*, Vol. 45, No. 219, November 10, 1980, pp. 74676–74677.

11. "Dealing with Harassment," *Colorado Business*, July 1983, p. 11.

12. Ibid.

13. Beth Brophy, "At Work: Employers Still Liable," *USA Today*, July 31, 1985, p. 2B.

14. Diane Feldman, "Sexual Harassment: Policies and Prevention," *Personnel*, September 1987, pp. 12–17.

15. Donald J. Petersen and Douglas Massengill, "Sexual Harassment: A Growing Problem in the Workplace," *Personnel Administrator*, October 1982, p. 85.

16. Andrew S. Grove, "Mind Your Own Business, Boss!" *The Wall Street Journal*, September 19, 1988, p. 26.

17. Steven H. Appelbaum and Barbara T. Shapiro, "The ABCs of EAPs," *Personnel*, July 1989, pp. 39–46.

18. Cathy J. Brumback, "EAPs—Bringing Health and Productivity to the Workplace," *Business*, April–June 1987, pp. 42–45.

Recommended Reading _____

Applebaum, Steven H. "A Human Resource Counseling Model: The Alcoholic Employee." *Personnel Administrator*, August 1982, p. 35.

——, **and Barbara T. Shapiro.** "The ABCs of EAPs." *Personnel*, July 1989, pp. 39–46.

Bacon, Donald C. "See You in Court." *Nation's Business*, July 1989, pp. 16–26.

"Dealing with Harassment." *Colorado Business*, July 1983, p. 11.

Champagne, Paul J., and R. Bruce McAfee. "Auditing Sexual Harassment." *Personnel Journal*, June 1989, pp. 124–138.

"Final Amendment to Guidelines in Discrimination Because of Sex (EEOC)." *Federal Register*, Vol. 45, no. 219, November 10, 1980, pp. 74676–74677.

Flax, Steven. "The Executive Addict." *Fortune*, June 24, 1985, p. 24.

Greiff, James. "When an Employee's Performance Slumps." *Nation's Business*, January 1989, pp. 44–45.

Jacobs, Paul. "Validity of Alcoholism Treatment Aids Doubted." *The Los Angeles Times*, December 14, 1981, pp. 1–3, 20, 23.

Kupfer, Andrew. "Is Drug Testing Good or Bad?" *Fortune*, December 19, 1988, pp. 133–135.

Linenberger, Patricia. "What Behavior Constitutes Sexual Harassment?" *Labor Law Journal*, April 1983, pp. 238–247.

Masi, Dale A., and Seymour J. Friedland. "EAP Action and Options." *Personnel Journal*, June 1988, pp. 61–67.

Massey, Steve. "Fake Speed Causes Almost as Much Fear as the Real Thing." *The Wall Street Journal*, September 8, 1981, p. 1.

"On the Job Against Drugs." *Nation's Business*, July 1989, pp. 29–31.

Peterson, Donald J., and Douglas Massengill. "Sexual Harassment: A Growing Problem in the Workplace." *Personnel Administrator*, October 1982, p. 85.

"Privacy." *Business Week*, March 28, 1988, pp. 61–65, 68.

Rout, Lawrence. "Pleasures and Problems Face Married Couples Hired by the Same Firms." *The Wall Street Journal*, May 28, 1980, pp. 1, 21.

U.S. Department of Justice. *Drug Enforcement Administration, Fact Sheets.* Washington, D.C.: GPO, 1973. Later editions available.

Wrich, James T. "Beyond Testing: Coping with Drugs at Work." *Harvard Business Review*, pp. 120–127, 130.

Group and Role Behavior

After studying this chapter, you should be able to:

1. Understand groups and their characteristics.
2. Appreciate propositions about group dynamics.
3. Understand consensus building, its advantages and disadvantages.
4. Discuss the difference between an impermeable and a permeable class society.
5. Explain the advantages and disadvantages of a permeable class society.
6. Cope with inconsistencies and ambiguities of group and role behavior.
7. Understand role prescriptions and role behaviors.

TO START YOU THINKING . . .

Here are some more questions to stimulate your thinking and open avenues of discussion before you read the chapter.

- What is a group? What determines if it is effective?
- What attracts you to another person or group of people?
- How do you obtain consensus in group behavior and decision making?
- Do you believe that you will remain in the same class as your parents, or do you have aspirations to move upward? What is the difference between earned status and donated status?
- Does being born into the "right" family assure one of future success?
- Can eventual earnings and success be predicted from high test scores in school?
- Are social values changing?
- Is success or failure in any particular endeavor predictive of all behavior?

GROUP DYNAMICS

The demands of meeting individual challenges are minuscule compared to being effective in groups. Sheer numbers and the accompanying arithmetic or geometric interactions possible among groups make the task of managing groups challenging. Groups, like individuals, have and develop their own personalities.

This chapter explores classes of our society, reasons for group formation and role behavior as well as success and failure within those groups. Let's start with the basics of group formation and dynamics.

What Is a Group?

A group is a collection of people who either meet personally or in absentia for the purpose of accomplishing a social or work objective. This definition is more contemporary than those traditionally used but with modern communications techniques, it is quite possible to have a meeting or other interactions with individuals separated by thousands of miles.

Interaction, interdependence, and communication are the keys to group activity. There must be some commonality of objectives and interdependency of individuals to accomplish those objectives. Thus, communication among those individuals is imperative to successful fulfillment of group goals.

Groups are usually involved in meetings, task forces, or teams. All these activities are affected by many variables, including the size of group and the predisposition to work together to accomplish an objective. Figure 6-1 shows the various factors that influence group task accomplishment.

Major determinants of group effectiveness are norms of the individuals, size of the group, and degree of cohesiveness in the group. Status of group members also affects effectiveness and success of the group and will be discussed in the chapter on power and status.

Norms

Norms are ideas or values that a group has regarding expected behaviors of individuals and group members. Both individuals and groups have values. Individuals bring their values to the group, which in turn, develops group norms.

Norms are usually unwritten but are powerful devices for assuring group conformity. Feelings run strong about right and wrong conduct of group members. In one sense, the group norms are summations of the individual members' values, but they are larger than the sum. They are, in effect, synergistic or larger than the sum of the parts. They can be very strong or less effective depending on the character, morals, and integrity of the individuals comprising the group.

Consider the example of a team who assembles aircraft or automotive products. The values that individuals attach to money, human life, and congeniality of a group all affect the speed and quality of production output. If the members are on a pay-for-piecework basis, their output may be guided by numbers of products they can produce and other variables. If the product is safety related and might endanger its end user if not properly produced, their output may be more balanced with concern for quality and safety. Similarly, and perhaps most important, if an individual wants to be a part of the group, he or she must cooperate with the group members. These individual values all contribute to the formation of a group norm and standards of behavior.

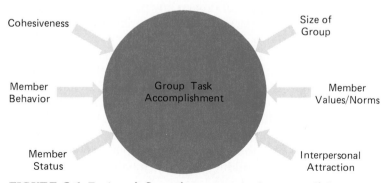

FIGURE 6-1 Factors influencing group task accomplishment.

Group Composition

Why are we attracted to some individuals? Certainly the task goals of the workplace may almost force attachment if not attraction. More likely, and in voluntary associations, we are attracted to work with others because of similar attitudes, opinions, behavior, goals, age, education, and personality. Continued exposure and frequent interaction are also reasons for interpersonal attraction.[1]

Another reason groups are composed the way they are is *perceived* attractiveness or desirability of association. If "we perceive an individual as having desirable characteristics, we anticipate that an interpersonal relationship with that individual will be rewarding."[2] If we grow to like an individual through association and interaction, the relationship becomes mutually rewarding.

Size of Group

The overall effectiveness of a group is influenced significantly by its size. Two-person groups can be very effective depending upon interpersonal attraction and task goals. But groups are more commonly thought of as having more than two people. Group size minimums are not so important as maximums. Two to five individuals may function very effectively as a group.

The ideal size of a group is from five to seven persons

The size of a group is important, and the desirable number seems to be five, although some experts would say it is seven members. Below five, for the most part, each person in the group says something to each other person. In groups over seven, the low participators tend to stop talking to each other and speak more to the leader. Subconsciously this situation becomes more formal, and real interaction generally declines. The tendency for stronger directive leaders generally increases visibly as size increases.

There also must be recognition by each group member that each way of thought has its own validity. The failure of group members to grant these recognitions to each other results inevitably in the failure to communicate. Successful communication among the different members of a group depends on something more than a common language. Experts trained in using precise technical vocabularies have difficulties in communicating with lay persons. Even in ordinary everyday language, different words have different meanings for different people.

Figure 6-2 compares communication and complexity of interaction in small (6 members) and large groups (16 members).

As group size increases from 5 to 12 or more members, consensus becomes increasingly difficult to achieve. Thus, consensus will be facilitated by limiting the size of the group working on any particular project and maximizing each person's opportunity to participate and contribute. Otherwise, if the group is too large, a "false consensus" (nominal agreement only) is obtained.

There is an inverse relationship between group size and the ability of the group to function efficiently and effectively. Factors influencing optimal size of a group include the group's purpose and individuals' needs for influence, interaction, and interdependency. As group size is increased, up to a point, the skills and resources of the total group are increased. Unique skills and status may be added if a person with perceived high prestige is added to the group. If prestige or status differences are too great among group members, there may be a negative effect on cohesiveness of adding group members.

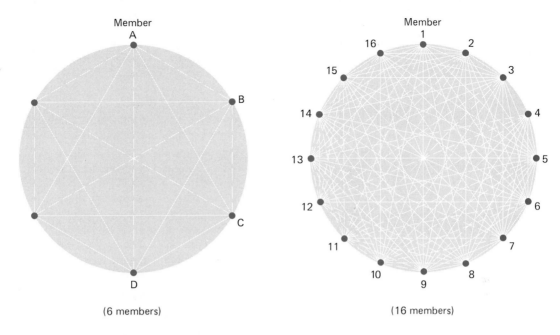

FIGURE 6-2 Complexity of interaction in small and large groups.

Group Cohesiveness _____

Group cohesiveness is both a cause and effect of group size and ability to reach consensus. A highly consensual group exhibits high group cohesiveness; similarly, a highly cohesive group (where group members are mutually attracted and desire to remain a part of the group is high) can reach consensus more readily because of their mutuality.

Related to the group's cohesiveness are the types of decisions and emotions affecting the group. Emotional or affective conflict results in consensus being reached largely due to avoidance or withdrawal from group processes—the "I don't care" and "Anything, just to get this over with" syndromes—even in important decisions affecting group members. Difficult decisions or particularly troublesome decisions are handled on an ad hoc basis rather than as part of a cohesive, well-functioning group. Figure 6-3 summarizes some propositions about group dynamics.

HOW TO OBTAIN GROUP CONSENSUS _____

How do you obtain consensus among group members? You communicate and work at it—and it is hard work. It requires management guidance and some processing, that is, working with and through the group on the decision making, communication, or process as well as the end product.

Obtaining consensus requires extensive communication, especially, but not limited to, interpersonal dialog either between two or a small number of individuals, or within a group. The process requires a lot of give and take: the giving and taking of advice and the giving and taking of constructive criticism.

The communicative behaviors of group members can either facilitate or hinder

1. *Groups really exist.* One view is that groups are an artificial construct or a product of a distorted thought process. In fact and practicality, they do exist. They are a practical state of affairs. All of us, from childhood, are normally associated with various groups and consequently have a strong sense of belonging.

2. *Groups are omnipresent.* In normal society, groups are everywhere. Anthropologically, we form groups to accomplish tasks. In doing so, we form sentiments, attitudes, values, and behaviors that reflect the quality of the group.

3. *Groups have power.* What we do in groups has far-reaching impact on us as individuals. What a person does in a group may also influence his or her future behavior and the way others behave toward them. Exclusions of individuals from or enforced group membership may have an almost permanently damaging effect.

4. *Groups produce good and bad consequences.* The conformity dimensions of groups can be either good or bad in business. As noted earlier, there is reason to conform in business dress and interpersonal relationships. But there are also reasons for rugged individualism and entrepreneurship. Carrying either conformity or individualism to extremes can be detrimental to both the individual and the group.

5. *Group consequences can be enhanced.* Understanding how and why groups operate permit using the group for desirable consequences. Notwithstanding the charge of "social manipulation," there is a Machiavellian purpose to be achieved by using groups. Groups *can* be made to be more effective and to serve better ends.[3]

FIGURE 6-3 **Propositions about group dynamics.**

group consensus. If the communications are group oriented, they will have a positive effect on group consensus. Highly opinionated or "me" statements—"I'm an expert, and if you don't agree with me, you're wrong!"—have a negative effect on the group.

Even the terminology employed can affect the group's behavior. Efforts need to be made to secure agreement, adaptation, and compromise instead of getting "locked in" or becoming defensive about one's position. A very practical approach to this is to ask group members to describe *their process* not "What do you think should be done?" The latter locks them onto a position or solution, and they become defensive of their decisions.

As noted in the previous section on cohesiveness, decisions can become emotional, ad hoc, and hurried. In contrast, when the discussions, decisions, and even differences of opinion take place on a higher and rational plane, it is much more possible to achieve true consensus for a decision.

Group rapport and trust develop high morale

If a group is composed of five persons, each contributing his or her own personality, soon a new personality develops—that of the group. Group rapport and trust in each other develops. The growth encouraged by all relates to the height of the morale that can be achieved by the group. However, the larger the group, the more elusive the feeling of group morale and the harder it is to determine.

CHANGING SOCIAL VALUES

Individuals and groups are influenced by changing social values. The upheaval of the 1960s and the evolution of the 1970s—the civil rights movement, the women's liberation movement—had a tremendous effect on our society. The individualism of the 1980s also changed the character and destiny of American organizations. People continue to question the routine paths that their careers are expected to take. Women realize that they have new options and men can also grow and develop in new ways in their work lives.

Need for personal growth

The individual looking for personal growth and development these days is no longer satisfied to stay in one job for years on end, no matter how large the paycheck or secure the situation. We hear of many instances of people who are driven by sheer boredom to try something different.

Two-career couples are more common

The two-career couple is now a norm. Husbands and wives may alternate in job changing. The author knows a young, former bank president who is now "Mr. Mom" at home with his pre-school children while his wife works outside the home. Both are enjoying the relationship.

Early Career Changes

The "trying twenties"

There are life decisions to be made in the "trying twenties." People in this age group are preparing for a career, marriage, a family, and many of their intimate dreams. There seems to be the idea that during this age people can overcome all if they apply their minds and wills to life—that destiny is within their control. Perhaps this is a necessary self-deception that can help them to achieve their goals and to succeed.

The great majority of young people in America still believe in the work ethic, the idea that hard work and getting ahead are essential for a full and satisfying life. It is with this spirit of enthusiasm that many young people begin working at their first "real" jobs.

Midcareer Adjustments

Higher up the ladder competition becomes greater

Career consultants often help clients by encouraging them to review their backgrounds in terms of what they have to offer prospective employers. Three important aspects are experience, education, and breadth of background. A person midway in his or her career can usually offer experience, but may find education lacking. Formal education may be a determining factor in the choice between two experienced persons for a position or a promotion.

As an employee moves up the ladder of success, the competition becomes stiffer, and reeducation is one answer. Returning to the classroom may scare the middle-aged person, but more persons of all ages are returning to further their education. The evening college classroom or industrial programs have two features: (1) providing the means by which to learn up-to-date methods of handling work problems and (2) offering new vantage points through which the individual can perceive himself or herself in relationship to the world.

The breadth of one's background can show that a person is willing to accept greater responsibility. Such experience can prove at a later time to a potential employer that this applicant has accepted responsibility, either in a company or in the community. The employer who hires workers older than 40 years of age usually perceives these qualities:

1. Stability that comes with maturity

2. A serious attitude toward the job

3. More reliability, less absenteeism, and proven steady work habits

4. A sense of responsibility and loyalty

5. A tendency not to be distracted by outside interests or influences

Noting these advantages, many employers now make it a practice to include older workers in every working unit. They find that mature employees have a stabilizing influence on the group as a whole. McDonald's restaurants provide classic examples of this change in social values and work groups.

THE FIXED OR IMPERMEABLE SOCIAL CLASS _____

Inherited Class _____

One view of social structure is that people are unable to change their social status. When a child is born, it inherits, along with its genetic makeup and ethnic origin, a social class to which its family belongs. Its family's orientation to life can be viewed in certain ways and then classified into large categories of behavior and thought. Social scientists have found it convenient to designate three major classes in Western industrial nations: the lower, middle, and upper classes. Further divisions occur within these three classes.

Children have the class of their parents

Typically, children grow up to become solid members of the class into which they are born. They learn the aspirations and life styles particular to their class upbringing. Class lines overlap: our class system is not a stable one nor is it at all comparable to a caste system, in which a person is born into a class from which it is impossible to depart. However, class lines are strong enough so that "rising above one's class" is considered a feat, demanding devotion and skill. Class origins are not erased easily, even when the upward struggle has been won.

Self-rating is high

People have a tendency to rate themselves higher than would the general public. This tendency to have a strong feeling of self-worth may be very natural and perhaps stronger than the view that society as a whole may have of us when it compares us with the rest of the working force.

Social Class and Economic Success _____

Christopher Jencks did a five-year national study on the traits of an economically successful male. His findings seem to indicate that some can find economic success or greater status more easily than can others.[4]

Early expectations by others

1. Test scores, even in the sixth grade, shape a person's own expectations and those of others toward him.

College degree is a big key

2. Those with a college degree have a key to the gate of success. The degree is more important than what you have learned. For blacks this can be even more important.

3. Be born in the "right family." The father should occupy a high-status position and earn an excellent income. The father and mother should have received good educations. Family size should be small.

Leadership makes a difference.

4. Leadership ability is worth as much as cognitive skills, especially if accompanied by a college degree.

5. Jews, WASPS (White, Anglo-Saxon Protestants), and German Catholics have a small economic edge over other ethnic groups.

THE STRIVER AND THE PERMEABLE SOCIETY _____

A permeable society is one in which people can move from one social class to another. Social class subcultures differ from one another in several ways. Some people are contented or resigned to their social status; some are striving to achieve a better social status. Basically there are three personality traits that distinguish the difference between them as shown in Table 6-1.

The status climber is active and individualistic and plans for the future. These three are more characteristic of higher social status groups in our society than of groups lower in the socioeconomic spectrum.

Middle-class person or higher plans for a career

Those in professional and managerial occupations, as well as in semiprofessional and white-collar occupations, are more likely to believe that their lives are under their own control and that occupational achievement and success are a result of their own efforts. The upper-middle-class person fits himself or herself for a career. The notion of a career implies self-actualization. The lower-middle-class person is exposed to experiences that may make him or her look for a job and not a career. Such a person has learned that the values of security, stability, and respectability are his life-style.

Economic Prosperity _____

The talented and the ambitious are rewarded

Strong people with humble origins can climb up the social ladder; as a result the whole social structure is apportioned according to talent and ambition. An open class society facilitates economic prosperity and more rapid social progress. An open class society provides society with many talented individuals; it does not waste any of society's "brains." These fulfilled individuals contribute greatly to the technological and scientific advances of society.

Facilitates Creativity _____

A permeable society encourages the inventor

The environment of a permeable society provides a more diversified and greater combination of ideas, values, and things productive of inventions in the minds of the people. Here there is an incentive for individuals to think, to invent, and to discover.

TABLE 6-1 Personality Differences Between Strivers and Nonstrivers

	INDIVIDUALS DESIRING TO CHANGE THEIR SOCIAL STATUS (STRIVERS)	INDIVIDUALS WHO ARE RESIGNED OR CONTENTED WITH THEIR SOCIAL STATUS (NONSTRIVERS)
Attitude	*Active:* Believe that they can manipulate physical and social environment to their own advantage	*Passive:* Accept situations as they are.
Approach	*Individualistic:* Need not subordinate personal wants to those of the group or the family.	*Collectivistic:* Believe that much can be accomplished through group effort.
Outlook	*Future:* Willing to forgo short-term pleasure or accomplishments in the interest of better long-term gains.	*Present:* Willing to accept present joys, because future pleasures seem too distant, vague, or unattainable.

Less Discriminatory and Narrow-Minded Attitudes

One who has lived in several classes may be more broad-minded

When an individual works at the same occupation and has the same economic and social status for life, that person is doomed to think and to look at the world through his or her social "standpoint" or "social box." The person naturally cannot understand the standpoint of those in other positions and therefore must evaluate and think in terms of permanent social status. One who has been in several social, occupational, and economic situations acquires different "mental vistas." A person who has been both a millionaire and a working person is not a stranger to either group.

Increases Individualism

When an individual is a member of a particular social stratum for most of his or her life, it is likely that the person identifies himself or herself not so much as a particular personality but as a component of a group to which he or she belongs. In passing from stratum to stratum (and encountering several overlapping groups), the attachment to the "social box" becomes less intense. This participation in many groups awakens one's personality and transforms one from a component of a group to an individual.

GROUP BEHAVIOR AND UPWARD MOBILITY

Occupations provide the major channels for rising in social status. Two factors are essential for a low-status person to acquire a high-status job: (1) education and (2) the ability to break through the barriers of class prejudice. By acquiring skill, training, and the status that educational degrees automatically confer, it is possible to knock on the doors of employers who can unlock future status possibilities. For the doors to be opened, however, those in power must accept those who come knocking. Since people of a higher class often feel threatened when members of a lower class attempt to penetrate their ranks, antidiscrimination and fair employment laws have been enacted to help force open the doors of opportunity.

No matter how much people aspire to membership in another group, they must meet that group's standards in order to be admitted. If a person is to rise in any system, the values of the system must be understood and applied. Here is how one individual moved from the "back office" into the "front office":

Associate with the right people

I began to watch the front-office people more closely. They seemed calm and unaffected by their jobs, and I started to realize that it wasn't accumulated knowledge that would get me out. It was a certain way of speaking—polite, cool and calm. A cheerful friendly look on my face, no stray hair out of place or that tight, frantic look that comes with pressure. And above all, association with the right people.[5]

Occupational status can be seen in the shape of a pyramid, with lower-status jobs at the base and higher-status jobs at the peak. This work structure is supported by the class structure of the larger society:

What matters is that in a class society there is a financial "top" to every area of work; admission to the top is granted largely on the basis of money and class; and the reward for having a top position is still more money and status. The system is closed and self-perpetuating; the privileged position of the managers and professionals—not to mention the ruling class—is built into it.[6]

This pyramidal status design is shaped according to the capitalistic mold: money, opportunity, and position beget more of the same, just as lack of money, opportunity, and position beget less of the same. People's class destinies depend a great deal on the kind of encouragement they receive to develop talents holding status values.

There tends to be more loyalty toward higher groups

People are more likely to feel loyal to higher-status groups. Social climbers are careful to conform to the norms of the group to which they aspire rather than to comply with the norms of the group from which they want to escape. Workers who develop strong attachments to individuals of higher status may regard themselves as only temporary members of their own status group. For example, lower-status white-collar workers often identify with their higher-status managers.

One set of authors summarize behavior as a result of status differentiation.

In general, at least in the United States, there are strong expectations about how high- and low-status people are supposed to behave. In a given situation people who are clearly higher status are expected to be "nice" and not lord it over others. It is a form of noblesse oblige, with expressions of the person's higher status being subtle and designed not to make others feel bad even though they are lower status. In turn, lower-status people are expected to "know their place" and not presume on the privileges of those with higher status; those who do not properly defer are considered "uppity." Because of the democratic ideals in the United States, little of this is talked about directly; but if you have trouble believing it try testing it in a social or work situation.[7]

Intelligence and Success

Is drive more important than IQ?

Lewis Terman conducted one of the longest-term studies ever undertaken on the backgrounds and personality characteristics of 1,528 people with IQs of over 135 when they were in grammar school. In 1980, *Psychology Today* reported on how these people fared in their careers.[8] The important part of the follow-up was that exceptional intelligence does not guarantee extraordinary accomplishment. Some of Terman's subjects did markedly better in life than did others, but the most successful members from the group shared a special drive to succeed, a need that had been with them from grammar school onward. The high achievers had felt a greater parental pressure to excel. Finally, a feeling of choosing one's career, not drifting into it, was an important part of job and status satisfaction.

STRIVERS FALL PREY TO THE "PETER PRINCIPLE"

Strivers may earn or have their place in a group donated. *Earned place* is the social reward for achieving something that others consider useful. *Donated* or unearned status is not earned but is the willingness of somebody else to believe that we have earned our position by the exercise of ability.

Peter principle means raised to level of incompetence

Once one's place has begun to be conferred because of demonstrated ability, it tends to be donated. One potential result of this willingness to confer status is the *Peter principle*, which states that employees are raised to their highest levels of incompetence.[9] The rise may have been earned, but we do not know that a person has the ability to accomplish a job until it is done.

J. S. Minion was a maintenance foreman in the public works department of Excelsior City. He was a favorite of the senior officials at City Hall. They all praised his unfailing affability.

"I like Minion," said the superintendent of works. "He has good judgment and is always pleasant and agreeable." When the superintendent of works retired, Minion succeeded him. Minion continued to agree with everyone. He passed to his foreman every suggestion that came from above. The results were conflict in policy and the continual changing of plans, which soon demoralized the department. Complaints poured in from the mayor and other officials, from taxpayers, and from the maintenance-workers' union. In short, Minion, a competent foreman, became an incompetent superintendent.

DISADVANTAGES OF A PERMEABLE CLASS SOCIETY

There are several reasons why accepting one's own "birthright" or place in society and the class structure is justified. A fluid society can diminish intimacy, disrupt group relationships, and cause status anxiety.

Diminished Intimacy

A striver can lose intimacy

A person needs close social ties with others. This does not mean so much formal contact with others as an intimacy, a close friendship, a "togetherness." Increased mobility reduces considerably the chances of such intimacy. Permanency of social position in an immobile society also means a permanency of the people among whom one lives, whereas individuals who are shifting from group to group, from place to place, experience many fewer chances for intimacy and greater sociopsychological isolation and loneliness.

Disruption of Primary Group Relationships

Strivers fail to keep their roots

Shifting from position to position, and from locality to locality, disrupts established primary group relationships. Mobility means estrangement of one's parents and threatens patterns of friendship and residence. Frequent movement means that it is difficult to develop roots in a neighborhood or work environment. The old family home, the familiar neighborhood, all give way to an adjustment to new roles, new friends, and new places. The loss is reflected in superficial temporary relationships.

Personal morals become fuzzy

We are dependent for moral health upon the intimate association with some sort of group, usually our family and friends. It is the interchange of ideas with these groups that makes standards of right and wrong seem real to us. When an individual moves from status to status, a common result is moral isolation and an atrophy of the moral sense.

Marriage Disruption

Even the marriage of the mobile couple is sometimes threatened. Often two mates are not equally interested in shifting from position to position or may differ in their ability to learn the new role adjustments. One may resent the implied insult of being constantly prodded, polished, and improved, and the other may resent the mate's lack of cooperation.

Express Your Opinion

You have now read advantages and disadvantages for a permeable and an impermeable society. Some of the attitudes expressed are sociological and some are psychological. Based on what you have read and knowing yourself, which method do you favor for yourself—the permeable or the impermeable society? What reasons can you give for your opinion? Try to give your personal feelings.

GROUP ROLES

Group roles are shared expectations of how group members are to perform in their positions. Group roles are developed because of activities, interactions, and sentiments of others in a group as well as self-expectations. There is an informal testing of each group member to see if there is a good fit. How well an individual fits into a group depends on the factors discussed earlier: norms, social class, interpersonal attraction, group cohesiveness, and size.

Roles of group members may be divided into task-related and maintenance-related roles. *Task-related roles* are those behavioral expectations that directly aid in the accomplishment of group objectives. *Maintenance-related roles* are those behavioral expectations directly related to the well-being and development of the group. Examples of task-related and maintenance-related roles are shown in Figure 6-4.

Group roles are also a function of role prescriptions and roles behaviors.

Role Prescriptions and Role Behaviors

Doing as others expect you to do is playing the role

What we say and do are largely matters of expectations, role prescriptions, and role behaviors. The things that people are expected to do are known as *role prescriptions;* the things that they actually do are known as *role behaviors.* To the extent that role behaviors match the appropriate role prescriptions, within a company, for example, an individual is said to be effective or successful. It is assumed that the individual is in fact contributing to company goal achievement.

The role prescription is the set of expectations that affect a particular role, such as a manager's position. All the different people with whom one comes into contact collectively form one's multiple role.

Performance evaluation is essentially a matter of determining the degree to which the role prescription and role behavior match. It is an attempt to equate

Examples of Task-Related Roles	*Examples of Maintenance-Related Roles*
Objective(s) clarifier	Consensus seeker
Planner	Encourager
Organizer	Mediator
Seeker of information	Gatekeeper, relevant to group norms
Leader	Compromiser
Coordinator	Communicator
Energizer	Standard setter
Evaluator	Observer

FIGURE 6-4 Task and maintenance roles of group members.

organizational goal attainment with the individual contribution. What is really important insofar as an organization is concerned is not how much an individual does but how much of what he or she does is organizationally relevant as determined by his or her role.

The role is thus the sum total of expectations placed on the person by the supervisors, subordinates, peers, customers, vendors, and others, depending on the person's particular job.

Role Conflict and Ambiguity

When self-expectations and others' expectations differ, role conflict develops

One must be able to integrate these expectations, as well as one's own, into a coherent psychological pattern if one expects to perform successfully. If, however, the individual lacks a clear understanding of these expectations and if they conflict with one another or his or her own expectations, the individual has *role conflict* and will be unable to satisfy some of these expectations. *Role ambiguity* exists when a person is not too sure how to act or perform in a given situation.

Research suggests that, when there is a sizable discrepancy between a manager's concept of his or her role and the employees' role expectations of that job, motivation and efficiency tend to be poor. For example, if managers see themselves as mediators and developers of compromises between management and labor, but both management and union expect them to be hard-nosed negotiators, role conflict develops.

Lack of role expectation leads to uncomfortable feelings

Even when top management has learned to live with varying role expectations, many employees find their function in a company much easier when their role prescription is defined clearly. The lack of a job description or role definition sometimes accounts for employees saying, "Oh, I don't know, I just feel uncomfortable on the job. I guess I really don't know what the boss expects of me."

BEHAVIOR OF SMALL GROUPS

The behavior that goes on in a committee or other small group can be viewed as positive and negative reactions to questions and answers. Such negative reactions include showing disagreement, tension, or antagonism. The positive reactions include showing agreement, tension release, and friendly solidarity.

A successful meeting needs a balance between positive and negative reactions

There are about twice as many positive reactions in most meetings as there are negative reactions. One might suppose that the more successful the meeting, the more positive the reactions. But evidence does not support this view. Rather, there appears to be a kind of optimum balance between disagreements and agreements. Too few disagreements may be an indication of the lack of involvement and interest in the task, or that the atmosphere is so inhibited and constrained that nobody dares to disagree. When ill feelings rise about some critical point, a chain reaction tends to set in, and logical or practical demands of the task may cease to be governing factors.

Groupthink

There is a downside to group cohesiveness, the harmony and consensus approach: there is a risk that everyone in the group starts to think alike. "Groupthink" sets in. Groupthink is a "deterioration of mental efficiency, reality testing, and moral judgment that results from ingroup pressures."[10]

Irving Janis, communication consultant, has been studying the symptoms of groupthink for many years. A strong sense of group unity and a feeling that "we" are on the right track can lead to finding the quickest, but not the best, answer, according to Janis. Closely knit groups sometimes suffer from the illusion of unanimity—that is, no one wants to break up the cohesiveness of the group. Group leaders may also assume, wrongly, that silence on the part of a member means consent or agreement.

Members of a group may indulge in self-censorship, failing to mention a legitimate idea contrary to the group's direction. They feel that the idea is not really what the group wants to hear. Many of us want so much to be a member of the team that we will not oppose the general trend.

Groupthink can also generate the illusion of invulnerability. "After all, we have been a leader in the field for many years; why shouldn't people accept our results?" The idea that our group cannot be wrong because we think alike leads to feelings of grandeur and infallibility. Very successful companies are likely to find that their committees fall into the groupthink syndrome. Do you have a strong leader of your committees who states his opinion before others, setting the stage for groupthink? Such group leaders expect the committee to rubber stamp predetermined decisions.

Task Leaders or Social Leaders

When people are active in a group meeting, they may be characterized by actions of two types: the task leader and the social leader. The *task leader* feels that the accomplishment of the task is important. The ability to define the problem, the best way to handle it, and the time restriction become of paramount importance. The feelings of the individual members are of lesser concern. Task leaders are willing to "forgive and forget" if someone's feelings are hurt or if someone tramples on their emotions. The accomplishment of the goal, success, and self-ego are their trademarks. The *social leader* is concerned with the feelings of each member and that each has an opportunity to participate. An agreement on a solution to a problem is only possible if there is compatibility among the members. The social leader will resent the "takeover" tactics of the task leader and will move in for a reassessment, compromise, or evaluation.

Summary

Groups have powerful influences on the success or failure of our organizations. If the group perceives itself as being cohesive, it will be much more likely to succeed. On the other hand, the perception of the group as an habitual failure naturally affects the outcome of further efforts and a vicious cycle of cause-and-effect failure is created. Athletic teams are classic examples of this phenomenon.

The success of groups are influenced by group size and cohesiveness, interpersonal attraction, as well as individual behavior, status, values, or norms of members. Changing social values contribute to the makeup of work groups; increasingly, there are many midcareer changes and a mix of age, gender, and other demographic groups in the workplace.

Those who believe in the permeable society feel that such a system increases individualism, encourage economic prosperity, and facilitates creativity—and even lessens discrimination. Such people tend to associate with the "right people," and have more loyalty toward higher-status groups. However, the strivers can easy fall prey to the Peter principle.

The more one wants to move up the social ladder, the less accurate that person's communications are likely to be. The striver is more likely to minimize disagreements with a supervisor, filter out problems, and stick to "business talk." The less respect you give a supervisor, the more likely you will perceive a chat as advice or information rather than as an order.

One last key to effective group behavior is the ability of the group to reach consensus. And the key and the challenge to obtaining consensus, is keeping discussions on a high, rational plane. Concerted effort by the group leader and group members (limited to a small, cohesive group) to be fair, open, and trusting will help achieve consensus. Above all, universal participation and contribution by *all* group members will enhance the quality of the process and the decisions.

Case Study 12

Who's the Boss?

Sam and Sarah Cerenti are a husband-and-wife team who operate a small manufacturing facility in Riverside, California. Sam is in charge of design and production of their printed T-shirts, sweatshirts, and other novelty items—many of which are related to the ski and other sports industries. Sam's background includes working as a mechanical engineer for a major manufacturing company.

Sarah is responsible for marketing and public relations for the small firm. Unlike Sam, Sarah does not have a formal education in business or engineering but is "picking up the business as she goes along."

When a major contract customer presents an idea for a unique, marketable T-shirt and sweatshirt to Sarah, she replies that "We just don't have time in the schedule to produce it." The customer knows that the product will sell because he has done the market research at a chain of health clubs and has orders in hand for several hundred shirts.

The customer is put off by Sarah and is ready to take his business elsewhere.

1. What is the problem here? Are there role conflicts?
2. Has Sarah overstepped her authority? Are any of the following factors contributing problems?
   a. Authority definition
   b. Group or role behavior
   c. Management style
   d. Consensus decision making
3. What would you suggest that Sarah, Sam, and the customer do?

Charlie Has a Chance to Get Ahead

Charlie is employed as an accountant in a small assembly plant in the Midwest. In his seven years at Astro-Technology, he has become acquainted with most of the 200 employees and enjoys the atmosphere of his office and the company attitude toward him. However, in the past three years, he has not received a promotion, and there is little chance for one in the near future. The raises he has received have not kept up with inflation. He has discussed the situation frequently with his wife, Rita, who is working as a personnel officer at a research firm in town.

Although Rita has never told Charlie, she feels that her job has more status than his. Even though Charlie earns slightly more income, she has more flexible hours, more holidays with pay, better company fringe benefits, and apparently more status when the two companies' organizational charts are compared. Rita enjoys her present position and the salary she receives.

Their two daughters are doing well in grammar school and are active in the Girl Scouts and the 4-H Club.

A month ago Charlie heard of a new position for an accountant in their home office in Dallas. He knows that his company has a practice of promoting from within, and his supervisor feels that he would have a good chance of getting the position. It would mean an immediate 15 percent raise in pay; more prestige, because he would have a private office; and more opportunities for promotions. He applied for the position, but was afraid to tell his wife. When the interview was scheduled, he informed Rita that he had to go to Dallas for a seminar.

Charlie was impressed with Dallas and the possible neighborhoods his family could select to make their home. The home office was impressive! Dark walnut and chrome were everywhere, and the personnel in the office were very friendly. After a tour of the facility he had an interview with five managers.

A week later he was informed that he was one of the three finalists. He was excited and eager to accept the position if it was offered him. That night, when he told Rita, she was upset. The move would mean they would have to leave their lovely home that they had been remodeling over the last seven years. The girls would have to find new friends.

Finally, and most important, could Rita find a job as good as the one she has? It seemed unfair to force her to move and give up a good job, just so Charlie could satisfy his own ego. It turned into a real argument. Charlie wanted to move and Rita did not. Charlie was saying that he is a striver and Rita was saying she is happy with their status in life.

1. What points can Charlie use to justify the move and his attitudes as a striver?

2. What points can Rita use to justify staying where they are? What points can she make to say that the status quo is satisfactory for them?

3. What do you think the family should do?
4. Would the situation and the results be different if the roles were reversed?
5. Do you think Charlie is a striver? Do you think Rita is a nonstriver?

Terms and Concepts

class structure or social stratification the ranking of people within the society, by others, into higher and lower social positions to produce a hierarchy of prestige or respect.

group roles shared expectations of how group members are to perform in their positions.

groupthink the condition of everyone adopting the ideas and views of the group.

impermeable social structure a social structure in which people are unable to change their social status.

maintenance-related roles behavioral expectations directly related to the well-being and development of the group.

permeable social structure a social structure in which people can move from one social class to another.

role ambiguity the condition that exists when a person is not too sure how to act or perform in a given situation.

role behavior the things people actually do.

role conflict if an individual lacks a clear understanding of expectations or if there is conflict among the expectations.

role prescription the things people are expected to do. Greater correlation between prescription and behavior lead to perceptions of greater success.

strivers individuals who attempt to achieve a better economic and social status.

task-related roles behavioral expectations that directly aid in the accomplishment of group objectives.

Notes

1. Robert Albanese, *Management* (Cincinnati, Ohio: South-Western Publishing, 1988), p. 524.

2. Ibid.

3. Adapted from Dorwin Cartwright and Ronald Lippitt, "Group Dynamics and the Individual," in *Organizational Psychology: A Book of Readings*, eds. David A. Kolb, Irwin M. Rubin, and James M. McIntyre (Englewood Cliffs, N.J.: Prentice-Hall, 1971), pp. 177–179.

4. Daniel Yankelovich, "Who Gets Ahead in America," *Psychology Today*, July 1979, pp. 28–39, 90–91.

5. Lynn O'Connor, Walter Russell, and Pat Mialocq, *The Office Worker's Manifesto* (New York: Freeway Press, 1973), p. 17.

6. Ibid., p. 32.

7. Allan R. Cohen and others, *Effective Behavior in Organizations*, 3rd ed. (Homewood, Ill.: Richard D. Irwin, 1984), p. 111.

8. Daniel Coleman, "1528 Little Geniuses and How They Grew," *Psychology Today*, February 1980, pp. 28–32.

9. Laurence Peter and Raymond Hull, *The Peter Principle* (New York: William A. Morrow, 1969).

10. Irving Janis, *Victims of Group Think* (Boston: Houghton Mifflin, 1972), p. 9.

Recommended Reading

Casey, David. "When Is a Team Not a Team?" *Personnel Management*, January 1985, pp. 26–29.

Cohen, Allan R., and others. *Effective Behavior in Organizations*, 3rd ed. Homewood, Ill.: Richard D. Irwin, 1984.

Fox, William M. *Effective Group Problem Solving: How to Broaden Participation, Improve Decision Making, and Increase Commitment to Action.* San Francisco: Jossey-Bass, 1987.

Fry, Louis W., Steven Kerr, and Cynthia Lee. "Effects of Different Leader Behaviors Under Different Levels of Task Interdependence." *Human Relations*, December 1986, pp. 1067–1081.

Homans, George C. *The Human Group.* New York: Harcourt Brace Jovanovich, 1950.

Putti, Joseph M. "Leader Behavior and Group Characteristics in Work Improvement Teams—The Asian

Context." *Public Personnel Management,* Fall 1985, pp. 301–306.

Schein, Edgar H. *Organizational Psychology,* 3rd ed. Englewood Cliffs, N.J.: Prentice-Hall, 1980.

Smith, Kenwyn K., and David N. Berg. *Paradoxes of Group Life.* San Francisco: Jossey-Bass, 1987.

Weisbord, Marvin R. "Team Effectiveness Theory." *Training and Development Journal,* January 1985, pp. 27–29.

Interpersonal Communication

After studying this chapter, you should be able to:

1. Restate in your own words the idea that "meanings are in us, not in messages."
2. Describe the communication process and discuss barriers to effective communications.
3. Describe the importance of the following elements in communication:
   a. Attitudes
   b. Emotions
   c. Roles
   d. Nonverbal behavior
   e. Feedback
   f. Perception
4. Describe why listening is an active, not a passive, activity. List six general guidelines for more effective listening.
5. Define and give examples of the four basic levels of communication:
   a. Conventional
   b. Exploratory
   c. Participative
   d. Intimate
6. Describe how proxemics affects our actions.
7. Describe at least five ways by which we can interpret people's feelings through body language.

TO START YOU THINKING . . .

Here are a few questions that you might think about as you read this chapter. The answers to some of these questions can be found in your reading; others can only be answered based on your own experiences. Your feelings and ideas about these questions might well be shared with others.

♦ Is it easier for you to speak or to listen?
♦ Do you have to work just as hard listening as preparing a speech?
♦ Does body language contradict your verbal messages?
♦ Which is more honest? Why?
♦ What are some examples of ways in which we communicate our feelings visually?
♦ What is the mysterious "inner circle" and is your inner circle larger than that of your friends?

- What are some ways to make the written word easier to read?
- What are some of the international symbols that all people seem to understand?

THE MEANING OF COMMUNICATION

Communication is simple, isn't it? It's just a matter of A saying to B, "Do this or that activity," and B hearing what A said. Rarely is it that simple—and even then note that B only *hears* A; nothing was said about understanding or acting upon what A said. Over 70 to 80 percent of our work lives are spent receiving messages, but we are usually not trained to be listeners. We receive education and training in sending verbal messages—speech—but very little in receiving them.

This chapter is about the not-so-simple interpersonal communication processes, including sending and receiving—listening and understanding—as well as nonverbal communication. We will explore several fundamental principles for helping us to be better communicators, especially better listeners. The next chapter addresses the more formal types of communications in organizations.

Communication is the process of transferring information and understanding *from* one or more persons *to* one or more persons. In the simplest form of communication, one person transfers information to another. In more complex kinds of communication, members of a group transfer information to other members of a group. Comprehension is the only test of a message's success as communication. If the message is *understood,* communication has succeeded. If it is not, communication has failed.

Communication of all types is so common but so complex that it continues to justify study. We think because we all communicate so frequently in one way or another that we have expertise in communication processes. It is surprising that we don't do a better job, given our experience. But we have a tendency to concentrate on the transmittal process (speaking and writing) rather than receiving (listening, reading, and understanding). We think we know more than we do about communication.

There is an old story about three Englishmen riding on a bus. The bus stops. The first man says, "I say there, is this Wembley?" "No," says the second man, "this is Thursday." "So am I," says the third, "let's have a drink." Moral: All too often we hear only what we want to hear!

Meanings Are Within Us

The meaning of words exists within ourselves

How many times have you asked someone, "What do you mean by that?" How many times have you had to answer that question yourself? How do you answer it? Consult a dictionary? Probably not. Most people confronted with that question assemble their thoughts into new combinations of words and phrases and try to get the meaning across in different words. The meaning doesn't change, but the words do. *Meaning* exists *within ourselves,* not in the words we use to express that meaning. The meaning of a message is also called its *semantic* content.

Meaning is that which is intended to be understood. Except in the case of mathematical and some scientific communications, meaning is always *subjective.*

Objective meaning in mathematics and science can be communicated because, in those "language systems," one term is never allowed to have more than one meaning. Nor can a term have an ambiguous meaning. "Plus" can never mean "minus," nor can it ever imply "equal to." The rules of mathematical language leave absolutely no room for disagreement, but the word "happy" can mean 100 different things to 100 different people. It can also mean 10 different things to the same person in 10 different sets of circumstances.

Subjective meaning has multiple meanings

A word's *subjective* meaning is the personal *significance* that that word has for an individual. To some people, "rock music" means stimulating, exciting rhythms, singable melodies, and amusing or provocative lyrics. To others, it means a noisy assault on human ears, with no discernible melodies and inaudible or asinine lyrics. Almost every word we use has different emotional and intellectual meanings for each of us. Even the most ordinary, everyday term will have an astonishing variety of meanings attached to it because the *meaning attached to any object or experience is always experienced personally.*

Semantic meanings can never be fixed

The more our messages relate to and overlap the other person's mental and emotional experiences, the more effectively we communicate with each other. And, just as experiences are constantly changing, so are meanings. Thus, meaning can never be fixed permanently. Since no two people can ever give *exactly* the same meaning to anything, good communication demands a high tolerance for ambiguity, especially because the more abstract the term, the more meanings it can have. Consider some of the different meanings that words such as "justice," "freedom," and "faith" have for different people.

Because so many words have ambiguous meanings, to understand someone's meaning fully requires paying as much attention to the *person* speaking as to the words being spoken. Voice tones, facial gestures, and body language communicate as much meaning as do words, sometimes more. Effective communicators are *person oriented, not word oriented.* They know that, although one word may have many meanings, people always give their own meanings to all words.

THE COMMUNICATION PROCESS

Communication is largely a matter of style. Psychologist Robert Hecht says that:

> Paying attention to *communication styles* when you do business can help you avoid people problems. As the old song title explains, "It Ain't What You Do, It's the Way That You Do It." Becoming a student of communication styles can help you be more persuasive, working with other people's natures rather than against them. . . .
>
> Each of us, it seems has a preferred way of approaching people, tasks, and time. Adapting occasionally to another's communication style can yield impressive results.[1]

Hecht recognizes four basic styles of communicators and advocates using different styles to meet the needs of the intended receiver:

- *Forecaster* is interested in ideas; is imaginative, visionary, innovative.
- *Associator* is interested in personal relationships; is agreeable, adaptable, perceptive.

- *Systematizer* is impressed by details, plans, order; seems rational, steady, methodical.
- *Energizer* is results-*now* oriented; is spirited, dynamic, decisive, impatient.[2]

If we are to speak coherently, we select 10 percent of the words and thoughts in our minds and discard or "put on hold" the remaining 90 percent *at the same time* that we are speaking. It is an amazingly complex process.

When we listen, we can hear and comprehend at least double the number of words that we can speak. Therefore, it would seem that listening to and understanding a message would be easier than speaking it, because listening requires less mental activity than does speaking. However, in our culture verbal messages frequently are received inaccurately, understood poorly, and garbled in retelling. If you have played the "Pass It Along" whisper game, you know how garbled the message may become.

The keys to effective verbal communication are speaking more quickly, active listening, and ample feedback supplemented when necessary by "getting it in writing."

Models

One way to find out what takes place during any changing process is to construct a model of the process. A model is a visual representation that names, describes, and classifies the separate parts of the process. It also shows how the separate parts connect, interact, and influence one another. Figure 7-1 shows a simple model of the communication process. In it a speaker (sender) transmits a message to a listener (receiver), who sends back another message.

This simple model omits so many parts of the communication process that it could be applied just as logically to a temperature control system. Figure 7-2, although still quite simple, shows a more sophisticated model of human communication. In Figure 7-2 the clarity of the transmission is shown as a function of the speaker's attitudes, emotions, role relationships with the listener, and nonverbal behavior. Similarly, the clarity or the reception is shown as a function of the listener's attitudes, emotions, role relationships with the speaker, and nonverbal behavior. The listener is shown as responding to the message by either positive or negative feedback or by a combination of both.

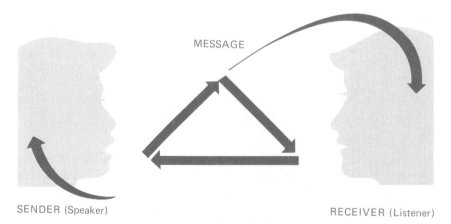

MESSAGE

SENDER (Speaker)   RECEIVER (Listener)

FIGURE 7-1 **Simple Communication.**

PERCEPTION

Perception is an individual view of facts and emotions, but our organizational and total worlds are more complex than one person's view. Perceptions are the way in which we interpret circumstances to be—either accurately or in a distorted manner.

Our value systems have a profound effect on what we see or hear happening. We are also influenced by our needs for economic, social, and psychological fulfillment: recognition, love, and self-worth, among others. In other words, we frequently see and hear what our backgrounds would have us perceive.

A classic example of this phenomenon is the famous drawing of the woman shown in Figure 7-3. Look carefully. What do you see first—a fashionably dressed young woman or a much older woman with a scarf over her head? Actually, both figures are present. The younger woman is looking away from you, to your left at an angle. The older woman is also looking to your left but toward you at an angle. Do you see them both? Which one you see first and whether or not you can see them both is a matter of perception—your view of facts, age, and physical characteristics.

SPEAKING

Speaking is a form of communication that should be confirmed in writing if it is lengthy, complex, or technical. Studies have shown that college freshmen, immediately following a ten-minute lecture, retain only 50 percent of it and forget half of that material within 48 hours.

Matters important to a subordinate are particularly susceptible to misinterpretation and should be confirmed in writing. The most common example is the spoken promise of a raise or promotion, which is often misinterpreted after a lapse of time.

About 30 percent of a message is lost or distorted after having passed through the first two recipients. If a communication is important, intermediate layers of communication should be skipped and the message given directly to the person affected.

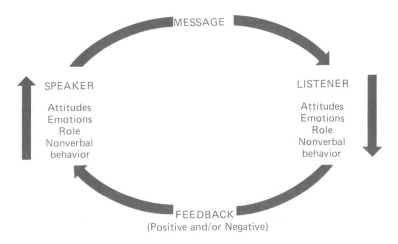

FIGURE 7-2 Complex Communication.

FIGURE 7-3 What do you see—a young woman, an old woman, or both?

Voice Tone

"There are no dull subjects . . . only dull ways of talking."[3] The basic point and purpose of our communication must be clear. But our intent and enthusiasm for the subject matter must also be clear.

Often the tone of our voice will indicate our emotional state to others even if we are not aware of it. To those who know how to interpret them, voice tones can transmit as much or more emotional information as words. Loudly pitched voices can communicate anger no matter how emotionally neutral the dictionary meanings of the words being shouted. Anger can also be conveyed by very intense whispering. The same emotion can be expressed by different tones of voice, and people differ in their reactions to these tones.

Emotions

Emotions can make it hard to listen accurately

Perhaps the most important emotional factor in good communication is desire. If the desire to understand one's self and others is strong, then understanding usually results. However, one of the largest drawbacks to effective communication is that, as humans, we do not separate ourselves from our emotions. In fact we identify with them. We *become* our emotions. We say, "I am angry" or "I am sad." The intensities of our feelings color everything we think and talk about. When we talk about a problem we cannot help seeing it in terms of our own past experience and in terms of how we feel at that very moment. Naturally, this can make it more difficult to see the other person's point of view—especially if he or she is also in the throes of some strong emotion.

Sensitivity to Others

Sensitivity to others begins with the *desire* to communicate, which involves the desire to perceive other people's meanings as well as the desire to express one's own. Sensitive people are willing to make the necessary effort to try to understand other frames of reference and other sets of values. Sensitivity to others also requires the ability to recognize and identify one's own responses and perceptions as well as those of others. It is impossible to be sensitive to other people if you are not sensitive to yourself.

Self-Disclosure

When people communicate with each other, especially face to face, their physical and emotional states of being are to some degree exposed. This exposure is sometimes disturbing, because our culture places a high value on self-conceal-ment. In a competitive society, concealment is frequently more useful than is self-exposure or self-revelation. If we were to reveal more of ourselves to each other, we would understand each other better.

When people wish to reveal themselves to each other, they talk about *personal* matters such as loves and hates, beliefs and fears, worries and anxieties, and perceptions about work, about themselves, and about each other. Of course, the atmosphere for self-disclosure must be one of mutual acceptance and goodwill, or mutual self-defense systems will automatically switch our psychic "early-warning systems" on to "red alert," thereby raising "defensive barriers" and short-circuiting communication.

LISTENING

Listening is an active, not passive, activity. Listening can be described as a combination of (1) *hearing*—the physical reception of sound; (2) *understanding*—the interpretation and comprehension of the message; (3) *remembering*—the ability to retain what has been heard; and (4) *acting*—responding by either action or inaction. It is not enough to hear. It is necessary to understand, remember, and act.

The "echo chamber" is not worthwhile feedback

Henry Thoreau once wrote, "It takes two to speak the truth—one to speak and another to hear." Sometimes people think that they are communicating when all they are really doing is talking a lot and taking some time to get the feedback on what they have said. This has been called the "echo-chamber approach to communication." Feedback is important, but there is much more to listening than just feedback.

Bad listening can result in people being injured or killed. The sinking of the *Titanic*, the attack on Pearl Harbor, the Jonestown, Guyana incident, and some recent disasters such as Bhopal, India are classic examples of breakdowns in communication and judgment. Messages were sent and listening broke down.

We are a wasteful society compared to other cultures; we waste our natural resources and energy. And we waste our communication abilities compared to other cultures: we waste our words both in sending and receiving.

In primitive societies, where writing is unknown and *all* messages are transmitted by speech, the accuracy of the transmission is much higher than in countries with high literacy rates. This indicates that illiterate people know how to listen and remember messages better than do literate people.

THE ECHO CHAMBER AT WORK

A PERSON WHO DOESN'T ALLOW
ENOUGH FEEDBACK SOON HAS
A NONLISTENER.

We just don't listen carefully. Two researchers have suggested that one of the reasons that we are not more careful is because we don't view communication from different listening perspectives. Bennett and Wood say that there are three perspectives or listening styles called results, reasons, and process. Results-style listeners want to hear the bottom line only. Process-style listeners want to be led into a subject with some background on how it all came about, before getting to the bottom line. Finally, reasons-style listeners must be convinced that whatever is being proposed is reasonable, logical, and correct for the situation.[4]

Good listening is paying attention to what is said

How many times have you had a conversation with someone and not heard a word that was said? Have you ever wanted to shake anyone and force him or her into "paying attention" to you while you were speaking? Most people have these experiences from time to time. Listening is a form of *paying attention*, which is an active process involving much more than hearing and seeing. When we pay attention to each other, we are *focusing* our awareness on what is being said and are excluding other external and internal stimuli. This is not always easy, since our senses are constantly scanning the environment for incoming stimuli, much like switched-on radar screens, and our minds are often preoccupied with our own thoughts.

Under normal circumstances, people listen with only about 25 percent efficiency.[5] Good management requires listening more. People who force themselves to talk less begin to lose the desire to talk too much and, in turn, begin to enjoy listening instead. The ability to listen well is not an inherent trait. It is a learned behavior. When we come into this world, we don't have a built-in knowledge of how to listen. That skill must be developed. Unfortunately, it is not developed well systematically in our school systems. We teach reading, writing, speaking, and numerous other abilities, but not listening. In the business world Steil has found that, as one advances in management, listening ability becomes increasingly critical.

Problem of preoccupation

Nation's Business magazine has reported that most of us can speak at about 140 words per minute but that we can comprehend at a much faster rate.[6] This permits us to take mental excursions into other areas as we listen. If we are preoccupied, we can slip away from the conversation quickly to think of another topic. Later we return, hoping not to have missed anything important.

Problem of prejudgment

Opinions and prejudices can also cause poor listening. The style of the speaker's clothes, facial expression, posture, accent, color of skin, mannerisms, or age can cause a listener to react emotionally and tune out. Trying to put aside preconceived ideas or prejudgments when a person is speaking allows us to open our minds to worthwhile listening.

One sales manager tried to judge the percentage of the sales presentation dialog that was carried out by his own salesperson and the percentage done by prospects—generally hospital purchasing agents, heads of housekeeping, and hospital department heads. He found that there was usually an inverse correlation between the amount of talking by his salesperson and the amount of the resulting order. The "high-percentage talkers" tended to be the newer people in the field, whereas the "low-percentage talkers" were the more experienced and successful ones.

There are no specific rules to follow for effective listening, because what might work well for one person might not work for another. There are, however, some general guidelines that will help you to construct your own rules for more successful listening.

BARRIERS TO COMMUNICATION

The communication process is complex enough by itself, but there are many barriers that block or distort communication. These include distortion, language/semantics, defensiveness, noise, mistrust, and other emotional responses. Let us now examine each of these barriers.

Distortion

There are so many distractions to the communication process. Environmental considerations, other demands on our time, thought processes are just a few of the things that can distract and consequently distort the communication process as defined earlier. For example, one experiment shows that at any given time in a college classroom, 20 percent of both men and women are thinking about sex, 60 percent are off on a mental trip of their own, and the remaining 20 percent are paying attention to the lecture! No wonder there is distortion and we fail to hear, let alone understand, what is being said.

Figure 7-4 shows an area of distortion common in most communication. The area or arc of distortion is a function of what the sender intends to communicate, and what both the sender and receiver actually do communicate. There may always be some distortion, but effort should be made to minimize the area and to avoid deceitful practices that increase misunderstandings.

Stereotyping is another, unfortunate type of distortion. Our preconceived notions or ideas about people, situations, or cultures get in the way of the truth. Remember the wag who said: "Don't confuse me with the facts, my mind is made up!" As noted, we hear and perceive what we want to hear.

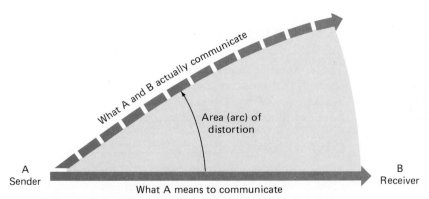

FIGURE 7-4 Area of communication distortion.

Here are two topics that might develop some strong contrasting feelings between people. Pair off with another student and take opposite views on the topic. Argue for 5 minutes for your special viewpoint; then engage in the Carl Rogers's *Repeat My View* game. See if you don't develop a new appreciation or understanding for the other person's point of view.

Thousands, perhaps even millions, of illegal aliens are in the United States, and many are working in our industries. They are depriving our citizens of potential employment; they are not paying taxes; yet they are receiving welfare.

Many businesses feel that they must compete in the open marketplace. If they can pay the illegal alien less than the prevailing wage rate, they can in turn sell a product cheaper to the public. By such a method the public benefits. It is certainly cheaper than sending our raw goods or parts to a foreign country to be processed or assembled and then bringing them back to the United States to sell. Are you for or against aliens in the United States?

Is nudity pornographic? Do you consider a nude model in an advertisement to be in bad taste? A well-known cosmetic company is advertising a beauty skin product. The ad tells women to compare facial skin with breast skin. It explains that women should use the firm's skin product. The ad claims to use the "adult approach" and to be above sexiness. Here we have a beauty product company employing nudity in its campaign. Is it pornographic? Should it be used in family magazines? Is it all right to have nude women in a family magazine? Is it all right to have nude men in a family magazine? Where do you stand?

Language/Semantics

There are honest differences in language, among cultures, and even within families. Semantics are the meanings given to individual words. Each of us may give different meaning to the same word. We may even give different meaning to the same word under different circumstances. The word "love" has many different meanings. Another example is that a parent may ask teenagers what they are going to do with their lives—meaning, what occupations, what job expectations, and so on are contemplated. The teenagers, on the other hand, may perceive the question to mean life-style expectations—and there will probably be a different time perspective as well. That is, the parent probably means for a career or lifetime; the teenager probably means the next five years at the most.

Defensiveness

Good communication depends on the organizational and communication climate or culture. If there are not too many undiscussables in the organization or between boss and subordinate, we can expect an entirely different climate than if all transactions are conducted at arm's length, that is, with a suspicion or at least a wariness on the part of both sender and receiver. Such a climate can be described as a defensive climate where the characteristics shown in Figure 7-5 exist.

The defensive climate can be distinguished from a supportive climate where there is more mutuality of objectives, openness, and understanding. The supportive climate means that people:

1. Seem interested; they listen.
2. Don't seem hurried; they imply by body movements that they are not bored/not busy, and that they want to hear what an individual has to say.

DEFENSIVE CLIMATE		SUPPORTIVE CLIMATE
Evaluation	Communication that appears to "judge" the other person increases defensiveness.	Description
Control	Communication that is used to control the receiver evokes resistance.	Problem orientation
Strategy	Perception of the sender engaging in a strategy involving ambiguous motivations causes receivers to become defensive.	Spontaneity
Neutrality	Perception that neutrality in communication indicates a lack of concern for the receivers' welfare causes receivers to become defensive.	Empathy
Superiority	Communication that indicates superiority in power, wealth, or in other ways arouses defensiveness.	Equality (as human beings)
Certainty	Dogmatic speakers who seem to know the answers, to require no data, tend to put others on guard.	Provisionalism (willing to listen)

FIGURE 7-5 A contrast of communication climates. Source: Adapted from Jack R. Gibb, "Defensive Communication," *Journal of Communication,* September 1961, pp. 141–148.

3. Who are receivers invite the sender to proceed by asking questions that are directly tied to preceding statements.
4. Who are receivers don't judge or criticize what is being said for the sake of criticism but request clarification and allow time to correct misunderstandings.

Noise

The sender must often compete with a number of other stimuli in getting the message through to the receiver; that is, there is physical noise or other externally generated sensations in the system or process. "Noise is . . . an irritant that can prevent employees from working efficiently, and which can prevent managers from being able to collect their thoughts."[7] Physical noise is but one of the many sources of confusion and therefore a barrier to effective communication. So-called background noise may include loud or even soft music or noise in an office, and, depending on the ears of the listener, either hard-rock or "elevator" music may be distracting to people trying to work in nearby environments.

Machinery or some other physical noise is a bad enough distractor, but when human-generated noise like loud conversation takes place nearby, it can be equally or even more distracting because of the irregular peaks and valleys of decibels. Some organizations have attempted to cope with the problem by restricting phone calls during certain hours of the day or by providing "think tanks" where employees can go to work in a stress-free environment. Employees who work in offices where noise control is not institutionalized can reduce noise by not using the telephone at certain hours, coming early to the office or staying late, or even by using earplugs or earphones that mask sporadic noise.[8]

Mistrust

There may be a distinct mistrust between the sender and receiver of a message. That mistrust will also be a barrier to effective communication. In the workplace, such a condition can be very negative and telling in explaining poor performance and productivity. Pollster Lou Harris surveyed 1,500 office workers and bosses and found that a climate or organizational restructuring, mergers, and acquisitions may be contributing to the workers' mistrust of management. The survey revealed that top executives, when questioned about worker feelings, do not always show a thorough understanding of their employees.[9]

There is a direct link between employee communication and the trust relationship between management and employees. Understanding the goals of the organization and the results of their work give meaning to employee efforts. Valorie McClelland finds that five factors are essential in building communication trust: openness, feedback, congruity, autonomy, and shared values. Mistrust can arise from mixed signals sent by management. Managers need to consider the consistency of their communication to their audiences. Finally, to achieve better communication and less mistrust, managers must consider emerging issues and plan together to make decisions consistent with long-term goals.[10]

FEEDBACK

Have you ever heard the three principles of real estate marketing/selling? Location, location, location! Or financing, financing, financing! Likewise, there are three similar principles of communication: feedback, feedback, feedback! Our communications are only as good as the message that gets through—and the sender needs to know that; that is, the sender needs feedback.

Feedback connects, influences, and interacts with all the other parts of the communication process. Originally, the term *feedback* was used by engineers to refer to the transfer of electrical energy from the output to the input of the same electrical circuit. In computer technology, feedback is used to describe a computer's coded responses or answers to messages. These responses are usually very simple. "Correct," "incorrect," and "not enough data" are the most common. In this manner the computer "tells" the source of the message whether the message has been received accurately or not. In similar fashion, people tell one another whether their messages are being received correctly or not.

Feedback is verbal and visual

In face-to-face communication, both the listener and the speaker continuously give feedback to each other (1) nonverbally, by nodding agreement or disagreement, frowning or smiling, yawning or engaging in or avoiding eye contact, and (2) verbally, by the relevance of their questions and responses in relation to what is being discussed.

Those responses likely to be perceived as rewarding (smiles or nods of agreement) are called *positive feedback.* Those perceived as punishing (yawns, signs of inattention) are called *negative feedback.* Feedback enables us to recognize misunderstandings while they are happening so that the messages can be modified and redefined until the confusions are cleared away.

Feedback in its broadest usage includes *all* the verbal and nonverbal responses to a message that are perceived by the sender of that message. In its narrow usage, feedback means only those specific responses that correct misunderstandings.

Feedback should be constructive and responsible; it should be:

1. Specific, *not* general
2. Focused on behavior, not the person
3. Considerate of the needs of the receiver
4. Focused on something the receiver can *act* upon
5. Solicited, not imposed
6. Shared information, not advice
7. Well-timed and not overloading
8. Concerned with "what" and "how," not "why"
9. Checked for accuracy

Silence

Have you ever decided to let silence speak for you? Silence is a type of feedback. Some experts feel that it is never good to rush in and break the silence in a small conversation. Remember, the more secure the person, the less fearful he or she is of silence. This technique appears to be contrary to what you have learned in speech classes. However, here are some reasons for believing that "silence is golden."

Silent power is used frequently by interviewers and others to force a person to speak. Another example of silence is the *silence of uncertainty*; if a person has a thoughtful look of concentration, it may be risky to break the concentration if you are trying to convince someone or to communicate a specific message. The more important the subject, the greater the patience required: *silent accord* accompanied by a smile or a nod is a good way in which to respect their choice of communication. *Silent disapproval* may be accompanied by a studied frown, pursed lips, or a shake of the head. Don't rush to speak—wait for the person to verbalize his or her feelings. If you wait for the person to verbalize those feelings, then you can direct your comments to the misgivings rather than to a mere guess.

LEVELS OF VERBAL COMMUNICATION

The first level is to get acquainted

There are four levels of verbal communication. (See Figure 7-6). We communicate with strangers and casual acquaintances on the *conventional* level. Conversation on

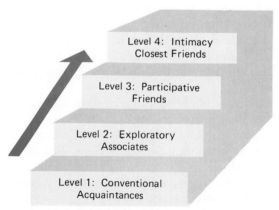

FIGURE 7-6 Levels of communication in building a relationship.

this level is fairly impersonal. It consists of conventional attempts to be polite, to get acquainted, to fill silences, or to seek or convey incidental information or relieve tensions. Remarks such as "Hi, there!" "Do you have the time?" and "Good morning, Homer" show only that we acknowledge the presence of the other person. They may open the door to further communication, but they are minimal in attempts at communicating.

The second level is for business

On the second, *exploratory*, level, communication is fact and problem oriented. Here, too, conversation is usually impersonal. Many times our relationships with our coworkers, neighbors, and business contacts are developed on this level and remain on this level for many years. Your relationship is friendly, but not open to very much self-disclosure. The topics of conversation are almost always related to business, not to personal matters. Classroom lectures are usually conducted on the exploratory level. Often in personal transactions a relationship must be established on this level before the participants can move on to the third level.

The third level is for self-disclosure

The third level is *participative*. Here people talk about themselves and engage in self-disclosure. They express their own feelings, describe their own experiences, and discuss their own ideas. While these are *personal subjects,* they are expressed in fairly *safe ways:* "I feel happiest with people my own age" or "I would say that I am more conservative now than I was five years ago." (See Figure 7-7.)

The fourth level is for intimate conversations

The fourth, *intimacy*, level we reserve for only a select few. Here again people reveal themselves, but now they expose themselves intimately to one another in ways that involve risk: "I get the feeling that you don't really care about me" or "I want you to know I've been on drugs." Intimate relationships are characterized by communication of this kind, which evolves from deeply felt mutual understanding.

FIGURE 7-7 If we believe that our messages are being received with warmth, respect, and concern, we tend to become more relaxed and more articulate. Barbara Rios/Photo Researchers

NONVERBAL COMMUNICATIONS

Body Language

Body language can convey the opposite of our words

Body language, or in more scientific terms, *kinesics,* is using your eyes to understand how a person feels without depending on verbal communication. Any nonflexive or reflexive movement of the body can communicate something to the outside world and often more honestly than can verbal communication.

Studies show that at least 70 percent of what is really being communicated between individuals is done nonverbally.[11] This type of communication involves various dimensions: body posture, eye contact, gestures, distance and proximity, among others.

We imitate people we admire through body movements

Our eyes, and hands, and bodies send and receive communication signals constantly. Some 33 separate major head and facial movements that communicate specific messages have been isolated. When engaged in nonflirtatious conversation, nearly all men and women and boys and girls tend to imitate the sitting and standing postures of someone they admire. People may cross their arms and legs and orient their bodies in specific "withdrawal" postures to shut out people who are perceived as threatening. And most people, regardless of sex or age, will touch each other when they are deeply moved by strong emotions.

Here is a tip: You might consider deliberately mirroring movements to enhance rapport when you feel that would be useful. And remember to avoid rigid interpretations of nonverbal clues. Never make an interpretation based on a single clue or read too much into the body language. Maybe some people just fold their arms a lot!

Posture

Studying a person's posture is a good clue as to how an individual feels about himself or herself. Stooping indicates that the person has the burden of the world on his shoulders, whereas a rigid walk or stance may indicate emotional stress.

Body language speaks to muggers

Body language even speaks to muggers. Two researchers secretly videotaped people walking in Manhattan's garment district on three working days between 10 A.M. and 12 noon.[12] Each pedestrian was taped for 6 to 8 seconds. The researchers assembled 60 taped segments of an equal number of men and women of varying ages. Then 12 prisoners who had been convicted of assaults on persons were asked how "muggable" the people videotaped were. More than half the convicts rated the same 20 people as either easy or very easy victims. Movements that characterized easy victims included their strides, which were either very long or very short, and their postures, which were awkward. Overall, the people rated most muggable walked as if they were in conflict with themselves.

Eye Contact

Everyone knows that a few seconds of eye contact can transmit meanings that might require hundreds of words if spoken. Such idioms as "to make eyes at," "to keep an eye on," or "if looks could kill" reflect the importance of eye contact in many kinds of communication. Someone who sits at a crowded lunch counter looking straight ahead and an airplane passenger who sits with tightly closed eyes are both communicating that they do not wish to speak or be spoken to. And their message is usually interpreted correctly without any need for words.

Sometimes eye contact is a clue as to whether someone is lying. The liar tends not to make eye contact. The direction of a person's gaze is also an important clue as to whether information or instructions are being absorbed. A wandering gaze plus a shifting posture usually are evidence that the individual has stopped listening.

Space or Proxemics

Proxemics is the distance between people

There are two types of space as a form of communication: social and public. In the social type, for example, the proxemics between a housewife and a repairman or the distance in a normal business transaction would be 4 to 7 feet. This distance is used for casual social gatherings, but it can be used as a manipulative tool by a salesperson as well. As the salesperson steps closer to the client, he or she invades the client's inner circle, making the customer feel uncomfortable. The salesperson pressures the client psychologically into a sale. The social space of 7 to 12 feet is used for more formal business relations. It is the distance between the "big boss" and you—a way of showing the boss's authority. This distance also allows other activity with another person around without being rude. Public space of 12 to 25 feet, as in a teaching situation, allows many to focus their attention on one or more persons.

You will discover that, the closer an individual chooses to sit to another, the more comfortable that person feels about the relationship. In business, the more confident a person is, the closer he or she will decide, even subconsciously, to sit to a partner or associate. Notice that two coworkers sit closer to each other than do the employee and the "boss."

SUBCONSCIOUSLY WE WATCH HOW MUCH SPACE WE PUT BETWEEN OURSELVES AND OTHERS.

Touching

When we allow ourselves to touch and be touched, we become more open and vulnerable to one another. This openness, in turn, creates a greater sense of receptivity and, consequently, a greater willingness to listen attentively and try to understand the other person's point of view. In recent years, the nontouching taboo has lost much of its strength, although it is still strong in some cultures.

There is an interesting relation between the words "touch" and "tact." The word *tact* derives from the Latin word for "touch." The psychological relationship between the two terms has not been lost altogether, for every day we say of a tactless person that he or she has a "heavy touch." We do not *trust tactless* people because they are likely to wound or betray us. We do trust those whom we allow to touch us and those who we feel it is safe to touch. Trust, or the lack of it, often determines the kind of feedback that is generated during a conversation.

Neurolinguistic Programming

Body language has now become part of the study of communications. Richard Bandler and John Grindler, a Gestalt therapist and a linguist, respectively, have packaged the art of establishing rapport and nonverbal language into a program known as NPL or *neurolinguistic program learning.* Observation and intuition along with verbal and nonverbal language have become the modus operandi of neurolinguistic programming.[13]

NLP is a communication technique that is easily learned. *Neuro* refers to the human nervous system and the way it receives and uses communication. *Linguistic* refers to the manner of communication including the words, tone, inflection, and timing. The *programming* aspect refers to the mechanisms for achieving consistency of responses, given the message and manner of communication. It is becoming increasingly important in obtaining the total message of communications.

WRITTEN WORD

The most durable of all means of communication is the written word. Perhaps when facts need to be presented, nothing surpasses the written word, for it provides an historical document for future reference. A few of the factors used to determine the readability of material are the number of syllables and words in a sentence, the number of sentences in a paragraph, and the number of personal references.

The three averages (sentence length, syllables, and personal references) are applied to a scale that gives the reading-ease score. (See Table 7-1.) For example,

TABLE 7-1 Guidepost for Effective Writing

READING LEVEL	FAIRLY EASY	STANDARD	FAIRLY DIFFICULT	DIFFICULT
Average sentence length in words	14	17	21	25
Syllables per 100 words	142	150	158	166
Personal references per 100 words (I, you, us)	10	6	4	3
Typical publications	Newspaper	Magazine	Literary	Scholarly

SOURCE: Rudolph Flesch, *The Art of Plain Talk* (New York: Harper & Row, 1949). See also Robert Gunning, *The Technique of Clear Writing* (New York: McGraw-Hill, 1952).

an average sentence length of 17 words, with about 150 syllables for each 100 words and 6 personal references per 100 words, would be considered average. The greater the number of syllables and words in a sentence, the more difficult the sentence is to read and understand. The greater the number of personal references in a passage, the easier the passage is to read. From these studies the Prudential Insurance Company developed guideposts for more effective writing. Shorter sentences do not mean duller or degrading sentences but, rather, sentences that are more easily understood by more people.

Another index of clear writing measures "fog" and pomposity, as shown in Figure 7-8.

VISUAL SYMBOLS

Besides the written word, we communicate in other graphic ways—and more universally. The world speaks a babel of a thousand tongues, but wouldn't it be nice to travel anywhere in the world and be able to find the restroom or the ticket agent in any airport? Or wouldn't it be nice for a 3-year-old in Gambia and a 3-year-old in Indiana to recognize "Danger—Don't Touch!" instantly? Some signs are "instant communications." The biological symbols for man and woman are known in many countries. The symbol for man is a circle with an arrow going up, easy to remember if you think of Mars as a shield and a spear. The symbol for woman, the circle with a cross going down, is Venus or a woman with a hand mirror. However, a figure in a skirt and a figure in pants are usually used on restrooms. Assume you are working on pictographs for a dictionary that can be used the world over for international understanding. How would a pictograph of a man in trousers and a woman in a skirt go over in India, where men often wear skirts and women trousers?

Traffic symbols are more or less standard in Europe, thanks to an intercountry agreement that makes it possible to drive from Italy to Denmark with nothing more than a smile and a map (Figure 7-9). But there are still some problems

How does one gauge the value, if any, of euphemisms and circumlocutions? Is longer and more circuitous really better than short and straightforward and, if so, by how much? For the statistically minded, Hugh Rawson has developed the Fog and Pomposity Index, or FOP.

The index compares the length of a euphemism to the word or phrase for which it stands. It tallies the letters in both expressions and awards an extra point for each additional syllable and word in the substitute that is used. Since "medicine" has 8 letters and 3 syllables, while *medication* has 10 letters and 4 syllables, the latter gets a point count of 11. Dividing 8 into 11 yields a FOP index of 1.4. Similarly, replacing "drop" (4 letters) with *adjustment downward* (18 letters, 4 extra syllables, and 1 extra word) gives an index of 5.75.

The highest FOP uncovered by the author is 17.8 for a *Personal Assistant to the Secretary (Special Activities)* hired by former HEW Secretary Joseph Califano. He turned out to be a "cook."

FIGURE 7-8 Measuring fog and pomposity. Source: Adapted from John Hein, "Measuring Fog and Pomposity," *Across the Board*, April 1982, p. 72.

INFORMATION HOTEL INFORMATION NO SMOKING

RAIL TRANSPORTATION COFFEE SHOP TOILETS

FIGURE 7-9 International symbols help people communicate. The United States is now using symbols the rest of the world has been using for decades.

worldwide. A triangle, which means "caution" in France, means "stop" in England, "yield" and "helicopter landing" in America, and "birth control" in India.

We find that we react to symbols or pictures and draw certain inferences from them. The color red or black may derive positive or negative responses. The use of these colors in a sign may invoke actions that were not intended by the signmaker.

Summary

Communication is the process by which information and understanding are transferred from one person to another. Effective communication enables people to exercise control over their environment. It is an essential tool for the establishment and maintenance of good social and working relationships. If the messages being communicated are not understood, then communication is poor or nonexistent. Effective communication is a dynamic process that involves constant change and interaction among all the elements that comprise it.

The meaning of a message is always subjective, because meanings reside in people, not in words. A word's meaning is the significance that that word has for both speaker and listener, and that significance is likely to vary greatly from person to person. Good communication requires paying as much attention to the person speaking as to the verbal message itself, because so many words have such ambiguous meanings.

Barriers to effective communications include distortion, language/semantics, defensiveness, noise, mistrust, and other emotional responses. Failure to listen is another major barrier.

Effective listening depends on paying attention and focusing. It requires understanding, remembering, and acting, as well as hearing. Although there are no specific rules that everyone must follow to become a good listener, there are some general guidelines for acquiring good listening habits.

The communication process can be described in terms of a model in which attitudes, emotions, roles, nonverbal behaviors, perceptions, and feedback are interacting constantly.

There are four levels of communication that depend on the degree of intimacy existing between speaker and listener: conventional, exploratory, participative, and intimate.

Body language, or kinesics, is interpreting a person's attitudes by observing his or her body movement. Nonverbal cues are usually more honest than are verbal cues. But remember to avoid rigid interpretations of nonverbal clues, particularly those based on a single clue. Proxemics is the distance people put between themselves. The closer they are to each other, the more comfortable they are in their relationship.

We are more informative in written language if we keep our average sentences between 15 to 18 words.

Case Study 14

There's a Rumor about My Promotion

Bill Hackaday has worked for the Denver branch of the Tamlon Corporation for three years and is now a junior executive in the Engineering Department. Bill has just returned from a two-week vacation.

This morning Randy Meyers, a coworker and good friend, stops Bill on his way into the building. "Congratulations, Bill. From what I hear, you will apparently be in your own office soon."

"What are you talking about, Randy? I'm not due for a promotion yet."

"I didn't think you were, but the rumor is that Mr. Lundquist is going to promote you."

This information has Bill puzzled. He knows that there are others in line for promotion before him. But then again, he knows that his work is good and that a promotion at this time would be ideal for he is about to be married. With the promotion he could consider purchasing a new home.

When Bill entered the plant, he was not approached by anyone else about the promotion. When he passed Mr. Lundquist in the hallway he mentioned nothing about a promotion. That evening, as Bill prepared to leave work, Mary Stewart, a coworker in the department, asked, "Is it true that you'll be leaving us soon, Bill? I heard that you were being transferred to the Atlanta branch this summer."

"I haven't been told anything about it. Where did you hear about it?"

"Oh, I don't know, someone mentioned it last week and said to keep it quiet until you got back. The word is that either you'll be promoted or transferred to the Atlanta branch."

"But don't you think someone would have said something to me by now?" inquired Bill.

"It sure seems so. I suppose it could be another false rumor. Do you remember the one that was going around last month?"

This information has Bill concerned. He'd like a promotion, but the last thing he wants right now is a transfer.

1. What would you do if you were Bill?
2. What kinds of signs is Bill getting? Are there hidden agenda here?
3. Should you try to track down the source of the rumor, or ignore it and go ahead with your future plans?
4. Should you discuss the rumor or your personal plans with Mr. Lundquist?
5. Are there other ways of checking the validity of the rumor?

Case Study 15

Visual Communications Speak Loudly in the Escrow Office

An escrow department of a large national bank recently hired a new employee. Monica Chatman is 25 years old and single, and prior to being hired as an escrow officer worked as a teller and later as a secretary of an escrow office in another firm. Before leaving her former location, Monica was given some training in escrow procedures. Monica is an attractive woman, and this is highlighted by her stylish, yet conservative, method of dress, as seen in her preference for coordinated pantsuits and dress suits.

Although Monica has had previous on-the-job training in escrow, she has not yet reached complete proficiency. In some areas she is still in need of further training and advice. The person closest to Monica, both in physical distance and job responsibilities, is John Baxter—the only other escrow officer. When Monica was hired, she was informed by the department supervisor that John would be the person to go to for help and advice, primarily because both she and John would be working on the same tract of homes for some time.

Being a rather shy person Monica has not made a habit of asking John for his help. She has tended to keep to herself for the most part, and John has not gone out of his way to help break the ice between them. At any rate, Monica doesn't really know if John is capable of giving her any worthy advice, let alone taking the time to help her. Judging from appearances, she feels that John is a pretty sloppy individual both in appearance and in his work. He seems to have trouble handling his own duties. It looks as if he is always a week behind in his work. His desk is constantly a mess. Besides, John's clothes look almost as if he slept in them.

In spite of his overly casual appearance and method of handling his work, John is competent and qualified in the escrow business. When Monica began working in the department a few weeks back, John had planned on giving her any assistance she would need in handling her new position. However, John soon began to feel that Monica really didn't want his help. Even though Monica seems shy, John believes that she is more stuck up and cold than anything else. To friends, John will readily admit that he is a little chauvinistic when it comes to women, and he has admitted to a close friend in the bank that he is somewhat jealous of Monica's promotions all the way from teller to escrow officer by the age of 25. He also finds it irritating that Monica manages to type so quickly and has her desk clean at the end of each day. It is also John's opinion that Monica looks down upon his appearance. As a family man he cannot afford the quality of clothes that Monica, as a single woman, wears each day. As far as John is concerned at the present time, if Monica wishes any help from him, she will have to come and ask for it.

As the supervisor of the escrow department, you have become aware of the problem existing between Monica and John. They should be working together and yet they are not.

1. Given the information supplied, what would you identify as the main problem?

2. What steps would you take to improve the situation?

3. From the description of Monica, what other assumptions might you make about her personality? Could these assumptions lead to faulty conclusions?

4. From the description of John, what other assumptions might you make about his personality? Could these assumptions lead to faulty generalizations?

5. How can you, as supervisor, help both Monica and John overcome their misconceptions of each other?

Terms and Concepts

body language   the ability to observe body movement of a person and interpret the person's attitude and feelings.

communication   a process by which senders and receivers of messages transfer information and understanding.

feedback   the process of reacting to a person's message either verbally or nonverbally. It can be either positive or negative.

kinesics   another term for body language, the study of body movement.

listening   the receiving half of the communication equation; not a passive activity. Involves hearing, understanding, remembering, and acting upon information.

neurolinguistic programming   a combination of total rapport and verbal and nonverbal language in communicating a particular message.

perceptions   the way in which we interpret things to be—either accurately or in a distorted manner. Our perception of things is usually based on our past experiences.

proxemics   the distance that people put between themselves. The closer they are to each other, the more comfortable their relationship tends to be.

self-disclosure   the act of opening up your personality to others; your weaknesses as well as your strengths.

semantics   the meaning given to individual words. Each of us may give different meaning to the same word. We may even give different meaning to the same word under different circumstances. Example: love.

Notes

1. Robert M. Hecht, "Key Words: Use the Right 'Communication Style,'" *Success*, December 1989, p. 14.

2. Ibid.

3. Ralph Proodian, "There Are No Dull Subjects," *The Wall Street Journal*, January 4, 1985, p. 18.

4. Ruth T. Bennett and Rosemary V. Wood, "Effective Communication via Listening Styles," *Business*, April–June 1989, pp. 45–48.

5. Glenn Pearce, "Doing Something About Your Listening Skills," *Supervisory Management*, March 1989, pp. 29–34.

6. "Listen to What You Can't Hear," *Nation's Business*, June 1979, p. 24.

7. J. H. Foegen, "Quiet, Please!" *SAM Advanced Management Journal*, Winter 1987, p. 17.

8. Ibid.

9. Louis Harris cited in Stanley J. Modic, "Whatever It Is, It's Not Working," *Industry Week*, July 17, 1989, p. 27.

10. Valorie McClelland, "Employees We Trust," *Personnel Administrator*, September 1988, pp. 137–139.

11. C. Barnum and N. Wolniansky, "Taking Cues from Body Language," *Management Review*, June 1989, pp. 59–60.

12. Betty Grayson and Morris Stein, "Body Language That Speaks to Muggers," *Psychology Today*, August 1980, p. 20.

13. Daniel Goleman, "People Who Read People," *Psychology Today*, July 1979, pp. 66–67.

Recommended Reading

Adler, Mortimer J. *How to Speak, How to Listen.* New York: Macmillan, 1983.

Adler, Ron, and Neil Towne. *Looking Out, Looking In,* 2nd ed. Corte Madera, Calif.: Rinehart Press, 1979.

Burley-Allen, Madelyn. *Listening: The Forgotten Skill.* New York: John Wiley, 1982.

Fielden, John S. "Why Can't Managers Communicate?" *Business*, January–February–March 1989, pp. 41–44.

Flesch, Rudolf. *The Art of Plain Talk.* New York: Harper & Row, 1946. Also *The Art of Readable Writing.* New York: Harper & Row, 1949.

Gunning, Robert. *The Techniques of Clear Writing.* New York: McGraw-Hill, 1952. Gunning also developed the "Fog index."

Hulbert, Jack. "They Won't Hear If You Don't Listen." *Administrative Management*, February 1979, pp. 55–57, 62.

Loeb, Michel. *Noise and Human Efficiency.* New York: John Wiley, 1986.

Marcus, Eric H., M.D. "Neurolinguistic Programming." *Personnel Journal*, December 1983, pp. 972–978.

Nierenberg, Gerald I., and Henry Calero. *How to Read a Person Like a Book.* New York: Pocket Books, 1971.

Odiorne, George S. "Ethics for the Nineties." *Manage*, April 1988, pp. 8–14, 33.

Rogers, Carl. "Active Listening." In *Effective Behavior in Organizations*, 3rd ed., edited by Allan R. Cohen and others. Homewood, Ill.: Richard D. Irwin, 1984, pp. 242–243.

Rosenthal, Robert, ed. *Skill in Nonverbal Communication: Individual Differences.* Cambridge, Mass.: Oelgeschager, Gunn & Hain, 1979.

Stewart, John, and Gary D'Angelo. *Together: Communicating Interpersonally.* Reading, Mass.: Addison-Wesley, 1975.

Organizational Design and Communication

After studying this chapter, you should be able to:

1. Compare and contrast tall and flat organizational structures.
2. List the advantages and disadvantages for each of the three types of organization: line, line-staff, and matrix.
3. Describe the kind of information that vertical communication usually conveys, both upward and downward. Describe the basic elements involved in improving upward and downward communication.
4. Understand the Pygmalion (self-fulfilling prophecy) effect.
5. Explain the importance of good horizontal communication in coordinated group effort and how it can be improved.
6. Define the difference between formal and informal communication channels in business.
7. Argue for the importance of the "grapevine" in business organizations and describe:
   a. The people who use it
   b. Its accuracy
   c. Its uses
8. Identify and discuss examples of electronic communications, including:
   a. Electronic mail
   b. Personal computers
   c. Facsimile machines

TO START YOU THINKING . . .

Here are some more questions to challenge your reading and to stimulate your thinking. Not all the answers to these questions will be found in the chapter. Some can only be answered from your own perspective.

♦ What are staff and line functions, and why are they sometimes confused with each other?
♦ Would you rather work for a tall or a flat organizational-type firm?
♦ How do formal communications differ from informal ones?
♦ How are organizational structures changing, and what impact are they having on communication?
♦ Are the contents of vertical messages likely to be the same if they are moving up or down?
♦ Why do some supervisors distort messages?
♦ How can you use the "positive sandwich" technique? Is the positive sandwich technique phony?

- Should companies try to "stamp out" the grapevine? Can the grapevine have any useful purpose? Is it ever accurate?
- How have electronic communications changed organizational communication?

COMMUNICATING IN ORGANIZATIONS

So many of the "human relations problems" that we encounter today have their origin in organizational communication or miscommunication. This chapter explores the differences in communication among various types of organizations, including more formal types of communications—channels, charts, and groups—within the organizational structure. If a group is to cooperate in accomplishing a common purpose, that purpose must be known to all group members, and to be known to all, it must in some way be communicated. All cooperative activities take place within a framework of communication. Without effective communication, there is no cooperation.

An organization comes into being when (1) there are individuals able to communicate with one another (2) who are willing to act (3) to accomplish a common purpose. These are the three basic elements necessary for any organization, and all are equally important for the effective functioning of the organization.

Good communications unify group behavior

In today's work organizations, communication is the foundation upon which all other functions rest. Communication serves not only to transfer information and to help *understanding among individuals and groups,* but it also *unifies group behavior.* Unified behavior provides the basis for *continuous* group cooperation. The simplicity of the organizational structure itself can facilitate good communication.

THE NEED FOR ORGANIZATIONAL STRUCTURE

The organization's structure must be built around the firm's long-range goal

An organization's structure limits the freedom of individuals to achieve a larger goal. That goal may be questionable or it may conflict with other larger goals. Workers who object to the organization's purposes will not accept the structure of the organization, because they do not accept the objectives.

Furthermore, a company may become bureaucratic—its structure may become unwieldy and so complicated that it actually obstructs its original purposes. Most people have had unpleasant experiences, at best humorous and at worst tragic, with bureaucratic organizations.

TALL AND FLAT ORGANIZATIONAL STRUCTURES

In complex organizations, there are usually several levels of management, but only one or two levels of workers. Supervisors interact with the employees daily and manage their work closely.

Fewer controls are found in flat structures

A flat or short organizational structure, with widely distributed authority and fewer strict controls, is a good environment for people who like to work independently. A successful flat organization depends primarily on alert supervi-

Problems develop faster
in a flat structure

sors who make good decisions and take responsibility. Poor supervision in a flat organization can lead quickly to management problems because of fewer divisions of labor.

Flat structure allows for
a wider span of
management

Entrusting each supervisor with a greater number of subordinates reduces the number of supervisors needed and thus reduces supervisory salaries, which may constitute a large part of the firm's operating costs. If efficiency can be maintained, then the organization will benefit financially through the use of this broader span of control or span of management.

The greater the number of management levels, or the taller the structure, the longer it takes for a message to reach the proper level for action and the more numerous the possibilities for communication breakdown. Some companies, as a result, have been trying to reduce the number of their intermediate management levels without overloading the managers.

The taller the structure,
the poorer the
communications

Given an equal number of persons in each organization, an axiom concerning the tall and flat organizational structures is evident: the taller the structure, or the more numerous the levels of management, the poorer the communication; the flatter the structure or the fewer the levels of management, the better the chances that accurate information is being transmitted. (See Figure 8-1.)

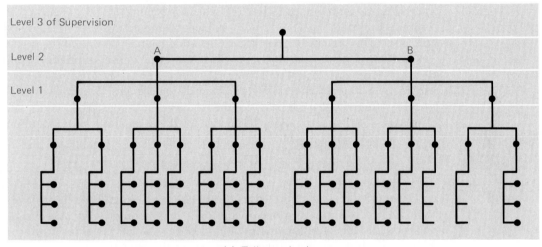

(a) Tall organization
(Maximum span of management: 3 subordinates. Four levels of management)

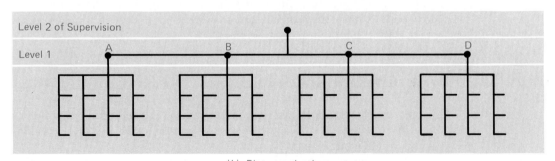

(b) Flat organization
(Maximum span of management: 12 subordinates. Two levels of management)

FIGURE 8-1 Organizational differences caused by different spans of management for the same number of operative employees (48).

Span of Management

The number supervised is the span of management

Studies on organizational structure suggest that one person can supervise from 12 to as many as 21 with little difficulty. This number is called the *span of control* or *span of management*. If most workers are doing the same tasks, and the variety of demands is not too great, a manager can supervise many people. As managers ascend the company hierarchy, the number of persons they can supervise effectively diminishes because of the complexity and diversity of the jobs supervised. The span of management is also defined as the number of people with whom one can have meaningful daily face-to-face contact.

Limiting the Span of Management

When a supervisor has extensive responsibilities, the workers may feel that no personal attention is being given to their work and their problems. The supervisor may also have difficulty in training, communicating, and controlling the workers if the span is too wide. To remedy the situation, a supervisor can break up the span, either by delegating some authority to informal team leaders or by asking experienced people to serve as trainers. It is important to organize the work so that there is more time for the human relations aspect so vital to any company.

Stretching the Span of Management

Enlarging the span and producing a flatter organization facilitates communications. Bottlenecks caused by too many levels can then be eliminated.

Broadening the span of control lessens the red tape

The advantage of broadening the supervisory span is less red tape. The structure is compacted, so that operations require a shorter chain of command. A broader span also encourages more extensive delegation and more general, rather than close, supervision. All these factors can raise employee morale.

Express Your Opinion

Consider how many persons each supervisor must manage in your company and whether you consider the span of control is more typical of a tall or a flat organization. Would you consider your company as having a tall or a flat organizational structure? Now that you have made such a determination, do you feel that it is the best type of structure for your company?

Do you feel that the number of people in the company is likely to determine the type of organizational structure? Is the nature of the business or the leadership more important as to the type of organizational structure that will be developed within the company? Rank these three factors in terms of importance in developing an organizational structure: the size of the company, the nature of the business, and the leadership style used.

STAFF AND LINE ORGANIZATIONS

The words *staff* and *line* are the classical terms used to define the traditional divisions of labor in complex organizations. They stem from nineteenth-century military usage and are still employed by the military. In business and industry, generally speaking, a line function is one that contributes directly to the main activity of the business; a staff function is one that assists the line function in an advisory or administrative capacity.

Line Structure

The supervisor usually functions according to a *line structure* of authority. In other words, authority is delegated downward in a clearly defined line, from the individual who is the supreme authority, to a subordinate, to a lower subordinate, and so on. The military is a prime example of a tightly structured line organization.

In this type of organizational structure, authority is delegated from the top management to the middle managers, who delegate it to the supervisors, who exercise it over their workers. Many more levels may be included, but the basic chain of command remains the same.

General Staff and Specialized Staff

There are two separate types of staff: general and specialized. General staff personnel usually assist division managers in a variety of ways. Specialized staff usually contribute specific skills in very *narrow* areas of expertise. Examples of general staff include accounting and human resource management. Market research and production planning are examples of specialized staff.

Staff persons are usually better informed of company activities

General staff are much more mobile than are line personnel because of the nature of their jobs, especially in factories. Their jobs tend to cut across horizontal divisions and consequently they are much better informed about company affairs than line managers. In recent years, there has been a reduction in corporate staff. Many companies are downsizing and attempting to save money and increase efficiency by clearing out staff members at headquarters. "Corporate staff is becoming an endangered species," according to some experts.[1]

Staff persons have a greater motivation to communicate

Staff must sell ideas, not give commands

Specialized staff personnel often find themselves in conflict with line managers because the line managers fear that new production methods will render their jobs obsolete. Poor communications, hostility, and even sabotage are not uncommon between line and staff personnel. While many specialists lack command or line authority, they have greater motivation to communicate because they realize that their success is dependent upon selling their ideas to others. A specialist has a shorter communication chain to higher management, which, as a result, usually gives him or her more mobility than operating workers. (See Figure 8-2.)

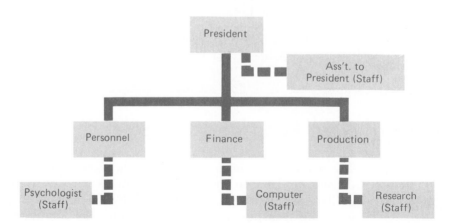

FIGURE 8-2 Types of staff positions.

The concept of group work teams has become an important aspect of modern organizational theory. Traditional organizations utilized a pattern of one-to-one relationships between organization members in which supervisors dealt with subordinates individually. Modern concepts emphasize group relationships and task force teams in accord with the new emphasis on better human relations and fuller participation among and by all employees. The manager must have a good grasp not only of group dynamics but of each person involved.

Group participation is, in fact, sometimes referred to as human relations because its primary function is to give employees a voice in what they do and how they do it. Available evidence indicates that, when a solution to a problem is worked out by the group to be affected by the change, it is accepted much more readily than when it is superimposed from above.

PROJECT MANAGEMENT

There are some unique communication problems in project management. Project management is a method for managing short-term, specific tasks. Most projects are completed by use of project teams or a special type of matrix organizations.

Project Teams or Matrix Organizations

Under a team project, a boss may report to an employee

Teams of people are brought together from different departments to work on a single specific project. The project manager may have no permanent authority in the organizational structure, but be an expert in the specific project and as such coordinate, direct, and control the various members of the project team. In effect, a matrix organization is a second form of organization overlaid on the line chain of command (Figure 8-3). Computer engineers, those who install electronic data processing equipment or automated machinery, often function in this capacity. As short-term programs are established, special groups are created to handle them.

A matrix is often a temporary structure

The chairman may find that he has persons reporting to him who are above, below, or at the same hierarchical level as he. Temporarily, for only hours a day, or for months at a time, a person may find that he has a superior from another department working under his direction. This can put a strain on the relationship, or it can help to break down the rigid barriers of formal communications.

Integrated machine production and data processing can be developed into

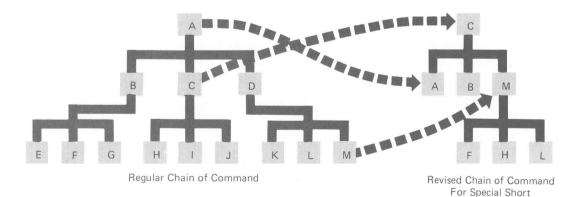

Regular Chain of Command

Revised Chain of Command
For Special Short
Term Projects

FIGURE 8-3 A matrix organization or project team as related to the regular chain of command.

what might be called a "horizontal plane." Such a combination of two different units into a workable team cuts across superior-subordinate relationships that may be affecting the jobs of employees in different areas. This new matrix plan superimposes a new vertical structure whose chain of command can help to solve or cause obvious difficulties.

Project managers who have to solve *new* problems must learn to deal horizontally with their peers and diagonally with workers at different levels. Following established, formal, vertical routes is costlier, takes more time, and is too disruptive.

Problems and Their Prevention in Matrix Organizations

The matrix design has many benefits, but to reap them managers need to know how to prevent and treat its problems.[2]

No leader

1. Problem. There is a tendency toward anarchy or no recognizable boss. This can happen quickly if the project is about to confront a crisis. The solution is to establish more structure and to have one person oversee the project until the situation can be resolved.

Power struggle

2. Problem. A power struggle can take place early in a matrix organization. One answer is to develop a balance of power or dual command. Strong statements of equal strength and friendly competition must be stressed. If this method does not work, then an overseer must be appointed.

Group makes all decisions

3. Problem. Severe "groupitis" or groupthink can emerge. That may lead to many meetings at which only group decisions are made. Such an attitude could be fatal to a project. Responsibilities must be established as to work loads and decisions that can be made by individuals as well as to duties that can be decided only by the group.

Keeping the channels of communication open and clear, especially in a matrix organization, can make the difference between an effective and ineffective organization.

COMMUNICATION CHANNELS

Formal communication is a part of all organizations

Communication channels are the paths along which messages travel from one person to another, or from one group to another, or both. All organizations use both formal and informal channels of communication. Formal channels are the communication chains and networks that determine the direction and flow of official messages to all the different members and divisions of an organization. Formal communication channels are an integral part of organizational structure. They stem from the rules and customs that govern the distribution of authority, rank, and type of work within the organization.

FORMAL CHANNELS

Figure 8-4 is an organization chart illustrating the internal structure of a complex factory in terms of its work divisions and power hierarchies. It also illustrates the formal channels that official messages must travel between and within the separate divisions. Official communications usually move along structural paths.

In complex organizations, there are usually several levels of management, but only one or two levels of workers. Management levels tend to increase in number and complexity, but worker levels tend to remain stationary. The greater the number of levels of managers, the longer the communication chain and the greater the possibilities for communication breakdowns. The move toward "lean and mean" organizations has the positive benefits of reducing levels of communication.

Organization Charts

A chart or table showing an organization's structure is a kind of anatomical drawing indicating the formal, *official* channels through which messages must travel, as shown in Figure 8-4. Flowing around the formal structure are complicated, ever-changing networks of informal, *unofficial* channels. Informal channels are not shown on a table of organization because they are by nature *unstable*, whereas the structure of an organization is more often stable.

An organization chart cannot indicate *all* the formal channels, only the *major* ones. A chart that showed all the formal paths that messages must travel would look more like a maze or a Chinese puzzle than a chart. For example, secretaries and receptionists are seldom shown on charts, but in large organizations most messages are routed through these individuals. The efficiency of a communication system often depends on how well the secretaries of vice presidents are relating to one another.

The organization chart is not sacred. Charting the organization makes sense to give some continuity for management and other employees. But new organization theory suggests that "we are not hapless beings caught in the grip of forces we can do little about. . . . Organization has been made by man; it can be changed by man. . . . The fault is not in organization, in short; it is in our worship of it."[3]

Chain of Command

An organization chart shows the chain of command, but again, those formal channels should not be set in stone. Experience has suggested that, by following the principle of the chain of command, with accountability following one level at a time from the top of the company to the bottom, an organization can have a more efficient, productive operation and a more cohesive work force. The main purpose of the organizational chain of command is to establish responsibility and effective communication at every level. This approach offers several advantages, including having decisions made on the spot.[4]

HORIZONTAL CHANNELS

Horizontal, or lateral, channels are of increasing importance in today's workplace. They are used when members at the same level in the hierarchy of authority communicate with one another; that is, one worker to another or one manager to another. Horizontal channels operate both formally and informally, and officially and unofficially. A sales manager who tells a plant manager to increase production next month because a clever advertising campaign has paid off and sales are pouring in would use formal channels for the message. But the plant manager might have given the sales manager a great idea for the advertising campaign over a drink a few months previously—surely an informal situation. Many workers and managers use informal horizontal channels often and with great success. They rely

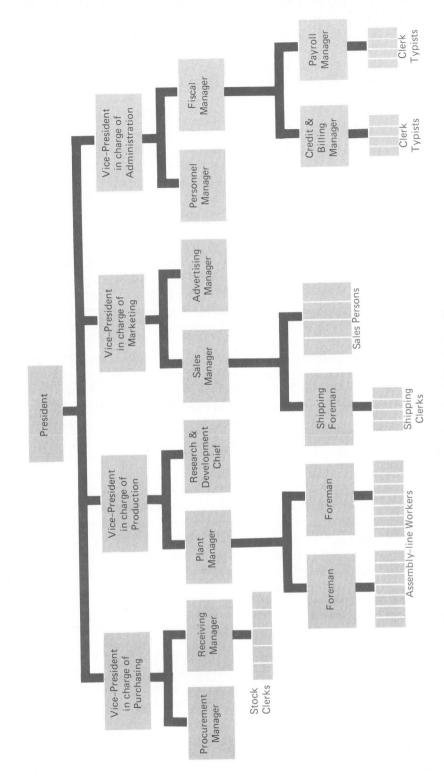

FIGURE 8-4 The organizational structure of an industrial plant illustrates the formal communication channels.

on friendships and favors given and owed as a way to ignore or expedite requests, to evade rules, or to change the work flow.

The problems associated with horizontal communications seldom stem from a lack of messages among individuals or groups but, rather, from the large numbers and various types of messages that are sent and received. Work is often duplicated unnecessarily or is delayed inordinately because information needed in one department is available only in another, and sometimes no one in the department needing the information knows that it exists.

The lack of horizontal communication is becoming more pronounced. Despite efforts such as MBWA (discussed in Chapter 2) there continues to be less candor and information in our communications.

VERTICAL CHANNELS

It is easier to communicate downward than upward

Messages moving along vertical channels flow in two directions, up and down. However, although downward and upward communications travel along the same paths, the content, nature, and problems of the two vary considerably. The differences between them can be compared with the force of water when it flows up or down. Downward communication is like water streaming down from a waterfall or a showerhead. It pours down easily with great force and wets a large area; upward communication is like a small spurt of water shooting up from a fountain *against* the pull of gravity. The higher it travels, the more it loses its force. Official top-to-bottom communication channels flow down with great force and reach a great many people, but official bottom-to-top channels flow up with difficulty and reach relatively few people.

Seven trends developing in organizations today will have a significant impact on communication and its practitioners. These trends are:

1. Rewards and recognition systems are more closely reinforcing corporate values and individual behavior.
2. As organizations become more small-team oriented, communication is being facilitated.
3. Bureaucracy that presents obstacles to excellence is being eliminated; this includes unnecessary busywork and paperwork.
4. The responsibility for communication is flowing toward line management and away from the staff departmental level.
5. Organizations are adopting more participatory management styles, which is causing communication to focus more on listening, ownership, teamwork, and involvement.
6. Perquisites that create barriers between employee groups are being replaced by behavior that promotes teamwork.
7. Among the qualities people want most in their jobs, individual fulfillment and quality of life still outrank pay, benefits, and job security.[5]

DOWNWARD COMMUNICATIONS

To increase the effectiveness of their firms, many executives have decided to shift decision making related to everyday operations downward to middle-level em-

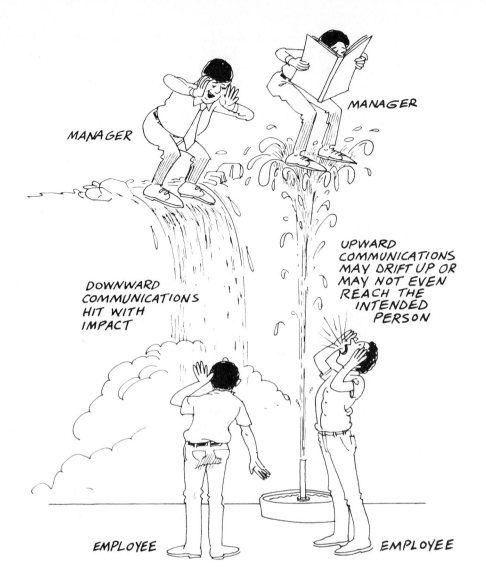

MANAGER

MANAGER

DOWNWARD
COMMUNICATIONS
HIT WITH
IMPACT

UPWARD
COMMUNICATIONS
MAY DRIFT UP OR
MAY NOT EVEN
REACH THE
INTENDED
PERSON

EMPLOYEE

EMPLOYEE

ployees, who are closer to operations and to the customer. In many firms, this decision to decentralize is not working. This "gap" in the middle—that is, the existence of a more negative view held by people at a particular organizational level than those below and above them—exists across a broad range of issues.[6]

Among the factors contributing to the gap are the growing complexity of cross-functional coordination, the increasing reliance on data-based information systems, and the trend toward organizational downsizing. The gap reflects a narrow, local perspective and poor lateral, cross-functional cooperation and teamwork at the middle level. Firms also need to introduce lateral mechanisms to ensure that information sharing and coordination exists at the middle level. Finally, management should reorder information flows to facilitate real communication, not just more data.[7]

Downward communication is the fastest form of communication

Downward communication is the fastest form in the vertical chain of communication, is accepted more at face value, and is reacted to more vigorously. Matters that affect employees directly, such as salaries, job security, and fringe benefits, are of real interest to them. Studies show that this type of information ranks highest with employees, whether they are managers, supervisors, or shop workers. Therefore, a basic approach toward more effective communication is to use words that are understandable and simple.

Managers only *think* they know the problems of their employees!

Another problem of downward communiqués is that many managers think they understand the problems of their employees; however, their employees are not likely to agree. This fundamental difference in perception tends to exist at each level in an organization, thereby making communication more difficult.

Often managers become overconfident and take less care with their downward communications. Some companies hold regularly scheduled meetings of their management personnel each Monday morning where everyone is required to stand up. Things tend to get accomplished in a hurry. Many banks, savings and loan associations, and retail stores do this during the 15-minute period just prior to the morning opening. There is an increasing use of short meetings that include warm-up exercises and singing of company songs—spinoffs of Japanese management ideas.

Written Versus Oral Downward Communications

Written communications traveling along downward channels range from handwritten messages pinned to bulletin boards, to typed interoffice memos, to printed job descriptions, circulars, handbooks, and job manuals. The number of internal publications and memoranda as well as external publications continues to increase. Electronic mail is influencing these numbers, but its impact is still too early to quantify.

Research suggests that those who rely principally on memos, letters, and manuals for communicating messages downward not only fall short of achieving understanding, credibility, and acceptance, but they actually contribute to new problems of misunderstandings, disbelief, and rejection. Incredible amounts of time, money, and materials are wasted on written communications that serve little purpose.

Saving information for a brief verbal meeting can serve at least two purposes: (1) less paperwork and (2) better interpersonal communication, relationships, and overall understanding.

When emotions are "high," tell it to them

Some employees are informed best in writing, some orally, and some both in writing and orally. And there are those who must be told repeatedly for the message to have any substantial impact. Any tender topics are best handled orally rather than in writing. Firing an employee or arbitrating conflicts among workers is best handled in person. When emotions are high or financial stakes are great, face-to-face communications are a must.

Oral messages for quick decisions

Many companies have begun to change their basic views about internal communication systems. One corporation banished its "Never say it—Write it!" slogan and replaced it with "Talk it over—Jot it down." No one denies that written, downward communication serves an extremely important function when complex, hard-to-remember facts and details must be transmitted precisely and preserved with care. But paper is often the wrong medium for the "getting-things-done" kind of message that demands quick decisions in response. Information on a CRT screen allows action more quickly than information on a piece of paper.

Self-Fulfilling Prophecy

Pygmalion management

Do you believe in self-fulfilling prophecy? What you expect of others determines the reactions of others. If you expect low achievement, people will produce little. If treated as inferior, lazy, materialistic, or irresponsible, people become so. People in different organizational settings, if treated as responsible, independent, understanding, goal achieving, and creative, tend to become so. The term *Pygmalion management* is derived from this concept. Management can expect elegant performance from an employee if the training is good and, most important, if the expectations and responsibilities are high enough. Is there some truth in this theory that is expressed by leaders through their actions and attitudes?

Express Your Opinion

Do you believe that there is some truth to the self-fulfilling prophecy or the Pygmalion theory? Do you believe that your parents or teachers may have influenced you either in a positive or negative way? Can you name people who have influenced you in your accomplishments or career direction? It is usually easier to see how others have influenced us, but harder to see how we have influenced others. Whom do you feel you have influenced through the self-fulfilling prophecy? Have you expressed such feelings subtly to a co-worker or to those at home?

Do you suppose that such an attitude or belief in the Pygmalion theory might be an excuse for not being successful? "I am not successful, because my father didn't expect much out of me!" Can we overcome such a negative influence?

How to Handle Bad News

Managers are frequently called on to transmit negative messages, such as denying salary raises, job promotions, or transfers.

The "positive sandwich" is bad news between two slices of good feelings

Basically, the *positive sandwich technique* should be used in handling negative news. Start with a good slice of bread spread generously with good news and information that is true and supportive. Then express the bad news quickly and simply as a slice of thin ham, followed up with another piece of bread bearing supportive reasons and assurances.

Whether the message is written or oral, you have to prevent the disappointing news from turning your subordinate against you. The opening remarks or sentences should strengthen whatever good feeling exists. Certainly, by asserting the bad news right at the beginning, you would be giving too much emphasis to it and jeopardizing existing goodwill. Equally vital to bad news situations is the last third of the positive sandwich, a positive ending. A positive closing can tip the scales toward the retention of the employee's goodwill.

There is another viewpoint on delivering bad news. Get it out of the way first and then positively reinforce the recipient of the bad news. Advocates of this approach say the "positive sandwich technique" is phony and only prolongs the inevitable. What do you think?

UPWARD COMMUNICATION

Upward communication occurs when someone in a lower position in the company communicates information, ideas, suggestions, opinions, or grievances to someone higher. When a typist drops a suggestion in the company suggestion box, or a supervisor reports a breakdown in the machinery to the plant manager, or a copy editor suggests a sales campaign to the advertising manager, or the results of a survey about workers' attitudes are distributed to the vice president—all these communications travel by upward routes.

The first step toward building a successful upward communication program is to gain the endorsement of top management. Next, employee surveys with open-ended questions should be taken to gauge how employees understand the goals of the business and to understand the concerns of the employees themselves. Open-ended questions provide a better opportunity for employees to express their true concerns.[8]

Other mechanisms that are available for encouraging upward communications include (1) employee-management meetings, (2) speak-out sessions, (3) quality circles, (4) employee ombudsmen positions, (5) newsletters, and (6) the open-door policy. Employees consider access to upper management, involvement in decision making, information about the business, feedback to suggestions, and a climate of trust as the most effective methods of communication.[9]

For upward communications to be effective, managerial staffs and their subordinate employees must work together in a spirit of trust and goodwill. Suppose that a company maintains a conspicuously placed suggestion box that gets a great deal of use but that the employees never receive managerial feedback on any of their suggestions; they will probably take a cynical view of management's sincerity. On the other hand, when workers know that their messages are treated with respect and attention, the company benefits in at least four important ways. The acronym OPEN gives good reason why upward communications are of value.

The Open-door Policy

In recent years, many companies have tried to revive the tradition of the "open-door policy." Theoretically, this policy allows low-level workers the privilege of walking into any manager's office to register a complaint or to make a suggestion. In most cases, however, the policy exists only on paper. The door may be open, but somehow, hourly workers are seldom seen crossing the threshold.

The open-door policy works better in theory than in practice. Physical layout of most office complexes isolate executives from other employees. And then, there is organizational resistance to bypassing first-line supervisors or midlevel managers.

The best "open door" is when the supervisor walks out to the workers

It seems, therefore, as if the most practical open-door policy today would be one in which managers tried to recreate some of the conditions of the nineteenth century. The open door appears to work most effectively when supervisory

---

Being OPEN Provides Good Reasons for Good Upward Communications

O *Offers ideas.* Employees often have valuable ideas and suggestions about increasing product quality and production rates. The research and design department does not have a monopoly on all good ideas.

P *Prevents problems.* When messages travel upward easily, managers can stay informed about potentially troublesome situations and prevent union problems.

E *Encourages acceptance.* Effective upward communication reveals to management the degree of acceptance and credibility that company policies have among employees.

N *Notable participation.* Free, open upward communication stimulates employees to work more willingly when they have some say in planning or evaluating those policies.

personnel walk through it *out* to the workers instead of waiting for workers to come in to them. This is another manifestation of management by walking around.

INFORMAL CHANNELS

Although informal organizations are bound by no chart on the wall, they are bound by convention, custom, and culture. Informal communications grow out of the *social* interactions among people who work together. These communications do not appear as formal patterns of relationships on organization charts. Most theorists believe that informal relationships cannot be charted because they change so rapidly and are so complex. One of the major functions that informal channels serve is that of providing communication routes for members of small groups. Every successful business has at least one healthy, if invisible, communication channel through which to conduct the messages of the informal organization. One major source of employees' information about their companies is the grapevine.

The Grapevine

The grapevine is the unofficial news carrier

The term *grapevine* is believed to have come into use during the Civil War when the first telegraph lines, used to carry military intelligence, were strung from tree to tree in the pattern of a grapevine. Often messages were garbled or interfered with, and so all rumors, or unofficial messages, came to be known as carried "by the grapevine."

In a complex organization, depending on its size, there can be dozens or hundreds of grapevines. They carry information that is not, or cannot be, transmitted by formal means. Information of this sort includes "I wouldn't ask for that raise today, if I were you. The boss is in a foul mood, and you'd better wait until her mood changes."

You can't eliminate the grapevine

However, it is impossible to predict the direction, speed, accuracy, or final content of a message carried by the grapevine. Messages may be abbreviated, magnified, restructured, elaborated, or generally twisted out of shape. Sometimes official messages must be issued to counteract the inaccuracies of the grapevine. At other times it can spread information very quickly and accurately.

Even though the grapevine's reliability can never be determined with complete certainty, it does serve some useful functions.

Develops relationships

1. It satisfies a need that employees have to enjoy friendly relations with their fellow employees.

2. It helps workers make sense out of their work environment, especially in interpreting unclear orders from supervisors.

Releases anxieties

3. It acts as a safety valve. When people are confused and unclear about what is going to happen to them, they use the grapevine to release their anxieties. When they feel powerless to direct their destinies, passing a rumor along the grapevine is a way of expressing and releasing negative energy.

A way of dealing with uncertainty

4. When people gossip about someone who is not present, they often pass judgment. Some people pass judgment on others to find out where they stand. It is a way of dealing with self-doubt and insecurity.

Rumor

Rumor has no standard of evidence, no basis but feelings

The grapevine is the channel through which information is disseminated and is based on limited information. A rumor, by contrast, is information based on speculation, wishes, or imagination. Rumor is sometimes used as a synonym for the grapevine, but a rumor is not a grapevine message. A rumor has no secure evidence or reliable person's word behind it. Rumors can be correct, but more often they are not. Generally, rumors are spread by people who are very interested in the subject. In the course of a day, the details of a rumor may change, but the theme will remain the same. Sometimes rumors are agents for wish fulfillments. Why would Mary and Herman start a rumor that everyone in the office is going to get a $25 monthly raise?

Rumor is more often untrue

Probably just saying it out loud makes them feel good, and they may think that, if the words are said long enough and loud enough to enough people it just might come true. The problem with rumors is that they are especially subject to distortion because people *are* interested in the subject matter and distort those details that don't interest them. They enlarge and elaborate the ones that do.

Stop rumors quickly

Managers who wish to stop rumor mongering should try to stop only those that are important—rumors that affect morale and productivity. Those should be nipped in the bud as quickly as possible. Face-to-face conversations or group meetings are the best methods for stopping dangerous rumors from spreading. But the person denying the rumor must be known for honesty and be willing to answer questions on the subject.

Rumors express a feeling, may indicate insecurity

Upwardly moving rumors can provide managers with an understanding of feelings among the work force. Managers who learn to ask questions such as "What does that rumor mean—is someone insecure and afraid of being fired?" or "Is someone really quitting?" are often provided with truthful answers via the grapevine. Labor relations mediators always make it their business to listen to the rumors that union and company officials spread about each other. They believe that such rumors are projections of fears and that, if they can learn what each side is afraid of, they can achieve a better understanding of complex issues.

SMALL-GROUP COMMUNICATIONS

Groups satisfy needs

Most people spend a great deal of time communicating in small groups. Our lives revolve around our families, classes, work teams, quality circles, athletic teams, and committees; and this list could be extended much further. The groups that most influence peoples' behavior become their reference groups: the groups with whom values, attitudes, and beliefs are shared. Groups also provide people with opportunities to satisfy their needs for recognition and achievement. They satisfy other wishes too, such as those for dominance and autonomy.

A person with high credibility has great influence

Small-group interaction is dynamic and involves a lot of feedback. The social relations within a small group influence the kind of communication that takes place, and, in turn, the nature of the communication will influence social relations. For example, a person who has high credibility will have much more influence than will someone of high status but low credibility. High credibility confers a kind of power on the person who has it.

In business organizations especially, the power relations within a group determine to a large extent the kind of communication that exists. When power is concentrated in too few high-status people, lower-status group members will feel that their needs are not being met, and communication will be less than effective. Communication is also affected within a group by the degrees of cooperation and competition among the group members.

Additional information on group behavior and dynamics was presented in Chapter 6.

ELECTRONIC COMMUNICATION

As we move into the twenty first century, computers and electronic media have transformed organizational communication. Mainframe computers and technologically sophisticated electronic switching systems first made transfer of information easier. Then, minicomputers and personal computers, and now networking make this information transfer an everyday occurrence.

The electronic revolution is promising that business at the turn of the century will be fast, more efficient, and challenging. Now is the time to prepare to adjust to that environment. Handwritten symbol recognition, which allows a person to write directly onto a flat display screen and then convert the handwriting into text, will put an end to paper handling.[10]

Other technologies include personal computer interface and digital video interactive technology. There are many obstacles that must be surmounted if technological advancements are to be used on a widespread basis.

Electronic Mail

Electronic messaging systems (EMSs) are computer-based telecommunications systems combining any of the following: (1) E-mail, (2) electronic mailbox, (3) electronic data interchange, (4) facsimile transmissions, (5) telex, (6) voice mail, and (7) alphanumeric pager.

Electronic mail is a quicker and cheaper means of sending messages and documents than postal services. An advantage of E-mail is that it does not require real-time connections but is a store-and-forward communications medium. EMSs are changing the way businesses negotiate and enter into contracts, and this raises legal issues regarding delayed communications.[11]

There has been a rise in defensive strategies to avoid certain information and messages such as software to route unwanted calls to answering machines and call blockers to reject calls from unwanted numbers. The Information Lens, under development at MIT, scans and sorts incoming mail and can identify unwanted electronic mail.[12]

Facsimile and Other Telecommunications Machines

Facsimile, one of the oldest electronic communications media, allows clerical staffs to transmit entire documents over telephone lines in as little as 15 seconds. Improvements in fax technology, and reduced costs of equipment and long-distance charges, are expected to contribute to its increased use.

New scanning and printing technologies and maturing international standards have advanced facsimile (fax) machines to the point that worldwide communication is possible. The personal computer/fax machine is another variation on electronic communication. The chief advantages of personal computer (PC)-fax are cost, convenience, control, clarity, and consolidation. In many cases, the disadvantage of PC-fax is that it is designed to serve individuals, not groups. A stand-alone fax machine, on the other hand, can be shared by several people.[13]

Many companies use audio- and videotapes as well as teleconferencing instead of formal minutes and reports for their meetings. The application of telecommunications equipment (the combination of telephone and computer technologies) can improve the ease and efficiency of conducting business.

Seven advantages of telecommunications technology to enhance pure organizational communication are (1) avoiding intraoffice and intercompany communication delays by using voice messaging systems, (2) broadening market reach with portable computers and electronic mail, (3) accessing up-to-date information via online data bases, (4) keeping geographically dispersed units in touch with each other, using facsimile transmissions and electronic mail, (5) simplifying scheduling and facilitating ongoing business relationships, (6) making equipment more productive by linking more than one computer to a printer or workstation, and (7) increasing the quality of decision making by having complete and current information available when needed.[14]

Summary

Traditional concepts of staff and line have changed in recent years. With those changes have come innovations in communication techniques between the divisions. Integrated work teams composed of both line and staff personnel create much better human relations among employees and contribute greatly to better small-group communications.

Two kinds of communication channels serve to accomplish effective communication: formal and informal. Formal channels are the official paths by which official messages travel. They are called the vertical and horizontal channels because they relate to and grow out of the vertical and horizontal relationships pictured on an organization's structural chart. Informal channels stem from the unofficial, social relationships existing between individuals who work together, and they serve to transmit unofficial messages.

Although the downward and upward channels both move vertically, the nature, content, and volume of messages going up or down are completely different. The downward channel is dominated by orders from above dealing with policies and procedures. Vast amounts of printed matter are generated in the top-down channel in the form of memos, reports, and house organs.

Horizontal channels exist for members of the same organizational rank to communicate with one another. Horizontal communications can be observed on a formal organization chart, but they also exhibit a number of characteristics associated with the informal modes of communication. It has been demonstrated that open horizontal communication is essential for the success of any complex organization, from the managerial level to the assembly line.

The grapevine is used by nearly everyone in an organization at one time or another. It can carry accurate messages with amazing speed. It can also distort and filter messages beyond recognition. Rumor as well as facts are carried by the grapevine. Good managers pay attention to grapevine communications as a way of staying in touch with workers' thoughts and feelings. The 1990s are exciting times for telecommunications. The technology continues to develop rapidly and improve communication and the quality of our decisions.

Case Study 16

How Can the Staff Communicate More Effectively with Line Personnel?

Good communication between staff and line personnel is important in all organizations, and it can be said that effective communication plays a significant role in determining the overall success of any organization. However, when the communication process between staff and line personnel is less than effective, problems can develop, as seen in the following illustration.

Jay Galler, who manages the personnel department of a large industrial plant of about 200 employees, recently distributed to all employees a detailed questionnaire that required the employees to fill in information about their job title, number of years with the company, salary rate, and a description of their job responsibilities. The form stated that the purpose of the questionnaire would be to provide management with updated material concerning personnel classifications. The form stated that all employees should return the form on or before the coming Friday, which gave the workers five days in which to fill all the information needed. Jay announced to each department that he would tour the plant on Friday morning and pick up all the forms that had not yet been turned in to the personnel department.

The updating of the personnel classifications was requested by the plant manager. The reason was to review all the job duties with the possibility of reclassifying some of the positions, in some cases to provide a more equitable pay rate, which would mean a pay raise for some.

At the end of the week, before Jay's tour of the plant, fewer than 20 percent of the questionnaires had been returned to the personnel office. After touring the plant, Jay had collected only an additional dozen forms.

Obviously, an accurate study of the wages and salary schedules could not be done because of the lack of necessary data. There appears to be a problem between line and staff, more specifically the passing of information from the line personnel to the staff, a common problem.

1. How will the line personnel suffer as a result of not filling out the questionnaire?
2. How could Jay have made his communication more effective?
3. Was Jay's method the best way of distributing the forms? Is there a better way? Should Jay have departmental meetings to discuss the form?
4. What information should be included on the memo regarding the questionnaire?

Work Delegation and Dual Command

Frank Colella works in an aircraft plant as a dispatcher in production control. According to his immediate supervisor, Frank's duty is to determine the priority of shop orders for completion in each department. On this particular Saturday, Frank was assigned to the turret lathe department and only a few people were working. Frank was working this day under a lower-level supervisor by the name of Mike. Since Mike's department was behind in production, he told Frank to make an inventory of all the orders in his department, not just those that could be completed quickly to reduce the backlog. Frank told Mike he could not follow the order, since his immediate supervisor had given him specific instructions. Mike replied, "This is my department, I should know what is best; I am the supervisor, and I run the department." Frank again refused and Mike called his general supervisor, who told Frank that the matter would be referred to the superintendent on Monday and that Frank would be fired.

1. Who is right in this situation, Mike or Frank?
2. How would you resolve the problem of dual authority?
3. What action would you take if you were the superintendent, and why?
   a. Fire Frank.
   b. Reprimand him.
   c. Do nothing.
   d. Commend him for following the orders of his immediate supervisor.

Terms and Concepts

electronic mail a computer-based, store-and-forward communication medium for sending messages and documents.

facsimile an electronic communications medium for transmission of entire documents over telephone lines.

flat organizational structure an organization that has fewer levels in its hierarchy than a tall structure. There are fewer supervisors, and each one has more people to supervise.

formal communications structured, stable manner of communicating between people and their superiors or subordinates. Customs are followed in regard to authority, rank, and type of work.

grapevine the informal channel of communications between people. It serves to disseminate limited information. It is fast, selective as to who receives the information, and stays within its own area of influence.

horizontal communications communications between people of equal status.

informal communications a communication chain created by friendships and social associations within the work situation. It is unofficial and highly unstable.

matrix organization a team of people brought together from different departments to work together on a project. Temporarily, a person may have people report to him or her who are normally above or below him or her in rank.

positive sandwich bad news slipped in between two slices of good news "bread."

rumor a message that has no secure evidence or a reliable person's word behind it. More often it is not true and is based on wishes, needs, or wild imagination.

span of management the number of people that one person can supervise effectively and directly.

vertical communications communications both up and down the hierarchy of a firm. They are more likely to be formal, rather than friendly and open.

Notes

1. Thomas Moore, "Goodbye, Corporate Staff," *Fortune*, December 21, 1987, p. 65.

2. Stanley M. Davis and Paul R. Lawrence, "Problems of Matrix Organizations," *Harvard Business Review*, May–June 1978, pp. 34–37.

3. Jerry Buckley, "The New Organization Man," *U.S. News and World Report*, January 16, 1989, p. 50.

4. Andre Nelson, "A Supervisory Principle—Chain of Command," *Supervision*, May 1988, pp. 14–17.

5. James C. Shaffer, "Seven Emerging Trends in Organizational Communication," *Communication World*, February 1986, pp. 17–19.

6. Leonard W. Johnson and Alan Frohman, "Identifying and Closing the Gap in the Middle of Organizations," *Academy of Management Executive*, May 1989, pp. 107–114.

7. Ibid.

8. Valorie A. McClelland, "Upward Communication: Is Anyone Listening?" *Personnel Journal*, June 1988, pp. 124–131.

9. Ibid.

10. Karen Frech and Nicholas Wood, "The Brave New Office: Plugging into the Year 2000; The Future Isn't Now But It's on the Way," *Life Association News*, June 1989, pp. 40–48.

11. Brad Schultz, "Electronic Mail," *United States Banker*, February 1989, pp. 53–59.

12. David Churbuck, "Prepare for E-Mail Attack," *Forbes*, January 23, 1989, pp. 82–87.

13. Christopher O'Malley, "Where PC-Fax Pays Off," *Personal Computing*, June 1989, pp. 91–98.

14. Theresa Engstrom, "Seven Business Reasons to Turn to Telecommunications," *Working Woman*, August 1987, pp. 44–47, 84.

Recommended Reading

Baldwin, William. "Just the Bare Facts, Please." *Forbes*, December 12, 1988, pp. 233–238.

Chisholm, Donald. *Coordination Without Hierarchy: Informal Structures in Multiorganizational Systems.* Berkeley: University of California Press, 1989.

Davis, Stanley, and Paul Lawrence. "Problems of Matrix Organizations." *Harvard Business Review*, May–June 1978, pp. 46–52.

Fielden, John S. "Why Can't Managers Communicate?" *Business*, January–February–March 1989, pp. 41–44.

Hunt, Gary T. *Communication Skills in the Organization.* Englewood Cliffs, N.J.: Prentice-Hall, 1980.

Johnson, Leonard W., and Alan L. Frohman. "Identifying and Closing the Gap in the Middle of Organizations." *Academy of Management Executive*, May 1989, pp. 107–114.

McClelland, Valorie A. "Upward Communication: Is Anyone Listening?" *Personnel Journal*, June 1988, pp. 124–131.

Mueller, Robert K. *Corporate Networking: Building Channels for Information and Influence.* New York: Free Press, 1986.

Munter, Mary. *Guide to Managerial Communication.* Englewood Cliffs, N.J.: Prentice-Hall, 1982.

Naisbitt, John, and Patricia Aburdene. *Re-inventing the Corporation: Transforming Your Job and Your Company for the New Information Society.* New York: Warner Books, 1985.

Odiorne, George S. "Ethics for the Nineties." *Manage*, April 1988, pp. 8–14, 33.

Tomasko, Robert. *Downsizing.* New York: AMACOM, 1987.

Power
and Status

After studying this chapter, you should be able to:

1. Differentiate between personal and organizational or position power.
2. Understand the *norm of reciprocity* as it pertains to power relationships.
3. Know what types of people are powerful and what makes them powerful.
4. Understand the relationships between power, perception, and organizational politics.
5. Distinguish between various sources and types of power, including
   a. Referent power
   b. Connection power
   c. Reward power
   d. Expert power
   e. Information power
6. Explain how differences in job status are expressed by
   a. Task differentiation
   b. Professionalism
   c. Hours and pay
   d. Work environment
   e. Clothing and other belongings
   f. Communications
7. Explain the major determinants of status.

TO START YOU THINKING . . .

◆ How do you define power? Where does it come from?
◆ Is it important for individuals to perceive themselves as powerful if they want to exercise power?
◆ Is "playing politics" necessarily bad?
◆ How and why do you measure power in organizations?
◆ What determines your status?
◆ Do you agree with the following statement: "If people think they have status, they have status"?
◆ How would you rate different occupations in terms of status? Do some jobs have more prestige, even though they produce less income than other positions in the marketplace?

DEFINITION OF POWER

Absolute power is a person's ability to influence others, not just their behavior. The amount of power that an individual possesses is determined by his or her organizational and personal power.

Organizational power is derived from higher authority

Organizational power means the capacity of managers to exert influence over others. It is derived from higher-level authority and is delegated downward in an organization. The greatest organizational power is the power of doing a good job—the power of and authority of being right, having the knowledge, and being a proficient expert in one's discipline. Personal power, on the other hand, is obtained from the acceptance of followers, not from higher-level management.

Personal power is obtained from acceptance of followers

There is certainly an instinct for power in many of us. Most people do not like to admit that they want power, which is why they never get it. Those who do have power may go to endless lengths to mask that fact. The contemporary American style of power is to pretend that one has none, because to confess that one has power is to make oneself responsible for using it. The masters of power instinctively try to control every situation in which they find themselves and try to place as much of an obligation as possible on another person.

We have four reasons for working: (1) money (need), (2) pleasure, (3) force of habit, and (4) power.[1] Companies consciously or unconsciously have noticed that the opportunity to acquire and wield power motivates people. Therefore there tends to be a built-in or "house" power game that is established by the management. Most corporations find it in their interest to encourage power games, because providing an opportunity to obtain power is cheaper than giving raises.

Hedrick Smith, *New York Times* and PBS correspondent, writes in *The Power Game* that: "Power is the ability to make something happen or to keep it from happening." He continues:

> In short, the most vital ingredients of power are often the intangibles. Information and knowledge are power. Visibility is power. A sense of timing is power. Trust and integrity are power. Personal energy is power; so is self-confidence. Showmanship is power. Likability is power. . . . Winning is power. Sometimes, the illusion of power is power.[2]

Another definition is that power is the probability that a person can carry out his or her own will despite resistance. Power is only as useful as it is recognized by those over whom it is exercised. There is a quid pro quo for power; that is, individuals over whom it is exercised accept it. This is known as the acceptance of authority or power. There may be coercion or force to effect the acceptance, but it is nevertheless not really effective until it is accepted.

Norm of reciprocity creates an obligation

Related to the acceptance of power is another concept known as the *norm of reciprocity*. The norm of reciprocity states that people feel an obligation to return pay or other consideration to another for continuance of a mutually beneficial relationship.

WHO ARE THE POWERFUL?

Heads of private and public organizations including government wield a great amount of power. The stereotype of the powerful individual is the tycoon billionaire who can at will buy and sell properties, including the services of individuals. To be sure, many of the very powerful have amassed large private fortunes; even more are the heads of publicly held corporations. Figure 9-1 shows some of the most powerful people in corporate America according to one survey.

The individuals shown in Figure 9-1 and others like them are extremely powerful, but there are many others beneath the surface of these and similar private and public organizations who wield considerable power. What makes one person powerful and another not, even though they have both formal organizational and personal power? Before individuals can be considered powerful, they must possess the confidence and trust of the others over whom they would exercise power. They must also have the self-confidence that they can use power to the satisfaction of subordinates, bosses, and other coworkers.

Chief of staff position has power

Behind-the-scenes power brokers are common. The chief of staff position in many organizations possesses considerable power but does not always share the glory (or disdain!) from others. Consider the chiefs of staff for all the presidents of the United States that you can remember—do they not wield considerable power in who gets the ear of or who gets to see the president? Just the recent presidents, Ford, Carter, Reagan, and Bush have had powerful individuals in Dick Cheney (later secretary of defense), Jodi Powell, Don Regan, James Baker (later secretary of state), and John Sununu, to name a few.

Sometimes the power is hidden even further from view. James Baker and Don Regan were both active chiefs of staff, but the real power broker behind President Reagan was his wife, Nancy—who ultimately arranged the ouster of Regan. Parallel situations exist in other organizations, including city governments, educational institutions, and the military where the chief of staff role has achieved formal status.

John Akers	IBM
Edward Brennan	Sears, Roebuck & Co.
Warren Buffett	Berkshire Hathaway Corporation
Robert Crandall	AMR Corporation
Michael Eisner	Walt Disney Corporation
Robert Goizueta	The Coca-Cola Company
Katherine Graham	Washington Post Company
John Gutfreund	Salomon Inc.
Lee Iacocca	Chrysler Corporation
Rupert Murdoch	New Corporation Ltd.
John F. "Jack" Welch	General Electric Corporation
John Young	Hewlett-Packard Co.

FIGURE 9-1 Some of the most powerful people in corporate America. Source: "The 797 Most Powerful Men and 3 Most Powerful Women in Corporate America," *Forbes*, June 15, 1987, pp. 145–216 and "The Power and the Pay: Corporate America's Most Powerful People," *Forbes*, May 28, 1990, pp. 199–317.

POWER AND PERCEPTION

Power is a function of perception

Are perception and power strange bedfellows? Not really, for power is more a function of perception than anything else. The strengths of both personal and organizational power are a matter of perception. Important perceived questions are: Can the boss or any other powerful individual reward or punish me? Is the boss competent? Does he or she have the formal position or earned respect from me to exercise power?

Perception is a matter of individuals' beholding what others believe, think, or see to be truly representative of a situation. If an individual is perceived as having power, he or she has power—at least in the eye of the beholder. If they are not perceived as having power—they have a serious flaw in conducting business effectively for their organizations. Self-confidence and self-perception are part of this process as well.

Leadership Power Is Derived

Leaders are given power by group consensus

It is common practice to grant leadership power to people who already have some authority. But leaders are given their power *only* by *group consensus*, without necessarily having any special status, such as position, skill, or education, to recommend them. Leaders gain power within a group gradually, by establishing trust and recognition.

Power is largely a matter of perception. If the leader is perceived to have power, then that leader's ability to lead and otherwise exercise influence over a group is enhanced. The distinguishing difference between a leader and an authority figure is that the group chooses the leaders (see Figure 9-2). We will examine those leadership processes in greater detail in Chapter 10.

FIGURE 9-2 Groups need leaders to reduce confusion and uncertainty, but it must be remembered that authority is conferred and leadership must be earned.
Gilles Peress/Magnum Photos, Inc.

Express Your Opinion   What are the attributes of leaders/managers that make them powerful? Are they considered to have the following attributes? envisioner? empowerer? champion? encourager? listener? person with knowledge? others?

SOURCES AND TYPES OF POWER

What are the real sources of power? Power is derived from various sources, including personal expertise and from informal leadership skills that enable managers to obtain the loyalty and support of others. You do not have to take power away from others to increase your power base.[4]

You do not have to be the highest-ranking individual to be the most powerful. The power of the informal group is strong—and just because a person has formal organizational power does not make him or her more powerful than someone else who has strong personal power.

Let's examine the sources. Figure 9-3 shows a continuum of the sources and types of power.

Expert Power

The power of expertise is a most important source. Does the person who exercises the power know what he or she is talking about? If the answer is "yes," he or she has the authority or power because of their knowledge and competence. Such

Expert		Referent		Reward		Coercive
	Information		Legitimate		Connection	

FIGURE 9-3 A continuum of types of power.

power is important in organizations where there may not be a direct boss-subordinate relationship between individuals but cooperation is essential to achieving objectives.

Information Power

He or she who holds the information, has the power—at least the power of information. If someone else—a boss, subordinate, or other decision maker—needs certain information and you have that information, you also have power.

Information power is similar to but different from expert power in that they are both sharing knowledge or information, but the power of expertise is based more on education and knowledge held than is the latter, which is based on information held. For example, a person may be very smart and know a subject backward and forward, but he or she may lack essential skills and information in passing that knowledge along. In a sense, they may not know where the "skeletons in the closet" are located.

Referent Power

Influence based on referent power reflects faith in and following of the leader. A person has referent power if others identify with him or her. This type of power comes as close as any to the charismatic approach or following that is so often talked about. People like to be with or follow this type of powerful person.

People like and follow individuals in whom they see characteristics they admire. They are emotionally attached—perhaps even mesmerized—by this kind of power. They are probably liked personally and may be perceived as a role model or mentor. Individuals with referent power are just plain liked better than others.

Legitimate Power

Legitimate power is based on position and exists because people believe a person has a legitimate right to influence them. It is power delegated from within an organization. Employees feel obligated to follow the power because of the formal position.

Response to legitimate power is almost automatic. The power is so entrenched that a response is routine. If power is exercised over something that is standard operating procedure, a routine response can be expected. There are cultural and social expectations by peers that legitimate power will be followed.

Reward Power

Reward power is just what it sounds like—the holder has the power to reward. A person is influenced by the powerholder who can or does offer a reward and whether that reward satisfies a fundamental need. If people think that their efforts will meet the powerholder's objectives and if they think their efforts will be rewarded, they will follow.

Not all rewards are tangible; a leader can exercise reward power by complimenting another. Reward power is positive reinforcement using various types of incentives such as pay raises, promotions, praise, and recognition. Reward power is most closely related to motivation: it is a matter of finding out what motivates others and attempting to reward them accordingly.

Connection Power

Closely related to rewards, connection power allows the holder to reward others through a network of connections with influential people. As noted before, power is largely a matter of perception, and if the holder is viewed as having powerful connections, the holder has power. An individual may not have strong personal or organizational power, but, if he or she has connections with people who do, that individual can exercise that connection power.

Coercive Power

On the continuum of personal to organizational power, coercive power is most typical of organizational power. Here the powerholder has the power to punish. Like reward power, it is largely a matter of perception but also fact if it is the boss who holds the power. The threat of punishment is as strong as the actual act of punishment as we know from the study of discipline and disciplinary action. Punishment or the threat of it works better in law than in management; it is advisable to minimize the use of coercive power because it hurts human relations and productivity.[5]

Figure 9-4 offers several summary suggestions for eliminating negative reactions to the exercise of power.

1. "It is better to be liked than feared." The general rule is, in most situations, *referent* power is preferable to *coercive* power.

2. Always know what you're doing. It is crucial for persons wishing to exercise power over others to establish a high level of expertise. To the extent that they do, this may enhance their performance.

3. Be legitimate: don't overstep the bounds. Managers have legitimate power over their subordinates to change subordinates' behavior in some ways but not others. It is very important that these boundaries not be overstepped.

4. Style counts: always use the velvet glove. Many managers are unsure how to give directions to their subordinates; most people strongly dislike being told what to do; it makes them angry. Instructions that are phrased as requests rather than commands can prevent employees from feeling that their egos have been squashed.

FIGURE 9-4 **Steps for minimizing negative reactions to power.** Adapted from Robert Baron, "Power in Organizations: Using It Wisely," *Behavior in Organizations,* 2nd ed. (Boston: Allyn & Bacon, 1986, p. 353).

POLITICS

The manifestation of power is a series of political trade-offs. There is always present the idea of "you scratch my back, and I'll scratch yours," or a reciprocal agreement to help one another.

"Playing politics"

Some groups and individuals have formal power to control others directly. Other groups have power to impact others by slowing performance and productivity. Any group can impact others by advancing or withholding power in the form of services rendered, or economic sanctions. This is known as "playing politics."

Politics is a way of distributing power

Fortunately, playing politics is not all bad. It is a positive way of distributing power in offices and other organizations.

Office Politics

Business, or the conduct of any transaction, is by definition a process of give-and-take. If we are to be successful in our transactions, we have to be sensitive to others, their needs and aspirations.

Office politics means tuning into others and their reactions. Specific examples of office politics activities are:

- Congeniality toward coworkers, including bosses and subordinates
- Unusual praise for bosses' or subordinates' work
- Helping a coworker who is struggling with a work-related problem
- Taking action solely to satisfy the boss
- Sharing information in articles or reports
- Communicating positively and selectively, that is, knowing when to say nothing

Do you see any compromises in your values if you engage in these activities?

Organizational Politics

Positive strategies for becoming more powerful

There are various pragmatic strategies for becoming more politically powerful and effective. When all else fails, do what is right—in your own mind, or seek the advice of a trusted counselor. Help others to achieve their objectives and thereby build up your own power. Find a mentor who has connection power. Make alliances and work from a position of strength in numbers. Finally, practice power by example—the action of work well done will speak more loudly than all the status symbols in the world.

Illegitimate strategies may backfire

There are also illegitimate strategies that include blackmail, character assassination, and physical force. These unscrupulous methods are self-serving, and no matter how nasty you may be or think you are, there is always someone who can make you look like an amateur!

Power Plays

How can you recognize the power plays at work? A person shows outward signs of power. There is a solid presence suggesting that the person belongs where he or she is, with a certain immobility, steady eyes, and quiet hands. Nothing can substitute for the combination of self-control and personal magnetism.

Rocklike immobility in times of crisis gives an impression that a person is in control. People who sit still acquire a reputation for common sense and reliability. If you wish to develop such a posture, try not to shift your eyes or blink a lot. Look straight at the person with whom you are conversing and keep your gaze on the person longer than he or she does on you. A relaxed mouth is very helpful, because locking lips, biting lips, or twitching the corners of the mouth can show frustration or nervousness. Perspiration is usually considered a sign of tension or lying.[6]

High-stakes players never ask for favors, but grant them willingly and make sure that there is no way of returning them. They take advantage of these situations in their favor. Such persons establish territorial imperatives by pushing their things gradually toward you or leaving their possessions around. They often ask to use your phone, and, while you politely leave, they will sit at your desk.

The power players are careful to work behind the scene; they don't want publicity. It is better to set things up quietly and patiently, so that what they want is offered to them. Confrontation produces friction and friction slows progress.

POWER RELATIONSHIPS _____

Good leaders obtain authority from groups

People who have authority are not necessarily leaders. All leaders have authority, but all authoritarians are not leaders. Good leaders derive their authority *from* the group.

External Power Is Derived _____

Authority, or externally derived power, usually stems from *position* or rank. Heads of small firms and managers of departments have authority because of their job positions. The director of a corporation will influence numbers of people because of the considerable authority he or she has in the organization. Because of the power vested in the position of the presidency of the United States, a president's policies influence the destinies of the nation and all its people.

External power may also come from *knowledge* or *expertise*. For example, a group applying for a grant may turn for leadership to someone who has applied for grants successfully in the past. A company interested in building a nuclear power plant will look to the most educated and experienced experts in the field of nuclear physics for leadership. Our leaders need—must have—the autonomy and power to lead if they are to be effective.

Michael Korda, author of *Power: How to Get It and How to Use It*, has said we don't have power brokers any longer. He cites Ronald Reagan as a charismatic, powerful individual but states that:

> Those who are not willing to delegate at least some power will eventually lose their own (power)—and their freedom. People who cannot *take* orders are in no position to give orders when they themselves are placed in positions of authority. We have gradually transformed our system of government into a town meeting of over 250 million people in which everyone has an equal right to *prevent* things from being done, but in which no one person can effectively control or begin anything.[7]

A frequent criticism heard of organizations today is that it takes too long to get some things done. Korda tells us why, in part, and leads to the suggestions that we need to capitalize on our power sources and exercise power to produce effective goods and services in a timely fashion.

POWER MEASUREMENTS

How do we know if we are doing a good job? How do we know if we are getting things done effectively? We measure it. Measurements of power include:

- Estimate potential influence by examining the outcomes of contested decisions in an organization.
- Assess power by examining each party's available sources of power and the constraints on its use.
- Examine reputational indicators of power. This approach assumes that a relatively stable power distribution exists at a given point of time, that organization members know who has how much power, and that they are willing to talk candidly about the power distribution.[8]

Other, more objective indicators of power include status symbols such as a person's position title, office location and furnishings, and salary. Special privileges provide an indication of the person's power in the organization. A weakness in this kind of measure is the possibility that status symbols may lag shifts in power or that some powerful persons may prefer to avoid obvious status symbols.[9]

THE SOCIAL BASIS OF STATUS

Definition

Status is ranking by prestige as seen by others

Status is the term applied to the *ranking or ordering of people into relative positions of prestige and the social rewards offered with such positions*. Status involves a two-way transaction that must include at least two people. One person may claim status, but status is not achieved unless the other person confers it. In other words, status is earned.

People of similar social status recognize one another by their social similarities, such as speech, mannerisms, and ways of dressing. People of the same rank consider one another equals. The various status levels are acknowledged and maintained on the basis of social differences that separate people from one another. In the assignment of status roles, certain differences are emphasized, whereas other differences—as well as similarities—are ignored. Which characteristics become the bases for social position depends on what is considered important to a particular society.

Some of the most common characteristics used to classify people are: (1) wealth and possessions; (2) education; (3) appointed authority; (4) ethnic background, religion, or race; (5) ancestry; (6) income; (7) occupation; and (8) political and economic power. The significance of ancestry, ethnic origin, or kinship is more important in some countries than others. In China, Great Britain, Kenya, and other African countries these factors are more important than in the United States. Similarly, level of education has more significance in European countries than it does in the United States.

Express Your Opinion	Does it make sense to classify or stereotype people by any means? Do you have ethical or moral reservations about such classifications?

Social Stratification

Social stratification is the ranking of people within society, by others, into higher and lower social positions to produce a hierarchy of respect or prestige. The things that people want, such as money, position, or security, are all in short supply and are distributed unevenly.

The status system is a way of recognizing this uneven distribution of social values; that is, it is a way of according the people at or near the top the respect due them for having the most of what society wants.

We can do little to change our heredity, race, or ethnic background, but if we desire, we can change our education, income, occupation, or power. Some may be able to upgrade themselves through a form of status over which they have some control; for example, those who try to enhance their prestige or status by using power.

STATUS SYMBOLS

The attainment of power and rank are considered normal work goals, and this process plays an important role in organizational incentive systems. In fact, the privileges attached to high-status positions are sometimes even more important to workers than is the money they earn.

The more observable the tasks, the easier it is to discern status. In physical or manual work, the levels of skill and responsibility a job requires are readily

Importance of jobs is often determined by the symbols

apparent. In offices, however, everyone shuffles papers, and, because jobs tend to look similar, more obvious external signs of status are needed. The importance of jobs, then, remains to be judged by the symbols attached to them.

Generally, the larger the organization, the more preoccupied are its workers with status symbols. Large organizations operate much like the military, with highly visible status symbols serving as a way of communicating authority. Because of the close personal contacts usually present in small companies, where everybody knows who has the power, symbols of authority are not as necessary.

Hours and Pay

Salary has more status than wages. Why?

Hourly workers who are required to punch time clocks do not have the same amount of status as those who receive fixed salaries—even though the hourly employees may earn more money.

Fixed working hours have less prestige

Working during fixed daily hours usually carries less prestige than being paid to complete specific projects. Only "important" employees are given the freedom to work around the clock or to not show up at all. Employees often indicate their high status by being casual about the hours they work: arriving late, leaving early, taking long lunch hours and breaks, and randomly leaving work stations to chat with other workers. Lower-status employees must observe rigid work schedules and strict eating and resting periods. So-called "hourly" employees can actually be paid for minutes worked and may even have to request permission to go to the bathroom.

An office worker has more status than a laborer

Relative pay standards within organizations do not apply consistently within the larger society. A relatively high wage may indicate monetary *compensation* to make up for low status. For example, a construction worker doing manual labor usually has less social prestige than does an office clerk. Yet construction workers make two to three times more money than do office clerks.

Despite the difference in pay, certain people wish to change from being a blue-collar worker to a white-collar worker. Why? (1) Supervision is more relaxed. (2) If the white-collar job is nonunion, there is less likelihood of being harassed and having to follow the many rules of unions. (3) Informal dialogue replaces the formal interview in the hiring process. (4) Grievances are likely to be handled through counseling by the supervisor rather than through a rigid grievance system.

Work Environment

Status can be conferred by any agreed-upon formula. The placement of a machinist's machine, the location of a parking spot, the location of a personal locker—all can carry status significance. Working near the end of the production line usually carries more status than does working near the beginning because the finished product is more valuable. Working on the eighth floor with the salespeople can imply less status than working on the tenth floor near the manager's office. Do you agree with these implications?

The aspects of the work environment that go beyond meeting utilitarian needs are usually placed there for the sake of status. Just about any environmental factor can be incorporated into creating a desired image: size of facility, layout and size of work areas, furniture, colors, decorations, temperature, humidity, ventilation, noise, and lighting are all status indicators.

Table 9-1 lists the furnishings allowed the various occupations in a small

TABLE 9-1 Office Furniture Allotment

1. Department head or equivalent	Desk, table, credenza, swivel chair, four to six arm chairs, 12′ chalkboard, files as required
2. Section head	Desk, table, swivel chair, four to six side chairs, 8′ chalkboard, two bookcases, files as required
3. Supervisor	Desk, table, swivel chair, two side chairs, bookcase, chalkboard space, four-drawer file
4. Scientist or engineer	Desk, swivel chair, side chair, chalkboard space, bookcase, four-drawer file cabinet
5. Secretary, clerical, etc.	Desk, swivel chair, file, furniture as authorized by department head
6. Draft, tech, hourly, etc.	No furniture

research firm in California. In this company the furnishings obviously indicate precise levels of status.

Within organizations, the value of certain status symbols depends on high demand and limited supply. If all the offices are already plush, then the size and location of work areas will indicate the status. For example, in most companies the few corner offices have premium status, followed by the rarely available offices with windows. Windowless offices are more numerous and, hence, lower in status. In offices with no windows, lighting is often used as a status criterion.

Corner offices have a higher premium

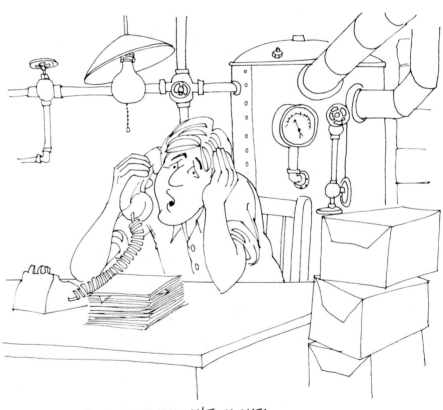

"HONEY, I WASN'T KICKED UPSTAIRS AFTER ALL!"

Normally, higher status is attached to the people having better working conditions. The better the working conditions, the higher the status. That is why white-collar jobs usually carry more status than blue-collar jobs of equal skill and pay. The status value given to different conditions has a supply-and-demand effect similar to that in economics. When supply is adequate relative to demand, the status value will be less than when demand exceeds supply. For example, if there were a great demand for plumbers and carpenters and few trained, their status would go up; likewise, if the demand for nurses and druggists were low, the status of these professions would drop.

Clothing and Cars

Throughout history, dress has been an important way in which to determine people's status. The mass production of clothing in the twentieth century has eliminated many traditional status distinctions based on dress. Today, "dirt" rather than fashion is the determining factor in the different attitudes that white- and blue-collar workers have about their work clothing. The basic dress distinction between the two groups is that white-collar workers can wear fashionable street clothes to work and blue-collar workers must wear clothes to protect them from dirt.

Lab technicians, nurses, waiters and waitresses, police personnel, and many other people employed in service industries wear uniforms to work every day. People expect the police, airline stewardesses, and nurses to wear readily identifiable clothing on the job. (See Figure 9-5). Some banks, public utilities, and insurance companies also provide "work clothes" for employees. The advantage of career apparel is that it tends to boost employee morale for a while, it improves the public image, it is tax deductible for the employer or the employee, and the cost is

Career apparel can affect morale

FIGURE 9-5 **Many people expect some government employees and others to wear readily identifiable clothing on the job.** Spectra.

small when compared with what a person would normally pay for a work wardrobe during a year. The disadvantage is the significant cost. There is also a loss of individuality, and the apparel program either becomes old and dull after a few years, or must be revamped.

Some American workers seem to like the convenience of uniforms. Honda provides each worker with eight and launders and mends them. "It saves deciding what to wear to work," said one worker. Company uniforms are a cultural value in Japan. "In Japan, what counts most is the group relationship and one's ability to conform to it." Individualism is frowned upon. An old Japanese aphorism holds that, "the nail that sticks out usually gets hammered down."

Janet Guthrie, the first woman to compete in the Indianapolis 500, writes that "In an age of individual affluence and mobility formerly unknown, the automobile rivals clothing as a statement of social, professional and political position, philosophical affiliation and wealth."[10]

HOW STATUS AFFECTS COMMUNICATION _____

The more one wants to move up, the less accurate the communication

Status affects the manner in which people communicate with one another. (See Figure 9-6.) The ability to move upward in the organizational hierarchy greatly

FIGURE 9-6 Status conferred can affect communications. Respect or status you give your supervisor may determine how you react.

affects the nature of communication. (See Figure 9-7.) Talking with a·supervisor, even about the job, is a form of socialization often used to gain favor with supervisors. Employees may minimize actual disagreements with their supervisors to put themselves in favorable light.[11] A study done in three large industrial organizations found that information communicated to supervisors is heavily filtered when it reflects incompetence and thus threatens the security or progress of subordinates. The study discovered that the more people aspire to move upward, the less accurate is their communication upward.[12] Another study concluded that, when low-ranking members of an organization are in a position to move upward, they are exceedingly guarded in their relations with those of higher rank who can interfere with their progress.[13]

Good communicators have a better chance of having their ideas accepted by the boss than noncommunicative individuals. The ability to communicate well can itself be status producing.

JOB STATUS

Titles and Positions

Job titles promote status distinctions. An executive has more job status than a shipping clerk; a secretary more status than a typist; a journeyman more status than an apprentice.

Status distinctions sometimes make us forget that many different kinds of work are necessary to the smooth functioning of our total society. They tend to separate us and to add to existing social and political tensions, particularly in large cities.

Little change in occupational status in 30 years

In 1981, *Gallup Report* found that relative rankings of certain professions had not changed appreciably in 30 years. In descending order of prestige or status, 12 professions ranked were MDs, judges, clergy, bankers, lawyers, public school

THOSE DESIRING PROMOTION MOST
1. ARE MORE GUARDED WITH THEIR COMMUNICATIONS.
2. MINIMIZE DISAGREEMENTS WITH SUPERVISORS.
3. FILTER OUT OR MINIMIZE THEIR PROBLEMS.
4. STICK MORE TO "BUSINESS" TALK
5. COMMUNICATE MORE WITH SUPERIORS.

FIGURE 9-7 **Those who want promotions have different speech patterns.**

principals, business executives, public school teachers, funeral directors, local political office holders, advertising practitioners, and realtors.[14]

The secretary's status is determined by boss's status

The same job title can carry differences in status caused by the status of the organization or the supervisor. The salesperson for an international company has a "better" job than does the salesperson working for a local manufacturer. The secretary to the senior vice president has more status than does the secretary to the sales division manager. The architect who designs huge office buildings can be more influential with colleagues than can the architect who designs only small dwellings.

Professionalism

Professionals are experts

Sometimes the only difference between an "occupation" and a "profession" is the social status accorded to various jobs. Attempts to "upgrade" or "professionalize" occupations are attempts to gain greater social recognition for certain kinds of work. Sometimes the nature of the work warrants such desires to raise status, sometimes it does not.

Aspects of a Profession

1. Career is restricted to credentials and professional training: more requirements limit the number who will enter the field; examples: law school, medical school.
2. Activities that do not enhance one's prestige are dropped.
3. Tasks that already have status are claimed as part of the profession.
4. The profession is consulted early in the decision making.
5. The words of the more professional "experts" are challenged less.

Express Your Opinion

Today as more and more people attend college in hopes of upgrading their status and more career fields are requiring more professional training, some interesting things are developing. In many areas of the United States, over 50 percent of the high school graduates will continue their education by going to college.

Many fields state that they are professionals or experts. Such career areas are requiring that people pass more tests or take more college courses to be accepted into the realm of the professionals. For example, in the past twenty years the real estate field in California has gradually required more and more professional or college coursework to receive the designation of "realtor."

With more people attempting to become "professional," will the term have less meaning in the next century? Further, as more people are becoming more educated, are they challenging the words of the "experts" or professionals now more than they did five or ten years ago? Should the public question professionals, such as lawyers, doctors, dentists, engineers, and educators more or less than they do now? Why? Is this questioning authority? What is your opinion?

Status Inconsistency and Ambiguities

If all roles have the same status, life is consistent

The indicators of status include title, pay position, and symbols. Each of these is a barometer that measures a different aspect of status. As long as all these status indicators give approximately the same readings, status is not likely to cause trouble to the individual or the organization. But when such indicators of status give inconsistent measures, personnel unrest and dissatisfaction will ensue.

Ambiguous situations in which the status position of an individual or group has not been established clearly can be troublesome. In a sense, status symbols are characterized by a "culture lag," as they do not keep up with technological and organizational changes. Newly created groups obviously suffer status identification, because there is no easy placement using the present status indicator.

At work, people with seniority do *not* always have the highest-status jobs or earn the most money. Office jobs may pay less than factory jobs, even though it is generally agreed that office workers enjoy higher occupational status. Sometimes supervisors earn less than the employees under them.

Several roles have similar expectations

But different status rankings for roles lead to inconsistencies

As noted, inconsistent measures may result in personnel unrest and dissatisfaction. The more prestigious group members expect to occupy the more prestigious jobs. The longer-service, better-educated employee expects extra respect, but may not receive it. The employee with a prestigious family background and education who works in a low-status job may feel uncomfortable and may demonstrate aggression. Employees who enjoy status consistency are less likely to feel the stress and difficulties than are those who do not.

"Status anxiety"

One can anticipate that "status anxiety" would show itself when an employee is unable to cope with his or her expected status. Certainly status anxieties are not helped by the fact that the indicators of status are often complex and not easily discerned. When there is status inconsistency in the various roles that a person is asked to perform, one can see how status anxiety is likely to be higher.

SUCCESS AND FAILURE

Success breeds success—confidence is gained when enterprises meet with favorable responses and feelings of accomplishment. Similarly, failure breeds failure—unless realistic goals are set and adequately met, individuals can come to believe that they do everything wrong—all the time. The perception of the self as a habitual failure affects the outcome of further efforts and a vicious cycle of cause and effect is created.

In most cases, high status is a symbol of success, and many people assume that they will feel successful when they attain a higher status. In fact, however, achieving higher status brings feelings of true success only when feelings of genuine achievement are experienced. Genuine achievements require constant challenge. Success is based on a *continuum* of changing goals that can be envisioned and then met. When *successive* challenges are not offered, only stagnation and frustration result.

Genuine achievement requires constant challenge

The levels of job status influence the *ability* to achieve feelings of success. Usually, the lower the job status, the greater the specification of the work routine. This means that there is relatively little opportunity for creativity, judgment, and initiative to come into play. Usually, the higher the job level, the greater opportunity to tackle new problems. The motivation to experience increased self-esteem through dealing successfully with *new* problems should not be underestimated. And it is probably best to remember that success is never final and that failure is seldom fatal.

Failure is seldom fatal

Summary

There are basically two sources of power: personal and organizational. Organizational power means the capacity of managers to exert influence over others. It is derived from higher-level authority and is delegated downward in an organization. Personal power, on the other hand, is obtained from the acceptance of followers, not from higher-level management.

Power is only as useful as it is accepted and recognized by those over whom it is exercised. Increasingly, in today's organizations, the people who have the knowledge and information, have the power.

Other types of power include legitimate power, which is based on organizational position; referent power, which is based on personal power; expert power based on skill and knowledge; and reward and coercive power based on the ability of the powerholder to reward or punish others. Connection power is based on the powerholder's ability to relate to influential people.

Politics is one means of gaining and using power. "Playing politics" is advancing or withholding power in the form of services rendered, or economic sanctions. It is a way of distributing power in offices and other organizations.

Status is rated according to relative rank. Status positions are rewarded in different ways according to rank. While higher status can be claimed by someone, it does not actually exist unless it is acknowledged by others. Society establishes specific behaviors and symbols by which status is acknowledged.

A salary has more status than wages, and fixed working hours have less prestige than flexible hours. Likewise, office workers have more status than laborers, because office work is "clean," even though the pay may well be less than that of the blue-collar worker. The location of offices, the clothes that people wear, and people's perceived height seem to affect the status people are given.

The ability to succeed affects self-esteem. Achieving higher status is perceived as a sign of success only when the individual has set a goal and met it, gaining status in the process. Self-worth is so important that workers in the most mundane jobs find ways in which to achieve a sense of success.

Case Study 18

The Powerful Professor

Max Stillwell is a senior professor in the College of Applied Sciences at the State University of New Hampton. He has been on the faculty for over 20 years and served as dean of the college for 10 of those years. After his "retirement" from the dean's job 5 years ago, he went back to full-time teaching.

As a dean, Max exercised considerable monetary control over his own and other college budgets. Nevertheless, he never thought of himself as particularly powerful. He continues to serve on a number of universitywide committees and is frequently called upon in his area of expertise—training and development. In fact, colleagues in the College of Extended Learning (CEL) frequently ask him to serve as a committee member on graduate students' committees. One of Max's friends who is a CEL faculty member, John Dickinson, asked Max to serve as a speaker at a summer conference sponsored by CEL. John made it clear initially that there would be no honorarium or other remuneration, but Max still agreed to give the talk.

One of the reasons Max accepted was that he wanted to learn more about the particular subject that he was asked to talk about. He rationalized that this experience would give him the opportunity to learn. In fact, he did conduct research and learn quite a bit about the subject before giving the talk, which was acclaimed successful by both John and the participants at the conference.

Another reason that Max accepted was that he and John, among others in CEL, were friends. He wanted to maintain that friendship. He told John he was accepting for the friendship reason, but he also knew that John might be able to repay the favor at another time.

1. What kinds of power has Max had in the past?
2. What kinds of power did Max exercise in giving the talk?
3. What kinds of power did John exercise in asking Max to give the talk?
4. Do you see the different sources and types of power at work?
5. Do you see an example of the norm of reciprocity at work?
6. Do you think most of Max's power is from personal or organizational sources? informal or formal sources?

Case Study 19

Status Reversal

How would you feel if a person who had worked under you for a long time suddenly became your boss, taking a job you had wanted and for which you felt qualified? Doubtless you would have feelings of disappointment, competitiveness, anger, and insecurity.

Status reversal is a frequent problem at all levels in organizations. But when it occurs at the pinnacle of a complex organization, which badly needs the optimum talent and experience of both people involved, it represents a problem of considerable consequence.

A difficult relationship problem between two key officers need not be felt with the same intensity by both parties for it to cause damage. In this case, each executive was highly ambivalent about the other prior to the reversal of their status. When the status reversal was announced, Alan McLean, the man who had been senior, generated negative attitudes. By contrast, the new superior, Norman Menninger, became more positive, tolerant, understanding, and caring toward his former boss.

In this instance both parties concerned recognized that they had to do something. Their experience and norms of their organization were such that they felt that in the best interests of human relations and the company something should be done. So they came to you, a coworker.

1. Is this a short-term or a long-term problem?
2. Is it best to bring in an outside consultant on the problem?
3. Should counseling take place and, if so, what kind of counseling?
4. What specific steps can be taken to solve this problem?

Terms and Concepts

class structure or social stratification the ranking of people within the society, by others, into higher and lower social positions to produce a hierarchy of prestige or respect.

connection power based on the powerholder's ability to relate to influential people.

expert power personal power based on skill and knowledge.

legitimate power organizational power based on position.

norm of reciprocity an obligation to return consideration to another for continuance of a mutually beneficial relationship.

occupational prestige ranking occupations in terms of status. Income is not the most important trait to consider. Creativity, responsibility, variety of tasks, and special education are the greatest determinants in placing an occupation within the ranking.

organizational power the capacity of managers to exert influence over others; derived from higher-level authority.

personal power obtained from the acceptance of followers, not from higher-level management.

professional a career type that is recognized by others as a profession. It is determined primarily by a college degree and/or special licensing.

referent power a following based on personal power; almost charismatic.

status anxiety difficulty in changing role behavior to each of the status roles.

status inconsistency inconsistencies due to different status assignments awarded by society.

Notes

1. Michael Korda, *Power, How to Get It and How to Use It!* (New York: Random House, 1975), p. 16.
2. Hedrick Smith, *The Power Game: How Washington Works* (New York: Random House, 1988), pp. xxii, 42.
3. Adapted from J. Kenneth Matejka, D. Ashworth, and Diane Dodd-McCue, "More Power to Ya!" *Management Quarterly*, Winter 1985–1986, pp. 33–36.
4. Hugh Taylor, "Power at Work," *Personnel Journal*, April 1986, p. 48.
5. Fernando Bartholome and Andre Laurent, "The Manager: Master and Servant of Power," *Harvard Business Review*, November–December 1986, p. 81.
6. Korda, *Power: How to Get It and How to Use It!* p. 35.
7. Michael Korda, "The Gradual Decline and Total Collapse of Nearly Everyone," *Family Weekly*, August 29, 1982, p. 5.
8. Gary A. Yukl, *Organizational Behavior and Personnel Psychology*, rev. ed. (Homewood, Ill.: R. D. Irwin, 1984), p. 221.
9. Ibid.
10. Janet Guthrie, "Scaling Down Status," *Working Woman*, December 1983, p. 74.
11. Phillip B. Applewhite, *Organizational Behavior* (Englewood Cliffs, N.J.: Prentice-Hall, 1965), p. 60.
12. Ibid.
13. Ibid., pp. 95–96.
14. "Professions: Contributions to Society, Stress, Prestige," *Gallup Report* No. 193, October 1981, p. 17.

Recommended Reading

Aschenbrenner, Gary L., and Robert D. Snelling. "Communicate with Power." *Business Credit*, April 1988, pp. 39–42, 54.

Blanchard, Ken, and Norman Vincent Peale. *The Power of Ethical Management: It's Smart to Be Ethical.* New York: William Morrow, 1988.

Cohen, Allan R., and David L. Bradford. *Influence Without Authority.* New York: John Wiley, 1990.

Conger, Jay A. "Leadership: The Art of Empowering Others," *The Academy of Management EXECUTIVE*, February 1989, pp. 17–24.

Cunningham, Mary, with Fran Schumer. *Powerplay.* New York: Linden Press/Simon & Schuster, 1984.

Francis, Dave, and Mike Woodcock. *Unblocking Organizational Values*. Glenview, Ill.: Scott, Foresman, 1990.

Greiner, Larry, and Virginia E. Schein. *Power and Organization Development: Mobilizing Power to Implement Change*. Reading, Mass.: Addison-Wesley, 1988.

Halberstam, Joshua. "The Allure of Power: A Visit with Arnold A. Hutschnecker, MD," *CV Magazine*, February–March 1989, pp. 71–72.

Korda, Michael. *Power: How to Get It and How to Use It!* New York: Random House, 1975.

Kotter, John P. *Power in Management*. New York: AMACOM, 1979.

Mangham, Iain L. *Power and Performance in Organizations: An Exploration of Executive Process*. New York: Basil Blackwell, 1986.

Mintzberg, Henry. *Power in and Around Organizations*. Englewood Cliffs, N.J.: Prentice-Hall, 1983.

Molloy, John T. *Dress for Success*. New York: Warner Books, 1975.

Pfeffer, Jeffrey. *Power in Organizations*. Marshfield, Mass.: Pitman, 1981.

Vincent, David R. "Understanding Organizational Power," *Journal of Business Strategy*, March–April 1988, pp. 40–44.

Weiss, Alan. *Managing for Peak Performance: A Guide to the Power (and Pitfalls) of Personal Style*. New York: Harper & Row, 1989.

10

Leadership

After studying this chapter, you should be able to:

1. Discuss the roles that a task leader and a social leader play in groups.
2. Discuss the relevance of technical skills, human relations, and conceptual skills to leadership.
3. Explain each of the following functional roles that leaders play to keep a group unified:
   a. Identifying goals
   b. Making decisions
   c. Resolving differences
4. Explain the advantages and disadvantages of the following styles of leadership behavior and how they relate to McGregor's theories of leadership:
   a. Autocratic
   b. Participative
   c. Free rein
5. List the eight features of Theory Z.
6. Discuss Fred Fiedler's "contingency model" and give examples of its theory in practice.
7. Explain the path-goal process of leadership and subordinate effectiveness.
8. Distinguish between leadership and management.

TO START YOU THINKING . . .

Look at these questions before reading the chapter. Some answers may be found in the chapter; others can only be answered by personal opinion.

♦ Is there an ideal leader for all situations?
♦ What are the personality traits of leaders?
♦ What kind of leader is needed for a crisis?
♦ Do leaders have more intelligence than their followers?
♦ What is the function of a leader in a group?
♦ How can the leader create a win-win environment?
♦ When is close supervision or general supervision best for most Americans?
♦ What traits of Theory Z could Americans adopt in their culture?
♦ What is the best type of leader in classroom or group discussion?
♦ What type of leader are you? Why?
♦ Free-rein leadership means almost no control by the leader; therefore it should not be used by supervisors. Do you agree?

WHAT IS LEADERSHIP?

Breaking through the Myths

Leadership, like common sense, is somewhat elusive and not so common. Boards of directors of business organizations complain, "What we need are more leaders!" Whole nations cry, "If only we had a great leader, we would be on the way to solving our major problems." Tom Peters and Nancy Austin suggest that what we need in American business is *leadership*, not management.[1] They argue that leadership is crucial to a "Back to Basics" revolution in American business. But what is a leader?

Leadership is such an elusive concept partly because people do not define themselves in leadership terms. Someone coming home from a community meeting might say, "I sure got them to come around to my point of view." Or "I was surprised at how carefully they listened to what I had to say." But if asked, "Did you *lead* the group?" that person would be apt to answer, "Well, not really." Furthermore, followers are unclear about their reasons for choosing leaders.

Leadership is not so mysterious

Researchers interested in defining leadership continue to have new ideas about it. One safe generalization, based on studies that have been made in the past 40 years, is that leadership is not nearly as mysterious as has been commonly thought. Warren Bennis, former university president and prolific author on leadership, believes you can do a lot to teach executives to be more imaginative, to communicate better, and to be more self-aware. But, beyond that, he says instilling leadership gets tougher: "Can you teach judgment, taste, wit? . . . You can't teach curiosity, energy, and resonance"—the ability to set something sympathetic vibrating around you. Noel Tichy and others agree: "Everyone can improve, but not everyone can become world class." Tichy estimates that 80 percent of a leader's growth comes form his or her job experience, but that the remaining 20 percent can be shaped by training and study.[2]

Defining Leadership

Inspiration, sales ability, and persuasion cannot have any impact unless there is some measure of *influence* over the audience or group. A person may be good at making dramatic speeches but not inspire anyone to become a follower. The best propaganda in the world may not convince anybody. The most persuasive arguments may fall on deaf ears. Only if a group *wishes* to be influenced can a leader function. Leadership can be defined as the ability to influence the actions of others. Leaders are going places and have the ability to inspire others to go along. The ability to cause others to follow a common goal is one sure way of recognizing leadership.

Leaders initiate change

Leaders initiate change, either by making decisions or by encouraging others to make them. A group's trust in its leader is affected by the quality of his or her decisions. Whether or not the decisions are good, people who follow leaders must accept the decisions made and the process used in making them.

Following Leaders

There is nearly always an element of uncertainty or confusion that prompts people to choose and follow a leader. Sometimes followers are attracted to a leader who represents their values. They are willing to place themselves under the leadership of someone who can help them to refine and act on values. Those values must be made attractive and acceptable to the followers. A good leader must be able to develop and work with subordinates.

Groups need leaders to reduce confusion and uncertainty

Groups need leaders to reduce uncertainty and confusion. If a group is functioning smoothly, very little leadership may be required. Leadership can have an important effect on a group's morale, especially since one of its chief functions is to keep the group focused on its goals. When it becomes necessary to stabilize unstable situations, aggressive leadership is required.

Being a Leader

Well-functioning groups never remain leaderless, but a group doesn't necessarily have only one leader. A group *can* have one leader, but *every* member of a group can also be a leader. Some leaders prefer to monopolize power; other leaders rely on all or several members of the group to display leadership individually. Group members who trust one another can mutually influence group decision making. People may hold back their abilities to lead for many reasons—perhaps because they lack confidence in themselves, perhaps because the situation does not allow leadership. However, *all people are potential leaders.* And, given the desire and the opportunity, people can develop into effective leaders.

All people are potential leaders

Another essential attribute of a leader is the ability to follow. A good leader must give and take depending upon the situation. As group goals and tasks change, new leaders and shifts in power result. As work is delegated, authority roles change. Leadership in a group depends on the group standards and the leadership rules that are acceptable.

When Is a Leader Best?	A leader is best When people barely know he exists, Not so good when people obey and acclaim him, Worst when they despise him. Fail to honor people They fail to honor you; But of a good leader, who talks little, When his work is done, his aim fulfilled, They will all say, "We did this ourselves." Lao-tzu, 6th century B.C., Chinese philosopher

A classic example of the type of leader who also follows is Peter Ueberroth. Ueberroth organized the 1984 Olympics in Los Angeles and then became major league baseball commissioner. During the one-and-a-half-day baseball strike in 1985, Ueberroth was credited by club owners and players with keeping the talks going even after the strike began. Keeping the talks going prevented gridlock and an impasse.[3] Ueberroth himself, however, denied any role in solving the strike.

> I want you to know very clearly that I had no role. This was done by these two teams of people headed by (union chief) Don Fehr and (management negotiator) Lee MacPhail. They put baseball back on the field. They had to be sure they did it right and they did do it right. Now they have a success. I was glad I could help them keep going, but I was of no consequence when it came to the actual negotiations.[4]

LEADERSHIP TRAITS _____

For many years, social scientists tried to isolate and analyze the personal characteristics necessary for effective leadership. Most of these attempts were found to be unsound because the research conclusions were based on predetermined models of leadership. Many of the lists of traits were anecdotal—that is, based on one "great man" or another who exhibited certain traits. Then respondents would draw up a list of what they thought leaders should be.

Today, researchers have examined more aspects of the human personality than were even conceived of 20 years ago. And remarkably few consistent leadership traits have been isolated. Lester Bittel lists the following desirable traits of successful leaders based on interviews with both executives and employees:

Energy	Personality
Perseverance	Self-confidence
Education and scholarship	Creativity and initiative
Intelligence	Objectivity and balance
Good judgment	Enthusiasm and optimism[5]
Stature	

Surprisingly, such traits as height, weight, appearance, self-control, dominance, alertness, cheerfulness, and geniality have little relation to leadership. Nevertheless, remember that some of the reasons for selecting leaders and spokesmen for the 1985 airline hostages in Beirut were their height, physical appearance, and dominance. Later, the leadership of these individuals was repudiated by some. See Figure 10-1 for a checklist that addresses more substantive measures of leadership.

Leader's IQ is usually higher than the average of the group

Intelligence has only a relative relationship. The leaders usually have a higher intelligence than the average of those they lead, regardless of the group, be it a group of manual laborers or a group of professional technicians. Intelligence as we know it is based in part on environmental factors such as formal education and past experience. The intelligence of a leader may not be much greater than that of his or her peers, but the leader is able to see the relationship between the task at hand and the personalities of those who must perform it. A leader's perception of the followers enables him or her to motivate group members into action. A leader also tends to have more abstract reasoning ability than his or her peers.

The leader reflects the group's values

A leader's personality traits tell just as much about the group as they do about the leader because the leader reflects the group's standards and values. For example, the members of a chamber of commerce might choose to be influenced by the president of a large bank, whereas the members of a group studying crime in the cities might accept the leadership of a person living in a ghetto. Again, the hostages of the airline hijacking and their "leaders" or spokesmen provide a good example of leaders reflecting group norms.

Social Popularity _____

Being popular implies a desire for friendly personal interaction. A leader can be very decisive and even unpleasant during a group discussion and very amiable among friends in a social setting.[6]

The desire to be well liked may inhibit certain leadership abilities. For

1. Have you assessed the degree to which others perceive your status as leader, the extent of formal authority granted your position, and the informal authority others grant to you in recognition of your knowledge, experience, and demonstrated effectiveness?

2. Are you aware of the various norms that your work group has developed? Do you know the workers' standards of behavior—especially those affecting the quality and quantity of work?

3. Have you decided how much freedom you will extend to employees in establishing work standards, how far they can go collectively without interfering with the attainment of the organization's goals?

4. Can you tolerate the dual loyalty of others—to their friends or work group as well as to you?

5. Have you identified the informal leaders in your organization, those individuals to whom others look for guidance or approval, even though they have no formal authority?

6. Have you established a communications network that serves the leadership needs in the most effective fashion?

7. Do you prepare your subordinates for organizational changes that will affect their status, security, or job responsibilities?

8. Have you taken appropriate steps to win the confidence of others in your ability to handle change by demonstrating the reliability of your previous decisions?

9. Do you provide sufficient opportunity for others to participate in plans for implementing change so that they will accept the rationale of new standards of performance?

10. Do you maintain a watch over new standards during the settling-in period that follows change, regularly reinforcing or adjusting the standards to accommodate unanticipated circumstances?

FIGURE 10-1 **Leadership Checklist.** Source: Lester R. Bittel, *Leadership: The Key to Management Success* (New York: Franklin Watts, 1984), pp. 49–50.

instance, at a two-week training session at the National Training Laboratory in Bethel, Maine, one observer noticed that out of the 20 people in a group, the most popular person did not contribute very much at all to formulating group goals. "The individual in question was, in everybody's opinion, a 'nice guy.' He was pleasant to everyone. But he never suggested what the group should do, nor did he give strong support to any position stated by any other member of the group."[7]

"Risk-taking" in leadership

Well-liked people do have an advantage in that they can bring group members "around" and help achieve consensus. Group members concerned with social relations often act as leaders in attempting to keep the group unified.

The group leader is not always the most popular group member. Assuming leadership by presenting new ideas and helping to make decisions may make a person admired but not liked. Part of "taking the risk" of leadership is that "taking a stand" does not always make a person popular with all group members.

Group Relationships

The "social leader" and the "task leader"

A group might develop two types of leaders, the "social leader" and the "task leader," each one having his or her own function and each complementing the other in achieving the goal with a minimum of conflict. The task leader contributes most to the achievement of the task, but difficulty may arise, because, in playing this role, the task leader may irritate people and injure the unity of the group. It is the social leader's role to restore and maintain group unity and satisfaction. Seldom can one person fill both roles, so it is important for the task leader to recognize the social leader and to achieve a coalition.[8]

The social leader maintains group unity

Dr. Thomas Gordon emphasizes the importance of the group in making the leader.

> Being a leader doesn't make you one. For after you get to be the leader of a group, you're going to have to do a lot to earn the acceptance of the group members and have an influence on their behavior. Even more important, the acquisition of a leadership title—supervisor, department head, president, manager, or just plain boss—soon brings unexpected disappointments and uninvited problems. Undoubtedly you'll see evidence of jealousy on the part of some of your group members. Others may show resentment because they didn't get your job; in their eyes *you* didn't deserve the position, *they* did.[9]

Leaders must create a win-win environment. A win-win environment is one where all parties—the organization, the leader, and the followers—win. There can be benefits to all parties.[10]

Functional Roles

There are times when leaders must make decisions. The leader's wishes certainly have weight in making choices—the extent depends on the distribution of power within the group. Leaders can help to clarify possible alternatives of action and prevent groups from stalemating or turning into debating societies.

In some cases, the leader may make the decision by default. The chances of the decision being acceptable to the group is enhanced if the group participates in the decision.

A leader can act as an arbitrator for the group. In this function, the leader does not usually participate directly in the group process, as when group decisions are being made, but tries to stay uninvolved and neutral. In this arbitration role, the leader listens to all sides of the argument and helps group members to arrive at a solution or, ultimately, takes action to decide the issue alone. A leader is often put in the position of arbitrator to *prevent* serious group splintering.

LEADERSHIP STYLES

Along with different leadership traits and functions, the *styles* in which leaders perform can also be described. The various styles are based on types of *control* that leaders exercise in a group and their behavior toward group members.

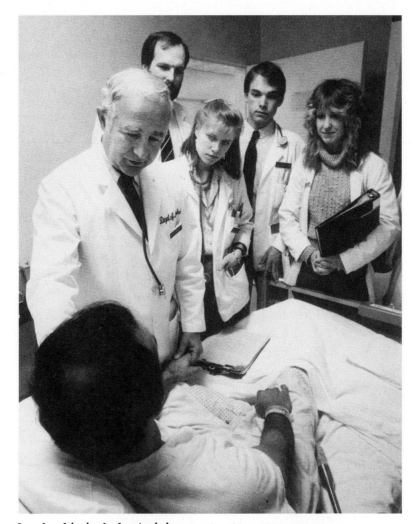

Leadership includes training. David Witbeck/The Picture Cube

Theorists of behavior styles did not dismiss the force of leaders' personalities, but they found that leaders use leadership styles consistent with their personalities. For example, someone who has trouble trusting other people's judgment will tend toward an authoritarian leadership style. Someone else will choose to be authoritarian simply as a way of saving time. One person's lack of trust and the other's desire for efficiency are both consistent with the authoritarian leadership style. Many different styles dependent on the situation lie between the authoritarian and, at the other extreme, highly participative styles discussed in the next section.

TEST YOURSELF LEADERSHIP QUIZ

Take the following quiz and find out something about yourself and your leadership capabilities.

1. People work mostly for money and status rewards.
   a. I agree.

b. I disagree.

c. I feel the statement is sometimes true, sometimes not.

2. People need to be "inspired" (pep talks) or pushed or driven.
    a. I agree.
    b. I disagree.
    c. I feel the statement is sometimes true, sometimes not.

3. People are naturally compartmentalized; work demands are entirely different from leisure activities.
    a. I agree.
    b. I disagree.
    c. I feel the statement is sometimes true, sometimes not.

4. People naturally resist change; they prefer to stay in the old ruts.
    a. I agree.
    b. I disagree.
    c. I feel the statement is sometimes true, sometimes not.

5. Jobs are primary and must be done; people are selected, trained, and fitted to predefined jobs.
    a. I agree.
    b. I disagree.
    c. I feel the statement is sometimes true, sometimes not.

6. The main force keeping people productive in their work is the desire to achieve their personal and social goals.
    a. I agree.
    b. I disagree.
    c. I feel the statement is sometimes true, sometimes not.

7. People are naturally integrated; when work and play are separated too sharply, both deteriorate.
    a. I agree.
    b. I disagree.
    c. I feel the statement is sometimes true, sometimes not.

8. People naturally tire of monotonous routine and enjoy new experiences; in some degree everyone is creative.
    a. I agree.
    b. I disagree.
    c. I feel the statement is sometimes true, sometimes not.

9. People are primary and seek self-realization; jobs must be designed, modified, and fitted to people.
    a. I agree.
    b. I disagree.
    c. I feel the statement is sometimes true, sometimes not.

10. People constantly grow; it is never too late to learn; people enjoy learning and increasing their understanding and capability.
    a. I agree.
    b. I disagree.
    c. I feel the statement is sometimes true, sometimes not.

Now is the time to score your quiz.

SCORING

1. a. X	2. a. X	3. a. X	4. a. X
b. Y	b. Y	b. Y	b. Y
c. neither	c. neither	c. neither	c. neither

5. a. X	7. a. Y	9. a. Y
b. Y	b. X	b. X
c. neither	c. neither	c. neither
6. a. Y	8. a. Y	10. a. Y
b. X	b. X	b. X
c. neither	c. neither	c. neither

If you answered more than five questions with the letter "c," it is probably because you have not given too much thought to leadership. Perhaps this chapter will give you more to think about concerning leadership. Some people might think that they are playing it safe by answering "c," but they are not really giving leadership in terms of direction and solution. If you answered "a" for the first five questions and "b" for the second five questions you would be considered an X leader. By contrast, if you answered "b" for the first five quejstions and "a" for the second five questions you could be considered a strong Y leader. Question 1–5 identify with the X leader and questions 6–10 identify with the Y leader. Are you more of an X leader or a Y leader? Read on to find out more about this theory of leadership and yourself.

THEORY X AND THEORY Y LEADERS

McGregor's X and Y theories

Behavior theorists have developed a scale of leadership qualities based on (1) the forces at work within a leader, (2) the forces at work within followers, and (3) the arena in which the leader and followers interact. This outline, developed by Douglas McGregor, is known popularly as the X and Y theories of leadership.[11] During the period of "sweat shop" labor in the early twentieth century, the leadership style demonstrated by supervisors was primarily autocratic or X type. And many still hold this view—that people work mostly for money and status rewards. However, McGregor believed that leaders can have a feeling for the employee as well as for the accomplishment of the company goal. The participative, or Y, leader, believes that many people naturally aspire to independent responsibility and self-fulfillment and, further, that people need to feel respected as being capable of assuming responsibility and correcting mistakes on their own. In brief, the X leader is interested in production; the Y leader is interested in employees. It remains a challenge to combine the two extremes.

Autocratic Leaders

Autocratic, or X, leaders leave no doubt about who is in charge. They use the power they have acquired by their rank, knowledge, or skills to reward and punish as they see fit. Their ability to command is the major or sole method by which things get done. This posture does not imply hostility or negativity but, rather, sureness of will. Authoritarian leaders give orders and assume that people will respond obediently. This style is usually perceived as "hard sell," and subordinates are permitted little freedom.

A spinoff of the autocratic leader is the benevolent autocrat. This person is still an autocrat but uses his or her reward power to manipulate or sell the subordinates on the goals of the autocratic leader. Do you see a degree of phoniness in the benevolent autocrat? Which would you rather work for—an autocrat or a benevolent autocrat?

Participative and Democratic Leaders

Participative leaders decide after group input

Participative, or Y, leaders invite decision sharing. Their style calls for subordinates to exercise high degrees of responsibility and freedom. They use as little authoritarian control as possible and are concerned with group interrelationships as well as with getting the job done.

There are two types of participative leaders: *consultive* leaders, who require a high degree of involvement from employees but make it clear that they alone have the authority to make final decisions, and *democratic* leaders, who confer final authority to the group and abide by whatever the group decides, with no exceptions.

True *democratic* leaders confer final authority to the group

Participative leaders do not try to disguise their power to make the final decision, particularly when faced with crises. But they also encourage employees to contribute opinions and information and to participate in the decision-making process as much as possible.

Participative leaders request and expect constant feedback, a practice that provides them with the best available information, ideas, suggestions, talent, and experience. When people participate in making the decisions that affect their lives, they support those decisions more enthusiastically and try hard to make them work. Most people demonstrate high productivity when they are given a fair amount of freedom. They maximize their potential in creative and productive ways and experience personal satisfaction and accomplishment in their work tasks. Further, when most people are given a little leeway, they develop and grow, both personally and in job competence. Often, they will take on more responsibility than called for in their job descriptions because of the pleasure they take in their work.

Ambiguities of the Y theory

There are certainly ambiguities attached to participative leadership, for it certainly does not mean that one considers the employee first and the company second. The employee-centered supervisor who gets the best results tends to recognize that high production is also among his or her responsibilities. The major difference between participative leadership and autocratic "leadership" is that participative leaders give their subordinates a share in decision making and communicate more openly with employees than the autocrat.

Table 10-1 compares the two leadership styles. Which one is the more comfortable for you?

Free-Rein Leaders

Free-rein leaders are also referred to as *laissez-faire* leaders or *group-centered* leaders. Free-rein leaders are almost completely nondirective. They communicate goals and guidelines and then allow employees to meet them without issuing further directions, unless specifically requested. One goal is to involve all nonleaders in participating as equally as possible in a project.

This leadership system offers the most effective use of time and resources. The highest possible degree of authority is vested in the group—it is almost as if the group were leaderless. This *laissez-faire* atmosphere can motivate people to initiate and carry out complex work plans efficiently and responsibly. Guidelines are established by a good free-rein leader, but a day-to-day direction is seldom used.

Examples of the free-rein leadership system are route sales representatives; certain professional workers, such as engineers, scientists, and teachers; and research and development personnel.

THEORY Z

Taking the leadership alphabet one more step, William Ouchi of UCLA has written a book entitled *Theory Z*. As American firms struggle with high employee turnover, declining productivity, and generalized worker alienation, Ouchi pointed to a management style used in Japan. Some ideas are founded in contemporary ideas and others in a strong Japanese cultural tradition.

Long-Range Planning

The basis of Theory Z is futurism. Businesses and governments look 5, 10, even 20 years ahead to try to build a prosperity that can last. One reason that some companies are not under constant pressure for fast profits is that much of Japanese

TABLE 10-1 Traits of Autocratic and Participative Leaders

AUTOCRATIC STYLE: X THEORY TRAITS	PARTICIPATIVE STYLE: Y THEORY TRAITS
Task oriented	Employee oriented
Interested in details	Interested in generalizing
Efficiency minded	Democratic to very permissive
Time and motion studies	Sensitive to individual's needs
Product oriented	People oriented
Interested in promoting oneself	Aware of morale
Fast in making decisions	Slow in making decisions
Somewhat extroverted	Somewhat introverted
Self-appointed or company appointed	Group appointed
Close supervision	General supervision
Task specialist	Maintenance specialist
Paternalistic	Democratic

The Backbone of Theory Z[12]	1. Long-range planning
	2. Consensus decision making
	3. Mutual trust and loyalty between management and worker
	4. Nonspecialized careers
	5. Strong company image and direction
	6. Quality over quantity
	7. Subsistence-level wages, but real bonuses
	8. Few promotions and lifetime employment

industry is owned by banks and not by individual shareholders. Major holdings of many of the country's largest firms, such as Toshiba, Fujitsu, and Nippon Steel, rest with banks that are less interested in short-range profits than in seeing their firm's profits reinvested for future growth.[13]

Consensus Decision Making

Corporate decisions are reached by a tedious process of collective compromise that can sometimes involve as many as 60 to 80 individuals, each of whom holds a potential veto. The process of consensus building is slow, but once an agreement is reached, no one attempts to sabotage or slow down the project.

Mutual Trust and Loyalty

Companies are developed for a powerful bond between the workers and their firms. Managers are famous for inspiring loyalty, long hours, and high-quality production in their workers. Time clocks are banned, managers and workers converse on a first-name basis, and all have lunch together in the company cafeteria. A top executive briefs the employees once a month on sales and production goals and employees are encouraged to air their complaints. Four times a year the workers attend company-paid parties. These are features of Sony, not in Japan, but in the plant in San Diego, California. Betty Price, an assembly-line worker, said "Working for Sony is like working for your family."

Nonspecialized Careers

Personnel are moved regularly from one department to the next. In the process, they become experts in the structure and the internal workings of the company, not specialists in marketing, finance, or production. It sounds like a way to develop conceptual skills.

Strong Company Image and Direction

A strong company image and a strong sense of direction often means a weak union organization. Japan has fewer strikes and less labor unrest than any other major industrial power.[14]

All Japanese employees wear the company "costume." Even employees of Japanese companies within the United States wear the company uniforms. At Sony the universal blue-gray jacket is the firm's way of saying that Sony is a working company, a blue-collar company all the way from top to bottom.

Quality over Quantity

Japanese workers are not only encouraged but are actually expected to make quality control their top priority. At Matsushita Electric, the country's second largest producer of electronics, workers are instilled with the notion that each one of them is a quality-control inspector. If they spot a faulty item in the production process, they are encouraged to shut down the whole assembly line to fix it.[15] There is even furious competition between Hitachi and Sony in statistical battles to achieve the lowest defect rate for products. The Deming quality-control award, named after an American, is now one of the most sought-after prizes among Japanese firms.

Subsistence-Level Wages, but Real Bonuses

Adequate wages are paid, but real bonuses are given to all workers if the company is successful each year. When a recession or other problem affects a firm, the company does not threaten the employees with layoffs, but will pare down paychecks for everyone, including top executives.

Few Promotions and Lifetime Employment

In Japan upwards of 35 percent of the work force is covered by a paternalistic employment practice. Since few people job hop, there are fewer promotions. Yet since no one else is promoted, no one feels that he or she is falling behind.

Promotions may come as infrequently as once every ten years in Japan, and such a glacial pace would drive any fast-moving U.S. manager crazy. Employees in Japan view their company as an extension of their family lives. Indeed many of them equate the importance of their company with that of their own life.

Although individualism and self-reliance have been the very basis of our American culture since the founding of our nation, some U.S. companies are looking to integrate theory Z style into their operations. IBM, Intel, Procter & Gamble, and Hewlett-Packard are examples.

Which features of Theory Z match the X or Y concept? Is Theory Z more like X or more like Y?

Express Your Opinion

Many people will be saying "Let's get on the bandwagon and use Theory Z in our company. If Japan can use it successfully, why can't we?"

Do you think that we can adopt Theory Z within our culture? Looking at the theory, analyze where you think we as a nation, or your company, can adapt most easily to each major idea. Where are we as a culture least likely to accept such ideas?

1. Long-range planning
2. Consensus decision making
3. Mutual trust and loyalty between management and worker
4. Nonspecialized careers
5. Strong company image and direction
6. Quality over quantity
7. Subsistence-level wages, but real bonuses
8. Few promotions and lifetime employment

CONTINGENCY MODEL

It is easier to change the company than the leader

Another leadership theory, the *contingency model*, was developed by business and management psychologist Fred E. Fiedler, at the University of Washington.[16] According to Fiedler, anyone can become a good leader, given the right circumstances. Effective leadership is not the function of any one particular management style but, rather, of matching the right style to the right job at the right time (Figure 10-2).

It is easier to mold the organization than it is to change the personality of a leader. By making an organizational change, it is possible to create a circumstance that will stimulate a person's positive leadership potential. Fiedler writes:

> The evidence suggests that neither the directive nor nondirective approach is consistently more effective. Each approach works better under certain conditions. You cannot run a committee in a completely directive and autocratic manner unless it consists of "yes" men and women. Nor would it make much sense to be very participative in working on an assembly line.[17]

To use the contingency model, we must first identify a manager's leadership style. We must then analyze the job situation and determine the best possible combination of leader and job for that particular moment in time.

Relationship-motivated leader is interested in people

In the contingency model, there are two basic leadership styles: the relationship-motivated style and the task-motivated style. The *relationship-motivated* leader is motivated primarily by relating to people. These leaders are stimulated by forming and maintaining good work relationships with their subordinates and in doing this can get jobs done very well—in certain situations.

In a certain stage of its development, a company needs relationship-motivated leadership. The company is established enough to know its goals and work routines but is many years away from reaching its final growth. For the present and the foreseeable future, the company requires a good, steady forward drive to be maintained. It thus needs leaders who can find their motivation in people rather than in pursuing high-risk goals or saving an organization on the verge of collapse.

Task-motivated leaders will not baby-sit an organization

At the other end of the scale are the *task-motivated* leaders, who "could never just baby-sit a company." These leaders need many task challenges to be stimulated. The companies and situations that need task-style leaders involve risk taking and crises.

Identifying the Style

Least-Preferred Co-Worker Test identifies style

Identifying a leader's style can often be difficult. To make the task easier, Fiedler devised a Least-Preferred Co-Worker Test, in which people are asked to characterize their least preferred coworker, past or present. From over 15 years of test data, Fiedler found that relationship-motivated leaders usually describe their least-preferred coworker as "untrustworthy" or "unreliable personally," whereas task-motivated leaders describe their least preferred coworker as "lazy," "unintelligent," or one who inhibits the completion of difficult jobs. In this test, leaders

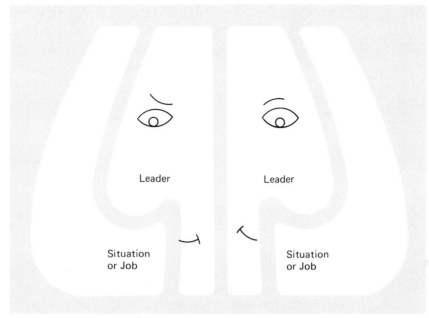

FIGURE 10-2 Fiedler's contingency model. Match the leadership personality and the job requirements.

usually fall somewhere between the two extremes, but in a manner that still allows us to identify their styles.

Analyzing the Job—Matching the Style

Fiedler analyzes job situations to discover (1) to what extent the job situation will call for a strong work relationship and (2) to what extent it will call for the completion of difficult jobs. His conclusion is that relationship-motivated leaders do best in situations that are relatively difficult—but not too difficult—to lead, whereas task-motivated leaders do best in situations that are either very difficult or very easy to lead. (See Table 10-2.)

Frequent evaluations of jobs should be encouraged. And leaders should not be afraid to change leadership positions. Such changes are called *organizational engineering*, which is a method of creating and maintaining effective leadership. The approach is a lot easier than firing or trying to change supervisors who lose their effectiveness because the leadership needs of their job situation have changed.

TABLE 10-2 Matching the Leader to the Situation, According to Fiedler's Contingency Model

SITUATION	LEADER NEEDED
Very difficult to lead	Task leader
Relatively difficult to lead	Relationship-motivated leader
Very easy to lead	Task leader

Companies Are Selecting Personalities to Fit Positions

Again, remember that it is easier to change the company than the leader's personality. Based on such a premise, some companies are striving to match a manager's personality style with the operating strategy. For example, the entrepreneurial type of manager may not be the right person to continue managing a product line after it is established; the idea of cost cutting and pushing production may be revolting to that person.

In an effort to develop a more aggressive growth strategy, Chase Manhattan Bank hired a manager from IBM instead of someone from the banking profession.[18] Likewise, a former head of a retail banking firm, a cost-cutting person by nature, took a bank's lagging European financial operation and worked it into a profit center. In the case of Heublein's United Vintners, Inc., which was split into two divisions—a premium wine division to stress quality over volume and a standard division to emphasize aggressive pricing and efficient volume production—a particular type of leader was selected for each. And General Electric, which has categorized its products as "grow," "defend," and "harvest," depending on the product life cycle, is attempting to categorize the best type of manager for each product as "growers," "caretakers," and "undertakers."[19] The purpose of selecting personalities for certain positions is to match managerial type with the product's status. In fact, the whole meaning of the contingency approach is to match the job and the leader for effective management.

THE PATH-GOAL APPROACH

According to the path-goal approach to leadership, the leader's behavior is based on two classes of factors: subordinate characteristics and environmental factors. The subordinate characteristics include ability, locus of control, authoritarianism, needs, and motives. Characteristics of the work environment include subordinates' tasks, the primary work group, and the formal authority systems.

Figure 10-3 illustrates the path-goal process. Note that each of the three behaviors or environmental factors interacts with the others to reach eventually the target goals: motivated behavior, satisfied employees, leader acceptance, and effective performance. Like any other leadership approach, the purpose of studying the path-goal process is not to build a monument to the leader but to put the emphasis on total organizational effectiveness—by both leaders and subordinates.

Some of the findings of path-goal studies are:

1. When the task or work situation is ambiguous, a directive style of leadership is desirable. When task demands are clear, directiveness is a hindrance.

2. Supportive leadership has its most positive effect on satisfaction for subordinates who work on stressful, frustrating or dissatisfying tasks.

3. In nonrepetitive ego-involving tasks, employees are more satisfied under a participative style of leadership than a nonparticipative style.[20]

As the label implies, the path-goal approach lays out a path by which to achieve the goal. If the goals, and the tasks necessary to accomplish them, are well defined, then a motivating and rewarding situation exists. The leader's behavior is

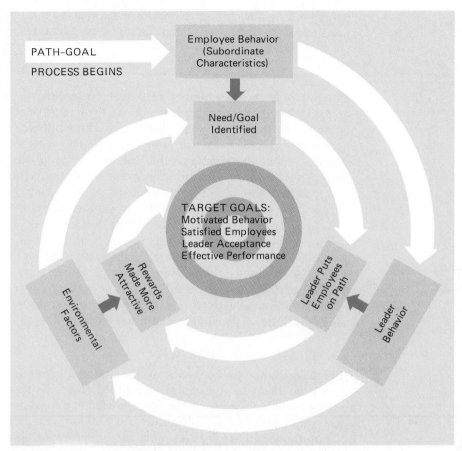

FIGURE 10-3 A path-goal spiral with emphasis on both leader and employee effectiveness.

effective because of its impact on a subordinate's perception of the goals and the paths to those goals.

> A leader through the use of positive and negative task and interpersonal rewards can have a major impact on these perceptions. The leader can specify goals that are more or less attractive to a subordinate and can make it easy or difficult to attain the goals. Thus, a leader can influence both the type of outcomes experienced by the subordinate as well as clarify the behavior-outcome relationship.[21]

Management by Objectives

Management by objectives (MBO) is a goal-setting and performance appraisal process where boss and subordinate mutually determine specific goals for the employee to meet within a given time frame. MBO is discussed in Chapter 12 as an appraisal method, but it has had limited success in its goal-setting applications. If an autocratic leader tries to impose his or her objectives or goals on the organization, and calls that MBO, no wonder it doesn't work.

The failure of MBO may be a result of a poor fit between the process itself and the organizational environment in which it is implemented. The traditional, highly participative, and permissive MBO process will fail if it is introduced in organizations whose leaders are not inclined to be participative or permissive.[22]

DELEGATION

Assignment and acceptance make a contract

Delegation is the assignment of a task to another person and that person's acceptance of the task. As with a contract, there must be an offer and an acceptance according to the terms of an agreement. The employee who accepts a job also accepts the responsibility for completing it. The acceptance of an assignment is thus two sided, carrying both the responsibility and the authority to do the job, although the two sides are not always equal in weight. For example, a subordinate may not have the authority to order the parts or employ the number of people necessary to complete a job that he or she has agreed to do.

To have the responsibility but not the authority to complete a task is an aggravating and depressing experience. It is like trying to shear a sheep, but needing permission to use the clippers every time you take a clip of the wool. Employees will eventually resent and resist supervisors who withhold authority when they delegate responsibility. No one wants to do a job unless he or she has some authority to carry it out. Remember, if you do not delegate the authority along with the responsibility, employees will do the job their way, not yours.

Delegation of Authority

The delegation of authority means the granting of enough power to subordinates to enable them to accomplish a defined task. In the delegation process, the manager still retains overall authority and can, if need be, revoke all or part of the authority that he or she has granted to a subordinate.

Authority gives rise to an equal amount of responsibility. Responsibility arises with the acceptance of delegated authority, but the responsibility itself cannot be delegated, neither with or separate from authority. The chief executive officer (CEO) of an organization has the ultimate responsibility for everything that happens in the organization. As that CEO or other leader delegates authority and it is accepted, then responsibility arises.

LEADERSHIP COMMUNICATION

Speech Patterns

Some researchers began to wonder if they could detect or predict leaders' communication skills. One experiment studied speech behavior. Twenty-two groups made up of three people each discussed a human relations case study for 20 minutes and then chose a representative (leader) from each group to continue to discuss the same problem with other representatives. Members chosen talked on the average of 44.8 percent of the meeting time; nonrepresentatives talked an average of 27.6 percent of the time. Those chosen to be leaders made a significantly high number of suggestions, asked for suggestions from the two others, and gave background information to the case study.[23]

Another researcher found that the communication patterns leaders use serve different purposes. If the purpose is to influence attitudes, the content of the communication will be highly redundant, stressing a few points over and over again, but it will be expressed in slightly different ways. In this strategy, the form varies, but the message stays the same. If the purpose is to achieve action, the communication will offer much more content in a single style. The strategy here is that the form stays constant, but the message keeps changing.[24] For example, someone running for public office has essentially *one* message: "Vote for me." The message may be delivered in many different ways and backed up by many different reasons, but it is always the same. The same person, having been in office for two years and required to make a speech about why the budget isn't adequate to pay municipal employees, will deliver a very different sort of speech. The tone will stay constant, probably sweetly reasonable, but the message will vary enormously in content as reasons and rationalizations pile up.

LEADERSHIP TRAINING

An age-old question is: Can leadership be taught? As noted, much of what we know and can learn about leadership can be taught. Everyone can improve in some aspects of his or her jobs, including leadership.

There are two schools of thought regarding leadership training. *Leadership awareness training* is based on the belief that self-awareness, insight into how behavior affects others, is the catalyst for fostering leadership. *Leadership skills training,* on the other hand, holds that leadership is a series of behaviors grounded in skills including communication. Leaders exhibit skills that attract followers. By identifying these skills, the leadership abilities of individuals can be enhanced and improved through training.[25]

"LEADERLESS" GROUPS

Finally, there is growing evidence that *some* groups may not need leaders, or more properly, that there are substitutes for leadership. It is still too early to know how many groups fit into this category. The emphasis in the 1980s on "lean and mean" organizations and quality circles has stimulated interest in reducing the number of formal leaders.

Steven Kerr and J. M. Jermier have suggested that a number of factors can serve as substitutes for certain aspects of leadership. These factors are tasks with direct feedback, cohesive work groups, able and experienced subordinates, and indifference toward organizational rewards on the part of subordinates.[26] Another substitute is self-leadership and self-control, requiring less direct intervention on the part of a formal leader.

Finally, more often than in the private sector, public sector managers tend to be leaderless and receive little policy guidance. This is true for both brief appointees and career officers serving long periods. Some rules for maintaining effective operation of an agency in the absence of leadership include:

1. Make normal decisions normally.
2. During leaderless periods, strive for greater cooperative bureaucratic efforts than would be normal during easier times.
3. Promote open information exchanges.
4. Do not permit process mechanics and red tape to take over the agency and its functions.

5. Do not permit petty turf and authority issues to assume undue importance.

6. Remember that a leader will eventually arrive to return things to normal.[27]

Summary

Many people admire or fear leadership and do not recognize the leadership potential in themselves. Leaders initiate and facilitate change by interacting with members of groups to make decisions about matters having a high-risk or uncertainty factor. Followers follow because they already agree with the changes that the leader is initiating or because they want to be changed.

Leadership is not always aggressive or autocratic; often the best test of effective leadership is how smoothly a group functions. In fact, every situation calls for different leadership responses. Because of the many functional variables inherent in each situation, there are plenty of opportunities to demonstrate different leadership traits and styles.

Much research into the personality traits of leaders has led to the conclusion that leadership is directly attributable to relatively few traits, such as self-confidence, energy relative intelligence, perseverance, and enthusiasm. In fact, a leader's traits are not out of the ordinary, although they are highly developed. Being well liked socially and being well respected as a leader are two different things; they sometimes go together and sometimes not. Often, social leaders and idea leaders are mutually supportive.

There are two major leadership styles according to Douglas McGregor: the benevolent autocrat or X leader and the participative leader or Y leader. There are many situations where one style works more effectively than the other. Theory Z, developed in Japan, is based on long-range planning, consensus decision making, company image, quality over quantity, and lifetime employment.

Fred Fiedler has developed a contingency model to identify a manager's leadership style and then analyze the job situation and match the best leader for the job at that particular moment in time. Providing a goal and a path for achieving that goal are also major parts of a leader's responsibility.

Leaders communicate differently from nonleaders. They talk more, and their speech is characterized by suggestions, information, and encouragement for others to participate. Effective leadership unifies group goals, evidenced by less group discussion and an increase in efficiency.

The effectiveness of a leader is not always determined by the person's personality traits; effectiveness can also be measured in terms of the composite relationship of the group to the problem, the environment, the feasibility of the solution, and the leader. All situations do not require the same type of leader, and maybe some do not require a formal leader at all.

Case Study 20

Conflict Between Two Styles of Supervision

Fire Station 13 is commanded by Captain Eric Collings. He has been in charge of the station for a period of six months, following his promotion and transfer from another fire station. Station 13 is located in foothills outside a large community. The station's location, along with some additional factors, has led to the confrontation between Collings and the battalion chief, David Marx.

Chief Marx: "I don't care, Captain Collings, what the reasons are. There are rules and regulations that must be followed. As long as I am the battalion chief, it is my duty to see that the fire stations under my supervision perform properly, and that means these rules and regulations will be followed."

Captain Collings: "It is my opinion, with all due respect, Mr. Marx, that your insistence upon following fire department regulations to the letter is hindering my men in their job performance and hurting their morale. I can't help but feel that in this case the regulations should be eased or modified for the benefit of this station and its men."

Chief Marx: "We have a good public image as a result of our uniform rules. The public sees us as a neat, clean, efficient fire-fighting unit. You're asking me to bend the rules to make it easier for your own men. If I were to bend the rules for you, I'd be obligated to bend the rules for everyone, and that I won't do."

Captain Collings: "But sir, ours is the only station that is removed from the community. We fight brush fires, not structural fires. We seldom come into contact with the public and we are constantly in the dust. I can't help but feel that you're being too strict with the men about appearances. I agree that appearance is important, but keeping uniforms spotless and shoes highly shined is next to impossible here. And I don't think your reprimanding Johnson this afternoon was fair. We don't even have a cement floor beneath our trucks here. How can you expect him to remain clean when he has to lie in the dirt to make his safety checks of the truck?

"While I'm at it, sir, I would also like to say that I think your haircut and television policies are too strict. Ours is the only department that is forced to wear our hair this short. In comparison to many other fire departments, we look bald. I feel this, and the fact that you won't allow the men to watch television while relaxing on duty, is unfair to the men. These men are professionals, and they should be treated as such. They have asked me to speak to you about this, and I myself am in total agreement with them. As their captain, I am asking that you relax the regulations that are clearly too severe."

Chief Marx: "Captain, we have a good public image. We shall continue to have a good public image in spite of your protests. If you and your men find the situation unbearable, transfers can be made available."

1. If you were Captain Collings, would you accept things as they are or would you continue to protest the rules and regulations imposed upon your station?

2. If you accepted the battalion chief's wishes for a strict code, how would you handle the supervision of the firemen? Would you inform your men of how you feel and how David Marx feels?

3. If your men then encouraged you to ignore the rules established by the chief, what would you do?

4. If you disobey the chief's orders, are you showing the firemen that it's all right for you to disobey, even though you expect them to obey you? Is this a situation of cognitive dissonance for the firemen—that is, are they being asked to hold two mutually contradictory viewpoints at the same time?

Who Leads: The Chosen Leader or the Informal Leader?

The Landau Construction Company recently contracted to erect the frames of houses as part of a federal housing project. Loren Franks is the supervisor for the company on this project, and the 12 people working for him were hired from the local union hall. Loren receives bonuses that are based on how rapidly projects are completed. The faster the project is completed, the more money he will get. Because of rain he is falling a little behind his schedule.

Loren has supervised most of the workers in the past and, on the whole, he considers them good, skilled carpenters. One of the men, a young and relatively new carpenter named Brian Baxter, has not worked for Loren before.

Soon after work began on the project, Loren became aware of Brian and his popularity with the other workers. In the beginning, during coffee and lunch breaks, Brian was constantly asking the more experienced workers questions about the carpentry field. Because of his easygoing manner and his desire to learn, Brian soon became popular with all the workers.

After a few weeks, Loren noticed that Brian began to ask fewer questions about carpentry, and instead began to tell many humorous stories and jokes for the workers' entertainment, which presented no problem in itself. Loren became increasingly aware, however, that the workers were taking longer lunch hours and coffee breaks to listen to Brian. It seemed that Brian always had a story to finish or one last joke to tell before going back to work.

Loren counseled Brian twice about the problem, but this failed to produce results. During the two counseling conversations Loren got the impression that Brian was enjoying both his popularity and the situation, which worsened. Usually after an extended break, Loren would find many workers grouped around a single operation for which only one worker was needed, such as sweeping shavings. Loren found that the center of the group cluster would invariably be Brian. On these occasions, when Loren was forced to remind the carpenters that their work was not getting done, Brian would always laugh it off and have one last comment to make, which the men would wait to hear.

From all appearances, Brian has assumed informal control of the group. If you were Loren, how would you go about correcting the situation that exists?

1. Do you continue to counsel Brian or do you now go to the workers?
2. If you talk with the other carpenters, what do you say to them?
3. Are there other alternatives?
4. Would you "blacklist" Brian—that is, tell other supervisors not to hire him because he doesn't work hard enough?

Terms and Concepts

authority   power that is more often appointed from above, such as the authority to hire, promote, demote, or fire an employee. Authority is conferred; leadership is earned.

autocratic leaders   X-type leaders who are task oriented, quick in making decisions, look after company goals, and may believe in close supervision.

benevolent autocrat   an autocrat who uses reward power to manipulate or sell subordinates on goals of the leader

contingency model   a model developed by Fred Fiedler that attempts to identify a person's leadership style and then tries to analyze the job situation and determine the best possible combination of leader and job for that particular moment in time.

formal authority   appointed responsibility from above often stated in writing, as contrasted to informal authority, which is authority granted by mutual agreement between parties, either consciously or unconsciously.

free-rein leaders   leaders who allow people to govern themselves and base decisions on "one person, one vote." The French would call it *laissez-faire*.

leadership awareness training   based on belief that self-awareness is the catalyst for fostering leadership.

leadership skills training   holds that leadership is a series of behaviors grounded in skills.

organizational engineering   a method of creating and maintaining effective leadership by frequent evaluation and changes in leadership positions.

participative leaders   Y-type leaders who allow employees to express their feelings about situations but reserve the final decision for themselves. The decision may agree with the popular consensus or it may not.

path-goal leadership   based on subordinate characteristics (ability, needs) and environmental factors (formal authority systems, primary work groups).

social leaders   leaders in a group who are concerned with the group working together and everyone understanding the other's point of view. Progressing together as a group is important. Groups frequently have both social and task leaders.

substitutes for leadership   a series of attributes that permit less direct leadership. These factors include subordinate ability, responsibility, routine tasks, and specific organizational plans.

task leaders   leaders in a group who are more concerned with completing a task. The task takes priority over the group's or the individual's concerns.

X leaders   see *benevolent autocratic leaders*.

Y leaders   see *participative leaders*.

Notes

1. Tom Peters and Nancy Austin, "A Passion for Excellence," *Fortune*, May 13, 1985, p. 20.

2. Warren Bennis and Noel Tichy, quoted in Jeremy Main, "Wanted: Leaders Who Can Make a Difference," *Fortune*, September 28, 1987, p. 94.

3. Rick Ostrow, "Ueberroth Still Has That Golden Touch," *USA Today*, August 8, 1985, p. C1.

4. "Ueberroth Denies Role in Solving Strike," *The Coloradoan*, August 8, 1985, p. D2.

5. Lester R. Bittel, *Leadership: The Key to Management Success* (New York: Franklin Watts, 1984), pp. 15–23.

6. William Foote Whyte, *Organizational Behavior: Theory and Application* (Homewood, Ill.: Richard D. Irwin, 1969), pp. 176–177.

7. Ibid., p. 177.

8. Amitai Etzioni, "Dual Leadership in Complex Organizations," *American Sociological Review*, October 1965, pp. 688–698.

9. Thomas Gordon, *Leader Effectiveness Training, L.E.T.: The No-Lose Way to Release the Productive Potential of People* (n.p.: Wyden Books, 1977), pp. 12–13.

10. Gerard Nierenberg, "How to Develop Win/Win Techniques," *Management Review*, February 1983, pp. 48–49.

11. Douglas McGregor, *The Human Side of Enterprise* (New York: McGraw-Hill, 1960).

12. Christopher Byron, "An Attractive Japanese Export: The XYZ of Management Theory," *Time*, March 2, 1981, p. 74, and "What American Business Can Learn from Japan," *U.S. News and World Report*, October 12, 1981, p. 43.

13. "How Japan Does It," *Time*, March 30, 1981, pp. 54–60.

14. Ibid., p. 57.

15. Ibid.

16. Fred Fiedler and M. M. Chambers, *Leadership and Effective Management* (Glenview, Ill.: Scott, Foresman, 1974).

17. Fred E. Fiedler, "When to Lead, When to Stand Back: If You Want to Be a Directive Leader You'd Better Be Smart. Otherwise, Get Your Employees Involved," *Psychology Today*, September 1987, p. 26.

18. "Wanted: A Manager to Fit Each Strategy," *Business Week*, February 25, 1980, p. 166.

19. Ibid.

20. Robert J. House and Terence C. Mitchell, "Path-Goal Theory of Leadership," *Journal of Contemporary Business*, Autumn 1974, pp. 81–99.

21. Terence C. Mitchell, *People in Organizations*, 2nd ed. (New York: McGraw-Hill, 1982), p. 378.

22. Jan P. Muczyk and Bernard C. Reimann, "MBO as a Complement to Effective Leadership," *Academy of Management Executive*, May 1989, pp. 131–138.

23. Philip B. Applewhite, *Organizational Behavior* (Englewood Cliffs, N.J.: Prentice-Hall, 1965), p. 116.

24. Ibid., pp. 128–129.

25. Chris Lee, "Can Leadership Be Taught?" *Training: the Magazine of Human Resources Development*, July 1989, p. 19.

26. Steven Kerr and J. M. Jermier, "Substitutes for Leadership: Their Meaning and Measurement," *Organizational Behavior and Human Performance*, December 1978, pp. 375–403.

27. Richard E. Schmidt, "Management in a Leaderless Environment," *Bureaucrat*, Fall 1985, pp. 30–32.

Recommended Reading

Bennis, Warren, and Burt Nanus. *Leaders: The Strategies for Taking Charge.* New York: Harper & Row, 1985.

Bittel, Lester R. *Leadership: The Key to Management Success.* New York: Franklin Watts, 1984.

Britton, Paul R., and John W. Stallings. *Leadership Is Empowering People.* Lanham, Md.: University Press of America, 1986.

Conger, Jay A. "Leadership: The Art of Empowering Others." *The Academy of Management EXECUTIVE*, February 1989, pp. 17–24.

De Pree, Max. *Leadership Is an Art.* Garden City, N.Y.: Doubleday, 1989.

Fiedler, Fred E. "When to Lead, When to Stand Back: If You Want to Be a Directive Leader You'd Better Be Smart. Otherwise, Get Your Employees Involved," *Psychology Today*, September 1987, pp. 26–27.

M. M. Chambers. *Leadership and Effective Management.* Glenview, Ill.: Scott, Foresman, 1974.

Gordon, Thomas. *Leader Effectiveness Training, L.E.T.: The No-Lose Way to Release the Productive Potential of People.* (n.p.: Wyden Books, 1977).

Locke, Edwin A., and Gary P. Latham. *Goal Setting: A Motivational Technique That Works!* Englewood Cliffs, N.J.: Prentice-Hall, 1984.

McGregor, Douglas. *The Human Side of Enterprise.* New York: McGraw-Hill, 1960.

Ouchi, William. *Theory Z: How American Businesses Can Meet the Japanese Challenge.* Reading, Mass.: Addison-Wesley, 1981.

Peters, Thomas J., and Nancy Austin. *A Passion for Excellence.* New York: Random House, 1985.

Rasberry, Robert, and Laura F. Lemoine. "Management Traits and Styles: What Makes a Manager a Leader?" *Legal Professional*, July–August 1989, pp. 26–34.

Zaleznik, Abraham. "Managers and Leaders: Are They Different?" *Harvard Business Review*, May–June 1986, pp. 67–80.

Discipline
and Training

After studying this chapter, you should be able to:

1. Distinguish between discipline and disciplinary action. Discuss the relationship between discipline and training.
2. Distinguish between training and development.
3. Discuss training from the point of view of needs assessment, goals, methods, and follow-up.
4. Relate the need for employee orientation on a new job.
5. Describe the "simulation techniques" used in training. Discuss how they simulate business situations.
   a. In-basket method
   b. Case method
   c. Management games
   d. Role playing
6. Discuss the following "experiential" methods of training. Develop ideas that are for and against each experiential method.
   a. Sensitivity training
   b. Transactional analysis
   c. Assertiveness training
   d. Transcendental meditation
7. Distinguish between aggressiveness and assertiveness.

TO START YOU THINKING . . .

Take a look at these questions and check your reactions to them.

- Do you have some attitudes toward training programs already that may influence your review of the chapter?
- What is the difference between discipline and disciplinary action?
- What is the relationship between discipline and training?
- What is the difference between job training and general education?
- What are the differences between training and development?
- Do you know what transactional analysis means? Or such terms as transcendental meditation, assertiveness training, or sensitivity training?
- What are the differences between assertiveness and aggressiveness?
- Are you aware of how much a company's orientation can affect job attitudes?
- What are the differences among simulation, experiential training, and organizational training methods?

DISCIPLINE DEFINED

One of the most common mistakes made in both management literature and practice is to refer to discipline as disciplinary action. *Discipline* is a *noun* that refers to a state of order, positive morale, and readiness to achieve organizational objectives effectively. It is brought about by learning and training. The result of this state is self-control, orderliness, efficiency, and effectiveness of a group or individual. *Disciplinary action,* on the other hand, is only one method of achieving discipline and usually more punitive. We will examine disciplinary procedures in Chapter 12, but here we need to emphasize the positive state of discipline.

Order and consistency are so important to an organization that is trying to be productive that we must do everything possible to bring about that order. Another way of viewing discipline is to think of it as subordinates who have commitment to organizational objectives. Members of an organization are made ready through learning and training to accomplish their tasks.

Military and athletic organizations recognize the importance of discipline and commitment to fulfilling their missions. Only if they are well prepared and committed to those missions will they be successful. And the responsibility for discipline lies with the leaders. Discipline is what leaders make of it.

Not to address the positive aspects of discipline and training would be a serious shortcoming in any discussion of human behavior. They are at the very heart of what enhanced human relationships are about. How well a person is prepared for working within a group or organization is a function of discipline and training.

Emphasize Positive Discipline and Performance

The objective of positive discipline is to obtain top performance of organization members. Too much emphasis has been placed on negative disciplinary action that creates poor morale and low performance and productivity.

For supervisors to get top performance from their employees, the employees must be convinced that performance does make a difference. There are a number of ways to achieve this, including (1) reward performance, (2) "talk-up" performance, (3) coach and counsel on performance, (4) measure performance and results, (5) delegate clearly and follow up, (6) give rewards for suggestions that lead to improved performance, (7) hold meetings that focus on performance, and (8) make performance satisfying.[1]

Personal discipline to do what has to be done, when it has to be done, is often cited as a quality necessary to be successful.[2] Create a positive rather than a negative environment and discipline—the state of order and commitment to get tasks done—will be high.

Commitment

Traditional approaches to discipline, based on punishment, promote adversarial relationships between leaders and followers. A more effective approach now being used by many companies recognizes good performance and encourages employee commitment to the organization and its goals. Once employees see the discrepancy between actual and expected performance, the burden for change is theirs.[3]

General Electric uses a commitment-oriented performance approach where employees are treated as responsible adults who are specifically accountable for acceptable performance. Contributions and commitment are recognized, as are inappropriate actions or inactions. There is still disciplinary action, but the emphasis is on discipline. Misdeeds are handled by reminders of employee responsibility for meeting defined performance and behavior standards. Companies like GE, Pennzoil, and Procter & Gamble have found that the commitment approach fosters mutual respect between supervisors and employees, makes for smoother labor relations, and lets more employees be recognized for good performance.[4]

Before individuals can feel a commitment, they must know the desired expectations. The level of commitment and expected performance is based on their job knowledge, abilities, and training to do their jobs. Only with improved performance brought about through education, training, and development can our work forces and other group members be more committed and disciplined or ready to do their jobs.

TRAINING AND DEVELOPMENT RELATIONSHIPS ───────

Learning and development are fundamental to all behavior modification. A person's success in an organization is determined in large part by education, including orientation, training, and development on and off the job.

Misunderstandings are costly; they waste time and often material. These are times when supervisors must train and direct employees in areas in which they have no experience on materials that are expensive and on procedures that are complex. Therefore, the likelihood of errors because of communication problems becomes more common in our technical world. It is wise then to consider training programs.

Training is hard to measure

The effectiveness of training programs is difficult to measure, and there is no guarantee that a training program will enable an employee to perform a job successfully. However, the risk is even greater in the other direction: without training, mistakes in skill and judgment are more possible. Often, training is a small risk when compared with the potential errors that result from no training.

It appears that more company managements consider it an intelligent investment to send their managers to school. The American Management Association alone enrolls over 100,000 managers a year in training programs. University executive development programs continue to service large numbers of managers through their continuing education and extension activities.

Worker participation and training are important in the 1990s. There is a smaller supply of motivated workers who are trained to perform complex tasks. The Labor Department's Employment and Training Administration earmarks much of its annual research budget for developing the future labor force.[5]

What Is Training? ────────────────────────────

Training can change behavior

Training is the process of transmitting and receiving information related to problem solving. It can be used in changing behavior as well as in learning skills and concepts. Training is specific in improving the trainee's abilities to perform in particular jobs. Educational programs transmit information for its own sake, with no expectation of how and when the information will be used—if ever. The specific purpose of training is to communicate information that is applicable to practical situations. After training, trainees should be able to demonstrate changes in behavior or performance that contribute to their abilities to deal skillfully with specific problems. Training, however, implies a formal commitment of time—be it ten minutes or six months—set aside to learn specific, directly applicable information.

Training takes two forms: traditional and human relations. *Traditional* training is concerned with learning skills and theoretical concepts that can be applied to performing the mechanics of a job. Traditional skills are oriented to the "how to" aspects of work. *Human relations* training passes on skills dealing with the ability to interact with others: coworkers with coworkers and supervisors with subordinates. Human relations training is concerned with the attitudes and assumptions that people have about their jobs, about themselves, and about other people.

Many kinds of training are vital to today's working world. Without it, misunderstandings are likely to occur, which often result in wasted time, money, and human energy and emotion. Nowadays, employees are rarely expected to work at tasks for which they receive no training. A manager who does not know how to work with people is at as severe a disadvantage as is a drill press operator who does not know how to run a drill press. Without job training, employees are put in the position of having to "muddle through" as best they can.

Training is a cyclical process involving at least four steps: (1) analyzing needs, (2) designing and developing training materials, (3) delivering training and development programs/assistance or counseling, and (4) evaluating results and follow-up. (See Figure 11-1.) All four steps are important, but too often only step 3 is considered training. One of the reasons that so much training is ineffective is because it addresses only one point in the cycle. If the delivery system does not meet a need, or is improperly designed, or is not evaluated or followed up, it is little wonder that we do not know our jobs or whether training is effective.

What Is Development?

Development falls between specific training and general education. There is an expected payoff to the sponsoring organization but it is not always concerned with the participant's current job. Development activity puts emphasis on increasing the participant's abilities to perform effectively in other jobs as well as the current job.

The focus of training is on the present job and the almost immediate

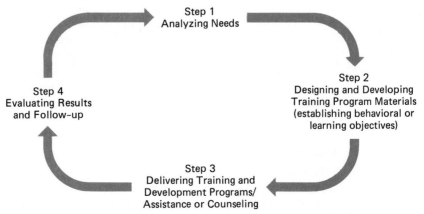

FIGURE 11-1 The Training and Development Process Cycle.

application of knowledge and skills to that job. The focus of development is on the general needs of the organization. Training is generally considered job specific and seeks to improve an individual's ability to perform a job or organizational role. Development is more oriented to the future and is broader in scope than training.[6]

Who has the responsibility for development? Just as managers and trainers have the responsibility for seeing that employees are trained, they both share the responsibility for development. Development is forward looking and requires forecasting future as well as current needs. The abilities to change in one's job and adapt to other jobs are brought about by development efforts.

Effort must be made to develop the discipline noted earlier, and to develop subordinates' capacities for and commitment to sharing responsibility for an organization's success. To be effective, the manager-as-developer must accomplish the following three major tasks:

1. Work with direct subordinates as a team to share responsibility collectively for managing the unit.
2. Determine and gain commitment to a common vision of the department's goals and purpose.
3. Work on the continuous development of individual subordinates skills, especially in the managerial/interpersonal areas needed to be an effective member of the shared responsibility team.

The manager-as-developer then seeks to develop in subordinates the willingness and ability to share the responsibility for departmental success. The manager must shape subordinates into a powerful, cooperative, hardworking, dedicated, and responsible team.[7]

Figure 11-2 shows a relationship between training, development, and education. One reason why the term *development* has come into more common usage in recent years is to cover the middle ground between training and education. Some, however, would argue that to define training as the imparting of more specific "how to" skills is too narrow a definition. What do you think?

What Is Learning?

To learn is to change. To demonstrate change, a person's capabilities must change. Learning has taken place when students (1) *know* more than they knew before, (2) *understand* what they have not understood before, (3) *develop a skill* that was not developed before, (4) *feel differently* about a subject than they have felt before, or (5) *appreciate* a subject that they have not appreciated before.[8]

Positive attitudes from everyone concerned with training and its spheres of potential influence help to make the learning process a worthwhile experience. But can you know too much? One study finds that learning more than you need can mean getting paid less. White male workers with substantially more schooling than others in the same occupation "often earn less than their adequately educated and undereducated counterparts."[9]

Goals and Methods

Whether an employee comes to a job with previous experience or is trained by the company after being hired, job training of some kind, formal or informal, must go on. Often the most difficult problem in job training is recognizing the *need* for it. Managers must be convinced to allow time and money for training endeavors.

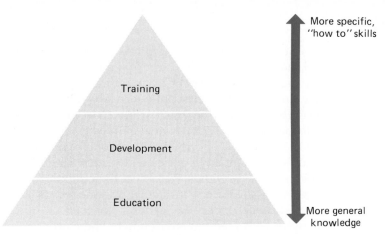

FIGURE 11-2 **The relationship of training, development, and education.**

The training director or a committee on training may select areas that need training programs and prepare a priority list of those areas selected. Such a list might look like this:

Areas of Training

1. New employee orientation
2. Stockroom
3. Reservation desk
4. Evaluation of programs

First select the goals—then the methods

A distinction must be made between training goals and the methods by which the goals are undertaken. Training methods are appropriate only according to the training goals. Methods can be compared only in terms of objectives. For instance, role playing does not help employees to learn more about running a drill, although it may help people to learn how to become better managers. Therefore, training goals must be defined clearly before a specific program is undertaken. (See Table 11-1.) Once the goals are well formed, the methods fall into place. The content of a training program might not be learned adequately if the appropriate methods are not used.

Human relations is learned by doing

It is, for instance, not enough to teach human relations without actually "doing" it. Instead of a lecture, some method involving interaction with other people must be employed. Case study and role playing are just two examples that we will examine under methods.

TABLE 11-1 Matching Areas of Training with Methods

AREAS OF TRAINING	METHOD OF TRAINING
1. New employee orientation	1. Classroom technique daily from 8 to 10 A.M. or 1 to 2 P.M.
2. Stock room training	2. Videotape
3. Reservation desk training	3. Programmed manuals
4. Evaluation of program	4. Survey of participants and management

ORIENTATION

When new employees decide to take a job, they already have some impressions about the company for which they plan to work. The job interview will have given them a sense of the company's environment. However, the on-the-job impressions of the first few days greatly influence and solidify attitudes toward their jobs and the companies for which they work. Orientation is the formal means by which employees learn about their new employer.

Orientation versus induction

Orientation is concerned with accomplishing two major tasks: (1) informing employees of company policies and benefits and (2) making employees aware of locations and procedures that affect their abilities to do their jobs. Formally, the first point is called *policy orientation,* and the second *procedural orientation.* Loosely, both tasks fall under the general concept of orientation—acquainting new employees with their job environment and coworkers and with company policies and procedures.

Policy Orientation

Another general area with which new employees must become acquainted is department and company policies and practices. These orientation subjects usually include absentee policies, vacation times and amounts, holidays, disciplinary procedures, and filling out of certain company forms. Employees will need to study the options for medical and other fringe benefits, use of the credit union, stock purchase plans, employee purchases and discounts, and retirement and insurance plans. Some companies find that detailed information should not be presented for about a week, or until after new employees have time to feel comfortable with more immediate concerns, such as the job, the coworkers, and the work environment.

Procedural Orientation

Important details—pay and restrooms

New employees must learn the locations of things that are pertinent to their working lives: parking spaces, employee entrances and exits, time clocks, lockers, restrooms, bulletin boards, cafeteria, coffee and smoking areas, and work-related departments. It is a sad comment on a company's orientation program to encounter a new employee wandering the halls in search of the restroom or the cafeteria. Further induction should include company procedures, uniforms, safety equipment, rest breaks, and details of pay.

Employee sponsors for the new recruit

Some managers consider it good management practice for an established coworker to sponsor a new employee, at least during the first few days. In this way, a new employee can establish immediate rapport with a person in the same department, which helps the newcomer to overcome feelings of shyness and strangeness. The coworker is available to answer questions and to introduce the new employee to others. In general, coworker orientation is a good method for easing the new employee into the company environment. But the manager must be careful when choosing an individual for this responsibility.

Two Approaches to Orientation

The inductive method

Orientation is approached in two ways: moving from part to whole (*inductive*) or moving from whole to part (*deductive*) (Figure 11-3). The inductive method favors expansion of orientation. Employees are first instructed in the details of their

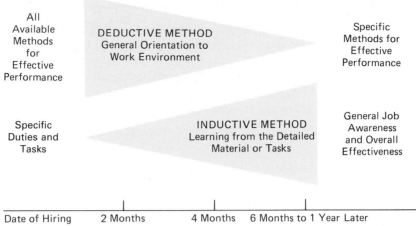

FIGURE 11-3 **Illustration of the Inductive and Deductive Methods of Orienting New Employees.**

jobs and necessary locations and procedures. Gradually, employees are exposed to more information. They learn the details of company benefits, the overall company objectives, how people and departments interrelate, and how the company relates to the community. Many new employees like to begin by learning their jobs and making themselves useful, and then gradually widen their scope. One disadvantage is that employees may form incorrect opinions about the company, opinions that are difficult to alter later on in orientation.

The deductive method   In the deductive method, employees are first introduced to the company as a whole. The company is treated as a family that employees must get to know before beginning their job duties. The deductive method is exemplified by the way in which two foreign firms orient their employees. It is a pleasure to work for Coats & Clark, a British buttons and fabric firm, or Mitsubishi, a large Japanese conglomerate, said several of their employees of these strongly paternalistic companies.

From the whole to the part   The deductive method is learning from the whole to the part. During the first week, a film on the company is often shown, which focuses on the firm's products but also emphasizes employee security and company success. Early in the employee orientation a new recruit is aware of the steps in production and what part he or she will play in the process. A disadvantage is that the newcomer may become anxious to get to work and learn his or her duties during this indoctrination period. However, the newcomer is learning to identify, associate, and feel comfortable with the firm. This approach may be more successful in reducing employee turnover. According to this view, it is better to train a good, productive, loyal employee first to become a statistician, a computer operator, or a labor relations specialist than to hire a highly trained outsider.

Express Your Opinion   Consider the company at which you work now or select a company you can relate to comfortably and determine whether you would use the deductive method or the inductive method of orientation. Consider not only the method that seems best for you but also the size of the company, the type of industry, and the turnover and longevity of the employees.

Justify your selection with three reasons.

DEVELOPING MANAGERS

Managers can do much to develop their subordinates by delegating small and large tasks. Of course it is difficult to delegate but one of the main purposes for doing so is employee development. Perhaps Y leaders more often encourage the development of people. If the department operates effectively while the supervisor is on vacation, people are being developed.

There are several reasons why managers fail to develop good subordinates.

1. Managers are chosen for their technical excellence, but they have little or no training in human relations.
2. Managers would rather avoid training and prefer to hire proven managers from other companies.
3. Managers are interested in enhancing their own status rather than in helping their subordinates.
4. Managers know very little about their subordinates' potential, preferring to select a carbon copy of themselves when a promotional opportunity arises.

These factors contribute to the reasons for accelerating management development efforts. Whether management development is done inside or outside of the organization, there are real benefits to be acquired from formalized programs. Primary among the benefits is increased performance and productivity. But the training and development efforts must be germane to both the human relations and technical aspects of jobs.

William S. Mitchell, director of human resources at Metropolitan Life Insurance Company, observes:

> If one reviews the content of many large corporations' management training programs, it is rare to find heavy skill-building in such areas as work-level forecasting; work scheduling; resource scheduling and allocation; resource quality improvement; work simplification; methods improvement; organization structuring; output monitoring and productivity control; and cost analysis, interpretation and control.[10]

Mitchell urges:

1. Build heavy technical productivity improvement skill building into management training.
2. Don't abandon the teaching of behavioral science–driven management skills, but place them in proper perspective and weight the curriculum toward the kind of management we need now.
3. Refocus reward systems to support that effort.
4. Return for guidance and inspiration to the management training used before the behavioral sciences approach came into vogue. But reinterpret and remodel the old subjects in light of advances in instructional technology and, of course, in work systems themselves.[11]

INSTRUCTIONAL METHODS

To instruct means to impart information, ideas, or skills so that they may be learned by others. On-the-job training is an example of applied instruction. Instruction can be made available not only through human teachers but also through literature, films, and computers—in fact, with any aid that provides students with materials from which to learn. The students' participation in this process is to learn what is presented to them.

On-the-Job Training

Good OJT requires a good trainer

No matter what skill training is necessary to acquire a job, some on-the-job training is helpful. Without it, new employees learn only through trial and error. On-the-job training, or OJT, can include informal comments and suggestions from others, but supervised OJT is more effective.

In OJT, the burden is on the trainer: it is generally assumed that, when a worker does not learn the job thoroughly, the teacher has not taught the job correctly. For an instructor to present material consistently, OJT should be preplanned. Information should be presented in manageable sections and in a logical sequence. To facilitate this process, the trainer should break down the job to be learned *on paper.*

A person new to a job is nervous, which makes it difficult to concentrate. The trainee must be put at ease and not feel rushed. Impatience, irritation, or criticism almost always terminate learning. The learner's accomplishments and efforts must be praised, helping to build self-confidence. A trainer should not interrupt when a trainee is performing correctly, because it will break the concentration. However, when a trainer sees that an error is going to be made, the trainer should interrupt, thereby preventing the error from occurring. A bad habit can be formed by doing something incorrectly just once. To correct an error, the trainer should return to the step immediately preceding the error.

Written Material

Probably the most popular way to disseminate general information is through the written word. Businesses like to keep employees informed of fundamental company background and policy. Well-designed pamphlets about company activities and job manuals containing specific job data often help employees to do their jobs more effectively.

Written material is good for details and easy access

One advantage of manuals is the ease with which they can be used over and over again. Also, job-relevant information can be accumulated so that maximum accessibility is assured. The mind is freed of learning many details when sources of information are available.

Written material, however, is often *not* read or is read superficially and soon forgotten. Writing is suitable for transmitting technical data, but it is not always useful for training that deals with emotions or attitudes.

Lectures

One of the most reliable ways to give information

Lectures can present a considerable amount of material to a considerable number of people. As with written material, the lecture method is employed best to convey ideas. It is used in company training programs as the most reliable way in which to pass on information. Lectures do not cater to individual needs and they provide little opportunity for feedback. Question-and-answer periods, interspersed throughout or following a lecture, allow for some individual participation and should be used whenever possible.

Whether or not lectures are interesting depends on the material presented and the presentation. Lectures can be presented by anyone familiar with the informa-tion, but the listening rate often depends on the lecturer's speaking style. The most accomplished lecturers are able to sense the overall moods of the crowd, to which they respond spontaneously and appropriately.

Programmed Instruction

Programmed instruction (PI), also called programmed learning, is a self-teaching method particularly useful for transmitting information or skills that need to be learned and placed in logical order. The "instructor" is replaced by an instruction booklet or a computer or both. It is possible to present programmed instruction entirely in written or computer form.

Programmed instruction presents what is to be learned in a brief, logical sequence, one step at a time. Two main approaches have been developed based on this concept: linear programming and intrinsic or branching programming. Of the two, the linear is the more common.

Programmed learning can be carried out by the use of computers or booklets, depending upon the need. The method is to present a small amount of information called a "frame," followed by a simple question that requires an answer on the part of the learner. The answer may be written or said silently, but in any case there is immediate feedback for each response as the learner finds the answer on the next page or elsewhere. The learner knows whether he or she is right or wrong immediately. Since the program is designed to have a low error rate, the learner is motivated further. The main advantage to such an individualized problem is that it is self-pacing. For remedial instruction, enrichment material, or short segments, this method works well.

Programmed instruction can reduce total training time appreciably and has the major advantage of immediate feedback. The major drawback is the cost of developing materials.

Computer-Assisted Instruction

With traditional training methods unable to keep pace with demand, computers have been called in to fill the gap. Computer-assisted instruction (CAI) has become the fastest-growing segment of the almost $10 billion training industry. While the costs of CAI are high, compared to costs for formulating and delivering teacher-led courses over a period of several years, the results favor CAI. Advantages of CAI include:

1. Consistency in teaching
2. A pace controlled by the learner
3. Response-driven lessons that provide immediate feedback
4. Lessons that are based on specific, measurable objectives
5. Easy administration and better information about the training program
6. Full multimedia capability when combined with videodisks
7. Participation and control of the training process by trainees[12]

Knowledge-based or expert computer systems, based on artificial intelligence, contain information on particular subjects and can give user-specific advice. Combined with interactive video, expert systems can be used as "intelligent" tutors to teach tasks and skills. The systems can also be used in the work environment as an aid to on-the-job decision making. Expert systems move training away from the transferal of knowledge to the application of the system to goal-oriented tasks in the actual work environment.[13]

Videotape

Video is good on assembly lines

Videotape is used to instruct new employees on how to perform their jobs. An assembly line can be filmed from several positions by a video camera, and the finished video cassette can be installed in a monitor or screen above the workstation. A well-timed tape recording describing a multistepped job can supply more job understanding than can supervised on-the-job training.

The new employee can watch the process on the screen several times before trying the project. The employee can start or stop the videotape at any point desired; in fact, the employee is learning at his or her own rate. Nervousness is minimized because the employee is not under the watchful eyes of an impatient supervisor. Likewise, supervisors can use their valuable time to attend to other duties, with only spot checks on the recruit for reassurance. Videotape can be used immediately after "shooting" the training sequence. Finally, it can be made "in house" with only a limited staff.

SIMULATION METHODS

The simulation method is used to develop in a controlled environment a situation that is as near to real life as possible so that people can learn from their mistakes without affecting the real world. Car and aircraft simulators recreate real-life situations (see Figure 11-4). Astronauts work thousands of hours in a simulator of the space shuttle before taking their first flights.

In-Basket Method

Problem solving under a time limit

In-basket training is structured around the familiar receptacle used for collecting incoming mail, memos, telephone messages, and reports. Materials that require problem solving are put into an in basket, and the student plays the role of a manager responsible for solving the problems found in the in basket. The students are given background information on the personalities and situations involved. Then, using their experience as a guide, students are asked to take the appropriate action within a short time period.

The in-basket method teaches planning and delegating

So far, the in-basket method has been used mostly to learn about effective management and supervision. The technique attempts to simulate real-life situations. Using a time limit helps to create the tension inherent in workaday problem solving. The problems are organized to approximate work experience as closely as possible.

One typical in-basket approach is to ask students to pretend they are a manager who has just returned from a business trip and must leave again shortly on another trip. The student managers have 20 minutes in which to make decisions on materials that have accumulated in the in basket. How well can the manager list priorities? What assumptions are made, and are they warranted? Is the work distribution planned adequately? Is the work delegated appropriately? Figure 11-5 gives two examples of in-basket exercises.

FIGURE 11-4 Car Safety Simulation. *Courtesy* of General Motors.

Case Study

In the case method, a problem, or case, is presented in writing to an individual student or group. Cases are intended to simulate real-work situations and therefore include descriptions of the organizational structure and personalities involved. Group members study the problem and then offer their solutions. Because of group participation, group members are able to get immediate reactions to their ideas, as well as react to the ideas of others. Although groups are often led by a teacher or trainer, the group sessions can be so informal that they get off the track. However, this experimental approach makes traditional management principles more meaningful to group participants.

Determining the problem, not the solution

The case method assumes that in business practice there is no one "right" way in which to accomplish an objective. It acknowledges that the "best" solutions often rely on personal preferences. The case method usually deals with problems that affect individuals in organizations. It involves the ability to *justify* management decisions, to give priorities to problems that are important to the company and its employees. For instance, a case study could involve an employee who was fired by a supervisor for using a company car for personal reasons. The employee has appealed to the grievance committee. As a member of the committee, each

MEMO:

TO: John Enwright, Manager

FROM: Joan Rider, Personnel Director

John, the approval came through for a facilities supervisor. Do you want to write up a formal job description for me? Do you want to have a panel interview candidates for the job or do you want to handle the interviews yourself?

1. Would you delegate the task of making out the job description? If so, to whom?
2. Would you use a panel interview or a personal interview? Why?

MEMO:

TO: John Enwright

FROM: Joel Peterson, Head Accountant

Helga Sue (the accounting clerk responsible for sending out bills) has not shown up for work the last three days. She cannot be reached by phone. There is a backlog in sending out statements to customers. You know how anxious the president is to maximize income and there is a large amount owed in the accounts receivable ledger. What shall we do?

1. Would you delegate this task?
2. What are the alternatives to the problem?

FIGURE 11-5 Samples of In-basket Forms.

student would receive pertinent information to decide whether to (1) sustain the firing, (2) suspend the employee for a period of time without pay, or (3) reinstate the employee with full rights.

Management Games

Groups compete

A management game is a form of problem solving. At least two teams, each of which represents an organization, make decisions concerning their company's operation. Decisions can be made about production, marketing, finance, human resource utilization, and other management challenges. Decisions are based on a set of specified economic theories, presented as a model of the economy.

Good judgment is the key

Simple management games are not based on analyzing complex problems. Instead, emphasis is placed on making good judgments in a minimum amount of time, based on specific problems and limited rules. In simple games, effective strategies can be reached without making too many decisions and without having to use large amounts of managerial know-how. These management games may oversimplify business relationships and give the impression that running a

THE 'IN-BASKET' METHOD IS REALLY
A GAME TO FORCE PEOPLE TO MAKE
DECISIONS.

company can be easy—when in fact, even the simplest management decisions require the consideration of many factors.

When the model is fairly simple, a referee can be responsible for calculating outcomes. When the model is complex, a computer must be used. The game can be continuous: teams receive all or part of the results of their decisions on which they make new decisions, thus continuing the game. Figure 11-6 is a diagram of the steps in a management game.

EXPERIENTIAL METHODS

There is an old saying: "Experience is the best teacher," but experience can also be very expensive if it is not conducted in a training environment. Training conducted to gain experience is what experiential learning is all about. Another and clever way of thinking about experiential training is that it means to learn from the mistakes of others—you can never live long enough to make them all yourself!

In experiential methods, participants do not pretend that they are solving anything. Their goal is to "be" who they are and to learn about themselves and others through the process of experiencing their relationship to others. Any kind of training in which participants interact and express their feelings is considered *human relations* training.

Human relations training

Psychology is the most popular game around. Each new "game" leaves a new imprint on our thoughts and language. Each wave etches in its own peculiar

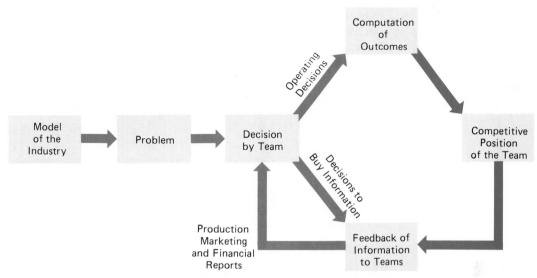

FIGURE 11-6 Steps in a management game—an important aid in teaching production, marketing, and financial concepts. Teamwork is the key in arriving at decisions.

vocabulary. The oldest game is role playing and close to it is psychodrama, followed by sensitivity training and encounter groups of the 1950s and 1960s; during the 1970s and 1980s we were presented with transactional analysis (TA), transcendental meditation (TM), and assertiveness training (AT). Experiential cases and computer-assisted training are becoming increasingly popular in the 1980s. Whether the participant will be caught up in the wave of TA, TM, or AT is hard to say, but all these methods are based on experiences that each individual will *feel*. The experience can be glowing or damaging to the ego, an afternoon happening that is soon forgotten or a mind-expanding event that will alter one's personality.

Role Playing

Act out a solution

Role playing is both a simulation and experiential exercise in problem solving, designed primarily to aid in understanding human relations. Role playing works in small groups of two to eight people.

A group is given a situation that requires a decision. Participants are then given descriptions of the attitudes of the people they are to represent, which they develop and dramatize as best they can. There are no lines to memorize—all the characterizations are improvised. The actors and actresses work on the problems until they arrive at a solution that satisfies most of the participants. Some members of the group may act as observers. After each role-playing session, the observers comment on the process, giving feedback on communication skills, supervisory techniques, and attitudes expressed between supervisors and subordinates.

Another variation is for one role to be played consistently by one person while another role is played successively by each group member. For example, a trainee plays a personnel director who interviews a particularly talkative job candidate. Application forms are provided and the talkative applicant is well versed in his or Videotape role playing her role. A video- or audiotape may be used during the role-playing session. Afterward, the trainer and group members discuss the process, thus beginning to change each trainee's attitudes and behaviors. Listening to or watching the tapes can help the trainees become more aware of their actions. The authors have found the videotape method to be the most successful way to provide students with helpful insights into interviewing techniques through role playing in job interviews.

Executives also watch themselves in action. To their distress, they see themselves mocking their teammates, issuing authoritarian orders, and exhibiting impatience. Although their goal is to beat other teams, they discover that most of the conflicts are with persons on their side.

The popularity of matrix management in which employees report to two bosses has reduced many executives' authority, thereby making their interpersonal skills far more important. The influx of women and minorities into the work force has caused problems that can rarely be resolved by fiat. All these reasons have caused an increase in role playing via videotape programs.

Sensitivity Training

How we function in groups

The goal of sensitivity training is for individuals to understand (1) how they function in a group setting and (2) how a group functions. Sensitivity training is concerned with "sensitivity" to one's feelings and the feelings of others. It differs from psychotherapy, whose purpose it is to delve deeply into inner motivations. The focus of sensitivity training is on observable "here and now" behavior rather than on assumptions about motives.

No stated goal

Leadership changes

The T-group, or training group, differs radically from more traditional forms of training because it lacks the demonstrable goal that exists in role playing. In this situation you play "yourself." The agenda in a sensitivity group or T-group is whatever people want to talk about. People who have been successful at "getting things done" find this experience frustrating and at first idiotic. With no problems to solve, participants are divested of their worldly status and authority. They are left to deal with other people without their formal relationships to back them up. Gradually group members learn to be more honest in their communication. As they become more open with one another, they trust one another more and accept other points of view. They learn to give and take leadership and make group decisions without using formal authority as a crutch.

All is not well with sensitivity training. The success of T-group techniques has been worse than expected for two reasons: (1) the groups gained a reputation for producing negative results by hurting individuals or damaging work relationships, and (2) even when groups had a good experience, the participants had difficulty applying what they gained to their work, possibly because the intensive group culture and conventional work culture tended toward opposite poles with regard to openness.[14]

Let feelings come to the surface

Another failure has been the use of untrained or inexperienced facilitators who sought to delve too deeply into feelings rather than simply bringing out sentiments for the sake of learning more about groups. Despite these failures, there is still much to learn about how openness can, and cannot, operate in organizations. The purpose of sensitivity training is to provide an environment in which feelings can be unmasked and shared—not where individuals are psychoanalyzed. People are conditioned culturally *not* to share true feelings; T-groups help people to learn how to do this. When feelings are withheld, or held onto, they become nurtured by the self. When they are released, or expressed, they can be "worked through." (See Figure 11-7.)

FIGURE 11-7 In sensitivity groups member learn to be more honest with each other—they learn to trust each other more and to accept other points of view. Robert D. Rubic.

Trainers can be important models with whom T-group members can identify. Ideally, a trainer should express feelings openly and honestly, should not become defensive and withdrawn under criticism, and should exhibit acceptance and trust of others. Trainers display different leadership patterns, from very directive to virtually nondirective and from a high expectancy of participants to accept emotional risk to a low expectancy. These variables should depend not only on the trainer's own preferences, but also on the constitution of the group itself. As a result, the styles and results of sensitivity groups vary greatly.

Transactional Analysis

Transactional analysis, or TA, was developed by the late Eric Berne, a psychiatrist who is best known for his book, *Games People Play,* and was popularized by Thomas Harris in *I'm OK—You're OK.* The leaders of TA believe that everyone's personality is made up of three parts, called ego states. An ego state is a pattern of behavior that a person develops as he or she grows up, that is based on a network of feelings and experiences he or she has.

The three ego states: child, adult, parent

The *child ego state* exists when people feel and act as they did in childhood. The spontaneous expression of internal feelings of joy, frustration, or creative ideas, as well as wishes and fantasies, are all examples of the child ego state. The *adult ego state* can be expressed when people are thinking and acting rationally, gathering facts, estimating outcomes, and evaluating results. The *parent ego state* is best likened to how a parent would handle young children. Rules and laws, tradition, demonstrations of the correct way to do things, and protection can be seen as examples of the parent ego state.

In any of the three states, one can adopt very different attitudes toward oneself and those with whom one works. In the *parent state*, a person can be an "OK" supervisor by giving critiques rather than criticism and knowing how to be supportive. Or one can be an "OK" supervisor in the *adult state* by being responsive and analytical. The *child state* can be seen as being a cooperative supervisor willing to help come up with creative ideas. Table 11-2 shows the TA of an adult, a parent, and a child.

I'm OK, you're OK

People really express how they feel about themselves and others as being OK or not OK, whether they are dealing with subordinates or superiors. They also reflect how they feel about others as being OK or not OK. Further, transactional analysis constructs the following classifications of the four possible life positions held with respect to oneself and to others.

1. I'm OK—you're OK.
2. I'm OK—you're not OK.
3. I'm not OK—you're OK.
4. I'm not OK—you're not OK.

By understanding ego states, as well as OK and not OK attitudes, we can make sense out of the different styles that people use. Some are so common that they are stereotypes. We may not like to use stereotypes, but like a mirror that distorts an image, it can still reflect some truth. The OK or not OK attitudes can be seen in the three ego states in Table 11-3.

Most supervisors have their own styles of handling their subordinates. Since all bosses have some measure of control over others, it is not uncommon for supervisors to adopt the *parental ego state* with their employees. This is no surprise, since parents are the first people we know with control over others.

At one time or another, we all act out each of the three ego states positively as well as negatively. It might be fun to tape a conversation and see whether comments can be detected as being from the parent, adult, or child state and whether they can be considered OK or not OK.

How would you rate the following statements?

1. How about a game of tennis?
2. How long will it take to get the data?

TABLE 11-2 Transactional Analysis of Parent, Adults, and Child

PARENT	ADULT	CHILD
Abides by rules and laws, do's and don'ts, truths, tradition	Is rational	Sees, hears, feels joy, frustration
	Estimates	
	Evaluates	Is creative
Avoids inconsistency	Stores data	Has wishes, fantasies, internal feelings
Uses how-to's	Figures out	
Teaches	Explores	
Demonstrates	Tests	

TABLE 11-3 Transactional Analysis of the Not OK and OK Attitudes

PARENT		ADULT		CHILD	
Not OK	*OK*	*Not OK*	*OK*	*Not OK*	*OK*
Dictator	Supportive	Computer	Communicator	Milquetoast	Negotiator
Do it my way	Informal critic	Always testing	Offering alternatives	Scatterbrain	Innovator

3. You'd better get the job done right!
4. Don't worry about it; it will be all right!
5. What do you think is wrong?
6. Yes, I am trying hard to finish it on time.

Some maintain that one of TA's values is its kindling of enthusiasm for many jobs that tend to be monotonous. TA cannot guarantee that human relations problems will disappear, but its role in future organization development programs is likely to be continued for some time.

Assertiveness Training

Assertiveness training (AT) teaches people to stand up for their feelings without resorting to one-upmanship. It encourages developing a straightforward, deliberate way of handling emotions and developing a personal authenticity. The teaching of assertiveness places as much emphasis on getting students to recognize how their own manners appear to others as it does on helping them deal with aggressiveness in others.[15] The ultimate goal is to keep communications flowing back and forth between people—even in the face of strong feelings.

Perhaps when someone mentions assertiveness training many people think of the "power boys that push people for payoffs." Robert Ringer and Michael Korda popularized the term and gave it a breezy bit of fresh "one-up-manship" in their books, *Winning Through Intimidation* and *Power: How to Get It and How to Use It.* Korda suggests jamming a visitor's chair into a small space to make him feel powerless and speaking softly to an elderly rival, as it may make him think he is going deaf. Other methods are learning to pick out the power seat at meetings and cultivating an appropriate air of mystery about yourself by hinting that you have powerful inside information.

A different feeling is expressed by others who believe in AT. The key words are *anxiety* and *authenticity.* Most humanistic behaviorists believe that teaching people the basic skills for handling difficult situations serves to alleviate immobilizing anxiety. Once people master those skills and feel that they have a cushion to fall back on, their self-confidence and spontaneity increase—anxious, scared persons are almost never spontaneous. William Dyer's *Your Erroneous Zones* and his later book *The Sky's the Limit* have helped people to deal with their anxiety and authenticity.

Assertiveness should not be confused with aggressiveness. Assertiveness allows you to express feelings constructively in a friendly manner. If both men and women would be warmer and more open, it would eliminate their anxieties about assertion. Straightforward, deliberate, and systematic rethinking is the first step toward a constructive change in our feelings and emotions.

How to Be Assertive

Overcoming the anxiety that prevents us from behaving assertively is the first step. It all comes down to your ability to size up a situation and tackle it without letting the other person's negative reactions sidetrack you. Here are a few rules.

Say It Directly.   It is natural to beat around the bush if you don't know how people will react. Recognize the other person's point of view, but be sure to get your own point across.

Express How You Feel.   If you have been asked to work overtime for at least three days a week for the last couple of months, express your feeling that *you are tired of it.* "I think I have done my part; perhaps it is time for others to put in their time."

Be Specific with a Solution.   "I don't mind working one night a week, but three is just too much. Besides, I feel that if I work overtime just one night a week I can do a better job all around." Ending with a strong positive note makes that request more reasonable and understandable to the listener.

TEST YOURSELF

How Assertive Are You?

Answer the following statements with *always, sometimes, seldom,* or *never.*

1. I usually make the first move to establish personal contacts with strangers at a party. _____

2. I would complain to the management about being overcharged or given poor service. _____

3. I would leave my usual amount of tip even if the waitress were slow and gave poor service. _____

4. When smoking bothers me, I would say so. _____

5. I can end the conversation comfortably when I think it is dragging on. _____

If the answers show that you seldom or never stand up for yourself, you may wonder about your assertiveness. In a training session your trainer may give you a long list of such questions. Responses to such lists might show that you are a tower of strength at work but a milquetoast at home or in social situations.

Transcendental Meditation

Eastern thought

There has been a trend in Western society to indulge in the Eastern esoteric psychologies of Zen, yoga, and transcendental meditation. In short, TM is a method used to learn how to be calm and alert through relaxing and concentrating on a single thought. It is a method of silent thinking, usually engaged in for a period of 20 minutes or so. It is a process that neutralizes anxiety and allows the body and the mind to feel alert after meditation. Certainly we can make better decisions if we are alert and calm. Proponents of TM believe that it can provide those qualities.

Benefits of Meditation

The reactions that occur when a person is practicing meditation are controlled mostly by the autonomic or involuntary nervous system, which produces movement in the cardiac and smooth muscle tissue and also controls the activation of the endocrine system. Some research shows that the major physiological change associated with meditation is a decreased metabolic rate, usually called *hypometabolism.* This research was taken further to illustrate that autonomic responses can be controlled.

Many behaviorists believe that the potentials of meditation without drugs or tobacco are great. We now need more research to prove these beliefs valid before the acceptance of meditation.

*Express Your
Opinion*

Now that you have studied the simulation methods (in-basket, case study, and management games) and the experiential methods (role playing, sensitivity training, transactional analysis, assertiveness training, and transcendental meditation), would you consider the simulation method or the experiential method the most important for your company? Why? Which technique (e.g., management games, TA, or TM) do you think would be the most beneficial for most of the employees in your company? Why?

Would you hire an outsider to conduct such training programs or would you have them conducted "in house" by your own personnel? Why?

Summary

Positive discipline is really what human behavior is all about. Discipline is the state of being orderly and ready to carry out a commitment. It is brought about by learning and training. The result of this state is self-control, orderliness, efficiency, and effectiveness of a group or individual. Training is the practical side of education because it has to do with transmitting information to improve problem-solving abilities. Traditional training is concerned with mechanical and intellectual knowledge; human relations training is concerned with emotions and attitudes. The main purpose of any kind of training is for learning to take place. Learning occurs when students change. Differences are demonstrated by changes in behavior. Development, including management education, takes place when the learning activity puts emphasis on increasing the participant's abilities to learn other aspects of jobs. Both employees and management have responsibility for development.

The effectiveness of training and development is determined in part by the attitudes of the participants: attitudes of students, teachers, and sponsoring companies. For training to be successful, companies must be clear about their training goals and then pick the training methods most applicable to these goals. The success of training programs is usually measured from the sponsoring company's viewpoint. Trainees may gain a lot personally, but if company goals are not met, the training has not "paid off."

Job orientation is a form of training that can greatly affect new employees' attitudes. Orientation familiarizes new employees with all the matters that don't pertain to performing the job itself. New employees must also receive some on-the-job training. Even when they have previous job experience, no two jobs are the same. The success of OJT is up to the trainers, who should have a clear idea of training procedures.

Instructional training methods include written material, correspondence courses, lectures, conferences, programmed instruction, and the many kinds of audio and visual aids. Well-known simulation techniques include the in-basket method, the case method, management games, and role playing. They share the goal of solving problems that are as close to real-life problems as possible. Simulation methods employ many different styles, but they are always at least one step removed from reality.

Experiential methods advocate learning about self to be more effective in solving problems in human relations. Members of sensitivity training groups, or T-groups, learn to experience themselves and each other in an unstructured group context. Transactional analysis, assertiveness training, and transcendental meditation all relate to self-awareness and behavior change as people see themselves in a new perspective.

Case Study 22

Training Gary for Promotion

Recently Don Taber, who is the supervisor of the Auto Repair Department of a large domestic and imported car dealership, was informed that he would be promoted to a position of higher management, that of the vice presidency of the dealership. He was also given instructions to select the most capable man in his department and to prepare him for taking over his current supervisory position.

There is one man in particular whom Don would like to promote, Gary Kurtz. He has been the lead mechanic for the company for a number of years. Gary is a reliable employee and has always performed his work with the utmost competence. Don feels that Gary possesses the ability to become a good leader. Along with Gary's knowledge of auto mechanics and his friendly attitude toward helping and training the other mechanics, he is always anxious to accept new responsibilities, and he is a man who enjoys working hard for the satisfaction of accomplishing goals that either he or others have set.

But it will be necessary to work with Gary first before placing him in charge of the department. Although Gary has many good leadership qualities, he does have certain weaknesses that need to be strengthened. In the past, when Don has been on vacation or away on company business, Gary has been placed in charge. On these occasions, when he was actually put in a position of authority, he was nervous and high-strung. When deadlines on repairs were required, he had a hard time scheduling his employees to finish the task. Under stress Gary has handled such situations poorly and has vented his unreasonable frustration upon employees—even customers. During these times he also tends not to listen fully to ideas of the other men and instead considers his own opinion as final and binding.

It is Don's opinion that these weaknesses can be overcome with proper training and that he will be able to develop Gary's good qualities to an extent that he will be considered an effective leader by both the company and the men who will be working for him.

1. How should Don go about developing Gary's good qualities and aiding Gary in correcting his poor ones?
2. What training aids or techniques might Don use in developing Gary's leadership ability?
3. Give reasons why certain techniques might develop certain leadership qualities.

Case Study 23

Should Training Be Required?

Jim Barnes had just finished going over the production reports and was getting ready to go home when Larry Williams, the assembly superintendent and Jim's immediate boss, walked into the office. He immediately came to the point of his visit. The company training director was starting a series of training sessions on improving communication skills, to be held late in the day on Thursdays. Larry wanted Jim to take the course.

The remark hurt Jim! Jim replied that he thought his communications had been all right. Larry explained that his suggestion had not been a criticism. He tried to present the idea of Jim's attending as an opportunity for Jim to develop himself and to broaden his understanding of communications. But there was still no change in Jim's expression.

"Jim, just the fact that I am having trouble making you see that I have your interest at heart illustrates the kinds of problems we have in communicating. I know what I want to say, but you are getting a different picture. We discussed things like that when I took the course. If you take the course, you might use this conversation for a case problem."

Jim said he was sorry he misunderstood and promised he would let Larry know in a day or two. On the way home, Jim reasoned that he should be grateful that the boss wanted him to take some further job training. But he was already having trouble keeping his work current, without leaving early on Thursday afternoons. He had always been careful to keep his boss fully informed. Where had he failed? Besides, this class would also interfere with his Little League games. "Damn, a suggestion from the boss is almost the same as an order," thought Jim.

The next day Jim met with Mark Watkins, a coworker, to discuss his concern. Mark said, "Relax, Larry probably made the same suggestion to other supervisors who report to him. Just forget the whole idea. Larry is from the new school, you know, forcing people to take management training programs, but they can't force you to take the class as long as you are producing. All they are interested in is profit."

Jim thought about this advice from a respected employee and decided he should take the course. However, some questions remained unanswered.

1. Should management expect a person to put in his or her own personal time on self-development?
2. If they want him or her to study, shouldn't they set it up on company time?
3. At what point are the demands on the supervisor's personal time for training programs excessive?

Terms and Concepts

assertiveness training (AT) a technique that teaches standing up for (one's) feelings without using one-up-manship; developing a straightforward, deliberate way of handling personal emotions to overcome anxiety and develop a personal authenticity.

deductive learning the ability to learn the general concepts followed by the more detailed aspects. You may learn about the general company policies before learning the specifics of your job.

development activity that puts emphasis on increasing the participant's abilities to perform effectively in other jobs as well as the current job.

discipline a state of order and readiness in an organization brought about by learning and training.

experiential methods any kind of training in which the participants interact and express their feelings. Assertiveness training, transactional analysis, and transcendental meditation are all experiential and are often called human relations training programs.

in-basket technique a technique of training designed to teach people to plan, organize, and delegate their responsibilities. In a given time period the trainees must decide how to handle problems written on memos in their in-basket.

inductive training learning from the part to the whole. More general information is added to the learning pattern once some specifics are learned. In business an employee learns how to do his or her specific job and later learns how the assembled piece fits into the total product manufactured by the company.

management games   games played by teams of employees that simulate departments or companies and engage in competition. Usually the games concentrate on making many decisions related to production, marketing, or finance. The object is to learn how to make better decisions and why some decisions were better than others.

programmed instruction (PI)   a self-teaching method whereby small amounts of information are presented in logical sequence to the learner. After being presented with a small amount of information, the learner is tested. The learner knows immediately if his or her answers are correct before going on to new information.

sensitivity training   a technique used to teach individuals to understand how they function in a group setting and how a group functions. It is a study of leadership and a person's hidden motives or needs.

There is seldom any structure or organization in the first sessions.

simulation   replication of a real-life situation in a controlled environment. Manufactured simulators are classic examples, but in-basket methods, case studies, and management games are all attempts to simulate real-life situations. People can learn from their mistakes without serious consequences.

training   the process of transmitting and receiving information related to problem solving; specific activity for improving the trainee's abilities to perform in particular jobs.

transactional analysis (TA)   a method of studying communication by learning of the three ego states of child, adult, and parent. It often helps one to better understand oneself.

transcendental meditation (TM)   a method of silent thinking used to learn how to be calm and alert through relaxing and concentrating on a single thought.

Notes

1. Phillip C. Grant, "The Do's and Don'ts for Getting Top Performance," *Management Solutions*, May 1988, pp. 22–26.

2. Leonard J. Goldstein, "Climbing the Corporate Ladder to Success," *Executive Speeches*, July 1989, pp. 1–6.

3. Eric L. Harvey, "Discipline vs. Punishment, *Management Review*, March 1987, pp. 25–29.

4. Ibid.

5. "Labor Letter," *The Wall Street Journal*, January 2, 1990, p. 1.

6. David E. Bartz, David Schwandt and Larry Hillman, "Differences Between 'T' and 'D'," *Personnel Administrator*, June 1989, pp. 164–170.

7. David L. Bradford and Allan R. Cohen, *Managing for Excellence: The Guide to Developing High Performance in Contemporary Organizations* (New York: John Wiley, 1984), pp. 70–87.

8. Robert F. Mager, *Developing Attitude Toward Learning* (Belmont, Calif.: Fearon, 1968), p. 8.

9. "Labor Letter," p. 1.

10. William S. Mitchell and others, "What Kind of Management Development Improves Productivity?" *Training and Development Journal*, January 1984, p. 17.

11. Ibid., p. 18.

12. Sandra K. Burleson, "Computer-Assisted Instruction," *Business & Economic Review*, October–December 1988, pp. 3–7.

13. Peter R. Kirrane and Diane E. Kirrane, "What Artificial Intelligence is Doing for Training," *Training: the Magazine of Human Resources Development*, July 1989, pp. 37–43.

14. Robert E. Kaplan, "Is Openness Passe?" *Human Relations*, March 1986, pp. 229–243.

15. Walter Kiechel, III, "Getting Aggressiveness Right," *Fortune*, May 27, 1985, p. 180.

Recommended Reading

Craig, Robert L., ed. *Training and Development Handbook: A Guide to Human Resource Development.* 3rd ed. American Society for Training and Development. New York: McGraw-Hill, 1987.

Hardy, Owen B., and R. Clayton McWhorter. *Management Dimensions: New Challenges of the Mind.* Rockville, Md.: Aspen, 1988.

Harris, Thomas. *I'm O.K.—You're O.K.: A Practical Guide to Transactional Analysis,* New York: Harper & Row, 1969.

Kiechel, Walter, III. "Getting Aggressiveness Right," *Fortune,* May 27, 1985, p. 180.

Kirkpatrick, Donald L. "Effective Supervisory Training and Development," Part 2. *Personnel,* January 1985, pp. 52–56.

——— "Effective Supervisory Training and Development," Part 3. *Personnel,* February 1985, pp. 39–42.

Kolb, David A. *Experiential Learning: Experience as the Source of Learning and Development.* Englewood Cliffs, N.J.: Prentice-Hall, 1984.

Mager, Robert F. *Analyzing Performance Problems.* Belmont, Calif.: Lake Publishers, 1984.

Milbourn, Gene, Jr. "The Case Against Employee Punishment." *Management Solutions,* November 1986, pp. 40–43.

Porter, Lyman, and Lawrence E. McKibbin. *Management Education and Development: Drift or Thrust into the 21st Century.* New York: McGraw-Hill, 1988.

Robinson, Dana Gaines, and Jim Robinson. *Training for Impact.* San Francisco: Jossey-Bass, 1989.

Sherman, Ellen. "Back to Basics to Improve Skills." *Personnel,* July 1989, pp. 22–26.

Sherwood, John J., Susan N. Faux, and Donald C. King. *Management Development Strategies.* New York: Pergamon, 1983.

Vaught, Bobby C., Frank Hay, and W. Wray Buchanan. *Employee Development Programs: An Organizational Approach.* New York: Greenwood, 1985.

12

Appraisals,
Promotions,
and Dismissals

After studying this chapter, you should be able to:

1. Discuss the importance of the three basic purposes of performance appraisals.

2. Describe how, ideally, an interviewer should prepare for and conduct an appraisal interview.

3. Define and give the advantages and disadvantages of the following types of appraisal methods:

   a. Essay
   b. Graphic rating scale
   c. Critical incident behavior
   d. Field review
   e. Ranking
   f. Management by objectives (MBO)
   g. Self-evaluation
   h. Behaviorally anchored rating scales (BARS)

4. Discuss the following errors that supervisors make when appraising employees:

   a. Halo effect
   b. Personal bias
   c. Central tendency
   d. Recency bias

5. Discuss the difference between merit and ability promotions.

6. Describe how to handle demotions and firings.

7. Describe the various incentive plans.

8. Discuss the increasing importance of benefits in establishing better employee-employer relationships.

TO START YOU THINKING . . .

Here are some more questions to think about while reading the chapter.

- Why is a job description important?
- What are some of the advantages of appraisals?
- What type of appraisal is the most difficult to conduct?
- What is meant by management by objectives? BARS?
- What are some of the "human errors" in rating employees?
- What are the various forms of employee benefits?
- What benefits are the most important to you? Why?
- How do you avoid or at least minimize layoffs?
- What three forms of employee benefits are most important to you and your classmates? Why?

APPRAISAL OF PERFORMANCE

All workers need to know whether they are doing a good job or not. A performance appraisal is a method by which to measure a worker's performance and let him or her know how they are doing. However, it is much more than a report card. Tom Peters makes a plea to measure constantly the things that are important:

> Performance appraisals should be ongoing, based upon a simple, written "contract" between the person being appraised and his/her boss. . . . The following attributes can turn performance appraisal from a minus to a plus:
>
> 1. "Appraisal" must be constant, not focused principally on the big annual (or semiannual) appraisal "event."
> 2. Appraisal is—and should be—very time-consuming.
> 3. There should be a small number of performance categories, and no forced ranking.
> 4. Minimize the complexity of formal evaluation procedures and forms.
> 5. Performance appraisal goals ought to be straightforward, emphasizing what you want to happen.
> 6. Make the pay decisions public.
> 7. Make formal appraisal a small part of overall recognition.[1]

Throughout history, people have evaluated one another's performances, measuring them against the codes of behavior, morals, and values that form the very fabric of society. A process of evaluation is necessary for any sort of understanding and communication. In the job situation, the performance appraisal and interview are equally important to both the employer and the employee.

Perhaps the most famous and effective performance appraisal of all time was addressed by God to the corrupt, idolatrous King Belshazzar, written on the wall of Belshazzar's palace by a disembodied hand: "You have been weighed in the balance and found wanting" (Daniel 5:27). The poor rating so upset Belshazzar that "he turned pale, he became limp in every limb, and his knees knocked together." He was slain shortly thereafter.

Employees need to know if they are doing a good job

All workers must sometimes wonder whether their supervisors think they are doing a good job or not. They may feel that management is either comparing them with other employees or judging their performance against a standard, and the employees are unable to decide which of these methods of appraisal is more fair.

PURPOSES OF AN APPRAISAL

Performance appraisals serve many purposes, but they can be sorted roughly into three categories: the administrative purpose, the informative purpose, and the developmental purpose.

The Administrative Purpose

To see if the employee should be transferred, promoted, or terminated

Performance appraisals are useful for management because they provide a method of allocating the resources of the company. Specifically, they are the means of deciding who is to be promoted, who is to be transferred, and who is to be terminated. In some companies, salaries are also determined by performance appraisals, but most companies use a seniority system, not because it is any more fair but because it is easier to operate, usually more objective, and creates less resentment among the employees. Performance appraisals compel the supervisors to do some constructive thinking about both their subordinates and themselves.

The Informative Purpose

The informative purpose of a performance appraisal, which is more obvious than the administrative purpose, albeit not more important, is to let the employee know whether management thinks that the employee is doing a good job or not, to let the employee know what the company expects and what the employee can expect from the company, to let the employee know what aspects of the work his or her supervisor feels need improvement. It is also to bestow recognition for those aspects of the work that are outstanding. Finally, it is a way of helping each employee to perform his or her present job more efficiently and satisfyingly and also a way of helping each employee to prepare for possible advancement and promotion.

A Developmental Purpose

Notice that we use the term performance *appraisal* more than performance *evaluation*. Evaluation has a connotation of looking back; appraisal suggests forward-looking, future development needs. The developmental purpose of performance appraisal is the most important from the employee's viewpoint. Individuals need/want to know how they are doing so they can continue strengths and improve upon their weaknesses. A developmental plan should be an integral part of any performance appraisal. How strengths and weaknesses are discovered is the subject of the methods section which follows later in this chapter.

First, it is important to seek some assurance that people know on what bases their performance is appraised. Performance appraisal is just that—appraisal of job performance, and, if it is to be successful for any of the purposes discussed here, the job must be defined.

Job Description

The number of people who do not know what their job responsibilities are is amazing. If an employee does not know what is supposed to be done, the job cannot be performed successfully, and if a supervisor does not know what an employee is supposed to be doing, any appraisal will be meaningless.

The best way—and the legal way—in which to evaluate an employee is to decide how well the employee's assigned duties are being carried out. Before an appraisal can be made, a job description must exist. Job descriptions are often written, spelling out in a general way the responsibilities and tasks of a position. The job description of a mail clerk might read: "Receives and opens the mail; stamps the date received on each item; distributes the mail to the proper department or individual; picks up the mail from each department; prepares and stamps the necessary envelopes; wraps, addresses, and stamps packages; delivers the mail to the post office." Usually the job description is written, but it must be understood by both the employee and the supervisor before any meaningful performance appraisal can be made.

Advantages and Disadvantages of Appraisals	1. Performance appraisal programs provide a basis upon which the employee knows that he or she will be evaluated.
	2. They motivate the employee by providing feedback on how he or she is doing.
	3. They provide backup data for management decisions concerning merit increases, promotions, transfers, and dismissals.
Advantages of Appraisals	4. They can be constructive rather than critical.
	5. They allow for quicker discovery of good and bad performance.
	6. It is believed that a required periodic appraisal will force the supervisor to face up to the problems of poor performance and deal with them.
	7. Performance appraisal programs force superiors to communicate to subordinates their judgments of employee performance.
Disadvantages of Appraisals	1. Performance appraisal programs may demand too much from supervisors, but then that's their job.
	2. Standards and ratings tend to vary widely and often unfairly.
	3. Personal values and biases can replace organizational standards.
	4. Because of lack of communications, employees may not know how they are rated.
	5. Managers tend to resist and avoid the task of making formal appraisals, particularly when critical judgments are involved.

THE APPRAISAL INTERVIEW

Performance appraisals cannot simply be handed to employees or put in their boxes or mailed to their homes, since they serve as the formal basis for a discussion of the employee's performance between the employee and the supervisor. This discussion is known as the appraisal interview. It can be one of the most unpleasant tasks of a supervisor, or it can be one of the most satisfying. Which it is depends to a great degree upon how good the employee's performance has been. But it also depends on how well the supervisor is prepared and conducts the interview.

Preparing for the Interview

The supervisor should put down in writing as much as possible pertaining to the employee's performance. The appraisal forms should be filled out and the supervisor should be prepared to justify each item. Time should be spent in reviewing the past reports of performance and in trying to recall what was covered in previous interviews. The supervisor should also remind the employee to prepare for the interview, to think about it ahead of time, and to jot down thoughts. A supervisor should consider what questions might be asked if he or she were in the employee's place and be prepared to answer those questions. The interview, however, should not be planned too rigidly. It should be flexible, for it is actually as much a discussion as it is an interview.

Plan for a half-hour interview

Inform the employee in advance

The supervisor should pick the right day, time, and place and allow at least half an hour for the interview, after notifying the employee well in advance. It is usually best not to have the interview immediately after a disciplinary action or a reprimand. The supervisor should select a time when neither the supervisor nor the employee is likely to be under stress or tired; mornings are usually best. (See Figure 12-1.) The supervisor should arrange not to be interrupted and should provide a private and comfortable place in which to meet. Comfort for both supervisor and employee probably means no barriers such as desks.

How to Open the Interview

If it is the employee's first appraisal interview, he or she should be told about the general purpose of the appraisal and the interview.

If an employee has been doing well, let it be known immediately

If the performance of an employee has been outstanding, it is often a good practice to make this known at once, because the employee will accept more readily any suggestion or minor criticisms that the supervisor may want to make. If, however, the performance is something less than outstanding, it may be best to avoid a discussion of the employee's overall rating at the beginning. Indeed, it is often best to avoid starting with the past at all.

Let the interview be future oriented

It is very important to emphasize the future development needs of the employee. If the supervisor opens with a discussion of the employee's future goals and plans, the interview will naturally go on to areas of improvement in the worker's present performance, and from there it will return to and cover the past. If, however, the supervisor opens the appraisal interview with a discussion of the employee's past performance, the interview may bog down in a detailed discussion of a particular item and never get beyond the past.

Discussion Methods

Directive or permissive interview

An appraisal interview can be *directive* or *permissive;* that is, either the supervisor or the employee will direct its course. The ideal interview, however, will be neither,

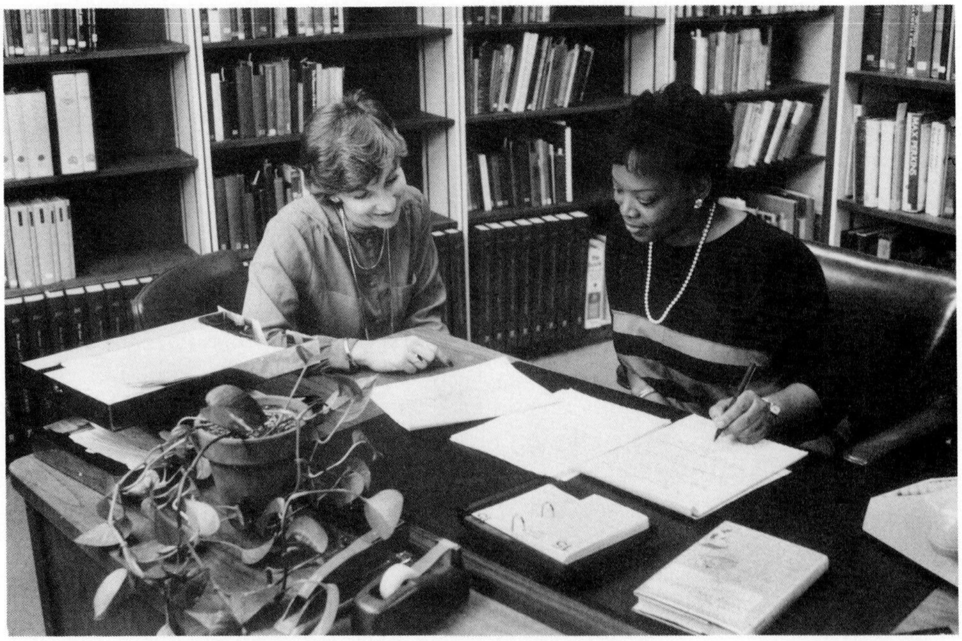

FIGURE 12-1 The supervisor should select a time for the appraisal when neither the supervisor nor the employee is likely to be under stress or tired. Barbara Alper/Stock, Boston

for both the supervisor and the employee have something to contribute; the whole discussion is about how the *supervisor and the employee* judge the performance of the *employee,* and therefore the participation of both is vital to a successful interview. The supervisor should encourage the employee to talk about himself or herself and the job. If possible, the employee should self-analyze the performance; people tend to believe what they have determined for themselves more readily than what they are told. If necessary, the supervisor can check his or her understanding of what the employee is saying by summarizing and clarifying the points in question.

The interview is partly a self-evaluation

At times, however, the supervisor does enter into the discussion in a more assertive way, letting the employee know how the performance is being viewed and whether it meets these standards. The supervisor must let the employee know in what ways performance falls short and how it can be improved.

The supervisor must be assertive

In the final analysis, the appraisal interview is a joint problem-solving effort, to which the supervisor and the employee both have something to contribute.

The interview is a joint effort

Ending the Interview

The interview should close when the supervisor has clarified what he or she intended to cover and the employee has likewise had a chance to review the issues that concern him or her. Company practices vary, but most supervisors give a copy of the performance appraisal to the employee immediately after the interview. If, however, the appraisal and the interview have dealt with the employee's objectives and plans for achieving specific goals, that information is put into the report when the employee is given his or her copy. The employee should also be reassured as to the supervisor's interest and willingness to take up the discussion at another time.

TECHNIQUES OF APPRAISALS

A number of appraisal methods are available, each with its own particular advantages and drawbacks.

Essay Appraisal

The essay appraisal requires the supervisor to write a paragraph or more about the employee's strengths and weaknesses, the quality and quantity of work, present skill and knowledge, and potential value to the company. Although this method probably gives a better and more fully rounded picture of the employee, it is likely to be more subjective than a simple graph or form. For this reason, an essay is not of much value for the purposes of comparison. In addition, essay writing is difficult and time consuming for the average supervisor, and more emphasis may be put on writing ability than other performance characteristics. The method is seldom used except to appraise employees in middle- and top-management positions.

Graphic Rating Scale

The graphic rating scale or profile rating sheet usually lists the factors to be considered and the terms to be used. Figures 12-2 and 12-3 are examples of such forms.

The supervisor simply fills out the form, and when all supervisors are using the same form and all employees are being judged in the same terms, comparisons can be made more easily and will probably be fairer. Although the opinions and

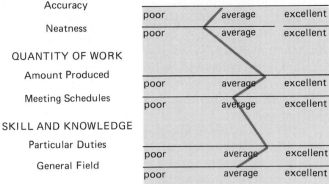

QUALITY OF WORK

Accuracy

| poor | average | excellent |

Neatness

| poor | average | excellent |

QUANTITY OF WORK

Amount Produced

| poor | average | excellent |

Meeting Schedules

| poor | average | excellent |

SKILL AND KNOWLEDGE

Particular Duties

| poor | average | excellent |

General Field

| poor | average | excellent |

FIGURE 12-2 **Graphic rating scale (or profile rating sheet) showing visually how well an employee is performing on the job (partial rating sheet).**

prejudices of the appraiser will still influence the rating, this is not necessarily a drawback, because the only way in which the element of subjectivity can be removed from an appraisal method is to eliminate the appraiser.

There are some important disadvantages, however. The categories and factors listed often tend to overlap, which makes it difficult for the conscientious supervisor to use the form (e.g., if the quantity and quality of an employee's work are excellent, how can the appraiser say that the employee's skill and knowledge are anything but excellent?) The method is also rather rigid and does not give a complete picture of the individual's past performance and future development potential. For these reasons, the method is often employed in conjunction with the essay appraisal.

Critical Incident Technique

Record incident that has happened

When the critical incident technique (CIT) method is used, the supervisor records the actual behavior observed, noting examples of insubordination or tardiness and instances of the employee using good or bad judgment. The method is used often when a supervisor has already more or less decided to recommend that an employee be fired or promoted. Keeping such records of all employees, however, demands much of the supervisor's time.

Dennis, a new deep-sea diver, was talking to a hard-hat worker on the oil platforms in the North Sea. "You know, Joe, I don't understand how little notes about my actions have popped up in my personnel folder back in Aberdeen, Scotland. Why, that's more than five hundred miles away!" Phone calls can put the CIT to work in the appraisal of employees—at a distance of 500 miles away and out at sea. The behavioral accounts are recorded as anecdotes and put in the employee's personnel file. There is the negative connotation of "keeping a little black book" on the employees.

NONEXEMPT
HOURLY REVIEW FORM

Employee _____ Job Assignment _____

Supervisor _____ Dept. _____

Date Hired _____ Prior Appraisal Date _____

AREAS OF PERFORMANCE	Outstanding 9–10	Above Average 6–8	Average 3–5	Below Average 1–2	Unsatisfactory 0	N/A
JOB KNOWLEDGE: Comment:						
QUALITY OF WORK: Ability to meet standards.						
QUALITY OF WORK: Ability to effectively use time and materials.						
SAFETY: Result of work under safe/unsafe practices.						
ATTENDANCE: Indicate hours off the job since the date of last appraisal due to: Personal _____ Illness _____ Punctuality (tardiness) _____ Comment:						

PERSONAL FACTORS	5	4	2–3	1	0	N/A
INITIATIVE: How person handles new skills or improvements. Comment:						
ADAPTABILITY TO CHANGE: Ability to adjust to new situations. Comment:						
COOPERATION: Ability to get along with employees and supervisor. Comment:						
DEPENDABILITY: Ability to complete the job. Comment:						

FIGURE 12-3 Sample appraisal form for an hourly employee (page one).

EMPLOYEE'S PRESENT JOB DUTIES: _____

_____

_____

<u>COUNSELING SUMMARY</u>

EMPLOYEE'S STRENGTHS   SUGGESTED IMPROVEMENTS

1. _____   1. _____

2. _____   2. _____

3. _____   3. _____

_____

<u>Improvement Activity</u>
Consider how this employee has reacted to the counseling and suggestions that were prompted by the last
formal appraisal. What has been accomplished toward the goals and objectives established in the previous
interview? If the person has failed to follow through, indicate why.

Comment: _____

_____

_____

_____

_____

OVERALL RATING:
_____ Results achieved far exceed the requirements
of the job in all areas.
_____ Results achieved are above average.

_____ Consistently performed the job to the requirements of the position.
_____ Results did not always meet the requirements
of the position.
_____ Results frequently did not meet the requirements of the position.

OVERALL RATING Comment: _____

_____

_____

_____

Company-related activities (Safety Committee, Christmas party, picnic, etc.): _____

EMPLOYEE'S COMMENT:

_____

_____

_____   _____   _____
Employee's Signature   Date   Supervisor's Signature

Comments by next level of supervision: _____

_____

_____
Manager's Signature

FIGURE 12-3   **(continued)**

The speech bubble reads: ADAMS, YOU LOOK LIKE A PERSON WHO'S GOING PLACES. THE PROBLEM IS, IT ALWAYS SEEMS TO BE THE MEN'S ROOM, THE LUNCHROOM, OR THE WATER COOLER.

Ranking

Ranking should only be done for promotions or layoffs

Ranking compares the employee with other employees. This method is useful and justifiable in cases when several employees are being considered for promotion to a single position. It may also be used when it is necessary to lay off a part of the work force, although seniority more often determines who is laid off. For any purposes other than these, however, a method of appraisal should be used that compares an employee with a job standard and not with fellow employees. Comparing a person with his or her peers will almost invariably create jealousy and bad feelings in a company's work force.

Field Review

Field review or group appraisal is used for middle management

Field review involves appraisal by a group rather than by an individual. The group can consist of fellow employees or several supervisors or a combination of these. It is sometimes used when there is reason to suspect prejudice or bias on the part of the employee's supervisor or when an employee wishes to appeal an appraisal.

The judgment of the group will usually be more fair and valid than will that of an individual, but field review is excessively time consuming, and it is not always easy to find a second supervisor who has any real firsthand knowledge of the employee. Some companies use the field method for all middle-management personnel on the grounds that they will arrive at a fairer evaluation and will overcome the personal biases of supervisors. Peer evaluations are a type of group review and also contribute to fairness and validity of the appraisals.

Peer and Subordinate Appraisal

There is strength in numbers. What this means regarding performance appraisal is that it makes sense to diversify the raters. It would probably be a mistake for an organization to adopt exclusively any method of appraisal. Putting all the appraisal responsibility with peers or subordinates would be as narrow and potentially biased as the typical system of having the boss exclusively appraise the subordinates.

Peer systems are gaining acceptance. The results of one study showed higher user acceptance if peer appraisals were used for developmental rather than evaluative purposes.[2]

Subordinate appraisals of their bosses are also on the increase. Professor John Bernardin of Florida Atlantic University surveyed 140 companies and found that about 10 percent had tried this process. When Bernardin did a follow-up study in 1988, the figure was nearly 20 percent.

> People at the highest level in a company typically do not get much feedback . . . (but don't try upward appraisal) in a primitively authoritarian organization, one being downsized, or anyplace with minimal communication up or down: It will only feed the general paranoia. Administered incorrectly, the process may leave subordinates open to reprisals from (the boss).
>
> The process works best if you can survey at least four immediate subordinates per manager. Otherwise, you run the danger of what the experts . . . term reciprocal leniency: "Rate me high," the boss insinuates, "and I'll do the same for you on your next appraisal. . . ."[3]

Another caveat is expressed by Steward Black at Dartmouth's Tuck School: Once you've collected appraisals from subordinates, don't just sit on them. "You've raised expectations. . . . By doing nothing you dash those expectations. . . . Better for employees to think the boss doesn't care than for them to think that he betrayed them."[4]

Self-Evaluation

Self-evaluation of job performance is also being adopted by more employers.[5] The idea is to get employees to participate in their job reviews and create a dialog with the boss on performance evaluation. Self-appraisal provides timely, focused feedback, eliminating the anxiety of performance ambiguity and motivating the individual to take more responsibility for performance and growth.[6] More frequent evaluations are possible; in fact, the individual is in a position to appraise his or her performance monthly or even more often if he or she is working on a special project.

One system recommended is to have at least two separate appraisal meetings —one to find ways for the employee to do the job better and the other to determine if any improvement has actually occurred since the developmental meeting. The experience gained from discussing job performance with a supervisor during a performance feedback discussion helps employees learn to accept constructive criticism as the basis for personal and professional growth. The experience in the developmental appraisal process will help employees overcome the apprehension associated with the formal evaluation process.[7]

Management by Objectives

MBO are goals set by
both supervisor and
employee
Future evaluations are
based on MBO

Specific goals

Measurable goals

Time frame

Employee responsible

MBO must be
measurable

Management by objectives (MBO) is a widely used appraisal system. Under this method the employee and the supervisor set common goals, discuss together what the employee can accomplish during the next evaluation period, and agree on what is expected of the employee. This method follows four rules:

1. Both the superior and the subordinate together set specific objectives to be accomplished for which the subordinate is held directly responsible.

2. Both decide how the performance will be measured.

3. Both develop short-term targets to be accomplished within a given time frame.

4. The appraisal focuses on the results that have been achieved in accomplishing these goals. (See Figure 12-4.)

Difficulties in using this method often arise when implementing the second rule, which is, of course, the basic problem of all the appraisal methods. How does one measure performance? Most goals are not easily measurable. Because it is an achievement-oriented method, management by objectives would seem to be a better instrument for measuring top- and middle-management performance than for measuring the performance of a clerk-typist.

The supervisor and the subordinate may have occasional progress reviews and reevaluation meetings, but at the end of the set period of time, the subordinate is evaluated on the accomplishment of the agreed-upon goals. Employees may be rewarded for their success by promotion or salary increase, and if they have failed, they may be fired or transferred to a job that will give them needed training or

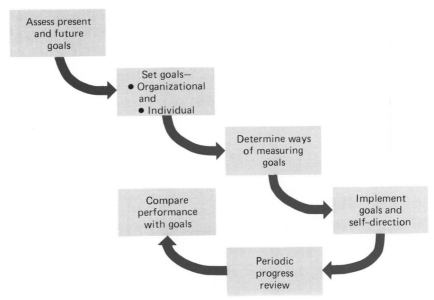

FIGURE 12-4 The path taken to establish and follow a management by objectives program.

supervision. Whatever the outcome, it will be based on the employees' accomplishment of the goals *they* had some part in setting and to which they had committed themselves.

Behaviorally Anchored Rating Scales

Behaviorally anchored rating scales (BARS) identify expectations of performance in specific behavioral terms. The absence or presence of behaviors rather than subjective ratings or rankings become the basis for the appraisal. Figure 12-5 is an example of BARS for an office support clerk. The possible outcomes of specific behaviors become part of a linear graphic scale where dimensions of job performance are the anchor points.

The BARS system is designed using a combination of the graphic rating scale and critical incident technique. To develop BARS scales, records are kept of critical incidents and performance dimensions are developed and scaled to the incidents producing the final instrument.

FREQUENT ERRORS MADE IN RATING EMPLOYEES

Supervisors make a number of mistakes when they fill out performance appraisals, most of them being the sorts of mistakes we all make when we misjudge friends and acquaintances.

Halo Effect

One area of performance influences other areas

The halo effect exists when a supervisor or other rater assumes that if an employee is above average in one area, the employee is above average in all areas. Many people attribute nonexistent virtues or accomplishments to those to whom they are attracted. Another term for this assumption is *constant error*: considering the employee to be excellent in one particular area, the supervisor goes on to say that he or she is excellent in all areas. It is similar to another natural tendency, that of

---

Job: Office Support Clerk
Dimension: Interpersonal Relations

PERFORMANCE	BEHAVIORAL ANCHOR
1. Unacceptable	Clerk is rude, sharp, and intolerant of others, their opinions, and questions.
2. Very poor	Talks aimlessly with clients; may argue with rude customer.
3. Poor	Exhibits poor followthrough when answering requests for information.
4. Average	Maintains communication with co-workers in a timely manner.
5. Good	Facilitates communications through effective questioning and listening.
6. Very good	Consistently provides high-quality treatment and acceptance of unusual clients and/or situations.
7. Outstanding	Always polite and courteous with others regardless of what difficulties arise.

FIGURE 12-5 Behaviorally Anchored Rating Scale.

rating a person as "excellent" rather than "above average" or flattering a worker rather than leaving room for improvement. The halo effect can also work in reverse. If a person strikes us as unpleasant, we may assume that he or she is an inefficient worker.

Personal Bias

Personal bias is difficult to avoid. Every human being has prejudices of one sort or another. Preference may be given to employees of the same race or the opposite sex or to workers who belong to the same club as the supervisor. Intelligent or good-looking persons may receive better ratings than their actual job performances deserve. On the other hand, supervisors are often aware of their prejudices and may attempt to compensate for them, actually giving individuals against whom they are biased better performance appraisals than they really merit.

Favoritism to certain groups, races, or sex

Central Tendency

When central tendency prevails, the supervisor completes all the forms in about the same way for all the employees under him and all the employees come out about average. In an attempt to be fair, the supervisor does not discriminate among different workers or among the different areas of performance of an individual. In fact, treating everyone as average is unfair to the outstanding performers especially. It is also unfair in the long run to the substandard performer who needs constructive criticism and to change performance behavior.

All people are average

Recency Bias

Supervisors have a tendency to judge an employee's performance for the whole rating period based on the employee's actions within the week just before the appraisal. The good or bad incidents of the last week are fresh in mind; the achievements or failures of a year ago are forgotten. There is also a natural and quite proper hesitation to rehash a recent incident, particularly when it is one in which the employee looked bad. Nevertheless, the performance appraisal is a rating for an entire period.

Your performance on the day of evaluation is most important

Mr. Smith is a supervisor for the Crummy Concrete Company. The team he supervises consists of Nick, Pedro, and Donald. Nick is the outstanding employee on the team, but last week he and Mr. Smith had a bitter argument. Donald, on the other hand, is only an average worker, but during the past week he has volunteered several times to stay a little late and help clean the machinery. Smith is about to submit his semiannual performance appraisal of his work team to top management. He wants to be a fair supervisor, but he will have a natural tendency to rate Donald higher than his overall performance during the past six months deserves and to rate Nick lower. If he had kept records of the actual performance of the men on the job through a critical incident or other technique and reviewed them prior to filling in the appraisals, his ratings might have been more accurate.

PROMOTIONS

Tradition, laws, and the availability of qualified candidates within a company influence whether a position becomes "open" to the general public or is filled by an in-house promotion. First-level management positions are usually filled by in-house promotions, which are often determined by the immediate supervisor. For middle-management positions, competition is also opened to people outside the organization.

It is common practice for companies to check for internal talent first before searching elsewhere. You should remember this when you are given expanded duties. It may be a method of testing you for a promotion.

Managers often need a way to determine who should be promoted and who can be terminated. A simple tool, known as a promotable people or replacement chart, can make it easier to identify and analyze employee potential. The first step is to sketch out a chain of command with each job title in a separate box; then color boxes blue for employees with excellent growth potential, green for those with moderate growth potential. Questionable employees, or those too new to evaluate, or marginal performers can be colored yellow. Poor producers, due or overdue for termination, would be colored red. At a glance, the completed chart will point out critical employee problems.[8]

What Promotion Means

To many people, job improvement or promotion means regular wage increases, more security, and perhaps an easier job. However, this is not always true. An easier job is not possible in some industries because of the fast-paced demand for new technology, and increased security is never guaranteed. As for wage increases, some people turn down promotions because the increase in pay does not seem to equal the increase in responsibilities.

Promotion does not always mean more money. Some individuals can outearn the boss and still keep their jobs by working on commissions and other means. One writer suggests: "Find a position with a secure chief executive, work on commission, and as Babe Ruth said, 'Have a good year.'"[9]

Promotion Based on Merit or Ability

Merit is based on performance

If promotion is to be an incentive for an employee, the best performing employee should be advanced. However, differences in employee merit may not be readily measurable, so that, when you make a promotion based on merit, the person who was not promoted may feel that favoritism was involved. Another difficulty with merit promotions is that it is hard to evaluate many on-the-job performances, such as that of the salesperson trying to sell a product that is in short supply.

Ability is based on potential

In awarding promotions, there is also the question of ability—the potential to perform well in advanced jobs. Larry is doing a good, even a great, job in his present position, but on the surface he does not show the potential for additional responsibility. Charlie, however, is doing only adequate work, but he has poor supervision and the job is not challenging. A promotion to a more difficult assignment may cause him to blossom.

The Employee Who Doesn't Want to Be Promoted

Our culture encourages promotion

In our culture a person who doesn't want a promotion is considered to be either weird or lazy. People who really do not want to be promoted may come to feel that failure to show interest in advancement is a black mark against their records. Thus, some individuals accept a promotion when they are not suited for it, thereby putting the "Peter principle" into practice. Unfortunately, it is at a high cost to

Promotion doesn't satisfy everyone

themselves and to the organization. For these reasons, a clear recognition of each employee's psychological needs is valuable both to the person and to the company.

DISCIPLINARY ACTION

In Chapter 11, we defined disciplinary action as one method of achieving discipline, the desired state of order and readiness in an organization. Disciplinary action has traditionally been punitive—punishment for an infraction of rules or violation of an accepted group norm.

The connection between discipline and training was also made in Chapter 11. A similar link exists between training and performance appraisal. The Performance Assessment Review (PAR) system attempts to link training to employee performance and development for New Jersey state employees. PAR, a performance appraisal system, is used to identify major work assignments by establishing a written and objective work performance agreement between subordinates and their supervisors. State training personnel review aggregated improvement data to plan training opportunities and forecast training needs. Supervisors and managers are forced to focus on the improvement of employee capacity and actual job performance rather than on punitive sanctions for those not "up to PAR."[10]

The importance of having a procedurally correct performance appraisal system is strengthened by recent court and administrative rulings. There is a need to adopt procedural due process for performance appraisal systems to rate employees' job performance accurately because their ratings may be challenged.

Legal problems regarding employee disciplinary measures can be prevented by making sure that employee disciplinary actions follow prescribed guidelines. Before imposing disciplinary actions, employers should make sure that:

- Employees have been given advance notice of disciplinary action
- Disciplinary rules are reasonable
- Offenses have been properly investigated
- Investigations are conducted objectively
- Rules are enforced equally
- Penalties are related to the severity of offenses[11]

DEMOTIONS AND DISMISSALS

Warnings

Must provide written warnings for a dismissal

Employees should be given written warnings of demotion or dismissal. In cases involving unsatisfactory performance, particularly for permanent employees, warnings in *addition* to the scheduled evaluation reports should be given before action is taken.

In most cases, permanent employees may not be dismissed for reasons of unsatisfactory performance unless there is documented evidence. Performance evaluation reports—scheduled and unscheduled—provide a written record of specific deficiencies. *Employees' deficiencies affecting job performance that are not recorded on performance evaluation reports cannot be used properly as a basis for dismissal.*

How to Handle a Demotion

A demotion is required when an employee does not have the ability to perform specific tasks or when economic conditions within the company dictate staff changes. In the former case, an employee is usually aware that he or she is not performing to expectations. There is no need to be abusive about the poor performance, especially if you have given encouragement to perform better and have issued written warnings of the impending demotion. Your best approach is to be *firm*.

Be firm, be honest

Make clear statements about the poor performance, using actual incidents. If you are not clear, the employee may feel that the demotion is your fault, not his (or hers), and attribute the demotion to personality problems between the two of you. Remember, it is the performance that is unacceptable, not the employee. An assignment that is less taxing physically or emotionally or one that requires less current technology may be the answer. Remember, a demotion is not a firing.

The "sandwich technique" is ideal in a demotion situation, as in the following example:

The positive sandwich technique

"Charlie, you have been with us about six months now. You have been able to adapt to the company and the employees seem to like you. You have a sincere desire to put out an honest day's work. That I like, Charlie!

"However, I wouldn't be fair if I told you that your performance has been up to par. We can't have so many mathematical errors in your docking and loading reports. As you have discovered, it has a domino effect all the way up to the accounting department.

"Now, we don't want to let you go because we feel you have potential, but not in your present position. I was thinking, Charlie, perhaps things would work out better for both you and the firm if we moved you to another position. Here is a description of the job I had in mind. I feel it is the type of job that is more suited to your nature and ability.

"Unfortunately, the pay is a little less, but if you can do the job well you can be making as much in three months as you are now. They have a good crew over there and you would still be reporting to me. I want you to know I have confidence in you, Charlie."

This approach leaves Charlie with some self-respect and also gives him the alternative of either accepting the demotion or leaving the firm. Using this technique, you seem to put Charlie, in this case, in charge of his destiny, although you as the supervisor have decided that Charlie is no longer going to continue in the present position.

How Do You Fire an Employee?

Don't fail yourself, the employee, and the company

Place yourself in a typical supervisory situation. When you analyze your department realistically and plan for its future goals, you come to the conclusion that loyal people in your department are shouldering the responsibility for one person who is not producing. You can see that it is unfair over a period of time for others continually to support the burden of the freeloader. In time, both morale and production will be lower if the problem continues. The solution to your problem is to "unhire" an employee.

Before you reach the decision to terminate a person's employment, ask yourself some questions:

1. Did I give ample warning? You are not being fair with the individual unless in performance reviews you have given constructive criticism on how to improve his or her work or mend his or her ways.

2. Do I have a qualified replacement ready to step into the vacancy? You must be certain that the change will bring about a significant improvement. At least the *potential* for improvement must exist.

3. Is the *primary* responsibility for failure the employee's—or mine? Did you pick the right person for the job? Did the person receive the necessary training and supervision? Perhaps all the person needs is a new manager, not a new employer.

The release of an employee should be handled delicately for the good of the company's image and the morale of the other employees. Care in firing can also head off a lawsuit that may charge discrimination because of age, sex, or race. But don't sugar-coat the problem, because the fired employee may be unaware that he or she has been fired.

Timing of the firing is very important, and it should never be done near the employee's birthday or anniversary. Some experts suggest that such an interview should be done at the beginning of the week. Ironically, some advisors recommend that several weeks before Christmas is a better time for dismissals than waiting until after the first of the year. According to this theory, the holidays are a good time to give notice because people are naturally networking at that time of year during parties and other festivities. It's much better than in January when they are left out in the cold, both literally and figuratively.

Express Your Opinion

What do you think—if the decision has been made, is it more humane to give notice of dismissal several weeks before Christmas, or should you wait until after the first of the year?

Certainly the supervisor shoud do the firing personally and not rely on a stranger from personnel, and the bad news should be communicated in a conference room or the employee's office, so that the boss can exit easily once the message is delivered. The location of the meeting room should also be off the beaten path, in case the employee erupts when told that he or she is through.

Tell the employee his or her ability and job don't match

Being fired can be a creative experience for an employee, despite its initial pain. Let an employee go in a way that lets him or her maintain self-esteem. There may be other areas in which the individual can perform more effectively and be happier. Thus, on the positive side, you may help an employee to recognize the opportunities involved in being fired and open new avenues to be explored.

Layoffs

With increasing economic uncertainties and technological advances, the number of layoffs is increasing. There is an uncertainty inherent in human resources forecasting that makes careful work force reduction planning a necessity. There are several ways that the work force can be reduced:

1. Attrition
2. "Induced" retirements
3. Selective dismissals
4. Layoffs

Attrition, the loss of employees in the normal course of events, may not reduce the work force rapidly enough. Induced retirements such as (1) "the Golden handshake," where an employee under 70 is given a financial inducement to retire, and (2) "window plans" where employees have a fixed period of time to resign, are costly. Layoffs, too, may be costly but their negative impact can be reduced by contingency and outplacement planning. Layoffs assume the possibility of recall.

The organization should make plans for reductions, and communicate the existence of those plans to their employees, no matter how good business and economic times may seem.

> Sound human resources planning suggests that personnel administrators should always know not only what the job needs are, but also where the personnel surpluses are located. These should be available at any given time in the form of some type of personnel data base. . . . The plan should be a part of published company policy.[12]

Whether reductions are determined by seniority, performance, potential appraisal records, or some other means, the reduction plan should be communicated to employees before the plan needs to be implemented. Finally, outplacement services provided by the company as an employee benefit can help soften the blow for the individual and the company. The "survivors" of a layoff will judge the company harshly and experience very low morale if the cuts are made without an understandable plan.

SALARIES AND WAGES AS REWARDS

Just as we have seen that a good performance appraisal is a way of telling the employee that the employer appreciates his or her work, a reward is another way of communicating the same information. That reward is usually monetary but can also be in the form of important nonmonetary recognition.

Ford Motor Company and others follow this practice of rewarding with various types of reinforcement reminders. Consider six rules for using reinforcement and rewards through operant conditioning:

1. Don't give the same level of reward to all.
2. Failure to respond to behavior has reinforcing consequences.

3. Tell a person what behavior gets reinforced.

4. Tell a person what he or she is doing wrong.

5. Don't punish in front of others.

6. Make the consequences equal to the behavior.[13]

On most levels of an organization, the usual procedure followed when a supervisor recognizes superior performance is developing a good performance appraisal followed by a promotion, bonus, or a raise or a combination of these. The supervisor rewards a high level of achievement over a short period of time with a substantial pay raise that the employee will likely receive for the rest of his or her working life. The supervisor does this in the hope that the high level of achievement will continue.

Salaries consist of base pay and benefits. The base pay is more important than benefits, in both practical and psychological terms. An employee must feel that his or her base pay is fair and adequate: an employer cannot make up in benefits for what is lacking in the basic wages, because a below-average wage plan with good benefits provides security but little substance for immediate necessities.

Salary can mean purchasing power, status, respect, and appreciation

Workers need the reassurance that wages can give them; although the company may have been good to them in the past, they need to have their feelings of worth updated periodically. Thus most companies give yearly raises. Indeed, in a great many organizations, except for general pay raises, these are the only raises that an employee receives unless he or she is promoted to a higher position. The employee may be practically guaranteed a raise, but status, appreciation, respect—all the intangible benefits that are bestowed with a merit raise—are virtually eliminated; the raise simply means that the employee has been there for another year. Because of the limited number of positions to which workers can be promoted, other rewards, such as performance appraisals, become all the more important.

INCENTIVE PLANS

Each of the four wage incentive plans outlined in this section has certain advantages and disadvantages. Many such plans have been devised only to be abandoned and replaced by others. No matter which wage incentive plan is adopted, all must take several factors into consideration:

1. The wage paid must be related to the individual's output.

2. The wage plan must make adequate provision for learners and new employees.

3. The plan must be easy to administer, easy to understand by the employees, and easy to relate to costs.

Andrall E. Pearson, former president of PepsiCo, advocates paying for the best:

> Make sure every unit rewards its best achievers appropriately. Sometimes, better performers get bigger raises than less-accomplished people, but the differences are so slight as to be demotivating. . . . Top performers relish the challenge of ever-higher goals. What demoralizes them is a climate that rewards mediocrity and excellence equally.[14]

Commissions

In this system, which is generally used for salespeople, income received is based on a percentage of sales. Many salespeople receive a base salary in addition; others have a guaranteed minimum wage.

A commission pay structure is a classic example of an incentive pay system: the more you produce, sell, or otherwise work, the more you get paid. There is a downside to a pure commission structure: there may be some external variables affecting production or sales. Perhaps the salesperson is working very hard in the short-term, tending to business and taking care of customers, but the sales just aren't coming. Compared to someone who is not working hard but enjoys the benefits of a healthy salary, salespeople may perceive an inequity. Equity is what compensation and rewards are all about. It behooves management to find a balance between commission pay and retaining good employees.

Profit-Sharing Plans

These plans are simply a method of distributing a portion of a company's profits among its employees. Such plans provide an incentive for efficiency, innovation, and cooperation among an organization's work force. Usually the profits are distributed annually, sometimes in the form of a Christmas bonus. Profit sharing is a way of enabling a company to give a pay increase to all its employees without being saddled with such an increase indefinitely. It has the disadvantage, however, of rewarding all workers indiscriminately, just as the group incentive raises reward all employees in a particular group without attempting to differentiate between the efficient and the inefficient.

Merit Increases

Merit increases are wage increases awarded for excellent performance

These are increases in pay given to employees who have received excellent performance appraisals. The system has the advantage of being uncomplicated, and the raises received under such a method probably communicate more of the intangibles (status, appreciation, respect) than do raises received under any other system. Unfortunately, the method also can produce considerable ill will and jealousy; and, because the employee receives raises almost entirely at the discretion of a supervisor, the system is only as fair or unfair as the supervisor is.

Cash Bonuses

A bonus is a reward for outstanding performance over a short period

Cash bonuses are money given to employees for outstanding performance, as a sort of one-time merit increase. As a practical matter, raises, once granted, cannot be rescinded. Bonuses, on the other hand, can vary from year to year with an employee's performance. It is far better to give bonuses for good performances over a short period. Theory Z companies rely heavily on the cash bonus system.

EMPLOYEE BENEFITS

Sacrifices and loyalty are two-way streets

Employees will make sacrifices for and be loyal to a company when they feel that the company, in turn, will make sacrifices for and be loyal to them. Thus a utility crew may take great personal risks to keep telephone service open during a flood, or the employees of a store might accept a pay cut when the store is faced with a financial crisis. Less dramatic, but no less important, is the worker who will stay on the job for an extra 10 to 15 minutes to explain something to a supervisor. On the other hand, when employees are in trouble, they rightly expect the company to make sacrifices also. It is here that benefits come in, for the greater part of such benefits is in the form of insurance: medical plans, sick pay, group life insurance, pensions, and credit unions.

Although the most common benefits seem to be vacations, group life insurance, and medical plans, they range all the way from organ transplants to group auto insurance to company-paid legal fees. The list in Table 12–1 is only partial. Can you think of others?

"Cafeteria-style" compensation

Because of the many benefits available, organizations have been able to offer "cafeteria-style" packages from which employees can select the benefits they want. Such packages are tailored to the needs of the individual employee. Different people have different needs and desires. For example, younger employees prefer higher salaries to extensive retirement plans. Female employees, married employees, and employees with children usually consider a medical plan to be the most desirable benefit, especially if it includes maternity benefits.

Stock options appeal primarily to single employees and professional employees. A psychological advantage to these benefit packages is that, by participating in the formulation of their own packages, the employees are more satisfied with their own roles in the programs, and thus the benefits they receive are more "visible" and tangible.

Average benefits are over 35 percent of total pay

If employees do not know what they are being paid, they cannot appreciate it. Benefits can often amount to somewhere between 30 and 50 percent of a worker's base salary. These benefits ought to be communicated to them. One means of communicating this information is shown in Figure 12–6.

Summary

Performance is what's important in performance appraisal—personality idiosyncrasies are not. Performance appraisals serve many purposes. They let management know the quality of the company's personnel, they compel the supervisor to think constructively about subordinates and about himself or herself, and they inform the employee of what management thinks about the job that he or she is doing.

There are several types of appraisal methods. The essay appraisal requires the supervisor to write a paragraph about the employee's performance. The graphic

TABLE 12-1 Types of Benefits Provided by Companies

Social security	Workers' compensation
Group life insurance	Supplemental unemployement benefits
Medical plans	Credit unions
Pension plans	Annuity programs
Stock purchase plans	Education aid
Recreational aid	Vacation with pay
Paid holidays	Paid birthday off
Company discount stores	Profit sharing
Loans	Group dental plans
Flexible time schedules	Child care centers

```
Dear_____

        After preparing your W-2 this year, we thought you
might be interested in knowing the total amount paid to you
by the firm for salary, incentive compensation and benefit
programs during the year.

Your annual salary amounted to $_____ plus incentive

compensation of $_____ for a total of $_____

The firm also paid the following amount for a comprehensive
program of benefits:

        1. Medical/dental insurance              _____
        2. Life insurance                        _____
        3. Accidental death and
           dismemberment                         _____
        4. Disability                            _____
        5. FICA (social security)
           employer's share                      _____
        6. Workers' compensation                 _____
        7. Unemployment insurance                _____
              Total benefits paid             $_____

Also last year the following amount was contributed to your
pension plan by the company:

                                               $_____




The total annual compensation paid to you during the year
amounts to:

        Salary                                  _____
        Incentive                               _____
        Benefits                                _____
        Pensions                                _____

        Total                                $_____

On behalf of all of us, thank you for your fine
contributions. We look forward to working with you during
the coming year.

                        Sincerely,
```

FIGURE 12-6 A letter showing employees what they earn in salary and benefits.

rating scale is a form listing a number of performance factors; the supervisor states on the form whether the employee is poor, average, or excellent in a number of performance areas. In critical incident technique, the supervisor keeps track of incidents and examples as they occur. The field review is the appraisal of an employee by a group of persons. Ranking is a method whereby the employee is compared with fellow employees. Management by objectives places the emphasis upon the employee's goals and the methods whereby those goals can be achieved. A system using behaviorally anchored rating scales (BARS) permits performance to be measured against predetermined standards that have been set mutually by boss and subordinate. The use of peer, subordinate, and self-appraisal is increasing rapidly.

There are also a number of errors that supervisors can make when appraising employees. With the halo effect, a boss assumes that because an employee is outstanding in one particular field, the employee is outstanding in other ways too. Supervisors can let their own personal bias influence them. Another kind of error involves placing too much emphasis on recent behavior.

Tradition, laws, and the availability of company candidates influence whether a position becomes open to the general public or promotional from within the company. Some promotions are based on merit and ability; others are based on seniority.

Demotions can usually be made only after oral and written warnings have been issued. Written warnings of substandard performance should be given before recommending a demotion or a dismissal. Before firing an employee, you must think of the employee, the department, the company, and yourself as a supervisor. If you don't release an incompetent worker, you are failing yourself, your department, and the company. Planning for layoffs and employing outplacement counselors can reduce the trauma associated with cutbacks for both those dismissed and the "survivors."

Rewards in the form of salaries and wages satisfy much more than simply the basic material needs of employees. They represent status, respect, and appreciation. In addition to ordinary wages of one sort or another, most companies offer their employees benefits that can amount to as much as 50 percent of their base salaries. Most, but not all, of these provide employees with security in case of sickness, old age, or other emergencies. They include sick pay, group medical and dental plans, group life insurance, and vacations. Many large companies allow their employees to choose from a cafeteria of benefits.

Case Study 24

What Rewards Should Be Given Now?

Bruce Levin is the sales manager of the Amcox Corporation, which sells sewing notions to distribution and retail outlets. Bruce has 23 employees in his department, and all are paid on commission for their sales in their territories. For the past three years, the market for the company's goods has been growing steadily, and the majority of Bruce's men and women have met this growth with increased sales. However, one employee in particular, Jerry Lawson, has not kept up with the pace.

Jerry has been with Amcox for 15 years and is now 59 years old. Jerry is a friendly man and is well liked by both his peers and those to whom he sells notions on a regular basis. The company has always considered Jerry dependable and loyal. Through the years Jerry has been counted as an asset to the company, but at the age of 59 he has gone into a state of semiretirement. Jerry's sales have not increased as the others have, and he doesn't have the determination to acquire a significant increase in sales.

Bruce Levin wishes to change this situation. He wants to motivate Jerry into increasing his sales to match that of his younger peers. To accomplish this, Jerry must begin to do more than put in his time, but Bruce is not sure how to go about trying to motivate him. Unlike the majority of the new employees, Jerry is an older man, who within a few years will reach the age of retirement.

If you were Bruce what would you do?

1. Would you threaten to fire him?
2. Does your solution involve the feelings of others in your staff?
3. Would you increase his commissions?
4. Would you increase the retirement benefits for Jerry rather than offer him the increased commission rate?
5. Would you offer him more status in the way of a new title or new company car or place his desk in a better position in the office?
6. Is there some way in terms of appraisal and rewards that you can motivate Jerry?

Case Study 25

Promotion Based upon Supervisory Characteristics

You are asked by your superior to recommend someone in your department to supervise the staff of ten salespersons. You think of three people in the department and you consider their backgrounds. Which person would you choose? What characteristics (either demonstrated or inferred) will help you make the choice?

John McVean has been a sales representative for five years and shows initiative and drive. He is friendly, loves to tell stories, and is basically easy to understand. He has exceeded his sales quota for the last four years. The major disadvantage is that he is overaggressive. Fellow salespeople have recently complained about his aggressiveness or rudeness in front of customers, and customers have complained about John's inability to deliver what he promises.

Kathy Crevier, a sales representative for three years, is very personable and outgoing and tends to be the life of the party when she is in a group. However, when discussing business with you, she tends to become quiet and reserved. Her contribution to the discussion is often limited and you wonder if you are doing something wrong. Kathy's sales record is outstanding, and her peers believe that she is a valuable member of the crew.

Bob Koyne has been with the company for seven years. The last six years have been outstanding sales years. Bob, in contrast to John and Kathy, is a steady, quiet producer. He is a "team man" in his conversations with you, and he feels uncomfortable when the discussion turns to him as an individual.

1. How do you feel the new supervisor should relate to the employees?
2. Is it important for a first-line supervisor to have technical competence?
3. Does the fact that a first-line supervisor has initiative and drive have any effect on subordinates?
4. Is emotional stability important for a supervisor? Why?

Terms and Concepts

ability promotion   a promotion based on the potential that an employee has to hold an advanced position; it is not based on past merit or performance of the prior job.

central tendency   the tendency of the evaluator to rate all of an employee's abilities and performance as average. Also it may be the tendency to rate all the employees as average.

critical incident technique   the written documentation of an employee's behavior, good or bad, which is put in his or her personnel file to be used later during the appraisal period.

disciplinary action   one form of discipline that usually involves punishment for an infraction of rules.

essay appraisal   an essay in which a supervisor writes a paragraph or more about the employee's strengths and weaknesses as well as potential value to the company.

field review   a multiple appraisal or review. An evaluation done by several people of an employee's performance.

graphic rating scale   an appraisal form that is checked to show how well an employee is doing in various aspects related to his or her job.

halo effect   a supervisor or other rater assumes that, if an employee is above average in one area, the employee is above average in all areas.

management by objectives   a method of measuring achievement. The supervisor and the employee determine specific goals for the employee to meet within a given time frame.

merit promotion   a promotion based on past performance rather than on the ability to perform the duties of the advanced position. See ability promotions.

outplacement   professional counseling and other assistance provided to terminated employees to help them locate new jobs.

ranking   the practice of comparing an employee with others and ranking the employees' evaluations. Ranking should only be done for purposes of promotions or layoffs. An appraisal should be used to compare an employee with a job description or job standards and not with fellow employees.

recency bias   one error made frequently by supervisors in appraising employees. An employee may receive a higher or lower evaluation depending on his or her most recent performance. The critical incident technique helps to overcome such an error.

work force reduction planning   contingency plans drawn up to provide for layoffs.

Notes

1. Tom Peters, *Thriving on Chaos: Handbook for a Management Revolution* (New York: Alfred A. Knopf, 1988), pp. 494–498.

2. Glenn M. McEvoy and Paul F. Buller, "User Acceptance of Peer Appraisals in an Industrial Setting," *Personnel Psychology*, Winter 1987, pp. 785–797. See, also, Glenn M. McEvoy, "Evaluating the Boss," *Personnel Administrator*, September 1988, pp. 115–120.

3. Walter Kiechel III, "When Subordinates Evaluate the Boss," *Fortune*, June 19, 1989, pp. 201–202.

4. Ibid.

5. "Labor Letter," *The Wall Street Journal*, June 25, 1985, p. 1.

6. John W. Lawrie, "Your Performance: Appraise It Yourself!" *Personnel*, January 1989, pp. 21–23.

7. G. Stephen Taylor, Carol Lehman, and Connie Forde, "How Employee Self-appraisals Can Help," *Supervisory Management*, August 1989, pp. 32–41.

8. Charles H. Gray, "Charting Your Employees' Potential," *Management World*, May–June 1988, pp. 11–12.

9. John Paul Newport, Jr., "How to Outearn the Boss and Keep Your Job," *Fortune*, May 27, 1985, p. 73. See also Janet Bamford, "The Babe Ruth Syndrome," *Forbes*, June 2, 1986, pp. 145–148.

10. Charles Nanry, "Performance Linked Training," *Public Personnel Management*, Winter 1988, pp. 457–463.

11. Kenneth R. Gilberg, David McCarthy, and Jacqueline Shulman, "Disciplinary Guidelines," *Supervisory Management*, July 1989, pp. 16–17.

12. Douglas A. Benton, "A Guide to Work Force Reduction Planning," *Personnel Journal*, April 1980, p. 283.

13. W. Clay Hamner and Ellen P. Hamner, "Behavior Modification on the Bottom Line," in *Organization and People*, 3rd ed., eds. J. B. Ritchie and Paul Thompson (St. Paul: West, 1984), pp. 87–88.

14. Andrall E. Pearson, "Muscle-Build Your Company," *Success*, July–August 1989, p. 10.

Recommended Reading

Baker, Joe. *Causes of Failure in Performance Appraisal and Supervision.* Westport, Conn.: Greenwood Press, 1988.

Eyres, Patricia S. "Legally Defensible Performance Appraisal Systems." *Personnel Journal*, July 1989, pp. 58–62.

Goodard, Robert W. "Is Your Appraisal System Headed for Court?" *Personnel Journal*, January 1989, pp. 114–119.

Gottschalk, Peter T. "Employer-Initiated Job Termination." *Southern Economic Journal*, July 1982, pp. 35–44.

Hymowitz, Carol. "Small-Business Owners Discover Giving Up Authority Isn't Easy." *The Wall Street Journal*, May 23, 1985, p. 37. (Entrepreneurs feel compelled to promote long-term employees even when they aren't qualified.)

Kiechel, Walter, III. "When Subordinates Evaluate the Boss." *Fortune*, June 19, 1989, pp. 201–202.

Lehr, Richard I., and David J. Middlebrooks. "Work Force Reduction: Strategies and Options." *Personnel Journal*, October 1984, pp. 50–54.

Patten, Thomas H., Jr. *A Manager's Guide to Performance Appraisal.* New York: Free Press, 1982.

Peters, Tom. *Thriving on Chaos: Handbook for a Management Revolution.* New York: Alfred A. Knopf, 1988.

Spruell, Geraldine. "Say So Long to Promotions." *Training and Development Journal*, May 1985, pp. 70–75.

Taylor, G. Stephen, Carol Lehman, and Connie Forde. "How Employee Self-appraisals Can Help." *Supervisory Management*, August 1989, pp. 32–41.

Whitney, James L. "Pay Concepts for the 1990s," *Compensation & Benefits Review*, March–April 1988, pp. 33–44.

Innovation in Decision Making

After studying this chapter, you should be able to:

1. Distinguish between innovation and creativity.
2. Discuss the relationship of innovation to decision making.
3. List the four P's of creativity and various theories behind those ideas.
4. Describe the following four stages of the creative process:
   a. Perception
   b. Incubation
   c. Inspiration
   d. Verification
5. Explain the differences between unstructured, heuristic decisions and structures, logical decisions.
6. Explain the steps used in decision making.
7. Explain the differences between short-term and long-term decisions in relationship to risk and uncertainty.
8. Discuss the advantages and/or disadvantages of decisions made by
   a. Individuals
   b. A powerful few
   c. Groups
9. List the advantages and disadvantages of group decision making using the following methods:
   a. Brainstorming
   b. Statistical method
   c. Delphi technique
   d. Nominal group techniques

TO START YOU THINKING . . .

Look at these questions before reading the chapter. Perhaps you can use the questions to start a discussion after studying the chapter.

- How critical is innovation to American industry?
- Do creative people perform better under rigid or relaxed managers?
- Is creativity inherited or can it be developed?
- What makes a person an entrepreneur?
- What can be done in the workplace to make the environment more conducive to creativity?
- What are the benefits and variations of brainstorming?
- Do you ever make decisions based on intuition? Do you think people in responsible positions might make decisions based on intuition? Is there justification for such actions?

- Who tends to seek advice more in determining a decision, lower management or top management? Why?
- Are corporate boards of directors just as likely to succumb to "group-think" as community committees?
- Is an average person or a millionaire more likely to take risks or be fearful of failure when a decision is to be made? Is the difference long-term versus short-term decisions? dollar magnitude?

WHAT IS INNOVATION?

Innovation is the end product of creative activity. Innovation can take place in policies, processes, and techniques as well as in people's activities and behaviors.

Management has the responsibility for innovation and creativity in an organization just as it does for other managerial functions such as communication. Harry J. Gray, chairman and CEO of United Technologies, says: "Innovation begins with example. When management acts in an innovative way, and managers at every level show appreciation for good ideas you have a climate that attracts and nourishes creative people, and you will always have innovation."[1]

Creative activity is a means to the end of innovation. Creative effort is more of a mental activity; innovation is more active. The "do-it, fix-it, try-it" mentality that authors Tom Peters and Robert Waterman, Jr., talk about is evidence of innovation. Peters writes that to get the constant innovation necessary for survival, managers must:

- Personally symbolize innovativeness in their daily affairs.
- Seek out opportunities to stand foursquare with innovators.
  . . . It is essential that managers make a constant effort to recognize innovators (and applaud the details of their victories over organizational inertia), at all levels and in all functions.[2]

Tremendous pressures to innovate confront organizations. While pursuing their mission or corporate objectives in the mainstream, they must also generate "newstreams." Mainstream businesses can quickly dry up or stagnate. Thus, companies must explore opportunities to pioneer in new directions, seek innovations that will improve and even transform the mainstream.[3]

WHAT IS CREATIVITY?

How Is Creativity Defined?

Nothing new under the sun? Maybe there is not, but there are new ways of putting things together. Mark Twain said, "The man with a new idea is a crank until the idea succeeds."

As with justice, democracy, and liberty, "creativity" is a word with many different meanings for many different people. Basically, it is the ability to develop novel and useful ideas from diverse resources.

The diverse resources are the sum total of our cultural heritage. What is new is *the combination of these elements into new patterns of association.* Einstein could never have postulated the theory of relativity if the patterns of Newtonian physics had not been established so firmly.

Who Has It?

Can creativity be taught? One view is that it cannot. One of the most common criticisms of Japanese education is that too little time is spent in developing creativity and thought processes. The principal of a Japanese high school says that these talents cannot be taught.[4]

Another view is that everyone has the potential for creativity. Some people develop that potential more than others. From childhood, people have vivid imaginations that, when cultivated and allowed to grow, become productive mechanisms for performing a job. "Creativeness often consists of merely turning around what is already there.

If creativity is defined as the ability to combine already existing elements in new ways, we can see clearly that a child's creative energies do not disappear with the onset of adulthood. They are simply expressed in different ways in many aspects of daily life: in homes, schools, offices, and factories. A secretary who designs a new, more efficient filing system, a factory worker who uses an unconventional tool to perform a familiar task more easily, a needy student who uses cement cinder blocks to build a bookcase—all are acting creatively.

TEST YOURSELF

- How many squares are in the box?
- Now, count again.
- Only sixteen?
- Take away your *pre*conception of how many squares there are.
- Now, how many do you find?   You should find thirty!

THE FOUR P'S OF CREATIVITY

Perhaps one of the best ways in which to approach the complex area of creativity is by looking at the four "P's" of creativity: *the person, the process, the pressure,* and *the product.* See the following illustration for a more complete breakdown of the four points. First, let us study a creative person and compare the personality traits with those of a direct opposite—the custodial person.

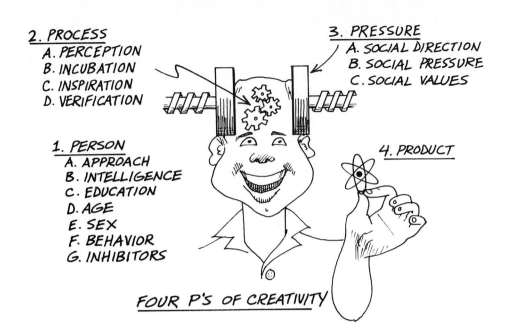

2. PROCESS
   A. PERCEPTION
   B. INCUBATION
   C. INSPIRATION
   D. VERIFICATION

3. PRESSURE
   A. SOCIAL DIRECTION
   B. SOCIAL PRESSURE
   C. SOCIAL VALUES

1. PERSON
   A. APPROACH
   B. INTELLIGENCE
   C. EDUCATION
   D. AGE
   E. SEX
   F. BEHAVIOR
   G. INHIBITORS

4. PRODUCT

FOUR P'S OF CREATIVITY

THE PERSON

Although all people have a creative spark, the potential is not always utilized fully. How does one recognize those who are developing their creative energies to the fullest? Mad painters and tormented poets are only comic stereotypes of the creative personality. The essential traits of creativity are found among a wide variety of less conspicuous creators: scientists, carpenters, social reformers, teachers, gardeners, business people, politicians, doctors, parents—people in all walks of life. The potential for creativity resides within us all. Unfortunately, the structure of our social and educational environment does not always promote its growth.

Approach

A creative person distrusts "pat" answers

Highly creative people are apt to make "leaps of reasoning" from one fact to a seemingly unrelated fact and construct a bridge of logic across the chasm. The creative temperament distrusts pat answers and implicit assumptions. It has a tendency to break problems down into their most basic elements and then reconstruct them into whole new problems, thereby discovering new relationships and new solutions. Table 13-1 contrasts the two opposite types: the creative and the custodial person.

The curiosity of a child

Highly creative people aren't afraid to ask what may seem to be naïve or silly questions. They ask such questions as: "Why don't spiders get tangled up in their own webs?" and "Why do dogs turn in circles before lying down?" Such questions may seem childlike, and in a way they are. Children have not yet had their innate creative energies channeled into culturally acceptable directions and can give full rein to their curiosity—the absolute prerequisite for full creative functioning, in both children and adults.

TABLE 13-1 Differences Between the Custodial and the Creative Person

CUSTODIAL	CREATIVE
Enjoys routine and details	Enjoys variety
Works for simplification and streamlining	Speculates, guesses
Predictable personality	Unpredictable personality
Enjoys the status quo	Cannot understand people who are reluctant to try something new
Firm, fair, friendly	Enthusiastic
Microorientation (details)	Macroorientation (the whole)

Intelligence

According to many popular theories, great advances in creative thought were attributable to extraordinary intelligence, altered states of consciousness, and a "special" thought process that is available only to geniuses. Albert Einstein denied having any of these special talents or gifts.

One of the most common misconceptions about the highly creative personality is that there is a positive correlation between creativity and intelligence. The problem here is that *intelligence* is another word that means many different things to different people. If we mean by intelligence simply the ability to learn a lot of facts and relationships by rote memory and to put that knowledge into useful service, then there appears to be little correlation between intelligence and creativity. On the other hand, if we mean by intelligence the ability to solve complex and unusual problems, then there is a high correlation.

There has been some study and speculation as to which side of the brain houses the creative portion of one's personality. There is some speculation that the creative process of dreams, free association, and fantasies belong to the right hemisphere of the brain, whereas the logical, analytic, and reality-oriented process derive from the left side of the brain.[5]

Age and Gender

Contrary to popular myths that glorify youth, more creative achievements are likely to occur when people grow older. One researcher made a list of 1,000 ideas that have been important to the world and found that the average age of the innovators when they actually had those ideas was 74.[6] Genius may flare early and die young, but imagination generally grows by being used. Another researcher has found that mental ability grows until about age 60, then decreases—but so slowly that, at age 80, it is as if you are 30.[7] While memory may falter with senility that seems to come with age, but more likely because of a faulty diet, creativity seems to be ageless.

Dr. E. Paul Torrance has found no significant relationship between creativity and gender.[8] It does appear that less rigid male and female role identification increases the chances for creativity. For instance, the group of architects who were studied for intelligence were also given the Minnesota Multiphasic Personality Inventory (MMPI) to inquire into their psychological natures. The most striking aspect of the MMPI profiles was the tendency for creative males to score high on the femininity ratings.

Curiosity is more important than intelligence

There is little correlation between IQ and the creative quotient

Creativity is housed on the right side of the brain

Age does not seem to decrease creativity

Neither males nor females are more creative

Behavior

Creative people are sometimes more interested in ideas than in people

Creative people are more concerned with the world of ideas and images than with the world of society. As a result, they tend to be somewhat antisocial. In their personal lives they may appear to be highly sensitive and self-centered. Their life-styles may seem chaotic, but inner directed as they are, it doesn't matter to them what their lives look like to others. Their rewards are the joys of discovery, not the approval of society.

Table 13-2 outlines research on personality traits that often appear in creative personalities. Not all these traits *must* be present, however, for a person to be creative. All of them rarely appear together, and their presence does not always indicate creativity. The table is presented to familiarize you with possible indicators of creative ability.

Inhibitors

Early training and environmental influences can discourage natural curiosity and stifle impulses to explore and experiment. Schools still stress acquiring information rather than learning how to think. In many ways, the educational system tends to foster imitative rather than creative behavior.

Finding fault and "labeling" are also inhibitors

Some states of mind are less conducive to creativity than others. *Emotion-mindedness* is the habit of allowing feelings to distort reasoning and block objectivity. *Judicial-mindedness* is the tendency to find fault immediately with a new and different thought, thereby inhibiting further thoughts in that vein. *Label-mindedness* filters thought by finding the names for things rather than evaluating the facts about them.

Inhibitors to creativity include perceptual and cultural blocks. Emotional blocks to creativity include:

- Difficulty in rejecting a workable solution and searching for a better one
- Difficulty in changing set (no flexibility) depending entirely on biased opinion
- Lack of drive in carrying a solution through to completion and test
- Refusal to take a detour in reaching a goal
- Inability to relax and let incubation take place[9]

TABLE 13-2 Possible Personality Traits of a Creative Person

IN RELATION TO OTHERS	JOB ATTITUDES	ATTITUDES TO SELF
Not a joiner	Preference for things and ideas to people	Introspective
Few close friends	High regard for intellectual interests	Open to new experiences
Unconventional morality	Less emphasis on job security	Inner maturity
Independence of judgment, especially under pressure	Less enjoyment in detail work and routine	Less emotionally stable
	High level of resourcefulness	Spontaneous adventurous, compulsive, anxious
	Skeptical	
	High tolerance for ambiguity	
	Persistence, capacity to be puzzled	

SOURCE: Adapted from John W. Haefele, *Creativity and Innovation* (New York: Reinhold Publishing Corp., 1962).

THE PROCESS

The unfolding of the creative process is still mysterious. Many attempts have been made to analyze it, but it remains little understood. However, there are certain obvious *stages* in the process that can be identified. One classification notes five stages: the preparation stage, which lasts for years and includes education and experience; the concentration stage, which focuses on individual problems; the incubation stage; the illumination stage; and the verification stage.[10]

Another practical innovation model incorporates the major parts of the creative thinking process:

1. Discovery—identifies decisions that are accompanied by weak alternatives, uncovering dissatisfaction with the status quo, forcing a search for solutions, guiding the search for threat and opportunities.

2. Generation—requires the ability to move chameleonlike from logical to intuitive problem-solving modes.

3. Definition—seeks clarification of the solution developed in step 2.

4. Experimentation—is achieved by a limited application of the idea, a pilot test, or the development of a prototype.

5. Evaluation—now the idea is out in the open in the organization.

6. Implementation—plans how the new idea will be launched.[11]

We will look at four steps in the process: *perception, incubation, inspiration,* and *verification.*

Perception

As introduced in Chapter 7, perception is a powerful factor in communication and motivation. Likewise, it affects how creative we are.

Because of differences in temperament and environment, everyone sees the world in a slightly different way. Some people perceive the world as orderly and just; others see only disorder and injustice.

The creative person often sees problems where others see none and questions the validity of even the most widely accepted answers. Creative personalities are compulsive problem seekers, not so much because they thrive on problems, but because their senses are attuned to a world that demands to be put together, like a jigsaw puzzle scattered on a table.

The person with originality tends to view society from a different perspective than the custodial person. An analogy might be that the creative person sees the forest, whereas the custodial person sees the trees. A creative person is able to see problems that others are not able to see or do not want to see.

Creative problem solving involves formulating new ideas or alternatives rather than relying on old ones for making decisions. Creative problems require more "divergent" than "convergent" thinking.

In divergent thinking, the mind is encouraged to travel in many different directions to search for answers and try a variety of approaches. Convergent thinking includes the more logical, fact-finding, judgmental side of problem solving. Eventually, both types of thinking go into solving problems. The unstructured, intuitive process that is used to come up with the ideas will at some point give way to making a logical choice between them—using analysis, reason, and experience.

We all see the world slightly differently

A creative person brings together isolated ideas into a fused whole

"Divergent thinking is sidetrack thinking"

Convergent thinking is logical, quick solutions

Some change is a desire of creative people and sometimes their viewpoint is
seen as radical. But as Ralph Waldo Emerson said, "Every reform was once a
private opinion." *A creator is willing to dare to be different.* The creative person is
more likely to be a "Jonathan Livingston Seagull" than just another member of the
flock.

Incubation

The mysterious part of the creative process that takes place subconsciously is called
incubation. It is rather like a bird sitting quietly for days on end to hatch an egg.
There appears to be no activity whatever occurring, when, in fact, the creative
action is astonishing. In the egg, the embryo of a chick is developing, and in the
innovator's mind a massive amount of data is being sorted, filed, classified,
discarded, combined—in short, developed into a meaningful whole. During this
stage the process continues, even in dreams. The second law of thermodynamics
came to Johannes Kepler in a dream—after 20 years of conscious searching. This
stage can last anywhere from a few hours to many years, depending on the
complexity of the problem.

In the incubation stage, the mind creates remote associations leading to the
formation of new ideas. Major concerns now in the incubation stage at many
companies and in the minds of many individuals are "How to solve a food
shortage," "How to find new fuel substitutes," "How to reorganize the transportation system," and "How to solve the water shortages that prevail in certain areas of
the world."

Inspiration

The payoff for all this conscious and subconscious mental activity is usually
experienced as a flash, an instant insight, a slap on the forehead, and an astonished
"Aha!" or "Eureka, I found it!" as the answer comes bursting through to
consciousness. After days of patient, silent sitting, the incubated egg cracks and a
live chirping chick emerges. This stage is called *inspiration* or illumination (Figure
13-1). It is the moment representing the culmination of hours, days, or years of
thought, although in actual time it lasts for just a few moments. It is a release of
psychic tensions that have been building up all through the incubation period.

There is no way to predict when this moment of illumination will occur. Often
it comes when least expected—say, in the middle of a conversation about a
seemingly unrelated subject. A particular phrase or image or idea will ring a bell,
provide the final link in the puzzle, and bring the parts together to a new whole. It
is the moment that cartoonists represent by a light bulb suddenly flashing on over
the head of the character.

Remember our mentioning the problem of water shortages in the stage of
incubation? Some "nutty" creative person asked what is wrong with the idea of
towing an iceberg to a country like Saudi Arabia to supply fresh water. There are
enough icebergs that form each year, and they are all going to waste. Taking one to
a dry place seems a plan of elegant simplicity.

Verification

In a sense illumination represents only the end of the beginning of the creative
process. As Thomas Edison said, "Creation is 1 percent inspiration and 99 percent
perspiration." Now the innovator must elaborate on the idea. It must be tested,

FIGURE 13-1 There is no way to predict when the moment of inspiration will occur. Often it comes when least expected.
Aronson Photographics/Stock, Boston

evaluated, reworked, retested, and reevaluated. The idea must be stacked up against the real, practical world—and it must be foolproof: no leaks, no loopholes, no weaknesses. If such problems do arise, then the idea must be transformed and the solution mended.

It is during this stage that the innovator should, and often must, work closely with others of a more practical nature. Scientific discoveries must be tested thoroughly in the laboratory, and innovative ideas in business must be tested against all aspects of the enterprise, from production costs to marketability.

In verification the creative person needs the help of the custodial person

PRESSURE OF SOCIETY

Social Direction and Necessity

Our culture can lead us to be creative artists or creative mechanics

All children everywhere are born with some degree of innate creative energy, but the channels into which the energy will flow are determined by the values of a particular culture. In some parts of the world, such as the island of Bali, artistic ability is valued very highly, and almost every child grows up to be skilled in at least one art form. Most of us, if asked, would say, "I'm not a creative person: I don't paint or write poetry." But this is a very narrow view of the scope of the creative force.

There is an old saying, "Necessity is the mother of invention." In America, technological change is valued very highly, and in every new generation many children grow up to be skilled practitioners of at least one technological innovation. In the 1920s, if you wanted to own and drive a Model T Ford, and hundreds of thousands did, the odds were that it was necessary to repair it yourself. There were very few skilled auto mechanics outside the largest cities, and thousands of patents for automobile improvements were granted in those years to self-taught, *creative* auto mechanics. Computer programming, software development, and applications are modern-day examples of the pressure for change.

Social Pressure

Society often puts a great deal of pressure on creative people to channel their energies into specific areas to solve specific problems. Pollution, clean and abundant sources of fuel, and mass transportation, to name but three of the most pressing of today's social problems, require solutions as quickly as possible. The necessities of the society as a whole generally govern the inventions of creative people.

The more pressing the problem is on society, the more effort is made to find solutions. Today, in the research departments of many major industries, experimental work is underway to find a cleaner fuel than gasoline, and many chemists of a creative bent are drawn to such departments because the need is obvious and the pay is good.

Society can pressure us to find solutions to today's problems

Or society can create a "rebel spirit" to force the society to see new creative ways

THE PRODUCT

As a rule, it is easy to identify the end product of artistic creative energy, although as modern life grows more difficult, identification is not always a simple task. Still, as a general rule, poems, plays, musical compositions, and sculpture leave little room for confusion as to *what* they are. Identifying the products of scientific or industrial creativity is not always as easy. Fortunately, the U.S. Supreme Court has helped to settle the issue. An *invention*, says the Court, is an *idea.* Inventions are not poems, or symphonies, or machines; they are the ideas behind things.

An invention is an idea, not an object

Product development is not the only way in which the innovator contributes to business success. Some businesses, for instance, don't deal with products at all. A management consulting firm would have little use for an inventor, but it would value the creative person who could devise a bold reorganization plan for a failing business.

One of the areas in which creativity makes a big difference is advertising. Anyone can see the difference in effectiveness between a competent but dull, run-of-the-mill TV ad and one that excites comment and interest. Behind every successful advertisement there is at least one creator, someone who has sensed that there was a new and better way of presenting a product.

Creative personnel can contribute to better business office management or business systems analysis. An innovative office manager, for example, may discover new methods of operating the office for maximum efficiency. A creative systems analyst can take a fresh look at the accounting system used by a business for 50 years and in one swoop eliminate 75 percent of the busywork. Computer programming is popular among creative people, as witnessed by the many unofficial clubs of "computer freaks" who find countless ingenious ways to use mechanical brains for fun and profit.

In fact, there is virtually no aspect of business that can't be improved by a creative worker. Management itself must become more creative to see what is needed and where.

Do you think that you are more creative than the average person? Many experts believe that creativity can be developed to a greater extent in each of us—if we try. Many feel that we clutter our way with too many inhibitors, which tends to hamper our creative ability. Think of the times when you are the most creative. Do you tend to be more creative when you are with someone or when you are alone? Are you more creative early in the morning or late in the evening? Do you write down your ideas, or do you only express them verbally, or do you only express them to yourself?

Creative ideas need to be expressed orally, in written forms, and often, so that other individuals or groups can help in the verification.

Do you believe that creative people can develop more alternatives to problems but have a more difficult time deciding on a final selection?

Would you rather be considered creative or practical? Why?

BUSINESS AND THE CREATIVE EMPLOYEE

The patent office files bulge with ideas that are too costly, have no market value, or have too many hidden technical problems. The discoveries of new business ideas are often an inspiration sparked by a chance encounter, maybe something read in the newspaper.

Management Attitudes

While the creative temperament has much to offer to business and industry, it has special needs and does not always fit smoothly into an organization. Because of their sometimes unorthodox ways of doing things, creative people can create serious problems for organizations that aren't designed to accommodate them.

A satirical ad that has appeared in a number of different magazines presents a humorous, but all too accurate, view of the ambiguous attitudes held by many American businesspeople toward their creative employees:

Creative person wanted but not encouraged

> WANTED: TOP EXECUTIVE—Unusual opportunity for an imaginative (but not unconventional) planner who thinks quickly (but isn't impatient), acts aggressively (but ruffles no fur), and can get things done (through channels without stepping on toes). Should have an A.B. in Business Administration (preferably from an Eastern University), but the equivalent in experience will be considered (for blood relatives of management). Applicant should have varied and broad background (yet be a specialist) and have a work record demonstrating job stability (without being a "job-hopper," he must nevertheless have acquired a varied and broad background). The man chosen will be a member of an executive committee (team) jointly responsible (he'd better fit in) for company policy.

This parody of how American business deals with creativity highlights a basic contradiction: an organization may encourage creative behavior while at the same time establish policies that prevent the use of independent judgment, discretion, and innovation.

Management often prefers efficiency to unproven ideas

Management tends to prefer the efficiency that results from using proven methods. It fears that the innovator will cause unrest in the organization, challenge the status quo, and generally disrupt what has been a successful company policy. At the same time, most managers give at least token recognition to the need for the creative employee.

This basic contradiction is often a reason why some small companies never quite get off the ground and some large companies stagnate and stop growing. Creativity, although acknowledged as being necessary, is continually stifled, and the company goes its merry way toward mediocrity, led by the boss and followed by legions of "yes men" and "yes women."

Entrepreneurial Characteristics

Traditionally, the entrepreneur has been defined as a risk taker, who usually anticipates some type of profit. A more modern definition holds that the entrepreneur is a person who *creates* or perceives new kinds of demands and applies innovative techniques for meeting those demands. This definition includes individuals such as government officials, other public servants, and educators, who may not be anticipating monetary profit.

An entrepreneur creates

Regardless of whether entrepreneurs are economically motivated, they have certain strong needs. They need to (1) achieve, (2) accomplish or improve on something, (3) take responsibility, and (4) receive frequent feedback. Entrepreneurs are usually enthusiastic and perseverant—maybe even abrasive to their work associates. They are probably better off self-employed than working for someone else.

For a large organization to be effective, it must include individuals with these characteristics. These individuals are referred to as *intrapreneurs* or entrepreneurs within large organizations. The key to their effectiveness is not to let them get lost in the bureaucracy. They need the freedom to function more autonomously and must be rewarded for their performance.

Brainstorming

Various techniques that encourage creativity can and should be used in almost any business situation. One of the most successful and best known of these is called "brainstorming"—using the *brain* to *storm* a problem. Brainstorming sessions are designed to generate ideas to solve specific problems.

The following four rules provide the basis for a good brainstorming session.

1. *Criticism is ruled out.* Comments such as "That's stupid" are not allowed.

2. *"Freewheeling" is welcomed.* The more outlandish the idea, the better. It's always easier to tame down an idea than think it up.

3. *Quantity and variety are welcomed.* The greater the number of ideas expressed, the greater the likelihood of there being a winner.

4. *Combinations and improvements are welcomed.* Modifying, elaborating, and combining ideas is very productive, and combinations often generate totally new ideas. Hitchhiking on another person's ideas is encouraged.

Brainstorming can be done individually, but sessions seem to work best with about five to seven participants. *Quality circles* are classic examples of this type of group, which meets voluntarily, on company time, to brainstorm, solve problems, and receive training that will improve effectiveness.

"Hitchhiking" is fun and productive

Group brainstorming has the further advantage of producing many ideas quickly. When ideas are shared in a group, they stimulate more ideas, just by the power of association. Pooling thoughts has a chain-reaction effect. Ideas that are triggered by the suggestions of others are called "hitchhikes." Just the atmosphere of acceptance and friendly rivalry has a way of reinforcing the desire to make suggestions, but remember rule 1 and the others earlier.

Initial sessions may be as short as 5 minutes, later ones as long as an hour or more. Because ideas usually come so fast that many are lost, be sure to tape record all ideas, no matter how zany or impractical they seem. The chairperson enforces the "no-criticism" rule by using a bell to signify an infraction of the rule. Keep the meeting in a light, humorous spirit. The leader can repeat phrases and add to them as ways to stimulate action and motivation and close the session when fatigue or long periods of silence are encountered.

Once all the ideas are accumulated, it is time for judgment. The information can be reviewed, and the panel can evaluate the material with hopes that a couple of excellent ideas are available out of more than 20 or 30 that were generated. The appraisal session can even come a day or two after the brainstorming session rather than immediately following. At this meeting, *all* the ideas should be reviewed in expectation that several usable ideas can be derived from them.

Chairpersons reject their own ideas too

The chairperson should remind participants in brainstorming sessions that they should not feel badly about having their ideas rejected. The purpose of brainstorming is to generate alternative solutions to a problem. The chairperson will need to remind coparticipants that his or her own ideas are frequently rejected.

Rewards

A serious problem in dealing with creative personnel is finding adequate ways in which to reward successful effort. Monetary rewards alone are not the answer. Creative people are often satisfied to receive a merely comfortable salary as long as the job offers the freedom and time that they feel they need to work well.

Perhaps the best reward for a good idea is recognition and immediate use

Perhaps the greatest possible reward that can be bestowed for a creative effort is enthusiastic recognition and immediate application of the idea.[12] Witnessing the application of an idea is often the highest form of reward. Other avenues may be explored, such as granting greater degrees of freedom or equipping the scientific researcher with his or her own private laboratory. More money is seldom frowned upon. But what the true innovator responds to most is neither money nor status, but the enthusiastic "Hurrah" for the difficult problem that has been solved.

Possibly the major contribution that management can make to creative effort is bringing creative people together and providing them with the materials they require for their work. The ability to do this demands an unusually deep understanding of creative personalities and a degree of creativity in the manager. Introducing one innovator to another creates a new pattern of association of existing elements—in this case, people—and is thus itself a creative act.

WHAT IS DECISION MAKING?

The previous sections on innovation and creativity were designed to help you be better decision makers by creatively defining problems and seeking alternative solutions to problems. While creativity focuses on solving problems, decision making also implies a problem demanding a solution. Creativity requires an unstructured, heuristic approach, whereas decision making uses more structured, logical thinking. A *heuristic* approach to decision making and problem solving is intuitive, self-discovery oriented. Both the logical and heuristic approaches are necessary to solve problems, and they can be used together, alternating between the two kinds of thinking.

Almost everything we do involves making decisions. A decision is a commitment—a resolution to do or stop doing an act, or to adopt or reject an attitude. Because attitudes often develop unconsciously, they are hard to see as part of the decision-making process until decisions are actually made.

Decision making is a process of several steps, not a single step of deciding. The first step is correctly defining the problem.

Problem Definition

Spend time on defining the problem. A problem precisely defined is already half solved. Sometimes we have difficulty in isolating the problem. The difficulty in isolating a problem is often due to spending the minimum amount of effort on problem definition, so we can get to work quickly on solving it. More time spent in correctly identifying a problem has a big payoff in the timeliness and quality of the ultimate solution.

Look for the "right" question before you look for the "right" answer

Problems can be defined as the obstacles that prevent the achievement of goals or purposes. Often, the surface problem is only a symptom of a more important problem. For example, having a fever is a symptom of something more serious—perhaps a cold, the flu, or even pneumonia. Similarly, in a company with rapid employee turnover, the turnover itself is not the real problem; it is a symptom of more serious trouble. The question that needs to be asked is: "Why is there so much employee turnover?" Attempting to cure a symptom usually does not cure the cause. An aspirin may bring down the fever, but it will not cure the illness. Similarly, a supervisor may believe that he or she is confronted with a problem of conflicting personalities in the department. The symptom is that two employees are continually bickering. After checking into the situation, the supervisor may find that the problem is not one of personalities at all; rather, the work functions and specific responsibilities of each employee may never have been outlined clearly.

Look to find the real problem first, not a symptom or the solution. You may find a solution to a symptom and ignore the real problem. Once the problem is defined, there are several "ACTION" steps to take.

Steps in Decision Making after Problem Definition	What steps must be taken to yield the highest probability of successful decisions? The acronym ACTION indicates six fundamental ones:
	A ANALYZE the problem and gather data.
	C CONSIDER the alternative solutions.
	T TAKE action—select a solution.
	I IMPLEMENT the solution.
	O ONGOING EVALUATION. Conduct an ongoing evaluation of the solution: encourage feedback from employees.
	N NEED for change. After you have tried the solution, consider the need for modifications of the original decision.

Analyze the Problem

Collecting accurate information for decision making is crucial. (See Figure 13-2.) Using wrong or irrelevant data as the basis for a solution to a problem can be more detrimental than not solving the problem at all. Often the ability to collect useful information depends on how good the communication is within the firm. People sometimes hold back information to play it safe or to look good. Also, all information is filtered through individual perceptions, which are, by definition, subjective. Facts don't speak for themselves; people speak them.

Information related to a problem's solution is not always easy to acquire. A problem in real life is unlike a classroom case study in which most of the facts relevant to the case are available. In real life it is necessary to search thoroughly for the various facts that may illuminate a problem. Some of the ways of collecting these facts are (1) personal interviews, (2) review of records, (3) flowcharts, (4) organizational charts, (5) consultation of previous studies, and (6) outside information. Each method provides a specific kind of information. Often a balanced combination of the appropriate methods will yield a fairly objective and broad spectrum of data to use in assessing a problem.

Consider the Alternative Solutions

Decision makers must learn to stretch their minds

Decision makers need to learn to stretch their minds to develop all possible alternatives, even in the most discouraging situations. Even when one of the available alternatives is desirable, it is better to have choices than to be left with no choice at all. Doing nothing is also a decision—and can be worthwhile or it can be fatal. Brainstorming is one of the best known methods for developing alternatives to problems. The freewheeling, receptive atmosphere of a brainstorming session often produces workable solutions.

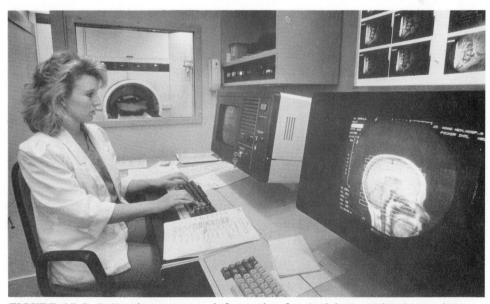

FIGURE 13-2 Collecting accurate information for decision making is crucial. Wrong data can be more detrimental than not solving the problem at all. Spencer Grant/Monkmeyer Press

At Minnesota Mining and Manufacturing Company every division is expected to generate 25 percent of its sales each year from products that didn't exist five years earlier. The goal forces managers to use 3M's skills to come up with new products. The yellow "sticky" note pads (Post-its) for which 3M has been famous were the product of a failure because the adhesive did not adhere well. Developing alternatives—even from a failure—has made 3M millions of dollars.

A 3M product from a failure

| **We Seek Out Positive Alternatives (choosing among negative choices seems like no choice at all)** | NEGATIVE: The pipe under your kitchen sink springs a leak and you call in a plumber. A few days later you get a bill for $40. At the bottom is a note saying that if you do not pay within 30 days, then there will be a 10 percent service charge of $4. You feel trapped with no desirable alternatives. You pay $40 now or $44 later.

POSITIVE: The same case, but with two changes. The plumber sends you a bill for $44, but the note says that if you pay within 30 days you will get a special $4 discount. The difference is that you will save $4. |

Choosing between negatives is no choice at all

We like a moderate number of hard, positive choices

People are happy when they have freedom of choice in making a decision, but choosing between negative alternatives seems like no choice at all. People tend to search for other, more positive, alternatives. Individuals prefer a number of alternatives, and they like hard choices between positive, closely similar alternatives. The law of diminishing returns applies to the number of alternatives, for too many can overwhelm people and make them feel trapped. When this happens, there is a higher possibility they will make an impulsive decision or no decision at all.

The question of *timing* will often make one alternative preferable to another. Noted sociology professor, Amitai Etzioni, asks "How do you make a decision when there's too much data and too little time?" His answer: "Good managers, like doctors, know how to make decisions based on sketchy information."[13]

Take Action—a Solution

After the alternative solutions have been developed, the probable desirable and undesirable consequences of each should be tested. The selection must be the best solution from the point of view of time and energy as well as money. The decision maker's selection will probably be based on a combination of factors, such as experience, intuition, advice, experimentation, and computer forecasts.

Alternatives can lead to experimentation

In the scientific world, many decisions are based on experimentation. When experimentation is not too costly, it is worth following. Even on a small scale, experimentation is almost always justified by good results. Moving machinery around in a factory to change the work flow, or changing the location of desks in a department to see if production rises or falls, are examples of small-scale experimentation, which can sometimes yield surprising results. Using a paper-and-pencil or computer simulation of the changes would be desirable and less costly.

Strategic analysis clarifies goals, assumptions, and expectations

Another experiment that companies have acted upon and like is staggering the work shifts of different departments by 15 minutes so that the parking lot will be less crowded at 9 A.M. and 5 P.M. When experimentation is not possible, the decision maker must select an alternative based on the most objective forecasting possible—the premise of strategic analysis, for example, that decisions are different because the initial objectives, assumptions, and expectations are different.

Implement the Solution

Good solutions must be backed up by good plans. Workable plans have four features in common: *unity, continuity, flexibility,* and *precision.* A plan may be divided into several parts, but those parts should be linked. The action of the plan should be continuous. Starting and stopping a new plan in the middle of the testing period can be disastrous for morale, but the plan should be flexible enough to bend to new pressures when necessary. A good plan exhibits as much accuracy as is compatible with the amount of risk attendant on all new plans. When a plan has been accepted, it must be put into action carefully and watched closely to ensure that it works.

General Foods Corporation provided a good example of planning for implementation when it decided to close down four plants in four states and combine operations in one new, larger plant in yet another state. About 1,800 employees were notified of the move by letter a year before the move was scheduled to take place. A few months later, a policy statement on transfer and termination was circulated to all employees, indicating the company's intention to transfer those employees who wished to move. Transferring employees were given job preferences over newly hired people. General Foods assisted those who did not wish to transfer in finding other employment. Such a carefully implemented, long-term approach not only eliminated many last-minute problems but kept employee motivation and morale at their maximum.

Ongoing Evaluation

All the ramifications of a chosen solution cannot be seen readily until the plan is put into action. Even as the solution is being tried, you and your subordinates will see ways in which to improve the implementation plan. Ongoing evaluation is a necessity in developing a plan, and the key concept in this stage is *feedback.* You will need to solicit feedback openly from employees working on the project as well as from your peers and your superior.

A system that is frequently used in marketing, advertising, and research and development is PERT. The *Program Evaluation Review Technique* evaluates each project at each step along the line in terms of each new input and how it may affect the final result. The cost of the program up to that step is determined both financially and in terms of human adjustment.

PERT or a similar program CPM (*Critical Path Method*) is particularly well adapted to control of major one-time projects. They have been used for revising accounting systems, instituting new inventory systems, installing a computer system, or establishing a new product. Figure 13-3 shows how several departments are involved in a simplified PERT network to introduce a new product. The quality

The key word is "feedback"

PERT

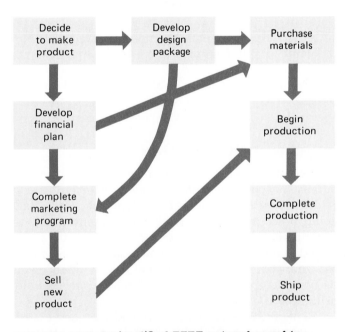

FIGURE 13-3 A simplified PERT network used to introduce a new product. The well-planned program shows timing is important and schedules must be constantly revised.

of a decision is influenced as much by the total process and acceptability of the decision as it is by quantitative measures.

Need for Change

A good decision maker must always be ready to consider new information and change a plan to satisfy new needs. If the solution is a good one, reevaluations and modifications will be concerned with details, and will not affect the intention and general nature of the solution. How many times have you made a decision to go to the library to read a reserve book, only to find when you arrived that the book you wanted would be out for another two hours? You may have had to change certain details of your day so that you could return in two hours to read the book, but the essential plan remains unchanged.

The best solution, and the most careful planning for implementing, will not insure against later flaws that almost always arise. When a particular solution is put into action, unthought-of difficulties will occur. As much time can be spent in refining our decision as we spend in analyzing the problem and collecting the data. Whether it involves a professional goal or new methods of routing manufactured goods, a decision can have a long-lasting effect on us. The time spent on the refinement of the decision is often well worth it!

LONG- AND SHORT-RANGE DECISIONS

Short-range decisions involve little risk

Short-range decisions are usually routine decisions that involve *little risk or uncertainty.* Many industries and business organizations try to create work environments in which as many decision-making functions as possible are standardized for greater production efficiency. The assembly line is the classic example of decisions made into a set of routinized behaviors involving risks. In a short-range decision, the outcome can be seen readily, if not immediately. A

Long-range decisions involve risk

long-range decision involves predicting and planning for the future. Whenever you plan for the future, you automatically encounter a certain amount of risk and uncertainty. (See Figure 13–4.)

Peter Drucker says that it's easier to define long-range decision making by what it is *not* than by what it is. First, it is not forecasting. People neither predict nor control the future. Long-range decisions do not deal with future decisions but, rather, with the probable results of present decisions. The long-range planner does not ask "What should we do tomorrow?" but instead asks, "What do we do today to be ready for an uncertain tomorrow?" Organizations engaged in training programs for minorities and for women are preparing for the desirable working relationships of tomorrow.

TRAITS THAT INFLUENCE DECISIONS

Decisions may be helped or hindered by the basic philosophies that decision makers have about life and how they interrelate with the people around them. People react to problems in many different ways; the solutions chosen reflect some of the assumptions that the person makes. Some of the personality traits that are particularly influential in the decision-making process are discussed now.

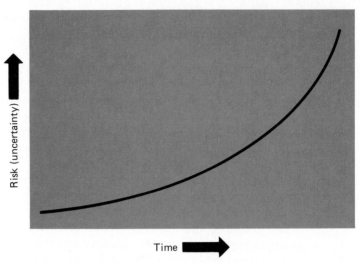

FIGURE 13-4 Risk and uncertainty in decision making increase over time.

Taking Risks

50:50 chance gambles

There is no such thing as a riskless decision, but the degrees to risk vary. Many decision makers have an aversion to risk taking. Most people, when offered a 50:50 chance that a gamble will succeed, would choose not to gamble, even if winning would bring in many times what the risk is worth. Most people do not want to jeopardize the gains they have made in the past.

A graphic way in which to illustrate the degree of risk would be to offer a decision maker a high payoff on an even-chance gamble. A majority would turn down such a proposition even if the payoff were ten times as high as the sum at risk. If the sum at risk involved all or most of the corporate resources, this attitude would be entirely rational. Mature corporations are not in business to gamble their corporate existences on a 50 percent chance of high returns.

To risk all funds on a 50 percent gamble is poor decision making

To risk a small fraction of total funds on 50 percent gambles for big returns is worthwhile

Most decisions, however, involve only a small fraction of total corporate resources. And the opportunities for them occur dozens of times every year. Taking several 50 percent chances every month to risk a small percentage of total resources for a tenfold return would appear to be very good business practice indeed and should pay off handsomely in the long run. Nevertheless, each decision maker tends to behave as though the fate of the company or his or her own were in balance with each decision.

Success and Failure Attitudes

Fear of failure gives little chance for great success

Fear of failure can stalemate the decision-making process. Worry about the unknown results of a decision can be paralyzing. As long as no decision is made, no judgment can be reached as to whether the decision is a good one or not. By not making decisions, people lose the opportunity to learn either from their failures or their successes. *Only by making decisions can one learn how to make successful decisions.*

Decisiveness

Failure to make decisions and to act are responsible for many of our national productivity problems, in both the private and public sectors. Sure, we want better information before making decisions. Some people are indecisive because they don't think they have adequate information. But we will never have enough information for most major decisions. Others just don't like to take the responsibility; the moment they see a problem, they become hopelessly confused.

To make a decision might be the first step to failure, so decisions may be delayed. Until a decision is made, judgments on individuals are often deferred. For the lack of decisions, little growth or experience can be obtained concerning success or failure.

Personal Biases and Experience

Systems of reason are influenced by habits, reflexes, prejudices, appetites, and emotions. All logic is biased by personal feelings and affinities. Sometimes these feelings are appropriate to the situation; sometimes they are not. When making decisions, it helps to know your personal biases.

Experience is only one input to decision making

Knowledge gained by experience is a helpful guide to decision making. The greater the number of successful decisions, the greater the confidence one has with dealing with more decisions. On the other hand, it is dangerous to follow experience blindly. It is too easy for the person with "many years of experience" to fail to listen to innovative ideas from others.

Biases inhibit decision making

Personal biases insulate the individual from anything new. For experience to be useful, a person must be flexible enough to see that it is just one of the many ingredients that goes into the decision-making process.

Intuition

Intuition is largely experiential

Intuition and hunches also help to determine decisions. Intuition is a way of knowing and recognizing the possible consequences of something without conscious reasoning. It is largely experiential; intuition and hunches are based on information or experience recorded in the subconscious.

Often, intuition can provide the essential direction for solving a problem in a certain way, while the justification comes later. Decisions based on intuition gain much more credibility when they are also supported by logic and experience. Unfortunately, it is often difficult to tell the difference between intuition and bias.

Weston Agor encourages unlocking your intuition and trust instincts to help you solve problems and make decisions. Agor writes

> Intuitive skills have a number of practical uses in management, and will come to be more important in the future. For example, intuitive managers are particularly adept at problem solving. Their intuition helps them generate new ideas and ways of looking at things—especially when they feel their input is valued. Such executives are especially effective in sales, purchasing, advertising, marketing and crisis management.[14]

Most executives will not admit to being clairvoyant, but they may see ways to solve business problems that defy computer logic. The bottom-line profit can be spectacular.

Seeking and Giving Advice

Compulsory advisory
service

The concept of *compulsory advisory service* states that the advice and counsel of others must at least be heard by decision makers. The advice may not be heeded, but the decision maker must take others' counsel and listen to it. Listening with an open mind to what other people have to say can greatly enlarge the potential of making a good decision. Other people can also act as sounding boards—providing a chance to hear how ideas sound.

Completed development
work

Completed development work is a corollary to compulsory advisory service. It means doing a thorough job of problem definition, analysis, weighing of alternatives, and recommending solutions. People who complete their work do not give half-baked advice.

People who make a practice of not consulting others take greater risks in making decisions because they isolate themselves from feedback. On the other hand, by seeking too much advice too much of the time, a person can not only appear to be incapable of making a decision independently but can also undermine his or her own confidence.

WHO MAKES THE DECISIONS?

The connection between individual decisions and organizational policy isn't always simple. A person who tries to shape an organization entirely to his or her thinking can expect to meet resistance. A strongly motivated person will form factions and cliques to work for the desired change. Those opposed will also band together. Adopting a policy is by no means the same thing as putting it into effect.

Individual Decisions

The owner-manager may have difficulty delegating decision-making power to subordinates because of a belief that power and prestige are lost when authority is delegated. However, in actuality, more work can be gained by delegation and more experience can be learned by the subordinate.

The supervisor who believes in more independent delegation spends less time checking up on the employees and thus has more time for more important work. Ideally, the employees get a chance to develop themselves by correcting their own errors. A climate of confidence results when the employees are allowed to check up on themselves, without the boss looking over their shoulders.

Decisions by a Powerful Few

Oligarchic decisions are
made by a powerful few

In decisions made by the few, or in oligarchic decision making, major decisions are made by a small group, usually at least three but no more than seven. In addition to participating in joint decisions, each person usually has an area in which he or she has the final say, such as in sales or production matters. Oligarchic control can create delay, or even bring action to a standstill, if there is a deadlock and no one has the final power to decide. In one large corporation, three executives with equal power were deadlocked over several important labor matters. The production specialist wanted to settle with the union to keep the plant operating. The other two opposed agreement for various reasons. The deadlock was broken only when a competing firm signed with the union, thus forcing the two executives who

"HOW MANY WANT TO STAND UP FOR THEIR PRINCIPLES AND HOW MANY WANT TO BACK UP?"

opposed settlement to capitulate. Since that time the corporation has been moving steadily toward one-person control.

Decisions by Groups

Decisions made by many people have been called integrative or participative decisions. These terms are preferable to democratic decision making because "democratic" implies an equality that usually does not exist—certainly not for income, or status, and usually not for the power to influence major decisions. Participatory action normally takes the form of informal consultation among top management and sometimes their subordinates.

Many firms use consultative decision making to bring those employees with technical backgrounds and know-how to the conference table. The technical staff is more likely to participate in making decisions when specific skills are involved than in those areas requiring long-range planning.

Group decision making can be an exceedingly complex affair, but two facts hold true. First, majority decisions usually represent something less than total

Few decisions have total group consensus

The more abstract the
matter, the greater the
chance for agreement

group commitment. Few groups operate with total group consensus. Second, the more abstract the matter being considered, the greater the chances of agreement. Put another way, the more concrete the matter, the less the chances for full agreement.

Group problem solving usually results in a synergistic relationship where $2 + 2 = 5$. Synergy means that the total outcome is greater than the sum of the individual parts. If too many parts are involved, the result may be $3 + 4 + 5 + 6 = 16$ instead of 18. Nevertheless, making decisions in groups can have the advantages previously noted. There are at least five group decision-making procedures: the ordinary group procedure, brainstorming, the statistical method, the Delphi technique, and the nominal group technique. Each is directed toward discovering the best solution for the problem. Each has particular advantages and disadvantages.

The *ordinary group procedure* entails calling a group together, presenting the problem, and asking for comments. The meeting is open ended, with the discussion being free-flowing with few controls. The chairperson controls the speakers so that everyone does not talk at once. Finally, the consensus is stated by the leader once one is reached.

Brainstorming is the technique described earlier in this chapter. It deals with the development of many alternatives to problems and not the evaluation or selection of one of the ideas.

The *statistical method* uses the ideas of a group of individuals, but does not ask these people to interact with one another in a group setting. The method is limited to quantitative problems. Simply, several people make individual estimates of the best answers to a problem. The estimates are collected, and one of a variety of aggregation procedures is used to determine the final solution.

Members of the Rand Corporation developed the *Delphi technique*, which extends the statistical method to include feedback and reestimates. The group does not need to meet face to face. In the Delphi procedure, the chairperson acts as the administrator of an estimate-feedback chain. The first of several questionnaires is constructed to state the problem as clearly as possible and is sent to the Delphi panel. Because the group never meets, there is no easy way to clear up any misunderstandings; thus, the problem statement must be particularly clear. Potential solutions are returned to the chairperson, who summarizes the solutions suggested and feeds them back to the panel by a second questionnaire. Preferences are again solicited in a third questionnaire-feedback report. By such a process, the supposed best solution is decided on by the panel of experts.

The *nominal group technique (NGT)* is a fairly structured decision process with the interpersonal characteristics of face-to-face groups. After the problem is stated clearly, group members sit together quietly and individually generate as many alternatives as they can. After about 15 minutes, ideas are presented in round-robin fashion. Each individual presents a single idea, taking turns, until all the group's ideas have been presented. The leader records them in full view at the front of the room. As in group brainstorming, individuals are encouraged to piggyback on others' ideas. Although each of the ideas is not strictly anonymous as in the Delphi technique, the round-robin recording process may reduce some social pressure.

After everyone is clear about the entire set of suggestions, a voting or rating process is used to reach a group decision. Each group member might vote for the five alternatives that he or she feels are best, rank ordering them from 1 to 5. Alternatively, each of the ideas can be rated on a ten-point scale, from good (1) to bad (10). Votes or ratings are done on private ballots. The chairperson tabulates the votes and announces them to the group. In most cases, the first ballot identifies a small set of possible solutions. If the vote should reveal a clear-cut winner, the group is finished. Also this procedure provides backup alternatives should the initially chosen solution fail to produce a desired outcome. A comparison of various decision-making methods is seen in Table 13–3.

Problems of "Groupthink"

"Groupthink"
Self-censorship

The idea of strong group unity and a feeling of "we are on the right track" can lead to finding the quickest answer and not the best answer. Closely knit groups sometimes suffer from the *illusion of unanimity*; that is, no one wants to break up the cohesiveness of the group. Members of a group may indulge in *self-censorship*, in other words fail to mention a legitimate idea contrary to the group direction. "This idea is not really what the group wants to hear." Such internal feelings, not verbalized, lead to self-censorship.

Shared stereotypes

Shared stereotypes of the opposition is another aspect of groupthink "Well all those people feel the same way, but what do they know?" "They really aren't that important. Actually, we have to discount the cranks." Such group behavior can even lead people to feel that, if you think differently from the group, you are of the opposition or you don't want to be part of the team. So many of us want to be members of the team that we will not oppose the general trend.

Illusion of invulnerability

The final idea is expressed in the *illusion of invulnerability*. "After all we have been a leader in the field for many years, why shouldn't people accept our results?" The idea that the group cannot be wrong because we think alike leads to feelings of grandeur and a belief in the inability to make mistakes. Very successful companies are likely to find that their committees exhibit the "groupthink" syndrome. Do you have a strong leader of your committees that states his or her opinion forcefully before others, thereby setting the stage of "groupthink"?

TABLE 13-3 The Various Methods of Evaluating the Decision-Making Process

CRITERIA	ORDINARY	BRAIN-STORMING	STATISTICAL	DELPHI	NGT
Number of ideas	Low	Moderate	NA	High	High
Quality of ideas	Low	Moderate	NA	High	High
Time and money costs	Moderate	Low	Low	High	Low
Task orientation	Low	High	High	High	High
Potential for interpersonal conflict	High	Low	Low	Low	Moderate
Feelings of accomplishment	High to low	High	Low	Moderate	High
Commitment to solution	High	NA	Low	Low	Moderate

NA—Not applicable

Think of a national issue, a company decision, or a well-known local situation in which a group or committee has fallen into the trap of "groupthink." Consider an international situation (e.g., the selling of new cars) or competition between companies. Review the four aspects of "groupthink."

1. Illusion of unanimity
2. Self-censorship
3. Shared stereotypes of the opposition
4. Illusion of invulnerability

Give reasons to each point above for why the group, committee, or company has succumbed to "groupthink."

Key People in Decision Making

The people between the innovators and the major policy decision makers are often the key link in bringing about effective results. Several hundred scientists in a division of a NASA laboratory were asked to name the colleagues who had been most helpful to them in problem solving.[15] Those who were named most often were interviewed to identify character similarities and differences. The key people were found to share the following characteristics:

Enjoy helping others

1. They derived a greater feeling of accomplishment from helping people to grow and develop than did nonkey personnel.

Talk more to each other

2. They enjoyed working with others. They communicated more often with more people, in their own labs and outside their own units.

Would rather work with competent than with congenial people

3. They placed less importance on working with congenial workers and more emphasis on working with competent workers.

4. They enjoyed a greater feeling of accomplishment from doing creative work rather than from exceeding expected standards of job performance. Practical problems and top management were the main sources of stimulation.

5. They used an environmental more than a humanistic approach, preferring to work with others on technical rather than social grounds.

Key people are not more creative, but have more formal education

6. They scored no better and no worse than their colleagues on a test of creative ability, but they had more formal education.

To summarize, key people in decision making can be predicted with reasonable accuracy. They are apt to be concerned with the broad features of problems and with the innovative aspects to their work. Key people prefer to interact with other workers, but on a professional rather than on a social basis. Their performance record is usually good, and they probably have been influential in shaping their job goals.

MAKING DECISIONS DURING CONFLICT

Two views, two right answers

When more than one person is involved in making a decision, it is often a challenge to arrive at a solution with a minimum of conflict. For example, suppose that the sales personnel of a cosmetics firm insist on a particular kind of packaging for a new product because of its eye-catching appeal. The production department, however, is firmly opposed to it on the grounds of expense and difficulty of manufacture. Both groups are right, at least within their respective areas of concern. This is the kind of situation that calls for developing and evaluating alternatives. Solutions to this kind of conflict are usually plentiful as soon as the parties involved agree to explore alternative choices together.

Polarizations

Polarization is strong opposing views

Making decisions always involves people—either they participate in the process of problem solving or they are affected by the decisions made. Decisions often involve disagreements, which sometimes can be resolved through discussing and understanding the different points of view. But deep-seated conflicts are not easily resolved. When such terms as "confrontation" and "nonnegotiable" are used in describing a situation, the resistance to argument may be so firm that effective decision making seems impossible.

One typical pattern in polarized conflict is called *nonexistence*. This occurs when one side refuses to listen to the arguments of the other side. Nonrecognition is often a ploy to force the antagonist to quiet down or to go away. You may be able to recognize this tactic in such circumstances as the "freeze out" in a lovers' quarrel or the temporary banishment of a "difficult" child from the family. Russia has

Nonperson status

institutionalized the practice of treating people as nonexistent by creating a specific "nonperson" status.

The universal plot

Universal plot theories can be used to explain just about anything. "It's a Communist plot" is a famous example of a conspiracy theory that can gain immediate support in some circles. It is a very human response to treat behavior we dislike as the work of our adversaries. By this tactic, the leaders of one group make the problem part of a larger, more sinister plot.

Win-lose approach

The *win-lose* approach to conflicts implies a "go-for-broke" attitude where something is at stake. It assumes that a person's contributions to group effort will result in a *personal gain* or loss in esteem, prestige, or responsibility. It also discourages the possibility of free expression and change of ideas. Consciously or unconsciously, people will feel that they personally are being tested, not their ideas.

The idea of winning or losing is so ingrained in the American character that some management personnel accept it as a natural part of the human condition. This assumption rules out the easy use of such methods as group brainstorming and group decision making. Some advocates of competitive games such as win-lose maintain that without such games, employees may become more content but that they also become less productive, and the quality of their work suffers.

Real Communication Leads to a Resolution

What can be done when two or more sides are polarized? How can a decision be reached that will prove effective and advantageous to all parties? As long as the hostile attitudes that frequently accompany conflict exist, it is difficult to arrive at a meaningful decision. Without *real* listening and a *real* desire to understand the other side's point of view, conflict cannot be resolved.

In a conflict situation, it is important to be able to recognize sincere efforts, as opposed to partial or superficial efforts, to communicate and agree. True communication is sometimes feared because of the changes that may follow in its wake.

Frequently, insincere efforts can be recognized by the *manner* in which the problem is stated. For example, the following does not indicate a sincere desire to reach accord: "We are ready to participate in reasonable discussions, but we will not submit to blackmail."

Two ways can help to promote a settlement. One is to bring in a neutral outsider. A mediator can more often talk to both sides from a conciliatory point of view—one that is not emotionally charged. Emotions add fuel to a fire; and calm facts extinguish the flames. Finally, and most important, the bargainer empathizes by placing himself or herself in the shoes of the adversary so that the final outcome does not disgrace the bargainer or the opponent publicly. Humiliating the opponent may only give a temporary victory. To allow the opponent to "save face" may be in the best interest of the company, the union, or the nation.

There is, of course, no simple solution to confrontation. Nevertheless, it is possible, through listening and through attending to the other communication techniques described in earlier chapters, to create an atmosphere in which, despite ongoing disagreement over details, the total process of decision making can continue. When this happens, solutions often emerge that neither side has envisioned.

Summary

The creative act combines old elements in new ways. Current concepts are the building blocks for new ideas. All people are born with the ability to create. This ability does not disappear with adulthood, but it takes many different forms. Although timeliness, usefulness, and originality are not always applicable criteria for recognizing a creative idea, they are frequently reliable indications.

While creative people are necessary to successful organizations, creative behavior can definitely conflict with the smooth running of a business. The ambiguous feelings that many managers have toward creative people can be stated as the reasonable desire for a balance between creativity and practicality.

The creative person is valuable to employers because it is through creativity that companies develop new products. Products may be tangible, or they may be ideas. An employee may not want status or more money as a result of a creative idea, as much as he or she wants recognition for it. The most direct rewards are acknowledgment of the creative act itself and encouragement for further creativity.

The creative process is still a mysterious one. Four stages have been recognized: perception, incubation, inspiration, and verification. Finally, the rewards for creativity and innovation must include psychological fulfillment and social recognition.

Creativity is an integral part of decision making—primarily in the selection of alternatives. A decision is a commitment to take action, not to take an action, or to accept or reject an attitude. No matter how routine the decisions are, their importance is often incalculable because they are all links in a larger process.

Long-range decisions require planning for contingencies, which automatically means that risk is involved. The future can only be predicted, whereas decisions are always based in the present. Decisions are often made as insurance against future events.

After problem definition, there are six ACTION steps to decision making: *a*nalyzing the problem; *c*onsidering alternative solutions; *t*aking action—selecting a solution; *i*mplementing it; making an *o*ngoing evaluation of the solution as it is being implemented; and making *n*ecessary changes.

Decisions affecting groups are made by one person, by a few, or by many; and each method has its own rewards and drawbacks. No matter who has the final word, key people are always involved. Key people are go-betweens—they help to get an idea proposed by one party to be decided upon by another.

Conflict situations have certain characteristics that indicate degrees of polarization. The only way in which to solve a polarized issue is through careful communication. Most of us like hard, positive choices. A choice between negative alternatives is really no choice at all. Too many choices can overwhelm us. We like to choose from among five alternatives, but not from among more than seven. When, as employees, we have an opportunity to participate in a decision, we are more likely to accept it.

Case Study 26

Achievement—Accomplished by Individual Creativity or by "Groupthink" Team Effort

In the United States today, individual achievement is highly valued. In our business setting, success or failure depends largely upon individual capability, and the road toward success is an individual effort. This is pretty much the way it has been for the first 200 years of our country's existence. But according to a poll of top corporate executives across the country, this characteristically American ideology is being replaced by an emphasis on group achievement rather than individual effort.

Ideology 2, our ideology of the future, will stress the use of teamwork in achieving goals. An effective team will be a group of people who work together noncompetitively to complete certain tasks. The members of the team will support one another, be receptive to new ideas coming from both within and outside the team, and be able to communicate well among themselves. Individuals within the effective team will be recognized for individual efforts and achievements, but the success will be credited to the group as a whole.

When considering the creative individual, which ideology—our ideology of today or our ideology of the future—will best aid creative potential?

Case Study 27

Missing Company Property

One of the most difficult problems that a personnel department can face is how to track down company property that it suspects was "lifted" by light-fingered employees. No matter how careful the management might be in searching for the culprits, its activities are likely to step on someone's toes.

Applied Computers was missing several things, from office supplies to small special hand tools. The office manager, Barbara Miller, was convinced that the pilferage was done by company employees.

"Our clients don't have access to our supplies, but many of our employees do. One problem may be our checkout system in our warehouse and toolroom," said Miller one day. Finally she was convinced that she should take a bold tack. She asked a representative of the local union, a shop steward, to meet her near the employees' locker room. You have overheard the conversation. As the company's personnel director you are torn between telling Miller, your superior, something about her possible action, and reporting to her superior, Jim Sanford, the vice president of the firm. You know that there is nothing in the company policies about such action.

1. What will you do? If you talk to Barbara Miller, what will you say? If you talk to Jim Sanford, what will you recommend?

2. Does the employer have the right to invade its employees' private lockers, where personal belongings are kept, without the employees' permission?

3. If the company takes items from the lockers that belong to the company, is this an unwarranted invasion of privacy and an illegal search and seizure?

4. If the company had requested permission of the employees, then would the company still have the same opportunity to find the missing property?

Terms and Concepts

brainstorming   a conference technique of developing new alternatives by unrestrained discussions.

completed development work   the concept of doing a thorough job of problem definition, analysis, weighing of alternatives, and recommending solutions.

compulsory advisory service   a concept in which decision makers are compelled to listen to the advice and counsel of others. The advice may not be heeded but the decision maker must at least listen to it.

creativity   the ability to produce original ideas, expressions, or products from diverse resources.

entrepreneur   a person who creates or perceives new kinds of demands and applies innovative techniques for meetings those demands.

groupthink   the theory that all members of a group learn to think alike and react alike. Members of the group will impose self-censorship, so they will not say something the group may not like to hear.

heuristic approach   an intuitive, self-discovery–orient-

ed approach to decision making and problem solving.

innovation   the action-oriented end product of creative activity. Innovation can take place in policies, processes, and techniques as well as in people's activities and behaviors.

intuition   a way of knowing and recognizing the possible consequences of something without conscious reasoning.

long-range decisions   from a company point of view, decisions that will affect the company one to five years hence. Such decisions are made by top management.

polarization   the establishment of two opposing views, with both parties unwilling to change their opinion as to how a problem should be solved.

risk taking   the willingness to chance a loss. The longer the time period, the greater the chance of risk. The first-line supervisor takes less risks than top management, from the company's point of view.

short-range decisions   decisions that cover a span of less than a year, usually a week or a couple of months.

Notes

1. Harry J. Gray, quoted in *Business Week,* July 27, 1981, p. 89.
2. Tom Peters, *Thriving on Chaos: Handbook for a Management Revolution* (New York: Alfred A. Knopf, 1988), p. 252.
3. Rosabeth Moss Kanter, "Swimming in Newstreams: Mastering Innovation Dilemmas," *California Management Review,* Summer 1989, pp. 45–69.
4. Byron R. Wien, "Japan's Nada High School: We've Nothing Like It," *The Wall Street Journal,* January 8, 1990, p. A10.
5. "What Makes Creative People Different," *Psychology Today,* July 1975, pp. 46–49.
6. Alex F. Osborn, *Applied Imagination* (New York: Scribner, 1963), p. 18.
7. Ibid.
8. Ibid., p. 22.
9. Chester H. Sinnett, "Emotional Blocks to Creativity," *Research/Development,* February 1973, p. 1.
10. Edward Glassman, "Creative Problem Solving," *Supervisory Management,* January 1989, pp. 21–22.
11. Michael McTague, "Tapping Creative Potential," *Training and Development Journal,* June 1989, pp. 36–41.
12. David DeLong, "Managing Creative People—Creative People Can Meet Deadlines," *Inc.,* December 1981, pp. 34–36.
13. Amitai Etzioni, "Humble Decision Making," *Harvard Business Review,* July–August 1989, p. 112.
14. Weston Agor, "Unlocking Your Intuition," *Management World,* May 1985, p. 9.
15. Robert Swain and George Farris, a study reported in *Innovation,* October 1971, p. 26.

Recommended Reading

Agor, Weston. *Intuitive Management: Integrating Left and Right Brain Management Skills.* Englewood Cliffs, N.J.: Prentice-Hall, 1984.

——— "Unlocking Your Intuition." *Management World,* May 1985, pp. 8–10.

Baily, Martin, and Alek Chakrabarti. *Innovation and the Productivity Crisis.* Washington, D.C.: Brookings Institution, 1988.

Botkin, James, Dan Dimancescu, and Ray Stata. *The Innovators.* Philadelphia: University of Pennsylvania Press, 1986.

Drucker, Peter. *Innovation and Entrepreneurship: Practice and Principles.* New York: Harper & Row, 1985.

Journal of Creative Behavior, various issues.

Kanter, Rosabeth Moss. *The Change Masters: Innovation for Productivity in the American Corporation.* New York: Simon & Schuster, 1983.

——— *When Giants Learn to Dance.* New York: Simon & Schuster, 1989.

Mastenbrock, William F. G. *Conflict Management and Organization Development.* New York: John Wiley, 1987.

Peters, Tom. *Thriving on Chaos: Handbook for a Management Revolution.* New York: Alfred A. Knopf, 1988.

Ray, Michael L., and Rochelle Myers. *Creativity in Business.* Garden City, N.Y.: Doubleday, 1986.

Sauser, William I., Jr. "Injecting Contrast: A Key to Quality Decisions." *Advanced Management Journal,* Autumn 1988, pp. 20–23.

Tanouye, Elyse. "Why Smart Managers Make Bad Decisions." *Working Woman,* August 1989, pp. 55–57, 96–97.

Managing Change Through Teamwork

After studying this chapter, you should be able to:

1. Discuss psychological resistance to change from the point of view of
   a. Occupational identity
   b. Fear of the unknown
   c. Status considerations
2. Explain in your own words why the idea of homeostasis is necessary in understanding how change takes place in groups.
3. List and understand the four basic economic reasons for fearing change.
4. Discuss the advantages and disadvantages of change through mandate as opposed to change through participation.
5. Describe the theory of behavior modification and how it can help supervisors to be more effective.
6. Describe the keys to a successful change.
7. Explain the characteristics of organization development and how it is related to group dynamics.
8. Discuss how to develop teamwork and trust.

TO START YOU THINKING . . .

Look at these questions before reading the chapter. Perhaps you can use the questions to start a discussion after studying the chapter.

♦ Is your first reaction "No!" when you are asked to change a procedure you are used to doing a certain way?

♦ Do certain kinds of change frighten you or threaten you?

♦ When it is clear that change must take place, do you try to hinder it or help it? Do you have any ideas about how to implement change?

♦ Is it right to change a person's behavior? When would it be ethical?

♦ What is the value of change?

♦ Can change really be managed?

♦ What makes change successful in some cases, but unsuccessful in others?

♦ What are some of the work environment changes facing us today?

♦ What are some diagnostic techniques for studying organizations and their people?

INNOVATIVE DECISIONS INVOKE CHANGE _____

Once a decision has been rendered, it then becomes necessary to implement it. Implementation requires changing individual attitudes, procedures, and skills. This chapter focuses on the changing of individual's behavior and then on organizational development.

Things change. Economic systems, technology, social systems all change. But, as the old saying goes "The more things change, the more they stay the same." Just when we think we have a situation under control, the variables change.

> At certain points in history, when we think we have political structures figured out and systems locked in, new winds begin to blow, changing what we thought was fixed. Ideologies surge and swirl, people and nations break out of boxes, attitudes change, our projections of what will and will not be are soon proven wrong, or at least incomplete. Our wisdom proves to be little.[1]

Most programs of innovation do not succeed because the process of change is not managed properly. The CET (Change equals Effort over Time) model makes it easier to consider change in a useful way. The abstract model separates change into four phases: (1) *excitement* phase, the pizzazz, the crashing cymbals; (2) *hard work* phase where existing habits, patterns, and the culture itself have to be fought; (3) *turning-point* phase where it is getting easier; and (4) *institutionalized* change where it takes no more effort to do things the new way than it did the old.[2]

It is important to note that phase 1 is usually overemphasized and that the effort in phase 2 is underestimated. To make the CET model work requires realistic analysis and more effective communication of needed change.[3]

People resist change. Some organizations and people are better at coping with change than others. Sometimes the Japanese adapt better to job changes than U.S. workers.[4] Both countries have experienced significant economic changes in recent years, but the U.S. companies laid off workers and closed plants while the Japanese tried to trim costs and transfer workers between plants.

PATTERNS OF CHANGE _____

The cliché that our technological society is rapidly changing expresses a truth that affects everyone. In the past, the progress of technology was measured by millenia, or at least by centuries. Today's technology has already outstripped the imaginations of the science fiction writers of a generation ago. Steel plants mass produce steel plates with the kind of minute precision that only computers can achieve. Freight trains are dispatched and rail car inventories are handled by computer banks. Instant credit checks are run in less than 20 seconds. Our increasingly sophisticated communication systems give us picture telephones and wireless telephones to carry in our pockets.

But some new technologies have not achieved their much acclaimed promise in the workplace. In the face of rapid change, many managers are preoccupied with the technical issues and neglect the equally important human resources element. Individuals who want to help achieve connections between people and technology should keep in mind eight key points:

1. Technological change is inevitable.
2. Resistance to change is natural.
3. Change must make sense to everyone involved.
4. Organizational settings vary.
5. Change takes time.
6. Change results in role overload.
7. Change requires ongoing technical support.
8. All change involves learning.[5]

Managers must take into account the inevitability of change and recognize that commitment to technology—something over which we have little choice—is a commitment to ongoing change. To make them successful, we need the symbiosis of people and technology.

Technological change has always been equated with progress, and who is against progress? Yet, when we examine the dynamics of change, we find that, although nearly everyone says that he or she is in favor of change, actual behavior patterns reveal contradictory and ambivalent feelings concerning its value.

We fear the unknown and the outcomes of change are unknown; so, in large part, we fear change. We all like to talk about the need for change, but there is tremendous resistance to doing it.

No matter how drastic our technological changes have been, are, or will be, social changes are even more dramatic. The power of information is great from a technological standpoint; it is even greater from a socioeconomic viewpoint. Peter Drucker notes that the social impacts may be greater than the technological impacts of information.[6]

Figure 14-1 describes a general model for change.

Initiating changes in the work environment may cause the development of

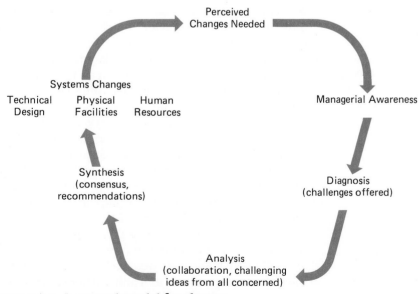

FIGURE 14-1 A general model for change.

similar patterns of resistance. Hostility may be expressed openly or only implied. It may be directed against supervisors or against the work activities. The manner in which it is expressed depends on how much hostility can be expressed safely without endangering job security. It may take the form of sloppy efforts, slowdowns, lots of lip service, or a subtle combination of apathy and apple polishing, but no actual change in behavior.

Lip service doesn't mean acceptance

When to Expect Resistance

Expect resistance to vague or unclear changes

If the elements of a proposed change are not made clear to the people who are going to be affected or influenced by it, resistance can be expected. People who dislike their jobs are particularly resistant to ambiguous or unclear orders to change. They want to know exactly what they have to do to minimize the unpleasant aspects of their jobs.

Various factors cause resistance to change: human nature, attitudes, anxiety, and insecurity, among many others. Human nature desires a change in status quo—whether humans are willing to effect or endure changes is another matter. Most people at all job levels in business and industry resist change for psychological, economic, and social reasons.

The amount of resistance can be related to the amount of participation that people have in the timing and direction of the innovation. Resistance will be least evident when workers *have the most to say about procedural matters and most evident when they have the least to say.*

CHANGING THE INDIVIDUAL

A supervisor who seeks to change an individual in some way faces the fact that an individual may resist the change. When we want to change an individual, we are seeking to modify one or more of the forces that make the individual behave as he or she does. For a model of an individual, consider the one shown in Figure 14-2. To change this individual, we can add or subtract one or more of the forces affecting his or her behavior, thereby perhaps producing a fundamental change in the individual's behavior.

The more pressures are in harmony, the more predictable the outcome

Naturally, pressure can invoke change, but the outcome cannot always be predicted. There are many forces on an individual, and the outcome of the various pressures can produce unexpected outbursts. The more forces working in harmony with each other, the more likely a predictable outcome can be generated.

Social adjustment to a new work environment can be difficult for those who belong to a tightly knit group. The process of breaking social ties with those at the old workstation and making new acquaintances can be threatening.

Conflict between individual goals and group loyalties produce unpredictable results

Studies have also shown that resistance to change often results from a conflict of individual and group loyalties (Figure 14-3). An individual may want to "please the boss" yet be restrained by group pressure to protect the slower members of the group who would be hurt most by a change. Group pressure may force a person to resist change even if that person believes in the innovation, because group acceptance is more important.

For every force of change there is a counterpressure. As shown by Figure 14-4 the group may pressure from above against the desires of the individual below. For

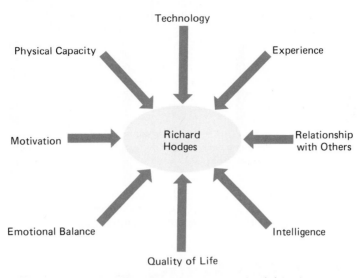

FIGURE 14-2 **Various influences on an individual.**

example, an employee who would like to make a bonus by producing more parts may be dissuaded from doing so by the other workers:

> Hey Charlie, we don't want a "rate-buster" in our shop. Sure, we can all produce more parts than is required, but why bust our butts? If we all did that, the guys in the head office would raise the standard and then where would we be? No bonuses, and we would have to produce more. Now, be a nice guy, Charlie, don't make waves. If you come in late, we will cover for you, so relax. Don't be an "eager beaver."

One of the important effects illustrated in Figure 14-4 is that the level of production can be raised either by increasing the forces below the line or by reducing the forces above the line. The greater the opportunity for a promotion for Charlie, the more likely he will become a "rate-buster." Likewise, the greater the turnover within the department, the less likely that group pressure will influence Charlie's production. See the Group Pressure—"Rate Busting" case at the end of this chapter.

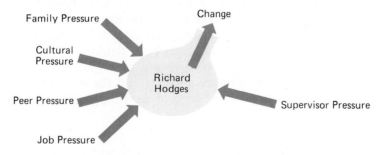

FIGURE 14-3 Various counterforces can produce an unpredictable change.

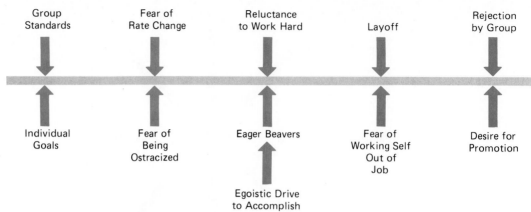

FIGURE 14-4 **Group pressures versus individual beliefs.**

PSYCHOLOGICAL RESISTANCE

Occupational Identity and Security

The stronger the occupational identity, the greater the security

Any environmental change that affects an individual always involves some loss of security. Change, by its very nature, forces confrontation with uncertainty. Familiar, predictable routines produce a sense of security that is pyschologically both necessary and satisfying. When there is a *strong sense of occupational identity*, there is also a *strong sense of psychological security*. If that occupational identity and the associated security are threatened, there will be resistance to change.

Consider the case of skilled factory workers who have had to relearn their jobs using automated machinery. Work that used to require skilled hand, eye, and brain coordination is now done by automated methods. Unless those workers have learned new skills, their sense of occupational identity has probably been damaged severely.

The recent changes in nurses' occupational status provide another example. For years, registered nurses (RNs) and licensed practical nurses (LPNs) have coexisted and provided basic nursing care services. Registered nurses have been able to attain their status via three educational channels: a hospital school diploma (usually three years), an associate arts degree (usually two years), or a baccalaureate degree (usually four years). There have been considerable educational and status struggles within the RNs' ranks alone, not to mention the status differentials with LPNs. The resistance to job responsibility changes associated with the various levels of LPNs and RNs have been detrimental to the general advancement of nursing and health care provision.

When stable patterns are disturbed, the feelings of pressure and dissatisfaction that result may take the form of direct opposition or subtle resistance to change.

Fear of Unknown Future

Factory and even white-collar workers have no monopoly on resistance based on feelings of insecurity. Members of management and other professions are especially notorious for wanting a change—and then retrenching or retreating from their positions when implementation of the changes are imminent. Congress has passed laws, only to repeal them a year later when they found out the true impact of the legislation.

We shoot ourselves in our feet by fearing to tread where others have not gone before. Donald Schon visited a small company that had been making foundry products since the turn of the century. It had established a good reputation built on old technology, but it was under severe competitive pressure from larger companies. For two years the company's managers had explored the possibilities of manufacturing various new products. What could they make in order to diversify? Their product director showed Schon a paper listing the criteria a new product had to meet. Any new product had to (1) promise a gross of $3 million within five years, (2) show a large profit margin, (3) be able to utilize present production facilities, and (4) be marketed and sold through the present sales force. Not one idea in two years had been able to pass those tests![7]

We can establish rules to deter change

Clearly, the criteria had been set up to make product innovation impossible, but from the company president on down, it was stated and believed that finding new products was both necessary and desirable. Peters and Waterman also saw innumerable examples of this type of resistance in their study.[8]

Fear of the unknown is potent

The difficulty of getting an idea through some systems suggests the NIH (Not-Invented-Here) syndrome: "If it's not my idea, it's probably no good." The insecurity demonstrated here is not as simple a matter as occupational identity, encompassing as it does complex financial, production, and sales aspects of the business. There can be no doubt, however, that fear of an uncertain future and possible failure played a large role in establishing rigid, impossible-to-meet criteria for change. The fear of the unknown is as potent a force in business as in any other realm of life.

Status Consideration

Another psychological factor leading to resistance to change is the feeling many people have, often justified, that change threatens their status within the organization.

Status always involves comparison, and major organizational changes usually bring in their wake the unintended side effect of lowering and raising the status of one or more individuals or work units. Naturally, the people who will be downgraded resist any such organizational change.

ECONOMIC RESISTANCE

Economic reasons for resistance to change are much easier to isolate than are psychological ones. How many blacksmiths are there in your community? Any steam locomotive engineers, stone cutters, or whale bone corset manufacturers? In the past century, perhaps as many time-honored occupations have disappeared from the economic sector as new ones have been born.

Economic reasons to fear change usually focus on one or more of the following: (1) fear of technological unemployment; (2) fear of reduced work hours and, thus, less pay; (3) fear of demotion and, thus, reduced wages; and (4) fear of speed-up and reduced incentive wages.

Unions can resist change

Consider the case of a hypodermic syringe manufacturer. The company's research and development staff introduced a machine that increased the production rate from 400 to 1,500 syringes an hour. At least, that was the machine's performance at the test site. Union representatives examined the machine and predicted that it would increase production to no more than 700 syringes per hour. They were right. Production rose to 700 an hour, leveled off, and stayed put. Of crucial importance to this story is the fact that the company's history of management-union relations was extremely bad, characterized for years by mutual distrust and hostility. No assurances from management would have been believed, so the workers took their job security into their own hands and kept production down at a "safe" level.

SOCIAL RESISTANCE

The Theory of Homeostasis

A clock is more than a collection of hands, cogs, and wheels because when it is assembled something new results: the registering and measuring of time. Similarly, a work group is more than a collection of individuals because when it is assembled something new results: important functions relating to establishing common standards, attitudes, goals, and leadership.

Homeostasis theory helps to maintain a balance or stability

Psychologist Kurt Lewin proposed a model of the dynamics of group behavior to support his theory that groups tend to maintain an equilibrium that allows them to behave pretty much the same way from day to day.[9] Whenever change threatens a group, the group acts to oppose it and to maintain the kind of balance it is used to. This balance-maintaining characteristic of groups is called *homeostasis*, that is, a state of stability of equilibrium.

For example, if management imposes new controls on a work group, the group may react with increased adherence to its own standards of group loyalty, as the workers at the syringe factory did. In that case, outside pressure did produce some changes in behavior, but it also caused a reaction that resisted change, and the group moved in the direction of homeostasis, or the maintenance of familiar routines.

Driving Forces and Restraining Forces

In Lewin's model, the forces that "up" production (new machinery and specific instructions and supervision in its use) are called *driving forces*. The forces that keep production down to a level deemed safe for job security are called *restraining forces*. (See Figure 14-5). Other driving forces to increase production in a work group might be the desire of some members to win promotions or higher salaries. These forces would be balanced by the group's fear of layoff—restraining forces that would make themselves known in the form of hostility to "eager beavers" or even ostracism of the offending group members.

An imbalance between forces "unfreezes" the pattern and permits a new homeostasis to develop

Lewin's studies show that change occurs when an imbalance develops between the restraining and driving forces. Such imbalance "unfreezes" the pattern, and the group struggles to achieve a new balance of equilibrium. Once found, the new pattern will be made up of different components. That is, the group refreezes at a new and different equilibrium level. These studies also show that, when efforts are made to change a work group by increasing the driving forces, the most common response of the group is to increase restraining forces to maintain the same balance. When a restraining force is weakened, the patterns are more

Pressure to Change	Resistance to Change
Changing technology	Habit
Knowledge explosion	Fear of unknown
Rapid obsolescence	Security and regression
New lifestyle	Loss of power and control
Wants new challenges	Organizational structure

FIGURE 14-5 Pendulum of change: there are pressures to bring about change and pressures of resistances. The equilibrium is homeostasis.

easily unfrozen and the group experiences little difficulty moving on to new and different patterns of balance.

Balancing the Forces

There is a good reason why it is difficult to bring about change through the increase of driving forces. When driving forces are increased, the tensions in the total system are likely to increase also. More tensions mean greater instability and a greater likelihood of irrational behavior on the part of group members.

The equilibrium of any group at any time is a balance of forces that work for and against change within the group. All groups are working simultaneously both for and against their ways of life. As noted earlier, resistance to change is a common and normal phenomenon. People have always objected to change when it threatens their accustomed ways of living. This applies to all groups: employees resisting change invoked by supervisors, companies opposing governmental regulations, and management objecting to union demands.

Change in Technology and "Quality of Life"

While it is true that technological innovation paved the way for the standard of living that we enjoy in the United States today, it is also true that the quality of our life has not always been enhanced by those changes. The environmental and ecology movements that have sprung up in the past decades are but one indication that growing numbers of people no longer believe that unchecked technological growth is the wisest course to follow.

Will it be technology versus "quality of life"?

It may be that in the near future we will see the entire direction of change focus less on technological innovation and more on technological "containment" and on interpersonal, intergroup changes in human behavior. Today, ideas being aired to preserve the environment call for changing our notions of the value of technological growth. Progressive social change may come to mean greater emphasis on the quality of life for the total population and less emphasis on the kinds and quantities of the goods we produce.

Conflict between the person's and the company's "life style"

We can see that sometimes there is a conflict between personal and social values. For example, our "life-style" is seen as an outward evidence of our own values, beliefs, and perspectives. Certainly, our own life-styles affect and are affected by company-related issues. Companies are aware of this influence, and many are careful to hire only those with compatible "life-styles," which can be contrary to equal opportunity principles. Large companies have installed "quality of work life" programs. It is an attempt to see to what degree members of the work force are able to satisfy important personal needs through their experiences in the company. The more satisfying the quality of work life, the more similar the employee and the company life-styles. The less similar the company's and the employee's life-styles, the greater the chance of resistance to change.

Work Environment Change

As the age of information develops, we recognize that it will never be possible to return to former industrial-based manufacturing, processes, and conditions. That is not all bad. The age of information brings with it a change in working conditions including working more at home than at the plant or in the office for some people.

Toffler predicts that work at home on a large scale could influence family structures and even redefine "love":

> Those who look ahead to working at home with a spouse, instead of spending the main part of their waking lives away, are likely to take more into consideration than simple sexual and psychological gratification—or social status, for that matter. They may begin to insist on Love Plus—sexual and psychological gratification *plus* brains (as their grandfathers once favored brawn), love *plus* conscientiousness, responsibility, self-discipline, or other work-related virtues. We may—who knows?—hear some John Denver of the future croon lyrics like:
>
> > I love your eyes, your cherry lips,
> > the love that always lingers,
> > your way with words and random blips,
> > your skilled computer fingers.[10]

The shift from an industrial to an information society is centered around five points:

- The information society is an economic reality, not an intellectual abstraction.
- Innovations in communications and computer technology will accelerate the pace of change by collapsing the *information float.*
- New information technologies will at first be applied to old industrial tasks, then, gradually give birth to new activities, processes, and products.
- In this literacy-intensive society, when we need basic reading and writing skills more than ever before, our education system is turning out an increasingly inferior product.
- The technology of the new information age is not absolute. It will succeed or fail according to the principle of high tech/high touch.[11]

"High tech/high touch" means that in the age of technological information, where individuals work alone at home or "telecommute," there must be corresponding human responses. There is, as Naisbitt says, "a need to be together."[12] How that need and the demands of the information age are to be reconciled remains to be seen.

Work environment changes are not all based around information technology. There are changes in the type of work that people *want* to do in the industrial manufacturing workplace. An example is a General Motors plant in Tennessee that gave its UAW union members the first choice at 50 custodial jobs—janitorial, clean-up, and routine maintenance work. The results were surprising:

> They expect ten or twenty applications from older workers who have not quite reached retirement age but have worn themselves out and are seeking a resting place. To the astonishment of both union and management, they receive not ten or twenty inquiries, but an overwhelming two thousand applications from men who hold higher-paying, higher-status jobs . . . most of the applicants are young, vigorous and far from retirement. The union doesn't know how to allocate the fifty jobs. Seniority rights were originally conceived with upward mobility in mind, giving the person with the longest service the right to higher-paying, not to lower-paying jobs. Who ever heard of bargaining for downward mobility rights?[13]

Express Your Opinion	Suppose your company is moving 50 miles away and you will probably need to be retrained to keep your job. What will bother you the most? Will you attempt to change employers? Will you move or commute? Will you resist being retrained? Why?

OVERCOMING RESISTANCE

Participation

There is a greater chance for success when all involved participate

Management theorists such as Kurt Lewin, Peter Drucker, and Leonard Sayles have created an impressive body of evidence indicating that, when all the parties to be affected by change participate in the planning of that change, the change has a real chance of succeeding. Groups everywhere tend to cooperate rather than to resist when presented with the opportunity to evaluate a situation and participate in planning for change. (See Figure 14-6). Social psychology theory has established that the least effective way in which to motivate for change is through discipline or the threat of punishment. In the past few decades, behavioral scientists have stressed the fact that force in human affairs, just as in physics, breeds counterforce.

Realistically, employees want to participate in change. Participation in the process of change motivates the individual by (1) fulfilling the developmental needs of a healthy personality, (2) promoting security through knowledge of the environment and exercising control over it, and (3) reducing basic fears of the unknown that cause resistance to change.

There is a sizable gap, however, between social psychology theory and practice in the business world. The author knows of several companies where changes have been effected without any involvement or participation on the part

FIGURE 14-6 Groups everywhere tend to cooperate rather than to resist when presented with the opportunity to participate in planning for the change. Laima Druskis/Photo Researchers

of the employees other than doing the physical work. Changes were conducted in such a way as to discourage all participation below the level of top management. Management refused to solicit ideas from people who were most affected by the changes. Predictably, there was animosity and ill will between management, supervisors, and employees. Changes in office arrangements and office moves are classic examples of these phenomena.

Another good reason for encouraging employees to take part in planning for change is that they usually have considerable useful information to contribute. Unfortunately, if they are not asked, they usually will not volunteer that information because they feel it will not be wanted or accepted.

Behavior Modification

In 1977 when President Carter announced his energy plan, few people got excited; energy was a subject that seemed to put people to sleep. The National Energy Act of 1978, which set up modest tax credits for conservation, the development of alternative fuel sources, and deregulating natural gas prices, was seen as a weak compromise by many observers. Effecting change and accepting changed attitudes can take a long time. By 1980 the public had realized there was an energy crisis. Yet there is still a resistance by Americans to drive slowly and make only necessary trips. Americans hate to be controlled.

Alternatives or changes should be made attractive. The more the new approach appears to appeal, the more likely people will change. Accenting the positive is the *behavior modification* approach to a better and more permanent change. Performance on a task generally improves when the performer is positively reinforced.

Behavior modification
requires keeping records

Behavior modification has worked well to change attitudes, but it does require people to keep records. Keeping records helps to clarify the behavior involved.

Supervisors who note on paper every time they criticize an employee or point to some mistake will see how much criticism they issue during the day. Supervisors who keep a record of every time they commend the employee will see the extent of commending. If more commendations are issued, the supervisor will likely see improved employee performance (Figure 14-7).

Mandating Change

In some cases, it may be better to introduce changes without consulting those to be affected. Often the effects of change cannot be assessed properly until well after the change has been installed. For example, it was not until department stores were forced, by federal mandate, to hire blacks as sales clerks that top management realized that customers and store personnel would accept the change as a matter of course.

Mandated change is fast

The main advantage of mandating change from above is that *change can take place quickly and efficiently.* It took less than a decade for the white populations of southern cities to become thoroughly accustomed to black sales clerks, a phenomenon that reversed 200 years of tradition.

Mandating change is a strictly authoritarian approach. The authoritarian is entirely responsible for major decisions. Resistance can be handled simply by firing or by transferring unruly employees. Resistance can be minimized because the authoritarian assumes the burden of risk—in fact, the authoritarian will often go to great lengths to protect employees from doubts or worries, fearing the resulting confusion. The authoritarian style of leadership appears to be strong because it appears to be able to overcome resistance. Nevertheless, resistance is to be expected when employees are pressured without a chance to contribute their own input.

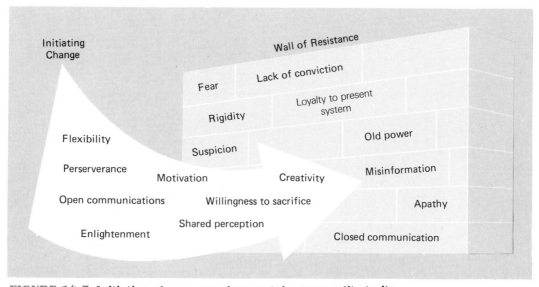

FIGURE 14-7 **Initiating change requires certain personality traits.**

Express Your Opinion

We have read of the pendulum of change and how there are pressures to bring about change and pressures to resist change. The equilibrium or the balance of the two is a state of homeostasis.

Mandating appears to effect changes suddenly, swinging the homeostasis pendulum dramatically to the left or right. By contrast, Skinner's behavioral modification method advocates making changes slowly, so that the pendulum moves more slowly to the left or right.

If situations change and a new direction is needed, which of the methods cited will encourage the fastest change? Do the laws of physics come into play? That is, if the pendulum is swinging quickly to the left or right, will a quick reversal cause it to move faster in the other direction? In other words, will change be faster in both directions under the mandating system as opposed to the behavioral modification system? Once behavioral modification has changed people's actions, will it work as a stronger pressure to resist change in the opposite direction?

Express your opinion with examples of changes that were mandated and changes that were effected by the behavioral modification method.

Time Allowance

Even if there is no resistance to the change itself, it takes *time* to put the change into productive use. If the supervisor loses patience with the amount of time that a subordinate needs to learn how to handle a procedural change, the subordinate will begin to feel pushed. And that feeling of being pushed can create a change in customary working relationships and breed resistance where there was none before.

Managers and supervisors need to become much more aware of how human relationships affect the rate at which change can take place. Often, in the name of speed and efficiency, and without understanding the rhythms involved in creating the necessary atmosphere for change, management simply creates obstacles that later take much time and labor to overcome.

Group Dynamics of Change

The process of implementing change in individuals requires subtle guidance. A slight change in words can cause certain actions to be interpreted as "enforced change." The influence of groups in bringing about change often yield equally amazing consequences. The term *group dynamics of change* refers to those forces operating in groups. Since change is an integral part of group life, it is desirable to study the group as a medium of change. You might want to review those properties of group dynamics studied in Chapter 6, namely, that groups are omnipresent, have power, and produce good and bad consequences.

KEYS TO SUCCESSFUL CHANGE

To achieve change, there are several stages or key steps to follow. One is to make clear the *need* for change. This step involves communication and understanding. Other steps are also shown in Figure 14-8.

Need	1. Make clear the *need* for change.
Objectives	2. State the *objectives* clearly.
Participation	3. Encourage relevant group *participation* to clarify the needed changes.
Broad guidelines	4. Establish *broad guidelines* to achieve the objectives.
Details by group	5. Leave the *details* to the group that will be most affected by the change.
Benefits of change	6. State the *benefits* or rewards expected from the change.
Give rewards	7. Keep the *promise of rewards* to those who helped in the change.

FIGURE 14-8 **Keys to a successful change.** Source: Goodwin Watson and Edward M. Glaser, "What We Have Learned About Planning for Change," *Management Review*, November 1965, pp. 34–36.

The changes must be systemwide in any organization. To begin a program of planned change, Ralph Kilmann, author of *Managing Beyond the Quick Fix*, says:

> The first step in developing a completely integrated program for improving organizations entails identifying at least three sets of elements: (1) all the controllable variables—pinpointed via a systems perspective—that determine organizational success, (2) all the multiple approaches—techniques, instruments, and procedures—that can alter these controllable variables, and (3) all the ongoing activities that drive organizationwide change.[14]

Various techniques and procedures for achieving organizational change include team building, studying the organizational culture, and reward systems. Implementation of a program must be flexible.

ORGANIZATION DEVELOPMENT

Whole company must change

Organization development (OD) assumes that an *entire* organization, not just select individuals in it, must work for change. Organization development also recognizes the vulnerability of new employees who enter established work environments.

Characteristics of Organization Development	Goal Setting	1. It subscribes to *goal setting*. It recognizes some purpose or direction for both the company and the individual.
	Time and Money	2. It is a dynamic ongoing process. It takes time to develop and requires a considerable investment of *time* and *money*. There is a strong belief in training programs.
	Psychology	3. It relies heavily on *psychological* ideas. If the company has a motivation problem, for example, management will investigate how other organizations have solved similar problems.
	Mutual Trust	4. It encourages the development of *mutual trust* between management and the employees.
	Team Building	5. It believes in *team building* and recognizes that one work group affects all others. One group cannot be changed without it affecting others. A development program must be a companywide effort.
	Experience Based	6. It is *experience based*. If the design is to improve intragroup communications, the group activity will provide opportunities for the members to obtain insight into developing effective communication skills.

OD can be defined as a long-term, systematic, and organizationwide change effort designed to increase an organization's total effectiveness. OD advocates maintain that the entire complex organization must be dealt with as a whole. This includes all the personalities and issues that continuously make the organization what it is.

Company development

Organization development has two major objectives: (1) to develop people's specific skills that make it possible for them to do their jobs well and (2) to develop people in interpersonal and group membership skills. Capacities are developed in giving and receiving assistance, listening and communicating, and dealing with people and organizational problems. As implied, this method aims at developing the organization.

Organizational goals

OD is based on the belief that, although organizations begin purposively, as they grow in size and in age, organizational goals give way to individual goals. When this happens, the organization begins to decay. OD theory also recognizes that people have needs and desires that must be considered part of organizational goals. If all members of the organization participate in forming group goals, and in the process subscribe to them, then a great deal of energy is released for employees to move toward a common purpose.

OD theory also assumes that, to ensure a healthy organization, individuals within the organization must have the opportunity to grow and be healthy.

Teamwork and Trust

How do you test for and further team development in an organization? Before you can help an organization to be more successful, you must know the state of the organization now. The first step in organization development is diagnosis of the organization. Unfortunately, too many times, "quick-fix" consultants reach into their bags of tricks and prescribe "fixes" for an organization's ills before they know what, if anything, is wrong with the organization. Remember: "Prescription without diagnosis is malpractice in management as well as in medicine."

Teamwork is where a cohesive group works to accomplish specific tasks in a supportive environment. One way of finding out how well a team functions is to observe communication and results patterns. One instrument that the author has used is shown in Figure 14-9. Knowing who is communicating with whom in an organization allows sociometric analysis of group interactions and provides evidence for later prescriptions. The reporting relationships also offer surprises in some organizations.

Another instrument that provides similar information is shown in Figure 14-10. Useful results are achieved by administering this instrument to various group members who are or have the potential of becoming team members.

The key to organizationwide change is a team effort. One or two individuals cannot change the organization appreciably, even from the top down, if there is not overall commitment to change. In turn, the key to a team effort is developing mutual trust and not misplacing that trust.

What is trust? Trust means that an individual can rely upon another with respect to a given situation. Specific manifestations of trust are status, self-esteem, mutual relationships, job, and career—even life itself. Trust is earned and experienced, not something instantly installed externally. (See Figure 14-11.)

MURPHY'S LAWS

In concluding this chapter, perhaps it is worthwhile to mention Murphy's laws. They have been written in a humorous fashion with several parts, yet there is a thread of truth in each:

To help in the *diagnosis* of your organization, please answer the following (the questions are *nonsensitive,* but please respond individually and CONFIDENTIALLY; your responses will be handled collectively and CONFIDENTIALLY):

1. Who are three people *to* whom you most frequently *send* communications—either verbally or written?

   _____

   _____

   _____

2. Who are three people *from* whom you most frequently *receive* communications—again, either verbally or written?

   _____

   _____

   _____

3. To whom *do* you report? _____ | 3a. To whom *should* you report? _____

4. How does your "boss" demonstrate concern for your job performance?

   _____

5. How does your "boss" demonstrate concern for you as a person?

   _____

6. Which work associates report directly to you?

   _____ _____

   _____ _____

   _____ _____

   _____ _____

6a. Which work associates *should* report directly to you?

   _____ _____

   _____ _____

   _____ _____

   _____ _____

7. What, on the management team, needs improving?

8. What are the barriers to your being a full participant on the management team?

FIGURE 14-9 **Diagnostic for communications and reporting relationships.** Source: Douglas A. Benton, "Team Development" consulting for federal agencies, AT&T, and small businesses.

1. Nothing is as simple as it looks.
2. Everything takes longer than it should.
3. If anything can go wrong, it will.

Take as an example a plan to change the date of monthly paychecks from the first of the month to the end of the month. Instead of receiving your check on the first of the next month, you would receive it at the end of the present month. Certainly everyone would like to be paid one day early. Surely there would be no resistance to such an administrative change. The school board in one county found out differently after informing the school employees of its plan.

Things will go wrong

Immediately, the county school office was informed of the income tax problem. Instead of receiving 12 paychecks the first year, each employee would

Please *rank* (1 = highest rank) the following potential OBJECTIVES OF A TEAM DEVELOPMENT PROGRAM:

		Who has primary/secondary responsibility
(1 = highest rank)		for accomplishing these objectives

_____ • Create an open problem-solving climate throughout the organization _____ _____

_____ • Supplement the authority associated with rank or status with the authority, knowledge, and competence. _____ _____

_____ • Locate decision-making and problem-solving responsibilities as close to the information sources as possible _____ _____

_____ • Build trust among individuals and groups throughout the organization _____ _____

_____ • Make activity more relevant to work goals and maximize collaborative efforts _____ _____

_____ • Develop a reward system that recognizes both the achievement of the organization mission (service?) and organization development (growth of people) _____ _____

_____ • Increase the sense of "ownership" of organization objectives throughout the work force _____ _____

_____ • Help managers to manage according to relevant objectives rather than according to "past practices" _____ _____

_____ • Increase self-control and self-direction for people within the organization _____ _____

FIGURE 14-10 **Diagnostic for objectives of a team development program.** Source: Douglas A. Benton, "Team Development" consulting for federal agencies, AT&T, and small businesses.

It takes longer than planned

receive 13, thereby having to pay income tax on a larger income. The solution: the teachers would be paid on the first day of January and the last day of February. Every month after that they would be paid on the last day of the month, except for December at which time they would be paid on January 1. Yes, everything takes longer than it should. This plan took two-and-a-half years to implement, and a few things did go wrong.

Summary

Once a decision has been rendered there is the task of implementing it. The implementation process often requires changing people's attitudes to bring about lasting effects. We hear, "Study change, praise it, but don't do it; we may resist." You can expect resistance to vague or unclear changes. Resistance will be least

Do:	Don't:
• Assume trust initially (until proven otherwise)	• Take cheap shots
• Communicate openly with one another	• Knowingly hurt another
• Share information—not evaluation	• Talk out of both sides of your mouth
• Display confidence in your own and others' abilities	• Talk behind backs
• Earn trust	• Scapegoat
• Make and keep commitments	• Second guess
• Respect one another	• Doubt when listening
• Operate with honesty and integrity toward one another	• Play games with my career
	• Take organizational matters personally

FIGURE 14-11 How to develop mutual TRUST in a management team. Source: Douglas A. Benton, "Team Development" consulting for federal agencies, AT&T, and small businesses.

evident when workers have the most to say about procedural matters and most evident when they have the least to say. Fear of the unknown is potent, but by encouraging participation in change, people can help to overcome this resistance monster.

When change is about to occur, the more the pressures are in harmony, the more predictable the outcome will be. If a striving worker is offered a promotion and transfer to another city and his family and friends are for it, then it is likely he will accept the move and promotion. The stronger a person's occupational identity happens to be, the greater the feeling of security. The greater the sense of security, the more likely there is to be resistance.

The theory of homeostasis developed by Kurt Lewin is a balance between those who are attempting to bring about change and those who are opposing change. Lewin's studies showed that change occurs when an imbalance develops between the restraining and the driving forces. Such imbalance "unfreezes" the pattern, and the group struggles to achieve a new balance of equilibrium. Once found, the new pattern will be made up of different components. That is, the group refreezes at a new and different equilibrium level.

Change can also be encouraged by behavioral modification. One premise of this method is that changes should be made attractive. People like to be commended on how well they are doing in achieving the new goal, and such actions should be done both orally and in writing.

To manage change, some key points should be remembered. The need for a change must be stated clearly. Encouraging relevant groups to participate helps to clarify the need for changes. Broad guidelines to achieve the objectives need to be stated, but it is important to leave the details to the groups that will be most affected to handle the changes.

Change throughout the entire organization is organization development. Concentrating on the entire organization allows many changes to occur at once rather than on a piecemeal basis, or putting-out-fires approach. It also allows the homeostatic processes of thawing, changing, and refreezing to operate. Keys to organization development are teamwork and trust.

Case Study 28

Group Pressure—"Rate Busting"

Engineer Frank Gonzales came to set up a new piece of equipment in the plant. According to Mr. Krieger, the plant manager, the new machine would improve the production rate of the assembly crew.

Leon Robbins, the informal group leader, doesn't like the idea of the new fancy machine. "What they're really after is a way to get more out of us without paying us any more than they have to. When they are done, you and I will be without a job. Just wait and see, one day this company won't need skilled people anymore; all they will need is a few button pushers."

When Frank completed the installation of the new machine he asked for a volunteer to operate it. With the approval of the supervisor of the assembly department, John O'Neil began operating the machine under Frank's supervision. At the end of the day the machine and the operator far exceeded Frank's anticipated increase in production.

"What effect will these new machines really have on our jobs?" asked one worker.

"According to the plant manager, if the system works out well, we'll all be either running the machines or we'll have some other related task," replied O'Neil.

"Well, we know we don't have to worry about losing our jobs, that's one of the first things we were told," said another worker.

"I've been around a long time, friend—you haven't. Let's wait and see what happens," retorted Leon Robbins in a disgusted way.

During the second day of testing, Frank chose another person to operate the new machine. After giving the operator instructions on how to run the machine, Frank began to supervise the employee's performance. Throughout the day Frank felt that the man was performing at less than an appropriate speed. In fact, Frank got the feeling that the man was stalling. At the end of the day, the operator's rate was only marginally higher than the average production rate using the old machine. Playing the role of Frank you are convinced that the machine is superior to those already in the plant. You also feel that some people do not want to learn the operation of a new machine and are quietly sabotaging any possibility of a really successful run on the machine. What would you do?

1. Go to the employee's supervisor?
2. Go to management and complain about your suspicions?
3. Spend more time with the employees through informal chats?
4. Call for a general meeting with the employees to explain the merits of the machine?

5. Keep trying in the same manner, but be sure that you are picking those employees to work on the machine who are willing to ignore the group pressure?

Case Study 29

The Overqualified Employee's Dilemma

Leslie Fisher has been employed as an administrative assistant in a large food service industry for nearly two years. Recently the chain suffered a serious financial crisis, and the Marketing Division where she works experienced an 80 percent layoff. Leslie was not laid off but was transferred involuntarily to the Corporate Planning and Development Division.

The new position has less responsibility and status, but her pay was not reduced. She has become bored by the new job, because the tasks involved offer less variety. She is also frustrated by the lack of opportunity for advancement within the division, and the company has a current "no-growth" policy.

To advance and stay within the corporation, Leslie applied and was selected for a promotional transfer into the Personnel Department. However, her supervisor was not aware of her request.

Mr. Sullivan, the vice president of corporate planning and development, refused to allow her to transfer to Personnel. He claimed that he had a rush project in his department that Leslie was handling and would not be able to complete it within the next few weeks.

This week Leslie had her annual review and had hoped for a merit increase. Her immediate supervisor told her that, although her job performance has been up to standard, since she is overqualified and overpaid for her job, she will not receive an increase in pay.

1. What are Leslie's alternatives?
2. Should Leslie ask Mr. Sullivan why her transfer was denied?
3. How can a corporation best handle a situation of this type?
4. Do you feel that the corporation should have a policy regarding transfers? If so, how should it be worded?
5. What is the best solution for Leslie?

Terms and Concepts

behavior modification   a technique to bring about behavioral change by frequently praising positive behaviors and ignoring negative behavior.

group dynamics   the effect that individuals collectively

have on each other. The sense of belonging, prestige, and shared perceptions can dramatically affect one's individual behavior.

homeostasis   the process whereby a group may make an

effort to develop change within an organization or, conversely, resist such a change. The balance between the two groups forms an equilibrium that is known as homeostasis. This state of equilibrium allows both groups to exist and to compromise.

mandated change a change demanded by someone of authority. Some policies are mandated because laws, safety, or health seem to require it. Company economics can mandate a factory closure.

Murphy's law nothing is as simple as it looks; everything takes longer than it should; and if anything can go wrong, it will.

occupational identity the identity that one has by virtue of his or her job. The longer an occupation has been in society the greater the likelihood of tradition, security symbols, and resistance to change.

organization development a long-term, systematic, and organizationwide change effort designed to increase an organization's total effectiveness.

teamwork a cohesive group who works to accomplish specific tasks in a supportive environment.

trust reliance upon another with respect to a given situation.

Notes

1. Roger C. Palms, "Change," *Decision,* October 1989, p. 22.
2. Clay Carr, "Following Through on Change," *Training,* January 1989, pp. 39–44.
3. Ibid.
4. "Labor Letter: Japan Does It Better," *The Wall Street Journal,* May 28, 1985, p. 1.
5. Lloyd P. Steier, "When Technology Meets People," *Training & Development Journal,* August 1989, pp. 27–29.
6. Peter Drucker, "Information and the Future of the City," *The Wall Street Journal,* April 4, 1989, p. A10.
7. Donald Schon, *Technology and Change* (New York: Delta Books, 1967), pp. 46–47.
8. Thomas J. Peters and Robert H. Waterman, Jr., *In Search of Excellence: Lessons from America's Best-Run Companies* (New York: Harper & Row, 1982), Chap. 7.
9. Kurt Lewin, "Frontiers in Group Dynamics," in *Field Theory in Social Science,* ed. Dorwin Cartwright (New York: Harper, 1951), pp. 188–237.
10. Alvin Toffler, *The Third Wave* (New York: William A. Morrow, 1980), p. 235.
11. John Naisbitt, *Megatrends: Ten New Directions Transforming Our Lives* (New York: Warner Books, 1982), p. 19.
12. Ibid., p. 45.
13. Daniel Yankelovich, *New Rules: Searching for Self-fulfillment in a World Turned Upside Down* (New York: Random House, 1981), p. xv.
14. Ralph H. Kilmann, "A Completely Integrated Program for Creating and Maintaining Organizational Success," *Organizational Dynamics,* Summer 1989, pp. 5–6.

Recommended Reading

Carr, Clay. "Following Through on Change," *Training,* January 1989, pp. 39–44.

Kanter, Rosabeth Moss. *The Change Masters: Innovation for Productivity in the American Corporation.* New York: Simon & Schuster, 1983.

Kilmann, Ralph H. "A Completely Integrated Program for Creating and Maintaining Organizational Success," *Organizational Dynamics,* Summer 1989, pp. 5–19.

Kirkpatrick, Donald L. *How to Manage Change Effectively.* San Francisco: Jossey-Bass, 1985.

Kulmann, Torsten M. "Adapting to Technical Change in the Workplace." *Personnel,* August 1988, pp. 67–69.

Lynch, Dudley, and Paul L. Kordis. *Strategy of the Dolphin: Scoring a Win in a Chaotic World.* New York: William A. Morrow, 1988.

Martel, Leon. *Mastering Change: The Key to Business Success.* New York: Simon & Schuster, 1986.

Naisbitt, John. *Megatrends: Ten New Directions Transforming Our Lives.* New York: Warner Books, 1982.

Odiorne, George S. *The Change Resisters: How They Can Prevent Progress and What Management Can Do about Them.* Englewood Cliffs, N.J.: Prentice-Hall, 1981.

Peters, Thomas J., and Robert H. Waterman, Jr. *In Search of Excellence: Lessons from America's Best-Run Companies.* New York: Harper & Row, 1982.

Sauser, William I., Jr. "Injecting Contrast: A Key to Quality Decisions," *Advanced Management Journal,* Autumn 1988, pp. 20–23.

Schon, Donald. *Technology and Change.* New York: Delta Books, 1967.

Stanislao, Joseph, and Bettie C. Stanislao. "Dealing with Resistance to Change." *Business Horizons,* July–August 1983, pp. 74–78.

Toffler, Alvin. *The Third Wave.* New York: William A. Morrow, 1980.

Yankelovich, Daniel. *New Rules: Searching for Self-fulfillment in a World Turned Upside Down.* New York: Random House, 1981.

Job and Pay Discrimination

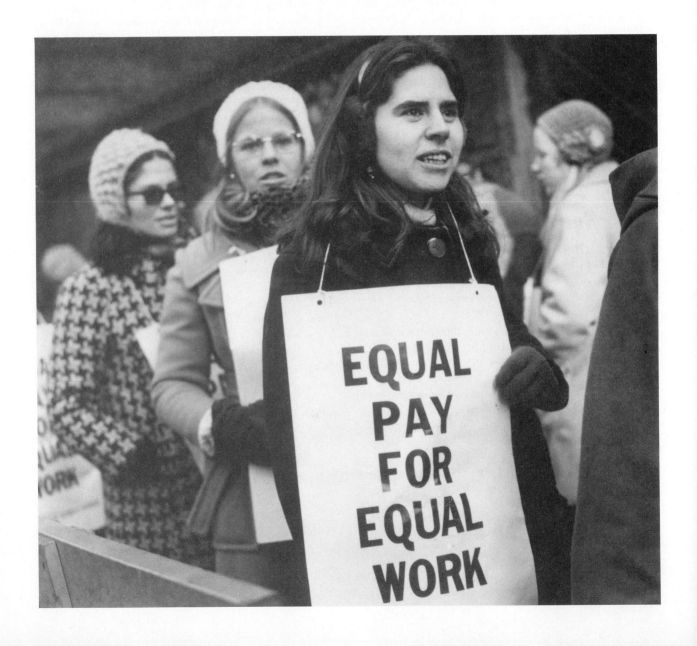

After studying this chapter, you should be able to:

1. Define and discuss the meaning of prejudice and discrimination.
2. Discuss the psychological and economic roots of prejudice.
3. Explain why women and minorities often have such poor self-images.
4. Discuss some of the ways in which it is possible to see and measure discrimination in the business world.
5. Describe and give examples of some of the ways in which discrimination can be overcome.
6. Discuss some of the ideas of "affirmative action" in relation to the following:
   a. Goals and objectives
   b. Hiring and promotion policies
   c. Recruitment
   d. Job restructuring
7. Appreciate why child care facilities make sense for both employers and employees.
8. Understand the protections for handicapped and other legally protected groups.

TO START YOU THINKING . . .

It might be well to discuss some of these questions with others before you read the chapter. Maybe some different feelings will develop as a result.

- What is meant by prejudice?
- What is meant by discrimination?
- Do we inherit or learn prejudice and how do we exhibit our discrimination in everyday life?
- What group is discriminated against most in your geographical area?
- Which social class exhibits the greatest discrimination?
- Does it seem to be a social class other than the one to which you belong?
- Is society giving more opportunities to minorities now as compared with three years ago?
- How do we discriminate against the physically and mentally handicapped?

BACKGROUND TO PREJUDICE AND DISCRIMINATION

Discrimination is by no means a dead or resolved issue. Progress has been made through better management practices and antidiscrimination laws, but there are still opportunities for better business and government practices with or without executive, legislative, or judicial intervention.

Discrimination is a continuing human relations problem for both management and workers. Most people are familiar with the overt, violent acts of political and racial discrimination that are reported by the media. Other kinds of discrimination, however, are often much less recognizable and, for this reason, difficult to overcome. Nevertheless, because it affects so many people in the job market, and because people need to work to live, even mild discrimination deserves serious attention.

Prejudgments

Prejudgment is normal

Making a prejudgment is normal, for we cannot handle every event freshly in its own right. If we did, what good would past experience be? Although prejudgments help to give order to our daily living, our mind has a habit of assimilating as much as it can into categories by which it prejudges a person or event. By overcategorizing, we tend to form irrational rather than rational categories, and this may lead us to prejudicial judgments and stereotyping.

We know that all women are not incompetent at math, that all Chinese are not inscrutable and industrious, and that all Afro-Americans are not suffering in exotic misery. People are more complicated, more varied, more interesting than that. They have more resiliency and survivability than we might think.

A person acts with prejudice because of his or her personality, which has been developed by socialization or learned behavior taught by family, school, and neighborhood environment. It is in one's environment that one's attitudes are shaped and can be reshaped.

What Is Prejudice?

Prejudice is an attitude, not an act

Prejudice has been defined as "being down on something you're not up on." Prejudice is an attitude, not an act; it is a habit of mind, an opinion based partially on observation and partially on ignorance, fear, and cultural patterns of group formation, none of which has a rational basis.

A prejudiced person tends to think of members of a group of people as being all the same, without considering individual differences. This kind of thinking gives rise to stereotypes. Stereotypes, like prejudices, are based partially on observation and partially on ignorance and tradition. For example, a person who assumes that most or all women are vain, illogical, and overly emotional is subscribing to a widely held stereotype of women.

Stereotyping on the basis of race or sex, even if unconscious, should not be part of the employment or promotion process. If it affects employment and promotion decisions, it is wrong and should be "unlearned" through education.[1]

Stereotypes are hard to overcome

Stereotypes are difficult to overcome because they have developed over long periods of time and because so many people share them, giving them an illusion of rationality. However, many people today are trying hard to rid themselves of stereotyped thinking about other people, and the effort shows in a general, growing consciousness that people are individuals who can and should be treated as such. For example, the film and television stereotype of the black person as servile, clowning, and stupid has vanished. We now have television programs that show independent, strong, capable blacks in leadership roles. Not just on television but in fact, the number and level of minority executives are increasing.[2]

What Is Discrimination?

Discrimination is the actual behavior that manifests a prejudice. What kinds of discrimination are most common in the United States? Sometimes it is not easy to tell, because at any given moment the public media may be emphasizing one kind or another.

Discrimination is an act; prejudice is a feeling

Perhaps to understand job discrimination we must look at the prejudice that lies behind it. We are all likely to have some feelings of prejudice against those who are different from us and even display our prejudice through actions in the form of discrimination. Therefore, by definition, prejudice is an attitude, and discrimination is an overt act demonstrating our prejudice.

Prejudice Works Both Ways

It is also important to point out that all people, not simply members of dominant cultural groups, are prejudiced. We all hold stereotypes about other groups. Furthermore, groups that are traditionally thought of as objects of prejudice and discrimination are usually also prejudiced themselves. Blacks, for example, hold stereotypical views about whites, and women hold stereotypical views about men. The prejudices that people hold are usually met with equal prejudices from the other side, like reflections in a mirror. This process is one of the reasons that prejudice tends to spread throughout society.

A person who holds a prejudice but who does not discriminate, is tolerant—capable of allowing other people to live freely. Our society values freedom of thought highly, which is why most efforts to deal with discrimination are directed toward persuading people to be tolerant—to avoid harming other people—not at legislating ways of thinking.

Prejudice and Self-Image

The minority may accept the attitudes of the "in groups"

Minority groups also develop prejudices, not only against the in groups and other out groups, but also against themselves. They tend to accept the image that others hold of them, to be ambivalent about their own self-worth, to fulfill the stereotypes, and to suffer from lack of confidence. An employer who wishes to change the situation must be prepared not only to avoid discrimination completely but to encourage employees to overcome it.

People's action may arise more from situation than from skin color

Employers and workers alike can become more sensitive to the problems of self-image that minority people and women face by "putting themselves in the other person's shoes." Role playing is a very useful technique for learning how discrimination affects people. A white supervisor (or, for that matter, a black) who is an object of discrimination, if only for a short training session, can experience real changes in attitude and action as a result of experiencing the change in role.

A white man traveled as a black man

One of the most interesting studies of such a role shift was made by a white sociologist, John Howard Griffin, who changed his skin color with a series of chemical and ultraviolet treatments. He passed himself off as a black man in the South and wrote a book about the experience called *Black Like Me*. His most vivid effect of the adventure was that he found the rejections accumulating in his self-image, until he found himself fearful, clumsy, and self-rejecting. His conclusion was: "You place the white man in the ghetto, deprive him of educational advantages, arrange it so he has to struggle hard to fulfill his instinct for self-respect, give him little physical privacy and less leisure, and he would after a time assume the same characteristics you attach to the Negro."[3]

The brief review of historical events and legislation affecting discrimination in Table 15–1 seems to show that our society is moving to overcome discrimination, but at a slow pace.

RELIGIOUS DISCRIMINATION

Our Founding Fathers set foot on American soil to establish freedom of religion; however, those of certain religions have had more difficulty in obtaining employment than have those belonging to the Protestant faith. Catholics, Jews, Mormons, Buddhists, all have been subject to ridicule in various parts of the United States and more violently during certain times in history. While the practice is still common, religious discrimination has not received as much attention of late as perhaps other more overt forms of discrimination.

TABLE 15-1 Historical Events and Legislation Affecting Job Discrimination

1863	Emancipation Proclamation frees slaves in rebel states.
1896	U.S. Supreme Court establishes "separate, but equal" doctrine.
1905–1910	Black Americans organize NAACP.
1938	Congress passes Fair Labor Standards Act, including Child Labor Laws, amended several times.
1954	Supreme Court rules that "separate education facilities are inherently unequal" and orders schools desegregated.
1963	Equal Pay Act passed.
1963–1965	Widespread civil rights demonstrations.
1964	Civil Rights Act of 1964 passed, establishing the Equal Employment Opportunity Commission (EEOC).
1967	Age Discrimination in Employment Act passed.
1968	Architectural Barriers Act (handicapped accessible) passed.
1970	Presidential Executive Order 11246 sets detailed guidelines for fair employment practices for all government contractors.
1972	Congress passes law strengthening power of EEOC.
1973	Vocational Rehabilitation Act (for the handicapped) passed.
1974	Vietnam-Era Veterans Readjustment Act passed.
1974	Congress passes Employee Retirement Income Security Act.
1978	Amendment to the 1967 Age Discrimination Act banning mandatory retirement at 65 years of age.
1978	Pregnancy Discrimination Act passed.
1984	Retirement Equity Act passed.
1985	Consolidated Omnibus Reconciliation Act (COBRA).
1986	Age Discrimination in Employment amendments removing upper limit of any age for retirement.
1987	Omnibus Budget Reconciliation Act affecting defined-benefits pension plans.
1990	Fair Labor Standards minimum wage amendments.

Religious fighting is more prevalent in other countries of the world than the United States. Riots and bombings in Ireland, India, and some Middle Eastern countries are just a few examples. Nevertheless, the United States does have religious discrimination problems. Each year, the Equal Employment Opportunity Commission (EEOC) receives up to 2,000 complaints about religious discrimination by employers, and 2,000 more complaints are lodged with state authorities.[4]

The concept of reasonable accommodation for religious preferences has been the source of some confusion between the courts and the EEOC. The EEOC assigns the primary responsibility to the employer to reasonably accommodate preferences. Courts have put the primary responsibility on the individual.[5] The challenge is to find a happy medium between the two extremes so that real reasonable accommodation of individual preferences and organization needs may take place.

RACIAL DISCRIMINATION

The United States was divided from the beginning by racial tensions. White settlers drove out the native Americans and set up a system of labor based on black slavery. These two types of racism are still with us today. The native Americans were decimated, so that statistically the problem is not as great as with Afro-Americans, who are the largest ethnic minority in the United States. However, the lot of today's native Americans is hardly better than that of many Afro-Americans.

The United States also expanded into areas held by Spanish settlers and extended discrimination to the second largest ethnic minority, the Hispanic Americans. Asians, who first came here in large numbers to serve as cheap labor in the West, also suffer from discrimination. Originally, many other ethnic groups who immigrated here, such as the Irish, the Germans, and the Italians, were the objects of ethnic prejudice as well.

Almost 12 percent of the population is black

The subject of racial discrimination is an emotional issue and perhaps a few facts may help to give us all a common ground for further discussions. Afro-Americans number more than 30 million, or almost 12 percent of the total U.S. population. (See Figure 15-1.) An additional 19,887,000 Americans, over 7 percent

Over 7 percent of the population is Hispanic

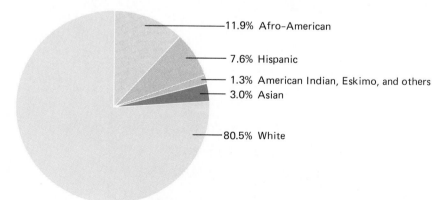

FIGURE 15-1 Distribution of races projected for 1990 in the United States according to the U.S. Bureau of the Census.

Source: Statistical Abstract of the United States, 109th Edition, 1989, pp. 14–15, 39. May include more than one ethnic origin.

of the total U.S. population, identify themselves as having an origin in a Spanish-speaking country.

Afro-Americans

Black pride is self-determination

The term *black pride* (see Figure 15-2) was used to bring self-respect to some and fear to others. One store owner in Watts said, "Black pride means self-determination. That a black can determine his own destiny and his own future. This in a way is a great slogan for blacks and instills a fear in some whites."

Myths make black bad

Certainly blacks cannot forget their color even if they wanted to. Individuals need not necessarily see something good or bad when they perceive an object with color, but they are likely to see color. Bill Cosby, in films and lectures, has pointed out how our myths and fairy tales are filled with "white knights" and "black witches of the North."

The riots of the 1960s came at a time of heightened aspirations for all blacks. Today, there is still anger and frustration in the ghetto, but also disillusionment. There is a lowering of expectations—the kind of despair that leads to more individual responses (such as crime) than to any sort of collective response (riots or protests).

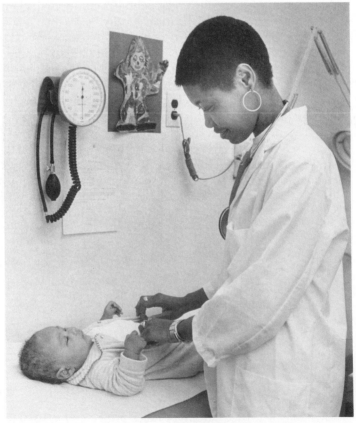

FIGURE 15-2 A new, stronger self-pride has helped the minority cause in the search for a better place in society and for job opportunities. Spencer Grant/Monkmeyer Press.

White attitudes about blacks have changed since the 1960s. Whites now see blacks in all sorts of settings they haven't seen them in before. Integration has faded as a primary goal of many. The "here and now" issue of jobs is more important. There is a growing realization that integration won't put food on the table.

Hispanic Americans

Over 8 million Mexican Americans in four border states

Of the over 17 million Hispanics officially residing in the United States, over 8 million are Mexican Americans. The four border states of California, Arizona, New Mexico, and Texas hold 90 percent of the Mexican Americans who live in the United States legally. Unless you live within this geographical area, you are not likely to know of the problems of discrimination that Mexican Americans may face, as 20 percent of them live below the government-drawn poverty line.[6]

Cesar Chavez and United Farm Workers

Agriculture was the strongest agent in bringing together Hispanics. The United Farm Workers Union formed by Cesar Chavez in 1965 became a focal emphasis for identification and enduring spirit. Mexican Americans may have ambivalent feelings about migratory workers in the farming community: allowing people to come from Mexico to work as aliens, either legally or illegally, does put more people on the employment rolls, but a large supply of workers can keep the wages down for all of them. In addition, the Mexican Americans who are U.S. citizens often want to bring their relatives into the United States and also want to keep them out.

Immigration reform and control legislation proposed in 1985 sought "to deter *illegal* immigration in order that we may continue our historically generous policy of *legal* immigration."[7] Father Ted Hesburgh, chairman of the Select Commission on Immigration and Refugee Policy, has often emphasized: "We must close the back door to illegal immigration in order that we may keep open the front door to legal immigration."[8]

The Indian Nation

A basic issue for many groups is how to integrate with the majority of society for the good of all but still maintain their unique individual cultures.

Many Indian leaders agree that unity of the native Americans or American Indians is in a large part the result of recent activism. Tribal officials indicate that there is a new determination among the nation's 1,500,000 Indians to "work within the system" through lawsuits to bring about legislation for their rights.

Three goals of native Americans

Their major goals include greater Indian control of the Bureau of Indian Affairs, establishment of an independent federal unit of lawyers to oversee Indian legal affairs, and more direct supervision of federal funds by local tribes.[9] The concept of Indian reservations is similar to government-sanctioned segregation. They remain political and socioeconomic hotbeds of crime and discontent.

Oriental View

Every major U.S. city has an Oriental section or a "Chinatown." However, the substantial Oriental population is more evenly distributed throughout the United States than are the native Americans and Hispanic Americans. They can be found in rural areas as well as in the big cities.

Orientals appear as a race to experience less discrimination than any other racial minority. Why? Certainly the "coolies" of San Francisco and the railroad builders of 1850 were treated much like slave labor. Can one reason be that as a group they are the most educated in America—even more educated than the Caucasians? The proportion of Japanese and Chinese men with college degrees is nearly 90 percent greater than it is for white men.

Social Problems of Race Mixing

The rise increase in Hispanic Americans has brought about rapid growth of bilingual and bicultural education in thousands of schools. A teacher in Los Angeles said that "English should be imposed only when the parents feel the child is ready for it, perhaps as late as the third grade. The child should learn in the language he *thinks* in. The child needs an approved emphasis on his own culture to feel good about himself." One minority member added, "I won't impose my culture on you, don't you impose your culture on me."

These conflicts could produce a backlash. Should an American taxpayer pay for bilingual education in schools, yet be denied a job because he or she is not bilingual? Further, should American taxpayers pay for welfare opportunities that are available to illegal immigrants?

Foreigners can get jobs U.S. citizens cannot

The heavy increase of Spanish-speaking Latins into southern Florida has been one factor in making southern blacks feel wronged even more intensely than blacks elsewhere in the nation. The Latin renaissance has left blacks in an unhappy place in their community. Often they cannot get jobs if they do not speak Spanish. They feel therefore estranged. Their questions present an almost unanswerable grievance. Why do Americans welcome strangers and mistreat their own, including the American Indian?

THE OLDER WORKER

Less than 8 percent of the aged suffer from senility

Agism exists and works like any other "ism." The troublesome truth is that the higher the age, the less dependable it is in revealing things about human beings. The aged may be more diverse and heterogeneous than any other group. One may be at different ages at the same time in terms of mental capacity, physical health, endurance, creativity, and emotions. Widespread failure to grasp such realities breeds agism. Such overdone myths as senility, memory loss, dependence, and rigidity are still associated with aging.

Almost 13 percent or 30 million of the population is over 65

Today over 30 million Americans, or 12.3 percent of the total population, are over age 65 and the size of that age group is rising sharply.[10] Certainly the number of older workers is increasing because of better health. Still the age of 40 arbitrarily seems to classify employees as older workers. And, whereas 35 is over the hill for most sports figures, age 60 can still be considered young for tool and die makers, and some executives. The age of retirement minus 10 or 15 years usually marks the beginning of the "older worker cycle." The attitude of the individual, his or her skill, and company policies are all factors that tend to fix the age range for the older worker.

The "older worker" is age of retirement minus 10 to 15 years

How Old Is Old?

Have you ever thought how old an "older worker" really is? How old *you* are might determine how old you think an older employee might be.

"Middle age" is relative

It is important to keep in mind that age affects each person differently. Its effect depends on many factors, such as heredity, physical condition, working conditions, climate, use of alcohol or drugs, and emotional and psychological strain. However, supervisors should look for signs of change due to age in any employee over 50 years of age. Working-class men describe themselves as middle-aged at 40 and old by 60. Business executives and professionals, in contrast, do not see themselves as reaching middle age until 50, and old age means 70 to them.

Psychologically, this period can be just as difficult for the older employee as the early years of employment are for the younger person. During this period he faces his last promotion. He may be motivated to work harder, up to the point at which he knows he cannot reach that last promotion. Thereafter motivation may operate to maintain the worker's status quo rather than to propel him toward self-realization. Some social behaviorists say this point is reached at retirement age minus three years.

When to Retire

Trend is toward early retirement

It is widely believed that there is a trend toward a longer working life for Americans, but no such trend has materialized. Indeed, all the data indicate that the long-term trend is toward retirement at earlier age.[11] A possible reversal in the early-retirement trend is still far down the road. The personnel officers of large companies haven't expected the law to disrupt company benefits programs or have much effect on their operations. In most companies, the typical retirement age is 62, despite the changes in social security and other laws.

Typical retirement is at age 62

One wonders how many retirees find new careers or part-time positions. Some say that many of the "aged" delay retirement or resume new jobs to beat inflation and the blues. Some plans have two retirees work half time to fill one position. The idea of hiring retired specialists or executives for one-year contracts affords companies a certain flexibility.

Supervising the Older Worker

In supervising an older worker, you are going to have to consider the physical and psychological differences between the young and old. You will have to consider how these factors affect productivity and how technological change may affect the older worker.

Quality often is more important than quantity to older workers

Errors are usually less acceptable to older workers than to younger ones. Efficiency and accuracy have become vital to them as evidence of their skill. The value of their contributions, too, is based more often on quality than on quantity.

Older workers are usually part of some type of departmental team. Each worker in the team should be capable of a certain amount of work set by the supervisor, and no member of the team should fall behind the work standard. The person who falls below this level of performance will become a marginal laborer. It is up to the supervisor to terminate the marginal laborer or to place him or her in a different position. If this is not done, either because of a labor shortage or because the supervisor is not willing to terminate a long-service employee from the position, problems may ensue.

Age Discrimination in Employment Act

The Age Discrimination in Employment Act (ADEA) protects employees aged 40 to 70 against employment discrimination because of their age. Historically, this legislation has been applied primarily to retirement, promotion, and layoff decisions but it applies to all human resource decisions and its use is increasing.

A federal appeals court ruling in the case of *Runyan* v. *NCR* held that employees could not waive their right to an age discrimination claim by signing a release form unless that form is approved first by a court or government anti-discrimination agency.[12] Runyan's counsel said that this prevents employers from taking advantage of employees.[13]

The main emphasis in avoiding ADEA and other discrimination complaints is to "make all personnel decisions on the basis of carefully collected data and systematically documented analysis of true worker competence."[14] Additional guidelines include:

- Formal and informal organizational communications prior to personnel action
- Current reading in journals and personnel periodicals covering ADEA
- Providing an employee with substantial early retirement benefits or other economic incentives is no guarantee that the employee who has resigned/ retired/been laid off will not file an ADEA complaint
- Ensuring that employers view older workers as a valuable resource rather than a probable liability[15]

How the Company Can Help the Older Worker

Job engineering and job reassignment

Job engineering and job reassignments are two things that companies can accomplish to help the older worker. Job engineering is redesigning the work-station so that work can be done in a way that is less taxing for the employee. It may be planning the work so that it can be done sitting down, providing different power equipment, reducing body movement, or changing the flow of work. Job reassignment is moving the person into a different position, in which the task does not demand so much in terms of dexterity or speed but is, it is hoped, just as rewarding. Older employees can become good trainers and setup workers and can rework rejects from the production line.

For assistance in programs for the aged contact the National Council on Aging, 1828 L Street, NW, Suite 306, Washington, D.C. 20036 and ask for a list of the National Association of Older Workers Employment Services. Another source is the Gray Panthers, Headquarters, 3635 Chestnut Street, Philadelphia, Pa. 19104. Don't forget that we elected Ronald Reagan president just before he turned 70. If a man can become president at 70, should a person be denied a position when he is 50 or 60?

Perhaps one of the best ways in which to end this segment is to relate a story of one man's zest for life and a company's confidence in the man: conductor Leopold Stokowski, at the age of 94, signed a six-year recording contract with Columbia Records.

TEST YOURSELF

Do you have the secret of staying young? Take the quiz, and perhaps the attitudes expressed will show you the way.

Test Your Psychological Youth!

1. Do young people often ask your opinion? _____

2. Do you exercise at least five times a week? _____

3. Do you have a clear idea of what you want from life five years from now? _____

4. Do you dress fashionably? _____

5. Do you read new books regularly? _____

6. Have you taken up a new hobby in the past year? _____

7. Have you made a new friend in the past year? _____

8. Does time seem to go fast for you? _____

9. Do you enjoy people who are younger than you are? _____

10. Do you enjoy traveling alone? _____

11. Are your friends a diverse group? _____

12. Would you consider a higher-paying job that was less secure than your present one? _____

13. Are you flexible about your daily schedule? _____

14. Do you have romance in your life? _____

15. Have you bought something in the past six weeks that you knew you could not afford? _____

16. Can you laugh when you make an unimportant mistake? _____

17. Do you like change? _____

18. Are you so deeply involved in a job or a cause that you wake up in the morning eager to get at it? _____

19. Do you pamper your five senses every day: the taste of delicious food and drink? the smell of flowers or perfume? the sight of a sunset? the sound of music? the touch of a human hand? _____

20. Can you recall two new ideas or bits of philosophy you have learned or thought of in the last week? _____

The more "yes" answers you gave, the more youthful you are psychologically. Fewer than ten "yes" responses might indicate that you need to take a closer look at your attitudes, your society, and your feelings about your work.

THE EMPLOYMENT OF WOMEN

Possibly the new era for women started January 5, 1976, when *Time* magazine selected "Women of the Year" instead of a man as having the most influence on history and everyday living for the year. The cover of the magazine pictured such people as Carla Hills, then head of the Department of Housing and Urban Development; Barbara Jordan, the black congresswoman from Texas; Billie Jean King of tennis fame; and Betty Ford, then first lady.

"It isn't how much time you spend with your children, but how well you spend it," says Mrs. Letting Cotting Pogrebin, author of *How to Make It in a Man's World*. She is convinced that, if you prefer working at a challenging job to doing housework, then by all means keep the job and you will be happier in the long run. (See Figure 15-3.)

Consider Sandra O'Connor, the first woman named to the Supreme Court, and the many women company presidents today. Many jobs are opening for women that were once taboo, such as truck driving and telephone line work. (See

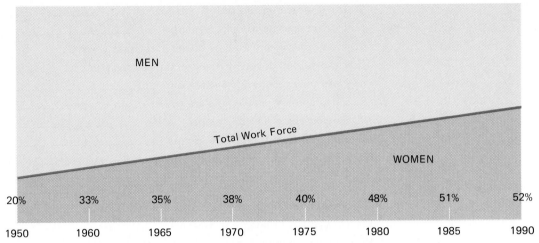

20%	33%	35%	38%	40%	48%	51%	52%
1950	1960	1965	1970	1975	1980	1985	1990

FIGURE 15-3 Over 50 percent of the *available* work force is composed of women.

Figure 15-4.) The greatest discrimination against women is most evident in industries such as steel, banking, finance, mining, and railroads. On the other hand, women have found little discrimination in advertising, high-fashion retailing, medicine, marine biology, dentistry, and physics.

The number of women professionals has grown significantly. Today, of course, a good job is as much a status symbol for a middle-class wife as it is for her husband, and even many affluent women now seek work for pay.

A working woman gains status

Over 40 percent of working women are single, widowed, or divorced

Over 40 percent of working women are single, widowed, or divorced and are responsible for their own support and often for others. Add to this figure another 10 to 25 percent of employed women who work because their husband's income is so low that the family cannot survive on one income. It is clear that few women go to work just for something to do or to buy luxuries. Perhaps because their work is important to them economically, they are reliable; studies have shown that they do not have higher tardiness or absentee rates than men.

Women's absenteeism and tardiness are no higher than men's

Women are holding onto jobs longer than formerly. Job turnover is only slightly higher for women than men at Cincinnati Bell and lower for women at Sun Company.[16]

Social Changes have Altered Women's Roles

New public attitudes toward the "pill" and other forms of birth control, divorce, housekeeping, child rearing, and abortion have all influenced women's self-concepts and have quickened their journey into the business world. Perhaps developments in the last 20 years have influenced women's roles in society more than the last hundred. Today, child support is a shared responsibility between husband and wife. In some states, a spouse seeking a divorce must charge specific cruelties such as abandonment, adultery, or mental abuse. But divorce laws have changed drastically. California, for example, passed a no-fault divorce bill whereby the court will grant divorce or a dissolution of marriage based on "irreconcilable differences"; there needn't be an accuser and an accused. Women are now more subject to paying alimony in divorce cases than ever before.

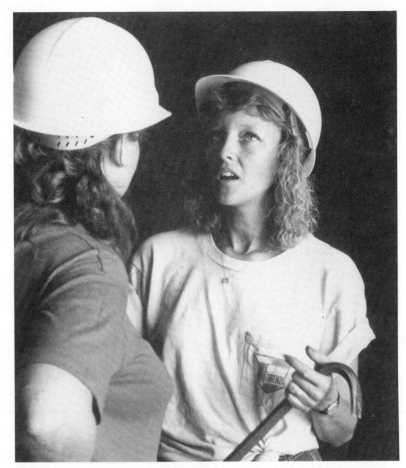

FIGURE 15-4 As yet no woman is playing halfback for the Los Angeles Rams, but many jobs are open for women that were once taboo, such as truck driving, telephone line work, and auto **repair.** Donna Jernigan/Monkmeyer Press.

Aims of Women's Action Groups

NOW leads the way for women

Some of the far-reaching attitudes of women that will influence business have been taken up by the women's action groups such as NOW (the National Organization for Women), the National Women's Political Caucus, and the Women's Equity Action League.

Equal Pay for Equal Work. The strongest demand is naturally equal pay for equal work, which is followed closely by equal opportunity for promotions. The reluctance to pass comparable worth legislation and adverse court decisions continue to hold back progress for equal pay made in recent years. Women's pay remains at about 60 percent of men's pay for comparable jobs, despite some slow movement to rectify the inequities.

Child Care Centers. There are over 10 million working mothers whose children are under 6 years of age. Further, over 8 million mothers in the labor force are divorced, separated, or widowed.[17] Over 1 million businesses and other establishments provide some type of child care benefits and/or varied work schedule policies.[18] Companies are getting involved because "many realize that childcare costs, ranging from $1,500 to $10,000 a year, are a major expense for working parents." and because existing tax laws have made child care a nontaxable employee benefit and a tax deduction for employers.[19]

Birth Control and Planned Parenthood   The widespread use of the "pill" and other birth control devices are only part of the issue of planned parenthood. Several companies are granting a day's leave for their male employees to have vasectomies.

Some women and men are taking up the cause of "maternity lib" and "paternity leave." They want to choose, without interference from the company, when they quit work to have a baby and when they will return. More and more career women are deciding to have children. More and more men are taking paternity leave.

Abortions.   Unwanted and unplanned childbirths have led to the acceptance of abortion by some women's groups. It should be noted that the abortion and birth control issues have caused many not to join the women's rights movement.

Education.   Many women are encouraged to further their education beyond high school, not in the traditional areas of secretarial skills, but in fields pursued by males, such as accounting, law, and medicine. In high-risk or inner-city neighborhood areas, special courses are offered to mothers during the day, so they are not faced with walking to school at night. Short-term programs and televised courses are all attempts at meeting the demand of women for more education.

Politics.   "It is time for women to make policies and not coffee." Rather than acting as hostesses for political candidates, women are moving to the forefront by running for political office. Shirley Chisholm was the first serious female candidate for the presidency in 1972, and Geraldine Ferraro was the first major party candidate to run for vice president of the United States. Today there are several women senators, representatives, and judges, as well as women generals in the armed services.

Problems for the Businesswoman

Several subtle factors face the working woman in her daily routine:

1. Women sometimes experience discomfort when buying lunch or a drink for a male client, or must deal with the male client's discomfort.
2. Women may be reluctant to ask their husbands to move when a promotion comes along.
3. Women find it difficult to travel and eat alone on business trips and are often deprived of female executive washrooms.
4. Women routinely have no credit rating following a divorce. Even if the husband drank and gambled while she maintained the credit, he gets the good rating and she gets none.

One of the problems for businesswomen is stereotyping. As one woman plant superintendent said: "If I do well, people will say I'm different. If I fail, they'll say that that's how women are. . . . Male executives have trouble saying the word 'woman,' preferring to use 'girls' or 'gals' for women at every level."[20]

Dual Careers

For the dual-career couple, there is never enough time. Time is a precious resource. It requires an understanding of how the couple prefers to use it. And, as strange as it seems for the two people living together, it is often necessary to schedule pleasurable time together. Too often togetherness of a dual-career couple is dictated solely by their having to face and solve mutual problems.

One busy couple schedules one lunch a week together to face difficult issues. This may not be recommended for the digestion, but it eases tension on the weekends.

Traditional Versus Neotraditional Roles. In the traditional dual-career marriage, the wife handles her career and virtually takes full care of the home as well. In the neotraditional relationship, both partners agree explicitly that the wife's career is important, possibly equally as important as the husband's. The husband is supportive and proud of his wife's accomplishments. Often the husband takes on some chores and feels quite good about it, even noble, as he does the weekly shopping or prepares the Monday night dinner.

Dual Overload. Dual careers can lead to anxiety and the feeling of being overloaded with responsibilities. A few suggestions on how to avoid overload for dual-career people follow:

1. Plan leisure time so that holidays and breaks in the routine come on a regular basis.

2. Delegate as many routine household tasks as possible to others. Rearrange other domestic duties more equitably.

3. Both work somewhat less. An ideal work schedule generally involves fewer hours of work than does an actual schedule.[21]

Express Your Opinion

In 1980 a corporate scandal made the headlines of newspapers and the covers of business magazines. Mary Cunningham, an extremely attractive Harvard MBA, and only 29 years old, was forced to resign from Bendix Corporation as a corporate officer.

The chairman of Bendix, William M. Agee, had elevated her in just 15 months after graduating from Harvard Business School to his top assistant in charge of planning. At a meeting of Bendix employees, Agee, age 43, remarked that Cunningham's rapid advancement in the firm had nothing to do with the "personal relationship we have." Cunningham had insisted that she and Agee were never anything more than good friends. That caused a furor, and two weeks later Bendix's directors accepted Cunningham's resignation.

As a woman, what feelings would you have if you were in her place? What comments would you release to the press before the resignation? As William Agee, and after the board of directors and the public had expressed their concern about your "cozy relationship," what would you reaction be? What comments would you release to the press?

Who is more at fault, Mary Cunningham, William Agee, the board of directors, or the public?

P.S.: Mary Cunningham has since taken a position as a strategic planning vice president at Seagram Distillers in charge of wineries (Paul Masson and Christian Brothers) and earns a salary in the "six figures." She and Agee were married after they left Bendix.

EMPLOYMENT OF THE HANDICAPPED ────────

Hiring the handicapped does not increase insurance premiums

While thousands of firms are willing to hire the handicapped, thousands are not. In the latter groups, reluctance to hire is based largely on the fear of extra expense. Here again there are fallacies about hiring people. One insurance company stated, "We believe, and our actuarial studies reinforce this belief, that physically handicapped persons who are full-time active employees not only do not increase Group Life, Disability or Medical Care insurance cost, but actually exert a slight but not measurable reduction in cost. We believe the reason for this is physically handicapped employees are aware of their condition, are somewhat more careful in their work and play habits . . . ".

Mainstream aids the handicapped

A second item of expense is remodeling. Mainstream, Inc., a nonprofit organization dedicated to getting handicapped persons into jobs, is finding that the costs of making a building free of architectural barriers are not that high. When Kaiser Aluminum & Chemical Corporation decided to revamp its 27-story headquarters building in Oakland, California, to help disabled workers, it was concerned that the cost would be in the hundreds of thousands of dollars. Mainstream, Inc., sent in architects who showed that the work could be done for less than $8,000. In the elevator, a blind person, for example, can be assisted by braille numbers installed on every selection button (at a cost of $10 to $50 per elevator) and a two-tone bell system that indicates whether the elevator is going up or down.

Rehabilitation Act of 1973

It is estimated that between 25 million and 40 million Americans have physical or mental disabilities that qualify them as handicapped. Since the passage of the Rehabilitation Act of 1973, any company that does more than $2,500 of business annually with Uncle Sam is required to take affirmative action to hire the handicapped. The law also applies to institutions, including schools and hospitals, that accept federal funds.

The wage gap between handicapped and other workers is too wide according to a study by William Johnson of Syracuse University and James Lambrinos of Union College: *ceteris paribus,* or "other things being equal," handicapped men earn 15% less than non-handicapped men in the same jobs; and handicapped women earn 30% less than non-handicapped women.[22]

AIDS ────────

In recent years, there has been much debate concerning the protected status under handicapped discrimination laws of such conditions as alcohol and drug addiction and acquired immunity deficiency syndrome (AIDS). The verdict is still out on whether AIDS will be considered a handicap or not.

Employees with AIDS have traditional tort claims of invasion of privacy, defamation, intentional (or negligent) infliction of emotional harm, and wrongful discharge. Federal laws may also prohibit discrimination against people with the AIDS virus. To date, they have been considered handicapped.[23]

PSYCHOLOGICAL ROOTS OF PREJUDICE ────────

C. G. Jung, one of the three founders of modern psychology, along with Freud and Adler, has suggested that prejudice is a projection onto other people of feelings we repress in ourselves. For example, if a person is angry and doesn't want to feel angry, he may repress it in himself and project it onto other people. Jung also suggested that projection most often occurred when the person involved was dealing with the unconscious part of himself or herself.[24]

Meerloo, another noted investigator in the field of prejudice, suggests that "Every war is a dramatization of man's [and woman's] inner war, the externalization of its own conflicts. Man feels temporarily relieved of tensions when there is outside trouble in the world. He can postpone finding a solution to his own conflicts as long as the outside world offers a more stirring emotional drama in which he can play a role."[25] Politicians know that one way in which to unite a constituency is to present the people with a common enemy. By providing oneself with an enemy to be feared, one can feel whole and not divided against one's self. In business, as in other aspects of life, we frequently meet individuals who blame their shortcomings on other people.

ECONOMIC ROOTS OF PREJUDICE

Prejudice and discrimination also have economic roots. Such fears are rational; obviously, if there are not enough jobs to go around, people will be competing for paying jobs, and people will compete for good wages. If one group of workers can be singled out, on the basis of some difference such as color, sex, ethnic background, or language, and if prejudice can be built up against such a group, then other workers will have a slightly better chance of getting the available jobs.

Competition for jobs feeds prejudice

There is also a macroeconomic gain for employers in aiding and abetting discrimination in the work force. Competition for jobs among workers can help employers to push down wages and working conditions. Employers often threaten striking workers with the prospect of being displaced. And there are always members of minority groups, having previously had little or no chance at jobs, and needing to survive like everyone else, who are willing to take jobs that pay poorly or who will even scab to make a living. The situation is then ripe for social unrest.

International trade

Finally, as the United States becomes more involved in the international market, business managers are increasingly becoming aware that discrimination can make a diastrous impression on potential buyers and sellers abroad. When we practice discrimination and preach democracy, our credibility is lost.

FIGHTING DISCRIMINATION

Discrimination can be fought on the individual level, by reexamining prejudice and discrimination in the light of modern psychological theory. Self-knowledge is one of the most powerful weapons against prejudice. This sounds like such benign advice; yet any ideas listed here are only guidelines and constitute no magical solution.

Education

Discrimination can also be fought through education. Much of the inertia that allows discrimination to exist is based on ignorance supported by tradition. Education is helping to break down old beliefs in the superiority of men over women, whites over nonwhites, one religion over another, and so on. Much of this battle against old patterns is taking place in the schools, but it is also affecting the public in the form of the public media, higher-level training and research, and on-the-job training.

Unfortunately, there is some sliding backward as the rate of college-bound blacks and Hispanics declines. One source says that over 50 percent of black graduating seniors enrolled in college in 1976, while that number shrunk to 36 percent in 1988.[26] The percentage of white college-bound students fluctuated between 50 percent and 55 percent over the same time period. According to an annual status report on minorities in higher education, blacks, Hispanics, and Native Americans continue to be underrepresented in four-year colleges and universities, and minority enrollments are either leveling off or declining.[27]

Programs of Awareness

If we distrust that which we know little of, then it is time to learn more of the cultural background of the disadvantaged. Increases in multicultural awareness are apparent in colleges, through, for example, ethnic study programs. Likewise, companies are attempting to educate employees through small study groups and sensitivity programs. Training programs for the hard-core unemployed as well as special supervisory training courses for minority groups are focusing on the need for a new awareness.

More Intergroup Contact

As more intergroup contact is achieved, the realities of how people think and act will tend to overcome the myths and pseudoscientific lingo that has formed people's prejudices. The movement of minority groups into the suburban areas has influenced white attitudes. Likewise, the flood of women into management positions has altered age-old myths of working females.

Legal and Legislative Action

The battle against discrimination is also being waged in the courts. Laws, of course, like education, do not substantially alter a society's general behavior—both systems reflect the trend of the majority and serve only to guide or coerce the minority into the general trend. It is important for business managers to understand the laws, to avoid prosecution.

Civil Rights Act of 1964 prohibits discrimination

EEOC enforces antidiscrimination laws

The most important antidiscrimination bill of the many that have been passed in the last two decades is the Civil Rights Act of 1964, which made discrimination illegal if it was based on national origin, ethnic group, sex, creed, age, or race. Many discrimination cases have been brought to the courts by the Equal Employment Opportunity Commission, the federal agency established to enforce such laws. These cases define the areas in which the federal law applies and serve to rectify situations in which discrimination is being practiced. Since the law is being clarified and modified continuously by the court decisions, employers need to be alert to changes in the laws at all levels of government.

A general overview of the kinds of judicial decisions that have been handed down may be helpful.

Griggs v. *Duke Power* relates to testing

One area clarified by the courts has been the testing of job applicants. The case of *Griggs* v. *Duke Power Company*, at Draper, N.C. (1971), resulted in a decision that "(1) If any employment test or practice has a disparate *effect* on persons on the basis of race, sex, religion, or national origin, for example a test with a higher percentage of black failures than white failures, *and* (2) that test has not been proven to be job-related and an accurate predictor of job performance, *then* that test constitutes an unlawful discrimination under Title VII of the Civil Rights Act of 1964.''

Bakke v. *University of California* did not destroy affirmative action programs

In *Bakke* v. *University of California*, the U.S. Supreme Court agreed with Bakke and held that special college admissions procedures were unconstitutional. However, the decision by the Supreme Court did not destroy the affirmative action program or the Equal Employment Opportunity Commission. Later decisions in 1979 upheld the affirmative action programs in employment situations.

Reverse discrimination argument

A classic case that cites reverse discrimination is *Firefighters Local Union No. 1784* v. *Stotts* (1984). The U.S. Supreme Court held that the seniority rights of white firefighters could not be disregarded in protecting them from layoff. The decision reversed the lower court's findings in a class action suit filed under Title VII that charged the Memphis, Tennessee, fire department with engaging in a pattern or practice of racial discrimination in hiring and promotion practices.

The Supreme Court cut back on affirmative action programs in 1989 when, in *City of Richmond* v. *J. A. Croson*, it held that a plan to set aside 30 percent of construction contracts for minority business enterprises was constitutionally suspect. They said there is no such thing as benign racial classification—even if it used as a tool to remedy past discrimination.[28]

Job Restructuring

One of the ways in which business has made room for minority members and women has been through the restructuring of jobs. Employees can be involved in this process in a way that can help to dispose them favorably toward the program. For example, if a secretary can take over excess work from an overloaded supervisor, and is given a promotion and raise in pay, he or she can restructure the job to give simpler jobs to a trainee. The promotion and pay raise serve to ease the fear of displacement, and the participation in the restructuring can involve the older worker in the success or failure of the program. Jobs can also be restructured to eliminate requirements such as the writing of English; for example, if a trucker's job normally involves the writing of reports, the establishment of a records clerk job to help fill out reports can make it possible to hire workers who do not write well but are excellent truckers.

What Is Affirmative Action?

Affirmative action is not neutrality but positive action

Affirmative action requires more than employment neutrality. An employer is required to make additional efforts to recruit, employ, and promote qualified members of groups formerly excluded. It recognizes the necessity for positive action to overcome the effects of systematic exclusion and discrimination, whereas neutrality in employment practices would tend to perpetuate the status quo.

Many companies have affirmative action plans that contain specific procedures to ensure equal opportunity for employees in recruitment, selection, and hiring; training and promotion; termination and layoff; salary, benefits, leave; job classification; and nepotism.

There has been agitation to get rid of affirmative action goals and timetables, or at least to make them voluntary. The chairman of the Equal Employment Opportunity Commission in the Reagan administration, himself a black, said ''I don't believe blacks should be treated differently because of historical discrimination. . . . We have to go forward from the present.''[29] But the courts, not a presidential administration, will ultimately decide the fate of affirmative action. And they are not likely to ban all goals and timetables.

Many businesses prefer having at least flexible goals. Hewlett-Packard used goals and timetables to raise employment of minorities and women from 7 percent and 39 percent in 1966, respectively, to 18 percent and 42 percent in 1985.[30] General Electric, AT&T, IBM, and others have successfully used flexible goals and timetables in their affirmative action programs.

Work Force Diversity

There is much positive to be said for cultural, ethnic, and gender differences. Each group has special abilities, skills, and talents. It makes sense to capitalize on each group's strengths.

Lennie Copeland, authority on valuing diversity, says work force diversity training is the step after equal employment opportunity (EEO) and affirmative action:

> EEO and affirmative action largely were the result of civil rights and, consequently, the moral and social impetus and legal basis for treating people fairly. *Valuing diversity* is about allowing individuals to make their maximum contribution and to succeed regardless of gender, color, race and so on. . . .
>
> If somebody was different from the white male standard, then it meant they weren't as good as white males. There was potential for real damage in saying that blacks are different from whites.
>
> Valuing diversity work is new in that it begins to talk about those things that have been taboo: the differences. It begins to address the fact that on top of stereotypes and prejudice, there are real cultural differences that cause miscommunication and conflicts, which then further compound the stereotype and the prejudice.[31]

The differences among people make our lives rich; it is important to remember that, as human beings, we have much in common but also significant diversity to contribute to our organizations and workplaces.

Termination at Will

An increasing concern in recent years has been the practice of termination at will. The termination-at-will doctrine holds that an employer can dismiss an employee at will for good cause, or for no particular cause, or even for morally wrong reasons.

The termination of poor performers is a particularly difficult problem in today's economic circumstances. Attention to employee rights discourages abuses and enhances employee's feelings of security, but it also can have a demoralizing effect on results-oriented managers.

Thus, it is important to get and keep our facts and records straight about who are good performers and who are not. Then when it becomes necessary to terminate employees, there are defensible reasons for doing so. Failure to follow a structured approach in dealing with problem employees can leave employers open to potential lawsuits and not allow them to salvage potentially good workers.

"Employment at will" (the reciprocal of termination at will) is grounded in the free enterprise system that leaves both the employer and employee free to terminate an employment relationship at will. Restrictions on that understanding have included laws that forbid firing based on discrimination or firing employees for organizing a union.[32]

Court decisions and other government agencies are beginning to set precedent for termination-at-will decisions. In the case of *Weiner* v. *McGraw-Hill, Inc.* (1981), the New York Supreme Court held that "Weiner's employment was 'at-will' and that he could be terminated at any time for any or no reason."[33]

Loyalty is a two-way street between employer and employee. Certainly there have been many examples in recent years of society granting more rights to individuals. It remains important for employers to respect the rights and human dignity of individuals with or without the law. As one author, the manager of personnel development for a large defense contractor, has stated:

> Management has an obligation to manage the enterprise efficiently and effectively and to provide fair procedures to employees. Rather than maintaining a reactive stance to new statutes and pressures, companies should be creative and active in dealing with the new sense of entitlement and its implications for changes in the employer-employee relationship.[34]

Summary

Prejudice is a feeling and discrimination is an action. In the last two decades, a social movement to combat discrimination has gathered force, especially in the area of employment.

The prejudiced individual may be trying to project internal tensions and self-doubts onto another person or a group of people. He or she may also gain a sense of group solidarity or individual identity by following cultural patterns of prejudice against other groups or individuals. But the personal costs of prejudice are also high: guilt, tension, and the fear of retaliation.

According to the projected 1990 census, approximately 12 percent of the population is black, 7.6 percent is Hispanic, and 3 percent is Asian. Discrimination is clear when we find that those percentages are not well represented in managerial and other professional areas.

Discrimination against the aged is common but often misunderstood. The aged may be more diverse, as one person may be at different ages at the same time in terms of mental capacity, physical health, and endurance. There are overdone myths as to the dependence, rigidity, and senility of the aged; for example, less than 8 percent of the "old people" suffer from senility.

About 52 percent of the total available work force is composed of women. Over 40 percent of working women are single, widowed, or divorced and are responsible for their own support and often for that of others. It is clear that few women go to work just for something to do or to buy luxuries. Studies have shown that women's tardiness or absentee rates are in line with men's and that women are reliable workers.

It has also been determined that physically handicapped persons who are full-time active employees do not raise the costs of group life, disability, and medical care insurance and actually may encourage better health and job-related habits in their coworkers. Moreover, the costs of eliminating a building's architectural barriers to the physically handicapped are relatively minor.

Since the Civil Rights Act was passed in 1964, several laws have been enacted to aid in overcoming discrimination: the establishment of the Equal Employment Opportunity Commission in 1964, the Fair Employment Practices Commission in 1972 (the law enforcement body of the EEOC), the Federal Rehabilitation Act for the handicapped in 1973, the ban on mandatory retirement age, as well as changes in minimum wage laws.

Affirmative action programs should be based on a thorough analysis of minority and female representation in various levels of the company, compared with their representation in the geographic area as a whole. Disparities should be remedied by the achievement of a set of specific goals and objectives over a given period of time, in stages. Pay equity and comparable worth pay remain areas of blight on equal opportunity and affirmative action.

Case Study 30

Discrimination against a Female Account Executive

Diane Patterson is employed as a registered representative by Johnson and Hunt, a large metropolitan brokerage firm. Diane was promoted to this position five months ago when the company lost a few of its brokers to a competing firm. Diane had worked previously for a number of years as a secretary to Scott Pitts, one of the partners in the firm, and he recommended her for a promotion when a vacancy arose.

Although Diane assumed her duties with enthusiasm, Cliff Stevenson, the office manager, soon felt it necessary to question Diane on her deteriorating performance. Cliff suspected the reason for Diane's poor performance. When Diane assumed her duties as a registered rep, Cliff had heard some of the men speak against her, as if they resented her taking on the job. He also knew that Diane was losing customers for no apparent reason other than the fact that she was female.

When Cliff questioned Diane on this, she replied, "I don't like being the only female in the department. I feel as if everyone is against me here." And she added, "Many of my male clients seem to think that because I'm a woman, I'm not qualified to be an account executive." Diane also mentioned that perhaps a new start in another department would enable her to carry out her duties more effectively.

Cliff knows that Diane is capable of performing her duties, even though she has few clients, and with the shortage of account executives in Cliff's department, he does not want to lose her. Cliff decides to ask Scott's opinion on the problem.

"The men feel threatened by Diane," Scott replied. "They feel that being an account executive is a demanding job and should belong to men only. One of the men said that she has no right to fill a position that may be needed by a man to support his family."

"I find that a bit hard to believe," replied Cliff.

"Believe it, Cliff. Even Harry Morgan mentioned something about not only having to worry about younger men taking over his job, but now he'd have to worry about his secretary."

Now, understanding the problem that exists, Cliff must decide what course of action to take. If you were Cliff, what would you do?

1. Would you let Diane go?
2. Would you discuss the problem with the men separately?
3. Would you discuss the problem with Diane present?
4. How could you as manager enhance Diane's status?
5. What is the best course of action for all concerned?

Case Study 31

Problems in Promoting a Minority

The executives of the Omega Computer Tape Company began to assemble for the bimonthly committee meeting. Wayne Baker, president of the Omega Company, knew that this particular meeting would be a touchy one. The first item on the agenda, the one that he was concerned about, dealt with the proposed promotion of Jad Lloyd, a black resident of the community, to the position of supervisor of the shipping and receiving department.

For some time, the Omega Company has been without a minority member in a management position. Although the company has had minority members in management positions before, the last member left the company more than five years ago for a higher-paying job in another city. When Brad Hall, the supervisor of the department under discussion, became eligible for promotion, this dispute began.

Bill Moore, head of the Personnel Department and former civil rights activist, feels that Jad Lloyd should be promoted to the supervisory position, because he is a minority member. He knows that Mr. Lloyd has been with the company for a good number of years, and from reports that he has received feels that Lloyd is qualified to handle a supervisory position.

Richard Speer, the administrative assistant of the shipping and receiving department, thinks otherwise. He feels that, regardless of the fact that the company needs minority members in management positions, the best qualified man should be promoted. It is his opinion that Mr. Lloyd is not the most qualified. He feels Mr. Manachek is more qualified and has more years with the company.

When the meeting begins and the discussion is opened on the topic, Bill Moore states, "If Mr. Lloyd is not promoted to this supervisory position, then we are failing in our obligation to ensure that minority members have an equal standing in this company."

"I'm all for giving minorities a fair shake," replies Mr. Speer, "but I won't stand for a man to be promoted over another just because of his color, black or white, as I feel you want done in this case."

"It's time that minority members were treated fairly around here, and it's high time we had one promoted to a management position!"

"Are you saying that regardless of ability, if it comes to promoting a black or a white, we should promote a black?"

"In this case, that is exactly what I am saying."

"That is reverse discrimination and I won't stand for it."

The meeting is obviously getting out of hand and Wayne Baker calls the discussion to a halt.

1. As president Wayne Baker, how would you handle the meeting?
2. Should he continue the meeting? If so, in what way?
3. Do you feel that Mr. Lloyd or Mr. Manachek should be promoted? Why?

Terms and Concepts

affirmative action a federal mandate requiring an employer to make efforts to recruit, employ, and promote qualified members of minority groups.

at-will termination an employer's practice of allowing dismissal of an employee at will for good cause, for no particular cause, or even for morally wrong reasons.

black pride determination by a black that he or she can determine his or her own destiny and own future.

Civil Rights Act the most comprehensive antidiscrimination legislation passed in this century. When the law was enacted in 1964, it established the EEOC.

cultural stereotypes general ideas or fixed opinions about groups of people that a society develops.

discrimination an act of prejudice against a person or a group of persons.

dual careers career commitments for both the husband and the wife.

EEOC (Equal Employment Opportunity Commission) a government agency that established guidelines for hiring, recruiting, and promoting minority groups.

FEPC (Federal Employment Practices Commission) the watchdogs of the EEOC or the enforcement arm that can levy fines or punishment for not following federal guidelines in recruiting, hiring, or promoting minority groups.

Hispanic Americans All Spanish-speaking groups including Cubans and Puerto Ricans as well as Mexican Americans.

job restructuring Changing the job qualifications and descriptions so that certain minorities can qualify for a position (e.g., not requiring the lifting of heavy objects, so that older people can be hired for the position).

NOW (National Organization of Women) leading organization for women's rights.

older worker usually, those over 65 years of age, but can mean those over 40 or 55, depending on the occupation; may also mean 10 to 15 years from retirement.

prejudice an attitude or habit of mind usually based on ignorance, fear, or cultural bias.

Rehabilitation Act of 1973 federal legislation that requires buildings of public and private organizations to be accessible to the handicapped (blind, deaf, and those in wheelchairs).

Notes

1. Anita Cava, "Evaluating the Professional: New Perils for Management," *Business and Economic Review*, July–September 1989, pp. 27–29.

2. James Braham, "Is the Door Really Open?" *Industry Week*, November 16, 1987, pp. 64–70.

3. John Howard Griffin, *Black Like Me* (Boston: Houghton Mifflin, 1960), p. 96.

4. James G. Frierson, "Religion in the Workplace—Dealing in Good Faith," *Personnel Journal*, July 1988, pp. 60–67.

5. Robert M. Preer, Jr., "Reasonable Accommodation of Religious Practice: The Conflict Between the Courts and the EEOC," *Employee Relations Law Journal*, Summer 1989, pp. 67–99.

6. "The Mexican Americans—A People on the Move," *National Geographic*, June 1980, pp. 781–808.

7. Statement of U.S. Senator Alan K. Simpson, State of Wyoming, "Immigration Bill," May 23, 1985, p. 1.

8. Ibid.

9. "An Indian Nation Is Gaining Unity, Respect—and Results," *U.S. News and World Report*, February 25, 1974, p. 60;

"America's Indians: Beggars in Our Own Land," *U.S. News and World Report*, May 23, 1983, pp. 70–72.

10. U.S. Bureau of the Census, *Statistical Abstract of the United States*, 109th ed., 1989, p. 17.

11. Anthony Ramirez, "Making Better Use of Older Workers," *Fortune*, January 30, 1989, pp. 179–187.

12. "Labor Letter: An Age-Bias Ruling," *The Wall Street Journal*, June 11, 1985, p. 1.

13. Ibid.

14. Robert A. Synder and Billie Brandon, "Riding the Third Wave: Staying on Top of ADEA Complaints," *Personnel Administrator*, February 1983, p. 45.

15. Ibid., pp. 45, 47.

16. "Labor Letter: Women Advance Further," *The Wall Street Journal*, June 11, 1985, p. 1.

17. Bureau of the Census, *Statistical Abstract*, p. 386.

18. Ibid., p. 673.

19. Beth Brophy, "80s Work Benefit: Child Care," *USA Today*, June 21, 1985, p. A-1.

20. Clair Safran, "Corporate Women: Just How Far Have We Come?" *Working Woman*, March 1984, pp. 102–103.

21. Nancy Lee, "The Dual Career Couple, Benefits and Pitfalls," *Management Review*, January 1981, pp. 46–52.

22. "Labor Letter," *The Wall Street Journal*, August 6, 1985, p. 1.

23. Louis K. Obdyke IV, "Interpreting AIDS Discrimination," *Personnel Administrator*, June 1989, pp. 83–89; see also,

James R. Redeker and Jonathan A. Segal, "The Legal Ramifications of AIDS Discrimination," *Business and Society Review*, Spring 1988, pp. 18–24.

24. Carl G. Jung and others, *Man and His Symbols* (Garden City, N.Y.: Doubleday, 1973), p. 172.

25. Joost A. M. Meerloo, *That Difficult Piece* (Great Neck, N.Y.: Channel Press, 1961), p. 16.

26. "Colleges Enroll Fewer Blacks and Hispanics," *USA Today*, January 15, 1990, p. D1.

27. Ibid.

28. "Now We're on Our Own," *Newsweek*, February 6, 1989, p. 64.

29. Anne B. Fisher, "Businessmen Like to Hire by the Numbers," *Fortune*, September 16, 1985, p. 28. See also, "Ed Meese Is Taking a Jackhammer to Affirmative Action," *Business Week*, September 2, 1985, p. 41.

30. "Labor Letter: Affirmative-Action Goals," *The Wall Street Journal*, September 3, 1985, p. 1.

31. Charlene Marmer Solomon, "The Corporate Response to Work Force Diversity," *Personnel Journal*, August 1989, pp. 43–53.

32. "Employment at Will: New Restrictions on the Right to Fire," *Small Business Report*, February 1988, pp. 60–63.

33. Maria Leonard, "Challenges to the Termination-at-Will Doctrine," *Personnel Administrator*, February 1983, p. 56.

34. Ibid.

Recommended Reading

Anderson, Howard J., and Michael D. Levin-Epstein. *Primer of Equal Employment Opportunity*, 2nd ed. Washington, D.C.: Bureau of National Affairs, 1982.

Eichner, Maxine N. "Getting Women Work That Isn't Women's Work: Challenging Gender Biases in the Workplace Under Title VII," *Yale Law Journal*, June 1988, pp. 1397–1417.

Hewlett, Sylvia Ann. *A Lesser Life: The Myth of Women's Liberation in America*. New York: Warner Books, 1987.

Howard, Cecil G. "Strategic Guidelines for Terminating Employees," *Personnel Administrator*, April 1988, pp. 106–109.

Hutchens, Robert M. "Do Job Opportunities Decline with Age?" *Industrial and Law Relations Review*, October 1988, pp. 89–99.

Jongeward, Dorothy, and Dru Scott. *Women as Winners.*

Reading, Mass.: Addison-Wesley, 1976.

Krett, Karen. "Maternity, Paternity and Child Care Policies," *Personnel Administrator*, June 1985, pp. 136, 218.

McEvoy, Glenn M., and Wayne F. Cascio. "Cumulative Evidence of the Relationship Between Employee Age and Job Performance," *Journal of Applied Psychology*, February 1989, pp. 11–17.

Scheibal, William J. "Title VII and Comparable Worth: A Post-AFSCME Review," *American Business Law Journal*, Summer 1987, pp. 265–284.

Solomon, Charlene Marmer. "The Corporate Response to Work Force Diversity," *Personnel Journal*, August 1989, pp. 43–53.

Susser, Peter A., and David A. Jett. "Accommodating Handicapped Workers: The Extent of the Employer's Obligation," *Employment Relations Today*, Summer 1988, pp. 113–120.

16

Employees and Unions

After studying this chapter, you should be able to:

1. Explain the various attitudes that management can exhibit toward unions.
2. Give reasons why people join unions.
3. Relate the functions and difficulties of the shop steward and the company supervisor in the labor-management relationship.
4. Define collective bargaining.
5. Compare the basic negotiating procedures in collective bargaining from the union's and management's point of view.
6. Explain the various tactics that unions and management can use to achieve their goals.
7. Discuss "grievance procedures" and the types of arbitration that are used when no decision can be reached.
8. Describe the impact of internationalism on unions.

TO START YOU THINKING . . .

Again here are some questions that you might think about as you read this chapter.

♦ Do you think that unions are as beneficial to society now as they were 10, 20, or 30 years ago?
♦ Are there more strikes now than 10 years ago? Why?
♦ What types of strikes are illegal?
♦ What is the difference between a mediator and an arbitrator?
♦ Do you think that public employees should be members of a union and be allowed to strike?
♦ What is the difference between a union shop and a closed shop?
♦ What is a yellow-dog contract? a boycott? a lockout?
♦ Are you a member of a union? How well does it represent you?
♦ How does a gripe become a grievance?

WHERE ARE UNIONS GOING?

Some would argue that labor unions as we know them are quickly becoming a thing of the past. Indeed the rough-and-tumble, sometimes violent unions of the mid–twentieth century are, for the most part, changing. Of course, some violence remains in isolated strikes and other actions. But is the labor union movement dead or simply changing?

There were thousands of employee strikes in the 1980s. Most, thank goodness, were nonviolent. The strike has always been a major weapon of most unions. Some public employees, like police and fire-fighters in some jurisdictions, are prohibited from using the strike weapon.

More fundamental than the right to strike, or otherwise get the attention of management, is the welfare of employees for which unions have fought. Many of the economic provisions have been obtained and the unions must change their strategy and tactics to a more conciliatory and cooperative stance if they are to survive. According to Peter Drucker, the single most important factor in the decline of labor unions is "the shift of gravity of the workforce from the blue-collar worker in manufacturing industry to the knowledge worker."[1]

Drucker believes that unions have three choices: (1) do nothing and disappear, (2) maintain themselves by dominating the political power structure, or (3) rethink their function:

> The union might reinvent itself as the organ of society—and of the employing institution—concerned with human potential and human achievement, and with optimizing the human resource altogether. The union would still have a role as the representative of the employees against management stupidity, management arbitrariness, and management abuse of power. . . . The union would work with management on productivity and quality, on keeping the enterprise competitive, and thus maintaining the members' jobs and their incomes.[2]

No, unions and their influences are not dead. They must be and are being restructured. Certainly their impact and membership have declined but new horizons and opportunities for cooperative action remain and, in some sectors, are growing.[3] Primary opportunities are in the services or so-called "white-collar sector." Management of traditionally unionized organizations and the blue-collar unions also have opportunities to effect changes working with rather than against one another.

WHO ARE UNION MEMBERS?

A labor union is an organization of employees formed for the purpose of furthering the interests of the workers. Most people think of unions in terms of the "blue-collar" movement, because most union members are in such fields. One of the largest unions today, however, is the American Federation of State, County, and Municipal Employees, which includes white-collar as well as blue-collar workers.

Other large unions include the Teamsters, the Food and Commercial Workers, and the National Education Association, an employee representation organization. The United Auto Workers is one of the largest unions affiliated with the AFL-CIO. It rejoined the AFL-CIO in June 1981 ending a 13-year separation. The Teamsters also affiliated with the AFL-CIO in the late 1980s.

Table 16-1 shows the percentage of union members in various employment sectors. Note that membership is declining in almost all sectors. The greatest potential for union development is in the retail, services, and financial sectors, and also among the medical and legal professions.[4] Public employee unions have been the fastest-growing of any segment of unionism. This sector includes teachers, police officers, fire-fighters, and county employees. Even middle-class workers

TABLE 16-1 Union Membership (as a percent of all workers in an employment sector of the U.S.)

	1980	**1985**	**1987**
Transportation and public utilities	48.4%	37.0%	33.5%
Government	35.9	35.8	36.0
Manufacturing	32.3	24.8	23.2
Construction	30.9	22.3	21.0
Mining	32.0	17.3	18.3
Wholesale and retail trade	10.1	7.2	7.1
Services	8.9	6.6	6.3
Finance, insurance, and real estate	3.2	2.9	2.3

SOURCE: U.S. Department of Labor, Bureau of Labor Statistics.

have rushed to join unions. More than 4 million white-collar workers are now represented by unions. Despite their growth, however, labor organizations have not kept up with the growth of the labor force. (See Figure 16-1.) This is due in part to management's offering the same benefits to nonunion employees that union members would receive.

A CLASH OF GOALS

The relationship between capital and labor is hand in glove. One cannot survive without the other, but a struggle between the two has been going on for years.

Management versus unions

With few exceptions, every company in the United States, regardless of size, has been faced with the fact that attempts at union organizing are here to stay. For

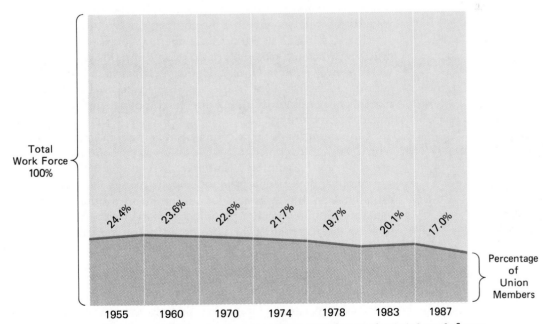

Total Work Force 100%

24.4%   23.6%   22.6%   21.7%   19.7%   20.1%   17.0%

Percentage of Union Members

1955   1960   1970   1974   1978   1983   1987

FIGURE 16-1 The percentage of union members relative to the total work force.
Source: Statistical Abstract of the United States, 1989 *(Washington, D.C.: G.P.O., 1989)*, p. 416.

managers, dealing with unions can be frustrating, tedious, and, in some cases, almost impossible. There are no precise formulas to make dealing with unions easy and no directions on the back of union contracts to help management come to an understanding of how a union works or why it is necessary in the first place.

Too often, both the company management and the union forget that the other is made up of people and that working with and understanding people takes more time and effort than does mastering a complicated computer language. Computer languages are logical and always consistent; people rarely are. Management sees the union as a corporate body, much like itself, a business that is in opposition to management goals. Unions see management as a profit monster that will take no time or expense to attend to the needs of the workers who feed it. A good example of this clash of goals is in the major league baseball and football owners and players' associations.

MANAGEMENT'S ATTITUDES TOWARD UNIONS

The goals of management, which are varied, include profit making, market development, and corporate efficiency. By concentrating on efficiency and profit, the managements of many American companies have neglected personnel problems for a long time, leaving such problems to the supervisors and shop superintendents. Faced with the union challenging their authority, employers have in the past generally been opposed to unions.

Relationship between unions and management

Many U.S. employers at the present time have come to accept unionism and forms of collective bargaining. But a few are bitterly opposed to the principle of unionism. The typical attitudes of employers can be classified from *exclusion* to *cooperation,* with intermediate steps of *containment, acceptance,* and *accommodation.*

Exclusion

When the employer's policy is that of union *exclusion,* management tries to discourage workers from joining unions by coercion or by trying to provide the wage and fringe benefits that the competitors grant through collective bargaining.

Containment

Faced with a law compelling them to deal with unions, many employers grudgingly act accordingly, but do everything possible to wean the loyalty of the workers away from the union. Under *containment,* all relations with the union are kept on a strictly "legal" basis, and the scope of collective bargaining is kept as narrow as possible. By doing so the company hopes to rid itself eventually of collective bargaining.

Acceptance, accommodation

Another attitude toward unionism is that of *acceptance* and *accommodation,* in which the employer recognizes the union as part of the industrial scene and tries to use collective bargaining to improve its relations with its employees.

Cooperation

Finally, there is the relationship of *cooperation,* in which the management actually seeks the assistance of the union in production problems that are not usually the subject matter of collective bargaining. Acceptance and accommodation are more prevalent than are exclusion or cooperation. (See Figure 16-2.)

UNION DEVELOPMENT

Today's wage earners often fear that the company holds all the keys to their well-being and, rather than lose what they have, will accept what the company offers on any ground to protect what they have won for themselves in the past.

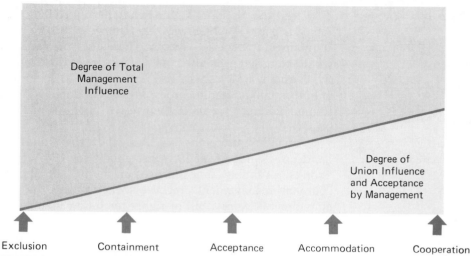

FIGURE 16-2 **Attitudes of employers toward unions and how they deal with them.**

Laborers, craftsmen, and skilled workers no longer own what they make, as many of them did in the Middle Ages. Their labor and only their labor is contracted out to the factory. The factory or company is sole owner of everything produced by the workers. The only thing they can claim is ownership of their labor. If they sell their labor to a company, most laborers feel that they have the right to bargain over the price of their labor, just as the company has the right to haggle with the buyers of their product over its wholesale cost. (See Figure 16-3.)

FIGURE 16-3 **Most crafts people and laborers feel their wages should reflect bargaining over the price of their labor.** Laima Druskis.

Until the National Labor Relations Act (NLRA), also known as the Wagner Act, was passed in 1935, workers had no legitimate means of bargaining with the company for increased wages. There was no guarantee that workers' salaries would be raised even after years of service to the company, and it was possible for the company to lower the workers' salaries to cover losses caused by production failure or financial difficulties. Workers wanted job and wage security, so they formed unions to protect themselves in the same way that the company was protected.

Amendments to the NLRA include the Taft-Hartley Act of 1947 and the Landrum-Griffin Act of 1959. Essentially the 1947 amendments provided a list of "don'ts" or unfair labor practices on the part of labor similar to the list of unfair company management practices spelled out in the original 1935 act. The 1959 amendments were a bill of rights for union members designed to protect them from abuses of their own unions. Corruption and misuses of union funds, racketeering, and other practices prompted passage of the amendments.

Executive Orders by Presidents Kennedy in 1961, Nixon in 1971, and others, brought to the public sector collective bargaining similar to that of the private sector. Many states as well as the federal government now authorize bargaining by government employees.[5] It seems that about every 10 or 12 years, major legislation or executive action has been taken to bring about changes in labor laws.

In 1985, the chairman of the Labor and Employment section of the American Bar Association said that U.S. labor policy was where the nation wanted it to be: conservative toward unionism but supportive of individual rights.[6]

DUAL LOYALTY

With employment and union membership comes a problem unique to workers. Their wages come directly from their employer, but the protection of their rights and privileges as employees comes from their union. Some personnel managers and union officials believe that employees will give their loyalties to the side that benefits the *individual* most, without considering the overall impact of their actions on society or on the economy.

No longer can unions or management count on blind support from their members or employees. So many more aspects of labor problems have been brought to public attention, that union employees cannot help but know the effects of their proposed actions even before they are taken. Workers are forced also to take public reaction into account now because the public, through television, may know about the strike or walk-out even before some of the workers do, and public reaction will be instantaneous. In the past, news of strikes wasn't heard until the following day or by word of mouth. Public sympathy for a strike for higher wages or increased fringe benefits cannot be gained by simply making the facts known, no more than management can get the public on its side by claiming low profits and increased costs.

Why Do People Join Unions?

Poor morale rather than
wages encourages
employees to join unions

On the surface, people join unions for economic advantage and security. They also gain some personal protection through the grievance procedures. But both unions and employers will more often agree that it is not wages alone but, rather, employee treatment that leads them to join unions. When union and nonunion companies of the same industry and locale compare wages, they are usually not that different.

Job satisfaction, job security, and positive attitudes toward unions are among major reasons why people join unions. If an individual does not receive job satisfaction on the job from management, then the union provides an attraction. Similarly, if an individual has no assurance of continued employment, he or she finds job security in belonging to a union.

Faced with the threat of unemployment in the 1980s, union members shifted their priorities from compensation issues to job security issues in the 1990s.[7] It is more difficult for management to get rid of a union employee than a nonunion employee because of formalized grievance procedures and other mechanisms built into a collectively bargained agreement.

Positive attitudes toward unions help attract and maintain union membership. A significant study by Getman, Goldberg, and Herman supports the idea that employees are more sophisticated about unions' roles than commonly thought. They are more influenced by attitudes that result from everyday experiences than by organizing campaign propaganda.[8]

Lack of worker participation and complaint system encourage union entry

When a company becomes highly structured and bureaucratic, it can create a breeding ground for unions. When all the rules have been written by the employer with no representation on the part of the employees, look out nonunion companies! Many large industries such as banking, insurance, and finance cultivate bureaucratic systems, partly due to size. If there is no effective "open-door" or complaint and grievance policy, the firm is encouraging unionization.

How Nonunion Companies Keep Unions Out

Steps that may discourage union organizing include the following:

1. Have supervisor push the company position and rebut the union talk on the plant floor.

2. Continue to manage fairly.

3. Hold frequent meetings with employees. Instead of telling or questioning employees, listen to them. Try to allay their hostility. You might just stand up and be honest by saying, "I blew it, help me." Ask where the company has gone wrong and what can be done to correct the problems.

4. Don't intimidate, interrogate, promise, or threaten. All these make the union seem like a good alternative.

5. Continue to inform employees with facts that favor your position.

6. Campaign against unions using visual aids as illustrated in Figure 16-4.

What Can Unions Promise?

1. Unions can reveal working conditions that are not equal to those for other employees in similar situations, but they cannot promise better wages, working conditions, or benefits.

2. They can usually deliver a job posting system that provides employees the opportunity for upward mobility. Every vacancy should be posted with a job description, salary range, and necessary qualifications.

3. They can usually develop a complaint system that can be monitored by the union to protect employees against jeopardy.

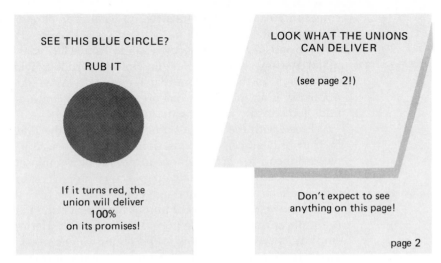

FIGURE 16-4 Campaign tactics used by companies to keep unions out. Such posters are seen on bulletin boards and in restrooms.

4. Most often, unions provide in their contracts for promotion by seniority where skills are equal, eliminating cutthroat competition and affording a feeling of regularity and justice.

AN ELECTION CAN VOTE A UNION IN OR OUT

Union Election Terminology

Recognition. If the employees of a company wish to be represented by a union and over 30 percent of the workers sign the recognition card, the cards will be submitted to the National Labor Relations Board (NLRB). Once the NLRB certifies the list, an election will follow.

Certification (election). Once an election is called, the union can request a list of all employees and their addresses. The union can contact them at home, but not on the company grounds. A simple majority, 50 percent plus one, of a substantial or representative number of eligible employees, can bring union representation into a company.

Decertification. At the end of a union contract, if the union members wish to terminate their relationship with the union, over 50 percent of the union members must vote for a decertification.

Deauthorization. If union conditions are so bad during the time of the contract, a deauthorization vote can be called. To deauthorize a union, over 50 percent of *all* the employees must vote to deauthorize a union. That includes employees who may be absent during the day of the vote.

UNION INTERACTION WITH MANAGEMENT

Union shop

The day-to-day relations of management and unions at the plant level center on the written collective bargaining agreement. The vast majority of contracts are written for a fixed period of time, usually three years. A provision of the contract is the "union security" clause that may provide for a *union shop* under which all employees covered by the agreement must join the union after a brief probationary period or lose their jobs. Federal law forbids the *closed shop* agreement under which only union members are hired, and the same federal law delegates to the states the authority, which some of them have exercised, to bar union shops. Twenty-one states, mostly in the South and West, have adopted *right-to-work laws* that are strongly opposed by organized labor.

Right-to-work laws

Another clause may provide that union membership must be maintained during the agreement. Many companies agree to deduct union dues from the workers' wages and pay them directly to the union treasurer. By this *checkoff* system, management avoids having dues collection taking place during work time and the union avoids the nuisance of seeking out individual members to get its income.

``Checkoff''

Some managements insist that agreements state clearly that management has the responsibility in directing the work force including the hiring and firing, assigning of jobs, and determining of production schedules.

Express Your Opinion

Analyze your own community in terms of union activity. Would you say that your community is becoming more union or more management oriented? For example, do you see much evidence of union activity around the company plants, or on main street, or in the local newspaper? Have you seen pro- or antiunion activity on bulletin boards, on the local television, or at street rallies? What main points are used by union or management to gain supporters? Are the political issues really clear? Can you relate to a particular company in town and identify which attitude it is using with the unions? Is it exclusion, containment, acceptance, accommodation, or cooperation? Are you happy that your community is becoming more union or management oriented?

THE TWO PERSONALITIES IN THE MIDDLE _____

The supervisor and shop steward are caught in the middle

There are two positions within the structure of the typical company whose occupants are answerable to more officials, managers, workers, and boards than any other positions, including company president (Figure 16-5). These two are the shop steward and the company supervisor. Although on opposing sides, their functions are similar, and each is situated in the hierarchy of either the union or the management so that each is one step above any worker on the floor. Each has the unenviable position of being answerable to higher-ups who sometimes have no *practical* knowledge of the work floor.

Shop Steward _____

The shop steward represents the employee

On the union side, the shop steward has direct contact with the workers and is generally elected by the workers in his or her department. The steward is an employee of the company and works by the side of the men and women represented. Provisions are usually made in the union contract that allow the shop steward time off to conduct union affairs. The steward's attitude toward management is a reflection of the attitude of the workers.

The steward's attitude reflects the attitudes of the employees

If the union is new and the members are militant, they may elect a person whose main quality is expertise in rallying support against the company. This antagonism, if recognized by management, can be dealt with by establishing

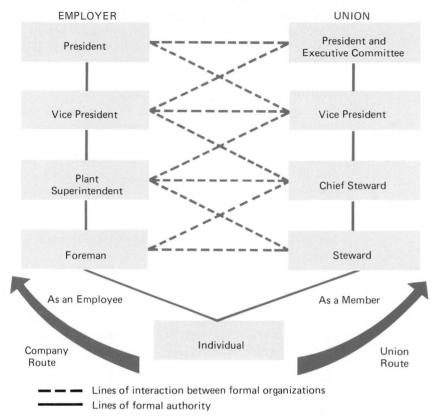

EMPLOYER   UNION

President   ← → ← → ← →   President and
                                  Executive Committee

Vice President   ← → ← → ← →   Vice President

Plant   ← → ← → ← →   Chief Steward
Superintendent

Foreman   ← → ← → ← →   Steward

As an Employee   As a Member

Company   Individual   Union
Route   Route

- - - Lines of interaction between formal organizations
───── Lines of formal authority

FIGURE 16-5 **The union adds an additional formal organization to the employment relationship.**

management credibility. Many of the problems coming from the growth of a new union are related to the workers' general suspicion of management. Tensions are high during periods of organizational change and lead to worker insecurity. Creating credibility may change the attitude of the steward or convince the workers to select a steward at the next election who is more open minded.

The shop steward functions as a safety valve in most cases. He or she represents individual employees in grievance hearings with management. The steward listens to employee complaints and advises whether an employee is justified in taking the complaint to management. On occasion, the supervisor may bring a problem to the shop steward that the steward forwards to the individual involved. The steward is more or less a lay lawyer, skilled or unskilled in the various articles of the union contract, and well versed in the fine points of grievance procedures. His or her effectiveness is based largely on the strength of the union itself within the company.

Company Supervisor

A realization of the importance of the supervisor in labor-management relations has brought about critical changes in the selection and training of supervisors by American management. Some time ago, supervisors were selected primarily for their ability to produce and for their industrial skill. The emergence of the union as a force in business has caused a reduction in the power of the supervisor, forcing the qualities of leadership and ability in personal relationships to take precedence over manual skill in the selection of new supervisors.

A training program for supervisors is needed

An increasing number of companies have instituted training programs to teach their supervisors elemental psychology, leadership skills, and group dynamics. Supervisors who were accustomed to absolute authority over the workers in their departments have found the transition to the demands of collective bargaining difficult. Even the most carefully designed training program sometimes fails to overcome the old system of unquestioned authority, and the supervisor must learn to satisfy the needs of management, as well as cope with the workers' new status as a bargaining force.

Union strength can undermine the supervisor's authority

Union power is, in many cases, so strong—involving discipline, work assignments, seniority, transfers, and so on—that frequently supervisors feel they don't have the authority to deal properly with the people under them. As they become better acquainted with the union and its functions, the supervisors may realize that shop stewards, who were once regarded as the uncooperative antagonists, can be useful in maintaining discipline, screening unwarranted complaints, counseling employees on personal problems and work habits, and communicating with management about employee problems.

Developing mutually beneficial communications can result in a supervisor-steward relationship that would alleviate many of the difficulties inherent in the labor-management conflict. The shop steward is also a leader and is often influential in determining the opinions of the wage earner concerning management. A mutual understanding as well as open lines of communication between the steward and the supervisor is imperative. While this is not always easy to attain, it should be worked for whenever possible.

COLLECTIVE BARGAINING

Bargaining agreement is legal, has time limits, and is complete

Although considered by some to be a legal contract, the collective bargaining agreement is much more flexible than a contract. It does have some of the properties of the contract, however: (1) it can be enforced by law, (2) it has a time limit, and (3) it is complete in itself. But provisions for change that are built into the agreement allow one or the other of the parties to interpret and apply the clauses on a continuing basis. It is a working document of resolution of conflict and, as such, is subject to renewed debate if conditions not covered by the agreement arise at a later date. Because the collective bargaining agreement is flexible, it is also interpreted in many different ways. In the opinion of some, it merely controls day-to-day union-management relations. This is a limited interpretation and covers only a small portion of the intended purpose of the agreement.

The collective agreement can be divided into three sections: (1) binding provisions, which include clauses in which little or no change is anticipated by either party (e.g., wages, union security, and the duration of the contract itself); (2) contingent clauses governing actions taken by union or management concerning new conditions not present at the time of agreement (e.g., promotion, transfer, change in operation techniques, governmental legislation); and (3) grievance procedures for use when disputes arise concerning interpretation of the agreement.

Management and Union Preparation

Understand the issues

1. A clear understanding of the issues is necessary. The issues may be wages, severance, conditions of work, the criteria for promotion, seniority rules, discipline, delays in the settlement of grievances, or disputes over interpretation.

2. If the dispute involves procedures, it should be made clear that the disagreement concerns the ways of attaining goals. Formulating criteria and agreeing on how to evaluate procedures must be spelled out clearly in operational terms.

3. Management should be acquainted with the unions, their leaders, structure, policies, and style of negotiation. The basic attitudes of how union leaders *or* managers accept or reject ideas, and trust or suspect each other, will directly determine the degree of success at the bargaining table.

Negotiators must know what to obtain and what to concede

4. Negotiators should estimate, as part of their preparation, what they want to get and what they are indifferent to getting. What they will concede, cannot concede, and could possibly concede are important tools of compromise. Negotiators should also be aware of the alternatives available to them in case agreement cannot be reached. They should be prepared to negotiate at a future time for employee benefits or changes that cannot be made at present.

Negotiating Procedures

Agree on time and place

1. Prior to the actual negotiations, both parties should agree on a time and place. There should be a central table for confrontation between the opposing sides as well as two separate areas so that each side can confer independently.

Use a round table

Because negotiations often begin in an atmosphere of distrust and hostility, attitudes of courtesy and reserve are important. The shape of the table may also have bearing on the negotiations. As in diplomatic confrontations, a round table is preferred because there is no head or foot and one party cannot seem to take precedence over the other.

Frequent recesses can minimize emotions

2. Either of the parties may make the opening statement on the matters in dispute. Unless copies of this statement are made available, a complete record should be kept by the other party. Frequent recesses may help to minimize emotional reactions and encourage a problem-oriented discussion rather than an angry debate, filled with charges and countercharges.

Negotiations are often tense

3. Negotiations are frequently tense and emotional, and strong feelings must be dealt with. Condescending attitudes can never be tolerated; they simply promote the feeling that the other party has the upper hand. Dealing with the issues and not with the emotions is generally best for the success of the entire procedure. Answering emotional outbursts with an attitude of reasoning and logic can sometimes lead to increased hostility from the emotional opponent, especially if reason and logic are offered in parental or superior tones. Withdrawing from negotiations for a short period of time may cool some tempers and allow both parties to take into full consideration the effects of their attitudes.

Bargaining is making trades

4. Never go up faster than the opponent comes down when discussing wages or demands. If one party gives in too easily on a particular issue, the other party may assume that the opponent is willing to agree to everything it demands. It should be remembered that, in a sense, bargaining is making a trade. Each demand may produce a counterdemand, so that, when it is accomplished, both parties eventually receive something from the bargaining process, even if it is only to trade higher wages for mandatory overtime.

In effect the negotiating process should not be a zero-sum game—the more I win, the more you lose. However, the negotiation process seems to be ruled more by human nature than by logic.

Sometimes experience and systematic observation can reveal the cues of serious commitment. A story is told of a union representative who always glanced at his watch when he had made his really final offer. His managerial opponent always lit a cigar when he had made his last offer.

A GRIPE CAN BECOME A GRIEVANCE

Consider each gripe a potential grievance

The company's handling of worker complaints is the same whether or not unions are involved. The essential difference in a union shop is that a dissatisfied worker may appeal the supervisor's decision by filing a formal charge, or grievance, against the company for a violation of one or more of the articles of the labor agreement. Consider every gripe as a potential grievance, as a complaint handled improperly can and often does become a grievance.

Unions can become involved

The contract between union and management spells out precisely workers' rights involving wages, hours, and working conditions. The contract is a formal, written document that limits the union's authority, as well as management's in general, for all must operate within the restrictions spelled out in the contract. The company should have management experts available to help interpret the contract and to answer questions that may arise. These specialists are usually found in the personnel department or, in larger companies, in the labor relations or industrial relations department.

HOW TO PREVENT GRIEVANCES

The only sound way to prevent grievances is to study the reasons behind complaints. Discontent among employees often stems from an accumulation of small, unresolved problems. Remember, supervisors get results through people.

1. Let each employee know how he or she is doing. Be honest and let people know what you expect. Help by pointing out how an employee can improve.

2. Give credit when credit is due. Look for the employee's extra performance and reward the person verbally during or shortly after the job.

3. If you think that a policy is unfair, express that opinion to your supervisor, not to your subordinates, and suggest changes to improve the policy.

4. Tell employees in advance about policy changes that will affect them and explain the reasons for each change. If possible get employees to participate in the change.

5. Make the best possible use of each person's ability. Instead of standing in a person's way, give him or her the opportunity for more responsibility and growth.

6. Solicit ideas from your employees. Employees often have great ideas for jobs or products that they should be encouraged to develop. Ask what can be done to eliminate bottlenecks and friction.

THE GRIEVANCE PROCEDURE

Where unions exist, a formal procedure for the processing of grievances will be spelled out in the union contract. A typical procedure follows. Some procedures may have more or fewer steps.

Step 1. If the supervisor cannot solve the complaint, it then becomes a grievance and the supervisor meets with the steward or grievance committee, while the employee files a written grievance. If the problem cannot be resolved at this level, it then moves to the second step (Figure 16-6).

Step 2. The supervisor's immediate superior and a representative from the labor relations department meet with the union grievance committee. At this point the problem usually involves more than one person and may relate to the individual rights of many. For example, a safety practice in the plant may have serious implications for all who work in the area. If the problem cannot be solved at this level, it moves to top management.

Step 3. Top management from both the company and the local union are now involved. The labor relations director and the plant or division manager meet with the union grievance committee. A representative from the local union may now represent the union's own grievance committee. Time and money begin to mount, and both sides usually want to solve the issue as quickly as possible.

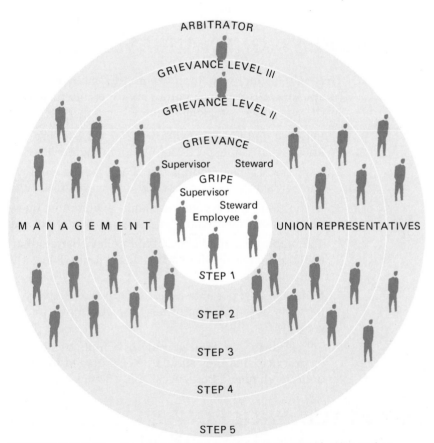

FIGURE 16-6 The five steps through which a complaint involving union and management can pass.

Step 4. Members of top management discuss the issues with a group from the national union. If the local union has no affiliation with a national union, an attorney or business agent meets with management representatives.

At this point, both parties could select a mediator. A mediator is a neutral third party who is called in to review both sides of the issue. The mediator is often a public official—for example, an attorney or college professor—who is respected by both sides. After hearing both points of view, the mediator recommends a solution. However, his or her decision is not binding on either party.

Step 5. At this point an arbitrator is usually called in on the dispute. The arbitrator, like the mediator, is a neutral third party. He or she is usually a professional arbitrator, recommended by the American Arbitration Association, the Federal Mediation and Conciliation Service, or one of the various state agencies. At this level, both sides have usually become polarized and the arbitrator often spends most of his or her time working with the disputing parties.

The arbitrator's decision is binding on management and union

The arbitrator will conduct hearings that are similar to legal proceedings. Witnesses are called, and testimony is recorded. The hearing may be quite informal, however, depending upon the arbitrator's style. The important difference between a mediator and arbitrator is that the decision announced by the arbitrator is *binding* on both the company and the union.

TACTICS OF THE UNION AND MANAGEMENT _____

If the union and management are unable to settle their grievances, one or both may resort to tactics that may be legal or illegal to force the other to come to a settlement. Such tactics are used when there appear to be no other alternatives.

Union's Weapons	
Strikes	1. *Primary strike.* Workers fail to show up for work.
	2. *Sympathy strike.* A strike is called by one union for the benefit of another union.
	3. *Sitdown strike.* Workers sit down on the job but fail to perform their duties.
	4. *Slowdown strike.* Workers simply perform their tasks at a slower rate.
	5. *Wildcat strike.* Some union members go on strike without the authorization or knowledge of the international union.
	6. *Jurisdictional strike.* Forcing the company to recognize one union over another. Sympathy, sitdown, wildcat, and jurisdictional strikes can be illegal.
Pickets	1. *Primary picket.* Union members walk around the place of employment with placards to inform the public of unfair practices of the management.
	2. *Mass picket.* So many union members are picketing around the company that it restricts entrance and exit of people into the company. Such activity is illegal.
Boycotts	A union tries to get the public to refuse to buy products or do business with the boycotted firm.

<table>
<tr><td>

Management's Weapons

</td><td>

1. *Lockout.* Employees are not allowed to come into the plant until they accept the employer's terms.

2. *Layoff.* Employees are released from employment for reason of lack of work. Employees are allowed to collect unemployment, but would not be able to if they were fired.

3. *Injunction.* A court order requiring certain action. A mandatory injunction requires performance of a specific act, such as requiring workers to return to work. A prohibitory injunction orders the other party to refrain from certain acts, such as ordering the union to stop mass picketing.

4. *Yellow-dog contract.* As a condition of employment a person agrees not to join a union. Outlawed by the Norris-LaGuardia Act, it is still practiced in some areas.

5. *Blacklisting.* A list of troublemakers that is available to other companies. Employment is not given to blacklisted union organizers. This activity is also illegal, but still used on occasion.

Other management weapons include inventory buildup for use during a strike, doing work at other plant locations, and subcontracting.

</td></tr>
</table>

All these tactics have been used by unions or management at some time in the history of the labor movement. Some are still being used and are "respectable" insofar as they are effective, if not always productive. The tactics used by unions today are generally aimed at production and, hence, the company's financial resources. Management uses tactics aimed at the resources and solidarity of the union or the bank accounts of the workers. With very few exceptions, labor disagreements today are relatively mild compared with the bloody confrontations of 50 years ago. Nevertheless, these disagreements can have powerful economic repercussions if not dealt with promptly and effectively.

TODAY'S UNIONS

The worker of today is vastly different from the worker of even ten years ago. American workers have opportunities for advancement and change that their parents couldn't have imagined. Today's workers are not particularly concerned with job permanence, are less inclined to conform to the decisions of higher authority, and are less likely to put up with uncomfortable working conditions. Workers' attitudes are in part responsible for current changes in unions, but there are other reasons.

Less than 20 percent of the work force are union members

Union membership was at a record high in 1970, with a total of more than 20 million members, a figure double that of 1960. Even though union membership was increasing during the 1960s, it was not increasing as fast as the work force. During the last half of the 1970s union membership dropped and by 1990 had fallen to less than 18 percent of the labor force. Still, unions have a great deal of influence in the United States.

Wages and Benefits

Union members are the offensive team

The part of the collective bargaining agreement of most concern to the employees, naturally, is wages. With few exceptions, the direction of wages has been upward, and the burden of the arguments for the change has been carried by the unions.

The employers are not usually arguing against wage increases but against the amount of union demands.

Leading unions set the trend for wages

The general amount of wage increases for an industry is usually determined by settlements arrived at by the leading unions and large companies. Whatever settlement is made between the United Auto Workers and whichever employer of the Big 3 automobile manufacturers they negotiate with first becomes the "pattern" for the industry. Sometimes one firm in a locality is recognized as the pace setter and other settlements follow it in much the same way.

At least 30 to 33 percent of the employer's wage cost is in benefits

Fringe benefits is a misnomer for the pension, hospitalization, supplementary unemployment, holidays, and vacation package, which now runs at least 30 to 33 percent of the per-employee wage cost paid by the employer. To make comparisons with what other employers and unions are doing, estimates of benefits are calculated as a per-hour expense, so that benefits have a dollar value. Such comparisons of employee costs among companies should include benefit expenses.

Mergers

The power of mergers

The unions' power will continue to grow if they consolidate into fewer and larger unions, with more centralized control. The same difficulties that are involved in corporate mergers are evident in union mergers as well. Old rivalries and animosities often combine with ordinary merger problems to cause further delay. However, since the merger of the American Federation of Labor and the Congress of Industrial Organizations in 1955, the realization that union strength can be increased by a broad political base has impressed more and more union leaders.

Social and Technological Change

More urban unions

There has been an increase in "urban unions" composed of teachers, hospital workers, police personnel, fire-fighters, and sanitation workers.

More blacks in unions

Trade unions and white-collar unions are becoming increasingly black, adding a different social base and political outlook, which is considerably different from the "traditional" union of 10 or 20 years ago.

Women are active in unions

Women are finding recognition in unions. Working women are wielding more clout in the labor movement these days, both at the local level and the national level, because union women are more numerous and active than ever before. Of every three union members one is a woman, meaning there are almost 6 million women union members.

Unions are begrudgingly accepting automation

The issue of automation has been around for almost 30 years, and for the most part, unions have become begrudging converts to automation. They recognize that business must become more efficient to compete in today's market. They recognize that industry must automate or they will be out of business. The key is to ensure that employees with 15 or 20 years of service are not let go. From this point of view

Unions and theory Z

the unions support Japan's Theory Z—paternalism and lifelong employment— discussed earlier.

Quality of Work Life

Cooperative efforts between union and management have led to several new programs. Depending on whom you talk with, union or management, both claim that they are responsible for many new programs. Few claim a shared responsibility for new ideas.

Yet unions and management have come to realize that they must work together for an enterprise to succeed competitively. Together, they have encouraged worker participation in business decisions and a greater emphasis on job security. The United Auto Workers, the Communications Workers of America, and many other unions, working with their counterparts in management, have reaffirmed their commitment to quality of work life (QWL).[9]

The goal of QWL programs is to make work more fulfilling and productive. They are implemented by semiautonomous work teams or management committees. The tasks of QWL are to:

1. Improve quality control
2. Improve work schedules
3. Improve compensation systems
4. Improve self-fulfillment

The growth of "quality of work life" programs

There seems to be an increased demand by workers for QWL programs. Companies such as GM, Procter & Gamble, Exxon, General Foods, TRW, and Polaroid are all trying such programs. However, the numbers of employees affected by such programs remain relatively small. Another issue is whether QWL programs are unfair labor practices on the part of management under the NLRA.

Union Losses

Because of slumping auto sales in recent years, the United Auto Workers (UAW) union has suffered declining membership. The robots now being used in the auto industry also seem to demonstrate to employees that unions can do little to protect their jobs.

Union leaders tend to be over 45

Today 91 percent of the employed adult population works for someone else. More of us are "employees" than ever before, and yet sympathy for unions is low. Finally, many union activists and leaders are over 45 years of age. Apparently, unions are finding it hard to recruit younger people to leadership jobs.

Union Gains

Union contract with J. P. Stevens opened up the South

In October 1980, J. P. Stevens signed its first labor contracts with the Amalgamated Clothing and Textile Workers Union. The signed contract heralded the end of one of the nation's longest and bitterest labor struggles. The big textile company had held its ground for 17 years despite the union's victories in representation elections, even despite National Labor Relations Board rulings against the company for unfair labor practices—and despite a national boycott of Stevens's products organized by the union.

The union pressured Stevens supporters

The union leader, Ray Rogers, used some unorthodox ways of fighting for workers' power, such as putting pressure on companies that did business with Stevens and members of the company's board of directors. The union's successful tactic of putting pressure on business partners of its antagonists may be adopted by other unions, undoubtedly causing a controversy in labor relations circles.

A union member on the board of directors of the company

During the early 1980s, both managements and unions realized that a more cooperative effort was needed by both for them to survive. Now a member of the United Auto Workers Union has a seat on the Chrysler board of directors. This was a major milestone for the unions. Interestingly, a member on the board will find himself or herself torn between the responsibility to the company and loyalty to the union members. A board decision to close a plant for example, might be necessary to ensure Chrysler's survival, but it could be denounced by union workers faced with losing their jobs.

Other examples of union gains in the 1980s are the experiences of Eastern and other airlines with pilots, mechanics, and flight attendants who honored picket lines and carried out economic boycotts.

Internationalism and Unions

Foreign unions are often more socialistic and lack strong central support

The new multinationalism has led American business managers to deal with foreign labor unions, and certainly they cannot be dealt with in the same way as American unions. By and large, foreign unions are more steeped in tradition, are more socialistically oriented, and lack strong centralized power. Workers have not always agreed with their union leaders on whether to stress collective bargaining or political action, but generally American unions have opted for collective bargaining, whereas unions in many other countries have relied more on political action.

The Japanese work ethic and unionism clash

The president of the Sharp (Japanese) plant in Memphis, Tennessee advocates that harmony is power and that difficulties should be tackled with a positive attitude but not to join a union.[10] In principle, Sharp is unopposed to unions. It hasn't prevented employees from joining blue-collar federations, but those federations generally seem less militant than many hard-driving American unions. The company fears that an American union could divide employees' loyalties and undermine the company's goals.

The European and Asian (Japanese) models of labor-management cooperation have had a positive and profound effect on U.S. labor relations. The New United Motor Manufacturing, Inc. (NUMMI), a joint venture of General Motors and Toyota, has adopted industrial relations practices emphasizing fewer job classifications, more teamwork and job rotation, and continuous improvement programs. These practices tend to replace direct supervision as the primary mechanism for obtaining high productivity and quality. There is much more union-management cooperation than commonly experienced in the automobile or other industries.[11]

SPIRIT OF COOPERATION

While the element of conflict is omnipresent between union and management, perhaps a spirit of cooperation can be developed. Sensitive observers increasingly call our attention to the fact that human beings are not machines, that they have feelings and emotions that must be respected to get the highest degree of cooperation in the workplace and in labor management relations. The present emphasis on the study of individual and group relationships is a recognition that, along with the solution of technical problems, there must be increasing concern for human elements in production.

Summary

Most people think of unions in terms of the blue-collar movements because most union members are in such fields. But, although most union members belong to the blue-collar unions, the white-collar and public employees sector has the greatest potential for unionization. The percentage of union members in the total work force has been decreasing since 1955. Today less than 18 percent of the work force are members of unions.

Managements' attitudes toward unions can range from total exclusion to cooperation with them. Many people feel that having a union on company grounds develops a dual or divided loyalty on the part of the employee. Sometimes those loyalties are in conflict. Poor morale and perceived low wages encourage employees to join unions. Certainly when a company becomes highly structured, it can be a breeding ground for unions.

The shop steward is sometimes a powerful adversary on the floor and can have a direct effect on the attitudes of the workers. The supervisor also affects the attitudes of the workers. If a supervisor misinterprets the relationship with either the shop steward or the workers, it can mean a serious breakdown in working relationships.

Good supervisors understand their relationship with the workers as one in which they have the authority to ensure that the work that has to be done is done, but not the authority to decide arbitrarily that some of the workers are transferred to other areas or shifts. Nor do they have the power to discipline an employee without that disciplinary action being questioned by the shop steward.

Collective bargaining is probably the most complicated area of labor-management interaction. The tensions involved are frequently excessive on both sides of the table. Without a good understanding of the demands of the other, neither of the opponents will be able to come to terms with the issues. In almost every instance where there are conflicting interests and goals, there will be arguments, excitement, tension, and fear. Cooperation on both sides may curtail a number of the problems, but cooperation is not the only attitude that plays a part in the effectiveness of the bargaining.

Negotiations occur on the average of every three years, depending on the length of the agreement. Important to the success of bargaining are the pains to which each party goes to meet the tensions and issues with fairness and intelligence.

The tactics used by both unions and management to express their dissatisfaction can be seen in many ways. Unions use strikes, such as the primary, sympathy, sitdown, slowdown, and wildcat strikes. They also use pickets and boycotts. Managements' methods are lockouts, layoffs, injunctions, yellow-dog contracts, and blacklisting. Many methods affecting both union and management are illegal, but it has not stopped some from using them.

Unions are making some gains despite declining membership. For the first time in the United States, a union member is serving on a company's board of directors. Chrysler was the first to take such action. Implementation of economic boycotts at Eastern Airlines and other companies have been effective. International influences are being felt in bringing about more cooperative union-management relationships.

Perhaps the element of conflict is always present between union and management, but maybe a spirit of cooperation can be developed. Sensitive observers increasingly call our attention to the fact that humans are not machines, that they have feelings and emotions that must be respected. Mutual respect must be brought about between union and management for higher production and mutual satisfaction.

Firehouse Union

Culver is a small and pleasant town with two modern and attractive fire stations. Most of the fire-fighters employed at these stations grew up together and now live within the city limits. They all get along well and frequently have family get-togethers. In spite of these conditions, the fire-fighters are far from happy.

For quite some time the fire-fighters have been in conflict with the city's Board of Administration over obtaining a wage increase. The men feel that their wages are too low and that the board is spending money unnecessarily. They feel that this money is being spent on fire equipment to impress the community instead of paying the men a reasonable salary in line with the amount being paid in neighboring communities.

Previous attempts to obtain a significant wage increase from the board have been futile. The only occasion when the fire-fighters managed to obtain an increase over 6 percent was when they hired a lawyer for an evening during negotiations at a cost of $400 of their own money.

Tomorrow the fire-fighters will go into negotiations with the board. There is talk among the ranks that, if their request for a 9 percent wage increase is turned down, as it is expected to be, they will contact the local Teamsters Union and request an election for union representation.

Those who speak in favor of joining the union state that the union would have a great deal more leverage in dealing with the board. If the board refuses to cooperate with the union, the fire-fighters could go on strike with the financial support of the union. In addition, the union could stop all trucking in the town to support a fire-fighters' strike if need be.

The fire-fighters who are speaking against joining the union point out that the union requires what they consider high fees and that the fire-fighters might be called upon to strike in support for other union members in the town. Additionally, a neighboring community fire station recently went on strike and, in that community, hostility was being expressed against the fire-fighters.

If you were one of the fire-fighters, what would you do?

1. Recommend accepting the wage increase offered by the board?
2. Recommend hiring another lawyer?
3. Recommend joining the union?
4. Quit and find a better fire station in some other community?

Unions Versus Minority Rights

Management decided that, due to a decline in business, the Rayon Furniture Plant would reduce the number of positions in the Finishing Department by 12 persons. After receiving the union's consent on the matter, the plant management gave the 12 workers with the least seniority their notice of termination.

Shortly after these events occurred, Tom Hale, head of the Personnel Department, contacted Bill Norton, the plant manager. Their discussion concerned the employees who received termination notices. Nine of these 12 were black, and they contacted the Fair Employment Practices Commission and filed a complaint against the company for discriminating against them. The complaint centered on the fact that only the Finishing Department was being forced to cut back and that only the Finishing Department was predominantly black. The workers saw this as discriminatory.

"I am aware that the majority of those to be laid off are black," stated Bill, "but we've been ordered to reduce that department, and we must follow the seniority provision of our union contract."

"Yes, I know," replied Tom, "but the seniority provision could well be contested. A few months ago, the Waltan Corporation laid off some workers based on seniority, and after a complaint of discrimination similar to our own, the FEPC won a case of discrimination in court."

"Well, what do you propose we do about it? Violate our union contract?"

"Can't we cut back in the Assembly Section and the Cutting Room too? That way, instead of laying off the 12 workers in one department, we could lay off 4 workers from each. Then it wouldn't seem discriminatory. There would be more whites laid off than blacks."

"But we don't need to cut back in the Assembly Section or the Cutting Room," Bill replied. "Besides, we have the workers with the greatest seniority of the entire company in the Assembly Section. Why, Fred has been with us for 12 years and he has the least seniority of anyone in the department."

"What do you think about transferring the majority of the 12 into other departments, then?"

"That doesn't solve the problem; the company is cutting back to save money, not to play musical chairs with the workers. As far as I'm concerned, the problem is out of our hands. Let's let the union handle it."

1. Whose solution to the problem do you think is best, Bill's or Tom's?
2. Should the union be asked for its views? Would this be a management attitude of exclusion, containment, acceptance, accommodation, or cooperation?
3. Should you accept the union's view as the right method? Then which attitude would management be accepting?
4. Are there other options to this problem?
5. Is there a compromise to this problem? Should there be a compromise?

Terms and Concepts

AFL-CIO the American Federation of Labor and the Congress of Industrial Organizations, a national federation of many craft and industrial unions.

arbitrator a neutral third party who hears the grievances of both the union and management. The decision announced by the arbitrator is binding on both the company and the union.

boycott an attempt by the union to get the public to refuse to buy products or to do business with the boycotted firm.

closed shop an agreement under which only union members are hired. Such an agreement is outlawed by the Taft-Hartley Act.

collective bargaining the process of negotiating a labor contract between union representatives and the employer. It is also an ongoing process of administering the existing contract. Contracts run from one to three years.

containment an attitude on the part of the management that tries to keep all relations with the union on a "strictly legal" basis, and the scope of collective bargaining is kept as narrow as possible.

cooperation an attitude on the part of the management that is opposite to exclusion. The company actually seeks the assistance of the union in production problems that are not usually the subject matter of collective bargaining.

dual loyalty employee loyalty felt for both union and management. Sometimes the employee must decide between the two just before a contract vote or other conflicting situations.

Fair Labor Standards Act a law that states the normal working week and requires time-and-a-half pay for all hours over 40 worked by an employee during a week. It also establishes the federal minimum wage.

grievance a complaint about an alleged violation of a collective bargaining agreement or the law as it applies to a worker.

injunction an order issued by a court that grants the employer the right to order employees to return to work or not to strike.

jurisdictional strikes strikes that force a company to recognize one union over another.

National Labor Relations Board a government body that investigates cases of unfair labor practices committed by employers or unions. Responsible for holding elections to determine whether or not a firm's employees want a union or not, and if so, which one.

Quality of Work Life a program developed by unions or management or both in an attempt to make the work more fulfilling and productive for the employees.

right-to-work laws state laws that outlaw union shops. In a union shop a nonunion worker may be hired, but must become a union member within 30 days or will be fired.

shop steward an employee of the company elected by the worker's peers to represent them in union activities. The principal activity is gripes and grievances. The shop steward will meet frequently with the shop supervisor to handle problems and to help prevent future ones.

shop supervisor the first-line supervisor; the lowest-level supervisor within a company.

union shop an agreement under which a nonunion worker may be hired by a company but must join the union within 30 days. May be outlawed in "right-to-work" states.

Notes

1. Peter F. Drucker, "Reinventing Unions," *Across the Board*, September 1989, pp. 12, 14.

2. Ibid., p. 14.

3. J. H. Foegen, "Labor Unions: Don't Count Them Out Yet!" *Academy of Management Executive*, February 1989, pp. 67–69.

4. Peter Waldman, "More Doctors and Lawyers Joining Unions to Fight Large Institutions," *The Wall Street Journal*, May 23, 1986, p. 21.

5. Raymond L. Hogler, *Public Sector Strikes: Employee Rights, Union Responsibilities, and Employer Prerogatives* (Alexandria, Va.: International Personnel Management Association, 1988), p. 3.

6. Jay S. Siegel, "A New Labor-Policy Consensus," *The Wall Street Journal*, September 4, 1985, p. 26.

7. Paul L. Blocklyn, "Labor Relations: Toward an Uncertain Future," *Personnel*, October 1988, pp. 18–24.

8. Julius G. Getman, Stephen B. Goldberg, and Jeanne B.

Herman, *Union Representation Elections: Law and Reality* (New York: Russell Sage Foundation, 1976).

9. Al Beck, "QWL and Unions in the 1990s," *Journal for Quality and Participation*, December 1988, pp. 20–24.

10. Eduardo Lachica, "Japanese Work Ethic and Unionism

Clash at Sharp of America's Memphis Factory," *The Wall Street Journal*, February 26, 1981, p. 25.

11. Clair Brown and Michael Reich, "When Does Union-Management Cooperation Work? A Look at NUMMI and GM-Van Nuys," *California Management Review*, Summer 1989, pp. 26–44.

Recommended Reading ———————————————

Beck, Al. "QWL and Unions in the 1990s." *Journal for Quality and Participation,* December 1988, pp. 20–24.

Bohlander, George W., and Harold C. White. "Building Bridges: Nonunion Employee Grievance Systems." *Personnel,* July 1988, pp. 62–66.

Drucker, Peter F. "Reinventing Unions." *Across the Board,* September 1989, pp. 12, 14.

Foegen, J. H. "Labor Unions: Don't Count Them Out Yet!" *Academy of Management Executive,* February 1989, pp. 67–69.

Freeman, Richard B., and James L. Medhoff. *What Do Unions Do?* New York: Basic Books, 1984.

Getman, Julius G., Stephen B. Goldberg, and Jeanne B. Herman. *Union Representation Elections: Law and Reality.* New York: Russell Sage Foundation, 1976.

Goldfield, Michael. *The Decline of Organized Labor in the United States.* Chicago: University of Chicago Press, 1987.

Heckscher, Charles C. *The New Unionism.* New York: Basic Books, 1988.

Hogler, Raymond L. *Public Sector Strikes: Employee Rights, Union Responsibilities, and Employer Prerogatives.* Alexandria, Va.: International Personnel Management Association, 1988.

——— *The Employment Relationship: Law and Policy.* New York, Ardsley House, 1989.

Jackson, Michael P. *Trade Unions,* 2nd ed. London: Longman, 1988.

Justice, Betty. *Unions, Workers, and the Law.* Washington, D.C.: Bureau of National Affairs, 1983.

Monthly Labor Review. Current issues.

Morgan, Reynolds. *Making America Poorer: The Cost of Labor Law.* Washington, D.C.: Cato Institute, 1987.

Parker, Mike, and Jane Slaughter. *Choosing Sides: Unions and the Team Concept.* Boston: South End Press, 1988.

Sloane, Arthur A., and Fred Witney. *Labor Relations,* 5th ed. Englewood Cliffs, N.J.: Prentice-Hall, 1985.

"Unions Have Future, If They Can Change," *USA Today,* August 30, 1985, p. 8A.

17

Intercultural Relations

After studying this chapter, you should be able to:

1. Discuss the importance of establishing good intercultural relations before embarking on an international business venture.
2. Describe the meaning of ethnocentrism, the pragmatic principle, cultural relativity, and reverse ethnocentrism as they relate to intercultural relations.
3. Discuss why intercultural relations is more important today in terms of imports and exports.
4. Discuss the importance of vertical and horizontal space in terms of cross-cultural business relationships.
5. Discover and discuss the hidden language of time difference between the United States and other cultures.
6. Recognize how the relationship of touch and friendship differs from one culture to another.
7. Discuss the language of agreements in relation to each of the three basic types of rules that usually apply to business contracts.
8. Discuss what is meant by high- and low-context cultures and give an example of each.

TO START YOU THINKING . . .

Again it is time to ask ourselves questions. This time it is about the field of intercultural relations—how do we feel about foreigners and those with cultural backgrounds that differ from ours? How can we relate and work effectively with people in foreign lands?

♦ Why do we feel uncomfortable with foreigners in this country—even if they speak English? Why do we feel overly comfortable with foreigners in their country when they speak English?

♦ Is time more important to Americans than it is to foreigners? Is space more important to us or to foreigners?

♦ Since we are one of the most technologically advanced societies in the world, should we teach other countries to handle sales contracts as we do?

♦ What nonverbal actions have you observed about a particular foreign group that is different from your group of friends?

♦ Our society has certain "rules" about touching people. When is it all right to touch people in public?

♦ What are some of the acceptable mores in our culture that are "off limits" elsewhere in the world?

♦ What impact will formation of the European Community in 1992 have on United States management and employee practices?

A LOOK AT A SHRINKING WORLD _____

This final chapter represents the culmination of the whole book—applied human relations not only in our microcosmic organizations but in the world at large. Our world continues to shrink, and the importance of intercultural relations increases. Are Americans going to have a "protective father," "ugly American," or "respected society image"? The answers to these questions depend on how we apply our human relations in foreign countries.

Cooperation with foreigners has now become imperative. Technology has made communication and travel not only easier, but essential for two reasons. First, technology has made it possible for nations to hold the threat of death over one another. Second, technology has made such demands on the world's material resources that scarcity of resources will result if the nations do not cooperate and share. Unfortunately the peoples of this world have a history of not being able to share and cooperate. The problems of war and scarcity directly involve the business world in intercultural relations.

Business becomes one of the first links between countries

First, many people look to business to satisfy their material needs. Business is often one of the first links established between peoples that have previously been separate and even antagonistic. Business was one of the first links between the United States and Japan in the nineteenth century; business was one of the first links between the United States and Japan after World War II. It is one of the first links between the United States and China, after years of antagonism. These business links have far-reaching effects on relations between American and other peoples by permitting the parties to offer each other material goods not available through other channels.

We must learn how to deal with other cultures

The fuel and precious metals crises that have plagued the United States in recent years have reminded people in this country that we have needs that can only be met by cooperation with other countries. For this reason, if business is to fulfill its job of providing material needs, it must learn how to deal with other cultures in a way that satisfies the material and social needs of both parties.

The fuel crisis of 1974 was an object lesson in many ways. It became apparent very quickly that people were dependent on fuel and that the world would have to recognize the Arab culture to deal with the suppliers of this needed commodity. Apartheid, the government-mandated economic and physical separation of races in South Africa, and our government's economic interest in South Africa have presented a similar cultural dilemma. We object to apartheid on moral grounds but, so far, acknowledge the sovereignty of South Africa's government to deal with the problem.

The international business manager must be prepared in a special way to overcome the obstacles to peaceful trade that are set up in the form of political, linguistic, social, religious, economic, and human differences. This book cannot provide the kind of intensive training that a business executive seeking to trade with foreign countries will need, but it can suggest the areas with which he or she must be concerned and in which he or she must be educated to be successful.

The real bottom line

In the discussion of cultural differences and intercultural relations that follow, the reader should not lose sight of the fact that we are all human—that beneath the external barriers to understanding, we are all people.

The Wave of New Americans

Over 600,000 immigrants into the United States every year

The arrival of more than 100,000 Cubans and thousands of Haitians in 1980 and 1981 coupled with the continuing admission of Asians brings the annual surge of immigrants into the United States to an average of over 600,000 a year. Asians and Latin Americans now represent 86 percent of the immigrants to this country; Europeans represent a little over 10 percent, down from the almost 40 percent in 1965.[1]

Since the 1970s, the United States has allowed more legal immigration than the rest of the world combined. The upshot is that by the 1990s, America will have a younger population than any of its major competitors—particularly Europe and Japan. Such rapid immigration will inject a continuous dose of dynamism into the economic system according to Joel Kotkin and Yoriko Kishimoto, authors of *The Third Century: America's Resurgence in the Asian Era.*[2]

OUR CULTURAL ATTITUDES TOWARD FOREIGNERS

Ethnocentrism

Events of this century have toppled our policy of isolationism, but they have not necessarily toppled our naïve ethnocentrism, that is, the feeling that our attitude is the only right attitude, the only way, the natural, normal way (Figure 17-1). Incidentally, this attitude is found all over the world, originating in the process of enculturation—learning cultural practices and values. As long as we are taught just one way, and know no other, we tend to accept that way as the right way.

We must become increasingly aware of our ethnocentric attitude. As we learn of the existence of other different ways, and become conscious of the impact of enculturation, we can recognize and understand the ethnocentric attitude in ourselves and others.

Ethnocentric attitudes usually surface in the form of patronization, superiority, disrespect, or stereotyping. "If a manager adopts a sincere attitude by patiently accepting a subordinate from another culture, that empathy will normally be received in a trusting, positive manner."[3]

Cultural relativity

Sometimes we develop a reaction against ethnocentrism—we discover the *principle of cultural relativity*, which holds that there are no absolute standards for judging customs, that a society's customs and ideas should be viewed in the context of that society's culture. A commonly drawn conclusion is that all cultures and cultural practices are equally valid, and therefore we should have tolerance and respect for other cultures and cultural practices, even if they happen to differ from ours.

Intercultural socialization involves becoming aware of another culture's habits, actions, and reasons behind behaviors. "Americans presume they are the safest, most sanitary culture in the world, but a large majority of the automobiles in the U.S. would not pass inspection in West Germany. The Japanese (and other cultures) think Americans are unhygienic for locating the toilet and bathing facility in the same area."[4]

The pragmatic principle

The *pragmatic principle* states: That which works is "better" than that which doesn't work. More accurately, when people are given a choice between two ideas, the one that works better to achieve certain valued ends is what most people end

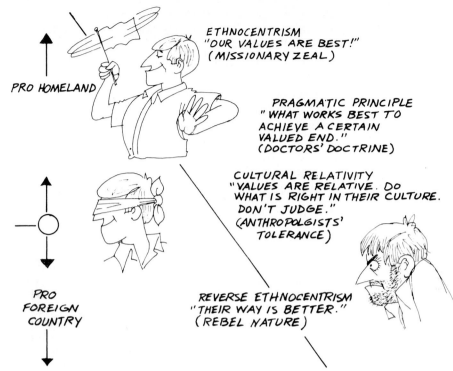

FIGURE 17-1 **Attitudes toward foreign cultures. Where do you stand on most of your attitudes to foreigners? What were your attitudes when you were in a foreign land?**

up choosing most of the time. "Such judging can be done in terms of the pragmatic *if . . . then*. If you value your children's life, and don't want them to die of smallpox, then vaccination is better than goat sacrifice."[5]

A stage sometimes occurs that we call *reverse ethnocentrism*; it holds that our ways, rather than being better than others, are actually *worse* than others.

THE UGLY AMERICAN OR THE PROTECTIVE FATHER IMAGE?

The image of the impolite, inarticulate, ill-mannered, patronizing "ugly American" barging through foreign countries like a barbarian at a tea party is legendary, and it contains some truth—and some falsity. But the image does tell us something about the problems associated with attempting to establish good business and human relations with the people of other countries. The Japanese are relatively successful in the Third World because of their cooperative efforts. The author has personally observed striking contrasts between brash, arrogant American executives and humble Japanese executives. And the Japanese got the business! If we are to continue to gain economically, we must modify our intolerance of others.

Growth of multinational corporations

The recent growth of multinational corporations, the majority of which are American owned, points up more than ever before the need to prepare the American business manager for dealing with foreign cultures and business practices. "Coca-Cola" is a word that has crept into almost every language spoken on earth, and "IBM" are initials that are understood in business conversation around the world.

The increasing interdependency fostered by the development of the multinational corporation and by the rapidly rising technological level of foreign economies has brought American business to realize that the image of the ugly American must be changed. How can they go about changing that image? How do they perceive other cultures? And how must they learn to interact with them to gain their cooperation?

To a degree, the United States enjoys a "respected society image." During the Armenian uprising against the USSR in early 1990, many signs were evident imploring, "America, help us." Others throughout the world also look to us for positive cultural, economic, and social examples.

Rose Knotts relates the following story:

> A man attending an international relations banquet was seated across from another man who possessed Asian physical characteristics. Wishing to advance international relations, he asked the Asian, "Likee foodee?" The man politely nodded his head. During the program, the Asian was introduced as an award-winning professor of economics at a prestigious university and was asked to make a few projections about world trade imbalances. After a brief discussion in perfect English, the Asian professor sat down, glanced across at his astonished neighbor, and asked, "Likee talkee?"

Knotts observes that "to avoid similar embarrassment situations, managers should not make assumptions from physical appearances, attributes, or superficial characteristics."[6] Good advice—domestically and internationally.

Subtle Differences

A gesture that is friendly in one culture may be interpreted as hostile in another; an innocent gesture can be an insult. These subtle *cues to action* complicate the problems of international business relations in a way that cannot be deduced from business experience in the United States.

Cultural differences go deep but are subtle

The business manager who is faced with such subtle cultural differences as gestures and tone of voice is participating in a frame of reference that is different from his or her own. Since communication always takes place within a frame of reference, international business managers must make sure that they can communicate in one that is not their own. The broad outlines of a culture are marked by the political and economic frames of reference, and these are the aspects with which business managers must familiarize themselves first.

The Political Frame of Reference

When we watch the stock market fluctuate with every major or minor crisis in our political lives, we are aware of the close relationship between politics and business. The political climate of our nation is determined largely by its economic well-being. Major decisions in business and industry affect political movements and vice versa. This is also true on an international scale.

Foreign political structure is more bureaucratic than in the United States

For example, with the fluctuating political détente with the communist world, American business managers have been establishing trade agreements with most of Eastern Europe and China. Now, Eastern Europe has disavowed communism as a sole political philosophy. One lesson that we have learned is that the political structure of those nations is far more bureaucratic than is the organizational structure of American business. Trade agreements must be passed through dozens of government bureaus and may take three times as long to complete as similar transactions among private firms.

Another politically related problem facing the multinational corporation has been the risk of nationalization, a problem that has been particularly acute in the Arab world and in South America. American oil companies were taken over or bought back by the Arab countries, and all American enterprises in Cuba except for the Guantanamo naval base were nationalized during the Cuban revolution. The multinational corporation frequently runs the risk of being considered imperialist by the countries in which it operates, and the international business manager must be alert to changes in the political atmosphere.

Tendencies toward nationalism have made it difficult for Americans to manage foreign workers, too. Some companies have sought to counter this problem by hiring managers from a third nation. This practice helps to reduce tensions arising from the presence of Americans in an emerging nation. The practice is augmented by hiring local managers from the country in which the corporation is operating, people who know the customs and the laws and who speak the language. Furthermore, when local nationals head up the branches of a multinational corporation, the company may be more immune from political expropriation or nationalization.

The Economic Frame of Reference

Have you ever heard of the SAMA (Saudi Arabian Monetary Agency)? It invests billions of dollars in oil exports for the Arab government every year. As a result, SAMA, the country's central bank, has loomed as one of the most powerful players in the international world of finance. If it chose to do so, SAMA could buy scores of large American corporations and millions of acres of prime U.S. real estate. Despite declining oil revenues and government spending, the European Management Foundation rates Saudi Arabia in first place for the lowest degree of "state interference in the economy." It ranks in second place, behind Japan, for its "outward orientation" or its attitudes toward foreign investment, trade, and aid.[7] Saudi Arabia, as the most conservative investor of the Arab world, has more than 85 percent of its holdings in U.S. investments, primarily in stocks and bonds and in fixed income instruments, such as U.S. Treasury notes.

One of the first things that American business managers traveling abroad may recognize is the difference between the standard of living to which they were accustomed and those that exist in the host country. These differences in economic capacity seriously affect the course of business dealings in foreign countries.

Our nation still enjoys a higher standard of living and productivity than most of Europe and the difference affects business relations there. Workers in Europe are accustomed to working longer hours for less money than are American workers. According to the International Labor Organization, the U.S. worker averages 35 hours a week, whereas French and West German workers work more than Japan's 40 hours a week. Japanese workers are also accustomed to taking less time off from work, working night shifts, and generally working at a more hectic pace.[8]

The underdeveloped nations, however, have little experience in highly developed technology and tend to have work forces that find it difficult to adapt to quality-control systems, tight schedules, and performance standards. The American managers of foreign workers who do not adjust their frame of reference frequently make the mistake of considering such workers lazy or sloppy. They are not; they simply have not experienced the development of technology and the consequent modifications of work behavior with which we are familiar here. Foreign workers may, in fact, feel—with some justification—that the American worker has been reduced to the level of a machine by efficiency and time-and-motion studies.

Countries with low income, but high inflation encourage spending now

The low level of economic development in many of the emerging nations is aggravated by high birth rates and even higher rates of inflation. Both factors discourage saving, which is one of the prerequisities for capital accumulation necessary for investment and expansion. The workers of such countries are essentially trapped by the cycle of low income, large families, and inflation that encourages spending rather than saving. Little money is available for local business and governments for training and relief of crisis situations, and foreign aid is usually inadequate for more than stopgap measures.

Training foreigners is one answer

The multinational corporation, however, has both the resources and the responsibility to help break the vicious circle in which such workers find themselves. In return for business profits realized from cheap labor and easy access to local natural resources, the multinational corporation can and should contribute massive training programs to help develop the human resources of its host nation. The ability of a nation to increase its productivity is directly proportional to the amount of training the work force receives. It is hoped, of course, that a trained work force will demand more money for its skills—but it will also bring in more profits for the corporation that trains and employs it.

Foreigners Are Bullish on America

Top-level foreign executives are accustomed to adjusting for double-digit inflation rates and are far more confident about the future of the U.S. economy than are their American counterparts. The executives, responding to a survey, agreed on three points.[9]

1. It makes no difference which political party is in power to direct the fight against inflation.
2. Americans seem somewhat naïve in their thinking about inflation.
3. There is a strong faith in the long-term strength of the U.S. economic and political system, including the American dollar.

Another more disturbing factor is that Americans do not seem to be as aware of their own country's political activities, let alone those of foreign countries.

Economic Tips for American Business Managers

A few economic factors should be mentioned when considering dealing with foreign countries.

1. During the decade of the 1980s, international relations continued to rest heavily on the shoulders of American business managers. The U.S. continues to run a trade deficit.

2. The United States exports only about 6½ percent of its gross national product, whereas several other nations export up to 50 percent of their gross national product, which makes them highly vulnerable to international crises.

3. A number of nations have less than a $600 annual income per capita. With income so low, a native employee is likely to spend his or her earnings as soon as it is received in an effort to subsist and to survive inflation. Inflation in some countries has been so high that saving seems impractical because the longer workers save their money, the less the money is worth.

The Cultural Frame of Reference

This chapter suggests that the many variables in the political and economic structures of both the developed and the underdeveloped nations are challenges that must be met by adaptation of American business methods to the foreign market. When "the American way" is transplanted to foreign soil, it must bend and twist, give and take, absorb and develop, according to local expectations and traditions.

A "third way"—compromise

In the process a third "way" to do business will be formed, one that borrows from both parties and aims at filling the needs of both. This process requires that the American business manager become versed not only in the economics and politics of a country but also in its culture and in its manners. We must steep ourselves in the language, religion, institutions, and personal relations of the host country. We must learn to understand and respect its way of life.

Language is a major barrier

Language is the foremost barrier to good international relations. Although English is still commonly accepted as the international business language, foreign business managers usually frown on the inability of Americans to converse in the native language. Mark Twain once observed, while traveling in France, that the French were astonishingly bright. "Even the smallest children speak fluent French," he remarked. Twain's satiric observation suggests that Americans feel that English should be the universal language, all others being secondary.

In fact Americans have found it difficult to acquire other languages easily, which has made people of other countries feel that Americans do not make an effort to communicate. It is perhaps understandable that Americans do not acquire languages readily because the United States is both homogeneous and isolated linguistically, and foreign languages are generally spoken only in small enclaves in the large cities and in some parts of the Southwest. Europeans, on the other hand, are in close and constant contact with people who speak other languages and sharply differentiated dialects. Switzerland, for example, has four national languages: French, Italian, German, and Romansch! In the future, American business managers will need to communicate in the language of their host countries, both by necessity and as a mark of goodwill.

"Cultural faux pas and foreign language translation errors are often the reason international business negotiations go sour."[10] Although considerable foreign business is conducted in English, and translators are readily available, managers wanting to do business in a foreign country should have a working knowledge of that country's language. Such knowledge will serve them well in dealing with social, political, legal, cultural, religious, and business systems in that market.

Semester-at-Sea

One aspect of international goodwill and a learning experience is the Institute for Shipboard Education's "Semester-at-Sea" program. Twice each year, approximately 600 college and university students, other adult passengers, faculty, and families go around the world on a ship, stopping for four to six days in ports of various countries. The formal classroom learning on the ship is supplemented by in-port field trips and other intercultural experiences. (See Figure 17-2.)

FIGURE 17-2 Young people are good intercultural communicators despite language barriers. Mona Beame/Photo Researchers.

Religion is reflected in one's culture

Protestant work ethic

In much of the world, formal religious observances have lost their power in the area of politics and trade, although religious and philosophical assumptions still play a role in determining the cultural interactions of peoples. The American work ethic, for example, is sometimes called the Protestant work ethic because it is associated with the simultaneous rise of capitalism and Protestantism in Europe. The idea at the time was that people who work hard are virtuous and are rewarded with material goods. We now view that idea as being rather harsh, but it remains an undercurrent in American business thought. Such an attitude can seriously undermine human relations with people from other countries who do not share in the Protestant tradition.

Express Your Opinion **Is the Protestant Work Ethic Dead?**	Are American work values changing? Do we still value the importance of work? Is work the central purpose of our lives? Is work an end in itself, or a means to an end? Do we put more emphasis on leisure time than on work? Or more than we formerly did? As we mature, do we put more emphasis on both "quality" work and leisure *time*? And on "quality" work and leisure output?

Most of us know little about the Islamic, Buddhist, or Hindu religions

Religious traditions are accompanied by various degrees of formal religious observance in most countries, including the officially antireligious communist nations. Therefore, religion may play a key role in determining how the business is transacted. This is particularly true in the Islamic nations of the Middle East and among the Buddhist and Hindu populations of the Far East and India.

Cultural change can be dramatic and severe in some countries. Americans knew of the upheaval in Iran, but less coverage was given during the same time to the civil war in Rhodesia, now known as Zimbabwe. The rebels overthrew white rule and established a black prime minister. The country boasts the second strongest economy in black Africa, after Nigeria. It is rich in gold, copper, nickel, coal, asbestos, and precious metals. Yet few Americans are even aware of where Zimbabwe is located.

The overthrow of governments in Eastern Europe and other parts of the world in the late 1980s and early 1990s are also examples of how dramatic and overdue changes can be.

Be Careful When Packaging in Red	In Africa, bold colors are fine—with the exception of red—the color of witchcraft. The wise old owl, a benign enough symbol in the United States, represents Satan to some Africans.

A LOOK AT TWO CULTURES

In Chapter 15 we studied the Hispanic Americans, African Americans, and Asian Americans. Here we examine two cultures that have had a distinct influence on our economy in the past: Japan and the Arab world. You should not be surprised if you have considerable contact with them in the years ahead.

Japan, Another Look at Theory Z

In 1981 William Ouchi created a stir in the management field by writing *Theory Z: How American Business Can Meet the Japanese Challenge.* Theory Z was discussed in Chapters 2 and 10, but additional ideas are presented here.

Much of Japan's success traces back to cultural past. It is a country that has few natural resources. It imports 100 percent of its aluminum, 98 percent of its iron ore, and 99 percent of its oil. Its only major natural resource is human ability. All sectors of the Japanese society are mutually compatible and supportive of each other. Illustrative of this point are the priorities of Japanese business, in the order of importance:

1. Mutual trust and benefits among employer, worker, and union.
2. The image of the company in the Japanese society.
3. Team effort over individual drive.
4. Maximization of profits.

The qualities admired in American managers—ambition, risk taking, independence—are handicaps in Japanese companies where group cooperation and strict decision-making hierarchy prevail.

Japanese managers generally choose a company for life, and they move up the corporate ladder very slowly and according to seniority rather than ability. Regimented in a multi-layered management structure, they are known for working long hours and piling up years of unused vacation time. Japanese companies have been described as Machiavellian bureaucracies where absolute loyalty is demanded and where one wrong political move can ruin a career— dumping a promising manager into what the Japanese call the madogiwa-zoka (the by-the-window tribe).[11]

Stable, dedicated work force

The major attribute of Japanese manufacturers is their stable and dedicated work force, which is committed totally to the success of the business and to customer satisfaction through quality production. Absenteeism, including vacation and sick time, runs very low relative to that in the United States. Work groups are an extension of the family and, in some cases, replace the family. People would rather come to work than to bring dishonor to their work group and to themselves.

Toyota adopts most ideas, GM accepts less than a third

All employees are totally dedicated to making the company successful. Employees are urged to submit suggestions for cost and quality improvements. Maximum awards of $500 are given, and it is common practice for the recipient to share his award with the other workers in his group. General Motors actively recruits productivity suggestions from employees and offers up to $10,000 for a proposal that is adopted. However, the company receives an average of less than one suggestion per employee a year and adopts less than one-third of the ideas. At Toyota's main plant near Nogoya, on the other hand, officials receive more than nine suggestions per worker per year and adopt the vast majority.[12]

Tatsuo Yoshida, managing director of the Industrial Bank of Japan, makes an analogy of hunting and rice farming to American and Japanese business. Japanese business culture is similar to rice farming while Western business culture is more like hunting. The Japanese culture evolved from rice farming where decisions are made from the bottom up, on-the-job training is valued, and everyone works together. Yoshida says "human relations must be pre-eminent in dealings with Japanese business. . . . Like it or not, you must play by the local rules of Japan. If you do not like the rice farming style of management, you will not be successful. In particular, we recommend that your top management visit Japan. Seeing is believing."[13]

A good company image attracts good workers

Because of the lifetime employment concept, great care is taken in the selection of a company for employment. And great care is taken among Japanese business concerns to maintain strong company image. If the image is poor, it will be difficult for the company to attract good young people.

There is another side to the human aspects of Japanese management. In *Japan in the Passing Lane*, Satoshi Kamata gives an insider's account of life in a Japanese auto factory.[14] Long hours, closely guarded conditions, safety and other problems are detailed in this diary of a worker beginning and ending a career in a Toyota plant. It still represents some of the conditions present in Japanese factories.

Group over individual need

Some Americans believe that at some point individuality must give ground to group needs. Perhaps it has taken a successful country to remind us that teamwork and basic cooperation are the prerequisites for a prosperous society.

A Marketing "No-No" in Japan

Golf balls were once sold in Japan in packages of four. The manufacturer's sales were well below anticipated volume. Research eventually targeted the packaging in fours as the principal factor in lagging sales. Four is the number of death in Japan.

Arabs Influence So Much, Yet We Know So Little _____

About 40 years ago, the Arab nations were isolated from the rest of the world, both politically and economically. Today, having realized the value of their oil to the economies of the Western world, the Arabs have opened trade routes that in turn have made them dependent upon the luxuries that can only be provided by the rich Western nations.

We should not consider every country in the Arab world (Morocco, Algeria, Tunisia, Libya, Sudan, Egypt, Jordan, Lebanon, Syria, Iraq, Iran, Saudia Arabia, Kuwait, Oman, and Yemen) as having similar attitudes, philosophies, or political ambitions, just as foreigners should not think all Americans are the same. Certainly the attitudes of Canadians, Americans, and Mexicans are not similar. However, all Middle Easterners are similar in one respect—they are all profoundly influenced by their religions. As proof of the strength of their religions, consider the fact that the faith of the Islamic culture is being used as the primary tool in the effort to unite Iran's 46 tribes and seven major groups.

In dealing with Middle Easterners, we must recognize the influence of their various religions. Because of a few basic religious beliefs, some Middle Easterners may view the world in a way totally alien to Americans. For example, the people of the Moslem world have strong feelings for the Koran, which says that society must come before the individual.

Pupils tend to dilate if you like something

One of the first things you will notice when dealing with an Arab is his concentration on your eyes. Arabs generally watch the pupils of your eyes, although not for long, to judge your responses to different topics. Eckhard Hess, of the University of Chicago, has discovered that the pupils are very sensitive indicators of how people respond to a situation. If you are interested in something, your pupils tend to dilate; if you encounter something you don't like, they tend to contract. The Arabs have known about the pupil responses for centuries, and many, like Yasser Arafat, wear dark glasses even indoors to protect their thoughts from others.

These people are reading the personal interaction on a second-to-second basis. By watching the pupils, they can respond rapidly to mood changes. That is one of the reasons why they use a closer conversation distance than we do. At about 5 feet—the normal distance between two Americans who are conducting business over a desk—we have a difficult time following eye movements. But if you use an Arab distance—less than 2 feet—you can watch the pupils of the eyes (Figure 17-3).

Express Your Opinion

You have now read about a few of the similarities and differences between the Japanese and Arabs. Certainly these few pages have only scratched the surface about the two cultures.

What other ideas and feelings can you add to these cultures, based on your own experiences and prejudices? Think of your attitudes that have been developed by watching television, reading the newspaper, or discussions you have had with friends. Write these thoughts down on paper. Which ones do you think are valid?

Based on your own personality, which culture would you prefer to deal with in terms of business negotiations? Considering the various cultures, who would you rather have as a coworker, a Japanese, a Saudi, a Persian, or an Egyptian? Would you like to go to Japan or to any of the Arab countries to learn more of their culture?

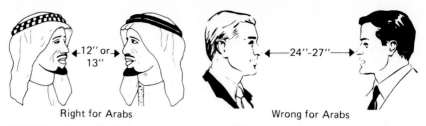

FIGURE 17-3 **Body language speaks. The normal conversational distance between Arabs is 12 to 14 inches, about half the distance that Americans use. When approached, don't flinch or laugh. Learn to like it. Don't expect long eye-to-eye contact; such a practice is not a comfortable one for them.** Source: Glen O'Brien, "How to Make It Nice with the Arabs," *Esquire,* August 1975, pp. 75–81.

THE CHANGING EUROPEAN COMMUNITY

The European Community is scheduled in 1992 (EC92) to permit the free movement of goods and services, as well as human and financial capital, within the 12-nation group that will make up the single economic market. Project 1992 would be a commonwealth of nations without economic borders. There would be 335 million consumers, people, capital, goods and services moving freely as they do within the United States. But the national and regional differences in Europe are very sharp. A common economic community is the kind of issue that can be very emotional, deeply ingrained and very difficult to reconcile.

One of the biggest concerns among the various European nations is job security. The emergence of the common market and the quest for job security by the often politically potent European labor unions is apt to lead to development of international labor standards that all corporations will be forced to meet even if they only operate in the United States.[15]

Perhaps the EC92 changes will not have a great direct impact on human relations in the United States. But indirectly, we are influenced in our style of international management and ultimately in our domestic relationships as well. EC92 will open many markets to U.S. business, and how we respond interpersonally to these opportunities will determine how successful we are.

There are negative views of EC92. Victor Kiam, owner of the New England Patriots and CEO of Remington Products, notes that he does not buy the idea that the European Community will impact the U.S. so negatively because of the many diverse characteristics of the countries.[16]

Another authority believes that 1992 will not automatically mean larger markets because wealthy demand will not be created overnight nor will the birth rate increase dramatically.[17] So, while there is reason for strong optimism regarding the European Community, there is some suggestion that it has been oversold and that demands for job security and differences among the countries may jeopardize its success.

HIDDEN LANGUAGES

Time, space, agreement, touch, and friendship

Language and religion are only two of the more obvious frames of reference in which business takes place. But basic understanding of them allows American business managers to negotiate on a roughly equal footing with their foreign associates and helps American managers of foreign workers to motivate and understand employees. There are many other languages in which people communicate, however, and knowledge of these may be more difficult to acquire. These are the unspoken, hidden languages of time, space, familiarity, agreements, touching, and friendship. These languages vary from culture to culture, are often incredibly complex, and are usually as important as the spoken language in establishing good communication and human relations abroad.

The Language of Time

Time is more important to Americans than any other cultural group

The unspoken language of time appears informal, but the rules governing its interpretation are surprisingly ironclad. In the United States a delay in answering a communication can mean to the person waiting that the decision is of low priority to the other person. In Ethiopia, the time required for a decision is directly proportional to its importance: the more money involved, the longer it will take to arrive at a decision. In the Arab East, the time that is required to accomplish something depends on the relationship between the two parties involved.

Deadlines can appear rude and pushy to Arabs

In the Arab world, close relatives take absolute priority; nonrelatives are kept waiting. Foreigners may be kept waiting for a long time. In the Middle East, assigning a deadline is a cultural trap, because a deadline in this part of the world is viewed as rude, pushy, and demanding.

In certain countries of the Orient—certainly not Japan—a delay of years does not mean that the people have lost interest in the project; only the urgency of time is not as important to them as it is to Americans. "Americans have one terrible weakness; if they are made to wait long enough they will agree to anything," said one Oriental businessman. The delays in arriving at agreements in the Vietnam Peace Treaty seem to show our sense of urgency versus the Orientals' patience. Indians and Buddhists think of time as circular whereas Americans and Europeans think of time as linear. We are always in a hurry to "get *it* over with."

February 1981 52 hostages were released after 14 months

Some will remember February 1981, the time that ended the 14 months Iran held 52 U.S. hostages, and the summer of 1985 when airline and other hostages in Lebanon were finally released. Maybe we learned patience, and the importance of understanding other cultures, their friends and enemies.

Other ethnic groups are not so fortunate. Asian Americans face a difficult task in ascending the corporate ladder. Because many of their cultural values don't always mesh with those of Americans, Asians are frequently viewed as passive and less social—qualities that are anathema to potential managers.[18]

Asian Americans comprise 8 percent of all professionals and technicians in the work force but only 1.3 percent of managers and officials. The ideas of networking and "playing politics" are not strong Asian values.[19] Networking and "taking time" are important factors to be learned.

From Microseconds to Antiquity

Foreigners feel we are rushing to our graves

There is no country in the world in which time is more important than in the United States. Telegrams were not fast enough for businessmen, so telephones became the most common form of communication. The automated society operates in microseconds (one-millionth of a second) and *nanoseconds* (one-billionth of a second). Such sophistication in time, in the words of one Chilean, is "rushing us to our graves."

A significant fact is that many cultures have had little opportunity to accept modern technology and its relationship to time, as we know it in the United States. People of agrarian cultures usually have a low tolerance for perfection, time, schedules, and performance standards, and they demonstrate little employee initiative. The acceptance of responsibility for work done by others rather than by themselves is a concept that some have not encountered before. The American demand for punctuality, regularity, and discipline on the job would find many foreigners quitting their jobs in a U.S. plant before they could become accustomed to the culture changes.

We have 200 years of history; the Orient has many centuries

Our country has just over 200 years of history, Europe has many hundred years of written history, and the Orient has thousands of years of recorded history. In the language of time, most cultures other than ours may seem to be tied to antiquity and the time lag that we may associate with it. The Indians of South Asia have an elastic view of time; indefiniteness does not mean they are evasive—just deliberate. The elasticity of time is the length of time it takes to accomplish a task. The less important time is and the longer it takes to accomplish the task, the greater the elasticity of time. Americans believe in a short elasticity of time where time is important. We must learn that time is not something fixed in nature but that it can be experienced in many different ways.

Americans have a short elasticity of time

The Language of Space

Americans always want more space

In everyday life, the manipulation and use of space have many meanings that vary considerably among different cultures. For instance, in the American business office, space is allocated according to status. Lower-echelon workers may have a small space in the middle of a crowded room shared with other workers. The top executive usually has a private office. The amount of space we receive is an indication of status.

Japanese rooms often seem uncluttered to Westerners, because they tend to place objects in the center of the room, whereas we tend to place objects around the edges and against the walls. The Japanese sense of privacy can be assured by the thinnest of paper screens, which do not give us any sense at all of being alone. Germans may require thick concrete walls that screen out the noise from other people's living space to feel private. If American business managers do not understand cultural differences in the use of space, they may feel very uncomfortable or may make their hosts very uncomfortable.

The office of an Arab businessman may seem small, crowded, and confused to an American; such a strange environment may cause the American to wonder if he can trust a man with a small, dirty office with a million-dollar contract.

U.S. status requires more space and less control

Supervision and Space. In the United States, India, and some other countries, tradition calls for the president or chairman of the board to have the largest office in the company. Each person's office space is determined by his or her status. The operations manager may have an area fenced in by a 4-foot barrier. If employees are deemed more important, they are given more space and their offices are walled in completely. A foreigner may wonder how managers can supervise when they are unable to see their subordinates. The ultimate, of course, is to move executives up to another floor, so they will not see their subordinates for days. The French are much more likely to lay out space as a network of connecting points of influence, activity, or interest. The French supervisor is usually found in the middle of his subordinates where he can control them. What Americans see as crowded, most foreigners would see as spacious.

Vertical Space.

In the United States the executive suites are on the top floor and the relative ranks of vice presidents are placed along "executive row." The top floor in Japan is frequently seen as the place for the average worker. Why should the executive spend his time going to the top floor? The privilege of class is for the first and second floors. Likewise, the top floor in a Japanese department store is not reserved for furniture, but the "bargain roof."

The hilltop home or the estate high on the mountain holds more prestige to Americans than the home down in the "flatlands." The concept of looking down on people is a part of our culture. Tall people have a psychological advantage in the United States because of this attitude. Rio de Janeiro, by contrast, is a city that represents an opposite attitude. The higher one lives up Sugarloaf Mountain, the poorer one is. The poverty stricken have the view, but the aristocrats have the conveniences of living in the heart of the city.

Familiarity Breeds Use in the United States.

In the United States, because of our tendency to zone our activities, nearness carries rights of ownership. As children, we view streets and vacant lots as community property, and children's games are frequently played there. People park their cars in front of our homes and few of us are concerned.

By contrast, in England nearness entitles you to nothing. You almost have to make an appointment for your child to play with the child next door. Frowns or verbal reprimands are given to those who park in front of a home without permission. The children of my late coauthor, to the dismay of some British neighbors, taught the local children the wonderful world of play outside their fenced yards, the world of "hop scotch" on the sidewalk, and doing "wheelies" on their bikes in the streets.

Our "Inner Circle" or Social Space.

Sociologists have also found that different cultures keep different social distances—the distances between people that correspond to the degree of comfort they feel in each other's presence. The distance we keep between ourselves and others is known as our "inner circle" or our personal space. We allow people to step into our space only if we want them. We frequently step backward to prevent someone else from coming too close to us and invading our social space. Americans normally keep a distance of about 5 to 8 feet during business conversations, but other cultures are more inclined to reduce the distance, sometimes to 3 or 4 inches.

Space speaks. When business managers arrive in a foreign country, they must try to be sensitive to what space tells them. Some useful advice to a newcomer: try to be aware of where people stand in relation to you and don't back up. This, in itself, can greatly enhance people's attitudes toward you.

The Language of Touch

We also communicate by the frequency and manner in which we touch each other, customs that differ radically from culture to culture. American men rarely go beyond a formal handshake. If they happen to be old friends, they may slap each other on the back. Infractions of these rules are fraught with tension: if someone refuses to shake a hand that is offered, he or she implies a serious insult or rejection. The man who is an indiscriminate back-slapper is usually viewed with either distaste or some fear, since the act implies intimacy without consent.

The taboos of touching in the American culture are very strict. American men avoid excessive touching, as it is seen as an expression of emotionalism or homosexuality. It is all right for an athlete to pat a fellow teammate on the back on the basketball court or the football field, but his behavior may not be acceptable elsewhere. An American father may no longer put his arm around his son after he reaches a certain age, yet in foreign cultures the holding of hands by members of the same sex is not uncommon.

In the United States when two men ride a motorcycle together, the rider will sit a few inches away from the driver and put his hands anywhere but around the waist of the driver. "The right masculine image seems more important than safety," said an Italian cycle driver of our culture. The various methods of tactile contact in countries along the Mediterranean Sea may seem too intimate or rude to us, but they are accepted ways of communicating there.

The relationships between men and women in other cultures are also sensitive to touching. The ease with which American women enter into touch may be interpreted as promiscuous by some cultures; in yet other cultures, American women may be seen as cold and unfriendly. The women of many Islamic and Hindu countries are only recently emerging from a tradition of purdah, the custom that a woman must be veiled in the presence of men. An involuntary or innocent infraction of social rules may result in serious consequences for both her and for the man involved. Anything in the realm of sexuality is sensitive and even dangerous for all cultures, including our own.

The Language of Context

How are Arabs different from North Americans? The basic difference is that Arabs are highly "contexted." They examine the entire circumstance in which events are happening to understand them. Everyone is aware that there is a relationship between the context of a statement and its meaning. If a man says "I love you" to a woman on the first date, she knows it doesn't mean the same thing that it might a year later.

The cultures of the world can be placed on a continuum, based on the amount of communication contained in the nonverbal context compared with the amount in the verbal message. A legal contract, for instance, is supposed to be context free—all the meaning is in the words of the contract. Some cultures, like our own, are low context; they tend to put more emphasis on the verbal message and less on the context. In a low-context culture you get down to business very quickly. The high-context culture requires considerably more time, simply because the people have developed a need to know more about you before a relationship can develop. You might say that they simply don't know how to handle a low-context relationship with other people.

In India, for example, merchants and others are more comfortable in doing business with you if they get to know you personally. In the Middle East, if you aren't willing to take time to sit down and have coffee or tea with people, you will have a problem. You must learn to wait and not be too eager to talk business. You can ask about the family or ask "How are you feeling?" But avoid too many personal questions about wives, because people are apt to get suspicious. Learn to make what we call chitchat. If you don't, you can't go to the next step.

In the United States, policy may have been to pay bribes so that people could do business with us. In this sense, we are naïve; we often think that price is

The custom of "nontouching" is common in the United States

Men touch each other less than women

Low context: you start business quickly

High context takes longer; learn to chit chat

Learn high context and you will pay less

everything and that every person can be bought. Clearly, there are reciprocal exceptions: some "camel jockies" in Egypt and similar "businesspeople" in other countries drive hard, profitable bargains for themselves. But for many people, profit isn't as important as a human relationship.

Once you are in a country and you have personal ties, it is possible to find a sort of cultural advisor, a friend who knows the place. For instance, Americans paid two or three times as much rent as they should have in Syria.

Many Americans hate to be coached

The trouble with high-context cultures is it's hard to get an American to take each step seriously and to be coached. Most Americans are too eager to buy and too reluctant to take coaching. Only actors and athletes are accustomed to being coached. Doctors, industrialists, and lawyers are difficult to coach. Even when you try to teach them to ski or fly an airplane, a lot of instructors tell me, they don't take directions very well.

In terms of high and low context, the United States is toward the middle of the scale. The low-context Swiss around Zurich don't even know their neighbors. The Swiss value their privacy so much that they may not develop a large circle of friends. The privacy of Swiss bank accounts is legendary. Look at Figure 17-4. Where would you place other cultures on the context line of continuum?

The Language of Friendship

Many Americans have offended others by refusing, or offering to pay for, items tendered as tokens of friendship. These types of encounters abroad have made some foreigners feel that Americans approach all human relations with the cynical and cold feeling that "everything has a price." The American abroad should be careful to distinguish between friendship and business relations and to find out what gestures are significant in matters of friendship and hospitality. The offering of food, for example, is a universal gesture of friendship—to protest that one is on a diet may be interpreted as an unwillingness to "break bread together," a rejection of friendships and good relations.

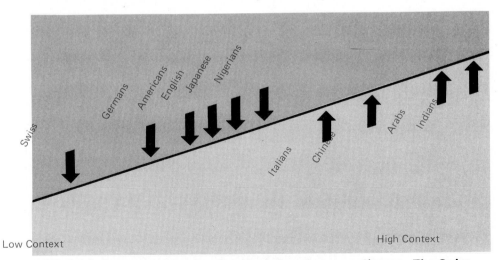

FIGURE 17-4 Cultural language of context placed on a continuum. The Swiss are basically low context and wish to "get down to business quickly." The Indians are high context; they want to get to know you, trust you, before they do business.

The philosophy expressed in the foregoing paragraph is one of giving freely of one's self and the good feeling that one has about one's own well-being after giving. Most often our culture manifests itself in the belief of reciprocity. When we give something or perform a favor, we expect one in return—at sometime in the future. There is usually a reciprocal relationship in other cultures, but it is not always done on a quid pro quo basis.

Tips for the World Business Traveler	**Women**	1. Women may be liberated in the United States, but remember that women have come further in the United States than in other countries. If a woman is out on the street unaccompanied by a man in certain areas of some countries *including the United States,* she is liable to be hassled.
	Unions	2. Unions in many developed countries are stronger, not from the national level but from the "grass-roots" level. National union leaders cannot encourage, predict, or direct their membership as well as they can here in the States. In England shop stewards and managers alike frequently spend half their day on labor disputes.
	Loyalties Change	3. People of the Third World find that their loyalties must change frequently, because of changes in government leaders. This often confuses U.S. business managers, because Americans feel that they understand the attitude of foreign contacts—when suddenly their attitudes change.
	Work Hours Vary	4. Remember, many work days begin around 8:00 A.M. Lunch and siesta are anywhere from 2:00 P.M. to 4:00 P.M. or 5:00 P.M. In the hot spots, people may not go back to work. Elsewhere, business goes on into the evening, and the streets are hopping till around ten o'clock, when dinner is served.
	U.S. Television	5. It must be remembered that all the world knows more about Americans than we do of any country. That is because of all the U.S. television shows, plus thousands of movies—not to mention such magazines as *Playboy* on every European newsstand—that are distributed abroad. Even the stock exchange in London displays the largest sign of all—the current U.S. dollar–British pound exchange rate. U.S. culture and influence is felt everywhere throughout the world.
	Pick an Interpreter	6. You need an interpreter. Don't pick the first bilingual person you meet in your foreign country. If you feel you need help in making a contact, there are hundreds for hire in the States. Get to know your interpreter before you need to rely on him or her. If you want to play it safe, consult the international department of a multinational bank.

The Language of Agreements

For any society to produce on a highly commercial level, a complex set of rules must be developed and widely accepted on which agreements can be reached. The language of agreements may be absolute or flexible, sophisticated or informal; in any event it must be understood clearly by both parties to the agreement.

Differences in cultural approaches to agreements can cause serious difficulties in business.

Usually, agreements are based on one or a combination of three types:

1. Rules that are spelled out technically as demonstrated by law or regulation.
2. Moral practices agreed on mutually and taught as a set of principles.
3. Information customs to which everyone conforms without being able to state the exact reason or rule.

Naturally, informal, unstated rules can cause a lot of trouble for an uninformed American.

Americans are particularly unfamiliar with the practice and unspoken rules of bargaining, since in our own economy, goods and services do in fact "have their price." In other economies, prices may be flexible—goods may have to be sold rapidly because there is no place to store them at the end of the market day, and therefore the price may come down. Americans confronted with a confusion of different prices for the same product have to deal with the situation of the moment, which may include a number of social variables. If they offer too low a price, the seller may be insulted. If the seller suggests an exorbitant price, the Americans must realize that the seller is probably willing to bargain downward.

A woman may have no legal right in a foreign country

In the Arab world, a man's word is considered as binding as his legal signature (a woman may not have certain legal rights in business). To require a Moslem to sign a formal contract runs the risk of violating his sense of honor. However, since 1974 many Arabs have adopted American customs regarding contracts.

A verbal contract may be more binding than a written contract

On the other hand, to a Greek, a contract may only represent a sort of way station along the route of negotiations to be modified periodically until the work is completed. If an American complains about such a procedure, the Greek may exclaim, "Take me to court." But there is no court to settle international business disputes, and mutual satisfaction is reached only through mutual respect and understanding of the various meanings of the agreement.

Americans are obsessed with the legal system. Maybe that is a function of high-context culture. Eugene Mendonsa, senior vice president of the International and Domestic Negotiating Institute, cites seven mistakes that professionals should try to avoid when negotiating contracts overseas:

1. Setting targets too high
2. Being too schedule-oriented and moving too quickly away from the opening position
3. Not taking the personal approach
4. Making *faux pas* or cultural gaffes
5. Being too open, too forthright, making disclosures
6. Making the first concession
7. Being ethnocentric and getting angry.[20]

Some written contracts have no value

Americans must not only understand that the laws governing trade in the United States no longer apply on the world market but that the laws of the host country may not protect them. The only security is in structuring a business deal so that guarantees of fulfillment are intrinsic and the terms of the agreement are based firmly on informal as well as formal rules. The best guarantee, of course, is good human relations, the building up of a relationship in which both parties willingly cooperate to reveal common goals of exchange.

Summary

Technology has made the world smaller by introducing rapid communication, travel, machines that boost productivity and hence allow for greater productivity, weapons that have enormous range and power, and the realization that the natural resources of the world have limits. We are now aware that, for our survival in matters of fuel and other resources, we must become a more outgoing nation.

The first unofficial ambassadors to other countries are frequently business managers, and the multinational corporation is becoming so common on the international market that it bears the brunt of establishing good intercultural relations abroad. American business managers must learn how to relate successfully to people from other cultures to fulfill the role of business in our economy—to procure for the United States the things it needs.

Our attitudes toward foreigners can vary from ethnocentrism to reverse ethnocentrism. Ethnocentricity is the view that our way of doing things is the only correct way. Another attitude is that of cultural relativity, which holds that there are no absolute standards for judging customs, that a society's customs should be viewed in the context of that society's culture. Another attitude is that of the pragmatic principle, which means that the idea that works best is the one that should be used if it achieves the necessary valued end. We find that Americans have varying attitudes about foreigners and how to do business with them.

Theory Z seems to tell us that Japanese culture reflects a great deal of mutual trust between the employee and employer. The company works hard at developing a strong company image, so as to attract the best workers for lifelong employment. Where Americans believe in strong individualism, the Japanese believe in group effort.

The Arab world is composed of countries that are principally of the Moslem faith. Arabs also have a strong belief in the power of society over the individual; therefore, individual status improvement is very difficult, if not impossible. Authority is not to be questioned, be it religious or governmental. Arabs can be strongly goal oriented and use a closer "inner circle" than Americans.

The European Community, an economic alliance to be formed in 1992, provides at once challenges and opportunities for U.S. human relationships. Job security and powerful European labor unions may dictate the relative success of the European economic community in world markets.

The language of time is an unspoken, but closely held, concept in many cultures. Time is very important to Americans, yet to be late in other countries not only is customary but to be expected. To establish deadlines can be rude and pushy for some Latins and Arabs. In the language of space, Americans almost always want the use of more space than foreigners, whether it is in terms of conversational space, office space, or vertical space. The phrase "familiarity breeds use" in the United States means that Americans tend to use or claim what they are near. The more you use a public item, the more you feel it is yours.

In the language of touch, touching is considered more taboo by Americans than by almost any other culture. Men touch each other less than women do in the United States except in sports. The language of context established the Swiss as low context, because they like to get down to business quickly and respect the privacy of others. The Indians by contrast are a high-context culture. They like to get to know someone well before negotiating a business deal. People in Latin America also exhibit high-context relationships. U.S. citizens tend to be more low context; for example the written contract is more important than verbal agreements or promises.

All of these cultural differences, however, can be worked out if we keep in mind the fundamental concepts of human dignity, empathy, and individual differences, among others. Keep in mind also the basic common bond of humanity, understand that one's own values are not universal, but local to one's own culture, and make a serious effort to respect and understand cultural differences.

Case Study 34

International Bribery

Henry Cordero works for Maytax Industries, a large multinational corporation with production and research facilities in several foreign countries. Henry is in charge of one of the facilities in a South American country.

Henry was recently informed by a member of the country's government that, if Maytax wished to remain operating in the country, it was strongly suggested that the corporation begin contributing to that country's medical research association. Somewhat shocked, Henry asked if the order was official. He was told by the individual that, although the order did not come officially from the government, it could easily be enforced.

Well aware that bribery payments were being demanded, Henry returned to the corporation's home office to discuss the matter with the corporation's vice president, Mr. Manoushek. After filling in Mr. Manoushek on the details of the demand, Henry was asked what should be done concerning the matter.

"It's my opinion," stated Henry, "that we shouldn't become involved in making bribery payments. Aside from the fact that such payments are against our moral ethics and our system of free enterprise, the American public and our government take a pretty dim view of such matters."

"I agree with you there, Henry," stated Mr. Charles Manoushek, "but I don't think you understand the realities of the problem. In countries such as the one we're dealing with, bribery has been an accepted custom for years and years. Although our country is against this type of thing, many countries abroad are not. We are a corporation that does the majority of our business abroad and we must deal with these countries on their own terms. If we don't, some other company will."

"But if we begin paying these bribery payments everytime someone suggests it, where will the demands end?" retorted Henry. "On the other hand, when we begin offering these payments on our own initiative, like Lockheed, Exxon, Gulf or ITT, and the public finds out, we will be no better off for it. I know company images suffer when the American public finds out about their affairs. If it was my choice, I'd back out of the country if necessary."

"Our duty, Henry, is to our shareholders first, and that duty is protecting our investments abroad. If we must contribute to a country's medical research association to protect our investment, then that is what we must do."

1. Whose side do you favor—Henry Cordero's or Charles Manoushek's?

2. Give reasons for your stand.

3. Is giving small gifts acceptable? When does it stop being a gift and become a bribery payment? At what point do you make the distinction? Is there a dollar value?

4. Should there be more government agencies to audit overseas operations? Can it legally be done?

5. If codes should be established, who will say what is ethical?

6. Companies have stated that there will be no "unusual payments." What is considered unusual?

Case Study 35

A Problem of Cultural Communication

Harold Underhill walked into the office of the Latin American country's commercial attaché for help. Harold has arrived two weeks earlier from the United States for the purpose of securing a several-million-dollar production order. Harold is the sales manager of a large corporation that produces communications systems.

When Harold first arrived in the country he had been under the impression that his business would take no more than a few days, and then he could take a few days vacationing before returning within his allotted seven-day period.

Upon arriving in the country Harold immediately contacted the minister of communications, whom he needed to have sign the production order. He was then instructed that Minister Muñoz would see him that afternoon. When Harold arrived he was forced to wait in the outer office for a considerable amount of time and then only to be greeted briefly, but politely, by the minister before being ushered out without any business being discussed. Harold was then informed that the minister would see him next Wednesday for lunch. Although upset about the delay Harold accepted the invitation.

When Harold and Señor Muñoz did meet the following week for lunch, Harold soon realized that the minister had no intentions of talking business. Somewhat in a panic he tried pressing the fact that he needed the order signed. As a result of this the minister politely cut short the business conversation and invited Harold to meet him again in a few days.

As a result of these events Harold asked the commercial attaché for his advice. "You must understand," stated the attaché, "that business relations are not the same here as they are in the United States. Things are not always done overnight here. Latin Americans feel a need to spend more time completing business transactions and to get to know who they are doing business with. You should not rush things—let them take the initiative. When you are in their country you must follows their rules of behavior."

When Harold met again with the minister of communications they took a walk in a memorial park near the minister's office. As Señor Muñoz commented on the beauties of the park Harold failed to recognize the statue of Simon

Bolivar, and then he compounded his error by stating that he had never heard of him. Insulted, the minister decided that the pushy, rude American was not the person with whom he wanted to do business and informed both Harold and his employer that he didn't wish to continue negotiations.

1. Identify the American's problem.
2. Name several errors in Underhill's approach.
3. How could Underhill's company have prepared him better for the business transaction?

Terms and Concepts

apartheid the government-mandated economic and physical separation of races in South Africa.

cultural relativity the idea that there are no absolute standards for judging customs and that society's customs and ideas should be viewed in the context of the society's culture.

elasticity of time the length of time it takes to accomplish a task. Americans believe in a short elasticity of time. Time is important.

ethnocentrism the feeling that our attitude is the only right attitude, the natural, normal way of doing things.

European Community a single economic market to be formed in 1992 to permit the free movement of goods and services, as well as human and financial capital, within a 12-nation group.

inner circle the distance we keep between others and ourselves; known as our personal space.

intercultural socialization becoming aware of another culture's habits, actions, and reasons behind behaviors.

isolationism the view that a person or a country can be self-sufficient and not dependent on others or other countries.

multinational companies companies that operate in more than one country. For example, Shell Oil is a Dutch company that operates in the United States and whose shares are owned by Americans.

nationalization the taking over of private companies, often under foreign control, by the host country. The company operations become under government control.

pragmatic principle the belief that the principle that works best is the one that should be used. The pattern of life that should be used is the one that works best to meet the valued ends.

Notes

1. *The World Almanac and Book of Facts, 1990* (New York: World Almanac, Scripps Howard, 1990), p. 560.
2. Joel Kotkin and Yoriko Kishimoto quoted in David M. Smick, "A Guide to the Pacific Rim Phenomenon," *The Wall Street Journal*, December 5, 1988, p. A12.
3. Rose Knotts, "Cross-Cultural Management: Transformations and Adaptations," *Business Horizons*, January–February 1989, pp. 32–33.
4. Ibid., p. 33.
5. Henry H. Bagish, "Confessions of a Former Cultural Relativist," Second Annual Faculty Lecture, Santa Barbara City College, Santa Barbara, California, 1981.
6. Knotts, "Cross-cultural Management," p. 32.
7. Norman Peagam, "Still a Land of Opportunity/The Accent Is on Saudization," *Euromoney*, Special Sponsored Supplement, September 1985, pp. 27–32.
8. Leslie Helm and Maralyn Edid, "Life on the Line: Two Auto Workers Who Are Worlds Apart," *Business Week*, September 30, 1985, pp. 76–78.
9. "Keeping Informed," *Management Review*, December 1980, p. 5.
10. Robert J. Kuhne, "Habla Usted Espanol?" *Business & Economic Review*, April–June 1986, p. 9.
11. Leah Nathans, "A Matter of Control," *Business Month*, September 1988, p. 46.
12. Christopher Byron, "How Japan Does It—And Can We Do It Too?" *Reader's Digest*, August 1981, p. 63.
13. Henry Eason, "In Japan, Make Haste Slowly," *Nation's Business*, May 1986, p. 48.
14. Satoshi Kamata, *Japan in the Passing Lane: An Insider's Account of Life in a Japanese Auto Factory* (New York: Pantheon, 1982), pp. 95–113.
15. Frank Swoboda, "Labor Rules Will Change During '90s," *The Fort Collins Coloradoan*, June 5, 1989, p. D6.

16. Victor Kiam, "Fortress Europe 1992? Don't Hold Your Breath," *The Wall Street Journal,* September 11, 1989, p. A22.

17. Philip Revzin, "Euro-Miracle or Euro-Fantasy?" *The Wall Street Journal Reports,* Special Supplement on World Business, September 22, 1989, p. R34.

18. Winifred Yu, "Asian-Americans Charge Prejudice Slows Climb to Management Ranks," *The Wall Street Journal,* September 11, 1985, p. 37.

19. Ibid.

20. Eugene L. Mendonsa, " 'Seven Deadly Sins' of Purchasing Overseas," *Purchasing World,* March 1987, pp. 90–91.

Recommended Reading

Butler, Michael. *Europe: More than a Continent.* London: Heinemann, 1986.

Ferguson, Henry. *Tomorrow's Global Executive.* Homewood, Ill.: Dow Jones-Irwin, 1988.

Goldenberg, Susan. *Hands Across the Ocean: Managing Joint Ventures with a Spotlight on China and Japan.* Boston: Harvard Business School Press, 1988.

Hall, Edward T. *The Hidden Dimension.* Garden City, N.Y.: Doubleday, 1969.

———. *Beyond Culture.* Garden City, N.Y.: Doubleday, 1977.

———. *The Silent Language.* Garden City, N.Y.: Doubleday, 1973; also Greenwood Press, Westport, Conn., 1980.

———, **and Mildred Hall.** *Hidden Differences: Doing Business with Japanese.* Garden City, N.Y. Anchor Press/Doubleday, 1987.

Harris, Philip R., and Robert T. Moran. *Managing Cultural Differences: High-Performance Strategies for Today's Global Manager,* 2nd ed. Houston: Gulf, 1987.

Institute for Shipboard Education. *Semester at Sea.* Pittsburgh: Institute for Shipboard Education, 1984.

Kotkin, Joel, and Yoriko Kishimoto. *The Third Century: America's Resurgence in the Asian Era.* New York: Crown, 1988.

Knotts, Rose. "Cross-cultural Management: Transformations and Adaptations." *Business Horizons,* January–February 1989, pp. 29–33.

Kuhne, Robert J. "Habla Usted Espanol?" *Business & Economic Review,* April–June 1986, pp. 9–11.

Lodge, Juliet (ed.). *The European Community and the Challenge of the Future.* New York: St. Martin's Press, 1989.

Morrison, Catherine. *1992: Leading Issues for European Companies,* Research Report No. 921. New York: The Conference Board, 1989.

Ricks, David A. *Big Business Blunders: Mistakes in Multinational Marketing.* Homewood, Ill.: Dow Jones-Irwin, 1983.

Terpstra, Vern, and David Kenneth. *The Cultural Environment of International Business,* 2nd ed. Cincinnati: South-Western Publishing, 1985.

Thompson, Roger. "EC92," *Nation's Business,* June 1989, pp. 18–26.

Walter, Ingo (ed.) *Handbook of International Management.* New York: John Wiley, 1988.

"World Business," *The Wall Street Journal Reports,* September 22, 1989, pp. R1–R36.

INDEX ————————————————————————

A

Ability, 68, 284, 288, 296
Absenteeism, 90, 93
Achievement, 22, 60, 68, 72, 211
Action orientation, 13, 312, 315, 326–27
Adult ego state, 259–60
Affiliation motive, 60
Affirmative Action programs, 373–74, 376, 378
AFL-CIO, 382, 403
Afro-Americans, 360–61
Age:
  and creativity, 303
  and job satisfaction, 87
Age discrimination, 362–65, 375
Age Discrimination in Employment Act of
      1967, 363
Agreements, 424–25
AIDS, 370
Alcoholics Anonymous, 106
Alcoholism, 106–8, 125
  extent of problem, 106–7
  signs of, 107–8
Alcohol treatment programs, 108 *see also*
      Employee Assistance Program (EAP)
Alternative schedule choice, 46
Ambiguity, 144, 210–11
  role of, 140
  training for, 250
American Federation of State, County, and
      Municipal Employees, 382
Anger, 32–33
Anxieties, 186, 261
Apartheid, 407, 429
Apple Computer, 90
Appraisal:
  of performance, 269–83, 292–94
  purposes of, 271–72
  techniques of, 275–82

Arab influences, 417–19, 423, 425–26
Arbitration, 394–95, 403
Argyris, Chris, 57
Assertiveness, 261–62, 266, 275
AT&T, 10, 374
Attitude, 33, 48, 133, 135
  management, 309–10, 384
  success, 318–19
  surveys, 93–95, 99
  work, 13
A-type behavior, 28–29, 52
Authority, 72, 202, 234, 239
  delegation of, 234
Autocratic leadership, 225, 239
Autonomy, 90

B

Bakke (U.S. Supreme Court decision), 373
Barriers to achievement, 68–70
Barriers to communication, 155–59
Behavior:
  exaggerated, 105–6
  of groups, 140–41
Behavioral sciences, 14
Behaviorally anchored rating scales (BARS),
      81–82, 282
Behaviorist school, 59
Behavior modification, 59, 342–43, 352
Behavior training, 244–45
Belonging needs, 62–63, 77
Bendix Corporation, 112, 369
Benefits, 67–68, 291–93, 396–97, 415
Bias, personal, 282–83
Blacklisting, 396
Black pride, 360–61, 378
Blue-collar job, 101
  satisfaction and morale in, 88–89

Body language, 162–64, 167, 169, 417–18, 421–22
Bonuses, 290–91
Boredom, 70–73, 92–93
Boycotts, 395, 403
Brain, right-side, 303
Brainstorming, 310–11, 322, 328
B-type behavior, 28–29, 52
Burnout, 35

C

"Cafeteria-style" compensation, 292
Career advancement, 44–46, 133–34
Career development, 26–53, 133–34
Career pathing, 43–44, 51
Case study, 254–55
Cash bonuses, 291
Catharsis, 117
Central tendency, 283, 296
Challenge, 71, 211
Change, 17, 218, 330–53
    driving forces, 338–39
    mandating, 343, 353
    model for, 333
    resistance to, 336–45
    restraining forces, 338–39
    social, 366, 397
    successful, 345–46
    technological, 332–33, 339–40, 397
Child care centers, 367–68
Chrysler, 398–400
Churchill, Winston, 30, 109
Civil rights, 372, 375–76, 378
Closed shop, 389, 403
Clothing, as status symbol, 207–8
Coaching, 423
Cognitive dissonance, 237
Collective bargaining, 391–93, 400, 403
Colors, 98–99, 415
Commissions, 291
Commitment, 9, 12, 91, 243–44
Communications, 15, 39–40, 146–92, 325–26
    barriers, 155–59
    channels, 178–87
    cross-cultural, 428–29
    defensive, 157–58
    downward, 181–83
    electronic, 188–89
    feedback, 83, 159–60, 169, 316
    formal, 178–79, 191
    horizontal, 179–80, 189, 191
    informal, 186–87, 189, 191
    interpersonal, 146–70
    leadership, 234
    levels, 160–61
    nonverbal, 162–64
    oral, 183
    small-group, 187–88
    upward, 184–86
    vertical, 181, 192
    written, 183
Company (alcohol and drug) treatment programs, 119–21
Company needs, 19–20
Company objectives, 24
Comparable worth, 367, 376
Compensation, as a defense mechanism, 70
Completed development work, 320, 328
Compulsory advisory service, 320, 328
Computer-assisted instruction, 252
Conceptual skills, 19
Conflict management, 324–26, 400
Congruency theory, 57–58
Consensus, 131–32, 197, 228, 321–22
Consolidated Omnibus Reconciliation Act (COBRA), 358
Containment, as method of dealing with unions, 384, 403
Context, international, 422–23
Contingency model, 230–32, 239
Contracts, 424–25
Control, personal, 32
Convergent thinking, 305
Cooperation, with unions, 384, 399, 403
Coping with stress, 31–34
Corporate renewal, 12
Counseling, 34, 114–21
    cooperative, 118–20, 125
    directive, 117, 120, 125
    nondirective, 117–18, 120, 125
Courtesy, 13
Coworkers, 84
Creativity, 135, 300–311, 328
Credibility, 187
Critical incident technique, 276, 296
Critical path method, 316

Cultural attitudes, 408–9, 426
Cultural differences, 407–10, 414–15, 426–27
Cultural relativity, 408–9, 429
Cultural stereotypes, 378
Cunningham, Mary, 112, 369
Curiosity, 302–3
Custodial person, 302–3

D

Day care centers, 367–68
Deauthorization, 388
Decertification, 388
Decibels, 101
Decisions, 298–329
   groups, 178, 321–24
   individual, 320
   long-range, 317, 328
   oligarchic, 320
   short-range, 183, 317, 328
Deductive orientation, 248–49, 266
Defense mechanisms, 69–70
Delegation, 72, 234
Delphi technique of decision making, 322
Demand, occupational, 42–43
Deming, W. Edwards, 19, 25
Democratic leadership, 225–27, 321–23
Demotions, 285–89
Development (vis-a-vis training and education),
   244–47, 266
Directive interview, 117, 274–75
Disciplinary action, 243, 285, 296
Discipline, 242–68
   within business curriculum, 3
Discrimination, 354–79
   fighting, 371–75
Dismissals, 285–89
Dissatisfiers, 65–66
Distress, 28, 52, 105
Divergent thinking, 305
Downsizing, 192
Drucker, Peter, 25, 317, 341
Drugs, 108–12, 122
   abuse, 108–12, 125
   designer, 111, 125
   users, polydrug, 109, 125
Drug treatment programs, 119–21
Dual careers, 132–33, 369, 378

Dual loyalty, to management and union,
   386–88, 403

E

EC92. *see* European (economic) community
Echo chamber, 153–54
Edison, Thomas, 306
Education, 246–47, 368, 371–72
   and job satisfaction, 88
Efficiency, 309–10
Ego states, 259–61
Einstein, Albert, 303
Elasticity of time, 420, 429
Electronic mail, 188, 191
Emery Air Freight Company, 59
Emotions, 152, 183, 258, 304
Empathy, 14–15, 24, 105, 427
Employee Assistance Program (EAP), 112,
   121–22, 125
Employee benefits, 67–68, 291–93, 396–97
Employee Retirement Income Security Act of
   1974 (ERISA), 358
Engineering, job, 364, 373
Entrepreneurial characteristics, 310, 328
Environment, physical, 95–98, 205–7
Equal Employment Opportunity Commission
   (EEOC), 372–73, 376, 378–79
Equal pay, 354, 367
Equal Pay Act of 1963, 358
Equity theory, 60, 76
Ergonomics, 95, 364
ERG theory, 60, 77
Errors, in rating employees, 282–83
Essay appraisal, 275, 296
Esteem need, 63, 76, 288
Ethics
   business, 11–12
   see also Values
Ethnocentrism, 408–9, 429
European (economic) community, 418, 429–30
Eustress, 28, 52
Executive orders, 386
Exercise, physical, 33
Exit interviews, 93–94, 99
Expectancy theory, 60, 76
Experiential training, 256–63, 266
Exports, 411–12
Extrinsic motivators, 67–68, 84

Extrinsic rewards, 67–68
Eye contact, 162–63

F

Facsimile (FAX) communication, 188–89, 191
Fair Labor Standards Act, 403
Favoritism, 283
Fear, of unknown, 336–37
Federal Employment Practices Commission, 378
Federal Mediation and Conciliation Service, 395
Feedback, 83, 159–60, 169, 271–72, 316
Fiedler, Fred, 230–31, 236, 240
Field review, 279, 296
Firing an employee, 286–88
Fixation, 69
Flexibility, 72–73
Flextime, 72–73
Followership, 218–19
Ford Motors, 289–90
Foreigners, 408–9, 419–20
Free-rein leadership, 227, 239
Freud, Sigmund, 58–59, 73–74
Friendship, 423–24
Fringe benefits. *see* Employee benefits
Frustration, 68
Future shock, 33

G

Gender:
   and age, 303
   and job satisfaction, 88
General Electric, 90, 374
General Foods, 72–73, 315–16
General Motors, 341, 416
Goal congruency, 57–58
Goals:
   individual, 3, 24, 334–35
   long-range, 46–47
Goal setting, 61, 281, 347
"Golden" handshake, 288
Grapevine, 186, 189–91
Graphic rating scale, 275–76, 296
Grievance, 393–95, 403
Griggs (U.S. Supreme Court decision), 372–73
Group:
   behavior, 127–45, 323–24
   cohesiveness, 131
   decision-making, 178, 321–23, 345, 352

dynamics, 128, 132
   norms, 129
   roles, 139–40
   size, 130
   values, 204, 220
Groupthink, 140–41, 144, 323–24, 327–28
Growth needs, 60, 63, 65–66, 76
   personal, 133

H

Halo effect, 282, 296
Handicapped, 370, 379
Hawthorne Study, 8, 24
Herzberg, Frederick, 9, 65–67, 80
Heuristic approach to decision making, 311–12, 328
Hewlett-Packard, 85, 113, 229, 374
Hierarchy of needs, 63–64
High context, 422–23, 426–27
"High-tech" society, 340–41
Hispanic-Americans, 361, 378
Hitchhiking, as brainstorming technique, 310–11
Holistic health, 28, 52
Homeostasis, 338, 344, 352–53
Honesty, 12
Horizontal channels of communication, 179–81, 191
Horizontal loading, 70, 74
Hours of work, 424
H-type behavior, 28–29
Human dignity, 14, 426–27
Human engineering, 95
Human relations:
   defined, 3, 24, 247
   problems, 3, 19–20
   skills, 18–19
Human resource information systems (HRIS), 80, 84
Humanist school, 59–60
Hygiene theory, 65–67, 76

I

Iacocca, Lee, 38–39, 53
IBM, 229, 374, 410
Iceberg theory, 58–59
Illness, 33–34
Illusion of invulnerability, 324

Illusion of unanimity, 324
Immaturity of American management, 11
Immigration, 361, 408
Impermeable social structure, 144
In-basket method, 253, 266
Incentives, 67, 74–75, 290–91
Incubation phase of creativity, 302, 306
India, 414, 423
Indians, American, 361
Individual differences, 15, 24, 56–57, 86, 136,
    334–35, 427
Inductive orientation, 248–49, 266
Industrial democracy, 10
Inflation, 412
Informal organization, 8, 59–60
Information society, 339–40
Inhibitors to creativity, 304
Injunctions, 396, 403
Inner circle, 421, 429
Innovation, 300–301, 328
  in decision making, 298–329
Inspiration, 302, 306
Integrity, 12
Intel, 121, 229
Intelligence, 137, 220, 303
Intercultural relations, 405–30
Intercultural socialization, 429
Internationalism, 399, 427 see also Intercultural
    relations
International trade, 371, 399
Interview:
  appraisal, 273–75
  corrective, 120–21
  directive, 117, 274–75
  exit, 93–94, 99
  non-directive, 117–18
Intimacy, 160–61
Intrapreneurs, 310
Intrinsic motivators, 67–68, 76, 85
Intuition, 164, 319, 328–29
Isolationism, 408, 429

J

Japan, 9–10, 44, 228–29, 415–16
Job cycle, 88–89, 101
Job description, 80, 101, 272
Job design, 70–73, 76, 85
Job discrimination, 354–79
Job engineering, 364, 373

Job enlargement, 77
Job enrichment, 72, 74, 77, 92–93
Job loading:
  horizontal, 70
  vertical, 71–72
Job performance, 78–102, 121
Job rotation, 72, 77
Job satisfaction, 48–49, 80, 86–93, 101
  and age, 87
  and education, 88
  and experience in an organization, 87–88
  and gender (sex), 88
  and occupational field, 88
  and organizational level, 88
  blue-collar, 88–89
  pink-collar, 89
  white-collar, 89
Job status, 209–11
Job structuring, 373, 378
Judgment, 255–56
Jurisdictional strike, 503

K

Key people, 324
Kinesics, 162, 169
Knowledge workers, 246–47
Korda, Michael, 215, 261

L

Labor unions, 7–8, 380–404, 424
Landrum-Griffin Act of 1959, 386
Language, 413, 418–26
Laughter, 31
Lawler, Edward, III, 80
Layoffs, 279, 288–89, 396
Leaderless groups, 235–36
Leaders, 178
  informal, 59–60, 238
  social, 141, 144, 222, 239
  task, 141, 144, 222, 239
Leadership, 16, 134, 216–40, 258
  autocratic, 225
  contingency, 230–32
  democratic, 225–27
  free-rein, 227, 239
  participative, 225–27
  path-goal, 232–33, 239
  style, 222–25, 236–37

Leadership (cont.)
  training, 235, 239
  traits, 220–22
  visionary, 13
Learning, 246
Least preferred co-worker, 230–31
Legislative action, to fight discrimination, 358, 372–74
Lewin, Kurt, 9, 341
Life charts, 33–34
Life cycle, 14
Life satisfaction, 340
Lifetime employment, 44, 229–30
Lighting, 8, 97–98
Line and staff relationships, 175–77, 189
Listening, 73, 115, 118, 148–51, 153–55, 166–67, 169
Listening supervisors, 73, 115–16
Lockouts, 396
Low context, 422–23, 426–27
Loyalty, 12, 73, 134, 137, 228, 291–92, 375
  dual or divided (with unions), 386–88
  group, 334
  mutual trust and, 228–29
  Third World, 424

M

Magnanimity, 48–49, 52
Maintenance theory, 65–67, 76
Management:
  and unions, 384
  attitudes, 309–10, 384
Management by objectives (MBO), 61, 233–34, 281–82, 296
Management by walking (or wandering) around (MBWA), 39, 85, 181
Management development, 250
Management games, 255–56, 267
Management skills, 17–18
Maslow, Abraham, 9, 61–65, 67
Matrix organization, 177–78, 191
Maturity, 48
Mayo, Elton, 8
McDonald's, 134
McGregor, Douglas, 9, 67, 225–26, 236
Mediation, 394–95
Mediator, 326
Meditation, 262–63
Meetings, 39–40

Mentor, 45
Mergers, 397
Merit increases, 284, 291, 296
Midcareer adjustment, 133–34
Middle age, 362–63
Middle management, 279
Midlife crisis, 133
Minnesota Multiphasic Personality Inventory (MMPI), 303
Minorities, 359–65, 402
Mirroring, 118–19
MIT Commission on Industrial Productivity, 6–7, 25
"Mommy track," 52 see also Alternative schedule choice
Monotony, of work, 92
Morale, 78–102, 386–87
  blue-collar, 88–89
  diagnosis, 93–95
  early career, 133
  mid-career, 133
  surveys, 93–95, 99, 101
  white-collar, 89
Morals, 138
Moslems, 417
Motivation, 15–16, 54–77
  growth, 60
Motorola, 72
Multinational corporations, 409–11, 429 see also Intercultural relations
Murphy's laws, 347–48, 353

N

Naisbitt, John, 25, 53
National Council on Aging, 362
Nationalization, 429
National Labor Relations Act, 9, 386
National Labor Relations Board, 403
National Organization of Women (NOW), 378
National Training Laboratory (NTL), 221
Needs:
  belonging and social, 62–63, 76
  esteem, 63, 287–88
  growth, 60, 63, 65–66, 76
  physiological, 62, 77
  safety and security, 62, 77
  self-actualization, 60, 63, 77
Negotiation, 392–93, 400
Neurolinguistic programming (NLP), 164, 169

Noise, 95–97, 158
Nominal group technique (NGT), 322
Nonverbal communication, 150–51, 162–66
Norm of reciprocity, 195, 214
Not-Invented-Here (NIH) syndrome, 337
Nurses, occupational status, 336

O

Objectives, company (organization), 24
Occupational identity, 336, 353
Occupational status, 136–37, 209–10, 214
Older workers, 362–65, 378
On-the-job training (OJT), 251
Open-door policy, 185–86
Organizational design, 171–92
Organizational engineering, 231, 239
Organizational structure, 173–81
Organizational theory, 59
Organization charts, 174, 176–77, 179–80
Organization development (OD), 346–47, 353
Oriental population, 361–62
Orientation, 248–49, 264
Ostracism, 334–36
Ouchi, William, 9, 44, 53, 415
Outplacement, 286–87, 296
Overload, 33
Overspecialization, 72

P

Participation, 10, 177, 341–45, 387
Participative leadership, 225–27, 232, 239
Patents, 309
Path-goal approach, 232–34, 239
Pay, 67–68, 84, 205
Pay discrimination, 354–79
Pay-for-performance, 84
Peer appraisals, 280
Perceptions, 148, 151–52, 169, 197, 302, 305–7
Performance, 16, 45–46, 68, 243, 284
    appraisal of, 90–91, 121, 285
    job, 78–102, 285
    measurement of, 83, 281
    reward for, 291
    standards of, 80–82
Permeable society, 135–36, 138–39, 144
Personal behavior, 3
Personal development, 27–53

Personal feelings, 22
Personal needs, 3–4, 20–21
Personnel Management, U. S. Office of, 80
Peter Principle, 137–38, 284–85
Peters, Thomas, 8, 11, 25, 218, 300
Pickets, 395
Planning:
    career, 33, 38–46
    long-range, 228–29
Polarizations, 324, 328
Politics, 201–2, 368
    office, 201
    organizational, 201
Popularity, 220–22
Porter, Lyman, 80
Positive sandwich technique, 184, 191, 286
Posture, 162
Power, 60, 178, 194–215,
    measurements of, 203
    relationships, 202
    types of power, 198–200, 214
Pragmatic principle, 408–9, 429
Praise, 84
Prejudgment, 155, 356
Prejudice, 356–58, 370–71, 375, 378
Preoccupation, 155
Priorities, 34–37, 50
Problem solving, 311–17
Problems, personal, 103–26
Procter & Gamble, 229, 398
Productivity, 79–80, 91–93
    improvement, 250
Professionalism, 210, 214
Profit-sharing, 291
Program Evaluation Review Technique (PERT),
    316–17
Programmed instruction, 252, 267
Project teams, 177–78
Projection, as defense mechanism, 70
Promotion, 28, 143–44, 229, 264–65, 283–84,
    295–96
    opportunities, 66, 86
Protestant work ethic, 414 see also Work ethic
Proxemics, 163, 169
Psychoanalytical school, 58
Psychological needs, 62, 77
Psychology, 5
    schools of, 58–60
Pygmalion management, 184 see also
        Self-fulfilling prophecy

Q

Quality, 14, 229
Quality circles, 10–11, 24, 93
Quality of life, 339, 397–98, 403–4
Questionnaires, 93–95
Quiet time, 35

R

Racial discrimination, 359–62, 375–76
Rand Corporation, 322
Ranking:
    as performance appraisal, 279, 296
    as social status, 203–4
Rapport, 132
Rationalization, 70
Recency bias, 283, 296
Reciprocity, 424
Recognition, 63, 84–85, 311
Referent others, 86, 101
Regression, 69
Rehabilitation Act of 1973, 370, 378
Reinforcement, positive principle of, 59
Religion, 414–15, 426
Religious discrimination, 358–59
Repression, 70
Resignation, as defense mechanism, 69
Resistance to change:
    economic, 337–38
    psychological, 336–37
    social, 338–41
Respect, mutual, 13
Responsibility, 16, 40–42, 71, 80, 90, 133–34,
    234
Retirement, 228, 363
Rewards, 67, 83–84, 289–90, 294–95, 311
Right-to-work laws, 389, 403
Risks, 120, 318–19, 328
Role behavior, 127–45
Role conflict, 140, 144
Role playing, 257–58
Role prescription, 144
Roosevelt, Theodore, 49
Rumor, 187, 191

S

Saab/Scania, 92
Safety needs, 62, 77

Safety reports, 93, 102
Salary, 212, 289–90
Salespeople, 155, 291
Satisfiers, 65–66
Saudi Arabian Monetary Agency (SAMA),
    411–12
Scientific management, 5–7, 24
Security needs, 62, 77
Self-actualization needs, 60, 63, 77
Self-awareness, 41
Self-censorship, 141
Self-disclosure, 153, 160–61, 169
Self-evaluation, 280, 297
Self-fulfilling prophecy, 183–84
Self-image, 357–58
Selye, Hans, 28, 53
Semantics, 157, 169
Semester-at-Sea, 413, 430
Senility, 362
Sensitivity, 153, 258–59
Sensitivity training, 258–59, 267
Sexism, 112
Sexual discrimination, 365–69, 376–77
Sexual harassment, 113–14, 125
Sharp Company, 399
Shop steward, 389–90, 403
Silence, 160–61
Simulation, 253–56, 267
Skin color, 357–58
Skinner, B.F., 59
Social center, (third place), 90
Social change, 366, 397
Social class, 134–36, 144
Social leaders, 141, 144, 222, 239
Social needs, 62–63, 77
Social pressure and creativity, 308
Social readjustment scale, 34
Social space, 421
Social stratification, 204, 214
Social values, 132–34 see also Values
Sociology, 5
Space, 163, 420–21
Span of management, 175, 192
Speaking, 151–52, 234–35
Staff, 175–77
Staff, general, 176–77
Staff specialized, 176–77
Standard of living, 411
Standards, performance, 80–82
Statistical method of decision making, 322

Status, 194–215, 290, 337
Status anxiety, 210–11, 213–14
Status symbols, 63, 204–8
Stereotypes, 323, 356–57, 378
Stevens, J.P., 398
Stotts (U.S. Supreme Court decision), 373
Stress, 28–34, 114–15
Strike, 395, 403
Striver, 135–36, 137–38, 144
Success, 46–49, 52, 211, 318
Supervisor(s), 113, 115–16, 390, 400, 403
    role in appraisals, 275–79
Supportive leadership, 232
Surveys, morale, 93–95
Symbols, visual, 165–67
Synergy, 322

T

Taft-Hartley Act of 1947, 386
Tardiness, 93, 276
Task leaders, 141, 144, 222, 239
Taylor, Frederick, 5–6
Team building, 347–49
Team projects (matrix), 177–78
Teamwork, 330–53
Technical skills, 18–19
Technological change, 332–33, 339–40, 397
Telephone paradox, 37–38
Tension, 28–31, 49–50
Termination at will, 374–75, 378
T-groups, 258–59, 267
Theory X, 225–27
Theory Y, 225–27
Theory Z, 9, 44, 227–29, 236, 397, 415, 426
Time, 51, 419, 426
    for change, 345, 348
    management, 31, 34–40, 49–52
Titles, 89, 209–10
Toffler, Alvin, 33
Tolerance, 33
Touching, 164, 421–22, 426
Toyota, 416
Training, 23, 244–47, 267
    of foreigners, 412
    of new employees, 248–49
    of supervisors, 391
Transactional Analysis (TA), 259–61, 267
Transcendental Meditation (TM), 262–63, 267

Trust, 132, 228, 347, 350, 353, 415
    mutual, 13
Turnover of employees, 93
Twain, Mark, 300
Type A behavior, 28–29, 52
Type A organizations, 44
Type B behavior, 28–29, 52
Type H behavior, 28–29, 52
Type J organizations, 44
Type Z organizations, 44

U

Ueberroth, Peter, 219
Ugly American, 409
Unfreezing, as part of change process, 338–39
Unions, 7–8, 380–404, 424
    internationalism and, 399
Union shop, 388–89, 403
Union tactics, 395–96
United Auto Workers (UAW), 341, 382, 398–99
United Farm Workers, 361
Upward communication, 182, 184–86
Upward mobility, 136–37

V

Valence, 60
Values, 24, 132–34, 414, 426
    organizational, 10–14, 21
Variety, job, 72, 88–89
Verification, phase of creativity, 302, 306–7
Vertical job loading, 71–72, 74
Videotape, 253, 257–58
Visionary leadership, 13
Visual pollution, 96
Visual symbols, 165–66
Voice tone, 152

W

Wages, 396–97
Wagner Act, 9, 386
WASPS (White, Anglo-Saxon, Protestants), 134
Waterman, Robert H., Jr., 8, 11–12
Wellness program, 90, 101
White-collar workers, 101
    job satisfaction and morale, 89
    unions, 382–83